# Saxon® ALGEBRA 1

# Solution Manual

ISBN 13:   978-1-6027-7500-8
ISBN 10:   1-6027-7500-1

## SAXON®

HOUGHTON MIFFLIN HARCOURT
Supplemental Publishers

www.SaxonPublishers.com
800-531-5015

ISBN 13:     978-1-6027-7500-8
ISBN 10:     1-6027-7500-1

17  18  19  20  2266  20  19  18

4500698900

# LESSON 1

## Warm Up 1

1. Venn diagram

2. $2 \div 9 = 0.\overline{2}$    Divide the numerator by the denominator.

3. $3 \div 8 = 0.375$    Divide the numerator by the denominator.

$$4\frac{3}{8} = 4 + \frac{3}{8}$$
$$= 4 + 0.375$$
$$= 4.375$$

4. $0.6 = \frac{6}{10}$    The decimal is in the tenths place, so use 10 as the denominator.

$\frac{6}{10} = \frac{3}{5}$    Simplify.

5. $0.75 = \frac{75}{100}$    The decimal is in the hundredths place, so use 100 as the denominator.

$\frac{75}{100} = \frac{3}{4}$    Simplify.

$5.75 = 5 + 0.75 = 5 + \frac{3}{4} = 5\frac{3}{4}$

## Lesson Practice 1

a. integers, rational numbers, real numbers

b. rational numbers, real numbers

c. irrational numbers, real numbers

d. whole numbers; Sample: There can be no people or any number of people.

e. irrational numbers; Sample: Area is equal to pi times the radius squared, so the answer will be irrational.

f. rational numbers; Sample: The value of the coins will have tenths and hundredths places.

g. $C \cap D = \{20\}$;
$C \cup D = \{4, 5, 8, 10, 12, 15, 16, 20\}$

h. $C \cap D = \{ \}$ or $\varnothing$;
$C \cup D = \{6, 7, 12, 14, 18, 21, 24, 28\}$

i. Verify the statement by multiplying two whole numbers.

$$3 \cdot 4 = 12$$
$$2 \cdot 0 = 0$$
$$1 \cdot 100 = 100$$

The product is always a whole number.
The statement is true.

j. Verify the statement by dividing two natural numbers.

$$\frac{4}{2} = 2$$
$$\frac{100}{10} = 10$$
$$\frac{1}{2} = 0.5$$

$\frac{1}{2}$ is a counterexample. The quotient is not a natural number. The statement is false.

## Practice 1

1.    26.1    Write the problem vertically.
   $\times\ 6.15$
   $\overline{160.515}$    Since the factors have a total of 3 decimal places, there should be 3 decimal places in the product.

2. Multiply to find a common denominator.
$7 \cdot 8 = 56$

$\frac{4}{7}\left(\frac{8}{8}\right) + \frac{1}{8}\left(\frac{7}{7}\right) + \frac{1}{2}\left(\frac{28}{28}\right)$    Multiply by fractions equal to 1.

$= \frac{32}{56} + \frac{7}{56} + \frac{28}{56}$    Add.

$= \frac{67}{56}$ or $1\frac{11}{56}$    Simplify.

3.   $\frac{1060}{9)9540}$    Multiply the divisor and dividend by 10 so the divisor is a natural number.

4. Combine like terms. Write the result in simplest form.

$\frac{3}{5} + \frac{1}{8} + \frac{1}{8} = \frac{3}{5} + \frac{2}{8}$

$= \frac{3}{5} + \frac{1}{4}$

Multiply to find a common denominator.
$5 \cdot 4 = 20$

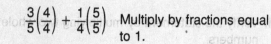

$$\frac{3}{5}\left(\frac{4}{4}\right) + \frac{1}{4}\left(\frac{5}{5}\right)$$ Multiply by fractions equal to 1.

$$= \frac{12}{20} + \frac{5}{20}$$ Add.

$$= \frac{17}{20}$$ Simplify.

5. $8\overline{)3.000}$ $0.375$ Divide the numerator by the denominator.

6. To eliminate the repeating decimal, subtract the same repeating decimal.

$n = 0.66\overline{6}$    Let $n$ represent the fraction equivalent to $0.66\overline{6}$...

$10n = 6.66\overline{6}$    Since 1 digit repeats, multiply both sides of the equation by $10^1$ or 10.

$10n = 6.66\overline{6}$
$-n = 0.66\overline{6}$    Subtract the original equation.

$9n = 6$    Combine like terms.

$n = \frac{6}{9}$ or $\frac{2}{3}$    Divide both sides by 9 and simplify.

$0.66\overline{6}$ is equivalent to $\frac{2}{3}$.

7. Multiply to find a common denominator for the fractional parts.

$2 \cdot 5 = 10$

$$\frac{1}{2}\left(\frac{5}{5}\right) + \frac{1}{5}\left(\frac{2}{2}\right)$$ Multiply by fractions equal to 1.

$$= \frac{5}{10} + \frac{2}{10}$$ Add.

$$= \frac{7}{10}$$ Simplify.

Add the integer parts to the sum of the fractional parts.

$$2 + 3 + \frac{7}{10} = 5 + \frac{7}{10}$$

$$= 5\frac{7}{10}$$

8. Choose any whole number. Multiply the numerator and the denominator by that number. Sample: $\frac{2}{5} = \frac{2 \cdot 2}{5 \cdot 2} = \frac{4}{10}$

9. Student B; Sample: Student A did not factor the 9 completely.

10. Choose any two factors of 144. Continue

to factor until each branch ends in a prime number.

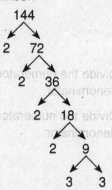

The prime factorization of 144 is $2 \cdot 2 \cdot 2 \cdot 2 \cdot 3 \cdot 3$ or $2^4 \cdot 3^2$.

11. Move the decimal two places to the right. 0.15 is equivalent to 15%.

12. Move the decimal point two places to the right. 7.2 is equivalent to 720%.

13. The natural numbers are the numbers used to count objects or things. Using braces and digits, the set of natural numbers can be written as {1, 2, 3,...}.

14. This is the set of whole numbers, because it is the set of natural numbers {1, 2, 3,...} and zero.

15. The elements of the set are 2, 4, 0, 6, 10, and 8. Use braces and digits to represent the numbers.

$K = \{2, 4, 0, 6, 10, 8\}$

16. B; Since $\sqrt{15}$ cannot be written as the quotient of two integers, it is an irrational number.

17. If $s$ is an integer, then $6s^2 = 6 \cdot s \cdot s$ is also an integer because the integers are closed under multiplication. All integers are rational numbers, so the surface area of a cube would be a rational number.

18. false; Sample: A right angle and an obtuse angle have a sum of more than 180°.

19. The baby's head is one fourth of its total body length, or one fourth of 19 inches. To find one fourth of 19 inches, multiply 19 by $\frac{1}{4}$ and simplify.

$19 \cdot \frac{1}{4} = \frac{19}{4} = 4\frac{3}{4}$ inches

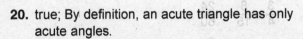

20. true; By definition, an acute triangle has only acute angles.

21. false; A trapezoid has only one pair of parallel sides.

22. Tyrone ran 7 laps on the quarter-mile track, or $7 \cdot \frac{1}{4} = \frac{7}{4}$ miles. This distance is in the form $\frac{a}{b}$, where a and b are integers and $b \neq 0$. Therefore, the set of rational numbers includes the distance Tyrone ran at practice.

23. true; By definition, a parallelogram has two pairs of parallel sides.

24. yes; The ones digit is even.

25. The length of the hypotenuse is $\sqrt{34}$ inches. Since $\sqrt{34}$ cannot be written as the quotient of two integers, the length of the hypotenuse is a member of the set of irrational numbers.

26. a. The area of the rectangle is equal to the product of its length and its width.

    (6 feet)(3 feet) = 18 square feet

    b. The number of square feet is a member of the sets of rational numbers, integers, whole numbers, and natural numbers.

27. Use the formula distance = rate · time.

    $$\begin{array}{r} 10.56 \\ \times\ 3.5 \\ \hline 36.960 \end{array}$$ Write the problem vertically.

    Since the factors have a total of 3 decimal places, there should be 3 decimal places in the product.

    The rover would travel 36.96 miles in 3.5 hours.

28. yes; The sum of digits is $2 + 0 + 7 = 9$, which is divisible by 3.

29. Multiply to find a common denominator.

    $5 \cdot 7 = 35$

    Write the fractions with a common denominator.

    $\frac{3}{5} \cdot \frac{7}{7} \bigcirc \frac{4}{7} \cdot \frac{5}{5}$

    $\frac{21}{35} > \frac{20}{35}$, so $\frac{3}{5} > \frac{4}{7}$.

30. The set of rational numbers best describes her balance. The balance could be positive or negative and may contain decimal amounts.

## LESSON 2

### Warm Up 2

1. product

2. Multiply to find a common denominator.

   $5 \cdot 3 = 15$

   $\frac{2}{5}\left(\frac{3}{3}\right) + \frac{1}{3}\left(\frac{5}{5}\right)$  Multiply by fractions equal to 1.

   $= \frac{6}{15} + \frac{5}{15}$  Add.

   $= \frac{11}{15}$  Simplify.

3. $\begin{array}{r} 654.1 \\ +\ 78.39 \\ \hline 732.49 \end{array}$  Write the problem vertically. Align the decimal points.

4. $\begin{array}{r} 4.5 \\ \times\ 0.23 \\ \hline 1.035 \end{array}$  Write the problem vertically.

   Since the factors have a total of 3 decimal places, there should be 3 decimal places in the product.

5. Multiply the numerators and denominators. Then simplify.

   $\frac{3}{8}\left(\frac{2}{9}\right) = \frac{6}{72}$

   $= \frac{1}{12}$

### Lesson Practice 2

a. The numbers 65 and 12 are constants because they never change. The letters q, r, s, and x are variables because they represent unknown numbers.

b. The numbers 4 and 71 are constants because they never change. The letters g, h, y, and z are variables because they represent unknown numbers.

c. The factors are 17, d, e, and f. The coefficient is 17.

d. The factors are $\frac{1}{4}$, u, and v. The coefficient is $\frac{1}{4}$.

e. The factors are − 3, s, and t. The coefficient is − 3.

**Saxon** Algebra 1

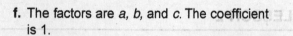

**f.** The factors are *a*, *b*, and *c*. The coefficient is 1.

**g.** The first term is 8*v*. The second term is 17*yz*. The third term is $\frac{63b}{4gh}$.

**h.** The first term is $\frac{(4 + 2x)}{38q}$. The second term is 18*s*. The third term is 47*jkl*.

**i.** There are three terms.

**j.** The constants are 6.50, 3.25, and 0.75.

**k.** The variables are *h* and *b*.

**Practice 2**

**1.** List the factors of each number to find the greatest common factor.
24: 1, 2, 3, 4, 6, 8, 12, 24
32: 1, 2, 4, 8, 16, 32
2, 4, and 8 are common factors.
The GCF of 24 and 32 is 8.

**2.** List the factors of each number to find the greatest common factor.
28: 1, 2, 4, 7, 14, 28
42: 1, 2, 3, 6, 7, 14, 21, 42
2, 7, and 14 are common factors.
The GCF of 28 and 42 is 14.

**3.** List the multiples of each number to find the least common multiple.
Multiples of 9: 9, 18, 27, 36, 45, 54, 63, 72, …
Multiples of 12: 12, 24, 36, 48, 60, 72, …
36 and 72 are common multiples.
The LCM of 9 and 12 is 36.

**4.** List the multiples of each number to find the least common multiple.
Multiples of 3: 3, 6, 9, 12, 15, 18, 21, 24, 27, 30, …
Multiples of 5: 5, 10, 15, 20, 25, 30, 35, 40, …
Multiples of 6: 6, 12, 18, 24, 30, 36, 42, 48, …
The LCM of 3, 5, and 6 is 30.

**5.** Multiply the numerators and denominators. Then simplify.

$$\frac{3}{4} \cdot \frac{8}{15} = \frac{24}{60}$$
$$= \frac{2}{5}$$

**6.** Write the reciprocal of $\frac{21}{25}$ and then multiply.

$$\frac{7}{15} \cdot \frac{25}{21} = \frac{175}{315}$$
$$= \frac{5}{9}$$

**7.** The coefficients are 1 and 12. The variables are *r*, *s*, *t*, and *v*.

**8.** The coefficients are 2 and 7. The variables are *x*, *y*, and *w*.

**9.** The coefficients are 47 and $\frac{2}{5}$. The variables are *s* and *t*.

**10.** false; Sample: Zero is a whole number, but it is not a natural number.

**11.** true; Sample: The set of integers is a subset of real numbers.

**12.** false; Sample: By definition, the sets of rational and irrational numbers do not have any members in common.

**13. a.** 1 two; 3 threes; 3 fours; 1 five; 4 sixes; 1 seven

**b.** Draw a number line that includes the minimum and maximum values. Use an *x* to represent each number. Title the graph and the axis.

**Frequency of Numbers**

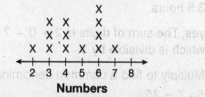

**Numbers**

**14.** All natural numbers are members of the sets of whole numbers, integers, and rational numbers.

**15.** Multiply to find a common denominator.
$8 \cdot 3 = 24$

$$\frac{3}{8}\left(\frac{3}{3}\right) + \frac{1}{3}\left(\frac{8}{8}\right)$$ Multiply by fractions equal to 1.

**Saxon** Algebra 1

$= \dfrac{9}{24} + \dfrac{8}{24}$   Add.

$= \dfrac{17}{24}$   Simplify.

Add the integer parts to the sum of the fractional parts.

$7 + 6 + \dfrac{17}{24} = 13 + \dfrac{17}{24}$

$= 13\dfrac{17}{24}$

The sum is $13\dfrac{17}{24}$ meters. The sum can be written in the form $\dfrac{a}{b}$, where a and b are integers and $b \neq 0$, so it belongs to the set of rational numbers.

**16.** Choose any two factors of 153. Continue to factor until each branch ends in a prime number.

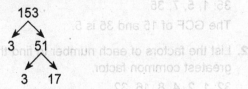

The prime factorization of 153 is $3 \cdot 3 \cdot 17$ or $3^2 \cdot 17$.

**17.** false; Sample: The sum of two obtuse angles is greater than 180°.

**18.** straight

**19.** no; The number formed by the last two digits is not divisible by 4.

**20.** Move the decimal two places to the right. 0.003 is equivalent to 0.3%.

**21.** The set of whole numbers is the set of natural numbers and zero. Using braces and digits, the set of whole numbers can be written as {0, 1, 2, 3, ...}.

**22.** It is the set of natural numbers, or the set of numbers used to count objects or things.

**23.** The second term is $\dfrac{gh}{5}$. The answer is **D**.

**24.** The constants are 2 and $\pi$. The variables are r and v. The coefficient is $2\pi$.

**25.** The variables are c and a.

**26.** Student B; Student A listed two terms.

**27. a.** The coefficients are 0.53 and $\pi$.

**b.** The variables are r and h.

**28.** A trapezoid has only one pair of parallel sides. The answer is **C**.

**29.** There are two terms in the expression: $5 and $2.25h.

**30.** The set of whole numbers best describes the number of students in attendance. The number may be no students or any number of students.

## LESSON 3

**Warm Up 3**

**1.** variable

**2.**   1.2     Write the problem vertically.
     × 0.7
     ——
     0.84    Since the factors have a total of 2 decimal places, there should be 2 decimal places in the product.

**3.** Work from left to right. Find the product of the first two factors.

     0.5     Write the problem vertically.
     × 11
     ——
     5.5     Since the factors have a total of 1 decimal place, there should be 1 decimal place in the product.

Write the problem again.

$(0.5)(11)(0.9)$

$= (0.5 \times 11)(0.9)$

$= (5.5)(0.9)$

Find the product of 5.5 and 0.9.

     5.5     Write the problem vertically.
     × 0.9
     ——
     4.95    Since the factors have a total of 2 decimal places, there should be 2 decimal places in the product.

$(0.5)(11)(0.9) = 4.95$

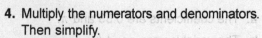

**4.** Multiply the numerators and denominators. Then simplify.

$$\left(\frac{2}{3}\right)\left(\frac{6}{7}\right) = \frac{12}{21}$$

$$= \frac{4}{7}$$

**5.** Multiply the numerators and denominators. Then simplify.

$$\left(\frac{1}{2}\right)\left(\frac{4}{5}\right)\left(\frac{15}{16}\right) = \frac{60}{160}$$

$$= \frac{3}{8}$$

## Lesson Practice 3

**a.** The exponent 4 indicates that the base is a factor four times.

$$6^4 = 6 \cdot 6 \cdot 6 \cdot 6$$

$$= 1296$$

**b.** The exponent 2 indicates that the base is a factor two times.

$$(1.4)^2 = (1.4)(1.4)$$

$$= 1.96$$

**c.** The exponent 3 indicates that the base is a factor three times.

$$\left(\frac{2}{5}\right)^3 = \frac{2}{5} \cdot \frac{2}{5} \cdot \frac{2}{5}$$

$$= \frac{8}{125}$$

**d.** The exponent 6 indicates that the base is a factor six times.

$$10^6 = 10 \cdot 10 \cdot 10 \cdot 10 \cdot 10 \cdot 10$$

$$= 1,000,000$$

**e.** Since each of the factors has the same base, the exponents can be added to find the power of the product.

$$w^3 \cdot w^5 \cdot w^4 = w^{3+5+4}$$

$$= w^{12}$$

**f.** The first two factors have $y$ as the base. The exponents can be added to find the product of those two factors. The last three factors have $z$ as the base. The exponents can be added to find the product of the last three factors.

$$y^6 \cdot y^5 \cdot z^3 \cdot z^{11} \cdot z^2 = y^{6+5} \cdot z^{3+11+2}$$

$$= y^{11}z^{16}$$

**g.** 1 EFLOPS = $10^9$ GFLOPS

1 GFLOPS = $10^9$ FLOPS

To find the speed in FLOPS, find the product of the number of GFLOPS, $10^9$, and the number of FLOPS in a GFLOPS, $10^9$.

$$10^9 \cdot 10^9 = 10^{9+9}$$

$$= 10^{18}$$

The computer performed at a speed of $10^{18}$ FLOPS.

## Practice 3

**1.** List the factors of each number to find the greatest common factor.

15: 1, 3, 5, 15

35: 1, 5, 7, 35

The GCF of 15 and 35 is 5.

**2.** List the factors of each number to find the greatest common factor.

32: 1, 2, 4, 8, 16, 32

48: 1, 2, 3, 4, 6, 8, 12, 16, 24, 48

2, 4, 8, and 16 are common factors of 32 and 48.

The GCF of 32 and 48 is 16.

**3.** List the multiples of each number to find the least common multiple.

Multiples of 8: 8, 16, 24, 32, 40, 48, 56, 64, ...

Multiples of 12: 12, 24, 36, 48, 60, 72, ...

24 and 48 are common multiples.

The LCM of 8 and 12 is 24.

**4.** List the multiples of each number to find the least common multiple.

Multiples of 2: 2, 4, 6, 8, 10, 12, 14, 16, 18, 20, 22, 24, 26, 28, 30, ...

Multiples of 4: 4, 8, 12, 16, 20, 24, 28, 32, 36, 40, ...

Multiples of 7: 7, 14, 21, 28, 35, 42, 49, 56, 63, 70, ...

The LCM of 2, 4, and 7 is 28.

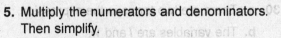

**5.** Multiply the numerators and denominators. Then simplify.

$$\frac{9}{16} \cdot \frac{12}{15} = \frac{108}{240}$$
$$= \frac{9}{20}$$

**6.** Write the reciprocal of $\frac{24}{30}$ and then multiply.

$$\frac{6}{15} \cdot \frac{30}{24} = \frac{180}{360}$$
$$= \frac{1}{2}$$

**7.** The coefficients are 6 and 4. The variables are $m$, $n$, and $b$.

**8.** The coefficients are 5 and 9. The variables are $j$, $c$, and $d$.

**9.** The coefficients are 23 and $\frac{4}{7}$. The variables are $t$ and $w$.

**10.** false; Sample: Fractions are real numbers, but they are not integers.

**11.** true; Sample: The set of whole numbers contains all the natural numbers and zero.

**12.** true; Sample: By definition, the set of irrational numbers is a subset of the set of real numbers.

**13.** $42.53 > 42.35$

**14.** Multiply to find a common denominator.

$9 \cdot 12 = 108$

Write the fractions with a common denominator.

$$\frac{5}{9} \cdot \frac{12}{12} \bigcirc \frac{7}{12} \cdot \frac{9}{9}$$

$$\frac{60}{108} < \frac{63}{108}, \text{ so } \frac{5}{9} < \frac{7}{12}.$$

**15.** Multiply to find a common denominator for the fractional parts.

$8 \cdot 5 = 40$

$\frac{1}{8}\left(\frac{5}{5}\right) + \frac{2}{5}\left(\frac{8}{8}\right)$ Multiply by fractions equal to 1.

$= \frac{5}{40} + \frac{16}{40}$ Add.

$= \frac{21}{40}$ Simplify.

Add the integer parts to the sum of the fractional parts.

$$1 + 7 + \frac{21}{40} = 8 + \frac{21}{40}$$
$$= 8\frac{21}{40}$$

**16.** The integers are the set of whole numbers and the opposites of the natural numbers. Using braces and digits, the set of integers can be written as
$\{\dots, -4, -3, -2, -1, 0, 1, 2, 3, \dots\}$.
The set of integers best describes temperature. Temperature can be positive, negative, or zero, but volume cannot be negative.

**17.** Choose any two factors of 98. Continue to factor until each branch ends in a prime number.

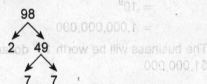

The prime factorization of 98 is
$2 \cdot 7 \cdot 7$ or $2 \cdot 7^2$

**18.** Student B; Sample: Student A multiplied the exponents instead of adding them.

**19.** false; Sample: A rhombus does not always have 4 right angles to make it a square.

**20.** yes; The number is divisible by 2 and 3.

**21. a.** The base is 3.
  **b.** The exponent is 6.
  **c.** $3^6 = 3 \cdot 3 \cdot 3 \cdot 3 \cdot 3 \cdot 3$
  $= 729$

**22.** 1 PFLOP = $10^3$ TFLOPS
1 TFLOP = $10^6$ MFLOPS
To find the number of MFLOPS in a PFLOP, find the product of the number of MFLOPS in a TFLOP, $10^6$, and the number of TLOPS in a PFLOP, $10^3$.
$10^6 \cdot 10^3 = 10^{6+3}$
$= 10^9$
There are $10^9$ MFLOPS in a PFLOP.
The answer is **B**.

**Saxon** Algebra 1

**23.** To find the number of recipes in $4^2$ issues, find the product of the number of recipes in one issue, $4^4$, and the number of issues, $4^2$.

$4^4 \cdot 4^2 = 4^{4+2}$

$\qquad = 4^6$

$\qquad = 4 \cdot 4 \cdot 4 \cdot 4 \cdot 4 \cdot 4$

$\qquad = 4096$

There are 4096 recipes in $4^2$ issues.

**24. a.** $10^3 = 10 \cdot 10 \cdot 10$

$\qquad = 1000$

**b.** To find the value of the business in five years, find the product of the value of the business this year, $10^6$, and the number of times more valuable the business expects to be in five years, $10^3$.

$10^6 \cdot 10^3 = 10^{6+3}$

$\qquad = 10^9$

$\qquad = 1,000,000,000$

The business will be worth $10^9$ dollars, or $1,000,000.

**25.** To find the population of Bridgetown in 2030, find the product of the population in the year 2000, 25,000, and the factor by which the population increases over the three decades between 2000 and 2030, $3^3$.

$25{,}000 \cdot 3^3 = 25{,}000 \cdot 3 \cdot 3 \cdot 3$

$\qquad = 675{,}000$

There will be 675,000 people living in Bridgetown in 2030.

**26.** By definition, a right triangle has one right angle. A right angle has measure 90°. The answer is **A**.

**27.** $1 \cdot (2)^8 = (2)^8$

$\qquad = 2 \cdot 2 \cdot 2 \cdot 2 \cdot 2 \cdot 2 \cdot 2 \cdot 2$

$\qquad = 256$

There will be 256 bacteria after one day.

**28.** The constant in the equation is $\frac{1}{2}$.

**29.** To find the volume of a prism, find the product of its three dimensions. Each side measures 3 feet, so the volume is $3^3$ ft$^3$ or 27 ft$^3$.

**30. a.** There are two terms in the expression.

**b.** The variables are $l$ and $w$.

## LESSON 4

### Warm Up 4

**1.** exponent

**2.**
$$\begin{array}{r} 28.75 \\ + 13.5 \\ \hline 42.25 \end{array}$$
Write the problem vertically. Align the decimal points.

**3.**
$$\begin{array}{r} 89.6 \\ - 7.4 \\ \hline 82.2 \end{array}$$
Write the problem vertically. Align the decimal points.

**4.** Multiply the numerators and denominators. Then simplify.

$\dfrac{2}{3} \cdot \dfrac{9}{16} = \dfrac{18}{48}$

$\qquad\qquad = \dfrac{3}{8}$

**5.** Write the improper fractions as mixed numbers.

$4\dfrac{1}{5} = \dfrac{21}{5}$

$3\dfrac{1}{2} = \dfrac{7}{2}$

Write the reciprocal of $\frac{7}{2}$ and then multiply.

$\dfrac{21}{5} \cdot \dfrac{2}{7} = \dfrac{42}{35}$

$\qquad\qquad = \dfrac{42}{35}$ or $1\dfrac{1}{5}$

### Lesson Practice 4

**a.** $45 - (2 + 4) \cdot 5 - 3$

$= 45 - 6 \cdot 5 - 3$    Simplify inside parentheses.

$= 45 - 30 - 3$    Multiply.

$= 12$    Subtract.

**b.** $9 \cdot 2^3 - 9 \div 3$

$= 9 \cdot 8 - 9 \div 3$    Simplify the exponent.

$= 72 - 3$    Multiply and divide from left to right.

$= 69$    Subtract.

Solutions Key

**c.** $\dfrac{15 - 3^2 + 4 \cdot 2}{7}$

$= \dfrac{15 - 9 + 4 \cdot 2}{7}$    Simplify exponents.

$= \dfrac{15 - 9 + 8}{7}$    Multiply.

$= \dfrac{14}{7}$    Add and subtract left to right in numerator.

$= 2$    Divide.

**d.** Use the order of operations to simplify the two expressions.

$\dfrac{1}{4} + 3^2 + 6 \qquad 5 - 2 + 2 \cdot 4 + 3 \div 9$

$= \dfrac{1}{4} + 9 + 6 \qquad = 5 - 2 + 8 + \dfrac{1}{3}$

$= 15\dfrac{1}{4} \qquad\qquad = 11\dfrac{1}{3}$

Since $15\dfrac{1}{4} > 11\dfrac{1}{3}$,

$\dfrac{1}{4} + 3^2 + 6 > 5 - 2 + 2 \cdot 4 + 3 \div 9.$

**e.** To find the volume of the model moon, substitute $\dfrac{3}{2}$ for $r$ in the formula for volume and simplify.

$\dfrac{4}{3}\pi \cdot \left(\dfrac{3}{2}\right)^3$

$= \dfrac{4}{3}\pi \cdot \dfrac{27}{8}$    Simplify the exponent.

$= \dfrac{108}{24}\pi$    Multiply.

$= \dfrac{9}{2}\pi$    Simplify.

The volume of the model moon is $\dfrac{9}{2}\pi$ in$^3$.

## Practice 4

**1.** Multiply to find a common denominator for the fractional parts.

$4 \cdot 2 = 8$

$\dfrac{1}{4}\left(\dfrac{2}{2}\right) + \dfrac{1}{2}\left(\dfrac{4}{4}\right)$    Multiply by fractions equal to 1.

$= \dfrac{2}{8} + \dfrac{4}{8}$    Add.

$= \dfrac{6}{8}$    Simplify.

$= \dfrac{3}{4}$

Add the integer parts to the sum of the fractional parts.

$2 + 4 + \dfrac{3}{4} = 6 + \dfrac{3}{4}$

$= 6\dfrac{3}{4}$

**2.** Write the mixed numbers as improper fractions.

$5\dfrac{2}{5} = \dfrac{27}{5}$

$3\dfrac{1}{4} = \dfrac{13}{4}$

Multiply to find a common denominator.

$5 \cdot 4 = 20$

$\dfrac{27}{5}\left(\dfrac{4}{4}\right) - \dfrac{13}{4}\left(\dfrac{5}{5}\right)$    Multiply by fractions equal to 1.

$= \dfrac{108}{20} - \dfrac{65}{20}$    Subtract and simplify.

$= \dfrac{43}{20}$ or $2\dfrac{3}{20}$

**3.** $1\dfrac{3}{4} + 4\dfrac{1}{8} - 2\dfrac{1}{2}$

$= \dfrac{7}{4} + \dfrac{33}{8} - \dfrac{5}{2}$    Write the mixed numbers as improper fractions.

$= \dfrac{7}{4}\left(\dfrac{2}{2}\right) + \dfrac{33}{8} - \dfrac{5}{2}\left(\dfrac{4}{4}\right)$    Write equivalent fractions using a denominator of 8.

$= \dfrac{14}{8} + \dfrac{33}{8} - \dfrac{20}{8}$

$= \dfrac{27}{8}$ or $3\dfrac{3}{8}$

**4.** Write the mixed numbers as improper fractions.

$4\dfrac{1}{3} = \dfrac{13}{3}$

$2\dfrac{1}{6} = \dfrac{13}{6}$

Write the reciprocal of $\dfrac{13}{6}$ and multiply.

$\dfrac{13}{3} \cdot \dfrac{6}{13} = \dfrac{78}{39}$    Multiply by $\dfrac{6}{13}$.

$= 2$

**Saxon** Algebra 1

**5.** 3)$\overline{35.19}$ (quotient 11.73)   Multiply the divisor and dividend by 10 so the divisor is a natural number.

**6.** 
$$\begin{array}{r} 4.16 \\ \times\ 2.3 \\ \hline 9.568 \end{array}$$
Write the problem vertically.

Since the factors have a total of 3 decimal places, there should be 3 decimal places in the product.

**7.** There are three terms in the expression.

**8.** Choose any two factors of 225. Continue to factor until each branch ends in a prime number.

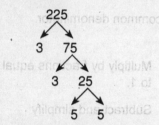

The prime factorization of 225 is $3 \cdot 3 \cdot 5 \cdot 5$ or $3^2 \cdot 5^2$.

**9.** 124,302 is divisible by 3; Sample: The sum of the digits is 12, which is divisible by 3.

**10.** The elements of the set are $-15, 1, 7, 3, -8, 0, 12,$ and $6$. Use braces and digits to represent the numbers.

$L = \{-15, -8, 0, 1, 3, 6, 7, 12\}$

**11.** true; Sample: The set of whole numbers is a subset of the set of integers.

**12.** Since $\sqrt{5}$ cannot be written as the quotient of two integers, the length of the hypotenuse is a member of the sets of irrational and real numbers.

**13.** 6)$\overline{1.000\ldots}$ (quotient 0.166...)   Find the equivalent decimal. Divide the numerator by the denominator.

Find the equivalent percent. Move the decimal two places to the right and round to the nearest tenth.

$0.16\overline{6} \approx 16.7\%$

**14.** 9)$\overline{5.000\ldots}$ (quotient 0.555...)   Find the equivalent decimal. Divide the numerator by the denominator.

Find the equivalent percent. Move the decimal two places to the right and round to the nearest tenth.

$0.55\overline{5} \approx 55.6\%$

**15.** Use the order of operations to simplify the two expressions.

$$\begin{array}{ll} 3 \cdot 4^2 + 4^2 & 3(16 + 16) \\ = 3 \cdot 16 + 16 & = 3(32) \\ = 48 + 16 & = 96 \\ = 64 & \end{array}$$

Since the value of the first expression, 64, is less than the value of the second expression, 96, $3 \cdot 4^2 + 4^2 < 3(16 + 16)$.

**16.** By definition, an obtuse triangle has one obtuse angle. A triangle with angle measures of 40°, 120°, and 20° has one angle that measures more than 90° and less than 180°. The answer is **B**.

**17.** Draw a number line that includes the minimum and maximum values. Use an X to represent each number. Title the graph and the axis.

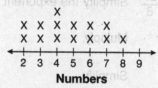

**Frequency of Numbers**

**Numbers**

**18.** true; A square has 4 right angles and its opposite sides are parallel and congruent.

**19.** Write the mixed numbers as improper fractions.

$15\frac{1}{3} = \frac{46}{3}$

$7\frac{4}{5} = \frac{39}{5}$

Multiply to find a common denominator.

$5 \cdot 3 = 15$

$\frac{46}{3}\left(\frac{5}{5}\right) - \frac{39}{5}\left(\frac{3}{3}\right)$   Multiply by fractions equal to 1.

**Saxon** Algebra 1

$= \frac{230}{15} - \frac{117}{15}$    Subtract and simplify.

$= \frac{113}{15}$ or $7\frac{8}{15}$

$7\frac{8}{15}$ yards

**20.** Student B; Sample: Student A has an extra factor of 3, which results in a product of 324.

**21.** yes; The sum of the digits is $1 + 1 + 1 + 6 = 9$, which is divisible by 9.

**22. a.** The variables are $n$, $x$, and $y$.

   **b.** The terms are $\frac{n}{6}$, $3xy$, and 19.

**23.** To find the average growth of the wolf population in one year, divide the change in the number of wolves by the number of years between 1976 and 2003.

$\dfrac{\text{number of wolves in 2003} - \text{number of wolves in 1976}}{\text{number of years between 1976 and 2003}}$

$\dfrac{2300 - 1100}{2003 - 1976} = \dfrac{1200}{27} \approx 44 \text{ wolves}$

**24.** Use the order of operations to simplify the expression.

$9 \cdot (\$1.75) + 5(\$1.50)$

$= \$15.75 + \$7.50$

$= \$23.25$

The answer is **B**.

**25.** Use the formula for the surface area of a cylinder, $S = 2\pi r^2 + 2\pi rh$, to find the surface area of the can. Use 3.14 for $\pi$ and round to the nearest tenth.

$S = 2\pi(3.8)^2 + 2\pi(3.8)(11)$

$= 2(3.14)(14.44) + 2(3.14)(3.8)(11)$

$= 90.6832 + 262.504$

$= 353.1872$

The surface area of the can is about 353.2 cm$^2$.

**26. a.** Write the sum of the products of the number of coins in Ashley's pocket and the respective value of each coin.

$12 \cdot 5¢ + 2 \cdot 10¢ + 4 \cdot 25¢$

$= 60¢ + 20¢ + 100¢$

$= 180¢$

**b.** Write the sum of the products of the number of coins in Beto's pocket and the respective value of each coin.

$10 \cdot 5¢ + 4 \cdot 10¢ + 3 \cdot 25¢$

$= 50¢ + 40¢ + 75¢$

$= 165¢$

**c.** Since $180 > 165$, Ashley has more money.

**27.** Use the order of operations to simplify the expression.

$8(10 - 3 \cdot 2)$

| | |
|---|---|
| $8(10 - 6)$ | Multiply inside the parentheses. |
| $8(4)$ | Subtract inside the parentheses. |
| 32 | Multiply. |

Anthony kept 32 markers for himself.

**28.** The volume of a prism is equal to the product of the area of its base and its height. The area of the base is $s \cdot s = s^2$ and the height is $s$. The volume of the cube is $s^2 \cdot s = s^{2+1} = s^3$.

**29.** Evaluate the expression for $F = 109$.

$\frac{5}{9}(F - 32) = \frac{5}{9}(109 - 32)$

$= \frac{5}{9}(77)$

$= 42.\overline{7}$

The temperature was approximately 42.8°C.

**30.** Evaluate the expression for $m = 223$.

$28 + 0.07m = 28 + 0.07(223)$

$= 28 + 15.61$

$= 43.61$

Mrs. Li was billed $43.61.

## LESSON 5

**Warm Up 5**

**1.** real numbers

**2.** $\begin{array}{r} 54.2 \\ -\,27.38 \\ \hline 26.82 \end{array}$    Write the problem vertically. Align the decimal points.

**3.** $\frac{1}{2}\left(\frac{4}{4}\right) + \frac{3}{8}$    Write equivalent fractions using a denominator of 8.

$= \frac{4}{8} + \frac{3}{8}$

$= \frac{7}{8}$

**4.**    1.09    Write the problem vertically.
    + 76.9    Align the decimal points.
      77.99

**5.** $\frac{3}{4}\left(\frac{2}{2}\right) - \frac{3}{8}$    Write equivalent fractions using a denominator of 8.

$= \frac{6}{8} - \frac{3}{8}$

$= \frac{3}{8}$

## Lesson Practice 5

**a.** The distance from $-3.4$ to 0 is 3.4. So the absolute value is 3.4.

**b.** The distance from $\frac{6}{7}$ to 0 is $\frac{6}{7}$. So the absolute value is $\frac{6}{7}$.

**c.** First simplify within the absolute-value bars. Then find the absolute value.
$|14 + (-22)| = |-8| = 8$

**d.** First simplify within the absolute-value bars. Then find the absolute value.
$-|7 + 16| = -|23| = -23$

**e.** Since the numbers have different signs, find the difference of their absolute values. The sum is negative because $|-23.4| > |18.72|$.
$(-23.4) + 18.72 = -4.68$

**f.** Since the numbers have the same sign, find the sum of their absolute values. The sum is negative because both addends are negative.
$\left(-\frac{2}{3}\right) + \left(-\frac{1}{6}\right) = \left(-\frac{4}{6}\right) + \left(-\frac{1}{6}\right) = -\frac{5}{6}$

**g.** The statement is true because the sum of any two rational numbers will be a rational number.

**h.** The statement is true because the sum of any two positive integers will be a positive integer.

**i.** A decrease of 12°F can be expressed as $-12$.

$34 + (-12) = 22$
The temperature at midnight was 22°F.

## Practice 5

**1.** $1\frac{1}{6} + 3\frac{1}{3}$

$= \frac{7}{6} + \frac{10}{3}$    Write the mixed numbers as improper fractions.

$= \frac{7}{6} + \frac{10}{3}\left(\frac{2}{2}\right)$    Write equivalent fractions using a denominator of 6.

$= \frac{7}{6} + \frac{20}{6}$

$= \frac{27}{6}$ or $4\frac{1}{2}$

**2.** $2\frac{3}{8} - 1\frac{1}{4}$

$= \frac{19}{8} - \frac{5}{4}$    Write the mixed numbers as improper fractions.

$= \frac{19}{8} - \frac{5}{4}\left(\frac{2}{2}\right)$    Write equivalent fractions using a denominator of 8.

$= \frac{19}{8} - \frac{10}{8}$

$= \frac{9}{8}$ or $1\frac{1}{8}$

**3.** $3\frac{2}{3} + 1\frac{5}{8} - 1\frac{3}{4}$

$= \frac{11}{3} + \frac{13}{8} - \frac{7}{4}$

$= \frac{11}{3}\left(\frac{8}{8}\right) + \frac{13}{8}\left(\frac{3}{3}\right) - \frac{7}{4}\left(\frac{6}{6}\right)$

$= \frac{88}{24} + \frac{39}{24} - \frac{42}{24}$

$= \frac{85}{24}$ or $3\frac{13}{24}$

**4.** Write the mixed numbers as improper fractions.

$3\frac{1}{3} = \frac{10}{3}$

$1\frac{3}{5} = \frac{8}{5}$

Write the reciprocal of $\frac{8}{5}$ and then multiply.

$\frac{10}{3} \cdot \frac{5}{8} = \frac{50}{24}$    Multiply by $\frac{5}{8}$.

12    **Saxon** Algebra 1

$= 2\frac{2}{24}$ or $2\frac{1}{12}$

5. 2)15.06 → 7.53   Multiply the divisor and dividend by 10 so the divisor is a natural number.

6. 2.89
   × 1.2
   ———
   3.468   Write the problem vertically.

   Since the factors have a total of 3 decimal places, there should be 3 decimal places in the product.

7. There are three terms in the expression.

8. Choose any two factors of 150. Continue to factor until each branch ends in a prime number.

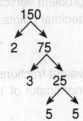

   The prime factorization of 150 is $2 \cdot 3 \cdot 5 \cdot 5$ or $2 \cdot 3 \cdot 5^2$.

9. yes; The ones digit is 0.

10. The elements of the set are −12, 0, −8, 4, −4, 8, and 12. Use braces and digits to represent the numbers.
    $L = \{-12, -8, -4, 0, 4, 8, 12\}$

11. true; All integers can be expressed as fractions.

12. Student B; Sample: The $\sqrt{2}$ is irrational.

13. 8)5.000 → 0.625   Find the equivalent decimal. Divide the numerator by the denominator.

    To find the equivalent percent, move the decimal two places to the right.

    $\frac{5}{8}$ is equivalent to 0.625 and 62.5%.

14. Write the mixed number as a decimal.
    $1\frac{1}{3} = 1.33\overline{3}$

    Convert 3 feet to yards.

3 feet = 1 yard

Since $1 < 1.25 < 1.33\overline{3}$, the lengths from least to greatest are 3 feet, 1.25 yards, and $1\frac{1}{3}$ yards.

15. To find the equivalent decimal, move the decimal two places to the left.

    7% = 0.07

    The decimal is in the hundredths place, so use 100 as the denominator. Then simplify.

    $0.07 = \frac{7}{100}$

    7% is equivalent to $\frac{7}{100}$ and 0.07.

16. The absolute value of −11 is the distance from −11 to 0 on a number line. Write an equation using absolute value.

    $|-11| = 11$

17. By definition, an acute triangle has three acute angles. The angle measures 55°, 45°, and 80° are all acute because they are less than 90°. The answer is **C**.

18. Estimate by rounding each value to the nearest $0.10.

    $1.48 + $0.12 − $0.27
    $1.50 + $0.10 − $0.30 = $1.30

19. The distance from −5 to 0 is 5.

20. true; The opposite sides of rectangles are congruent and parallel.

21. No, $a^2$ should be determined first.

22. An increase of 29°F can be expressed as +29. Since the numbers have different signs, find the difference of their absolute values. The sum is positive because $|29| > |-3|$.

    29 + (−3) = 26

    The day's high temperature was 26°F.

23. A gain of 8 yards can be expressed as 8. A loss of $13\frac{1}{2}$ yards can be expressed as −$13\frac{1}{2}$. Use addition to find the total number of yards lost or gained on the first two downs.

    $8 + \left(-13\frac{1}{2}\right) = -5\frac{1}{2}$

    The Tigers lost $5\frac{1}{2}$ yards on the first two downs.

**24.** The sum of any two integers will be an integer. The sum of any two rational numbers will be a rational number. The sum of any two real numbers will be a real number. The answer is **D**.

**25.** Write two expressions to represent and compare the current altitude of each airplane. A distance below sea level can be expressed as a negative number.

altitude of Airplane A $\bigcirc$ altitude of

Airplane B

$$-43 + 20{,}512 \bigcirc 1924 + 18{,}527$$

$$20{,}469 > 20{,}451$$

Since $20{,}469 > 20{,}451$, Airplane A is currently cruising at a higher altitude.

**26.** A withdrawal of $34.65 can be expressed as $-\$34.65$.

$$\$500 + (-\$34.65) = \$465.35$$

Martha's balance after the withdrawal was $465.35.

**27. a.** Use the order of operations to simplify the expression.

$$3 \cdot (\$15.25) + 4 \cdot (\$25)$$
$$= \$45.75 + \$100$$
$$= \$145.75$$

**b.** Use the order of operations to simplify the expression.

$$\$145.75 + (0.05) \cdot (\$145.75)$$
$$\approx \$145.75 + \$7.29$$
$$= \$153.04$$

**28.** The total change is the sum of the change in value Monday and the change in value Tuesday. A decrease in value can be expressed as a negative number.

$$(-12.67) + (-31.51) = -44.18$$

The total change in stock for the two days was $-44.18$ points.

**29.** The exponent, 5, indicates that the base, 1.6, is a factor five times. The answer is **A**.

**30.** $(-7) + 23 = 16$

The temperature at noon was $16°$F.

## LESSON 6

### Warm Up 6

**1.** absolute value

**2.**
$$\begin{array}{r} 86.9 \\ -\ 18.94 \\ \hline 67.96 \end{array}$$
Write the problem vertically. Align the decimal points.

**3.** $\dfrac{1}{3}\left(\dfrac{3}{3}\right) + \dfrac{4}{9}$  Write equivalent fractions using a denominator of 9.

$$= \frac{3}{9} + \frac{4}{9}$$
$$= \frac{7}{9}$$

**4.**
$$\begin{array}{r} 41.06 \\ -\ 83.7 \\ \hline 124.76 \end{array}$$
Write the problem vertically. Align the decimal points.

**5.** $\dfrac{5}{6}\left(\dfrac{2}{2}\right) - \dfrac{5}{12}$  Write equivalent fractions using a denominator of 12.

$$= \frac{10}{12} - \frac{5}{12}$$
$$= \frac{5}{12}$$

### Lesson Practice 6

**a.** $14 - (-22)$

$$14 + (+22) = 36$$

**b.** $(-7) - 16$

$$(-7) + (-16) = -23$$

**c.** $(-23.4) - 18.72$

$$(-23.4) + (-18.72) = -42.12$$

**d.** $\left(-\dfrac{2}{3}\right) - \left(-\dfrac{1}{6}\right)$

$$\left(-\frac{2}{3}\right) + \left(+\frac{1}{6}\right) = \left(-\frac{4}{6}\right) + \left(+\frac{1}{6}\right)$$
$$= -\frac{3}{6} = -\frac{1}{2}$$

**e.** false; Sample: counterexample:

$$5 - 12 = -7$$

**f.** The difference between any two rational numbers will be a rational number. The statement is true.

**g.** Write an expression that represents the January 7th record depth as the difference between the January 23rd record depth and the difference between the previously-set record depth. A distance below sea level can be expressed as a negative number.

$$-37,800 - (-13,800)$$
$$= -37,800 + (+13,800)$$
$$= -24,000$$

In relation to sea level, the record set on January 7th was −24,000 feet.

## Practice 6

**1.** Write the mixed numbers as improper fractions.

$$5\frac{1}{3} = \frac{16}{3}$$

$$2\frac{1}{3} = \frac{7}{3}$$

Write the reciprocal of $\frac{7}{3}$ and then multiply.

$$\frac{16}{3} \cdot \frac{3}{7} = \frac{48}{21} \quad \text{Multiply by } \frac{3}{7}.$$

$$= \frac{16}{7} \text{ or } 2\frac{2}{7}$$

**2.** $40\frac{1}{8} - 21\frac{1}{4}$

$$= \frac{321}{8} - \frac{85}{4} \quad \text{Write the mixed numbers as improper fractions.}$$

$$= \frac{321}{8} - \frac{85}{4}\left(\frac{2}{2}\right) \quad \text{Write equivalent fractions using a denominator of 8.}$$

$$= \frac{321}{8} - \frac{170}{8}$$

$$= \frac{151}{8} \text{ or } 18\frac{7}{8}$$

**3.** $5\frac{2}{3} + 2\frac{5}{6} - 2\frac{1}{6}$

$$= \frac{17}{3} + \frac{17}{6} + \left(-\frac{13}{6}\right) \quad \text{Write the mixed numbers as improper fractions.}$$

$$= \frac{17}{3}\left(\frac{2}{2}\right) + \frac{17}{6} + \left(-\frac{13}{6}\right) \quad \text{Write equivalent fractions using a denominator of 6.}$$

$$= \frac{34}{6} + \frac{17}{6} + \left(-\frac{13}{6}\right) = \frac{38}{6}$$

$$= 6\frac{2}{6} \text{ or } 6\frac{1}{3}$$

**4.** Write the mixed numbers as improper fractions.

$$1\frac{2}{3} = \frac{5}{3}$$

$$1\frac{1}{4} = \frac{5}{4}$$

$$1\frac{1}{2} = \frac{3}{2}$$

Write the reciprocal of $\frac{5}{4}$ and then multiply from left to right.

$$\frac{5}{3} \div \frac{5}{4} \cdot \frac{3}{2} = \frac{5}{3} \cdot \frac{4}{5} \cdot \frac{3}{2} \quad \text{Multiply by } \frac{4}{5}.$$

$$= \frac{5 \cdot 4 \cdot 3}{3 \cdot 5 \cdot 2}$$

$$= \frac{60}{30}$$

$$= 2$$

**5.** Use the order of operations to simplify the expression. First, find the quotient of 0.74 and 0.2.

$$\begin{array}{r} 3.7 \\ 2\overline{)7.4} \end{array}$$ Multiply the divisor and dividend by 10 so the divisor is a natural number.

Since $0.74 \div 0.2 = 3.7$, the original problem can be written as

$0.74 \div 0.2 \cdot 0.3 = 3.7 \cdot 0.3$. Find the product of 3.7 and 0.3.

$$\begin{array}{r} 3.7 \\ \times\ 0.3 \\ \hline 1.11 \end{array}$$ Write the problem vertically.

Since the factors have a total of 2 decimal places, there should be 2 decimal places in the product.

$0.74 \div 0.2 \cdot 0.3 = 3.7 \cdot 0.3 = 1.11$

**6.** Use the order of operations to simplify the expression. First, find the product of 5.4 and 0.3.

$$\begin{array}{r} 5.4 \\ \times\ 0.3 \\ \hline 1.62 \end{array}$$ Write the problem vertically.

Since the factors have a total of 2 decimal places, there should be 2 decimal places in the product.

Since $5.4 \cdot 0.3 = 1.62$, the original problem can be written as
$5.4 \cdot 0.3 \div 0.4 = 1.62 \div 0.4$. Find the quotient of 1.62 and 0.4.

$$\begin{array}{r} 4.05 \\ 4\overline{)16.2} \end{array}$$   Multiply the divisor and dividend by 10 so the divisor is a natural number.

$5.4 \cdot 0.3 \div 0.4 = 1.62 \div 0.4 = 4.05$

7. Use the order of operations to simplify the expression. First, find the product of 1.24 and 0.2.

$$\begin{array}{r} 1.24 \\ \times\ 0.2 \\ \hline 0.248 \end{array}$$   Write the problem vertically.

Since the factors have a total of 3 decimal places, there should be 3 decimal places in the product.

Since $1.24 \times 0.2 = 0.248$, the original problem can be written as
$1.24 \cdot 0.2 \div 0.1 = 0.248 \div 0.1$. Find the quotient of 0.248 and 0.1.

$$\begin{array}{r} 2.48 \\ 1\overline{)2.48} \end{array}$$   Multiply the divisor and dividend by 10 so the divisor is a natural number.

$1.24 \cdot 0.2 \div 0.1 = 0.248 \div 0.1 = 2.48$

8. $$\begin{array}{r} 35.125 \\ 32\overline{)1124.000} \end{array}$$   Multiply the divisor and dividend by 10 so the divisor is a natural number.

9. Choose any two factors of 592. Continue to factor until each branch ends in a prime number.

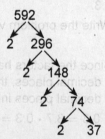

The prime factorization of 592 is
$2 \cdot 2 \cdot 2 \cdot 2 \cdot 37$ or $2^4 \cdot 37$.

10. Choose any two factors of 168. Continue to factor until each branch ends in a prime number.

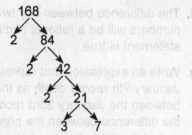

The prime factorization of 168 is
$2 \cdot 2 \cdot 2 \cdot 3 \cdot 7$ or $2^3 \cdot 3 \cdot 7$.

11. Draw a number line that includes the minimum and maximum values. Use an x to represent each number. Title the graph and the axis.

**Frequency of Numbers**

```
        X
        X     X
    X   X   X X
    X X X X X X
  +-+-+-+-+-+-+->
    4 5 6 7 8 9 10
```
**Numbers**

12. no; The sum of the digits is
$2 + 3 + 2 + 6 = 13$, which is not divisible by 3.

13. To find the equivalent decimal, move the decimal two places to the left.

$6\% = 0.06$

The decimal is in the hundredths place, so use 100 as the denominator. Then simplify.

$0.06 = \dfrac{6}{100} = \dfrac{3}{50}$

$6\%$ is equivalent to $\dfrac{3}{50}$ and 0.06.

14. The decimal is in the hundredths place, so use 100 as the denominator. Then simplify.

$1.25 = 1\dfrac{25}{100} = 1\dfrac{1}{4}$

To compare $1\frac{1}{4}$ to $\frac{5}{3}$, write $\frac{5}{3}$ as a decimal. Divide the numerator by the denominator.

$$\begin{array}{r} 1.66... \\ 3\overline{)5.00...} \end{array}$$

$\dfrac{5}{3} = 1.66\overline{6}$

Since $1.25 < 1.666$, $\dfrac{5}{3}$ is greater.

**Saxon** Algebra 1

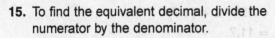

**15.** To find the equivalent decimal, divide the numerator by the denominator.

$$\frac{0.6}{5\overline{)3.0}}$$

To find the equivalent percent, move the decimal two places to the right.

$\frac{3}{5}$ is equivalent to 0.6 and 60%.

**16.** Use the order of operations to simplify the expression.

$$\frac{(3 \cdot 20 + 2 \cdot 20) \cdot 6 - 20}{10^2}$$

$$= \frac{(60 + 40) \cdot 6 - 20}{10^2}$$

$$= \frac{(100) \cdot 6 - 20}{10^2}$$

$$= \frac{(100) \cdot 6 - 20}{100}$$

$$= \frac{600 - 20}{100} = \frac{580}{100} = 5.8$$

The answer is **D**.

**17.** Use the order of operations to simplify the expression.

$$\frac{(45 + 39 + 47 + 40 + 33 + 39 + 41)}{(2 \cdot 2)^2 - 12}$$

$$= \frac{(284)}{(4)^2 - 12}$$

$$= \frac{284}{16 - 12}$$

$$= \frac{284}{4}$$

$$= 71$$

**18.** Evaluate each expression to determine which difference will be negative.

$-4.8 - (-5.2) = -4.8 + (+5.2) = 0.4$

$4.8 - 5.2 = -0.4$

$4.8 - 3.2 = 1.6$

$6.7 - (-7.8) = 6.7 + (+7.8) = 14.5$

The answer is **B**.

**19.** A loss of 15 yards can be written as $(-15)$.

$25 + (-15) = 10$

The team is now on the 10-yard line.

**20.** Use the order of operations to simplify the expression. Subtract from left to right.

$180 - 105.5 - 38.2$

$= (180 - 105.5) - 38.2$

$= 74.5 - 38.2$

$= 36.3$

The measurement of the third angle is 36.3°.

**21.** Write and simplify an expression that represents sixteen degrees fewer than the actual temperature of −5°C.

$-5°C - 16°C = -5°C + (-16°C)$

$\qquad\qquad\quad = -21°C$

It felt like −21°C.

**22.** Writing a check for $149.99 can be written as −$149.99. Depositing $84.50 can be expressed as +$84.50. Write and simplify an expression that represents writing a check for $149.99 and depositing $84.50.

$-\$149.99 + (+\$84.50)$

$= -\$149.99 + \$84.50$

$= -\$65.49$

The net change in Leila's account is −$65.49.

**23.** By definition, an equiangular triangle has three congruent acute angles. A triangle with angle measures of 60°, 60°, and 60° has three congruent acute angles. The answer is **B**.

**24.** Find the level of the lake after the recent rainfall. Write and simplify an expression that represents a level of $5\frac{1}{3}$ feet below normal and then an increase of $3\frac{1}{4}$ feet.

$$-5\frac{1}{3} + 3\frac{1}{4} = -\frac{16}{3} + \frac{13}{4}$$

$$= -\frac{16}{3}\left(\frac{4}{4}\right) + \frac{13}{4}\left(\frac{3}{3}\right)$$

$$= -\frac{64}{12} + \frac{39}{12}$$

$$= -\frac{25}{12} \text{ or } -2\frac{1}{12}$$

After the rainfall, the lake level is at $-2\frac{1}{12}$ feet, which is more than 2 feet below normal. No, the tour boat cannot leave the dock.

**25.** $|-18.5 + 4.75| \le |-18.5| + |4.75|$

$\qquad |-13.75| \le 18.5 + 4.75$

$\qquad\quad 13.75 \le 23.25$

**Saxon** Algebra 1

**26.** Student A is correct. Sample: Student B added 11 floors instead of subtracting.

**27. a.** Write 8 as the product of factors of 2.

$8 = 2 \cdot 2 \cdot 2 = 2^3$

**b.** Write 32 as the product of factors of 2.

$32 = 2 \cdot 2 \cdot 2 \cdot 2 \cdot 2 = 2^5$

**c.** The number of bits in 32 bytes is the product of the number of bits in one byte, $2^3$, and 32 bytes, or $2^5$.

$2^3 \cdot 2^5 = 2^{3+5} = 2^8$

**28. a.** The coefficients are 16, −4, and 21.

**b.** There are four terms in the expression.

**c.** $16c + (-4d) + \dfrac{8\pi}{15} + 21efg$

$= 16c - 4d + \dfrac{8\pi}{15} + 21efg$

Subtracting a number is the same as adding its inverse.

**29.** The number $-9.0909090\overline{909}$ can be written as the quotient of two integers, $-\dfrac{100}{11}$, so it belongs to the set of rational numbers. The answer is **D**.

**30.** Write and simplify an expression that represents the difference between the two depths. A distance below sea level can be expressed as a negative number.

$-11{,}730 \text{ ft} - (-12{,}925 \text{ ft})$

$= -11{,}730 \text{ ft} + (+12{,}925 \text{ ft})$

$= 1195 \text{ ft}$

# LESSON 7

## Warm Up 7

**1.** variable

**2.** $-1.5 + 3^2 - (3 - 5)$

$= -1.5 + 3^2 - (-2)$

$= -1.5 + 9 - (-2)$

$= 7.5 - (-2)$

$= 7.5 + (+2)$

$= 9.5$

**3.** $12 - 4 \cdot 0.5 + (3.4 - 1.7)$

$= 12 - 4 \cdot 0.5 + (1.7)$

$= 12 - 2 + (1.7)$

$= 11.7$

**4.** $\left(\dfrac{2}{3}\right)^2 - \left(\dfrac{1}{3}\right)^2 + \dfrac{5}{6} = \dfrac{4}{9} - \dfrac{1}{9} + \dfrac{5}{6}$

$= \dfrac{4}{9}\left(\dfrac{2}{2}\right) - \dfrac{1}{9}\left(\dfrac{2}{2}\right) + \dfrac{5}{6}\left(\dfrac{3}{3}\right)$

$= \dfrac{8}{18} - \dfrac{2}{18} + \dfrac{15}{18}$

$= \dfrac{21}{18}$

$= \dfrac{7}{6}$ or $1\dfrac{1}{6}$

## Lesson Practice 7

**a.** $12 + |5 - 11|$

$= 12 + |-6|$    Subtract inside absolute-value symbols.

$= 12 + 6$    Simplify the absolute value.

$= 18$    Add.

**b.** $5(8 + 4) \div (15 - 5 - 4)$

$= 5(12) \div (6)$    Simplify inside parentheses.

$= 60 \div 6$    Multiply.

$= 10$    Divide.

**c.** $5 + [6 \cdot (2^3 + 4)]$

$= 5 + [6 \cdot (8 + 4)]$    Evaluate the exponent.

$= 5 + [6 \cdot (12)]$    Add inside the parentheses.

$= 5 + [72]$    Multiply inside the brackets.

$= 77$    Add.

**d.** Sample:

$(1 + 2)^2 \div 6 + \dfrac{8 \cdot 3}{2}$

$= 4 \cdot 3^2 \div 6 + \dfrac{8 \cdot 3}{2}$    Simplify inside parentheses.

$= 4 \cdot 3^2 \div 6 + \dfrac{24}{2}$    Simplify the numerator.

$= 4 \cdot 3^2 \div 6 + 12$    Simplify the fraction

$= 4 \cdot 9 \div 6 + 12$    Simplify the exponent

$= 6 + 12$    Multiply and divide from left to right

$= 18$    Add.

**e.** Simplify each expression. Then compare.

$(13 + 5) - [5 \cdot 2^2]$     $[(7 + 11) - 5] - 2^3$

$= (18) - [5 \cdot 2^2]$     $= [(18) - 5] - 2^3$

$= 18 - [5 \cdot 4]$         $= [13] - 2^3$

$= 18 - 20$            $= 13 - 8$

$= -2$                $= 5$

Since $-2 < 5$,

$(13 + 5) - [5 \cdot 2^2] < [(7 + 11) - 5] - 2^3$.

**f.** Sample: Begin inside the parentheses. Square the height. Next, divide the weight by the new denominator. Then multiply the quotient by 703.

**Practice 7**

**1.** $(5 + 2)^2 - 50 = (7)^2 - 50$

                  $= 49 - 50$

                  $= -1$

**2.** $(3 - 5) + 7^2 = (-2) + 7^2$

                 $= (-2) + 49$

                 $= 47$

**3.** $3\frac{1}{3} - 1\frac{1}{6} - 5\frac{1}{4}$

    $= \frac{10}{3} - \frac{7}{6} - \frac{21}{4}$

    $= \frac{10}{3}\left(\frac{4}{4}\right) - \frac{7}{6}\left(\frac{2}{2}\right) - \frac{21}{4}\left(\frac{3}{3}\right)$

    $= \frac{40}{12} - \frac{14}{12} - \frac{63}{12}$

    $= -\frac{37}{12}$ or $-3\frac{1}{12}$

**4.** $2\frac{1}{3} \cdot 3\frac{1}{4} \cdot 1\frac{1}{2} = \frac{7}{3} \cdot \frac{13}{4} \cdot \frac{3}{2}$

                  $= \frac{273}{24}$

                  $= 11\frac{9}{24}$ or $11\frac{3}{8}$

**5.** $(0.56 + 0.3) \cdot 0.2 = (0.86) \cdot 0.2$

                      $= 0.172$

**6.** $3.25 \cdot 0.4 + 0.1 = 1.3 + 0.1$

                       $= 1.4$

**7.** $1.2 \div 0.1 \div 0.1 = 12 \div 0.1$

                       $= 120$

**8.** $20.2 \cdot 0.1 \cdot 0.1 = 2.02 \cdot 0.1$

                       $= 0.202$

**9.** false; 0 is a whole number but not a counting number.

**10.** The members are the set of whole numbers and the opposites of the natural numbers. The set represents the set of integers.

**11.** false; A triangle can only have one obtuse angle.

**12.** Choose any two factors of 207. Continue to factor until each branch ends in a prime number.

The prime factorization of 207 is $3 \cdot 3 \cdot 23$ or $3^2 \cdot 23$.

**13.** Choose any two factors of 37. Continue to factor until each branch ends in a prime number.

The prime factorization of 37 is $1 \cdot 37$.

**14.** yes; The number formed by the last three digits is divisible by 8.

**15.** The decimal is in the thousandths place, so use 1000 as the denominator. Then simplify.

$0.345 = \frac{345}{1000} = \frac{69}{200}$

To find the equivalent decimal, move the decimal two places to the right.

$0.345 = 34.5\%$.

**16.** To find the equivalent decimal, move the decimal two places to the left.

$0.07\% = 0.0007$

The decimal is in the ten thousandths place, so use 10,000 as the denominator. Then simplify.

$0.0007 = \frac{7}{10,000}$

$0.07\%$ is equivalent to $\frac{7}{10,000}$ and 0.0007.

**17.** $(|-3| \cdot 4) + \left| \left(\frac{1}{2} + \frac{1}{4}\right) \div \frac{1}{3} \right|$

**Saxon** Algebra 1

$= (3 \cdot 4) + \left| \left( \frac{1}{2} \cdot \frac{2}{2} + \frac{1}{4} \right) \div \frac{1}{3} \right|$

$= 12 + \left| \left( \frac{2}{4} + \frac{1}{4} \right) \div \frac{1}{3} \right|$

$= 12 + \left| \left( \frac{3}{4} \right) \div \frac{1}{3} \right|$

$= 12 + \left| \left( \frac{3}{4} \right) \cdot \frac{3}{1} \right|$

$= 12 + \left| \frac{9}{4} \right|$

$= 12 + \frac{9}{4}$

$= 12 + 2\frac{1}{4}$

$= 14\frac{1}{4}$

**18.** Use the order of operations to simplify the two expressions.

$\frac{1}{3} + \frac{1}{5} \cdot \frac{2}{15}$ ⎢ $\left( \frac{1}{3} + \frac{1}{5} \right) \cdot \frac{2}{15}$

$= \frac{1}{3} + \frac{2}{75}$ ⎢ $= \left( \frac{1}{3} \cdot \frac{5}{5} + \frac{1}{5} \cdot \frac{3}{3} \right) \cdot \frac{2}{15}$

$= \frac{1}{3} \cdot \frac{25}{25} + \frac{2}{75}$ ⎢ $= \left( \frac{5}{15} + \frac{3}{15} \right) \cdot \frac{2}{15}$

$= \frac{25}{75} + \frac{2}{75}$ ⎢ $= \left( \frac{8}{15} \right) \cdot \frac{2}{15}$

$= \frac{27}{75}$ or $\frac{81}{225}$ ⎢ $= \frac{16}{225}$

Since $\frac{81}{225} > \frac{16}{225}$,

$\frac{1}{3} + \frac{1}{5} \cdot \frac{2}{15} > \left( \frac{1}{3} + \frac{1}{5} \right) \cdot \frac{2}{15}$

**19.** Sample: The two formulas contain opposite operations.

**20.** Sample: $(2 \cdot 40) + \frac{1}{2}(2\pi \cdot 15)$

$= 80 + 47.1$

$= 127.1$ ft

**21.** $[(10 - 8)^2 - (-1)] + (5 - 3)$

$= [(2)^2 - (-1)] + (2)$

$= [4 - (-1)] + (2)$

$= [4 + (+1)] + (2)$

$= [5] + (2)$

$= 7$

The answer is **B**.

**22. a.** The surface area of Box A is the product of the number of sides, 6, and the area of the base, $12 \cdot 12 = 12^2$.

$6 \cdot 12^2 = 6 \cdot 144 = 864$ inches

**b.** Box B has two sides with dimensions 16 inches by 16 inches, and four sides with dimensions 16 inches by 6.75 inches. The surface area of Box B is the sum of the areas of the two 16-by-16 sides and the areas of the four 16-by-6.75 sides.

$(2 \cdot 16^2) + 4(16 \cdot 6.75)$

$= (2 \cdot 256) + 4(16 \cdot 6.75)$

$= (512) + 4(108)$

$= 512 + 432$

$= 944$ inches

**c.** Since $864 < 944$, Box A uses less material.

**23. a.** First bounce: $25.6 - 12.8 = 12.8$ ft

Second bounce: $12.8 - 6.4 = 6.4$ ft

Third bounce: $6.4 - 3.2 = 3.2$ ft

**b.** no; Sample: The ball is bouncing back up halfway each time.

**24.** $P = 2l + 2w$

$= 2(22.312) + 2(8.42)$

$= 44.624 + 16.84$

$= 61.464$ units

**25.** $|-250| + 78 = 250 + 78 = 328$ ft

**26.** The 11 planes that have taken off can be written as $(-11)$.

$7 + (-11) = -4$

The change in the total number of planes at the airport in the last hour is $-4$ planes.

**27.** Student B; Student A should have subtracted 10.

**28.** A water level of 2 feet below normal can be written as $(-2)$.

$5 - (-2) = 5 + (+2) = 7$ feet

**29.** The constant $\pi$ cannot be written as the quotient of two nonzero numbers, so the term $\frac{3\pi}{8}$ contains an irrational constant. The answer is **B**.

**Saxon** Algebra 1

**30.** Simplify the expression.

$$\frac{180(6-2)°}{6} = \frac{180(4)°}{6} = \frac{720°}{6} = 120°$$

## LESSON 8

### Warm Up 8

1. volume

2. Multiply the numerators and denominators. Then simplify if possible.

$$\frac{7}{12} \cdot \frac{36}{49} = \frac{252}{588}$$

$$= \frac{3}{7}$$

3. Multiply the numerators and denominators. Then simplify if possible.

$$\frac{8}{9} \cdot \frac{15}{36} = \frac{120}{324}$$

$$= \frac{10}{27}$$

4. Multiply the numerators and denominators. Then simplify if possible.

$$\frac{2}{5} \cdot \frac{15}{16} \cdot \frac{6}{7} = \frac{180}{560}$$

$$= \frac{9}{28}$$

5. Multiply the numerators and denominators. Then simplify if possible.

$$\frac{12}{13} \cdot \frac{1}{4} \cdot \frac{39}{48} = \frac{468}{2496}$$

$$= \frac{3}{16}$$

### Lesson Practice 8

**a.** Find a unit ratio and multiply.

$$\frac{35 \text{ mi}}{1 \text{ hour}} = \frac{? \text{ ft}}{1 \text{ hour}} \qquad \text{Identify known and missing information.}$$

$$35 \text{ mi} \rightarrow ? \text{ ft} \qquad \text{Write the conversion.}$$

$$5280 \text{ ft} = 1 \text{ mi} \qquad \text{Equate units.}$$

$$\frac{5280 \text{ ft}}{1 \text{ mi}} \qquad \text{Write a unit ratio.}$$

$$\frac{35 \text{ mi}}{1 \text{ hour}} \cdot \frac{5280 \text{ ft}}{1 \text{ mi}} \qquad \text{Write the multiplication sentence.}$$

$$= \frac{35 \text{ mi}}{1 \text{ hour}} \cdot \frac{5280 \text{ ft}}{1 \text{ mi}} \qquad \text{Cancel out common factors.}$$

$$= \frac{184,800 \text{ ft}}{1 \text{ hour}} \qquad \text{Multiply.}$$

$$\frac{35 \text{ mi}}{1 \text{ hour}} = \frac{184,800 \text{ ft}}{1 \text{ hour}} \qquad \text{Write the ratio of feet per hour.}$$

The Mourning Dove can reach speeds up to 184,800 feet per hour.

**b.** Find the area and convert the unit of measure.

Find the area of the wall.

$$4.5 \text{ yd} \cdot 3.25 \text{ yd} = 14.625 \text{ yd}^2$$

$$14.625 \text{ yd}^2 \rightarrow ? \text{ ft}^2 \qquad \text{Equate units.}$$

$$1 \text{ yd} = 3 \text{ ft} \qquad \text{Write a unit ratio.}$$

$$\frac{3 \text{ ft}}{1 \text{ yd}} \qquad \text{Write the multiplication sentence.}$$

$$14.625 \text{ yd} \cdot \text{yd} \cdot \frac{3 \text{ ft}}{1 \text{ yd}} \cdot \frac{3 \text{ ft}}{1 \text{ yd}} \qquad \text{Cancel out common factors.}$$

$$= 14.625 \text{ yd} \cdot \text{yd} \cdot \frac{3 \text{ ft}}{1 \text{ yd}} \cdot \frac{3 \text{ ft}}{1 \text{ yd}} \qquad \text{Multiply.}$$

$$= \frac{14.625 \cdot 3 \text{ ft} \cdot 3 \text{ ft}}{1}$$

$$= 131.625 \text{ ft}^2$$

The wall is 131.625 ft²

**c.** Convert mm³ to cm³.

$$\frac{46,300 \text{ mm}^3}{1} = \frac{? \text{ cm}^3}{1}$$

Identify known and missing information.

$$1 \text{ cm} = 10 \text{ mm} \qquad \text{Equate units.}$$

$$\frac{1 \text{ cm}}{10 \text{ mm}} \qquad \text{Write a unit ratio.}$$

$$\frac{46,300 \text{ mm} \cdot \text{mm} \cdot \text{mm}}{1} \cdot \frac{1 \text{ cm}}{10^3 \text{ mm}}$$

Write the multiplication sentence.

$$\frac{\overset{46.3}{46,300} \text{ mm} \cdot \text{mm} \cdot \text{mm}}{1} \cdot \frac{1 \text{ cm}}{10^3 \text{ mm}}$$

Cancel out common factors.

$$\frac{46.3 \text{ cm} \cdot \text{cm} \cdot \text{cm}}{1} = \frac{46.3 \text{ cm}^3}{1} \qquad \text{Multiply.}$$

Solutions Key

Since the planter has a volume of 46,300 mm$^3$ = 46.3 cm$^3$ and 46.3 < 50, Della has more than enough potting soil to fill the planter.

**d.** Convert the unit of measure.

16 pounds → ? dollars, Write the conversion.

2.016 dollars = 1 pound, Equate units.

$\dfrac{2.016 \text{ dollars}}{1 \text{ pound}}$, Write a unit ratio.

16 pounds $\cdot \dfrac{2.016 \text{ dollars}}{1 \text{ pound}}$

Write the multiplication sentence.

= 32.256 dollars, Multiply and cancel.

**Practice 8**

**1.** $4\dfrac{1}{3} \div 1\dfrac{1}{3} + 3\dfrac{1}{3} = \dfrac{13}{3} \div \dfrac{4}{3} + \dfrac{10}{3}$

$\qquad = \dfrac{13}{3} \cdot \dfrac{3}{4} + \dfrac{10}{3}$

$\qquad = \dfrac{39}{12} + \dfrac{10}{3}$

$\qquad = \dfrac{39}{12} + \dfrac{10}{3}\left(\dfrac{4}{4}\right)$

$\qquad = \dfrac{39}{12} + \dfrac{40}{12}$

$\qquad = \dfrac{79}{12}$ or $6\dfrac{7}{12}$

**2.** $2\dfrac{3}{8} - 1\dfrac{3}{4} \div 1\dfrac{1}{2} = \dfrac{19}{8} - \dfrac{7}{4} \div \dfrac{3}{2}$

$\qquad = \dfrac{19}{8} - \dfrac{7}{4} \cdot \dfrac{2}{3}$

$\qquad = \dfrac{19}{8} - \dfrac{14}{12}$

$\qquad = \dfrac{19}{8}\left(\dfrac{3}{3}\right) - \dfrac{14}{12}\left(\dfrac{2}{2}\right)$

$\qquad = \dfrac{57}{24} - \dfrac{28}{24}$

$\qquad = \dfrac{29}{24}$ or $1\dfrac{5}{24}$

**3.** $2\dfrac{2}{3} + 1\dfrac{5}{6} - 6\dfrac{3}{4} = \dfrac{8}{3} + \dfrac{11}{6} - \dfrac{27}{4}$

$\qquad = \dfrac{8}{3}\left(\dfrac{4}{4}\right) + \dfrac{11}{6}\left(\dfrac{2}{2}\right) - \dfrac{27}{4}\left(\dfrac{3}{3}\right)$

$\qquad = \dfrac{32}{12} + \dfrac{22}{12} - \dfrac{81}{12}$

$\qquad = \dfrac{-27}{12}$ or $-2\dfrac{1}{4}$

**4.** $3\dfrac{1}{3} \div 1\dfrac{1}{4} \cdot \dfrac{1}{2} = \dfrac{10}{3} \div \dfrac{5}{4} \cdot \dfrac{1}{2}$

$\qquad = \dfrac{10}{3} \cdot \dfrac{4}{5} \cdot \dfrac{1}{2}$

$\qquad = \dfrac{40}{30}$

$\qquad = \dfrac{4}{3}$ or $1\dfrac{1}{3}$

**5.** $0.37 \div 0.2 \cdot 0.1 = 1.85 \cdot 0.1$

$\qquad = 0.185$

**6.** $1.74 \cdot 0.3 \div 0.2 = 0.522 \div 0.2$

$\qquad = 2.61$

**7. a.** $A \cup B$ is the set of all elements that are in $A$ or $B$. The statement is true.

**b.** $A \cap B$ is the set of elements that are in $A$ and $B$. $A$ and $B$ do not have any common elements, so $A \cap B$ should be the empty set. The statement is false.

**c.** $B \cap C$ is the set of all elements that are in $B$ or $C$. It should contain all elements in $B$ and all elements in $C$. The statement is false.

**d.** $A \cap C$ is the set of elements that are in $A$ and $C$. The statement is true.

**8.** Simplify each expression. Then compare.

$8^2 \div 4 - 6^2 \qquad\qquad (6 \cdot 7 \cdot 5) \div 6 - 15$

$= 64 \div 4 - 36 \qquad = (210) \div 6 - 15$

$= 16 - 36 \qquad\qquad = 35 - 15$

$= -20 \qquad\qquad\quad = 20$

Since $-20 < 20$,

$8^2 \div 4 - 6^2 < (6 \cdot 7 \cdot 5) \div 6 - 15$.

**9.** Draw a number line that includes the minimum and maximum values. Use an x to represent each number. Title the graph and the axis.

**Frequency of Numbers**

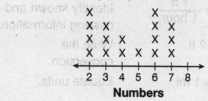

Numbers

**10.** $78\frac{2}{5} - 14\frac{7}{10} = \frac{392}{5} - \frac{147}{10}$

$= \frac{392}{5}\left(\frac{2}{2}\right) - \frac{147}{10}$

$= \frac{784}{10} - \frac{147}{10}$

$= \frac{637}{10}$ or $63\frac{7}{10}$

**11.** Choose any two factors of 484. Continue to factor until each branch ends in a prime number.

The prime factorization of 484 is $2 \cdot 2 \cdot 11 \cdot 11$ or $2^2 \cdot 11^2$.

**12.** no; The ones digit is not a 0 or a 5.

**13.** To find the equivalent decimal, move the decimal two places to the left.

$125\% = 1.25$

The decimal is in the hundredths place, so use 100 as the denominator. Then simplify.

$1.25 = 1\frac{25}{100} = 1\frac{1}{4}$

$125\%$ is equivalent to $1\frac{1}{4}$ and 1.25.

**14.** Find a unit ratio and multiply.

$\frac{105 \text{ km}}{1 \text{ hour}} = \frac{? \text{ km}}{1 \text{ min}}$  Identify known and missing information.

$1 \text{ hour} = 60 \text{ min}$  Equate units.

$\frac{1 \text{ hour}}{60 \text{ min}}$  Write a unit ratio.

$\frac{105 \text{ km}}{1 \text{ hour}} \cdot \frac{1 \text{ hour}}{60 \text{ min}}$  Write the multiplication sentence.

$\frac{\overset{7}{105} \text{ km}}{1 \text{ hour}} \cdot \frac{1 \text{ hour}}{\underset{4}{60} \text{ min}}$  Cancel out common factors.

$= \frac{7 \text{ km}}{4 \text{ min}}$  Multiply.

$\frac{105 \text{ km}}{1 \text{ hour}} = \frac{7 \text{ km}}{4 \text{ min}}$  Write the ratio of feet per hour.

$\frac{105 \text{ km}}{1 \text{ hour}}$ is equivalent to 1.75 km per minute.

**15.** Convert 74 m² to cm².

$\frac{74 \text{ m}^2}{1} = \frac{? \text{ cm}^2}{1}$  Identify known and missing information.

$100 \text{ cm} = 1 \text{ m}$  Equate units.

$\frac{100 \text{ cm}}{1 \text{ m}}$  Write a unit ratio.

$\frac{74 \text{ m} \cdot \text{m}}{1} \cdot \frac{100 \text{ cm}}{1 \text{ m}} \cdot \frac{100 \text{ cm}}{1 \text{ m}}$,
Write the multiplication sentence.

$= \frac{74 \text{ m} \cdot \text{m}}{1} \cdot \frac{100 \text{ cm}}{1 \text{ m}} \cdot \frac{100 \text{ cm}}{1 \text{ m}}$,

Cancel out common factors.

$= \frac{74 \cdot 100 \text{ cm} \cdot 100 \text{ cm}}{1}$  Multiply.

$= 740,000 \text{ cm}^2$

square meters is equivalent to 740,000 square centimeters.

**16.** Convert 72,576 in³ to ft³.

$\frac{72,576 \text{ in}^3}{1} = \frac{? \text{ ft}^3}{1}$, Identify known and missing information.

$1 \text{ ft} = 12 \text{ in}$  Equate units.

$\frac{1 \text{ ft}}{12 \text{ in.}}$  Write a unit ratio.

$\frac{72,576 \text{ in}^3}{1} \cdot \frac{1 \text{ ft}}{12 \text{ in.}} \cdot \frac{1 \text{ ft}}{12 \text{ in.}} \cdot \frac{1 \text{ ft}}{12 \text{ in.}}$,

Write the multiplication sentence.

$\frac{\overset{42}{72,576} \text{ in}^3}{1} \cdot \frac{1 \text{ ft}}{\underset{1}{12} \text{ in.}} \cdot \frac{1 \text{ ft}}{\underset{1}{12} \text{ in.}} \cdot \frac{1 \text{ ft}}{\underset{1}{12} \text{ in.}}$,

Cancel out common factors.

$= \frac{42 \text{ ft} \cdot \text{ft} \cdot \text{ft}}{1}$  Multiply.

$= 42 \text{ ft}^3$

72,576 cubic inches is equivalent to 42 cubic feet.

**17.** Evaluate each expression to determine which difference will be negative.

$-\frac{1}{2} - \frac{1}{8} = -\frac{1}{2}\left(\frac{4}{4}\right) + \left(-\frac{1}{8}\right) = -\frac{4}{8} + \left(-\frac{1}{8}\right)$

$= -\frac{5}{8}$

$\frac{9}{12} - 1 = \frac{9}{12} - \frac{12}{12} = \frac{-3}{12} = -\frac{1}{4}$

$\frac{5}{7} - \frac{3}{10} = \frac{5}{7}\left(\frac{10}{10}\right) - \frac{3}{10}\left(\frac{7}{7}\right) = \frac{50}{70} - \frac{21}{70} = \frac{29}{70}$

**Saxon** Algebra 1

Solutions Key

$-\frac{14}{15} - \left(\frac{14}{15}\right) = -\frac{14}{15} + \left(-\frac{14}{15}\right) = -\frac{28}{15}$

$= -1\frac{13}{15}$

The answer is **C**.

**18.** Student A; Sample: Student B incorrectly wrote the unit ratio, multiplying by 10 to cancel the units instead of dividing by 10.

**19.** The ratio $\frac{1 \text{ in.}}{2.54 \text{ cm}}$ has centimeters in the denominator, so it will convert 120 cm to an equivalent measure in inches. The answer is **B**.

**20. a.** The speed of the recorded wind gust is the product of the number of kilometers per hour in one knot, 1.852, and the number of knots of the wind gust, 38.

$\frac{38 \text{ knots}}{1} \cdot \frac{1.852 \text{ km/hr}}{1 \text{ knot}}$

$= 70.376 \text{ km/hr}$

**b.** Convert 70.376 km/hr to mph.

$\frac{70.376 \text{ km}}{1 \text{ hr}} \cdot \frac{1 \text{ mi}}{1.609 \text{ km}} \approx 43.74 \text{ mi/hr}$

**21. a.** By definition, the area of a triangle is the product of half the base and the height.

$A = \frac{1}{2}(b \text{ ft}) \cdot (h \text{ ft})$

$= \frac{1}{2}b \cdot h \text{ ft}^2$

**b.** Sample: $A = \frac{1}{2}b \cdot h \cdot \frac{12}{1} \cdot \frac{12}{1} \text{ in}^2$

**c.** Use $b = 3$ and $h = 2.2$ in the formula

$A = \frac{1}{2}b \cdot h \cdot \frac{12}{1} \cdot \frac{12}{1} \text{ in}^2.$

$A = \frac{1}{2}b \cdot h \cdot \frac{12}{1} \cdot \frac{12}{1}$

$= \frac{1}{2}(3)(2.2) \cdot \frac{12}{1} \cdot \frac{12}{1}$

$= 475.2 \text{ in}^2$

**22.** Convert 1 gram per cubic centimeter to grams per cubic inch.

$\frac{1 \text{ g}}{1 \text{ cm}^3} = \frac{? \text{ g}}{1 \text{ in}^3}$, Identify known and missing information.

1 in. = 2.54 cm   Equate units.

$\frac{2.54 \text{ cm}}{1 \text{ in.}}$   Write a unit ratio.

$\frac{1 \text{ g}}{1 \text{ cm}^3} \cdot \frac{2.54 \text{ cm}}{1 \text{ in.}} \cdot \frac{2.54 \text{ cm}}{1 \text{ in.}} \cdot \frac{2.54 \text{ cm}}{1 \text{ in.}},$

Write the multiplication sentence.

$= \frac{1 \text{ g}}{1 \text{ cm}^3} \cdot \frac{2.54 \text{ cm}}{1 \text{ in.}} \cdot \frac{2.54 \text{ cm}}{1 \text{ in.}} \cdot \frac{2.54 \text{ cm}}{1 \text{ in.}},$

Cancel out common factors.

$= \frac{1 \text{ g} \cdot 2.54 \cdot 2.54 \cdot 2.54}{1 \text{ in.} \cdot 1 \text{ in.} \cdot 1 \text{ in.}}$   Multiply.

$= \frac{16.39 \text{ g}}{1 \text{ in}^3}$

The density of water is approximately equivalent to 16.39 grams per cubic inch.

**23.** false; A right triangle contains one right angle and two acute angles.

**24.** Student A; Student B needed to simplify inside the parentheses first.

**25. a.** Use $s = 8$ in. and $h = 12$ in. in the formula $V = \frac{1}{3}s^2 h$.

$V = \frac{1}{3}s^2 h$

$= \frac{1}{3}(8 \text{ in.})^2 (12 \text{ in.})$

$= \frac{1}{3}(64 \text{ in}^2)(12 \text{ in.})$

$= 256 \text{ in}^3$

**b.** Sample: I simplified the $s^2$ first, because the order of operations tells us to simplify exponents before multiplying or adding.

**26.** A loss can be written as a negative number.

$6 million + (−$3.5 million)

$+ (−$2 million) + $5 million

$= $5.5 million

ABC Company had a total profit of 5.5 million.

**27.** Find the difference between each group's measurement and the actual length.

Error for Group A: $\left|56\frac{3}{4} - 57\frac{1}{2}\right|$

$= \left|\frac{227}{4} - \frac{115}{2}\right|$

$= \left|\frac{227}{4} - \frac{115}{2}\left(\frac{2}{2}\right)\right|$

$= \left|\frac{227}{4} - \frac{230}{4}\right|$

**Saxon** Algebra 1

$$= \left| -\frac{3}{4} \right|$$

$$= \frac{3}{4} \text{ in.}$$

Error for Group B: $\left| 57\frac{3}{4} - 57\frac{1}{2} \right|$

$$= \left| \frac{231}{4} - \frac{115}{2} \right|$$

$$= \left| \frac{231}{4} - \frac{115}{2}\left(\frac{2}{2}\right) \right|$$

$$= \left| \frac{231}{4} - \frac{230}{4} \right|$$

$$= \left| \frac{1}{4} \right|$$

$$= \frac{1}{4} \text{ in.}$$

Since $\frac{3}{4} > \frac{1}{2}$, Group B's measurement had the smaller error.

28. Student A; Sample: Student B incorrectly used $b$ as $b°$ and $c$ as $c°$.

29. Find a unit ratio and multiply.

| | |
|---|---|
| $\dfrac{32 \text{ mi}}{1 \text{ hour}} = \dfrac{? \text{ ft}}{1 \text{ hour}}$ | Identify known and missing information. |
| $32 \text{ mi} \rightarrow ? \text{ ft}$ | Write the conversion. |
| $5280 \text{ ft} = 1 \text{ mi}$ | Equate units. |
| $\dfrac{5280 \text{ ft}}{1 \text{ mi}}$ | Write unit ratio. |
| $\dfrac{32 \text{ mi}}{1 \text{ hour}} \cdot \dfrac{5280 \text{ ft}}{1 \text{ mi}}$ | Write the multiplication sentence. |
| $= \dfrac{32 \text{ mi}}{1 \text{ hour}} \cdot \dfrac{5280 \text{ ft}}{1 \text{ mi}}$ | Cancel out common factors. |
| $= \dfrac{168,960 \text{ ft}}{1 \text{ hour}}$ | Multiply |
| $\dfrac{32 \text{ mi}}{1 \text{ hour}} = \dfrac{168,960 \text{ ft}}{1 \text{ hour}}$ | Write the ratio of feet per hour. |

A giraffe can run 168,960 feet per hour.

30. a. The area of the square photograph is the square of the length of a side.

Area $= (8 \text{ in.})^2 = 64 \text{ in}^2$

b. The area of the photograph and frame is the square of the length of a side. The length of a side is the sum of the length

of the photograph, one side of the frame, and the opposite side of the frame.

Area $= (8 \text{ in.} + 1 \text{ in.} + 1 \text{ in.})^2$
$= (10 \text{ in.})^2$
$= 100 \text{ in}^2$

c. The area of the frame alone is the difference between the photograph with the frame and the area of the photograph.

Area $= 100 \text{ in}^2 - 64 \text{ in}^2 = 36 \text{ in}^2$

d. The area of the photograph and a 2-inch-wide frame is the square of the sum of the length of the photograph, one side of the frame, and the opposite side of the frame.

Area $= (8 \text{ in.} + 2 \text{ in.} + 2 \text{ in.})^2$
$= (12 \text{ in.})^2$
$= 144 \text{ in}^2$

The photograph in the larger frame will need $(144 \text{ in}^2 - 100 \text{ in}^2) = 44 \text{ in}^2$ more space.

## LESSON 9

### Warm Up 9

1. quotient

2. $x^5 b^2 \cdot 3b^3 x = 3 \cdot x^5 \cdot x \cdot b^2 \cdot b^3$
$= 3x^{5+1}b^{2+3}$
$= 3x^6 b^5$

3. $\dfrac{4^3}{2^3} + 7^2 = \dfrac{64}{8} + 49 = 8 + 49 = 57$

4. $\dfrac{5^3}{3^2 + 4^2} = \dfrac{125}{9 + 16} = \dfrac{125}{25} = 5$

5. $32 \div [2 \cdot (8 - 7)] = 32 \div [2 \cdot (1)]$
$= 32 \div [2]$
$= 16$

### Lesson Practice 9

a. Substitute 10 for $x$ and 2 for $b$ in the expression. Then simplify.

$3x - 4b + 2bx$
$= 3 \cdot 10 - 4 \cdot 2 + 2 \cdot 2 \cdot 10$
$= 30 - 8 + 40$
$= 62$

**b.** Substitute −1 for $a$ and 8 for $b$ in the expression. Then simplify.

$$2ab - 4a^2 + 10$$
$$= 2 \cdot (-1) \cdot 8 - 4 \cdot (-1)^2 + 10$$
$$= 2 \cdot (-1) \cdot 8 - 4(1) + 10$$
$$= -16 - 4 + 10$$
$$= -10$$

**c.** Simplify the expression on the left and then compare.

$$(6x^2 + y^3) - 3x^6 \qquad 8x^4 - y^3$$
$$(6 \cdot 2^2 + 5^3) - 3 \cdot 2^6 \qquad 8 \cdot 2^4 - 5^3$$
$$= (6 \cdot 4 + 125) - 3 \cdot 64 \quad = 8 \cdot 16 - 125$$
$$= (24 + 125) - 192 \qquad = 128 - 115$$
$$= (149) - 192 \qquad = 3$$
$$= -43$$

Since −43 < 3,
$$(6x^2 + y^3) - 3x^6 < 8x^4 - y^3$$
when $x = 2$ and $y = 5$.

**d.** Substitute −89.4 for $C$ in the expression and simplify.

$$\frac{9}{5}C + 32$$

$$= \frac{9}{5}(-89.4) + 32$$

$$= -160.92 + 32$$

$$= -128.92$$

The lowest recorded temperature is −128.92°F

**Practice 9**

**1.** $4\frac{1}{3} \div 2\frac{1}{3} = \frac{13}{3} \div \frac{7}{3}$

$$= \frac{13}{3} \cdot \frac{3}{7}$$

$$= \frac{39}{21}$$

$$= \frac{13}{7} \text{ or } 1\frac{6}{7}$$

**2.** $42\frac{3}{8} - 21\frac{3}{4} = \frac{339}{8} - \frac{87}{4}$

$$= \frac{339}{8} - \frac{87}{4}\left(\frac{2}{2}\right)$$

$$= \frac{339}{8} - \frac{174}{8}$$

$$= \frac{165}{8} \text{ or } 20\frac{5}{8}$$

**3.** $1\frac{2}{3} + 2\frac{5}{6} = \frac{5}{3} + \frac{17}{6}$

$$= \frac{5}{3}\left(\frac{2}{2}\right) + \frac{17}{6}$$

$$= \frac{10}{6} + \frac{17}{6}$$

$$= \frac{27}{6} \text{ or } 4\frac{1}{2}$$

**4.** $2\frac{2}{3} \div 1\frac{3}{4} = \frac{8}{3} \div \frac{7}{4}$

$$= \frac{8}{3} \cdot \frac{4}{7}$$

$$= \frac{32}{21} \text{ or } 1\frac{11}{21}$$

**5.** $0.75 \div 0.2$

$$\begin{array}{r} 3.75 \\ 2)\overline{7.50} \end{array}$$ Multiply the divisor and dividend by 10 so the divisor is a natural number.

**6.** $1.74 \div 0.3$

$$\begin{array}{r} 5.8 \\ 3)\overline{17.4} \end{array}$$ Multiply the divisor and dividend by 10 so the divisor is a natural number.

**7.** $\begin{array}{r} 1.25 \\ \times\ 0.2 \\ \hline 0.25 \end{array}$ Write the problem vertically. Since the factors have a total of 3 decimal places, there should be 3 decimal places in the product.

**8.** $\begin{array}{r} 12.2 \\ \times\ 3.2 \\ \hline 39.04 \end{array}$ Write the problem vertically. Since the factors have a total of 2 decimal places, there should be 2 decimal places in the product.

**9.** true; A square has 2 pairs of parallel sides and its sides are congruent.

**10.** $4[(6 - 4)^3 - 5] = 4[(2)^3 - 5]$
$$= 4[8 - 5]$$
$$= 4[3]$$
$$= 12$$

**11.** Convert 1.86 km² to m².
$$\frac{1.86 \text{ km}^2}{1} = \frac{? \text{ m}^2}{1}$$

Identify known and missing information.

1000 m = 1 km, Equate units.

$\dfrac{1000 \text{ m}}{1 \text{ km}}$, Write a unit ratio.

$\dfrac{1.86 \text{ km} \cdot \text{km}}{1} \cdot \dfrac{1000 \text{ m}}{1 \text{ km}} \cdot \dfrac{1000 \text{ m}}{1 \text{ km}}$,

Write the multiplication sentence.

$= \dfrac{1.86 \ \cancel{\text{km}} \cdot \cancel{\text{km}}}{1} \cdot \dfrac{1000 \text{ m}}{1 \ \cancel{\text{km}}} \cdot \dfrac{1000 \text{ m}}{1 \ \cancel{\text{km}}}$,

Cancel out common factors.

$= \dfrac{1.86 \cdot 1000 \text{ m} \cdot 1000 \text{ m}}{1}$, Multiply.

$= 1{,}860{,}000 \text{ m}^2$

$1.86 \text{ km}^2$ is equivalent to $1{,}860{,}000 \text{ m}^3$.

**12.** Substitute 4 for $c$ and 5 for $d$ in the expression. Then simplify.

$14c + 28 - 12cd$
$= 14 \cdot 4 + 28 - 12 \cdot 4 \cdot 5$
$= 56 + 28 - 240$
$= -156$

**13.** By definition, a straight angle measures exactly 180°.

**14.** Choose any two factors of 125. Continue to factor until each branch ends in a prime number.

$$125$$

The prime factorization of 125 is $5 \cdot 5 \cdot 5$ or $5^3$.

**15.** Substitute 72 for $t$ and 1 for $l$ in the expression. Then simplify.

$\dfrac{t - 36}{36} + l$

$= \dfrac{72 - 36}{36} + 1$

$= \dfrac{36}{36} + 1$

$= 1 + 1$

$= 2$

**16.** $14 + \dfrac{36}{9} \cdot (2 + 5)$

$= 14 + \dfrac{36}{9} \cdot (7)$

$= 14 + (4) \cdot (7)$

$= 14 + 28$

$= 42$

The answer is **C**.

**17.** $(3 + 12) + (|-4| - 2)^3 + 1$

$= (3 + 12) + (4 - 2)^3 + 1$

$= (15) + (2)^3 + 1$

$= (15) + 8 + 1$

$= 24$

**18. a.** Substitute 1 for $t$ in the expression and simplify.

$112 - 32t = 112 - 32 \cdot 1$
$= 112 - 32$
$= 80$

The rocket's speed after 1 second is 80 ft/sec.

**b.** Substitute 2 for $t$ in the expression and simplify.

$112 - 32t = 112 - 32 \cdot 2$
$= 112 - 64$
$= 48$

The rocket's speed after 1 second is 48 ft/sec.

**19.** Substitute 3 for $h$ in the expression and simplify.

$\$6.50 + \$1.75(3) = \$6.50 + \$5.25$
$= \$11.75$

**20.** Student B; Sample: Student A made an error in evaluating the negative number raised to a power.

**21.** Substitute 30 for $s$ and 12 for $n$ in the expression. Then simplify.

$\dfrac{s}{n} = \dfrac{30}{12} = 2.5$

**22.** Substitute 80 for $s$ and 53 for $a$ in the expression. Then simplify.

$80 + 0.5 \cdot 53 = 80 + 26.5 = 106.5$

The total-blocks statistic for the player is 106.5 total blocks.

**23.** no; The number is divisible by 2, but not divisible by 3.

**24.** To find the equivalent decimal, move the decimal two places to the left.

$35.2\% = 0.352$

The decimal is in the thousandths place, so use 1000 as the denominator. Then simplify.

$0.352 = \dfrac{352}{1000} = \dfrac{44}{125}$

3.52% is equivalent to $\dfrac{44}{125}$ and 0.352.

**25. a.** The area of the triangle is the product of its length and its width.

Area $= (88\text{ cm})(24\text{ cm})$
$= 2112\text{ cm}^2$

**b.** Convert 2112 cm² to mm².

$\dfrac{2112\text{ cm}^2}{1} = \dfrac{?\text{ mm}^2}{1}$,

Identify known and missing information.

10 mm = 1 cm,   Equate units.

$\dfrac{10\text{ mm}}{1\text{ cm}}$,   Write a unit ratio.

$\dfrac{2112\text{ cm}\cdot\text{cm}}{1}\cdot\dfrac{10\text{ mm}}{1\text{ cm}}\cdot\dfrac{10\text{ mm}}{1\text{ cm}}$,

Write the multiplication sentence.

$= \dfrac{2112\ \cancel{\text{cm}}\cdot\cancel{\text{cm}}}{1}\cdot\dfrac{10\text{ mm}}{1\ \cancel{\text{cm}}}\cdot\dfrac{10\text{ mm}}{1\ \cancel{\text{cm}}}$,

Cancel out common factors.

$= \dfrac{2112\cdot 10\text{ mm}\cdot 10\text{ mm}}{1}$, Multiply.

$= 211{,}200\text{ mm}^2$

2112 cm² is equivalent to 211,200 mm².

**c.** Write and simplify a ratio that compares the area in square centimeters to the area in square millimeters.

$\dfrac{\text{area in square centimeters}}{\text{area in square millimeters}} = \dfrac{2112}{211{,}200} = \dfrac{1}{100}$

**26.** Find the volume of the cylinder in square millimeters.

$V = \pi r^2 h$
$= \pi\cdot(56\text{ mm})^2\cdot(128\text{ mm})$
$= \pi\cdot(3136\text{ mm}^2)\cdot(128\text{ mm})$
$\approx 3.14\cdot(3136\text{ mm}^2)\cdot(128\text{ mm})$
$= 1{,}260{,}421.12\text{ mm}^3$

Convert 1,260,421.12 mm³ to cm³.

$\dfrac{1{,}260{,}421.12\text{ mm}^3}{1} = \dfrac{?\text{ cm}^3}{1}$,

Identify known and missing information.

10 mm = 1 cm,   Equate units.

$\dfrac{1\text{ cm}}{10\text{ cm}}$,   Write a unit ratio.

$\dfrac{1{,}260{,}421.12\text{ mm}^3}{1}\cdot\dfrac{1\text{ cm}}{10\text{ mm}^3}$,

Write the multiplication sentence.

$\dfrac{1{,}260{,}421.12\ \cancel{\text{mm}^3}}{1}\cdot\dfrac{1\text{ cm}}{10\ \cancel{\text{mm}^3}}$

Cancel out common factors.

$= \dfrac{1{,}260{,}421.12\text{ cm}\cdot\text{cm}\cdot\text{cm}}{10\cdot 10\cdot 10}$, Multiply.

$= 1260.42\text{ cm}^3$

1,260,421.12 mm³ is equivalent to 1260.42 cm³.

**27.** Divide $n$ by 12.

**28.** Write and simplify an expression for the difference between his final scores for the two tournaments.

$\big|[1 + (-2) + (-3) + 2]$
$\quad - [(-2) + (-1) + 1 + (-1)]\big|$

$= \big|[-2] - [-3]\big|$
$= \big|[-2] + [+3]\big|$
$= |1|$
$= 1$

**29.** Student A; Sample: Student B did not follow the order of operations and did not work inside the parentheses first.

**30.** Substitute 15 for $m$ in the expression. Then simplify.

$35m = 35\cdot 15 = 525$ words

# LESSON 10

## Warm Up 10

**1.** irrational

**2.** $(25 \div 5) - (30 \div 10) = (5) - (3) = 2$

**3.** $-4 + (-9) + (-6) = -(4 + 9 + 6) = -19$

Saxon Algebra 1

**4.** $(2.45 + 5.75) - (4.85 - 3.75)$

$= 8.2 - 1.1$

$= 7.1$

**5.** $(j^4k^5)(4kj^2)(3k^3)$

$= 4 \cdot 3 \cdot j^4 \cdot j^2 \cdot k^5 \cdot k \cdot k^3$

$= 12j^{4+2}k^{5+1+3}$

$= 12j^6k^9$

**Lesson Practice 10**

**a.** $\dfrac{4}{9} + \dfrac{2}{9} - \dfrac{5}{9}$

$= \dfrac{4}{9} + \dfrac{2}{9} + \left(-\dfrac{5}{9}\right)$    Write the problem as addition.

$= \dfrac{6}{9} + \left(-\dfrac{5}{9}\right)$    Add numbers with like signs.

$= \dfrac{1}{9}$    Add.

**b.** $16.21 - 21.54 + 12.72$

$= 16.21 + (-21.54) + 12.72,$
Write the problem as addition.

$= 16.21 + 12.72 + (-21.54),$
Group the terms with like signs.

$= 28.93 + (-21.54)$    Add numbers with like signs.

$= 7.39$    Add.

**c.** Convert the fractions to decimals.

$\dfrac{3}{4} = 0.75$

$\dfrac{5}{8} = 0.625$

Now order numbers from least to greatest.

$-1, 0.625, 0.75, 0.85$

$-1, \dfrac{5}{8}, \dfrac{3}{4}, 0.85$

**d.** Simplify each expression. Then compare.

$3.2 + (-2.8) - 5.2$

$= 3.2 + (-2.8) + (-5.2)$

$= 3.2 + (-8)$

$= -4.8$

$\dfrac{7}{12} - \dfrac{5}{12} + \left(-\dfrac{11}{12}\right)$

$= \dfrac{7}{12} + \left(-\dfrac{5}{12}\right) + \left(-\dfrac{11}{12}\right)$

$= \dfrac{7}{12} + \left(-\dfrac{16}{12}\right)$

$= -\dfrac{9}{12}$

$= -\dfrac{3}{4}$

Since $-4.8 < -\dfrac{3}{4}$,

$3.2 + (-2.8) - 5.2 < \dfrac{7}{12} - \dfrac{5}{12} + \left(-\dfrac{11}{12}\right).$

**e.** Gayle finished the race 3.01 seconds after Jonah, who completed the race in 32.68 seconds. Write and simplify an expression to find Gayle's time.

$3.01 + 32.68 = 35.69$

It took Gayle 35.69 seconds to run the race.

**Practice 10**

**1.** $\dfrac{1}{2} + \dfrac{3}{5} = \dfrac{1}{2}\left(\dfrac{5}{5}\right) + \dfrac{3}{5}\left(\dfrac{2}{2}\right)$

$= \dfrac{5}{10} + \dfrac{6}{10}$

$= \dfrac{11}{10}$ or $1\dfrac{1}{10}$

**2.** $15\dfrac{1}{3} - 7\dfrac{4}{5} = \dfrac{46}{3} - \dfrac{39}{5}$

$= \dfrac{46}{3}\left(\dfrac{5}{5}\right) - \dfrac{39}{5}\left(\dfrac{3}{3}\right)$

$= \dfrac{230}{15} - \dfrac{117}{15}$

$= \dfrac{113}{15}$ or $7\dfrac{8}{15}$

**3.** $3\dfrac{2}{3} \cdot 2\dfrac{1}{4} = \dfrac{11}{3} \cdot \dfrac{9}{4} = \dfrac{99}{12}$

$= \dfrac{33}{4}$ or $8\dfrac{1}{4}$

**4.** $3\dfrac{2}{5} \div 1\dfrac{2}{3} = \dfrac{17}{5} \div \dfrac{5}{3}$

$= \dfrac{17}{5} \cdot \dfrac{3}{5}$

$$= \frac{51}{25} \text{ or } 2\frac{1}{25}$$

**5.** $78\frac{2}{5} - 14\frac{7}{10} = \frac{392}{5} - \frac{147}{10}$

$$= \frac{392}{5}\left(\frac{2}{2}\right) - \frac{147}{10}$$

$$= \frac{784}{10} - \frac{147}{10}$$

$$= \frac{637}{10} \text{ or } 63\frac{7}{10}$$

**6.** $2\frac{1}{3} \cdot 1\frac{1}{4} = \frac{7}{3} \cdot \frac{5}{4}$

$$= \frac{35}{12} \text{ or } 2\frac{11}{12}$$

**7.** 10.2    Write the problem vertically.
$\underline{\times\ 3.15}$
32.130    Since the factors have a total of
          3 decimal places, there should be
          3 decimal places in the product.

**8.** 20.46 ÷ 2.2

         9.3    Multiply the divisor and dividend
22)204.6    by 10 so the divisor is a natural
            number.

**9.** 12.3    Write the problem vertically.
$\underline{\times\ 2.02}$
24.846    Since the factors have a total of
          3 decimal places, there should be 3
          decimal places in the product.

**10.** 0.8 ÷ 0.25

         3.2    Multiply the divisor and dividend
25)80.0    by 100 so the divisor is a natural
           number.

**11.** Write the fractions with a common
denominator of $3 \cdot 5 \cdot 7 = 105$ and
compare.

$$\frac{6}{7}\left(\frac{15}{15}\right) = \frac{90}{105}$$

$$\frac{3}{5}\left(\frac{21}{21}\right) = \frac{63}{105}$$

$$\frac{1}{7}\left(\frac{15}{15}\right) = \frac{15}{105}$$

$$-\frac{4}{3}\left(\frac{35}{35}\right) = -\frac{140}{105}$$

Since $-\frac{140}{105} < \frac{15}{105} < \frac{63}{105} < \frac{90}{105}$, the order
from greatest to least is $\frac{6}{7}, \frac{3}{5}, \frac{1}{7}, -\frac{4}{3}$.

**12.** By definition, an acute angle measures less
than 90°.

**13.** Convert 8673 g to kg.

$$\frac{8673 \text{ g}}{1} = \frac{? \text{ kg}}{1},$$

identify known and missing information.
1000 g = 1 kg,          Equate units.

$$\frac{1 \text{ kg}}{1000 \text{ g}}$$          Write a unit ratio.

$$\frac{8673 \text{ g}}{1} \cdot \frac{1 \text{ kg}}{1000 \text{ g}}$$    Write the multiplication
                          sentence.

$$= \frac{8673 \cancel{g}}{1} \cdot \frac{1 \text{ kg}}{\underset{1}{\cancel{1000 \text{ g}}}}$$    Cancel out common
                                       factors.

$$\frac{8.673 \cdot 1 \text{ kg}}{1}$$          Multiply.

$$= 8.673 \text{ kg}$$

8673 g is equivalent to 8.673 kg.

**14.** Convert 26 mi to km.

$$\frac{26 \text{ mi}}{1} = \frac{? \text{ km}}{1},$$

Identify known and missing information.
1.609 km = 1 mi,          Equate units.

$$\frac{1.609 \text{ km}}{1 \text{ mi}}$$          Write a unit ratio.

$$\frac{26 \text{ mi}}{1} \cdot \frac{1.609 \text{ km}}{1 \text{ mi}}$$    Write the
                          multiplication
                          sentence.

$$= \frac{26 \cancel{\text{mi}}}{1} \cdot \frac{1.609 \text{ km}}{1 \cancel{\text{mi}}}$$    Cancel out common
                                      factors.

$$\frac{26 \cdot 1.609 \text{ km}}{1}$$          Multiply.

41.834 km

To the nearest tenth, 26 mi is equivalent to
41.8 km.

**15.** Simplify each expression. Then compare.

| $(2+5)-(3\cdot4)$ | $2+5-3\cdot4$ |
|---|---|
| $=(7)-(12)$ | $=2+5-12$ |
| $=(7)+(-12)$ | $=7-12$ |
| $=-5$ | $=-5$ |

The value of each expression is −5. The statement is true.

**16.** $1.29 + 3.9 − 4.2 − 9.99 + 6.1$

$= 1.29 + 3.9 + (−4.2) + (−9.99) + 6.1$

$= 1.29 + 3.9 + 6.1 + (−4.2) + (−9.99)$

$= 11.29 + (−14.19)$

$= −2.9$

The answer is **A**.

**17.** Student A; Sample: Student B did not complete the operations in parentheses first.

**18.** Find the difference between the two lengths of time.

$\left| 2\frac{1}{4} − 1\frac{1}{3} \right| = \left| \frac{9}{4} − \frac{4}{3} \right|$

$= \left| \frac{9}{4}\left(\frac{3}{3}\right) − \frac{4}{3}\left(\frac{4}{4}\right) \right|$

$= \left| \frac{27}{12} − \frac{16}{12} \right|$

$= \left| \frac{11}{12} \right|$

$= \frac{11}{12}$ hour or 55 minutes

**19.** Draw a number line that includes the minimum and maximum values. Use an x to represent each number. Title the graph and the axis.

**Frequency of Numbers**

```
        X       X
  X     X  X    X
  X  X  X  X  X X
  X  X  X  X  X X
+--+--+--+--+--+--+--+
  9 10 11 12 13 14 15
```

**Numbers**

**20. a.** Sample: $1000b$

**b.** Substitute 0.04 for $b$ in the expression $1000b$ and simplify.

$1000b = 1000 \cdot 0.4 = 400$

The actual length of the block is 400 feet.

**21.** The area of a parallelogram is the product of its base length and its height.

Area $= z \cdot 2z = 2z^{1+1} = 2z^2$

Substitute 12 cm for $z$ in the expression $2z^2$ and simplify.

Area $= 2z^2$

$= 2(12 \text{ cm})^2$

$= 2(144 \text{ cm}^2)$

$= 288 \text{ cm}^2$

**22.** Student B; Sample: Student A only multiplied by the unit ratio once instead of twice.

**23.** Convert +4.5 mm to inches.

$\frac{+4.5 \text{ mm}}{1} = \frac{? \text{ in.}}{1}$,

Identify known and missing information.

$25.4 \text{ mm} = 1 \text{ in},$  Equate units.

$\frac{1 \text{ in.}}{25.4 \text{ mm}},$  Write a unit ratio.

$\frac{+4.5 \text{ mm}}{1} \cdot \frac{1 \text{ in.}}{25.4 \text{ mm}},$  Write the multiplication sentence.

$= \frac{+4.5 \cancel{\text{ mm}}}{1} \cdot \frac{1 \text{ in.}}{25.4 \cancel{\text{ mm}}},$  Cancel out common factors.

$= \frac{+4.5 \cdot 1 \text{ in.}}{25.4},$  Multiply

$\approx 0.177 \text{ in.}$

To the nearest thousandth, +4.5 mm of mercury is equivalent to +0.177 inches of mercury.

**24. a.** The area of the buildings is the sum of the area of the rectangular building and the area of the circular building. Substitute 9 yards for $l$ and 6 yards for $w$ in the formula for the area of a rectangle, $A = l \cdot w$. Substitute 4 inches for $d$ in the formula for the area of a circle, $A = \pi\left(\frac{d}{2}\right)^2$.

Area $= l \cdot w + \pi r^2$

$= 9 \cdot 6 + \pi\left(\frac{4}{2}\right)^2$

**b.** The area on the plot of land not being taken up by the buildings is the difference between the area of the rectangular plot of land and the area of the two buildings.

Area $= 16 \cdot 10 − \left[ 9 \cdot 6 + \pi\left(\frac{4}{2}\right)^2 \right]$

$= 16 \cdot 10 − \left[ 9 \cdot 6 + \pi(2)^2 \right]$

$= 16 \cdot 10 − \left[ 9 \cdot 6 + \pi \cdot 4 \right]$

$\approx 16 \cdot 10 − \left[ 54 + 12.56 \right]$

$\approx 16 \cdot 10 - [66.56]$

$\approx 160 - [66.56]$

$\approx 160 - [66.56]$

$\approx 93.44 \text{ yd}^2$

25. Student B; Sample: Student A added the absolute values of the numbers rather than subtracting them.

26. Writing checks for $157.62 and $43.96 can be written as (−$157.62) and (−$43.96), respectively.

$500 + (−$157.62) + (−$43.96) + $225

= $500 + $225 + (−$157.62) + (−$43.96)

= $725 + (−$201.58) = $523.42

Raul's balance after the three transactions was $523.42.

27. The rational and irrational numbers are mutually exclusive. Sample: By definition, the sets of rational and irrational numbers do not contain the same numbers.

28. Losses of 8.2 and 5.3 points can be written as (−8.2) and (−5.3), respectively.

(−8.2) + (−5.3) + 9.1

= −13.5 + 9.1

= −4.4 points

29. A loss of 6 yards can be written as (−6).

4 + (−6) + 14

= 4 + 14 + (−6)

= 18 + (−6)

= 12 yards

30. Write and simplify an expression that represents the difference between the elevation of the kite and the height of the person flying the kite.

(74 feet) − (5 feet 6 inches)

= (888 inches) − (66 inches)

= 822 inches

= $\frac{822}{12}$ feet or 68 feet 6 inches

## LAB 1

### Practice Lab 1

a. A single number cube generates numbers between 1 and 6. To simulate a number

cube, Jared would enter randInt(1, 6) into the calculator.

b. To simulate rolling two number cubes, Jared would enter randInt(1, 6) and press [ENTER] twice. Jared would add the two random numbers that were generated to determine how many spaces to move.

c. Sample: The total number of spaces moved for rolls of 8, 4, and 8 would be 8 + 4 + 8 = 20 spaces.

## INVESTIGATION 1

### Practice Investigation 1

a. Since half of the numbers on a number cube are even and half are odd, it is as likely as not that Gavin rolls an even number on a number cube.

b. It is generally hot in the northern hemisphere during the summer. It is likely that the temperature will get above 90°F in the month of July.

c. It is rare to be left-handed, so it is unlikely that Sonya meets a left-handed person.

d. A batting average of .875 is considered to be very good. It is likely that a player with a batting average of .875 gets a hit on his next at bat.

e. There are 9 + 6 + 10 = 25 total spins. The probability of landing on A is $\frac{\text{number of times the spinner lands on A}}{\text{total number of spins}}$, which is $\frac{9}{25}$ or 36%. The probability of landing on B is $\frac{\text{number of times the spinner lands on B}}{\text{total number of spins}}$, which is $\frac{6}{25}$ or 24%. The probability of landing on C is $\frac{\text{number of times the spinner lands on C}}{\text{total number of spins}}$, which is $\frac{10}{25}$ = $\frac{2}{5}$ or 40%.

f. Jamie will most likely spin a C. Sample: The letter C has the greatest probability of occurring.

g. The probability he will get a hit in his next at bat is $\frac{\text{number of hits}}{\text{total number of at bats}}$, which is $\frac{18}{50}$ or 360.

h. See student work.

Saxon Algebra 1

# LESSON 11

## Warm Up 11

1. opposites

2. $(-4) + (-4) + (-4) = -12$

3. $-8 - 8 - 8 - 8 - 8 - 8$
   $= (-8) + (-8) + (-8) + (-8) + (-8)$
   $= -48$

4. $5^4$
   $5 \cdot 5 \cdot 5 \cdot 5$
   .625

5. $2^5$
   $2 \cdot 2 \cdot 2 \cdot 2 \cdot 2$
   32

## Lesson Practice 11

a. $9(-0.8) = -7.2$
   Sample: Multiplying two numbers with different signs results in a negative product.

b. $-12(-2.5) = 30$
   Sample: Multiplying two numbers with like signs results in a positive product.

c. $(-4)^3$
   $= (-4)(-4)(-4)$
   $= -64$

d. $(-8)^4$
   $= (-8)(-8)(-8)(-8)$
   $= 4096$

e. $-5^4$
   $= -1 \cdot 5^4$
   $= -1[(5)(5)(5)(5)]$
   $= -1(625)$
   $= -625$

f. $-105 \div (-7) = 15$
   Sample: Dividing two numbers with like signs results in a positive quotient.

g. $63.9 \div (-3) = -21.3$
   Sample: Dividing two numbers with different signs results in a negative quotient.

h. $-\dfrac{4}{5} \div \left(-\dfrac{9}{10}\right)$
   $-\dfrac{4}{5} \cdot \left(-\dfrac{10}{9}\right)$
   $\dfrac{8}{9}$

i. $\dfrac{3}{8} \div \left(-\dfrac{3}{4}\right)$
   $\dfrac{3}{8} \cdot \left(-\dfrac{4}{3}\right)$
   $-\dfrac{1}{2}$

j. $2 \times -24°F$
   $2 \cdot (-24) = -48$
   The low temperature in Bethel was $-48°F$.

## Practice 11

1. true; Sample: $7 \times \dfrac{1}{7} = \dfrac{7}{1} \times \dfrac{1}{7} = \dfrac{7}{7} = 1$

2. $-(-4)^2$
   $= -1 \cdot (-4)^2$
   $= -1[(-4)(-4)]$
   $= -1 \cdot 16$
   $= -16$

3. Student A; Sample: Student B did not find a common denominator.

4. $\dfrac{2 \cdot 14 + 3 \cdot 7}{71 - 15} = \dfrac{28 + 21}{56}$
   $= \dfrac{49}{56}$
   $= \dfrac{7}{8}$

5.

**6.** obtuse

**7.** Evaluate $3(x + 4) + y$ when $x = 8$ and $y = 7$.

$3(8 + 4) + 7 = 3(12) + 7$
$= 36 + 7$
$= 43$

**8.** Evaluate $3x^2 + 2(x - 1)^3$ for $x = 6$.

$3 \cdot 6^2 + 2(6 - 1)^3$
$= 3 \cdot 6^2 + 2(5)^3$
$= 3 \cdot 36 + 2 \cdot 125$
$= 108 + 250$
$= 358$

**9.** $\frac{660}{15} = 44$; $\frac{645}{11} \approx 58.6$

$\frac{616}{12} \approx 51.3$; $\frac{1100}{30} \approx 36.7$

The answer is **B**.

**10.** $5 + \frac{9}{3}\left[4\left(\frac{1}{2} + 4\right)\right]$

$5 + \frac{9}{3}\left[4\left(\frac{9}{2}\right)\right]$    Add inside parentheses.

$5 + \frac{9}{3}[18]$    Multiply inside brackets.

$5 + 54$    Multiply.

$59$    Add.

**11.** The time 11 p.m. is 11 hours after noon. Since the temperature drops 2 degrees every hour, the temperature drops
$2 \cdot (11) = 22$ degrees.
$20 - 22 = -2$
The temperature at 11 p.m. is $-2°C$.
The answer is **B**.

**12.** Evaluate $a = \frac{v^2}{r}$, where $v = 35$ cm/s and $r = 200$ cm.

$a = \frac{(35 \text{ cm/s}^2)}{200 \text{ cm}}$

$= \frac{1225 \text{ cm}^2/\text{s}^2}{200 \text{ cm}}$

$= 6.125 \text{ cm/s}^2$

**13.** $(560 \text{ pt})(\$0.16/\text{pint}) = \$89.60$

**14.** First dive:

$$\frac{(\text{number of minutes}) \cdot (\text{rate})}{(10 \text{ min}) \quad \cdot (-400 \text{ m/min})}$$

$10 \cdot (-400) = -4000$
The submarine traveled $-4000$ m in the first dive.

Second dive:

$$\frac{(\text{number of minutes}) \cdot (\text{rate})}{(4 \text{ min}) \quad \cdot (-400 \text{ m/min})}$$

$4 \cdot (-400) = -1600$
The submarine traveled $-1600$ m in the second dive.

**15.** $-1.06 + 2.01 + 4.13$
$0.95 + 4.13$
$5.08$

**16. a.** Sample:

$0.99$ is about 1; $0.23$ is about $\frac{1}{4}$

$1 - \frac{1}{4} = \frac{3}{4}$

The difference is about $\frac{3}{4}$ m.

**b.** $0.99 = \frac{99}{100}$; $0.23 = \frac{23}{100}$

$\frac{99}{100} - \frac{23}{100} = \frac{76}{100} = \frac{19}{25}$

The difference is $\frac{19}{25}$ m.

**17.** Student B; Sample: Student A should have multiplied 4 and 17 together first.

**18.** Evaluate $2.6f + 65$ for $f = 40$.
$2.6(40) + 65 = 104 + 65 = 169$
The approximate height is 169 cm.

**19.** Student B; Sample: Student A subtracted 282 instead of $-282$. Since the lowest point is below sea level, the elevation is $-282$ feet.

**20. a.** Because there are as many even numbers as there are odd numbers, the event is as likely as not.

**b.** Because September only has 30 days, the event is impossible.

**c.** Because the basketball team has been winning most of its games, the event is likely.

**Saxon** Algebra 1

**21.** $5(-2) = -10$

**22.** $(-3)(-5) = 15$

**23.** $-|-15 + 5| = -1 \cdot |-10| =$
$-1 \cdot (10) = -10$

**24.** $(-3)(-6)(-2)(5) = (18)(-2)(5)$
$= (-36)(5)$
$= -180$

**25.** $(3)(5) = 15$

**26.** No, the perimeter of a rectangle cannot be a negative integer.

**27. a.**

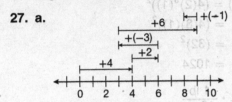

**b.** $4 + 2 + (-3) + 6 + (-1)$
$4 + 2 - 3 + 6 - 1$

**c.** $4 + 2 - 3 + 6 - 1 = 6 - 3 + 6 - 1$
$= 3 + 6 - 1$
$= 9 - 1 = 8$

Mary is 8 spaces away from the starting point.

**28.** Yes, Jan has enough.
$2 \text{ yd} = (2 \text{ yd})\left(\dfrac{36 \text{ in.}}{1 \text{ yd}}\right) = 72 \text{ in.}$
2 yards > 64 inches

**29.** $20 - (-5) = 25$
The temperature rose 25°F.

**30.** Evaluate $20 + 0.10m$ for $m = 200$.
$20 + 0.10(200) = 20 + 20 = 40$
The amount of the bill is $40.

## LESSON 12

### Warm Up 12

**1.** algebraic

**2.** $6 - |-6| + (-4)$
$6 - 6 - 4$
$-4$

**3.** $-\dfrac{4}{5} \div \left(-\dfrac{8}{9}\right)$
$-\dfrac{4}{5} \cdot \left(-\dfrac{9}{8}\right)$
$\dfrac{36}{40}$
$\dfrac{9}{10}$

**4.** $2|y| - 2|x| + m$
$2|(-3)| - 2|(-1.5)| + (-1.3)$
$2(3) - 2(1.5) - 1.3$
$6 - 3 - 1.3$
$1.7$

### Lesson Practice 12

**a.** Associative Property of Addition

**b.** Identity Property of Addition

**c.** Commutative Property of Multiplication

**d.** Identity Property of Multiplication

**e.** true; Associative Property of Multiplication

**f.** false; Commutative Property does not work for subtraction

**g.** true; Identity Property of Addition

**h.** $18 + 7x + 4$
$= 7x + 18 + 4$    Commutative Property of Addition
$= 7x + (18 + 4)$    Associative Property of Addition
$= 7x + 22$    Add.

**i.** $\dfrac{1}{3}d \cdot 3$
$= \dfrac{1}{3} \cdot 3 \cdot d$    Commutative Property of Multiplication
$= \left(\dfrac{1}{3} \cdot 3\right) \cdot d$    Associative Property of Multiplication
$= 1 \cdot d$    Multiply.
$= d$    Identity Property of Multiplication

**j.** $\$1.45 + \$3.35 + \$2.65$
$= \$1.45 + (\$3.35 + \$2.65)$    Associative Property of Addition

**Saxon** Algebra 1

= $1.45 + $6.00     Add within the parentheses.

= $7.45     Add.

## Practice 12

1. Identity Property of Multiplication

2. $-18 \div 3 = -6$

3. $|12 - 30| = |-18| = 18$

4. $(-3)(-2)(-1)(-8) = 48$

5. false; The Associative Property only applies when the operations are all addition or all multiplication

6. Sample: $\frac{4}{6}$

7. The statement is true by definition.

8. The equation $a + 0 = a$ demonstrates the Identity Property of Addition. The answer is **B**.

9. Write the fractions with a common denominator of 60.

$\frac{11}{15} + \frac{1}{30} + \frac{3}{60}$

$= \frac{11}{15}\left(\frac{4}{4}\right) + \frac{1}{30}\left(\frac{2}{2}\right) + \frac{3}{60}$

$= \frac{44}{60} + \frac{2}{60} + \frac{3}{60}$

$= \frac{49}{60}$

10. Student A; The quotient of a positive and a negative number is negative.

11. $x + 5 + 15$     Commutative Property of Addition

$= x + (5 + 15)$     Associative Property of Addition

$= x + 20$     Add.

or

$5 + 15 + x$     Commutative Property of Addition

$= (5 + 15) + x$     Associative Property of Addition

$= 20 + x$     Add.

12. $\dfrac{(5x + x)^2(6 - x)}{x} = \dfrac{(5(2) + 2)^2(6 - 2)}{2}$

$= \dfrac{(10 + 2)^2(4)}{2}$

$= \dfrac{(12)^2(4)}{2}$

$= \dfrac{144(4)}{2}$

$= 288$

The answer is **A**.

13. $(4x^3y^2) = (4(2)^3(1))^2$

$= (4(8)(1))^2$

$= (32)^2$

$= 1024$

14. $588 \; \cancel{oz} \cdot \dfrac{1 \text{ lb}}{16 \; \cancel{oz}}$

$= \dfrac{588 \text{ lb}}{16} = 36.75 \text{ lb}$

15. Sample: The Commutative Property of Multiplication says that the order of the factors does not change the product.

16. yes; Sample: The Commutative Property of Addition states that the order of the terms does not affect the sum.

17. Both are correct; Sample: The Commutative Property of Addition states that the order of the terms can be changed without changing the sum.

18. Area = length · width

Area = $2w \cdot w$

$= 2w^2$

$= 2(2.3)^2$

$= 2(5.29)$

$= 10.58$ sq. in.$^2$

19. $-15$; Sample:

$5(28) + 3(-41) + 2(-16)$

$140 - 123 - 32$

$-15$

20. In order from greatest to least are:

$\frac{1}{3}, \frac{1}{4}, 0.23, -0.24$

The answer is **D**.

**21.** $124 \text{ in.} \cdot \dfrac{1 \text{ yd}}{36 \text{ in.}}$

$\dfrac{124}{36} \text{ yd} = 3.4 \text{ yd}$

Maria needs 4 yards of ribbon.

**22.** Student B; Sample: Student A did not follow the order of operations.

**23.** Sample: First you have to work inside the parentheses and divide 9 by 3 to get 3. Next, take that 3 away from 8 to get 5. Then square 5 to get 25 and multiply by 4 to get 100.

**24.** $x^2 k x k^2 x^2 y k x^2$

$k^1 k^2 k^1 x^2 x^1 x^2 x^2 y^1$

$k^{1+2+1} x^{2+1+2+2} y^1$

$k^4 x^7 y$

**25.** Student A; Sample: Student B did not treat the constant and variable in the second term as factors. Instead of multiplying, Student B treated $x$ as a digit in the ones place.

**26.** $396.25 - 150.50 + 220.00 + 8.00$

$= \$473.75$

**27.** $3.5 - 5 + 8 = 6.5 \text{ ft}$

**28.** $2.5(60) = 150 \text{ mi}$

$2.5(63) = 157.5 \text{ mi}$

Bill's friend lives between 150 and 157.5 miles away.

**29.** Follow the order of operations.

$2^2 + 24 - (3 - 12)$

$= 2^2 + 24 - (-9)$    Simplify inside parentheses.

$= 4 + 24 - (-9)$    Evaluate exponents.

$= 37$    Add.

**30.** Sample: $7 + (-7) = 0$

## LESSON 13

### Warm Up 13

**1.** exponent

**2.** $(-3) + (-4) - (-8) = -7 - (-8)$

$= -7 + 8$

$= 1$

**3.** $\left[-(-4)^3\right] = -1 \cdot (-4)^3$

$= -1[(-4)(-4)(-4)]$

$= -1(-64)$

$= 64$

**4.** $a^3 \cdot x^4 \cdot x^8 \cdot a^4 \cdot z^4$

$a^{3+4} \cdot x^{4+8} \cdot z^4$

$a^7 x^{12} z^4$

**5.** $\left(-\dfrac{2}{6}\right) \div \left(-\dfrac{3}{8}\right) = \left(-\dfrac{2}{6}\right) \cdot \left(-\dfrac{8}{3}\right)$

$= \left(-\dfrac{1}{3}\right) \cdot \left(-\dfrac{8}{3}\right)$

$= \dfrac{8}{9}$

### Lesson Practice 13

**a.** Yes, 225 is a perfect square. Sample: $15^2 = 225$; The product of a number multiplied by itself is a perfect square.

**b.** No, 350 is not a perfect square: Sample: There is no number multiplied by itself that equals 350.

**c.** $\sqrt{37} \approx 6$; Sample: 37 is between the perfect squares 36 and 49. $\sqrt{36} = 6$ and $\sqrt{49} = 7$, so $\sqrt{37}$ is between 6 and 7, but closer to 6 because 37 is closer to 36.

**d.** $\sqrt{16} + \sqrt{441} \,\bigcirc\, \sqrt{81} + \sqrt{361}$

$4 + 21 \,\bigcirc\, 9 + 19$

$25 \,\bigcirc\, 28$

$25 < 28$

**e.** To find the side length, find the square root of the area.

$A = s^2$

$169 = s^2$

$\sqrt{169} = s$

$13 = s$

The side length is 13 feet.

### Practice 13

**1.** $-16 \div -2 = 8$

**2.** $\dfrac{4 + 7 - 6}{2 + 7 - 3} = \dfrac{5}{6}$

**Saxon** Algebra 1

3. $-2 + 11 - 4 + 3 - 8 = 9 - 4 + 3 - 8$
$$= 5 + 3 - 8$$
$$= 8 - 8$$
$$= 0$$

4. $(-2)(-3) + 11(2) - 3 - 6$
$$= 6 + 22 - 3 - 6$$
$$= 28 - 3 - 6$$
$$= 25 - 6$$
$$= 19$$

5. Substitute 2 for $p$, $-3$ for $g$, and 4 for $x$. Then simplify.
$3p - 4g - 2x$
$$= 3(2) - 4(-3) - 2(4)$$
$$= 6 - (-12) - 8$$
$$= 10$$

6. Substitute 3 for $x$, 4 for $y$, and 3 for $z$. Then simplify.
$3xy - 2yz$
$$= 3(3)(4) - 2(4)(3)$$
$$= 36 - 24$$
$$= 12$$

7. 40 is between the perfect squares 36 and 49. $\sqrt{36} = 6$ and $\sqrt{49} = 7$, so $\sqrt{40}$ is between 6 and 7.

8. 289 is a perfect square because $17 \cdot 17 = 289$. The answer is **B**.

9. Since $\sqrt{4} = \sqrt{2 \cdot 2} = 2$, $b = 2$.

10. A model for $\frac{5}{12}$ is a 3 by 4 grid with 5 squares filled in. A model for $\frac{1}{3}$ is a 3 by 4 grid with 4 squares filled in since 4 squares is a third of 12 squares.

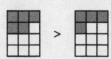

11. $\dfrac{25 \text{ feet}}{1 \text{ hour}} \cdot \dfrac{1 \text{ yard}}{3 \text{ feet}} = \dfrac{25 \text{ yards}}{3 \text{ hour}}$
$$= 8\frac{1}{3} \text{ yards per hour}$$

12. false; Sample: $\sqrt{9} = 3$ and 3 is a rational number.

13. area of second square
$$= \frac{1}{2} \cdot \text{area of first square}$$
$$= \frac{1}{2} \cdot 392 \text{ m}^2$$
$$= 196 \text{ m}^2$$
side length of second square
$$= \sqrt{196 \text{ m}^2}$$
$$= 14 \text{ m}$$
The answer is **A**.

14. true; Commutative Property of Multiplication.

15. a. $4^2 + 15 \cdot 20 = 16 + 300 = 316$
   The statement is true.

   b. $(4 + 5)^2 = 9^2 = 81$
   $4 + 5^2 = 4 + 25 = 29$
   Therefore, $(4 + 5)^2 \neq 4 + 5^2$
   The statement is false.

16. a. A common denominator for each measure is 16.
   The measures written with the common denominator of 16 are:
   $8\frac{4}{16}$ in, $8\frac{3}{16}$ in, $8\frac{10}{16}$ in, and $8\frac{1}{16}$ in.

   b. The measures ordered from least to greatest are:
   $8\frac{1}{16}$ in, $8\frac{3}{16}$ in, $8\frac{4}{16}$ in, and $8\frac{10}{16}$ in.

17. 1.05, 1.09, 1.11, 1.5

18. No, the expressions are not equivalent. Sample: Simplify the first expression.
   $(20k^3 \cdot 5v^5)9k^2 = 20 \cdot 5 \cdot 9 \cdot k^{3+2} \cdot v^5$
   $$= 900k^5v^5$$
   This is not equivalent to $900k^3v^5$.

19. The side length can be found by finding the square root of the area.
   $s^2 = 1,690,000$
   $s = \sqrt{1,690,000}$
   $s = 1300$
   The side length is about 1300 meters.

**Saxon** Algebra 1

**20.** Evaluate $t = \frac{\sqrt{d}}{4}$ for $d = 169$.

$t = \frac{\sqrt{169}}{4} = \frac{13}{4} = 3.25$ seconds

**21.** Evaluate $f = 120\sqrt{p}$ for $p = 169$.

$f = 120\sqrt{169} = 120 \cdot 3 = 1560$ gal/min

**22.** yes; Sample: Divide 210 by 12 to convert it into feet.

$\frac{210}{12} = 17.5$

So, the pie is 17.5 feet in diameter, and 17.5 is a rational number because it can be expressed as a quotient of two integers.

**23.** area of circle $= 3.14 \cdot 4^2$

area of square $= 4.25^2$

area of shaded portion $=$
$3.14 \cdot 4^2 - 4.25^2$

Use a calculator to evaluate the expression.

$3.14 \cdot 4^2 - 4.25^2 = 32.1775$

The area is 32.1775 in.$^2$

**24.** Sample:

$+\$105 + (-\$144) = -\$9$

Frank's account balance decreased by about $9.

**25.** $52 + (1 + 3)^2 \cdot (16 - 14)^3 - 20$

$= 52 + 4^2 \cdot 2^3 - 20$    Simplify inside the parentheses.

$= 52 + 16 \cdot 8 - 20$    Simplify powers.

$= 52 + 128 - 20$    Multiply.

$= 160$    Add and subtract.

**26.** Student A; Sample: Student B incorrectly used the Associative Property to add $2 + 3x$; $2 + 3x \neq 5x$.

**27.** $30 + 7x - 12$

$= 30 + 7x + (-12)$    Add inverse to subtract.

$= 30 + (-12) + 7x$    Commutative Property of Addition.

$= [30 + (-12)] + 7x$    Associative Property of Addition.

$= 18 + 7x$    Add.

**28.** In choice **A**, an even power of a negative number is positive. In choice **B**, the quotient of two negative numbers is positive. In choice **C**, the product of $-\frac{3}{4}$ and 6 is negative, and when the product is divided by $-4$, the quotient is positive. In choice **D**, the power is positive, and the product of $-1$ and the power is negative. The answer is **D**.

**29.** $\$1,295,800 \cdot \dfrac{1 \text{ drachma}}{\$0.004}$

$= 323,950,000$ drachmae

**30. a.** Because a standard number cube does not have a 10, the event is impossible.

    **b.** Because there are 899 incorrect guesses compared to one correct guess, the event is unlikely.

    **c.** Because heads or tails are equally likely, the event is as likely as not.

## LESSON 14

### Warm Up 14

**1.** probability

**2.** $5 \times 7 - 27 \div 9 + 6$

$= 35 - 3 + 6$

$= 32 + 6$

$= 38$

**3.** $6.3 + (-2.4) + (-8.9)$

$= 3.9 + (-8.9)$

$= -5$

**4.** $6 + |-72| + |-5|$

$= 6 + 72 + 5$

$= 78 + 5$

$= 83$

**5.** 12 represents "twelve floors up." The opposite is $-12$.

### Lesson Practice 14

   **a.** $\{1, 2, 3, 4\}$

   **b.** $\{2, 4, 6\}$

   **c.** $\{3, 4, 5, 6\}$

**d.** $P(\text{blue}) = \dfrac{3 \text{ blue marbles}}{10 \text{ total marbles}}$

$= \dfrac{3}{10}$

The probability is 0.3 or 30%.

**e.** $P(\text{not red}) = 1 - P(\text{red})$

$= 1 - \dfrac{3}{10} = \dfrac{7}{10}$

The probability is 0.7 or 70%.

**f.** 5 balls out of 8 have a number less than 6.

$P(\text{less than } 6) = \dfrac{5}{8}$

The probability is 0.625 or 62.5%. 5 balls out of 8 have a number less than 6.

1 ball out of 8 has the number 6. 2 balls out of 8 have the number 7.

$P(6) = \dfrac{1}{8}; \; P(7) = \dfrac{2}{8} = \dfrac{1}{4}$

You have a greater chance of drawing a 7.

**g.** total number of cards = 52

number of kings = 4

$P(\text{king}) = \dfrac{4}{52} = \dfrac{1}{13}$

The probability randomly drawing a king out of the deck is $\dfrac{1}{13}$.

**Practice 14**

**1.** $P(\text{greater than } 4) = \dfrac{2}{6} = \dfrac{1}{3}$

**2.** $P(\text{green}) = \dfrac{5 \text{ green marbles}}{14 \text{ total marbles}} = \dfrac{5}{14}$

**3.** $20 \text{ in.} \cdot \dfrac{2.54 \text{ cm}}{1 \text{ in.}} = 50.8 \text{ cm}$

**4.** $25 \text{ ft} \cdot \dfrac{12 \text{ in.}}{\text{ft}} \cdot \dfrac{2.54 \text{ cm}}{1 \text{ in.}} = 762 \text{ cm}$

**5.** $3 - 2 \cdot 4 + 3 \cdot 2$

$= 3 - 8 + 6$

$= 5 + 6$

$= 11$

**6.** $-3(-2)(-3) - 2$

$= -18 - 2$

$= -20$

**7.** $5(9 + 2) - 4(5 + 1)$

$= 5(11) - 4(6)$

$= 55 - 24$

$= 31$

**8.** $3(6 + 2) + 3(5 - 2)$

$= 3(8) + 3(3)$

$= 24 + 9$

$= 33$

**9.** When $z = 5$,

$\sqrt{31 + z} = \sqrt{31 + 5} = \sqrt{36} = 6$.

**10.** Write the fractions with a common denominator of 30.

$\dfrac{4}{5} = \dfrac{24}{30}$

$\dfrac{5}{6} = \dfrac{25}{30}$

Since $\dfrac{24}{30} < \dfrac{25}{30}, \dfrac{4}{5} < \dfrac{5}{6}$.

**11.** $A = x^2$

$49 = x^2$

$\sqrt{49} = x$

$7 = x$

The length of the side is 7 centimeters.

**12.** The answer is **A**.

**13.** If $-xy$ is positive, then $xy$ is negative, so either $x$ or $y$ is positive and the other is negative. If $-xy$ is zero, then either $x$ or $y$ is zero. If $-xy$ is negative, then $xy$ is positive, so either both $x$ and $y$ are positive or both $x$ and $y$ are negative.

**14.** $5 \cdot 6 = 6 \cdot 5$ illustrates the Commutative Property of Multiplication.

**15.** $P(\text{odd}) = \dfrac{3 \text{ odd numbers}}{6 \text{ total numbers}} = \dfrac{1}{2}$

The answer is **A**.

**16.** total number of letters = 11

number of letter b's = 2

$P(\text{letter b}) = \dfrac{2}{11}$

**17.** $P(\text{blue}) = \dfrac{4 \text{ blue marbles}}{16 \text{ total marbles}} = \dfrac{1}{4}$

The answer is **C**.

18. Student A; Sample: Student B found two different numbers that have a product of 16 instead of one number that, when multiplied by itself, equals 16.

19. Evaluates $= \sqrt{\dfrac{d}{0.04}}$, for $d = 4^2$.

$$s = \sqrt{\dfrac{4^2}{0.04}}$$

$$= \sqrt{\dfrac{16}{0.04}}$$

$$= \sqrt{400}$$

$$= 20$$

The speed was about 20 miles per hour.

20. Evaluate $\dfrac{mv^2}{r}$, for $m = 2$, $v = 50$, and $r = 25$.

$$\dfrac{mv^2}{r} = \dfrac{(2)(50^2)}{25}$$

$$= \dfrac{(2)(2500)}{25}$$

$$= \dfrac{5000}{25}$$

$$= 200$$

The centripetal force is 200 kg · cm/s$^2$.

21. $2.35 \text{ lb} \cdot \dfrac{16 \text{ oz}}{1 \text{ lb}} = 37.6 \text{ lb}$

Sample: 2.35 rounds down to 2 and $2 \cdot 16 = 32$. The answer 37.6 oz is reasonable, as it is close to the estimate of 32 oz.

22. no; Sample: Since $\pi$ is an irrational number and will never end, the program will never end.

23. Real numbers can be used to represent the elevations in Death Valley.

24. a. $\frac{5}{9}(F - 32)$ is one term.

   b. The constants in the expression are $\frac{5}{9}$ and 32.

25. $-7 + 3 - 2 - 5 + (-6)$

   $= -4 - 2 - 5 + (-6)$

   $= -6 - 5 + (-6)$

   $= -11 + (-6)$

   $= -17$

26. Student B; Sample; The weight of each piece is the weight of the cakes divided by 16. The weight of the cakes is $3 + 5$. Student B put parentheses around $3 + 5$, grouping 3 and 5. Student A did not put parentheses around $3 + 5$, and without these grouping symbols, $5 \div 16$ is the operation performed first.

27. $-9 + 15 = +6$

   The change in the number of people in the restaurant is $+6$.

28. $22 - (-11) - 11 - (-22)$

   $= 22 + 11 - 11 + 22$    Write subtraction as addition.

   $= 22 + (11 - 11) + 22$    Associative Property of Addition

   $= 22 + 22$

   $= 44$

29. Sample: If you don't complete the problem in the correct order, you get the wrong answer.

30. First find the length of a side.

   $$A = x^2$$

   $$144 = x^2$$

   $$\sqrt{144} = x$$

   $$12 = x$$

   The length of a side is 12 feet. Tanisha needs $4 \cdot 12 = 48$ feet.

## LESSON 15

**Warm Up 15**

1. term

2. $5 - 7 + 5(3) = 5 - 7 + 15$

   $= -2 + 15$

   $= 13$

3. $(-5) + (-2) + |(-5) + (-2)|$

   $= (-5) + (-2) + |(-7)|$

   $= (-5) + (-2) + 7$

   $= -7 + 7$

   $= 0$

4. $7x + 4y = 7(2.1) + 4(-0.7)$

   $= 14.7 + (-2.8)$

   $= 11.9$

Saxon Algebra 1

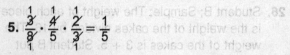

**5.** $\dfrac{1}{\cancel{8}} \cdot \dfrac{\cancel{4}}{5} \cdot \dfrac{\cancel{2}}{\cancel{3}} = \dfrac{1}{5}$

## Lesson Practice 15

**a.** $8(2 + 7) = 8(2) + 8(7)$
$\quad = 16 + 56$
$\quad = 72$

**b.** $4(6 - 2) = 4(6) + 4(-2)$
$\quad = 24 - 8$
$\quad = 16$

**c.** $-(9 + 3) = (-1)(9) + (-1)(3)$
$\quad = -9 - 3$
$\quad = -12$

**d.** $-14(4 - 2) = (-14)(4) + (-14)(-2)$
$\quad = -56 + 28$
$\quad = -28$

**e.** $-10(m + 4) = (-10)(m) + (-10)(4)$
$\quad = -10m - 40$

**f.** $(7 - y)8 = (8)(7) + (8)(-y)$
$\quad = 56 - 8y$

**g.** $4xy^3(x^4y - 5x)$
$\quad = (4xy^3)(x^4y) + (4xy^3)(-5x)$
$\quad = 4x^5y^4 - 20x^2y^3$

**h.** $-2x^2m^2(m^2 - 4m)$
$\quad = (-2x^2m^2)(m^2) + (-2x^2m^2)(-4m)$
$\quad = -2x^2m^4 + 8x^2m^3$

**i.** Find the product of the price per ticket and the total number of adults and children.
$\quad = 15(4 + 8)$
$\quad = 15(4) + 15(8)$
$\quad = 60 + 120$
$\quad = 180$
The total cost is $180.

## Practice 15

**1.** $-7(-8 + 3) = (-7)(-8) + (-7)(3)$
$\quad = 56 - 21$
$\quad = 35$

**2.** $5(-3 - 6) = 5(-3) + 5(-6)$
$\quad = -15 - 30 = -45$

**3.** $\sqrt{10,000} = 100$

**4.** Since $\sqrt{25} = 5$, $c = \sqrt{25} = 5$.

**5.** Sample:
$P(\text{egg breaking})$
$\quad = \dfrac{\text{number of broken eggs}}{\text{total number of eggs}}$
$\quad = \dfrac{b}{800}$

Since the probability is $\dfrac{2}{25}$,
$\quad \dfrac{2}{25} = \dfrac{b}{800}$
$\quad 2(800) = b(25)$
$\quad 1600 = 25b$
$\quad \dfrac{1600}{25} = b$
$\quad 64 = b$
64 eggs are likely to be broken in the shipment.

**6.** List the digits that are odd and greater than 5: $\{7, 9\}$.
$P(\text{odd and greater than 5})$
$\quad = \dfrac{\text{number of cards odd and greater than 5}}{\text{total number of cards}}$
$\quad = \dfrac{2}{10}$
$\quad = \dfrac{1}{5}$

**7.** $P(\text{number less than 7}) = 1$
Sample: An event that is certain to happen has a probability of one. All 10 of the balls have a number label less than 7, so the event is certain.

**8.** $-5(x + 6) = -5(x) + (-5)(6)$
$\quad = -5x - 30$
The answer is **D**.

**9.** When $x = -4$,
$y = 18 - x$
$\quad = 18 - (-4)$
$\quad = 22$

**10.** $5 - (-3) = 8$
The water level changed 8 feet.

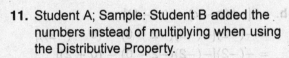

**11.** Student A; Sample: Student B added the numbers instead of multiplying when using the Distributive Property.

**12.** $-8(9 - 15) = (-8)(9) + (-8)(-15)$
$= -72 + 120$
$= 48$

Sample: I multiplied $-8$ by each number in parentheses and added the products.

**13.** $6(4 + 7)$
$= 6(4) + 6(7)$
$= 24 + 42$
$= 66$

There are 66 lots.

**14.** The statement is true. It illustrates the Identity Property of Addition.

**15.** $3.4 \text{ yd}^3 = 3.4 \text{ yd}^3 \cdot \dfrac{3 \text{ ft}}{1 \text{ yd}} \cdot \dfrac{3 \text{ ft}}{1 \text{ yd}} \cdot \dfrac{3 \text{ ft}}{1 \text{ yd}}$
$= 91.8 \text{ ft}^3$

**16.** Each child gets $\frac{c}{8}$ baseball cards. The value of each child's cards is 14 times $\frac{c}{8}$. An expression is $14\left(\frac{c}{8}\right)$.

**17.** $6 \times$ number of girls
$= 6g$
$= 6(b + 7)$
$= 6b + 6(7)$
$= 6b + 42$

**18.** $P(\text{number 5 or 6}) = \dfrac{2}{6} = \dfrac{1}{3}$

**19.** Student A; Sample: Student B incorrectly distributed over the square root.
$\sqrt{36 + z} \neq \sqrt{36} + z$

**20.** To simplify from right to left, use the Commutative Property of Multiplication.

**21.** $7 \cdot 8x$     Commutative Property of Multiplication
$(7 \cdot 8)x$     Associative Property of Multiplication
$56x$     Multiply.
or
$x \cdot 7 \cdot 8$     Commutative Property of Multiplication

$x(7 \cdot 8)$     Associative Property of Multiplication
$x \cdot 56$     Multiply.

**22.** $14\frac{1}{4} - 2\frac{1}{2} = 14\frac{1}{4} - 2\frac{2}{4}$
$= 13\frac{5}{4} - 2\frac{2}{4} = 11\frac{3}{4}$

Raymond is $11\frac{3}{4}$ years old.

$11\frac{3}{4} + 3\frac{3}{4} = 14\frac{6}{4} = 15\frac{2}{4} = 15\frac{1}{2}$

**23.** Sample: Substitute the value 3 for $f$ and the value 5 for $g$. Evaluate exponents from left to right. Multiply from left to right. Subtract and add from left to right.

**24.**

**25.** The difference from $-12.5$ to $-1.5$ is 11. The full moon is $2.512^{11}$ or about 25,131 times brighter.

**26.** Student A; Sample: Student B combined the two negative signs before taking the absolute value, but should have taken the absolute value first.
$-|-3| \neq |+3|$

**27.** When $x = -3$,
$y = x - |x - 2|$
$= (-3) - |(-3) - 2|$
$= -3 - |-5|$
$= -3 - 5$
$= -8$

**28.** Sample: It will be positive because every term is positive; the negative value in the absolute value symbols will become positive.

**29.** The total number of the results was
$3 + 5 + 9 + 8 = 25$.

    **a.** $P(\text{red}) = \dfrac{3}{25} = 0.12 = 12\%$

    **b.** $P(\text{green}) = \dfrac{8}{25} = 0.32 = 32\%$

**c.** $P(\text{not green}) = 1 - P(\text{green})$

$$= 1 - \frac{8}{25}$$

$$= \frac{17}{25} = 0.68 = 68\%$$

**30.** First find the length of a side.

$A = x^2$

$121 = x^2$

$\sqrt{121} = x$

$11 = x$

The length of a side is 11 inches. The perimeter of the square is $4 \cdot 11 = 44$ inches.

## LESSON 16

### Warm Up 16

**1.** integers

**2.** $-ax^2(dx^3 - a^5x)$

$-ax^2(dx^3) - ax^2(-a^5x)$

$-adx^{2+3} - a^{1+5}x^{2+1}$

$-adx^5 - a^6x^3$

**3.** $\sqrt{36} + \sqrt{81} - 4^2$

$6 + 9 - 16$

$-1$

**4.** $[-(-5)] - |-7|$

$[5] - 7$

$-2$

**5.** $\frac{9}{10}\left(-\frac{1}{12}\right)$

$= -\frac{9}{120}$

$= -\frac{3}{40}$

The answer is B.

### Lesson Practice 16

**a.** $ax[-a(a-x)]$

$= (2)(-1)[-2(2 - (-1))]$

$= (2)(-1)[-2(2 + 1)]$

$= (2)(-1)[-2(3)]$

$= (2)(-1)[-6]$

$= 12$

**b.** $-b[-b(b-c) - (c-b)]$

$= -(-2)[-(-2)(-2 - 0) - (0 - (-2))]$

$= -(-2)[-(-2)(-2 - 0) - (0 + 2)]$

$= -(-2)[-(-2)(-2) - (2)]$

$= -(-2)[-4 - (2)]$

$= -(-2)[-6]$

$= -12$

**c.** $(5y)(2z)4xy$

$= (5)(-1)(2)\left(\frac{1}{2}\right)(4)(3)(-1)$

$= 60$

**d.** $\frac{4rs}{6st}$

$= \frac{(4)(-1)(-3)}{(6)(-3)(-2)}$

$= \frac{12}{36}$

$= \frac{1}{3}$

**e.** $-b(a - 3) + a$

$= -ba + 3b + a$ — Distributive Property

$= -(-1)(2) + 3(-1) + 2$ — Substitute.

$= 2 + (-3) + 2$ — Multiply.

$= 1$ — Add.

**f.** $-a(-b - a) - b$

$= ab + a^2 - b$ — Distributive Property

$= (2)(-1) + 2^2 - (-1)$ — Substitute.

$= -2 + 4 + 1 = 3$ — Use order of operations to simplify.

**g.** $\frac{-b(a - 4) + b}{b}$

$= \frac{-25(-2 - 4) + 25}{25}$

$= \frac{-25(-6) + 25}{25}$

$= \frac{150 + 25}{25}$

$= \frac{175}{25}$

$= 7$

**Saxon** Algebra 1

**h.** $\dfrac{x^2 - x|y|}{x^3}$

$= \dfrac{(-4)^2 - (-4)|-2|}{(-4)^3}$

$= \dfrac{(-4)^2 - (-4)(2)}{(-4)^3}$

$= \dfrac{16 - (-4)(2)}{-64}$

$= \dfrac{16 - (-8)}{-64}$

$= \dfrac{24}{-64}$

$= -\dfrac{3}{8}$

**i.** Write the formula for the principal balance after 7 years.

$P_7 = 1.04(P_{7-1})$

$= 1.04(P_6)$

$= 1.04(\$1600)$

$= \$1664$

Write the formula for the principal balance after 8 years.

$P_8 = 1.04(P_{8-1})$

$= 1.04(P_7)$

$= 1.04(\$1664)$

$= \$1730.56$

The principal balance is \$1730.56 after 8 years.

**Practice 16**

**1.** $2 + 5 - 3 + 7 - (-3) + 5$

$= 2 + 5 - 3 + 7 + 3 + 5$

$= 19$

**2.** $3(7) + 5 - 3 + 7 - 9 \div 2$

$= 21 + 5 - 3 + 7 - 4.5$

$= 25.5$

**3.** $K = \{-5, -4, -3, -2, -1\}$

**4.** true; The product of any two whole numbers is contained within the set of whole numbers.

**5.** false; Sample: $-7$ is an integer, but it is not a whole number.

**6.** $-4y(d + cx) = -4yd - 4ycx$

**7.** $(a + bc)2x = 2xa + 2xbc$

**8.** $pa[-a(-a)]$

$= pa[a^2]$

$= pa^3$

$= (2)(-1)^3$

$= (2)(-1)$

$= -2$

**9.** $x(x - y)$

$= \left(\dfrac{1}{5}\right)\left(\dfrac{1}{5} - \dfrac{6}{5}\right)$

$= \left(\dfrac{1}{5}\right)\left(-\dfrac{5}{5}\right)$

$= \left(\dfrac{1}{5}\right)(-1)$

$= -\dfrac{1}{5}$

**10.** $\left(\dfrac{x - 3}{y}\right)^2$

$= \left(\dfrac{-5 - 3}{2}\right)^2$

$= \left(\dfrac{-8}{2}\right)^2$

$= (-4)^2$

$= 16$

**11.** $4(b + 1)^2 - 6(c - b)^4$

$= 4(2 + 1)^2 - 6(7 - 2)^4$

$= 4(3)^2 - 6(5)^4$

$= 4(9) - 6(625)$

$= 36 - 3750$

$= -3714$

**12.** $20x + 4$;

Sample: Since a square has four equal sides, $4(5x + 1) = 4(5x) + 4(1) = 20x + 4$ would be used to find the perimeter.

**13.** Associative Property of Addition

**14.** Substitute 20 for $t$ in the formula.

$v = 195 - 0.5t$

$= 195 - 0.5(20)$

$= 195 - 10$

$= 185$

The answer is **B**.

**15. a.** Substitute 2 for $r$ and 8 for $h$ in the formula.

$$V = \frac{1}{3}\pi r^2 h$$
$$= \frac{1}{3}\pi(2)^2(8)$$
$$= \frac{1}{3}\pi(4)(8)$$
$$= \frac{32}{3}\pi$$
$$\approx 33.49 \text{ cm}^3$$

**b.** Substitute 1 for $r$ and 4 for $h$ in the formula.

$$V = \pi r^2 h$$
$$= \pi(0.5)^2(4)$$
$$= \pi(0.25)(4)$$
$$= \pi$$
$$\approx 3.14 \text{ cm}^3$$

**c.** $V$ = volume of cone − volume of hole
$$\approx 33.49 - 3.14$$
$$= 30.35 \text{ cm}^3$$

**16.** Substitute 3 for $V_i$, 1 for $P_i$, and 6 for $V_f$ in the formula.

$$P_f = \frac{P_i V_i}{V_f}$$
$$= \frac{(1)(3)}{6}$$
$$= \frac{1}{2}$$

The final pressure is 0.5 atmosphere.

**17.** Substitute 2000 for $V_f$, 10 for $t$, and 0.02 for $I$ in the formula.

$$V_p = \frac{V_f}{(1+i)^t}$$
$$= \frac{2000}{(1+0.02)^{10}}$$
$$= \frac{2000}{(1.02)^{10}}$$
$$\approx \$1641$$

**18.** Each pair of $x$- and $y$-values makes the equation $y = |x^3 + 5|$ true.

$$|x^3 + 5| = |2^3 + 5| = |8 + 5| = 13$$

$$|x^3 + 5| = |1^3 + 5| = |1 + 5| = 6$$
$$|x^3 + 5| = |(-1)^3 + 5| = |(-1) + 5| = 4$$
$$|x^3 + 5| = |(-2)^3 + 5| = |(-8) + 5| = 3$$
The answer is **C**.

**19. a.** Substitute 50 for $N$ and 3 for $x$ in the equation.

$$A = Nx^2$$
$$= 50 \cdot 3^2$$
$$= 50 \cdot 9$$
$$= 450 \text{ in.}^2$$

**b.** Substitute 150 for $N$ and 3 for $x$ in the equation.

$$A = Nx^2$$
$$= 150 \cdot 3^2$$
$$= 150 \cdot 9$$
$$= 1350 \text{ in.}^2$$

**c.** Substitute 350 for $N$ and 3 for $x$ in the equation.

$$A = Nx^2$$
$$= 350 \cdot 3^2$$
$$= 350 \cdot 9$$
$$= 3150 \text{ in.}^2$$

**20. a.** $15b + 3r$

**b.** $2(15b + 3r) = 30b + 6r$

**21.** Student A; Sample: Student B only considered numbers greater than 5.

**22.** <; Sample:
$$\sqrt{36} + \sqrt{40} \bigcirc \sqrt{25} + \sqrt{80}$$
$$6 + 6 \bigcirc 5 + 9$$
$$12 \bigcirc 14$$
$$12 < 14$$

**23.** Each tile is 18 inches or
$$\frac{18 \text{ inches}}{1} \cdot \frac{1 \text{ foot}}{12 \text{ inches}} = 1.5 \text{ feet long.}$$

Each tile has an area of $(1.5 \text{ feet})^2 = 2.25$ square feet.

Therefore, John needs $\frac{81}{2.25} = 36$ tiles to cover the floor.

**24.** 8000 feet below sea level can be written as −8000. Write and simplify an expression that represents 2.6 times this distance.

$$2.6 \cdot (-8000) = -20{,}800 \text{ feet}$$

**Saxon** Algebra 1

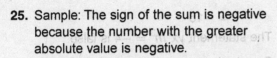

**25.** Sample: The sign of the sum is negative because the number with the greater absolute value is negative.

**26.** Sample: The French use metric measures in their recipes, but the United States uses customary measures.

**27.**

| $10 \cdot 2^3 + 4(7 + 2)$ | Simplify grouping symbols. |
|---|---|
| $= 10 \cdot 2^3 + 4 \cdot 9$ | Simplify inside parentheses. |
| $= 10 \cdot 8 + 4 \cdot 9$ | Simplify exponents. |
| $= 80 + 36$ | Multiply. |
| $= 116$ | Add. |

**28.** Student B; Sample: Student A added the two temperatures instead of subtracting to find the change.

**29.** The volume of the whole structure is the sum of the volume of the rectangular prism and the volume of the triangular prism.

$$V = (10 \cdot 5.8 \cdot 8) + \left[\frac{1}{2} \cdot (10 \cdot 5.8)\right] \cdot 4$$

$$= (10 \cdot 5.8 \cdot 8) + \left[\frac{1}{2} \cdot (58)\right] \cdot 4$$

$$= (10 \cdot 5.8 \cdot 8) + [29] \cdot 4$$

$$= 464 + 116$$

$$= 580 \text{ ft}^3$$

**30. a.** experimental probability

$$= \frac{\text{number of defective balls}}{\text{total number of balls produced}}$$

$$= \frac{10}{500}$$

$$= \frac{1}{50}$$

**b.** Find the product of the probability that a bowling ball will have a defect and the total number of balls shipped to Zippy Lanes.

$$\frac{1}{50} \cdot 250 = 5 \text{ balls}$$

# LESSON 17

## Warm Up 17

**1.** numeric

**2.**
$$5 - 7 + 5 - (-3) = -2 + 5 - (-3)$$
$$= 3 - (-3)$$
$$= 3 + 3$$
$$= 6$$

**3.**
$$(5 + 7)4 + 7(5 - 3)$$
$$= 20 + 28 + 35 - 21$$
$$= 48 + 35 - 21$$
$$= 83 - 21$$
$$= 62$$

**4.**
$$(x^3 + m^5)x^2m^2$$
$$= (x^2m^2)(x^3) + (x^2m^2)(m^5)$$
$$= x^5m^2 + x^2m^7$$

**5.**
$$-(-6)^3 = -1 \cdot [(-6)(-6)(-6)]$$
$$= -1 \cdot (-216)$$
$$= 216$$

The answer is **B**.

## Lesson Practice 17

**a.** $8x$

**b.** $18 - y$

**c.** $5x + 7$

**d.** If $x$ represents Monica's age, then $x + 2$ represents Raquel's age.

**e.** Sample: 10 divided by $s$; the quotient of 10 and $s$

**f.** Sample: $r$ less than 5; the difference of 5 and $r$

**g.** Sample: 7 more than 3 times $m$; the sum of 3 times $m$ and 7

**h.** Sample: three-fourths $x$ plus 9; the sum of three-fourths $x$ and 9

**i.** Sample: the quotient of three less than $x$ and 2; the difference of $x$ and 3 divided by 2.

**j.**

| dollars in savings account | dollars he withdraws each week | amount withdrawn after 15 weeks |
|---|---|---|
| $d$ | $x$ | $15x$ |

Therefore, the amount left after 15 weeks is $d - 15x$.

**Saxon** Algebra 1

## Practice 17

**1.** $(4 + 2y)x$
$= (4)(x) + (2y)(x)$
$= 4x + 2xy$

**2.** $-2(x - 4y)$
$= (-2)(x) + (-2)(-4y)$
$= -2x + 8y$

**3.** Sample: a part of an expression that is added to or subtracted from the other parts

**4. a.** $A \cap C = \{-3, -2, -1\}$
The statement is true.

**b.** $A \cap B = \{1, 2, 3\}$
The statement is false.

**c.** $B \cup C = \{-3, -2, -1, 1, 2, 3\}$
The statement is true.

**d.** $A \cup B = \{-3, -2, -1\}$
The statement is false.

**5.** $3(-x + (-7))$

**6.** $0.18x = 4.68$

**7.** $4.7 + (-9.2) - 1.9$
$= -4.5 - 1.9$
$= -6.4$

**8.** $\sqrt{36} + \sqrt{121} \bigcirc \sqrt{100} + \sqrt{49}$
$6 + 11 \bigcirc 10 + 7$
$17 \bigcirc 17$
$17 = 17$

**9.** 15 is between the perfect squares 9 and 16. $\sqrt{9} = 3$ and $\sqrt{16} = 4$, so $\sqrt{15}$ is between 3 and 4.

**10.** false; Identity Property of Multiplication states that $k \cdot 1 = k$.

**11.** When $a = -3$ and $x = -1$,
$(a + 4)^3 + 5x^2$
$= (-3 + 4)^3 + 5(-1)^2$
$= (1)^3 + 5(1)$
$= 1 + 5$
$= 6$

**12.** $yx^2m^3 = (2)(-1)^2(-2)^3$
$= (2)(1)(-8)$

$= -16$
The statement $yx^2m^3 = -4$ is false.

**13.** Sample: three times the sum of a number and 6

**14.** "4 times the sum of 9 and $g$" translates to $4(9 + g)$. The answer is **B**.

**15.** Let $p$ be Paul's age. Then twice Paul's age is $2p$. Mar's age is $2p - 1$.

**16.** Let $m$ be the amount Miles had. The amount he has after spending $7 is represented by $m - 7$. The amount Miles has now is represented by the expression $2(m - 7)$.

**17. a.** Sample: $a$ is the number of apples and $b$ is the number of bananas.

**b.** An expression to represent the total piece of fruit is $a + b$.

**c.** An expression to represent how much the fruit costs is $0.2a + 0.1b$.

**18.** Student A; Sample: Student B should have found that $(-2)^2 = 4$, instead of $(-2)^2 = -4$, when evaluating $x^2$ for $x = -2$.

**19.** The area of a half circle is given by the expression $\frac{1}{2}\pi r^2$. The length of the rectangle is twice the radius of the half circle or $2r$ and the width is 7, so the area is $(2r)(7) = 14r$. The total area, when $r = 7$, is
$\frac{1}{2}\pi r^2 + 14r$
$= \frac{1}{2}(3.14)(10)^2 + 14(10)$
$= 157 + 140$
$= 297$
The area is about 297 m$^2$.

**20.** Divide the wall into rectangles to find the area of the wall. The area (in feet) is
$30 \times 10 + 10 \times 10 + 11 \times 10$
$= 300 + 100 + 110$
$= 510$
To cover 510 square feet of wall, the painter will need 2 gallons of paint.

**21.** Student B; Student A multiplied the exponents of the variables instead of adding.

**Saxon** Algebra 1

**22.** P(tenth-grader)

$$= \frac{\text{number of tenth-graders}}{\text{total number of students}}$$

$$= \frac{120}{400}$$

$$= \frac{3}{10}$$

$$= 0.3 \text{ or } 30\%$$

**23.** Student B; Sample: Student A did not move the negative sign with the variable when the Commutative Property was used.

**24.** $-\frac{2}{3} \div \left(-\frac{8}{9}\right)$

$$= -\frac{2}{3} \cdot \left(-\frac{9}{8}\right)$$

$$= \frac{18}{24} = \frac{3}{4}$$

**25.** no; Sample: The variable $x$ and $y$ can have many different values, so the expression does not have to represent just one value.

**26.** $(85\ \cancel{lb}) \left[\dfrac{1\ kg}{2.2\ \cancel{lb}}\right] \approx 38.64\ kg$

**27.** Sample: Simplify the fraction, raise base numbers by their exponents, and multiply.

**28.** $174.52 - 186.15 = -11.63$
The net change is $-\$11.63$.

**29.** The first step is to subtract 2 from 23.

**30.**

| number of hours per week | | amount earned per hour by 1 employee and 1 executive |
|---|---|---|
| 40 | $\times$ | $x + y$ |

$$40(x + y)$$

$$= 40x + 40y$$

## LESSON 18

## Warm Up 18

**1.** variable

**2.** $(0.2)^5$

$$= (0.2)(0.2)(0.2)(0.2)(0.2)$$

$$= 0.00032$$

**3.** $y^3 \cdot x^4 \cdot y^2 \cdot x^5 \cdot y$
$x^{4+5}y^{3+2+1}$
$x^9y^6$

**4.** $2x + 6$

## Lesson Practice 18

**a.** $-2xy - 3x + 4 - 4xy - 2x$

$$= -2xy - 4xy - 3x - 2x + 4$$

$$= (-2 - 4)xy + (-3 - 2)x + 4$$

$$= -6xy - 5x + 4$$

**b.** $7m - (-8m) + 9m$

$$= [7 - (-8) + 9]m$$

$$= (7 + 8 + 9)m$$

$$= 24m$$

**c.** $3yac - 2ac + 6acy$

$$= 3yac + 6acy - 2ac$$

$$= 3acy + 6acy - 2ac$$

$$= 9acy - 2ac$$

**d.** $x^4y + 3x^4y + 2x^4y$

$$= (1 + 3 + 2)x^4y$$

$$= 6x^4y$$

**e.** $x^2y - 3yx + 2yx^2 - 2xy + yx$

$$= x^2y + 2yx^2 - 3yx - 2xy + yx$$

$$= x^2y + 2x^2y - 3xy - 2xy + xy$$

$$= (1 + 2)x^2y + (-3 - 2 + 1)xy$$

$$= 3x^2y - 4xy$$

**f.** $m^3n + m^3n - x^2y^7 + x^2y^7$

$$= (1 + 1)m^3n + (-1 + 1)x^2y^7$$

$$= 2m^3n + 0x^2y^7$$

$$= 2m^3n$$

**g.** $P = (x + 1) + x^2 + (x^2 + 1)$
$P = x + 1 + x^2 + x^2 + 1$
$P = x^2 + x^2 + x + 1 + 1$
$P = 2x^2 + x + 2$
$P = 2(2)^2 + 2 + 2$
$P = 2(4) + 2 + 2$
$P = 8 + 2 + 2$
$P = 12$

The perimeters of the display case is $2x^2 + x + 2$ feet or 12 feet.

## Practice 18

**1.** $5x + (-8)$

**2.** $m + 4 + 3m - 6 - 2m + mc - 4mc$
$= m + 3m - 2m + 4 - 6 + cm - 4cm$
$= (1 + 3 - 2)m + (4 - 6) + (1 - 4)cm$
$= 2m + (-2) + (-3)cm$
$= 2m - 2 - 3cm$

**3.** $xy - 3xy^2 + 5y^2x - 4xy$
$= xy - 4xy - 3xy^2 + 5y^2x$
$= xy - 4xy - 3xy^2 + 5xy^2$
$= (1 - 4)xy + (-3 + 5)xy^2$
$= -3xy + 2xy^2$

**4.** The expression $2x^2 + 3x$ does not contain any like terms, so it cannot be simplified. The answer is **D**.

**5. a.** $12x + 15y$ and $9x + 7y$

**b.** $12x + 15y + 9x + 7y$
$= 12x + 9x + 15y + 7y$
$= (12 + 9)x + (15 + 7)y$
$= 21x + 22y$

**6.** no; Sample: Many addition problems with negative numbers have positive answers. For example, $-2 + 3 = 1$ or $6 + (-2) = 4$.

**7.** Find the difference between the change over the five days and the water level after the five days.
$-40 - (-3)(5)$
$= -40 - (-15)$
$= -40 + 15$
$= -25$ inches

**8.** Convert the volume of a candlepin bowling ball to cm$^3$.
$\dfrac{48 \text{ in.}^3}{1} \cdot \dfrac{2.54 \text{ cm}}{1 \text{ in.}} \cdot \dfrac{2.54 \text{ cm}}{1 \text{ in.}} \cdot \dfrac{2.54 \text{ cm}}{1 \text{ in.}}$
$\approx 787$ cm$^3$

Find the difference between the volume of a ten-pin bowling ball and the volume of a candlepin bowling ball.
$V = 5274 - 787$
$= 4487$ cm$^3$ greater

**9.** $\dfrac{-16 + 4}{2(\sqrt{13 - 4})}$
$= \dfrac{-16 + 4}{2(\sqrt{9})}$
$= \dfrac{-16 + 4}{2(3)}$
$= \dfrac{-16 + 4}{6}$
$= \dfrac{-12}{6}$
$= -2$

**10.** $-7 - (2^4 \div 8)$
$= -7 - (16 \div 8)$
$= -7 - (2)$
$= -7 + (-2)$
$= -9$

**11.** $6abc - 7ac + 8acb$
$= 6abc + 8acb - 7ac$
$= 6abc + 8abc - 7ac$
$= (6 + 8)abc - 7ac$
$= 14abc - 7ac$

**12.** $2x^3y + 4x^3y + 9x^3y$
$= (2 + 4 + 9)x^3y$
$= 15x^3y$

**13.** $\left| -15 + \sqrt{81} \right|^2$
$= |-15 + 9|^2$
$= |-6|^2$
$= (6)^2$
$= 36$

**14.** $\dfrac{\sqrt{6 - 2}}{2 \cdot |-7 + 3|}$
$= \dfrac{\sqrt{6 - 2}}{2 \cdot |-4|}$
$= \dfrac{\sqrt{6 - 2}}{2 \cdot 4}$
$= \dfrac{\sqrt{4}}{2 \cdot 4}$
$= \dfrac{2}{2 \cdot 4}$
$= \dfrac{2}{8}$
$= \dfrac{1}{4}$

**Saxon** Algebra 1

**15. a.** $11 + 4x$; $8x$

   **b.** $11 + 4x + 8x$

$$= 4x + 8x + 11$$
$$= (4 + 8)x + 11$$
$$= 12x + 11$$

**16. a.** Sample: Marshall $= 2j + 3$;

     Hank $= 2j$; Jean $= j$

   **b.** If Jean is 12 years old, then substitute 12 for $j$ in each expression.

     Marshall is

     $2j + 3 = 2(12) + 3 = 24 + 3 = 27$ and Hank is $2j = 2(12) = 24$.

   **c.** If Hank was 14, then $2j = 14$. Then Jean's age, $j$, is 7.

**17.** $8x + 2x^2 + 5x$    Distributive Property

    $2x^2 + 8x + 5x$    Commutative Property of Addition

    $2x^2 + 13x$        Add

**18.** $\dfrac{8ak}{4k(2a - 2c + 8)}$

$$= \dfrac{8\left(\frac{1}{2}\right)(-2)}{4(-2)\left(2 \cdot \frac{1}{2} - 2 \cdot 3 + 8\right)}$$

$$= \dfrac{8\left(\frac{1}{2}\right)(-2)}{4(-2)(1 - 6 + 8)}$$

$$= \dfrac{8\left(\frac{1}{2}\right)(-2)}{4(-2)(3)}$$

$$= \dfrac{-8}{-24}$$

$$= \dfrac{1}{3}$$

**19.** true; $pm^2 - Z^3 = (-5)0^2 - (-3)^3 = 0 - (-27) = 27$

**20.** Student A; Sample: Student B substituted the wrong values for $y$ and $z$.

**21.** Finding a common denominator shows you that the first fraction is greater than the second fraction, and that a greater positive number minus a lesser positive number results in a positive number.

**22. a.** $x - 3$

   **b.** $10x + 12(x - 3)$

$$= 10x + 12x - 36$$
$$= (10 + 12)x - 36$$
$$= 22x - 36$$

**23.** $a^2 + b^2 = c^2$

**24. a.** $w + l + w + l$

$$= w + w + l + l$$
$$= (1 + 1)w + (1 + 1)l$$
$$= 2w + 2l$$

   **b.** Substitute $2w$ for $w$ and $3l$ for $l$ in the expression.

$$2(2w) + 2(3l)$$
$$= 4w + 6l$$

**25.** $7(10 - y)$

$$= 7 \cdot 10 - 7 \cdot y$$
$$= 70 - 7y$$

   The answer is **B**.

**26.** $m^2n^2 + m^3n$; Sample: Using the Distributive Property, each term is multiplied by $-m$: $-m(mn^2) - m(-m^2n)$.

**27.** probability

$$= \dfrac{1,\ 3,\ \text{or } 5}{\text{all possible outcomes}}$$

$$= \dfrac{3}{5}$$

**28.** The actual size of the room is $140 + 4 = 144$ square feet. Therefore, the office floor is 12 feet by 12 feet.

**29.** Sample: $24 \div 4 = 6$, $4 \div 24 = \frac{1}{6}$, and $6 \neq \frac{1}{6}$.

**30.** Student B; Sample: Student A squared the sum instead of finding the sum of the squares.

## LESSON 19

### Warm Up 19

**1.** opposites

**2.** $7.5 + (-1.25) = 6.25$

**3.** $12.75 - (-1.05)$

$$= 12.75 + (+1.05)$$
$$= 13.8$$

**Saxon** Algebra 1

**4.** $6(-3) + 3 = -15$ and $-2(-3) + 4 = 10$, so
$6x + 3 < -2x + 4$ when $x = -3$

**5.** $w - (wy - y)$
$= w - wy + y$
$= (-4) - (-4)(-1) + (-1)$
$= (-4) - (4) - 1$
$= -9$
The answer is **C**.

**Lesson Practice 19**

**a.**    $h - 14 = 2$
$(12) - 14 \overset{?}{=} 2$
$-2 \neq 2$
It is not a solution.

**b.** $-11 = j - 4$
$-11 \overset{?}{=} (-7) - 4$
$-11 = -11$
It is a solution.

**c.** Check: Substitute 22 for $x$.
$x - 5 \overset{?}{=} 17$
$(22) - 5 \overset{?}{=} 17$
$17 = 17$

**d.** $-30 = m - 12$
$\underline{+12 = +12}$
$-18 = m$
Check: Substitute $-18$ for $m$.
$-30 \overset{?}{=} m - 12$
$-30 \overset{?}{=} (-18) - 12$
$-30 = -30$

**e.** $p + 3 = 37$
$\underline{-3 = -3}$
$p = 34$

**f.** $-14 = y + 8$
$\underline{-8 \quad -8}$
$-22 = y$

**g.** $d + 4\frac{1}{2} = 3\frac{1}{6}$
$-4\frac{1}{2} = -4\frac{1}{2}$
$d = -1\frac{1}{3}$

**h.** Let $x =$ the score on the first test.
Write an equation.
$x + 13 = 87$
$\underline{-13 = -13}$
$x = 74$
Jagdeesh scored 74 on the first test.

**Practice 19**

**1.** $-3x^2ym + 7x - 5ymx^2 + 16x$
$= -3x^2ym - 5ymx^2 + 7x + 16x$
$= -3mx^2y - 5mx^2y + 7x + 16x$
$= (-3 - 5)mx^2y + (7 + 16)x$
$= -8mx^2y + 23x$

**2.** $x + 5 = 7$
$\underline{-5 = -5}$
$x = 2$

**3.** $x + 5 = -8$
$\underline{-5 = -5}$
$x = -13$

**4.** $x - 6 = 4$
$\underline{+6 = +6}$
$x = 10$

**5.** $7(x + (-5))$

**6.** $-3(-x - 4)$
$= -3(-x) - 3(-4)$
$= 3x + 12$

**7.** $xm^2xm^3x^3m$
$= m^{2+3+1}x^{1+1+3}$
$= m^6x^5$

**8.** Commutative Property of Addition

**9.** false; Sample: The answers are opposites;
$-5^4 = -1 \times 5^4 = -1 \times 625 = -625$;
$(-5)^4 = (-5)(-5)(-5)(-5) = 625$

**10.** A loss of 8 points can be written as $-8$. Write and simplify an expression that represents the sum of points Sandra lost and gained.
$-8 + 5 = -3$ points

**11.** Student B; Student A should have subtracted $\frac{1}{3}$ from both sides of the equation to isolate $x$.

52

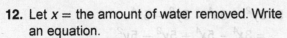
**12.** Let $x$ = the amount of water removed. Write an equation.

$$x + \frac{1}{3} = \frac{4}{5}$$

$$-\frac{1}{3} = -\frac{1}{3}$$

$$x = \frac{7}{15}$$

The maintenance man removed $\frac{7}{15}$ of the pool's total capacity. The answer is **C**.

**13.** Substitute 325.20 for $T_{kelvin}$.

$$T_{Celsius} + 273.15 = T_{kelvin}$$

$$T_{Celsius} + 273.15 = 325.20$$

$$\frac{-273.15 = -273.15}{T_{Celsius} = 52.05°C}$$

**14.** Let $x$ = the number of tickets the theater needs to sell over the rest of the weekend in order to make a profit.
Write an equation.

$$x + 1278 = 3500$$

$$\frac{-1278 = -1278}{x = 2222}$$

The theater needs to sell 2222 tickets over the rest of the weekend.

**15.** Jeremy must add 2.5 to both sides of the equal sign.

**16.** $-5 - b = -5 - (0) = -5$
$-5 - b = -5 - (-5) = 0$
$-5 - b = -5 - (-10) = 5$
$-5 - b = -5 - (5) = -10$

The table of values best represents $-5 - b = a$. The answer is **C**.

**17.** Student B; Sample: Student A added unlike terms.

**18.** $(200 - 2x) + (3x - 170) + (x - 35)$
$= -2x + 3x + x + 200 - 170 - 35$
$= (-2 + 3 + 1)x + 200 - 170 - 35$
$= 2x - 5$

**19. a.** $4t, 5t, 3t$

**b.** $4t + 5t + 3t = (4 + 5 + 3)t = 12t$

**c.** Substitute $\frac{1}{6}$ for $t$.

$$12t = 12\left(\frac{1}{6}\right) = \frac{12}{6} = 2$$

The family ran 2 miles.

**20.** Student B; Sample: Student A translated it into an expression using a quotient rather than the product.

**21.** $|x^2 + y^3|$
$= |(1.5)^2 + (-2)^3|$
$= |(2.25) + (-8)|$
$= |-5.75| = 5.75$

**22.** The number of cans in each level is equal to the square of the number of the level. Let $l$ = the lowest level of the display that is $l$ levels high. Then $l^2$ represents the number of cans in the lowest level. The answer is **C**.

**23. a.** The product of two negative numbers is positive. The product of a negative number and a positive number is negative. Therefore, the resulting value is negative.

**b.** The absolute value of a number is always positive, so the resulting value is positive.

**24. a.** $\dfrac{\text{number of 1250-ft tall buildings}}{\text{total number of buildings}} = \dfrac{1}{7}$

**b.** $\dfrac{\text{number of 1046-ft tall buildings}}{\text{total number of buildings}} = \dfrac{2}{7}$

**c.** $\dfrac{\text{number of buildings built between 1960 and 1980}}{\text{total number of buildings}}$

$= \dfrac{3}{7}$

**25.** Sample: a number that is the square of an integer

**26.** Substitute $500 for $P$ and 3% = 0.03 for $i$.
$P(1 + i)^2$
$= 500(1 + 0.03)^2$
$= 500(1.03)^2$
$= 500(1.0609)$
$= 530.45$

The value of the investment is $530.45.

**27.** Sample: First, I would divide $\pi$ by 4. Then I would simplify $b^2$. Finally, I would multiply to find the solution.

**Saxon** Algebra 1

**28.** The additive inverse of 12 is −12; Sample: When a number is added to its additive inverse, the sum is 0: $12 + (−12) = 0$.

**29.** $5(a + c) + (14a + 8c)$
$= 5a + 5c + 14a + 8c$
$= 5a + 14a + 5c + 8c$
$= (5 + 14)a + (5 + 8)c$
$= 19a + 13c$

**30.** Find the probability that an ace will be chosen from the full deck of cards.

$$\frac{\text{number of aces in the deck}}{\text{total number of cards in the deck}} = \frac{4}{52}$$
$$= \frac{1}{13}$$

If the first ace is not returned to the deck, then there are 3 aces and 51 total cards remaining.

$$\frac{\text{number of aces remaining in the deck}}{\text{number of cards remaining in the deck}}$$
$$= \frac{3}{51}$$
$$= \frac{1}{17}$$

## LESSON 20

### Warm Up 20

**1.** absolute value

**2.** $|3 + (−5) − (−7)|$
$= |3 + (−5) + (+7)|$
$= |5|$
$= 5$

**3.** $|(3 + −5) + (−7)|$
$= |(−2) + (−7)|$
$= |−9|$
$= 9$

**4.** $4(8 + c) + 5$
$= 4 \cdot 8 + 4 \cdot c + 5$
$= 32 + 4c + 5$
$= 32 + 5 + 4c$
$= 37 + 4c$

**5.** $5y^2 + 3x^4 − 5y^2 − 5x^4$
$= 3x^4 − 5x^4 + 5y^2 − 5y^2$
$= (3 − 5)x^4 + (5 − 5)y^4$
$= −2x^4 + 0y^4$
$= −2x^4$

### Lesson Practice 20

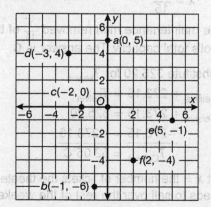

**a.** Point $(0, 5)$ is on the $y$-axis. It is located 5 units above the origin.

**b.** Point $(−1, −6)$ is located in the third quadrant, 1 unit to the left of the origin and 6 units below the horizontal axis.

**c.** Point $(−2, 0)$ is on the $x$-axis. It is located 2 units to the left of the origin.

**d.** Point $(−3, 4)$ is located in the second quadrant, 1 unit to the left of the origin and 4 units above the horizontal axis.

**e.** Point $(5, −1)$ is located in the fourth quadrant, 5 units to the right of the origin and 1 unit below the horizontal axis.

**f.** Point $(2, −4)$ is located in the fourth quadrant, 2 units to the right of the origin and 4 units below the horizontal axis.

**g.** independent variable: the number of toys purchased; dependent variable: the amount paid
The amount paid depends on the number of toys purchased.

**h.** independent variable: the number of yards mowed; dependent variable: the number of hours worked
The number of hours worked depends on the number of yards mowed.

**Saxon** Algebra 1

**i.** Substitute the *x*-values into the equation to determine the *y*-values.

$x = -3$

$y = 2x - 1$

$y = 2(-3) - 1$

$y = -6 - 1$

$y = -7$

$x = -2$

$y = 2x - 1$

$y = 2(-2) - 1$

$y = -4 - 1$

$y = -5$

$x = -1$

$y = 2x - 1$

$y = 2(-1) - 1$

$y = -2 - 1$

$y = -3$

| x | −3 | −2 | −1 |
|---|----|----|----|
| y | −7 | −5 | −3 |

**j.** Substitute 25, 50, 75, and 100 for *x*.

$y = 3(25) - 75 = 75 - 75 = 0$

$y = 3(50) - 75 = 150 - 75 = 75$

$y = 3(75) - 75 = 225 - 75 = 150$

$y = 3(100) - 75 = 300 - 75 = 225$

The amount of money raised when 25, 50, 75, and 100 flowers are sold is $0, $75, $150, and $225, respectively.

Graph the ordered pairs (25, 0), (50, 75), (75, 150), and (100, 225). Do not connect the points with a line because decimal numbers of flowers do not make sense.

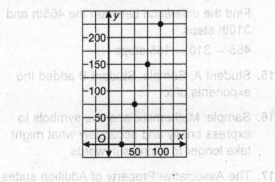

**Practice 20**

**1.** $(+3) + (-14) = -11$

**2.** $4xyz - 3yz + zxy$
$= 4xyz + zxy - 3yz$
$= 4xyz + xyz - 3yz$
$= (4 + 1)xyz - 3yz$
$= 5xyz - 3yz$

**3.** $3xyz - 3xyz + zxy$
$= 3xyz - 3xyz + xyz$
$= (3 - 3 + 1)xyz$
$= 1xyz$
$= xyz$

**4.** $x - 4 = 10$
$\phantom{x}\underline{+4 = +4}$
$\phantom{x}x = 14$

**5.** $x + \dfrac{1}{5} = -\dfrac{1}{10}$
$\phantom{x}\underline{-\dfrac{1}{5} = -\dfrac{1}{5}}$
$\phantom{x}x = -\dfrac{3}{10}$

**6.** Point (3, −4) is located in the fourth quadrant, 3 units to the right of the origin and 4 units below the horizontal axis.

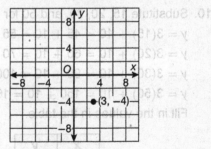

**7.** Point (0, 5) is on the *y*-axis. It is located 5 units above the origin.

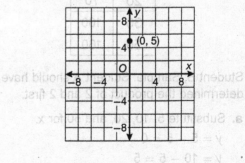

**Saxon** Algebra 1

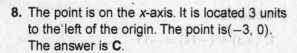
**8.** The point is on the *x*-axis. It is located 3 units to the left of the origin. The point is $(-3, 0)$. The answer is **C**.

**9.** Substitute 1, 2, 3, and 4 for *c*.

$r = 3 + c = 3 + (1) = 4$
$r = 3 + c = 3 + (2) = 5$
$r = 3 + c = 3 + (3) = 6$
$r = 3 + c = 3 + (4) = 7$

Fill in the values in the table.

| c | r |
|---|---|
| 1 | 4 |
| 2 | 5 |
| 3 | 6 |
| 4 | 7 |

Graph the ordered pairs (1, 4), (2, 5), (3, 6), and (4, 7).

**10.** Substitute 15, 20, 30, and 50 for *x*.

$y = 3(15) + 10 = 45 + 10 = 55$
$y = 3(20) + 10 = 60 + 10 = 70$
$y = 3(30) + 10 = 90 + 10 = 100$
$y = 3(50) + 10 = 150 + 10 = 160$

Fill in the values in the table.

| x | y |
|---|---|
| 15 | 55 |
| 20 | 70 |
| 30 | 100 |
| 50 | 160 |

**11.** Student B; Sample: Student A should have determined the product of 2 and 2 first.

**12. a.** Substitute 5, 10, 20, and 50 for *x*.

$y = 5 - 5 = 0$
$y = 10 - 5 = 5$

$y = 20 - 5 = 15$
$y = 50 - 5 = 45$

The profit in dollars when 5, 10, 20, and 50 cups are sold is $0, $5, $15, and $45, respectively.

Graph the ordered pairs (5, 0), (10, 5), (20, 15), and (50, 45). Do not connect the points with a line because decimal numbers of cups do not make sense.

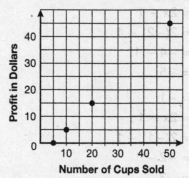

**b.** Sample: Substitute 30 for *x* in the equation.

**13.** $x + 8 + 10 = 24$

$x + 18 = 24$
$\underline{-18 = -18}$
$x = 6$ cm

**14.** Find the number of steps the guard walked during his morning rounds.

$\frac{1}{4}$(total number of steps)

$= \frac{1}{4} \cdot 1860$

$= 465$

The guard walked up 465 steps during his morning rounds.

Find the difference between the 465th and 310th steps.

$465 - 310 = 155$ steps

**15.** Student A; Sample: Student B added the exponents of *x*.

**16.** Sample: Mathematicians use symbols to express briefly and accurately what might take longer to express in words.

**17.** The Associative Property of Addition states that $(a + b) + c = a + (b + c)$. The answer is **D**.

**18. a.** $a^2 = (2)^2 = (2)(2) = 4$

     **b.** $-a^2 = -(2)^2 = -(2)(2) = -4$

     **c.** $-a^3 = -(2)^3 = -(2)(2)(2) = -8$

     **d.** $(-a)^3 = (-2)^3 = (-2)(-2)(-2) = -8$

     **e.** $\left|(-a)^2\right| = \left|(-2)^2\right| = \left|(-2)(-2)\right| =$

         $|4| = 4$

**19.** $\dfrac{3}{50}$

$$50\overline{)3.00}^{\,0.06}$$

The probability that a randomly selected student is type A is 0.06.

**20.** $\sqrt{441} + \sqrt{1089}$

     $= \sqrt{21 \cdot 21} + \sqrt{33 \cdot 33}$

     $= 21 + 33$

     $= 54$

**21.** Sample:

     $(3 \cdot 2) \cdot 4 = 3 \cdot (2 \cdot 4)$

         $6 \cdot 4 = 3 \cdot 8$

         $24 = 24$

**22.** A decrease in the number of deer can be written as a negative integer.

$$\frac{\text{total decrease in number of deer}}{\text{number of years}}$$

     $= \dfrac{-10 + (-7) + (-9) + (-10) + (-12)}{5}$

     $= \dfrac{-48}{5}$

     $= -9.6$ deer

**23.** A drop of 3 points can be written as $-3$.

     $79\dfrac{5}{7} - 3 = 76\dfrac{5}{7}$ points

**24.** Use 1 gram = 1000 milligrams.

     0.3 grams of protein is $0.3 \cdot 1000 =$ 300 milligrams.

**25. a.** A hexagon has 6 sides. Substitute 6 for $n$.

     $\dfrac{(6)^2 - 3(6)}{2}$

     $= \dfrac{36 - 18}{2} = \dfrac{18}{2} = 9$ diagonals

**b.**

**26.** $14 - \dfrac{(3)^2}{3 + 6}$

     $= 14 - \dfrac{9}{3 + 6}$

     $= 14 - \dfrac{9}{9}$

     $= 14 - 1 = 13$

**27. a.** false; Sample: The coefficient of $x$ is 1.

     **b.** The statement is true.

**28.** The coefficients are 1 and $-4$. The variables are $b$, $a$, and $c$. There are 2 terms in the expression.

**29.** Let $p =$ the number of pencils purchased and $e =$ the number of erasers purchased.

     **a.** $p + e$

     **b.** $10p + 5e$

**30.** Substitute 0, 1, 2, and 4 for $t$.

     $d = 5(0) = 0$

     $d = 5(1) = 5$

     $d = 5(2) = 10$

     $d = 5(4) = 20$

The distance the person has run in 0, 1, 2, and 4 hours is 0, 5, 10, and 20 miles, respectively.

Fill in the values in the table.

| $x$ | 0 | 1 | 2 | 4 |
|---|---|---|---|---|
| $y$ | 0 | 5 | 10 | 20 |

Graph the ordered pairs (0, 0), (1, 5), (2, 10), and (4, 20). Connect the points with a smooth line.

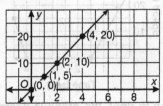

The graph is linear.

**Saxon** Algebra 1

## INVESTIGATION 2

### Investigation Practice 2

**a.** The graph is discrete because the data involve a count of items. Draw the graph using separate, disconnected points.

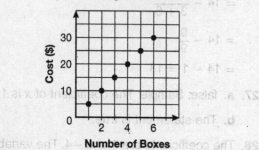

**Greeting Card Sales**

The graph is increasing.

**b.** The graph is continuous because numbers between any two data values have meaning. Draw the graph with a solid line.

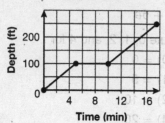

**Depth of Dive**

From left to right, the graph is increasing, has no change, is increasing, and then has no change.

**c.** The graph is continuous because numbers between any two data values have meaning. Draw the graph with a solid line.

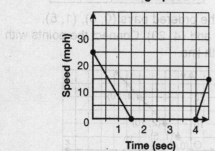

**Driving Speed**

From left to right, the graph is decreasing, has no change, and then is increasing.

**d.** From left to right, the graph should increase and then have no change. The answer is **A.**

**e.** Sample: The graph is an upside-down U.

**f.** Sample: The graph is a line that decreases from left to right.

**g.** Sample: The graph is a series of points that fall in a line that increases from left to right.

## LESSON 21

### Warm Up 21

1. variable

2. $\frac{4}{5} \cdot \frac{1}{2} = \frac{4}{10} = \frac{2}{5}$

3. $\frac{3}{4} \div \frac{1}{2}$

$= \frac{3}{\underset{2}{4}} \cdot \frac{\overset{2}{2}}{1}$

$= \frac{3}{2}$

$= 1\frac{1}{2}$

4. $8(0.5) + 2$
$= 4 + 2$
$= 6$

5. $5 + x = 7$
$x = 2$

The answer is **D.**

### Lesson Practice 21

**a.**  $\frac{k}{9} = 3$

$\cancel{9} \cdot \frac{k}{\cancel{9}} = 3 \cdot 9$

$k = 27$

Check:

$\frac{27}{9} = 3$

$3 = 3 \checkmark$

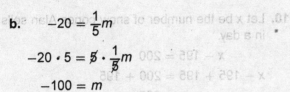

**b.** $-20 = \frac{1}{5}m$

$$-20 \cdot 5 = 5 \cdot \frac{1}{5}m$$

$$-100 = m$$

Check:

$$-20 = \frac{1}{5}(-100)$$

$$-20 = -20 ✓$$

**c.** $8y = 24$

$$\frac{8y}{8} = \frac{24^3}{8}$$

$$y = 3$$

Check:

$$8(3) = 24$$

$$24 = 24 ✓$$

**d.** $-15 = 3x$

$$-\frac{5\cancel{15}}{\cancel{3}} = \frac{\cancel{3}x}{\cancel{3}}$$

$$-5 = x$$

Check:

$$-15 = 3(-5)$$

$$-15 = -15 ✓$$

**e.** $\frac{3}{4}y = 11$

$$\frac{3}{4}y \div \frac{3}{4} = 11 \div \frac{3}{4}$$

$$\frac{\cancel{3}}{\cancel{4}}y \cdot \frac{\cancel{4}}{\cancel{3}} = 11 \cdot \frac{4}{3}$$

$$y = \frac{44}{3}$$

Check:

$$\frac{\cancel{3}}{\cancel{4}} \cdot \frac{44^{11}}{\cancel{3}} = 11$$

$$11 = 11 ✓$$

**f.** $8 = -\frac{5}{12}n$

$$8 \div \left(-\frac{5}{12}\right) = -\frac{5}{12}n \div \left(-\frac{5}{12}\right)$$

$$8 \cdot -\left(\frac{12}{5}\right) = -\frac{\cancel{5}}{\cancel{12}}n \cdot -\left(\frac{\cancel{12}}{\cancel{5}}\right)$$

$$-\frac{96}{5} = n$$

Check:

$$8 = -\frac{5}{\cancel{12}} \cdot \left(-\frac{\cancel{96}^8}{\cancel{5}}\right)$$

$$8 = 8 ✓$$

**g.** $A = lw$

$$140 = 16w$$

$$\frac{35\cancel{140}}{4\cancel{16}} = \frac{\cancel{16}w}{\cancel{16}}$$

$$\frac{35}{4} = w$$

$$8\frac{3}{4} = w$$

Check:

$$A = lw$$

$$140 = \cancel{16}^4 \cdot \frac{35}{\cancel{4}}$$

$$140 = 140 ✓$$

The pond is $8\frac{3}{4}$ feet wide.

**Practice 21**

**1.** $\frac{x}{4} = 7$

$$\cancel{4} \cdot \frac{x}{\cancel{4}} = 7 \cdot 4$$

$$x = 28$$

The ladder rises 28 feet.

**2.** Sample: The term in an algebraic expression is the part to be added or subtracted.

**3.** Sample: Multiply both sides by the multiplicative inverse of $\frac{2}{3}$, which is $\frac{3}{2}$, in order to isolate $x$.

$$\frac{\cancel{3}}{\cancel{2}} \cdot \frac{\cancel{2}}{\cancel{3}}x = \cancel{8}^4 \cdot \frac{3}{\cancel{2}}$$

$$x = 12$$

**4.** $\Delta v = v_f - v_i$

$$2 = v_f - 5$$

$$5 + 2 = v_f - 5 + 5$$

$$7 = v_f$$

Check:

$$2 = 7 - 5$$

$$2 = 2 ✓$$

The cart's final velocity is 7 miles per second.

**Saxon** Algebra 1

**5.** To graph $(-2, 6)$, start at the origin, move 2 units to the left, and then move 6 units up.

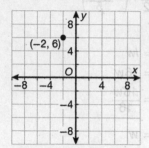

**6. a.**

$$3w$$

$w$ [rectangle]

**b.** $A = lw$

$\quad = 3w \cdot w$

$\quad = 3w^2$

**7.**

| x | −5 | 1 | 4 |
|---|----|---|---|
| y | −3 | 9 | 15 |

$y = 2(-5) + 7$

$\quad = -10 + 7$

$\quad = -3$

$y = 2(1) + 7$

$\quad = 2 + 7$

$\quad = 9$

$y = 2(4) + 7$

$\quad = 8 + 7$

$\quad = 15$

**8.** $\dfrac{x}{3} = 5$

$\cancel{3} \cdot \dfrac{x}{\cancel{3}} = 5 \cdot 3$

$\quad x = 15$

Check:

$\dfrac{15}{3} = 5$

$\quad 5 = 5 \checkmark$

**9.** $\qquad -\dfrac{x}{9} = -52$

$-\cancel{9} \cdot \left(-\dfrac{x}{\cancel{9}}\right) = -52 \cdot (-9)$

$\qquad x = 468$

Choice **B** is correct.

**10.** Let $x$ be the number of snow cones Alan sells in a day.

$\qquad x - 195 = 200$

$x - 195 + 195 = 200 + 195$

$\qquad x = 395$

Check:

$395 - 195 = 200$

$\qquad 200 = 200 \checkmark$

**11.** Sample: $3z^2y$ and $-z^2y$ can be combined. $2yz$ and $8yz$ can be combined. Each pair has the same variables and the same powers of variables. $-4y^2z$ cannot be combined with any other term because no other term has $y^2z$.

**12.** $2.364(4,500,000)$

$= 10,638,000$

The shuttle would weigh about 10,638,000 pounds on Jupiter.

**13.** $A = 8(2) = 16$

$A = 8(4) = 32$

$A = 8(6) = 48$

$A = 8(8) = 64$

| w | A |
|---|----|
| 2 | 16 |
| 4 | 32 |
| 6 | 48 |
| 8 | 64 |

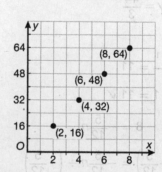

**14.** $-4 - 3 + 2 - 4 - 3 - 8$

$= -4 + (-3) + 2 + (-4) + (-3) + (-8)$

$= -20$

**Saxon** Algebra 1

**15.** $5p + 7 - 8p + 2$
$= (5p - 8p) + (7 + 2)$
$= -3p + 9$
$= 9 - 3p$
The answer is **A**.

**16.** Method 1:
$\frac{2}{3}\left(4 + \frac{3}{4}\right)$
$= \frac{2}{3}(4) + \frac{\cancel{2}}{3}\left(\frac{3}{\cancel{4}_2}\right)$
$= \frac{8}{3} + \frac{1}{2}$
$= \frac{19}{6}$

Method 2:
$\frac{2}{3}\left(4 + \frac{3}{4}\right)$
$= \frac{2}{3}\left(\frac{19}{\cancel{4}_2}\right)$
$= \frac{19}{6}$

**17.** The alphabet has 26 letters, 5 of which are vowels. The probability of randomly choosing a vowel is $\frac{5}{26}$.

**18.** Each side measures 10 feet. Sample: A square has equal sides and $A = s^2$, so the length of one side is $\sqrt{100} = 10$.

**19.** yes; The Commutative Property of Addition allows the order of the addends to be changed without affecting the result.

**20. a.** $y = 1200 - 150(1) = 1050$
$y = 1200 - 150(4) = 600$
$y = 1200 - 150(6) = 300$
$y = 1200 - 150(8) = 0$

| $x$ | $y$ |
|---|---|
| 1 | 1050 |
| 4 | 600 |
| 6 | 300 |
| 8 | 0 |

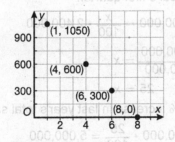

**b.** Sample: It takes her 8 minutes to get from home to school.

**21.** Yes; Sample: Dividing by a number is the same as multiplying by its reciprocal. Dividing by $-\frac{3}{4}$ is the same as multiplying by $-\frac{4}{3}$.

**22. a.** $4^3 = 64$
$\left(\frac{1}{4}\right)^3 = \frac{1^3}{4^3} = \frac{1}{64}$

**b.** $4^3 \cdot \left(\frac{1}{4}\right)^3 = 1$

$\cancel{4} \cdot \cancel{4} \cdot \cancel{4} \cdot \frac{1}{\cancel{4}} \cdot \frac{1}{\cancel{4}} \cdot \frac{1}{\cancel{4}} = 1$

$1 = 1$

**23.** No; Sample: A rational number can be expressed as a ratio of two integers.

**24.** Sample: metric units of measure, such as $cm^2$ to $mm^2$, or $dm^2$ to $cm^2$

**25.** $y = 4.5 - 0.25(4) = 3.5$
$y = 4.5 - 0.25(8) = 2.5$
$y = 4.5 - 0.25(12) = 1.5$
$y = 4.5 - 0.25(16) = 0.5$

| $x$ | $y$ |
|---|---|
| 4 | 3.5 |
| 8 | 2.5 |
| 12 | 1.5 |
| 16 | 0.5 |

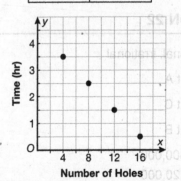

**Saxon** Algebra 1

**26.** $-|15 - 5|$

$= -|10|$

$= -10$

**27. a.** Let $s$ be the number of strawberries at the first stand. Let $k$ be the number of kiwis at the first stand.

The first stand has $s + k$.

The second stand has $2s + 4k$.

**b.** The total number of pieces of fruit is:

$s + k + 2s + 4k$

$= 3s + 5k$

**28.** At first, each increase in time leads to a small increase in height. After adding more sun and water, each increase in time leads to greater increases in height.

**Tomato Plant Growth**

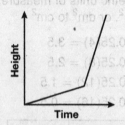

**29.** 0.21 of what number is 7.98

$0.21 \times n = 7.98$

The expression is $0.21n = 7.98$.

**30.** Student A; Sample; Student B should have added 5 to both sides of the equation to isolate $x$.

## LESSON 22

**1.** rational; irrational

**2.** point A

**3.** point C

**4.** point B

**5.** 12,300,000

$\quad\underline{-\ 20,000}$

$\quad$ 12,280,000

## Lesson Practice 22

**a.** Difference between Harry's and Sal's number of shops:

2001: $8 - 2 = 6$

2002: $10 - 5 = 5$

2003: $12 - 9 = 3$

2004: $14 - 14 = 0$

2005: $16 - 10 = 6$

2006: $18 - 7 = 11$

The greatest difference is in 2006, when Harry owned 11 more shops than Sal.

**b.** Number of shops opened:

2001–02: $5 - 2 = 3$

2002–03: $9 - 5 = 4$

2003–04: $14 - 9 = 5$

2004–06: Did not open any new shops.

The greatest number of shops Sal opened in one year is 5.

**c.** **Height of Jackson Grandchildren (in inches)**

| Stem | Leaf |
|---|---|
| 4 | 0 3 9 9 |
| 5 | 2 4 6 |
| 6 | 8 |
| 7 | 1 2 |

Key: $6|8 = 68$

**d.** Difference between deposits and withdrawals:

January: $|475 - 100| = 375$

February: $|200 - 275| = 75$

March: $|350 - 350| = 0$

April: $|425 - 400| = 25$

May: $|500 - 200| = 300$

June: $|150 - 225| = 75$

The greatest difference is $375 in January.

**e.** First quarter sales increased by $600,000 over last year's first quarter.

$3,000,000 - 2,400,000 = 600,000$

First quarter sales increased by 25% over last year's first quarter.

$$600,000 = \frac{x}{100} \cdot 2,400,000$$

$$\frac{60,000,000}{2,400,000} = x$$

$$25 = x$$

A 25% increase in last year's total sales is:

$$20,000,000 \cdot \frac{25}{100} = 5,000,000$$

Predicted total sales for this year:
20,000,000 + 5,000,000 = 25,000,000

**Practice 22**

1. False; Stem-and-leaf plots help organize data.

2. $y = -3(-1) - 9 = 3 - 9 = -6$
   $y = -3(0) - 9 = 0 - 9 = -9$
   $y = -3(1) - 9 = -3 - 9 = -12$

| x | −1 | 0 | 1 |
|---|----|----|----|
| y | −6 | −9 | −12 |

3. $2p(xy - 3k)$
   $= (2p \cdot xy) - (2p \cdot 3k)$
   $= 2pxy - 6pk$

4. $y - 3 = 2$
   $y - 3 + 3 = 2 + 3$
   $y = 5$

5. $x - \frac{1}{4} = \frac{7}{8}$
   $x - \frac{1}{4} + \frac{1}{4} = \frac{7}{8} + \frac{1}{4}$
   $x = \frac{7}{8} + \frac{2}{8}$
   $x = \frac{9}{8}$ or $x = 1\frac{1}{8}$

6. $4x = 2\frac{2}{3}$
   $4x \div 4 = \frac{8}{3} \div 4$
   $x = \frac{8^2}{3} \cdot \frac{1}{4}$
   $x = \frac{2}{3}$

7. $7x = 49$
   $\frac{7x}{7} = \frac{49^7}{7}$
   $x = 7$

8. line graph; Sample: Line graphs show changes in data over time.

9. a. false; 3 ÷ 4 in not an integer.
   b. false; $\sqrt{3} \div \sqrt{3}$ is a whole number.
   c. true

10.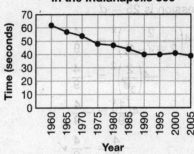

**Fastest Lap Times in the Indianapolis 500**

Sample: The lap times have become faster since 1960.

11. To graph (−4, −1), start at the origin, move 4 units to the left, and then move 1 unit down.

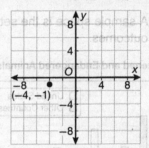

12. Student A is correct; Student B graphed the point (3, −4) by first moving vertically, then horizontally.

13. Choice **B** is correct. The sum of the number of eggs she has (12) and number of eggs she will buy (x) must equal 25.

14. $x = 14 - y$
    $x + y = 14 - y + y$
    $x + y = 14$
    $x - x + y = 14 - x$
    $y = 14 - x$

    a. If y must be greater than 14, x must be a negative number.
    b. If y must be equal to 14, x must be equal to zero.
    c. If y must be less than 14, x must be a positive number.

15. A double-bar graph is useful for comparing data values. The answer is **D**.

**Saxon** Algebra 1

**16.** The distance from home is 25 miles minus the $d$ miles the man has already driven. The expression is $25 - d$.

**17. a.** $-4\left(\dfrac{2}{2-(-4)}\right)^2 = -\dfrac{4}{9}$

$$-4\left(\dfrac{2}{3\cancel{6}}\right)^2 = -\dfrac{4}{9}$$

$$-4\left(\dfrac{1}{9}\right) = -\dfrac{4}{9}$$

$$-\dfrac{4}{9} = -\dfrac{4}{9} \checkmark$$

**b.** $\left|(-1-2)^3\right| = 27$

$$\left|(-3)^3\right| = 27$$

$$|-27| = 27$$

$$27 = 27 \checkmark$$

**18.** Sample: A sample space is the set of all possible outcomes.

**19.**

**Threatened and Endangered Animals**

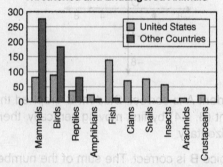

Sample: There are more threatened and endangered mammals, birds, and reptiles in other countries, but the total number of threatened and endangered animals in the United States is greater than the total for other countries.

**20.** Sample: The Commutative Property does not apply to subtraction. The order in which numbers are subtracted affects the result.

**21.** $A = \dfrac{1}{2}(b_1 + b_2)h$

$$= \dfrac{1}{2}(3 + 5.5)(6.2)$$

$$= 26.35$$

The area of the garden is 26.35 square feet.

**22.** $-7 + (-3) + 4 - 3 + (-2)$

$$= -7 + (-3) + 4 + (-3) + (-2)$$

$$= -11$$

**23.** The measure of the arc (16 inches) is $\frac{4}{9}$ of the circumference.

$$\dfrac{4}{9}c = 16$$

$$\dfrac{4}{9}c \div \dfrac{4}{9} = 16 \div \dfrac{4}{9}$$

$$\dfrac{\cancel{4}}{\cancel{9}}c \cdot \dfrac{\cancel{9}}{\cancel{4}} = \overset{4}{\cancel{16}} \cdot \dfrac{9}{\cancel{4}}$$

$$c = 36$$

The circumference is 36 inches.

**24. a.** Area is the product of length and width. The area of the new room is $15 \cdot 20$.

**b.** The new total area is the original area plus the area of the new room.

$$1200 + (15 \cdot 20)$$

**c.** The new total area is 1500 square feet.

**25.** Sample: A man makes 2 bank deposits of $d$ dollars and withdraws $w$ dollars.

**26.** $3ab^2 - 2ab + 5b^2a - ba$

$$= 3ab^2 + 5ab^2 - 2ab - ab$$

$$= 8ab^2 - 3ab$$

**27.** $\dfrac{380}{1187} \approx 0.32$

**28.** $x^2yyyx^3yx$

$$= (x^2 \cdot x^3 \cdot x)(y \cdot y \cdot y \cdot y)$$

$$= x^{(2+3+1)}y^{(1+1+1+1)}$$

$$= x^6y^4$$

**29. a.** Let $x$ be the sale price of each book. Six times the sale price of each book is equal to the total Enrique pays.

$$7x + 25 = 125$$

$$\underline{-25 = -25}$$

$$7x = 100$$

$$\dfrac{7x}{7} = \dfrac{100}{7}$$

$$x \approx 14.29$$

$$6x = 31.92$$

$$x = \dfrac{31.92}{6}$$

$$x = 5.32$$

The sale price of each book is $5.32.

**Saxon** Algebra 1

**b.** Let $x$ be the original cost of each book. The sale price of each book is $\frac{4}{5}$ of the original cost of each book.

$$\frac{4}{5}x = 5.32$$

$$\frac{4}{5}x \div \frac{4}{5} = 5.32 \div \frac{4}{5}$$

$$\frac{\cancel{5}}{\cancel{4}} \cdot \frac{\cancel{4}}{\cancel{5}}x = 5.32 \cdot \frac{5}{4}$$

$$x = 6.65$$

The original cost of each book is $6.65.

**30. a.** Out of 26 draws, Jose draws a heart 8 times.

$$\frac{8}{26} = \frac{4}{13}$$

The experimental probability of Jose drawing a heart is $\frac{4}{13}$.

**b.** Out of 26 draws, Jose draws a suit other than clubs 20 times.

$$\frac{20}{26} = \frac{10}{13}$$

The experimental probability of Jose not drawing a club is $\frac{10}{13}$.

## LESSON 23

### Warm Up 23

**1.** coefficient

**2.** $3(x - 4)$
$$= 3x - 12$$

**3.** $-2(x - 3) + 4(x + 1)$
$$= -2x + 6 + 4x + 4$$
$$= 2x + 10$$

**4.** $\frac{\cancel{3}}{2\cancel{4}}\left(\frac{\cancel{2}}{\cancel{9}_3}\right) + \frac{5}{6}$
$$= \frac{1}{6} + \frac{5}{6}$$
$$= 1$$

**5.** $\quad -7 + x = 14$
$$-7 + x + 7 = 14 + 7$$
$$x = 14 + 7$$
$$x = 21$$

The answer is **D**.

### Lesson Practice 23

**a.** Sample: Use the order of operations and first multiply 9 by 2.

**b.** Sample: Use the order of operations in reverse, and subtract to undo the addition. First subtract 6.

**c.** $8w - 4 = 28$
$$\underline{+4 = +4}$$
$$8w = 32$$
$$\frac{8w}{8} = \frac{32}{8}$$
$$w = 4$$

Check:
$$8(4) - 4 = 28$$
$$32 - 4 = 28$$
$$28 = 28 \checkmark$$

**d.** $-10 = -2x + 12$
$$\underline{-12 = -12}$$
$$-22 = -2x$$
$$\frac{-22}{-2} = \frac{-2x}{-2}$$
$$11 = x$$

Check:
$$-10 = -2(11) + 12$$
$$-10 = -22 + 12$$
$$-10 = -10 \checkmark$$

**e.** $\frac{1}{8}m + \frac{3}{4} = \frac{7}{12}$
$$\underline{-\frac{3}{4} = -\frac{3}{4}}$$
$$\frac{1}{8}m = -\frac{1}{6}$$
$$8 \cdot \frac{1}{8}m = -\frac{1}{6} \cdot 8$$
$$m = -\frac{4}{3}$$

Check:
$$-\frac{4}{3} \approx -1 \text{ and } \frac{7}{12} \approx \frac{1}{2}$$
$$\frac{1}{8}(-1) + \frac{3}{4} \approx \frac{1}{2}$$
$$-\frac{1}{8} + \frac{6}{8} \approx \frac{1}{2}$$

$$\frac{5}{8} \approx \frac{1}{2}$$

The solution is reasonable.

**f.** Let $x$ be the number of months it takes for the amount the Greens save to equal the amount they spend on the bulbs.

savings times months plus rebate equals cost

$$\quad \$7 \quad \cdot \quad x \quad + \quad \$25 \quad = \quad \$125$$

$$7x + 25 = 125$$
$$\underline{-25 = -25}$$
$$7x = 100$$
$$\frac{7x}{7} = \frac{100}{7}$$
$$x \approx 14.3$$

The Greens will have paid for the bulbs in about 14 months.

## Practice 23

**1.** $(3.5 - 2.5) - (3.5 - 2.5)$
$= 1 - 1$
$= 0$

**2.** Sample: Start at the origin. Go 2 units left and then 4 units up. Mark the point.

**3.** $3x + 5 = 32$
$$\underline{-5 = -5}$$
$$3x = 27$$
$$\frac{3x}{3} = \frac{27}{3}$$
$$x = 9$$

The answer is **B**.

**4.** Student B; Sample: Student A divided both sides of the equation by 12 instead of −12.

**5.** Let $x$ be the plane's altitude after 6 minutes.
350 m/min × 6 min + 750 m = $x$
$350(6) + 750 = x$
$2100 + 750 = x$
$2850 = x$

After 6 minutes, the plane's altitude is 2850 meters.

**6.** $3(9) - 8 = 22$
$27 - 8 = 22$
$19 \neq 22$
$x = 9$ is not the solution of the equation.

$$3x - 8 = 22$$
$$\underline{+8 = +8}$$
$$3x = 30$$
$$\frac{3x}{3} = \frac{30}{3}$$
$$x = 10$$

Check:
$$3(10) - 8 = 22$$
$$30 - 8 = 22$$
$$22 = 22 \checkmark$$

The correct solution is $x = 10$.

**7.** Sample: $\frac{3}{5} \cdot 5 = 3$

**8. a.** Comedy was the most popular.

**b.** $0.15(300) = 45$
45 people liked horror movies the best.

**c.** $0.30(300) = 90$
$0.20(300) = 60$
$90 - 60 = 30$
30 more people liked action movies than like dramas.

**9.** double-bar graph; Sample: Double-bar graphs can compare two different sets of data side by side.

**10.**

**Favorite Vacation Destinations**

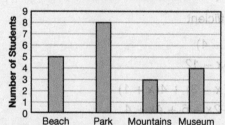

**11.** $C = 2\pi r$

$$\frac{8}{9}\pi = 2\pi r$$

$$\left(\frac{1}{2\pi}\right) \cdot \frac{8\pi^4}{9} = r$$

$$\frac{4}{9} = r$$

The radius of the circle is $\frac{4}{9}$ meters.

**12.** Check each point in equation D.
$(-1, 1)$ $\quad 1 = -2(-1)-1$
$\qquad\qquad 1 = 2 - 1$

**Saxon** Algebra 1

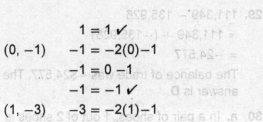

$$1 = 1 \checkmark$$

$(0, -1)$    $-1 = -2(0)-1$
$$-1 = 0 -1$$
$$-1 = -1 \checkmark$$

$(1, -3)$    $-3 = -2(1)-1$
$$-3 = -2 -1$$
$$-3 = -3 \checkmark$$

The $x$- and $y$-values of the three points satisfy $y = -2x - 1$. The answer is **D**.

**13. a.** The value of Jenny's coins is:

(value times #) plus (value times #)

(25    ·    $x$)  +  (10    ·    $y$)

$25x + 10y$

The value of Sam's coins is:

(value times #) plus (value times #)

(50    ·    $h$)  +  (5    ·    $z$)

$50h + 5z$

**b.** $25x + 50h + 10y + 5z$

**14.** $3x + 12$        $12 + 3x$
   $3(2) + 12$        $12 + 3(2)$
   $= 6 + 12$        $= 12 + 6$
   $= 18$        $= 18$

**15.** Evaluate each expression.

$$24 + \frac{16}{4} - (4 + 3^2) \cdot 2$$

$$= 24 + \frac{16}{4} - (13) \cdot 2$$

$$= 24 + 4 - 26$$

$$= 28 - 26$$

$$= 2$$

$$24 + \left(\frac{16}{4} - 4\right) + 3^2 \cdot 2$$

$$= 24 + \left(\frac{16}{4} - 4\right) + 9 \cdot 2$$

$$= 24 + (0) + 9 \cdot 2$$

$$= 24 + 18$$

$$= 42$$

$24 + \frac{16}{4} - (4 + 3^2) \cdot 2$ is less than

$24 + \left(\frac{16}{4} - 4\right) + 3^2 \cdot 2$

**16.** $y - \dfrac{1}{2} = -2\dfrac{1}{2}$

$$\dfrac{+\dfrac{1}{2} = +\dfrac{1}{2}}{y = -2}$$

Check:

$$-2 - \frac{1}{2} = -2\frac{1}{2}$$

$$-2\frac{1}{2} = -2\frac{1}{2} \checkmark$$

**17.** $2x + 3 = 11$

$$\dfrac{-3 = -3}{2x = 8}$$

$$\frac{2x}{2} = \frac{8}{2}$$

$$x = 4$$

Check:

$$2(4) + 3 = 11$$

$$8 + 3 = 11$$

$$11 = 11 \checkmark$$

**18.** $3x - 4 = 10$

$$\dfrac{+4 = +4}{3x = 14}$$

$$x = \frac{14}{3}$$

$$x = 4\frac{2}{3}$$

Check:

$$3\left(\frac{14}{3}\right) - 4 = 10$$

$$14 - 4 = 10$$

$$10 = 10 \checkmark$$

**19.** $2.2x + 2 = 8.6$

$$\dfrac{-2 = -2}{2.2x = 6.6}$$

$$\frac{2.2x}{2.2} = \frac{6.6}{2.2}$$

$$x = 3$$

Check:

$$2.2(3) + 2 = 8.6$$

$$6.6 + 2 = 8.6$$

$$8.6 = 8.6 \checkmark$$

**Saxon** Algebra 1

**20.** $\frac{801}{1789} \approx 0.45$

The probability of the player making his next shot is 0.45.

**21. a.** $\frac{3}{43}$

**b.** $\frac{4}{43} + \frac{4}{43} = \frac{8}{43}$

**c.** Of the first 43 presidents 17 (6 + 4 + 4 + 3) are named James, John, William, or George, and 26 (43 − 17 = 26) are not. The probability of choosing a president whose name is not in the table is $\frac{26}{43}$.

**22.** $A = s^2$

$361 = s^2$

$\sqrt{361} = s$

$19 = s$

Each side of the porch is 19 feet long.

**23.** The lowest temperature is about six times the highest temperature, so:

$t \approx 6 \cdot -13.6$

$t = 6 \cdot (-13.6)$

$t = -81.6$

The lowest temperature recorded is about −81.6°C.

**24.** −4 + 21 = 17

The high temperature was 17°F.

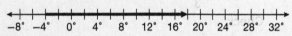

**25.** 138.24 − 46.59 + 29.83 + 1.87 = 123.35

Paula's new balance was $123.35.

**26.** $4 \div 2 + 6^2 - 22$

$= 4 \div 2 + 36 - 22$

$= 2 + 36 - 22$

$= 16$

**27.** $a^3 b^2 ac^5 a^4 b$

$= a^{(3+1+4)}b^{(2+1)}c^5$

$= a^8 b^3 c^5$

Sample: Use the Product Rule for Exponents by adding together the exponents of like bases.

**28.** $\frac{332 \text{ m}}{1 \text{ sec}} \cdot \frac{100 \text{ cm}}{1 \text{ m}} = 33,200$ cm/sec

**29.** 111,349 − 135,926

$= 111,349 + (-135,926)$

$= -24,577$

The balance of trade was −$24,577. The answer is **D**.

**30. a.** In a pair of shoes, 1 out of 2 shoes is for the left foot, so the event is as likely as not.

**b.** A standard number cube has the numbers 1, 2, 3, 4, 5, and 6, all of which are less than 7, so the event certain.

**c.** November never has 31 days, so the event is impossible.

## LESSON 24

### Warm Up 24

**1.** power

**2.** $\frac{5}{8} = 0.625$, so the order is:

$-2.85, -0.8, 0.58, \frac{5}{8}$

**3.** $4x - 3x^2 + 7x$

$= 4x + (-3x^2) + 7x$

$= -3x^2 + (4x + 7x)$

$= -3x^2 + 11x$

### Lesson Practice 24

**a.**
$$0.25 + 0.18y = 0.97$$
$$10(0.25) + 10(0.18y) = 10(0.97)$$
$$25 + 18y = 97$$
$$\frac{-25 \quad = -25}{18y = 72}$$
$$\frac{18y}{18} = \frac{72}{18}$$
$$y = 4$$

**b.**
$$0.05 = 0.5 - 0.15q$$
$$100(0.05) = 100(0.5) - 100(0.15q)$$
$$5 = 50 - 15q$$
$$\frac{-50 = -50}{-45 = -15q}$$
$$\frac{-45}{-15} = \frac{-15q}{-15}$$
$$3 = q$$

**Saxon** Algebra 1

**c.** $-0.5n + 1.4 = 8.9$

$$\underline{-1.4 = -1.4}$$
$$-0.5n = 7.5$$

$$\frac{-0.5n}{-0.5} = \frac{7.5}{0.5}$$

$$n = -15$$

**d.** decimal # of given # is what #?

| 0.6 | · | 24 | = | n |

$0.6 \cdot 24 = n$

$14.4 = n$

Check by estimating.

0.6 is a little more than one half. Half of 24 is 12, and 14.4 is a little more than 12, so the answer is reasonable.

**e.** (A to B) plus (B to C) is (A to C)

| x | + | 2x | = | 52.8 |

$x + 2x = 52.8$

$3x = 52.8$

$$\frac{3x}{3} = \frac{52.8}{3}$$

$x = 17.6$

The distance from Town B to Town C is $2x = 2(17.6) = 35.2$ kilometers.

**Practice 24**

**1.** $\frac{4}{5}x = -24$

$\frac{4}{5}x \div \frac{4}{5} = -24 \div \frac{4}{5}$

$\frac{\cancel{4}}{\cancel{5}}x \cdot \frac{\cancel{5}}{\cancel{4}} = -24^6 \cdot \frac{5}{\cancel{4}}$

$x = -30$

The answer is **A**.

**2. a.** $3(2x + 5x)$

$= 3(7x)$

$= 21x$

**b.** $3(2x + 5x)$

$= 6x + 15x$

$= 21x$

**3.** $0.45x - 0.002 = 8.098$

$$\underline{+0.002 = +0.002}$$
$$0.45x = 8.1$$

$$\frac{0.45x}{0.45} = \frac{8.1}{0.45}$$

$x = 18$

**4.** The solution remains the same. Sample: The Multiplication Property of Equality states that you can multiply both sides of an equation by the same number and the statement will still be true.

**5.** $/share times # plus fee is total $

| $6.57 | · | n | + | $25 | = | $846.25 |

$6.57n + 25 = 846.25$

$$\underline{-25 = -25}$$
$$6.57n = 821.25$$

$$\frac{6.57n}{6.57} = \frac{821.25}{6.57}$$

$n = 125$

She bought 125 shares of stock.

**6.** given # is decimal # of what #?

| 0.8 | = | 0.32 | · | n |

$0.8 = 0.32n$

$$\frac{0.8}{0.32} = \frac{0.32n}{0.32}$$

$2.5 = n$

The answer is **A**.

**7. Method I:**

$0.45x + 0.9 = 1.008$

$1000(0.45x) + 1000(0.9) = 1000(1.008)$

$450x + 900 = 1008$

$$\underline{-900 = -900}$$
$$450x = 108$$

$$\frac{450x}{450} = \frac{108}{450}$$

$x = 0.24$

**Method II:**

$0.45x + 0.9 = 1.008$

$$\underline{-0.9 = -0.9}$$
$$0.45x = 0.108$$

$$\frac{0.45x}{0.45} = \frac{0.108}{0.45}$$

$x = 0.24$

Both methods result in the same solution.

**8.** coefficient: $\frac{9}{5}$; variable: $C$; number of terms: 2. The two terms are $\frac{9}{5}C$ and 32.

**Saxon** Algebra 1

**9.** Method I:

$$0.25x + \frac{1}{2} = 0.075$$

$$0.25x + 0.5 = 0.075$$

$$\underline{-0.5 = -0.5}$$

$$0.25x = -0.425$$

$$\frac{0.25x}{0.25} = \frac{0.425}{0.25}$$

$$x = -1.7$$

Method II:

$$0.25x + \frac{1}{2} = 0.075$$

$$\frac{1}{4}x + \frac{1}{2} = \frac{3}{40}$$

$$\frac{-\frac{1}{2} = -\frac{1}{2}}{}$$

$$\frac{1}{4}x = -\frac{17}{40}$$

$$\cancel{4} \cdot \frac{1}{\cancel{4}}x = -\frac{17}{\cancel{40}_{10}} \cdot \cancel{4}$$

$$x = -\frac{17}{10}$$

Since $-1.7 = -\frac{17}{10}$, both methods result in the same solution.

**10.** Student B; Sample: The circle graph shows the number of students, not the percentages. Student A found the total number of students and wrote that number as a percent.

**11.** When it was 100 years old, the tree was about 20 inches in diameter.

$$C = \pi d$$

$$C \approx 3.14(20)$$

$$C \approx 62.8$$

The tree's circumference was about 62.8 inches.

**12.** % times total is cost per snack

$$0.01x \cdot \$12 = c$$

$$0.01 \cdot 10 \cdot 12 = 1.2$$

$$0.01 \cdot 20 \cdot 12 = 2.4$$

$$0.01 \cdot 30 \cdot 12 = 3.6$$

$$0.01 \cdot 40 \cdot 12 = 4.8$$

Will spent $1.20 on apples, $2.40 on juice, $3.60 on strawberries, and $4.80 on peanut butter.

**13.** Start at the origin. Move 2 units to the right, and then 1 unit up. Mark the point.

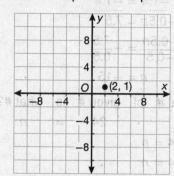

**14. a.** 5 out of the 8 sectors would be even numbers. The probability would be $\frac{5}{8}$.

**b.** 4 out of the 8 sectors would be odd numbers. The probability would be $\frac{1}{2}$.

**c.** 2 out of 8 sectors would be less than 20. The probability would be $\frac{1}{4}$.

**15.** Let $c$ be the number of counselors and let $d$ be the number of campers.

The total miles walked by counselors is $6c$.

The total miles walked by campers is $2d$.

The total miles walked is $6c + 2d$.

The total earned will be $0.50 times the total miles walked.

$$0.50(6c + 2d) = 3c + d$$

**16.** Yes; Sample: Using the Product Rule of Exponents the left side simplified is the same as the right.

$$(11w^4 \cdot 3z^9)(2w^7z^2) = 66w^{11}z^{11}$$

$$(11 \cdot 3 \cdot 2)(w^{(4+7)})(z^{(9+2)}) = 66w^{11}z^{11}$$

$$66w^{11}z^{11} = 66w^{11}z^{11}$$

**17.** $P(\text{no win}) = 1 - P(\text{win})$

$$= 1 - (0.12 + 0.18 + 0.20)$$

$$= 0.50$$

The probability that Miguel will not win any prize is 50%.

**18. a.** $P(\text{over } \$40) = \dfrac{\# \text{ who paid over } \$40}{\# \text{ who bought shirts}}$

$$= \frac{8}{100}$$

$$= \frac{2}{25}$$

**Saxon** Algebra 1

**b.** $P(\$30 \text{ or less}) = \dfrac{\text{\# who paid \$30 or less}}{\text{\# who bought shirts}}$

$= \dfrac{23 + 45}{100}$

$= \dfrac{68}{100} = \dfrac{17}{25}$

**19.** Yes; Sample: The Commutative Property of Addition allows the order of the addends to be changed without affecting the sum.

**20.** Sample: A fraction $\left(-\frac{3}{8}\right)$ multiplied by its reciprocal $\left(-\frac{8}{3}\right)$ equals 1; $\frac{4}{7} \div 1 = \frac{4}{7}$

**21.** $\dfrac{2}{5} \div \left(-\dfrac{7}{2}\right) \cdot \left(-\dfrac{5}{2}\right)$

$= \dfrac{2}{\cancel{5}} \cdot \left(-\dfrac{2}{7}\right) \cdot \left(-\dfrac{\cancel{5}}{2}\right) = \dfrac{2}{7}$

**22.** Sample: To simplify the expression, some of the bases would need to be the same in order to add the exponents.

**23.** $6(ab + ef) = 6ab + 6ef$; Distributive Property

**24. a.** Sample: After the decimal place a 1 is followed by an increasing number of 2s each separated by a 1; no

**b.** Sample: Irrational; No section of the decimal repeats, nor does it terminate.

**25.** $630 \text{ cm}^3 \cdot \dfrac{1 \text{ in.}}{2.54 \text{ cm}} \cdot \dfrac{1 \text{ in.}}{2.54 \text{ cm}} \cdot \dfrac{1 \text{ in.}}{2.54 \text{ cm}}$

$\approx 630 \text{ cm}^3 \cdot \dfrac{1 \text{ in.}^3}{16.39 \text{ cm}^3} \approx 38.44 \text{ in.}^3$

**26.** The temperature at 9 a.m. will be the temperature at 6 a.m. plus the rate of increase times the number of half hours elapsed.

$30 + 2(6) = 30 + 12 = 42$

The temperature will be 42°C at 9 a.m.

The temperature (50°C) at the unknown time will be 42°C plus the rate of increase times the number of half hours elapsed $h$.

$50 = 42 + 2h$

$\dfrac{-42 = -42}{8 = 2h}$

$\dfrac{8}{2} = \dfrac{2h}{2}$

$4 = h$

4 half hours, or 2 hours, have elapsed since 9 a.m. The temperature will reach 50°C at 11 a.m.

**27.** $-|10 - 7| = -|3| = -3$

**28. a.** $0.20(1{,}154{,}358{,}778) \approx 230{,}871{,}756$

About 230,871,756 people in North America use the Internet.

**b.** $0.35(1{,}154{,}358{,}778) \approx 404{,}025{,}572$

About 404,025,572 people in Asia use the Internet.

$\begin{array}{r} 404{,}025{,}572 \\ -230{,}871{,}756 \\ \hline 173{,}153{,}816 \end{array}$

About 173,153,816 more people in Asia use the Internet than do people in North America.

**29.** $A = s^2$

$\sqrt{784} = s$

$28 = s$

A tree was planted at 0 ft, 7 ft, 14 ft, 21 ft, and 28 ft. Five trees were planted.

**30. a.** $\dfrac{495}{500} = 0.99$

The experimental probability that a hair dryer will have no defects is 99%.

**b.** $0.99(20{,}000) = 19{,}800$

There should be 19,800 hair dryers with no defects in the warehouse.

# LESSON 25

## Warm Up 25

**1.** ordered pair; x-value; y-value

**2.** $(-4)^2 + 3^2 - 2^3$

$= 16 + 9 - 8$

$= 17$

**3.** $5y = -3(8) - 6$

$5y = -24 - 6$

$5y = -30$

$y = -6$

**Saxon** Algebra 1

Check:

$5(-6) = -3(8) - 6$

$-30 = -24 - 6$

$-30 = -30$ ✓

**4.** $x - 8(-0.4) = 1.6$

$x + 3.2 = 1.6$

$x = -1.6$

Check:

$-1.6 - 8(-0.4) = 1.6$

$-1.6 + 3.2 = 1.6$

$1.6 = 1.6$ ✓

**5.** The amount at the end of the year will be the starting amount plus the number of weeks in a year times the amount deposited per week.

$n + 52d$

The answer is **A**.

## Lesson Practice 25

**a.** domain: {1, 2, 3, 4, 7, 8}

range: {1, 2, 5, 6, 7, 10}

**b.** The ordered pairs represent a function. Each value in the domain is paired with only one value in the range.

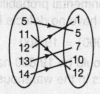

**c.**

| x | -2 | -2 | 0 | 1 | 2 |
|---|----|----|---|---|---|
| y | -7 | -4 | -1 | 2 | 5 |

$y = 3x - 1$ represents a function. For each value of the independent variable, the equation outputs exactly one value for the dependent variable.

**d.**

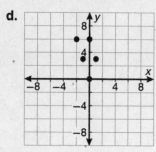

---

**A** vertical line drawn through the y-axis intersects the graph at more than one point, so the ordered pairs do not represent a function.

**e.** The cost of printing depends on the number of copies printed.

dependent variable: cost of printing

independent variable: number of copies

$y = \$0.07c$

$f(c) = \$0.07c$

**f.** Let $d$ be the number of days that the author has been writing.

$30d$       number of pages already written

$400 - 30d$   number of pages left to write

The number of pages left to write depends on the number of days the author has been writing.

$y = 400 - 30d$

$f(d) = 400 - 30d$

## Practice 25

**1.** $0.3 + 0.05y = 0.65$

$\underline{-0.3 \qquad\quad = -0.3}$

$0.05y = 0.35$

$\dfrac{0.05y}{0.05} = \dfrac{0.35}{0.05}$

$y = 7$

**2. a.** $103 + (-4) = 99$

$103 - 4 = 99$

$99 = 99$ ✓

**b.** $\dfrac{1}{2} - \left(-\dfrac{1}{4}\right) = \dfrac{3}{4}$

$\dfrac{1}{2} + \dfrac{1}{4} = \dfrac{3}{4}$

$\dfrac{3}{4} = \dfrac{3}{4}$ ✓

**3.**

| Domain (x) | Range (y) |
|:----------:|:---------:|
| -2 | -0 |
| 0 | -2 |
| 2 | 4 |
| 4 | 6 |
| 5 | 7 |

**Saxon** Algebra 1

$y = x + 2$ represents a function. For each value of the independent variable, the equation outputs exactly one value for the dependent variable.

4. dependent variable: time
   independent variable: miles
   $$y = 15m$$
   $$f(m) = 15m$$

5. $3.16 - 1.01 - 0.11$
   $= 3.16 + (-1.01) + (-0.11)$
   $= 2.04$

6. Each value in the domain is paired with only one value in the range. The answer is **A**.

7. dependent variable: perimeter
   independent variable: side length
   $$y = 4s$$
   $$f(s) = 4s$$

8. Yes; Sample: All functions also meet the criteria for a relation.

9. Relation: Sample: If you draw a vertical line through the circle it will show that several domain values have more than one range value. So a graph of a circle does not represent a function.

10. $C = \pi d$
    $\approx 3.14(0.45)$
    $\approx 1.413$
    The circumference is about 1.41 millimeters.

11. $5.2 \text{ AU} \cdot \dfrac{93{,}000{,}000 \text{ mi}}{1 \text{ AU}}$
    $= 483{,}600{,}000 \text{ mi}$
    Jupiter is about 483,600,000 miles from the Sun.

12. Sample: A subway train can hold up to 6 cars. Each car can hold 40 passengers.

13. Let $x$ be the number of DVDs Stephen rented. His annual fee plus the cost per DVD times $x$ is Stephen's total cost.
    $$39.95 + 0.99x = 55.79$$
    $$\underline{-39.95 \qquad\quad = -39.95}$$
    $$0.99x = 15.84$$

$$\dfrac{0.99x}{0.99} = \dfrac{15.84}{0.99}$$
$$x = 16$$
Stephen rented 16 DVDs.

14. Student A is correct; Student B did not use inverse operations to "undo" +4. Student A should have subtracted 4 from both sides instead of adding 4 to both sides.

15. In all but one game, Michaela scored more points than Jessie. The answer is **B**.

16. Sample: A double-bar graph would compare the amount of each beverage sold each month. A double-line graph would show the changes in the amounts of each beverage sold. A stem-and-leaf plot can help to quickly organize the data and show the middle of the data.

17. circle graph; Sample: Circle graphs best compare parts to a whole.

18. $3(4) - 2(4 - 1)^2 + 2$
    $= 3(4) - 2(3)^2 + 2$
    $= 12 - 2(9) + 2$
    $= 12 - 18 + 2$
    $= -4$

19.

| $x$ | 1 | 2 | 3 | 4 |
|-----|-----|-----|-----|-----|
| $y$ | 2.5 | 5 | 7.5 | 10 |

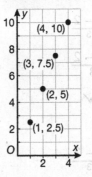

20. No; Sample: Subtraction is not commutative. The correct expression is $x - 3$.

21. $N_6 - N_4$
    $= N_i 2^6 - N_i 2^4$
    $= N_i(2^6 - 2^4)$
    $= 45(64 - 16)$
    $= 2160$

The sixth generation has 2160 more members than the fourth generation.

**22.** The expression $s^2$ represents the area of the mall.

$(4890)^2 = 23,912,100$

The mall will be about 24 million square feet in area.

**23.** false; Sample: The Associative Property applies only to multiplication and addition.

**24.** $1\frac{1}{2}y = 6\frac{3}{4}$

$\frac{3}{2}y \div \frac{3}{2} = \frac{27}{4} \div \frac{3}{2}$

$\frac{3}{2}y \cdot \frac{2}{3} = \frac{27^9}{4_2} \cdot \frac{2}{3}$

$y = \frac{9}{2}$

$y = 4\frac{1}{2}$

**25.** $\frac{1}{8}m - \frac{1}{4} = \frac{3}{4}$

$\underline{+\frac{1}{4} = +\frac{1}{4}}$

$\frac{1}{8}m = 1$

$\cancel{8} \cdot \frac{1}{\cancel{8}}m = 1 \cdot 8$

$m = 8$

**26. a.** $\frac{(5-2)^3 + 12}{(4 \cdot 2)} = \frac{41 - 2}{2^3}$

$\frac{27 + 12}{8} = \frac{41 - 2}{8}$

$\frac{39}{8} = \frac{39}{8} \checkmark$

The statement is true.

**b.** $\frac{(5-3)^3 + 12}{(4 \cdot 3)} = \frac{41 - 3}{3^3}$

$\frac{8 + 12}{12} = \frac{41 - 3}{27}$

$\frac{\cancel{20}^5}{\cancel{12}_3} \neq \frac{38}{27}$

The statement is false; The value of the first expression is $\frac{5}{3}$ and the value of the second expression is $\frac{38}{27}$.

**27.** Let $x$ be the distance from Town A to Town B.

(A to B) plus (B to C) is (A to C)

$x + 191.9 = 312.78$

$x + 191.9 = 312.78$

$\underline{-191.9 = -191.9}$

$x = 120.88$

The distance from Town A to Town B is 120.88 miles.

**28.** $2^6$ byte $\cdot \dfrac{2^3 \text{ bits}}{1 \text{ byte}}$

$= 2^{(6 + 3)} = 2^9 = 512$ bits

$2^6$ bytes contain $2^9$ or 512 bits.

**29.** $4x^2y - xy^2$; Sample: The area of the rectangle would be found using

$A = wl$

$= xy(4x - y)$

$= 4x^2y - xy^2$

**30.** $|-2 - 3| \cdot -4 + (-8)$

$= |-2 + (-3)| \cdot -4 + (-8)$

$= |-5| \cdot -4 + (-8)$

$= 5 - 4 + (-8)$

$= -7$

## LESSON 26

### Warm Up 26

**1.** reciprocal

**2.** $2x + 5y + 3x - 2y$

$= (2x + 3x) + (5y - 2y)$

$= 5x + 3y$

**3.** $2x + 5 = 12$

$\underline{-5 = -5}$

$2x = 7$

$\dfrac{2x}{2} = \dfrac{7}{2}$

$x = 3.5$

Check:

$2(3.5) + 5 = 12$

$7 + 5 = 12$

$12 = 12 \checkmark$

**4.** $3x + 6 = 33$

$\phantom{3x} \underline{-6 = -6}$

$3x = 27$

$\dfrac{\cancel{3}x}{\cancel{3}} = \dfrac{27^9}{\cancel{3}}$

$x = 9$

The answer is **B**.

**Lesson Practice 26**

**a.** $3x + 2 - x + 7 = 16$

| | |
|---|---|
| $2x + 9 = 16$ | Collect like terms. |
| $\underline{-9 = -9}$ | Subtraction Property of Equality |
| $2x = 7$ | Simplify. |
| $x = 3\frac{1}{2}$ | Division Property of Equality |

Check:

$3(3.5) + 2 - 3.5 + 7 = 16$

$10.5 + 2 - 3.5 + 7 = 16$

$16 = 16$ ✓

**b.** $6(x - 1) = 36$

| | |
|---|---|
| $6x - 6 = 36$ | Distributive Property |
| $\underline{+6 = +6}$ | Addition Property of Equality |
| $6x = 42$ | Simplify. |
| $x = 7$ | Divide both sides by 6. |

Check:

$6(7 - 1) = 36$

$6(6) = 36$

$36 = 36$ ✓

**c.** $5x - 3(x - 4) = 22$

| | |
|---|---|
| $5x - 3x + 12 = 22$ | Distributive Property |
| $2x + 12 = 22$ | Combine like terms. |
| $\underline{-12 = -12}$ | Subtraction Property of Equality |
| $2x = 10$ | Simplify. |
| $x = 5$ | Division Property of Equality |

Check:

$5(5) - 3(5 - 4) = 22$

$5(5) - 15 + 12 = 22$

$25 - 15 + 12 = 22$

$22 = 22$ ✓

**d.** $x + x + 90 = 180$

$2x + 90 = 180$

$\phantom{2x} \underline{-90 = -90}$

$2x = 90$

$\dfrac{2x}{2} = \dfrac{90}{2}$

$x = 45$

The measures of the angles are 45°, 45°, and 90°.

**Practice 26**

**1.** $\dfrac{3}{4} + \dfrac{1}{2}x + 2 = 0$

$\dfrac{1}{2}x + 2\dfrac{3}{4} = 0$

$\phantom{\dfrac{1}{2}x} \underline{-2\dfrac{3}{4} = -2\dfrac{3}{4}}$

$\dfrac{1}{2}x = -2\dfrac{3}{4}$

$\cancel{2} \cdot \dfrac{1}{\cancel{2}}x = -\dfrac{11}{\cancel{4}} \cdot \cancel{2}$

$x = -\dfrac{11}{2}$

$x = -5\dfrac{1}{2}$

**2.** The value of the quarters held in the machine depends on the number of quarters in the machine. Choice D is correct.

**3.** $2x(3 + 8)$

$= 6x + 16x$

$= 22x$

The answer is **B**.

**4. a.** Sample: A circle graph is used to show percentages of a whole.

**b.** Sample: A line graph would best represent the change in temperature over a period of time.

**5.** $2\,\cancel{GB} \cdot \dfrac{1024 \text{ MB}}{1\,\cancel{GB}} = 2048 \text{ MB}$

The player can hold up to 2048 MB.

Let $n$ be the total number of songs.

$5.5n + 16 = 2048$

$\phantom{5.5n} \underline{-16 = -16}$

$5.5n = 2032$

$n \approx 370$

The player can hold about 370 songs.

**Saxon** Algebra 1

6. Sample: You can either divide both sides of the equation by 12 or use the Distributive Property and then solve.

7.
$$-15x + 35 + 11 = 1 \quad \text{Distributive Property.}$$
$$-15x + 46 = 1 \quad \text{Combine like terms.}$$
$$-15x = -45 \quad \text{Subtraction Property of Equality}$$
$$x = 3 \quad \text{Division Property of Equality}$$

8. See student work. Students should draw vertical lines across their graphs to check that the lines do not intersect the graph in more than one place.

9. The relation is not a function. The graph fails the vertical-line test.

10.
$$0.4m + 2.05 = 10.45$$
$$\underline{-2.05 = -2.05}$$
$$0.4m = 8.4$$
$$\frac{0.4m}{0.4} = \frac{8.4}{0.4}$$
$$m = 21$$

11. Student B; Student A did not multiply each term by the correct power of ten, 100.

12.
$$7(8) - 12 = 44$$
$$56 - 12 = 44$$
$$44 = 44 \checkmark$$
$$x = 8 \text{ is a solution for } 7x - 12 = 44.$$

13. **a.** Let $h$ be the number of hot dogs in one package.
$$5h + 4 = 64.$$
**b.**
$$5h + 4 = 64$$
$$\underline{-4 = -4}$$
$$5h = 60$$
$$\frac{5h}{5} = \frac{60}{5}$$
$$h = 12$$
Check:
$$5(12) + 4 = 64$$
$$60 + 4 = 64$$
$$64 = 64 \checkmark$$

14. Let $x$ be the number of hops.
$$15x = 5280$$
$$\frac{15x}{15} = \frac{5280}{15}$$
$$x = 352$$
The kangaroo will take 352 hops to travel one mile.

15. The graphed point is $(-2, 5)$.
$$y = 2x + 9$$
$$5 = 2(-2) + 9$$
$$5 = -4 + 9$$
$$5 = 5 \checkmark$$
The point $(-2, 5)$ is a solution of the equation.

16. Simplify the second term.
$$2qdp \cdot -5d^2p$$
$$= -10p^{(1+1)}qd^{(1+2)}$$
$$= -10p^2qd^3$$
Sample: Yes, they can be combined. When the second term is simplified, they are like terms.

17. The probability of rain on Tuesday is two times the probability of rain on Monday.
$$P(\text{rain on Tues.}) = 2a$$

18.
$$V = \frac{4}{3}\pi r^3$$
$$\approx \frac{4}{3}(3.14)(2)^3$$
$$\approx \frac{4}{3}(3.14)(8)$$
$$\approx 33.5$$
The volume is about 33.5 micrometers.

19.
$$P(\text{waiter}) = \frac{\text{waiters interviewed}}{\text{total interviewed}}$$
$$= \frac{4}{2+2+3+1+2+1+2+3}$$
$$= \frac{4}{16}$$
$$= \frac{1}{4}$$

20.
$$\sqrt{324} - \sqrt{144} \bigcirc \sqrt{400} - \sqrt{289}$$
$$18 - 12 \bigcirc 20 - 17$$
$$6 > 3$$
So, $\sqrt{324} - \sqrt{144} > \sqrt{400} - \sqrt{289}$.

76

Saxon Algebra 1

**21.** $\frac{6}{2}[5(3 + 4)]$

$= \frac{6}{2}[5 \cdot 7]$

$= 3[35]$

$= 105$

**22.**

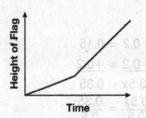

$-8 - (-4) - (-6)$

$= -8 + 4 + 6$

$= 2$

**23.** $2 \cdot (3 + 4)^2 + 15$

$= 2 \cdot (7)^2 + 15$

$= 2 \cdot 49 + 15$

$= 98 + 15$

$= 113$

**24.** $\frac{1}{4} - \frac{1}{3}$

$= \frac{1}{4} + \left(-\frac{1}{3}\right)$

$= \left(\frac{1}{4} \cdot \frac{3}{3}\right) + \left(-\frac{1}{3} \cdot \frac{4}{4}\right)$

$= \frac{3}{12} + \left(-\frac{4}{12}\right)$

$= -\frac{1}{12}$

**25.** $\frac{1}{6} \cdot \frac{1}{6} \cdot \frac{1}{6} \cdot \frac{1}{6} \cdot \frac{1}{6} = \left(\frac{1}{6}\right)^5$

**26. a.** The expression has one term.

**b.** There are 3 variables, $P$, $r$, and $t$.

**c.** The coefficient of $t$ is 4.

**27.** The coefficient is $\frac{1}{3}$, the variables are $B$ and $h$, and the expression has one term.

**28. a.** $6{,}574{,}481 \text{ acre} \cdot \frac{4840 \text{ yd}^2}{1 \text{ acre}}$

$= 31{,}820{,}488{,}040 \text{ yd}^2$

**b.** $31{,}820{,}488{,}040 \text{ yd}^2 \cdot \frac{1 \text{ mi}}{1760 \text{ yd}} \cdot \frac{1 \text{ mi}}{1760 \text{ yd}}$

$= 10{,}272.62656 \text{ mi}^2$

**29.** yes; Sample: The Commutative Property of Multiplication allows the terms to be multiplied in a different order without changing the product.

**30.** Let "1" = blue, "2" = red, "3" = yellow, and "4" = green. On graphing calculator press MATH, PRB, "5". Enter lower limit "1", upper limit "4", and 30 trials. Press ENTER.

$P(\text{blue}) = \frac{\text{number of 1s}}{30}$

## LESSON 27

### Warm Up 27

**1.** horizontal or vertical bars

**2.** False

**3.** Sample:

**4.** $2(2x + 3) = 24$

$4x + 6 = 24$

$\underline{-6} = \underline{-6}$

$4x = 18$

$\frac{4x}{4} = \frac{18}{4}$

$x = 4.5$

### Lesson Practice 27

**a.** The vertical scale does not begin at 0. The title does not specify whether the car or the driver traveled all the miles.

**b.** Sample: The large increments make the temperatures appear to be closer than they actually are.

**c.** The title does not specify that these were the only dogs the pet shop sold and may not represent all breeds sold.

**d.** Sample: The vertical axis has a broken scale, so it appears that the number of products sold throughout the year changed more than it actually did.

**Saxon** Algebra 1

**e.** The salesman may want it to appear that his sales increased a large amount from the beginning of the year to the end.

**f.**

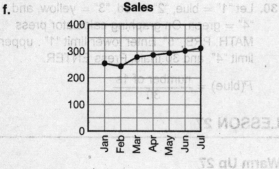

Sales

**Practice 27**

**1.** $(-2 + 3) \div (4 - 5 + 3)$

$= 1 \div 2$

$= \dfrac{1}{2}$

**2.** $0.5x - 0.2 = 0.15$

$\underline{+0.2 = +0.2}$

$0.5x = 0.35$

$\dfrac{0.5x}{0.5} = \dfrac{0.35}{0.5}$

$x = 0.7$

Check:

$0.5(0.7) - 0.2 = 0.15$

$0.35 - 0.2 = 0.15$

$0.15 = 0.15 \checkmark$

**3.** $\dfrac{1}{4} + \dfrac{2}{5}x + 1 = 2\dfrac{1}{4}$

$\dfrac{2}{5}x + 1\dfrac{1}{4} = 2\dfrac{1}{4}$

$\dfrac{-1\dfrac{1}{4} = -1\dfrac{1}{4}}{}$

$\dfrac{2}{5}x = 1$

$\dfrac{5}{2} \cdot \dfrac{2}{5}x = 1 \cdot \dfrac{5}{2}$

$x = \dfrac{5}{2}$

Check:

$\dfrac{1}{4} + \dfrac{2}{5}\left(\dfrac{5}{2}\right) + 1 = 2\dfrac{1}{4}$

$\dfrac{1}{4} + 1 + 1 = 2\dfrac{1}{4}$

$2\dfrac{1}{4} = 2\dfrac{1}{4} \checkmark$

**4.** $-0.4n + 0.305 = 0.295$

$\underline{-0.305 = -0.305}$

$-0.4n = -0.01$

$\dfrac{-0.4n}{-0.4} = \dfrac{-0.01}{-0.4}$

$n = 0.025$

The answer is **A**.

**5.** No; The graph fails the vertical-line test.

**6.** Associative Property of Multiplication; Changing the grouping of the factors does not affect the product.

**7.** The stopping distance depends on the speed of the vehicle.

dependent variable: stopping distance
independent variable: speed

$y = s^2$

$f(s) = s^2$

**8.** Sample: The title does not specify that the animals listed are only 5 of the 10 species in the petting zoo.

**9.** yes; $5(4) + 8 - 3(4) + 4 = 20$

$20 + 8 - 12 + 4 = 20$

$20 = 20$

**10.** false; about 65 people preferred Brand A and about 50 people preferred Brand D.

$65 \overset{?}{=} 2(50)$

$65 \ne 100$

**11.** Sample: The student could use a scale of 0 to 200 and state that the data is in thousands.

**12.** Sample: Machine 4 appears to produce about 3 times more parts than Machine 2 each day. Machine 2 appears to be less efficient.

**13.** true

**14.** Let $h$ be the number of hours spent kayaking.

Kayak rental: 3(4)h

Life jackets: 3(2)

Parking fee: 3

The total cost is the sum of the kayak rental, the life jackets, and the parking fee.

$3(4)h + 3(2) + 3 = 57$

$12h + 6 + 3 = 57$

$$12h + 9 = 57$$
$$\underline{-9 = -9}$$
$$12h = 48$$
$$\frac{12h}{12} = \frac{48}{12}$$
$$h = 4 \text{ hours}$$

**15.** $\left(2\cancel{4} \cdot \frac{1}{\cancel{2}}(5)h\right) + 5^2 = 150$

$$10h + 25 = 150$$
$$\underline{-25 = -25}$$
$$10h = 125$$
$$\frac{10h}{10} = \frac{125}{10}$$
$$h = 12.5 \text{ meters}$$

**16.** Sample: Work in reverse order of operations, subtracting 0.35 from both sides of the equation.

**17.** The ones digit that appears most often is 2.

**18.** Solve Equation 1 and then substitute the solution in Equation 2.

$$-\frac{3}{4}x = 12$$
$$\left(-\frac{\cancel{4}}{\cancel{3}}\right) \cdot -\frac{\cancel{3}}{\cancel{4}}x = \cancel{12}^4 \cdot \left(-\frac{4}{\cancel{3}}\right)$$
$$x = -16$$
$$\frac{5}{\cancel{32}_2}(-\cancel{16}) = -2\frac{1}{2}$$
$$-\frac{5}{2} = -2\frac{1}{2}$$
$$-2\frac{1}{2} = -2\frac{1}{2}$$

**19.**

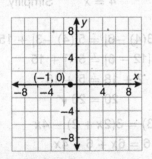

**20.** Let $r$ be the reference point.

$$r + 318 = 325$$
$$\underline{-318 = -318}$$
$$r = 7 \text{ millimeters}$$

**21.** $\$37 \cdot \dfrac{1 \text{ rupee}}{\$0.025} = 1480 \text{ rupee}$

**22.** Let $D$ be absolute deviation, $x$ be the data value, and $\bar{x}$ be the mean of the data set.

$$D = |x - \bar{x}|$$

For 8: $D = |8 - 11| = |-3| = 3$
For 9: $D = |9 - 11| = |-2| = 2$
For 11: $D = |11 - 11| = |0| = 0$
For 12: $D = |12 - 11| = |1| = 1$

**23.** The profit for the fundraiser is the profit per item times the number of items sold.

$$3(x + y) = 3x + 3y$$

**24.** $P(H) = \dfrac{\text{number of heads on the coin}}{\text{number of sides on the coin}} = \dfrac{1}{2}$

Sample: The probability that the results will be heads will remain the same.

**25.** $11 \cdot 3 + 7 = 33 + 7 = 40$

**26. a.** The value of the money in the vending machine is the value of 1 quarter times the number of quarters, plus the value of 1 dime times the number of dimes.

Sample: $0.25q + 0.10d$

**b.** $0.25(21) + 0.10(13)$
$= 5.25 + 1.30 = \$6.55$

**27.** $\dfrac{1}{3} + \dfrac{1}{5} \cdot \dfrac{2}{15} \bigcirc \left(\dfrac{1}{3} + \dfrac{1}{5}\right) \cdot \dfrac{2}{15}$

$\dfrac{1}{3} + \dfrac{2}{75} \bigcirc \left(\dfrac{5}{15} + \dfrac{3}{15}\right) \cdot \dfrac{2}{15}$

$\dfrac{25}{75} + \dfrac{2}{75} \bigcirc \left(\dfrac{8}{15}\right) \cdot \dfrac{2}{15}$

$\dfrac{27}{75} \bigcirc \dfrac{16}{225}$

$\dfrac{81}{225} \bigotimes \dfrac{16}{225}$

**28.** Sample: The number of stairs he ran up minus the number of stairs he ran down describes his position at the end of his run.

**29.** $10 \cdot 4^2 + 72 \div 2^3$

$10 \cdot 16 + 72 \div 8$    Simplify the exponents.

$160 + 9$    Multiply and divide from left to right.

$169$    Add.

**30.** Sample: rational number, because irrational numbers cannot be shown as fractions or ratios.

## LESSON 28

### Warm Up 28

**1.** like

**2.** $10 - 4(5 + 3) + 2^3$

$= 10 - 4(5 + 3) + 8$

$= 10 - 4(8) + 8$

$= 10 - 32 + 8$

$= -14$

**3.** $2(3 - x) = 10$

$6 - 2x = 10$

$-2x + 6 = 10$

$\underline{-6 = -6}$

$-2x = 4$

$\dfrac{-2x}{-2} = \dfrac{4}{-2}$

$x = -2$

Check:

$2(3 - (-2)) = 10$

$2(3 + 2) = 10$

$2(5) = 10$

$10 = 10 ✓$

**4.** $-3(1 + 2x) + x = 32$

$-3 - 6x + x = 32$

$-3 - 5x = 32$

$\underline{+3 = +3}$

$-5x = 35$

$\dfrac{-5x}{-5} = \dfrac{35}{-5}$

$x = -7$

Check:

$-3(1 + 2(-7)) + (-7) = 32$

$-3(1 - 14) + (-7) = 32$

$-3(-13) + (-7) = 32$

$39 - 7 = 32$

$32 = 32 ✓$

**5.** $3(x - 4) - x = 30$

$3x - 12 - x = 30$

$2x - 12 = 30$

$\underline{+12 = +12}$

$2x = 42$

$\dfrac{2x}{2} = \dfrac{42}{2}$

$x = 21$

The answer is **D**.

### Lesson Practice 28

**a.** $6x = 3x + 27$

$\underline{-3x = -3x}$  Subtraction Property of Equality

$3x = 27$  Simplify.

$\dfrac{3x}{3} = \dfrac{27}{3}$  Division Property of Equality

$x = 9$  Simplify.

Check

$6(9) \overset{?}{=} 3(9) + 27$

$54 = 54 ✓$

**b.** $2 + 3(3x - 6) = 5(x - 3) + 15$

$2 + 9x - 18 = 5x - 15 + 15$

Distributive Property

$9x - 16 = 5x$  Simplify.

$\underline{-9x = -9x}$  Subtraction property of Equality

$-16 = -4x$  Simplify.

$\dfrac{-16}{-4} = \dfrac{-4x}{-4}$  Division Property of Equality

$4 = x$  Simplify.

Check

$2 + 3[3(4) - 6] \overset{?}{=} 5[(4) - 3] + 15$

$2 + 3[12 - 6] \overset{?}{=} 5[1] + 15$

$2 + 18 \overset{?}{=} 5 + 15$

$20 = 20 ✓$

**c.** $2(x + 3) = 3(2x + 2) - 4x$

$2x + 6 = 6x + 6 - 4x$

Distributive Property

$2x + 6 = 2x + 6$  Simplify.

$\underline{-2x = -2x}$  Subtraction Property of Equality

**Saxon** Algebra 1

6 = 6          Simplify.

The equation is an identity.

**d.** $3(x + 4) = 2(x + 5) + x$

$3x + 12 = 2x + 10 + x$

$\qquad\qquad\qquad$ Distributive
$\qquad\qquad\qquad$ Property

$3x + 12 = 3x + 10$   Simplify.

$\underline{-3x = -3x}$   Subtraction
$\qquad\qquad\qquad$ Property of
$\qquad\qquad\qquad$ Equality

$12 = 10$          Simplify.

The equation has no solution.

**e.** Let $d$ = the number of work-out days

Member cost = $5d + 125$

Non-member cost = $10d$

$5d + 125 = 10d$

$\underline{-5d = -5d}$

$125 = 5d$

$25 = d$

After 25 work-out days, the cost is the same for members and nonmembers.

**Practice 28**

**1.** $\frac{3}{4}y = 4\frac{7}{8}$

$\frac{\cancel{4}}{3} \cdot \frac{\cancel{3}}{\cancel{4}}y = \frac{\cancel{39}^{13}}{\cancel{8}_2} \cdot \frac{\cancel{4}}{3}$

$y = \frac{13}{2}$

$y = 6\frac{1}{2}$

Check

$\frac{3}{4}\left(\frac{13}{2}\right) = 4\frac{7}{8}$

$\frac{39}{8} = 4\frac{7}{8}$

$4\frac{7}{8} = 4\frac{7}{8}$ ✓

**2.** $3p - 4 - 6 = 2(p - 5)$

$3p - 10 = 2p - 10$

$\underline{-2p = -2p}$

$p - 10 = -10$

$\underline{+10 = +10}$

$p = 0$

Check:

$3(0) - 4 - 6 = 2(0 - 5)$

$0 - 10 = 0 - 10$

$-10 = -10$ ✓

**3.** Let $n$ = the number of coins per pocket

Amount in first pocket = $3 + 0.05n$

Amount in second pocket = $2 + 0.10n$

$3 + 0.05n = 2 + 0.10n$

$\underline{-0.05n = -0.05n}$

$3 = 2 + 0.05n$

$\underline{-2 = -2}$

$1 = 0.05n$

$\frac{1}{0.05} = \frac{0.05n}{0.05}$

$20 = n$

You have 20 dimes and 20 nickels.

**4.** Student B; Sample Student A incorrectly distributed in step 1.

**5.** Let $p$ = number of pounds of apples

First worker's earnings = $0.03p + 486$

Second worker's earnings = $0.02p + 490$

$0.03p + 486 = 0.02p + 490$

$\underline{-0.02p = -0.02p}$

$0.01p + 486 = 490$

$\underline{-486 = -486}$

$0.01p = 4$

$\frac{0.01p}{0.01} = \frac{4}{0.01}$

$p = 400$

The workers are paid the same amount for picking 400 pounds of apples.

**6.** $(x + 15)\frac{1}{3} = 2x - 1$

$\frac{1}{3}x + 5 = 2x - 1$

$-\frac{1}{3}x = -\frac{1}{3}x$

$5 = \frac{5}{3}x - 1$

$\underline{+1 = +1}$

$6 = \frac{5}{3}x$

$\frac{3}{5} \cdot 6 = \frac{\cancel{5}}{3}x \cdot \frac{\cancel{3}}{\cancel{5}}$

$\frac{18}{5} = x$

The answer is **A**.

7. Student B; Sample: Student A didn't distribute properly.

8. Sample: $zx$ must be positive; therefore, $x$ must be a negative number.

9. **a.** Sheet 4 appears to be about 4 times greater in area than Sheet 3.

**b.** $A_3 = 8^2 = 64$
$A_4 = 11^2 = 121$

The area of Sheet 4 is about 120 square inches. The area of Sheet 3 is about 60 square inches. The area of Sheet 4 is about 2 times greater than the area of Sheet 3.

10. false; Sample: A broken scale makes data changes appear larger than they are.

11. **a.**

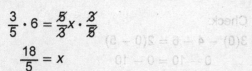

**Average Home Prices**

**b.** Sample: The average home price in Dunston is much greater than most others. On average a house in Dunston would cost about 2 times more than one in Reefville.

**c.** Sample: The clients are likely to conclude that home prices in Reefville are much less than in the other cities.

12. **a.** domain: $\{0 \le x \le 4\}$
range: $\{0 \le y \le 4\}$

**b.** The relation is a function; Sample: Each domain value is paired with exactly one range value.

13. The $x$-values represent years and the $y$-values represent numbers of elephants.

Choice **B** is correct.

14. 0.28 of what number is 18.2?
$0.28 \times n = 18.2$
$0.28n = 18.2$
$\frac{0.28n}{0.28} = \frac{18.2}{0.28}$
$n = 65$
Check:
$0.28(65) = 18.2$
$18.2 = 18.2 ✓$

15. **a.** Let $C$ be the cost of being online for $m$ minutes.
online fee = $3.95
charge for $m$ minutes = $0.05m$
$C = 0.05m + 3.95$

**b.** $1\frac{1}{2}$ to 2 hours is 90 to 120 minutes.
$C \approx 0.05(90) + 4$    $C \approx 0.05(120) + 4$
$\approx 4.50 + 4$      $\approx 6 + 4$
$\approx 8.50$        $\approx 10$

Working at the diner will cost about $8.50 to $10.00.

16. true

17. Sample: $(3, -1)$

18. Let $x$ be the amount Silvia deposited.
$247 + x = 472$
$\underline{-247 = -247}$
$x = 225$

Silvia deposited $225.

19. **a.** George: $6m + 1$
Frank: $4m + 16$

**b.** $6m + 1 + 4m + 16 = 10m + 17$

20. Let $g$ be the original grade. The new grade is $g + 13$.

21. $F = \dfrac{m_1 m_2}{d^2}$

$= \dfrac{(500)(1500)}{(1000)^2}$

$= \dfrac{750,000}{1,000,000}$

$= 0.75$

The gravitational force is about 0.75 newtons.

**Saxon** Algebra 1

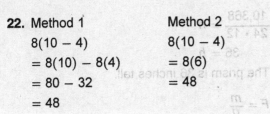

**22.** Method 1

$8(10 - 4)$

$= 8(10) - 8(4)$

$= 80 - 32$

$= 48$

Method 2

$8(10 - 4)$

$= 8(6)$

$= 48$

**23.** $\sqrt{49} + 4^2$

$= 7 + 16$

$= 23$

**24.** true; Associative Property of Addition says you can change the grouping of the addends without changing the sum.

**25.** $3(-3)^2(1)^5 + 4(-3 - 8)^2$

$= (3 \cdot 9 \cdot 1) + (4 \cdot 121)$

$= 27 + 484$

$= 511$

**26.** Any irrational number subtracted from itself will equal 0, which is not an irrational number; Sample: $\sqrt{3} - \sqrt{3} = 0$

**27.** $(3x + 3) + 1 + (4x + 2) + x + (2x + 6) + (7x + 1)$

$= (3x + 4x + x + 2x + 7x) + (3 + 1 + 2 + 6 + 1)$

$= 17x + 13$

**28. a.** rational numbers

**b.** yes; Sample: If an event is impossible its probability is 0, and if an event is certain its probability is 1.

**29.** Sample: 1 mi = 5280 ft, so the student will multiply because the conversion is from a larger unit of measure to a smaller unit of measure.

**30.** Sample: A graph that shows changes over time. For example: The salaries of women from 1990 to 2010.

## LESSON 29

### Warm Up 29

1. variable

2. $rt = 4 \cdot 7 = 28$

3. $3x - 24 = 6$

$\underline{+24 = +24}$

$3x = 30$

$\dfrac{3x}{3} = \dfrac{30}{3}$

$x = 10$

Check:

$3(10) - 24 = 6$

$30 - 24 = 6$

$6 = 6 \checkmark$

**4.** $4x + 14 = 2x + 20$

$\underline{-2x = -2x}$

$2x + 14 = 20$

$\underline{-14 = -14}$

$2x = 6$

$\dfrac{2x}{2} = \dfrac{6}{2}$

$x = 3$

Check:

$4(3) + 14 = 2(3) + 20$

$12 + 14 = 6 + 20$

$26 = 26 \checkmark$

**5.** $5x + 2 = 2x - 9$

$\underline{-2x = -2x}$

$3x + 2 = -9$

$\underline{-2 = -2}$

$3x = -11$

$\dfrac{3x}{3} = -\dfrac{11}{3}$

$x = -\dfrac{11}{3}$

Check:

$5\left(-\dfrac{11}{3}\right) + 2 = 2\left(-\dfrac{11}{3}\right) - 9$

$-\dfrac{55}{3} + \dfrac{6}{3} = -\dfrac{22}{3} - \dfrac{27}{3}$

$-\dfrac{49}{3} = -\dfrac{49}{3} \checkmark$

### Lesson Practice 29

**a.** $3m + 2n = 8$

$\underline{-3m = -3m}$    Subtract $3m$ to eliminate from the $n$ side.

$2n = -3m + 8$    Simplify.

**Saxon** Algebra 1

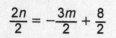
$$\frac{2n}{2} = -\frac{3m}{2} + \frac{8}{2}$$ Divide by 2 to eliminate the coefficient of $n$.

$$n = -\frac{3}{2m} + 4$$ Simplify.

**b.** $3x + 2y = 8 + x$

$$\underline{-x = -x}$$ Eliminate $x$ from the right side.

$2x + 2y = 8$ Simplify.

$$\underline{-2y = -2y}$$ Subtract $2y$ to eliminate from the $x$ side.

$2x = -2y + 8$ Simplify.

$$\frac{2x}{2} = -\frac{2y}{2} + \frac{8}{2}$$ Divide by 2 to eliminate coefficient of $x$.

$x = -y + 4$ Simplify.

**c.** $F = \frac{9}{5}C + 32$

$$\underline{-32 = -32}$$

$$F - 32 = \frac{9}{5}C$$

$$\frac{5}{9} \cdot (F - 32) = \frac{9}{5}C \cdot \frac{5}{9}$$

$$\frac{5}{9}(F - 32) = C$$

When temperature is 86°F:

$$C = \frac{5}{9}(86 - 32)$$

$$C = \frac{5}{9}(\overset{6}{\cancel{54}})$$

$C = 30$

86°F is equivalent to 30°C.

**d.** $V = lwh$

$$\frac{V}{lw} = \frac{lwh}{lw}$$

$$\frac{V}{lw} = h$$

Convert 6 ft³ to in.³.

6 ft³ $\cdot \frac{12 \text{ in.}}{1 \text{ ft}} \cdot \frac{12 \text{ in.}}{1 \text{ ft}} \cdot \frac{12 \text{ in.}}{1 \text{ ft}}$

= 10,368 in.³

Substitute to find height:

$$\frac{V}{lw} = h$$

$$\frac{10,368}{24 \cdot 12} = h$$

$$36 = h$$

The prism is 36 inches tall.

**e.** $F = \frac{m}{g}$

$$g \cdot F = \frac{m}{g} \cdot g$$

$$Fg = m$$

$$\frac{Fg}{F} = \frac{m}{F}$$

$$g = \frac{m}{F}$$

Substitute to find $g$.

$$g = \frac{350}{28} = 12.5$$

Felicia will need 12.5 gallons of fuel.

**Practice 29**

**1.** $3x + 2y = 5 - y$

$$\underline{-3x + y = -3x + y}$$

$$3y = -3x + 5$$

$$\frac{3y}{3} = -\frac{3x}{3} + \frac{5}{3}$$

$$y = -x + \frac{5}{3}$$

**2.** $-2y + 6y - x - 4 = 0$

$$4y - x - 4 = 0$$

$$\underline{+(x + 4) = +(x + 4)}$$

$$4y = x + 4$$

$$\frac{4y}{4} = \frac{x}{4} + \frac{4}{4}$$

$$y = \frac{1}{4}x + 1$$

**3.** Total cost without coupon:

107.50 + 35

Average cost per photograph w/o coupon:

$$\frac{107.50 + 35}{5} = 28.50$$

The average cost per photograph with the coupon is $28.50.

**4.** Area of a rectangle is the product of length and width. The answer is **C**.

**Saxon** Algebra 1

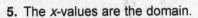
**5.** The *x*-values are the domain.

Domain: {6, 7, 8, 9}

The *y*-values are the range.

Range: {0, 1, 2, 3, 4}

**6.** Simplify terms with parentheses first.
Choice **B** is correct.

**7.** Add or subtract terms so that the terms with an *x*-variable are isolated on one side of the equation. Simplify the equation by collecting like terms. Multiply or divide so that the *x*-variable has a coefficient of 1.

**8.** Lee's average points per game: $3t + 2s$
Total points for season: $22(3t + 2s)$

**9.** Triangle A:

$$x + x + 90 = 180$$
$$2x + 90 = 180$$
$$-90 = -90$$
$$2x = 90$$
$$\frac{2x}{2} = \frac{90}{2}$$
$$x = 45$$

Triangle B:

$$3y + y + 90 = 180$$
$$4y + 90 = 180$$
$$-90 = -90$$
$$4y = 90$$
$$\frac{4y}{4} = \frac{90}{4}$$
$$y = 22.5$$

Triangle A has angles 45°, 45°, 90°
Triangle B has angles 22.5°, 67.5°, 90°
Triangle B has the smallest angle.

**10.** Student A; Sample: Student B in using larger increments does not emphasize the differences.

**11.** If *y* is negative, then $y^3$ will be negative. For $xy^3$ to be positive, *x* must be negative.

**12.** Sample: All categories of the data set should be represented.

**13.** $\sqrt{26} \approx 5.1$, or about 5

Check: $5 \cdot 5 = 25$, which is almost 26.

**14.** Triangle

$$A_t = \frac{1}{2}bh$$
$$A_t = \frac{1}{2}(x + 2)(10)$$
$$A_t = 5(x + 2)$$
$$A_t = 5x + 10$$

Rectangle

$$A_r = lw$$
$$A_r = 5(2x - 4)$$
$$A_r = 10x - 20$$

Since the areas are equal:

$$5x + 10 = 10x - 20$$
$$-5x \quad\quad = -5x$$

**19.** 

$$10 = 5x - 20$$
$$\frac{+20}{30} = \frac{+20}{}$$
$$30 = 5x$$
$$\frac{30}{5} = \frac{5x}{5}$$
$$6 = x$$

Substitute to find areas:

Triangle

$$A_t = \frac{1}{2}(6 + 2)(10)$$
$$= 40$$

Rectangle

$$A_r = 5(2(6) - 4)$$
$$= 5 \cdot 8$$
$$= 40$$

Each has an area of 40 square units.

**15. a.** $10c$

**b.** $5c + 15$

**c.**
$$10c = 5c + 15$$
$$-5c = -5c$$
$$5c = 15$$
$$\frac{5c}{5} = \frac{15}{5}$$
$$c = 3$$

If they each attend 3 classes in a month, they would have the same cost.

**16.** true; 
$$6(11) + 8 = 74$$
$$66 + 8 = 74$$
$$74 = 74 \checkmark$$

**17.** stem-and-leaf plot; Sample: Stem-and leaf plots are best for ordering data.

**18.** $i = 12(3) = 36$
$i = 12(5) = 60$
$i = 12(8) = 96$
$i = 12(10) = 120$

| *f* | *i* |
|-----|-----|
| 3 | 36 |
| 5 | 60 |
| 8 | 96 |
| 10 | 120 |

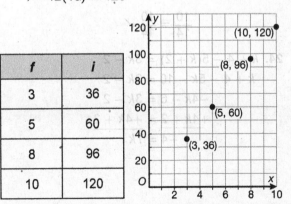

**Saxon** Algebra 1

**19.** false; Sample: Repeating decimals are rational numbers because they can be expressed as fractions. For example, $0.\overline{33}$ can be expressed $\frac{1}{3}$. A repeating decimal multiplied by a variable could be a rational number.

**20.** The difference between the highest and lowest temperatures is 148°F. Let $t$ be the lowest temperature.

$t = 23 - 148$

$t = 23 + (-148)$

$t = -125$

The lowest temperature is about $-125$°F.

**21.** cost of container $= 1$

cost of $s$ pounds $= 2s$

total cost $= 1 + 2s$

**22.** $x^2 - 3yx + 2yx^2 - 2xy + yx$

$= x^2 - 3xy + 2x^2y - 2xy + xy$

$= x^2 + 2x^2y - 3xy - 2xy + xy$

$= x^2 + 2x^2y - 4xy$

**23.** $-3y + \frac{1}{2} = \frac{5}{7}$

$\quad\quad -\frac{1}{2} = -\frac{1}{2}$

$\quad -3y = \frac{3}{14}$

$-\frac{1}{3} \cdot (-3y) = \frac{3}{14} \cdot \left(-\frac{1}{3}\right)$

$\quad\quad y = -\frac{1}{14}$

Check:

$-3\left(-\frac{1}{14}\right) + \frac{1}{2} = \frac{5}{7}$

$\frac{3}{14} + \frac{7}{14} = \frac{10}{14}$

$\frac{10}{14} = \frac{10}{14}$ ✓

**24.** $k + 4 - 5(k + 2) = 3k - 2$

$k + 4 - 5k - 10 = 3k - 2$

$\quad -4k - 6 = 3k - 2$

$\quad +4k + 2 = +4k + 2$

$\quad\quad\quad -4 = 7k$

$-\frac{4}{7} = \frac{7k}{7}$

$-\frac{4}{7} = k$

Check:

$-\frac{4}{7} + 4 - 5\left(-\frac{4}{7} + 2\right) = 3\left(-\frac{4}{7}\right) - 2$

$-\frac{4}{7} + 4 + \frac{20}{7} - 10 = -\frac{12}{7} - 2$

$\frac{16}{7} - 6 = -\frac{12}{7} - 2$

$-\frac{26}{7} = -\frac{26}{7}$ ✓

**25.** Sample: The number represented by $z$ is odd, and it is an integer.

**26.** $\frac{1}{3} - 1 \quad\quad\quad \frac{1}{2} - 1$

$= \frac{1}{3} - \frac{3}{3} \quad\quad = \frac{1}{2} - \frac{2}{2}$

$= -\frac{2}{3} \quad\quad\quad = -\frac{1}{2}$

Since $-\frac{1}{2} > -\frac{2}{3}$, $\frac{1}{2} - 1 > \frac{1}{3} - 1$.

**27.** $(3 + 5) - 2^3$

$= 8 - 2^3 \quad$ Simplify inside parentheses

$= 8 - 8 \quad$ Simplify exponents

$= 0 \quad\quad$ Subtract

**28.** $-(2) - (-2) = y$

$\quad -2 + 2 = y$

$\quad\quad\quad 0 = y$

**29.** $303,000,000 \times (1.015)^8$

$= 341,327,253.7$

about $341,327,254$ people

**30. a.** $P(\text{truck}) = \dfrac{\text{families with trucks}}{\text{total families}}$

$= \frac{5}{20}$

$= \frac{1}{4}$

**b.** $\frac{1}{4}(140^{35}) = 35$

**Saxon** Algebra 1

## LAB 2

### Practice Lab 2

**a.** Enter $2x - 2$ in the Y= editor. Press **2nd**. **TBLSET**. Enter TblStart = 2 and $\Delta$Tbl = 3.

Press **2nd** **TABLE**. When $x = 2, 5, 8$, and 11, $y = 2, 8, 14$, and 20 respectively.

**b.** Enter $4x$ in the Y= editor. Press **2nd** **TBLSET**. Enter TblStart = 1 and $\Delta$Tbl = 7.

Press **2nd** **TABLE**. When $x = 1, 8, 15$, and 22, $y = 4, 32, 60$, and 88 respectively.

**c.** Enter the equation that models the growth of the flower in the Y= editor.

**d.** Enter $y = 2x + 1$ for $Y_1$ and $y = 3x - 2$ for $Y_2$.

**e.** She should use TblStart = 1, because she will grow the flowers for at least one month.

**f.** $\Delta$Tbl = 1, because she will measure their height at the end of every month.

**g.** Flower A: 3 inches after 1 month, 5 inches after 2 months, 7 inches after 3 months;

Flower B: 1 inch after 1 month, 4 inches after 2 months, 7 inches after 3 months

**h.** yes; They will both be 7 inches tall in 3 months.

## LESSON 30

### Warm Up 30

1. relation

2. 3 units right of origin, 4 units up, (3, 4)

3. 3 units left of origin, 4 units up, (−3, 4)

4. 3 units left of origin, 3 units down, (−3, −3)

5. $2(4) + 3 = 8 + 3 = 11$

### Lesson Practice 30

**a.**

| x | 0 | 2 | -2 |
|---|---|---|----|
| y | 5 | 9 | 1 |

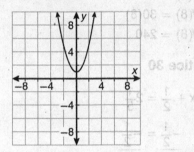

The graph is a function and it is linear.

**b.**

| x | 0 | −1 | 1 |
|---|---|----|---|
| y | 1 | 2 | 2 |

The graph is a function and it is not linear.

**c.** $x^2 \geq 0$, so $-2x^2 \leq 0$. Graph 2 shows all values of $y$ are less than or equal to 0. Graph 2 matches the equation $y = -2x^2$.

**d.** Graph 2 includes (−3, 0), which is only in the table for $y = \frac{1}{3}x + 1$, so Graph 2 matches the table.

**e.** Graph 1 includes (1, 4), which is only in the table for $y = 3x + 1$, so Graph 1 matches the table.

**f.** The domain is $x \geq 0$ and the range is $y \geq -1$.

**g.** The domain is all real numbers and the range is $y \geq 1$.

**Saxon** Algebra 1

**h.**

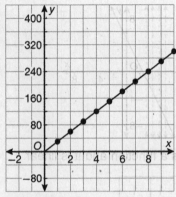

Eight classes sent 240 emails.

$f(x) = 30x$

$f(8) = 30(8)$

$f(8) = 240$

## Practice 30

**1.** $x + \dfrac{1}{2} = 2\dfrac{1}{5}$

$\dfrac{-\dfrac{1}{2} = -\dfrac{1}{2}}{x = \dfrac{17}{10}}$

$x = 1\dfrac{7}{10}$

Check:

$1\dfrac{7}{10} + \dfrac{1}{2} = 2\dfrac{1}{5}$

$\dfrac{17}{10} + \dfrac{5}{10} = 2\dfrac{1}{5}$

$\dfrac{22}{10} = 2\dfrac{1}{5}$

$2\dfrac{1}{5} = 2\dfrac{1}{5} \checkmark$

**2.** $0.4x - 0.3 = -0.14$

$\dfrac{+0.3 = +0.3}{0.4x = 0.16}$

$\dfrac{0.4x}{0.4} = \dfrac{0.16}{0.4}$

$x = 0.4$

Check:

$0.4(0.4) - 0.3 = -0.14$

$0.16 - 0.3 = -0.14$

$-0.14 = -0.14 \checkmark$

**3.** $\dfrac{1}{3} + \dfrac{5}{12}x - 2 = 6\dfrac{2}{3}$

$\dfrac{5}{12}x - 1\dfrac{2}{3} = 6\dfrac{2}{3}$

$\dfrac{+1\dfrac{2}{3} = +1\dfrac{2}{3}}{\dfrac{5}{12}x = \dfrac{25}{3}}$

$\dfrac{\cancel{12}}{\cancel{5}} \cdot \dfrac{\cancel{5}}{\cancel{12}}x = \dfrac{25^5}{\cancel{3}} \cdot \dfrac{\cancel{12}^4}{\cancel{5}}$

$x = 20$

Check:

$\dfrac{1}{3} + \dfrac{5}{\cancel{3}\cancel{12}}(\cancel{20}^5) - 2 = 6\dfrac{2}{3}$

$\dfrac{1}{3} + \dfrac{25}{3} - 2 = 6\dfrac{2}{3}$

$6\dfrac{2}{3} = 6\dfrac{2}{3} \checkmark$

**4.** $\dfrac{2}{3} - \dfrac{4}{9}x + 1 = 2\dfrac{7}{9}$

$-\dfrac{4}{9}x + 1\dfrac{2}{3} = 2\dfrac{7}{9}$

$\dfrac{-1\dfrac{2}{3} = -1\dfrac{2}{3}}{-\dfrac{4}{9}x = 1\dfrac{1}{9}}$

$-\dfrac{\cancel{9}}{\cancel{4}} \cdot -\dfrac{\cancel{4}}{\cancel{9}}x = \dfrac{10^5}{9} \cdot -\dfrac{\cancel{9}}{\cancel{4}_2}$

$x = -\dfrac{5}{2}$

Check:

$\dfrac{2}{3} - \dfrac{2\cancel{4}}{9}\left(-\dfrac{5}{2}\right) + 1 = 2\dfrac{7}{9}$

$\dfrac{2}{3} + \dfrac{10}{9} + 1 = 2\dfrac{7}{9}$

$\dfrac{25}{9} = 2\dfrac{7}{9}$

$2\dfrac{7}{9} = 2\dfrac{7}{9} \checkmark$

**5.** $x - 4(x - 3) + 7 = 6 - (x - 4)$

$x - 4x + 12 + 7 = 6 - x + 4$

$-3x + 19 = -x + 10$

$\dfrac{+3x - 10 = +3x - 10}{9 = 2x}$

$\dfrac{9}{2} = \dfrac{2x}{2}$

88

$$\frac{9}{2} = x$$

Check:

$$\frac{9}{2} - 4\left(\frac{9}{2} - 3\right) + 7 = 6 - \left(\frac{9}{2} - 4\right)$$

$$\frac{9}{2} - \frac{36}{2} + 12 + 7 = 6 - \frac{9}{2} + 4$$

$$-\frac{27}{2} + 19 = -\frac{9}{2} + 10$$

$$\frac{11}{2} = \frac{11}{2} \checkmark$$

**6.** false; A vertical line crosses the circle at two points, so the equation is not a function.

**7.** For $s = 1.5c + 50$

| c | 0 | 100 | 200 |
|---|---|-----|-----|
| s | 50 | 200 | 350 |

Graph 1 contains the points (0, 50), (100, 200), and (200, 350), so Graph 1 represents the equation.

**8.** The graph contains points (0, 10) and (10, 0). These points satisfy $y = -x + 10$. Choice **D** is correct.

**9. a.**

**Shrubs Planted**

**b.** yes; A vertical line will cross the graph at one point only.

**c.** no; This is not a linear function.

**10.**

yes; It is linear because the graph is a line.

**11.** Student A is correct; Sample: Student B did not subtract 6 on both sides.

**12.** The area of the shaded part is the difference between the area of the whole rectangle and the area of the unshaded part.

$$A_s = A_w - A_u$$
$$= 6(3x - 4) - 4x$$
$$= 18x - 24 - 4x$$
$$= 14x - 24$$

**13.** $\dfrac{x}{2} + \dfrac{y}{3} = 2$

$$-\frac{x}{2} = -\frac{x}{2}$$

$$\frac{y}{3} = -\frac{x}{2} + 2$$

$$3\left(\frac{y}{3}\right) = 3\left(-\frac{x}{2}\right) + 3(2)$$

$$y = -\frac{3}{2}x + 6$$

For $x = 3$:

$$y = -\frac{3}{2}(3) + 6$$

$$= -\frac{9}{2} + 6$$

$$= 1\frac{1}{2}$$

**14.** Solve for $r$.

$$i = prt$$

$$\frac{i}{pt} = \frac{prt}{pt}$$

$$\frac{i}{pt} = r$$

**15.**

$$\frac{3 + 7(-3)}{-7 - 2(-3)}$$

$$= \frac{3 + (-21)}{-7 + 6}$$

$$= \frac{-18}{-1}$$

$$= 18$$

**16.** Student B; Sample: Student A did not distribute the $-4$ and $-6$ over both terms.

**17.** $\dfrac{1\ cm}{50\ km} = \dfrac{x\ cm}{675\ km}$

$$675 = 50x$$

$$\frac{675}{50} = \frac{50x}{50}$$

89

**Saxon** Algebra 1

$13.5 = x$
The distance on the map between the cities is 13.5 cm.

**18.** The large interval minimizes the difference between the scores. Choice **D** is correct.

**19.** Sample: Changes in data appear less than they actually are.

**20.** Sample: The circle graph may make it appear that orange juice and fruit punch are the only drinks sold at the store and that fruit punch is the drink most sold by the store. A bar graph would be a more appropriate graph, as it does not represent parts of a whole.

**21.**

### Woodmont Temperatures (°F)

| Stem | Leaves |
|------|--------|
| 5 | 1, 3, 3 |
| 6 | 1, 2, 3, 3, 5 |
| 7 | 2, 4, 8 |
| 8 | 0 |

Key: 7|2 means 72

**22.**

| m | h |
|----|----|
| 4 | 4 |
| 6 | 5 |
| 10 | 7 |
| 20 | 12 |

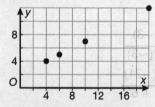

**23.** $P(5) = \dfrac{\text{number of "5" keys}}{\text{total number of keys}}$

$= \dfrac{1}{10}$

$= 10\%$

**24.** $18 \cdot \dfrac{1}{6} x$    Commutative Property of Multiplication

$= \left(18 \cdot \dfrac{1}{6}\right) x$    Associative Property of Multiplication

$= 3x$

**25.** $3.6 + 4.08 + 8$    Subtract from left to right.

$= 7.68 + 8$    Add from left to right.

$= 15.68$    Add from left to right.

**26.** Sample: When I use a unit as a factor $n$ times, I need to apply a unit ratio for converting that unit $n$ times.

**27.** $3 + \left(\dfrac{3}{4} + 2^2\right)$    symbol of inclusion

$= 3 + \left(\dfrac{3}{4} + 4\right)$    powers

$= 3 + 4\dfrac{3}{4}$    symbols of inclusion

$= 7\dfrac{3}{4}$    addition

**28.** $15 \cdot 2 + (23 - 15) \cdot \dfrac{1}{2^4} \cdot 2$

$= 30 + 8^4 \cdot \dfrac{1}{2}$

$= 30 + 4$

$= 34$

They will pay $34 for 23 visits in a month.

**29.** The value of $b$ will grow smaller; Sample: Any number less than one multiplied by itself will decrease.

**30.** Samples: An airplane descends at a steady rate. An item loses value steadily over time.

## INVESTIGATION 3

### Practice Investigation 3

  **a.** People who visit the complex

  **b.** Every fifth person who signs a lease

  **c.** Choosing every $n$th member of the population is a systematic sampling method. Choice B is correct.

  **d.** Sample: People who visit the complex but do not sign a lease will not be included.

  **e.** See student's work. For example, graphs might include a broken or unlabeled axis, an axis that does not start at 0, unequal intervals, or intervals that are inappropriately large or small.

**Saxon** Algebra 1

## LESSON 31

### Warm Up 31

1. simplify

2. $2.3 - 3.6 \div 4 - 1.7$
$2.3 - 0.9 - 1.7$
$1.4 - 1.7$
$-0.3$

3. $\dfrac{-0.4 + 1.3 \cdot 4}{0.5 - 5.1 \div 3}$

$\dfrac{-0.4 + 5.2}{0.5 - 1.7}$

$\dfrac{4.8}{-1.2}$

$-4$

4. $8x = 112$
$\dfrac{8x}{8} = \dfrac{112}{8}$
$x = 14$

5. $2.5y = 62.5$
$\dfrac{2.5y}{2.5} = \dfrac{62.5}{2.5}$
$y = 25$

### Lesson Practice 31

a. $\dfrac{\$4.96}{8} = \$0.62$

$\dfrac{\$3.25}{5} = \$0.65$

$0.62 < 0.65$

8 boxes for \$4.96 is the better buy.

b. $\dfrac{45°F}{1\ \text{minute}} \cdot \dfrac{1\ \text{minute}}{\overset{\overset{3}{}}{60}\ \text{seconds}} = \dfrac{3°F}{4\ \text{seconds}}$

c. $\dfrac{\overset{1}{20}\ \text{pages}}{2\ h} \cdot \dfrac{1\ h}{\underset{3}{60}\ \text{minutes}}$

$\dfrac{1}{6}$ of a page per minute

d. $\dfrac{c}{7} = \dfrac{3}{21}$
$c \cdot 21 = 7 \cdot 3$
$21c = 21$
$\dfrac{21c}{21} = \dfrac{21}{21}$
$c = 1$

e. $\dfrac{5}{n+2} = \dfrac{10}{16}$
$5 \cdot 16 = (n+2) \cdot 10$
$80 = 10n + 20$
$60 = 10n$
$6 = n$

f. $\dfrac{\text{number of blue chips}}{\text{total number of chips}} = \dfrac{b}{60}$

$\dfrac{5}{5+7} = \dfrac{b}{60}$

$\dfrac{5}{12} = \dfrac{b}{60}$

$5 \cdot 60 = 12 \cdot b$

$300 = 12 \cdot b$

$25 = b$

There are 25 blue chips, so there are 60 − 25 or 35 red chips.

g. $5.5 + 3.75 = 9.25$

$\dfrac{9.25\ \text{in.}}{x\ \text{mi}} = \dfrac{1\ \text{in.}}{100\ \text{mi}}$

$9.25 \cdot 100 = 1 \cdot x$

$925 = x$

The actual distance is 925 miles.

h. $\dfrac{4\ \text{miles}}{48\ \text{minutes}} = \dfrac{x\ \text{miles}}{72\ \text{minutes}}$

$48 \cdot x = 4 \cdot 72$

$48x = 288$

$x = 6$

Jeff can walk 6 miles in 72 minutes.

### Practice 31

1. $7 - 4 - 5 + 12 - 2 - |-2|$
$7 - 4 - 5 + 12 - 2 - 2$
$6$

**Saxon** Algebra 1

**2.** $-6 \cdot 3 + \left| -3(-4 + 2^3) \right|$
$-6 \cdot 3 + \left| -3(-4 + 8) \right|$
$-6 \cdot 3 + \left| -3(4) \right|$
$-6 \cdot 3 + \left| -12 \right|$
$-6 \cdot 3 + 12$
$-18 + 12$
$-6$

**3.** $\qquad -0.05n + 1.8 = 1.74$
$100(-0.05n) + 100(1.8) = 100(1.74)$
$\qquad -5n + 180 = 174$
$\qquad -5n = 6$
$\qquad n = \dfrac{6}{5}$ or 1.2

**4.** $-y - 8 + 6y = -9 + 5y + 2$
$\qquad 5y - 8 = 5y - 7$
$\qquad 5y = 5y + 1$
$\qquad 0 = 1$
Since $0 = 1$ is never true, there is no solution.

**5.** Solve for $x$.
$2x - 4.5 = \dfrac{1}{2}(x + 3)$

$2x - \dfrac{9}{2} = \dfrac{1}{2}x + \dfrac{3}{2}$

$2x = \dfrac{1}{2}x + \dfrac{12}{2}$

$2x = \dfrac{1}{2}x + 6$

$\dfrac{3}{2}x = 6$

$\dfrac{2}{3}\left(\dfrac{3}{2}x\right) = \dfrac{2}{3}(6)$

$x = 4$
The answer is **D**.

**6.** $4 + 2x + 2y - 3 = 5$
$\qquad 1 + 2x + 2y = 5$
$\qquad 2x + 2y = 4$
$\qquad x + y = 2$
$\qquad y = -x + 2$

**7.** $4k(2c - a + 3m)$
$4k(2c) - 4k(a) + 4k(3m)$
$8ck - 4ak + 12km$

**8.** $3x^2 + 2y$
$3(-2)^2 + 2(5)$
$3(4) + 2(5)$
$12 + 10$
$22$

**9.** $2(a^2 - b)^2 + 3a^3b$
$2[(-3)^2 - 2]^2 + 3(-3)^3(2)$
$2[9 - 2]^2 + 3(-3)^3(2)$
$2[7]^2 + 3(-3)^3(2)$
$2(49) + 3(-27)(2)$
$98 + (-162)$
$-64$

**10.** $\dfrac{42.50 \text{ dollars}}{10 \text{ boxes}} = \$4.25$ per box

**11.** Since the triangles are similar, corresponding sides are proportional.
$\dfrac{4}{n} = \dfrac{7}{10.5}$
$7n = 4 \cdot 10.5$
$7n = 42$
$n = 6$

**12.** $\dfrac{21}{x} = \dfrac{3}{13}$
$3x = 273$
$x = 91$
There are 91 foxes in the forest.

**13.** $s = 1.05\sqrt{w}$
$s = 1.05\sqrt{170 + 40}$
$s = 1.05\sqrt{210}$
$s \approx 1.05 \cdot 14$
$s \approx 15$
The falling speed is about 15 ft/sec.

**14.** $y = x^2 + 2$
$y = 1^2 + 2 \qquad y = 3^2 + 2$
$y = 1 + 2 \qquad y = 9 + 2$
$y = 3 \qquad\quad y = 11$

| $x$ | $-3$ | $-1$ | $0$ | $1$ | $3$ |
|---|---|---|---|---|---|
| $y$ | 11 | 3 | 2 | 3 | 11 |

**Saxon** Algebra 1

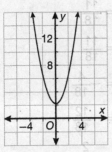

**15.** $\dfrac{4}{\$2800} = \dfrac{6}{x}$

$\qquad 4x = \$16,800$

$\qquad x = \$4200$

Six computers will cost $4200.

**16.** $12 + 8 = 20$

$\qquad \dfrac{20}{50} = \dfrac{2}{5}$

2 out of 5

**17. a.**

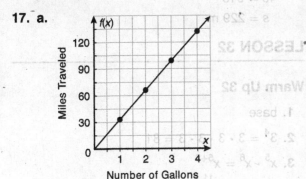

**b.** $f(x) = mx + b$

$\qquad = \dfrac{33}{1}x + 0$

$\qquad = 33x$

**c.** $f(10) = 33 \cdot 10$

$\qquad = 330$

330 miles

**18. a.** $3d + 6g, \ 5d + g$

**b.** $3d + 6g + 5d + g$

$\qquad 8d + 7g$

**c.** $8(5) + 7(4)$

$\qquad 40 + 28$

$\qquad 68$

$\qquad \$68$

**19.** The sum of the three angles of a triangle is 180°. Write and solve an equation for the value of $x$.

$$x + \dfrac{x}{2} + 90 = 180$$

$$\dfrac{3}{2}x + 90 = 180$$

$$\dfrac{3}{2}x = 90$$

$$\dfrac{2}{3} \cdot \dfrac{3}{2}x = \dfrac{2}{3} \cdot 90$$

$$x = 60$$

One angle is $x°$, or 60°.

$\dfrac{x}{2}$

$\dfrac{60}{2} = 30$

The other angle is 30°. The third angle is a right angle, so it is 90°. The angles are 90°, 60°, 30°.

**20.** The domain is all they $x$-values. The range is all the $y$-values.

The domain is {11, 12, 13, 18, 19}. The range is {0, 1, 2, 4, 10}.

**21.**

| $x$ | $-2$ | $-1$ | 0 | 1 | 2 |
|---|---|---|---|---|---|
| $y$ | 3 | 0 | $-1$ | 0 | 3 |

Domain: all real numbers

Range: $y \geq -1$

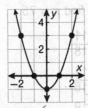

$\dfrac{1}{3}\left(-\dfrac{2}{3}\right) + \dfrac{5}{6} = \dfrac{11}{18}$

$-\dfrac{2}{9} + \dfrac{5}{6} = \dfrac{11}{18}$

$-\dfrac{4}{18} + \dfrac{15}{18} = \dfrac{11}{18}$

**Saxon** Algebra 1

**22.** $\frac{3}{2}x + 5 = 2x - \frac{1}{2}x + 5$

$\frac{3}{2}x + 5 = \frac{4}{2}x - \frac{1}{2}x + 5$

$\frac{3}{2}x + 5 = \frac{3}{2}x + 5$

$\frac{3}{2}x = \frac{3}{2}x$

$x = x$

In the equation $x = x$, $x$ can have any value.

**23. a.** $65 + \left(\frac{m}{5} - 10\right)$

**b.** $65 + n\left(\frac{m}{5} - 10\right)$

**c.** Divide $m$ by 5.

**24.** $4(x^2 - 4) + 3z^3(4z^7)$

$4x^2 - 16 + 12z^{10}$

The answer is **B**.

**25.** Student B; Student A did not multiply both sides by 6.

**26.** $A = P\left(1 + \frac{r}{1}\right)^t$

$A = 1500\left(1 + \frac{5.5}{1}\right)^{10}$

$A = 1500(1 + 0.055)^{10}$

$A = 1500(1.055)^{10}$

$A = 1500(1.7081444)$

$A = \$2562.22$

**27.** $\frac{3}{4} = \frac{x}{100}$

$3 \cdot 100 = 4 \cdot x$

$300 = 4x$

$x = 75$

Divide by 4 to find $x = 75$.

**28.** $\frac{1}{3}\left(\frac{2}{3}\right) + \frac{5}{6} = \frac{11}{18}$

$\frac{2}{9} + \frac{5}{6} = \frac{11}{18}$

$\frac{4}{18} + \frac{15}{18} = \frac{19}{18}$

Since $\frac{19}{18} \neq \frac{11}{18}$, it is false. Find the correct solution.

$\frac{1}{3}m + \frac{5}{6} = \frac{11}{18}$

$\frac{1}{3}m + \frac{15}{18} = \frac{11}{18}$

$\frac{1}{3}m = -\frac{4}{18}$

$m = -\frac{12}{18}$

$m = -\frac{2}{3}$

**29.** $20 \cdot \$9 + 10 \cdot \$13$

$\$180 + \$130$    Multiply from left to right.

$\$310$      Add.

**30.** The perimeter of the base is the distance around the base. The formula for the perimeter of a square is $4s = P$ since the sides are the same.

$4s = 916$

$s = 229$ m

# LESSON 32

## Warm Up 32

**1.** base

**2.** $3^4 = 3 \cdot 3 \cdot 3 \cdot 3 = 81$

**3.** $x^5 \cdot x^6 = x^{5+6}$

$= x^{11}$

**4.** Since the numbers have different signs, find the difference of their absolute values.

$26 + (-18)$

$|26| - |-18|$

$26 - 18 = 8$

The sum is positive because $|26| > |-18|$. So, $26 + (-18) = 8$.

**5.** $-34 - 19$

$-34 + (-19) = -53$

## Lesson Practice 32

**a.** $x^{-5} = \frac{1}{x^5}$

**b.** $\frac{p^{-8}}{q^4} = \frac{1}{p^8 q^4}$

**Saxon** Algebra 1

c. $\dfrac{1}{d^{-8}} = d^8$

d. $a^0bc^2 = 1 \cdot bc^2$

$= bc^2$

$= 6(3)^2$

$= 6(9)$

$= 54$

e. $4a^{-2} = \dfrac{4}{a^2}$

$= \dfrac{4}{4^2}$

$= \dfrac{4}{16}$

$= \dfrac{1}{4}$

f. $\dfrac{x^{10}}{x^4} = x^{10-4} = x^6$

g. $\dfrac{x^9}{x^{-2}} = x^{9-(-2)} = x^{11}$

h. $\dfrac{xy^{-3}z^5}{y^2x^2z} = x^{1-2}y^{-3-2}z^{5-1}$

$= x^{-1}y^{-5}z^4$

$= \dfrac{z^4}{xy^5}$

i. $\dfrac{10^1}{10^{-5}}$

$10^{1-(-5)}$

$10^6$ or 1,000,000 times more intense

**Lesson Practice 32**

1. $\dfrac{y^0y^6}{y^5} = 1 \cdot y^{6-5}$

$= 1 \cdot y$

$= y$

2. $\dfrac{m^3p^2q^{10}}{m^{-2}p^4q^{-6}} = m^{3-(-2)}p^{2-4}q^{10-(-6)}$

$= m^5p^{-2}q^{16}$

$= \dfrac{m^5q^{16}}{p^2}$

3. $9x - 2 = 2x + 12$

$9x = 2x + 14$

$7x = 14$

$x = 2$

4. $3y - y + 2y - 5 = 7 - 2y + 5$

$4y - 5 = -2y + 12$

$4y = -2y + 17$

$6y = 17$

$y = \dfrac{17}{6}$

5. $2y + 3 = 3(y + 7)$

$2y + 3 = 3y + 21$

$2y = 3y + 18$

$-y = 18$

$y = -18$

6. $5(r - 1) = 2(r - 4) - 6$

$5r - 5 = 2r - 8 - 6$

$5r - 5 = 2r - 14$

$5r = 2r - 9$

$3r = -9$

$r = -3$

7. The formula for the area of a circle is $A = \pi r^2$. The formula for the area of a square is $A = s^2$.

$\dfrac{\pi(2x)^2}{(4x)^2} = \dfrac{\pi 4x^2}{16x^2} = \dfrac{\pi}{4}$

8. $2x + 17 = 55$

$2x = 38$

$x = 19$

The number is 19.

9. Student B; Sample: Student B correctly found the cross products of the proportion.

10. Sample: The title of the graph does not specify that the data only apply to those who suffer from allergies. Someone may conclude that 75% of people suffer from indoor and outdoor allergies.

11. Sample: By combining like terms, the equation becomes simpler and easier to deal with. Combining contributes to the process of isolating the variable.

**12.** $-28 = -4n + 8$
$-28 = -4(9) + 8$
$-28 = -36 + 8$
$-28 = -28$
True, $n = 9$ is a solution for the equation.

**13.** Sample: No. For the input, 1, there are two outputs, 5 and 8. For the relation to be a function, each input would only have one output.

**14.** $\dfrac{60 \text{ dozen}}{12 \text{ cartons}} = \dfrac{x \text{ dozen}}{1 \text{ carton}}$
$12x = 60 \cdot 1$
$12x = 60$
$x = 5$
There are 5 dozen pencils in 1 carton.

**15.** $\dfrac{24 \text{ hours}}{1 \text{ day}} = \dfrac{? \text{ seconds}}{1 \text{ day}}$
$\dfrac{24 \text{ hours}}{1 \text{ day}} \cdot \dfrac{60 \text{ minutes}}{1 \text{ hour}} \cdot \dfrac{60 \text{ seconds}}{1 \text{ minute}}$
$\dfrac{86{,}400 \text{ seconds}}{1 \text{ day}}$
There are 86,400 seconds in 1 day.

**16.** Sample: The bar graph will show the exact number of roller coasters in each country and will compare the number of roller coasters in each country. The circle graph will show the relative number of roller coasters in each country to the total number of roller coasters.

**17.** $\dfrac{720 \text{ pencils}}{6 \text{ cartons}} = \dfrac{? \text{ dozen}}{10 \text{ cartons}}$
$\dfrac{\overset{10}{\cancel{720}} \text{ pencils}}{\underset{1}{\cancel{6}} \text{ cartons}} \cdot \dfrac{1 \text{ dozen}}{\cancel{12}} \cdot \dfrac{10 \text{ cartons}}{1}$
100 dozen pencils
There are 100 dozen pencils in 10 cartons.

**18.** $\dfrac{100 \text{ centimeters}}{1 \text{ meter}} \cdot \dfrac{1000 \text{ meter}}{1 \text{ kilometer}}$
$\dfrac{100{,}000 \text{ centimeters}}{1 \text{ kilometer}}$
There are 100,000 centimeters in 1 kilometer.

**19.** $\dfrac{1 \text{ inch}}{25 \text{ miles}} = \dfrac{2.5 \text{ inches}}{x \text{ miles}}$
$1 \cdot x = 25 \cdot 2.5$

$x = 62.5$
The two towns are 62.5 miles apart.

**20.**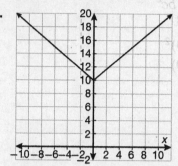

A vertical line intersects the graph at only one point, so the graph is a function.

**21.** The answer is **C**. Like terms are combined and it is written with only positive exponents and no zero exponents.

**22.** $\dfrac{10^{-24}}{10^{-28}} = 10^{-24-(-28)}$
$= 10^{-24+(+28)}$
$= 10^4$
$= 10{,}000$
It is 10,000 times greater.

**23. a.** $x + 4$
**b.** $x + x + 4 = 28$
$2x + 4 = 28$
$-4 = -4$
$2x = 24$
$x = 12$
The first side is $x$ feet long, so it is 12 feet long. The second side is $x + 4$ feet long. $12 + 4 = 16$, so the second side is 16 feet long.

**24.** $72 - 15 + x = 85$
$57 + x = 85$
$-57 = -57$
$x = 28$
She has to warm it by 28°F.

**25.** $x = M + 6$
$= 8 + 6$
$= 14$
Megan is 14 years old.

**Saxon** Algebra 1

**26. a.** ($3.25 − 0.32)$x$ = $73.25

**b.** ($3.25 − 0.32)$x$ = $73.25

$2.93$x$ = $73.25

$$\frac{\$2.93x}{\$2.93} = \frac{\$73.25}{\$2.93}$$

$x$ = 25

She bought 25 gallons of gas.

**27.** $(5p − 2c)4xy$

$5p \cdot 4xy − 2c \cdot 4xy$

$20pxy − 8cxy$

**28.** $\dfrac{7}{x} = \dfrac{1}{0.5}$

$1 \cdot x = 7(0.5)$

$x = 3.5$

**29.** $\dfrac{1}{x} = \dfrac{-3}{x + 2}$

$-3x = 1(x + 2)$

$-3x = x + 2$

$-4x = 2$

$x = -0.5$

**30. a.**

| x | 1 | 2 | 3 | 4 | 5 |
|---|---|---|---|---|---|
| y | 25 | 50 | 75 | 100 | 125 |

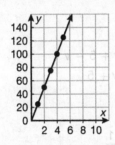

**b.** They all lie on the same line.

**c.** $\dfrac{1}{25} = \dfrac{x}{80}$

$25x = 80$

$x = \dfrac{80}{25}$ or 3.2

It will take him 3.2 hours or 3 hours and 12 minutes.

## LESSON 33

### Warm Up 33

1. sample space

2. The possible outcomes are 1, 2, 3, 4, 5, 6.

3. Three of the six numbers are prime: 1, 3, and 5.

$$\text{probability} = \frac{\text{quantity of prime numbers}}{\text{total possible outcomes}}$$

$$= \frac{3}{6} \text{ or } \frac{1}{2}$$

4. $\dfrac{4}{5} \cdot \dfrac{15}{22}$

$\dfrac{60}{110}$

$\dfrac{6}{11}$

5. $\left(\dfrac{18}{55}\right)\left(-\dfrac{33}{54}\right)$

$-\dfrac{594}{2970}$

$-\dfrac{1}{5}$

### Lesson Practice 33

**a.** The outcome of the first event does not affect the second event. They are independent.

**b.** The outcome of the first event does affect the second event. They are dependent.

**c.** The outcome of the first event does not affect the second event. They are independent.

**d.** The outcome of the first event does not affect the second event. They are independent.

**e.** First　Second　Outcomes

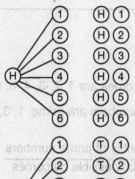

$P(\text{tails}) = \dfrac{1}{2}$

$P(\text{even number}) = \dfrac{1}{2}$

$P(\text{tails and an even number}) = \dfrac{1}{2} \cdot \dfrac{1}{2} = \dfrac{1}{4}$

**f.** There are 7 blocks to start. After one block is drawn, there are 6 blocks.

$P(\text{1st red block}) = \dfrac{4}{7}$

$P(\text{2nd red block}) = \dfrac{3}{6}$

$P(\text{1st red block}) \cdot P(\text{2nd red block})$

$= \dfrac{4}{7} \cdot \dfrac{3}{6}$

$= \dfrac{12}{42}$

$= \dfrac{2}{7}$

**g.** There are 7 blocks to start. After one block is drawn, there are 6 blocks.

$P(\text{blue block}) = \dfrac{3}{7}$

$P(\text{red block}) = \dfrac{4}{6}$

$P(\text{1st red block}) \cdot P(\text{2nd red block})$

$= \dfrac{3}{7} \cdot \dfrac{4}{6}$

$= \dfrac{12}{42}$

$= \dfrac{2}{7}$

**h.** There are 8 sections on the spinner. Two sections are black.

2:6 or 1:3

**i.** There are 8 sections on the spinner. Three sections are gray. Five sections are not gray.

5:3

**j.** $P(\text{pottery}) = \dfrac{1}{5}$

$P(\text{horsebackriding}) = \dfrac{1}{8}$

$P(\text{pottery and horseback riding})$

$= \dfrac{1}{5} \cdot \dfrac{1}{8}$

$= \dfrac{1}{40}$

**k.** Since one outside activity has been done and cannot be repeated, there are only 7 possible outside activities.

$P(\text{pottery}) = \dfrac{1}{5}$

$P(\text{swimming}) = \dfrac{1}{7}$

$P(\text{pottery and swimming})$

$= \dfrac{1}{5} \cdot \dfrac{1}{7}$

$= \dfrac{1}{35}$

**Practice 33**

**1.** $-5v = 6v + 5 - v$

$-5v = 5v + 5$

$-5v = 5$

$-10v = 5$

$v = -\dfrac{1}{2}$

**2.** $-3(b + 9) = -6$

$-3b - 27 = -6$

$-3b = 21$

$b = -7$

**3.** $-22 = -p - 12$

$-10 = -p$

$p = 10$

**4.** $-\dfrac{2}{5} = -\dfrac{1}{3}m + \dfrac{3}{5}$

$-\dfrac{5}{5} = -\dfrac{1}{3}m$

98

$-1 = -\frac{1}{3}m$

$m = 3$

5. $\frac{2}{x} = \frac{30}{-6}$

$30x = -12$

$x = -\frac{12}{30}$ or $-0.4$

6. $\frac{x-4}{6} = \frac{x+2}{12}$

$6(x+2) = 12(x-4)$

$6x + 12 = 12x - 48$

$6x + 60 = 12x$

$60 = 6x$

$x = 10$

7. $\frac{y^6 x^5}{y^5 x^7} = y^{6-5} x^{5-7}$

$= yx^{-2}$

$= \frac{y}{x^2}$

8. $\frac{w^{-5} z^{-3}}{w^{-3} z^2} = w^{-5-(-3)} z^{-3-2}$

$= w^{-2} z^{-5}$

$= \frac{1}{w^2 z^5}$

9. $\frac{4x^2 z^0}{2x^3 z} = 2x^{2-3} z^{0-1}$

$= 2x^{-1} z^{-1}$

$= \frac{2}{xz}$

10. The before draw picture has all of the marbles —10 little ones and 4 big ones. The after draw picture has all of the little marbles and one less big marble —10 little ones and 3 big ones, because 1 big marble was drawn and not replaced.

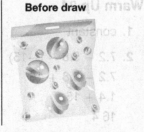

After draw          Before draw

11. Sample: Probability is the ratio of favorable outcomes to total outcomes (or sample space). Odds is the ratio of favorable to unfavorable outcomes.

12. True. The outcome of the second roll does not depend on the outcome of the first roll.

13. Verify the statement by subtracting two whole numbers. Then use a counterexample.

$5 - 3 = 2$

$3 - 5 = -2$

$-2$ is not a whole number so the set of whole numbers is not closed under subtraction.

14. $P(\text{blue stone}) = \frac{3}{10}$

$P(\text{white stone}) = \frac{2}{9}$

$P(\text{bluestone}) \cdot P(\text{white stone})$

$= \frac{3}{10} \cdot \frac{2}{9}$

$= \frac{6}{90}$

$= \frac{1}{15}$

The answer is **B**.

15. Write and simplify an expression that represents three times the change in value.

$3\left(-1\frac{3}{4}\right) = 3\left(-\frac{7}{4}\right) = -\frac{21}{4} = -5\frac{1}{4}$

16. $P(3) = \frac{1}{6}$

$P(3) = \frac{1}{6}$

$P(3) \cdot P(3) = \frac{1}{6} \cdot \frac{1}{6} = \frac{1}{36}$

17. Sample: A student who wants to make it appear that test grades have not dropped dramatically could use large intervals on the graph to persuade people to make this conclusion.

18. $x^3 \cdot x^{-3} = x^{3+(-3)} = x^0 = 1$

$x^n$ and $x^{-n}$ are reciprocals.

19. $\frac{10^{-9}}{10^{-6}} = 10^{-9-(-6)} = 10^{-3} = 1000$

The nanosecond is 1000 times faster.

**Saxon** Algebra 1

20. $\dfrac{30 \text{ quarts}}{1 \text{ mile}} \cdot \dfrac{1 \text{ gallon}}{4 \text{ quarts}}$

$\dfrac{30 \text{ gallons}}{4 \text{ miles}}$

7.5 gal/mi

21. Student A; Student B multiplied 9 by 225 instead of dividing 225 by 9.

22. $\$19.85 + \$0.20x = \$24.95 + \$0.17x$

$\$19.85 + \$0.03x = \$24.95$

$\$0.03x = \$5.10$

$x = 170 \text{ miles}$

23. Sample: No, the set cannot be a function because all functions are also relations.

24. Sample: First multiply each term by 100. Then add $-20$ to both sides of the equation. Finally, divide both sides by 9 to get the answer $n = 30$.

25. Use the values for $B$ and $w$ to find the length of the room.

$B = 377lw$

$12252.5 = 377 \cdot l \cdot 5$

$12252.5 = 1885l$

$l = 6.5$

Find the area as the product of the length and the width.

$A = lw$

$= 6.5 \cdot 5$

$= 32.5 \text{ m}^2$

26. a. $y = 30 \cdot 2 + 125 = 60 + 125 = 185$

$y = 30 \cdot 3 + 125 = 90 + 125 = 215$

$y = 30 \cdot 4 + 125 = 120 + 125 = 245$

$y = 30 \cdot 5 + 125 = 150 + 125 = 275$

| x | y |
|---|---|
| 2 | 185 |
| 3 | 215 |
| 4 | 245 |
| 5 | 275 |

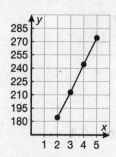

b. After 6 more games

27. Divide to find the qualifying average speed.

$26.2 \div 3\dfrac{2}{3} = 26.2 \div \dfrac{11}{3}$

$= 26.2 \cdot \dfrac{3}{11}$

$= \dfrac{78.6}{11}$

$= 7.15 \text{ miles per hour}$

She qualifies because the average qualifying speed is slower than her average speed.

28. a. Since the rectangles are similar, corresponding sides are proportional.

$\dfrac{4}{6} = \dfrac{2}{3}$

b. $\dfrac{2}{3} = \dfrac{6}{x}$

$2x = 18$

$x = 9$

29. $A = s^2$

$144 = s^2$

$\sqrt{144} = s$

$12 \text{ ft} = s$

30. False. Whole numbers are the set of natural numbers and zero. Whole numbers do not include negative numbers.

**LESSON 34**

**Warm Up 34**

1. constant

2. $7.2 - 5.8 - (-15)$

$7.2 - 5.8 + 15$

$1.4 + 15$

$16.4$

**Saxon** Algebra 1

**3.** $-0.12 - (-43.7) - 73.5$

$-0.12 + 43.7 - 73.5$

$43.58 - 73.5$

$-29.92$

**4.** $6(-2.5)$

$-15$

**5.** $(-15)(-4.2)$

$63$

## Lesson Practice 34

**a.** Since $6 - 7 = -1$, $5 - 6 = -1$, and $4 - 5 = -1$, the sequence is arithmetic with a common difference of $-1$. The next two terms are $4 + (-1) = 3$ and $3 + (-1) = 2$.

**b.** Since $12 - 10 = 2$ and $15 - 12 = 3$, there is no common difference and the sequence is not arithmetic.

**c.** $a_n = a_{n-1} + d$

$a_n = a_{n-1} + 4$

$a_1 = -3$

$a_2 = -3 + 4 = 1$

$a_3 = 1 + 4 = 5$

$a_4 = 5 + 4 = 9$

The first four terms of the sequence are $-3$, $1$, $5$, and $9$.

**d.** $a_4 = 14 + (n - 1)(-3)$

$= 14 + (4 - 1)(-3)$

$= 14 + (3)(-3)$

$= 14 - 9$

$= 5$

$a_{11} = 14 + (11 - 1)(-3)$

$= 14 + (10)(-3)$

$= 14 - 30$

$= -16$

The $4^{th}$ term is 5. The $11^{th}$ term is $-16$.

**e.** $a_1 = 1$ and $d = 9$

$a_n = a_1 + (n - 1)d$

$a_{10} = 1 + (10 - 1)9$

$= 1 + 9(9)$

$= 1 + 81$

$= 82$

**f.** $a_1 = \frac{2}{3}$ and $d = \frac{1}{3}$

$a_n = a_1 + (n - 1)d$

$a_{11} = \frac{2}{3} + (11 - 1)\frac{1}{3}$

$= \frac{2}{3} + 10\left(\frac{1}{3}\right)$

$= \frac{2}{3} + \frac{10}{3}$

$= \frac{12}{3} = 4$

**g.** $a_1 = 12$ and $d = 6$ so $a_n = 12 + (n - 1)6$

**h.** $a_n = 12 + (n - 1)6$

$a_{15} = 12 + (15 - 1)6$

$= 12 + (14)6$

$= 12 + 84$

$= 96$

## Practice 34

**1.** $\frac{2}{10} = \frac{x}{-20}$

$10x = 2(-20)$

$10x = -40$

$x = -4$

**2.** $\frac{32}{4} = \frac{x + 4}{3}$

$4(x + 4) = 3 \cdot 32$

$4x + 16 = 96$

$4x = 80$

$x = 20$

**3.** $a_1 = 24$, $d = 2$

$a_n = 24 + (n - 1)2$

$a_{15} = 24 + (15 - 1)2$

$= 24 + (14)2$

$= 24 + 28$

$= 52$

52 seats

**4.**

| x | y |
|----|----|
| -2 | 3 |
| -1 | -3 |
| 0 | -5 |
| 1 | -3 |
| 2 | 3 |

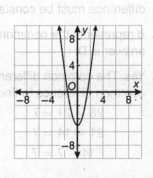

**Saxon** Algebra 1

**5.**
$$y = x + \frac{z}{3}$$
$$y - x = \frac{z}{3}$$
$$3(y - x) = z$$

**6.** $4x + 2 = 5(x + 10)$
$$4x + 2 = 5x + 50$$
$$4x = 5x + 48$$
$$-x = 48$$
$$x = -48$$
Check:
$$4(-48) + 2 = 5(-48 + 10)$$
$$-192 + 2 = 5(-38)$$
$$-190 = -190 \checkmark$$

**7.** $2\left(n + \frac{1}{3}\right) = \frac{3}{2}n + 1 + \frac{1}{2}n - \frac{1}{3}$
$$2n + \frac{2}{3} = \frac{4}{2}n + \frac{2}{3}$$
$$2n + \frac{2}{3} = 2n + \frac{2}{3}$$
$$2n = 2n$$
$$n = n$$
The solution is all real numbers.

**8.** The outcome of the first event does affect the second event. They are dependent.

**9.** Find the difference between each consecutive pair of numbers.
$$-0.5 - 0.3 = -0.8$$
$$-1.3 - (-0.5) = -0.8$$
$$-2.1 - (-1.3) = -0.8$$
Yes, it is an arithmetic sequence with a common difference of $-0.8$.

**10.** Sample: The first two terms have a difference of 2 and all the other terms have a difference of 4. To be an arithmetic sequence, the difference must be constant.

**11.** $d$ represents the common difference. The answer is **D**.

**12.** Yes. The common difference is 7. Use the common difference to find the next two terms.
$$28 - 21 = 7$$
$$21 - 14 = 7$$
$$14 - 7 = 7$$

$$a_n = a_{n-1} + d$$
$$a_5 = a_4 + d$$
$$= 28 + 7$$
$$= 35$$
$$a_6 = 35 + 7$$
$$= 42$$
The next two terms are 35 and 42.

**13.**
$$P(\text{yes}) = \frac{55}{100} = \frac{11}{20}$$
$$P(\text{yes}) = \frac{30}{100} = \frac{3}{10}$$
$$P(\text{yes and yes}) = \frac{11}{20} \cdot \frac{3}{10} = \frac{33}{200}$$

**14.**
$$P(2) = \frac{1}{6}$$
$$P(3) = \frac{1}{6}$$
$$P(2 \text{ and } 3) = \frac{1}{6} \cdot \frac{1}{6} = \frac{1}{36}$$

**15. a.** $28 - 22 = 6$
$$22 - 16 = 6$$
$$16 - 10 = 6$$
So $a_1 = 10$ and $d = 6$.
The rule is $a_n = 10 + (n - 1)6$.

**b.** $a_n = 10 + (n - 1)6$
$$a_{12} = 10 + (12 - 1)6$$
$$= 10 + (11)6$$
$$= 10 + 66$$
$$= 76 \text{ units}$$

**16. a.** $P(\text{pants}) = \frac{3}{8}$
$$P(\text{shirt}) = \frac{10}{10}$$
$$P(\text{tie}) = \frac{2}{3}$$
$P(\text{pants, shirt, tie})$
$$= \frac{3}{8} \cdot \frac{10}{10} \cdot \frac{2}{3}$$
$$= \frac{60}{240}$$
$$= \frac{1}{4}$$

**Saxon** Algebra 1

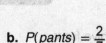 
**b.** $P(pants) = \frac{2}{7}$

$P(shirt) = \frac{9}{9}$

$P(tie) = \frac{2}{3}$

$P(pants, shirt, tie)$

$= \frac{2}{7} \cdot \frac{9}{9} \cdot \frac{2}{3}$

$= \frac{36}{189}$

$= \frac{4}{21}$

**17.** $d = 6 \cdot \frac{1}{c^{-2}}$

$= 6 \cdot \frac{1}{(2)^{-2}}$

$= 6 \cdot \frac{(2)^2}{1}$

$= 6 \cdot \frac{4}{1}$

$= 24$

**18.** $10^{-3} = \frac{1}{10^3}$

$10^{-1} = \frac{1}{10}$

$\frac{1}{10}$ m to $\frac{1}{10^3}$ m

**19.** $\frac{36 \text{ cookies}}{45 \text{ minutes}} \cdot \frac{60 \text{ minutes}}{1 \text{ hour}}$

$\frac{144 \text{ cookies}}{3 \text{ hours}}$

$\frac{48 \text{ cookies}}{1 \text{ hour}}$

She can make 48 cookies in 1 hour, so she can make $48 \cdot 3 = 144$ cookies in 3 hours. The answer is **D**.

**20.** Sample: Yes, for every value of $x$, there is only one value of $y$. Also, a vertical line drawn through the graph of $y = x^2 + 2$ only strikes the graph once.

**21.** $\frac{1 \text{ inch}}{20 \text{ feet}} = \frac{15 \text{ inches}}{x \text{ feet}}$

$x = 20 \cdot 15$

$x = 300 \text{ feet}$

**22.** Solve for $a$.

$\frac{2}{b} = \frac{1}{a}$

$2 \cdot a = 1 \cdot b$

$2a = b$

$a = \frac{b}{2}$

**23.** Sample: The increments are large, making the increase in tuition costs seem less than they actually are.

**24.** $x + 5 = x - 5$

$5 = -5$

The resulting equation $5 = -5$ is a false statement, so the equation has no solution.

**25.** $16x + 4(2x - 6) = 60$

$16x + 8x - 24 = 60$

$24x - 24 = 60$

$24x = 84$

$x = 3.5$

Check:

$16(3.5) + 4(2(3.5) - 6) = 60$

$56 + 4(7 - 6) = 60$

$56 + 4 = 60$

$60 = 60 ✓$

**26.** false; Sample: $\sqrt{5} \div \sqrt{5} = 1$. Any number divided by itself, even an irrational number, will equal 1.

**27.** $612.50x - 250x + 400 = 5500$

$362.50x + 400 = 5500$

$-400 \quad -400$

$362.50x = 5100$

$x = 14.1$

14.1 weeks is about 4 months, so it will take him about 4 months.

**28.** $d = rt$

$t = \frac{d}{r}$

$t = \frac{50}{8}$

$t = 6.25$

It will take him about $6\frac{1}{4}$ hours.

**29.** $45(7) + 0.23x = 395.50$

$315 + 0.23x = 395.50$

$-315 = -315$

$0.23x = 80.5$

$x = 350$

The family drove 350 miles.

**30.** Student A; Student B confused the dependent and independent variables.

## LESSON 35

### Warm Up 35

1. ordered pair

2. $3x + 14 = 3(-9) + 14$

$= -27 + 14$

$= -13$

3. $7.5w - 84.3 = 7.5(15) - 84.3$

$= 112.5 - 84.3$

$= 28.2$

4. $7x - 18 = -74$

$7x = -56$

$x = -8$

5. $57 + 19y = -76$

$19y = -133$

$y = -7$

### Lesson Practice 35

**a.** To find the intercepts, make a table.

Substitute 0 for $y$ and solve for $x$.

Substitute 0 for $x$ and solve for $y$.

$-6x + 9y = 36 \qquad -6x + 9y = 36$

$-6x + 9(0) = 36 \qquad -6(0) + 9y = 36$

$-6x + 0 = 36 \qquad 0 + 9y = 36$

$-6x = 36 \qquad 9y = 36$

$x = -6 \qquad y = 4$

| x | y |
|---|---|
| 8 | 0 |
| 0 | 6 |

The $x$-intercept is $-6$. The $y$-intercept is 4.

**b.** To find the intercepts, make a table.

Substitute 0 for $y$ and solve for $x$.

Substitute 0 for $x$ and solve for $y$.

$4x + 7y = 28 \qquad 4x + 7y = 28$

$4x + 7(0) = 28 \qquad 4(0) + 7y = 28$

$4x + 0 = 28 \qquad 0 + 7y = 28$

$4x = 28 \qquad 7y = 28$

$x = 7 \qquad y = 4$

| x | y |
|---|---|
| 6 | 0 |
| 0 | -5 |

The $x$-intercept is 7. The $y$-intercept is 4. To graph the equation, plot the intercepts and draw a line through them.

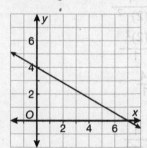

**c.** The $x$-intercept is the $x$-coordinate of the point where the line crosses the $x$-axis, $(-8, 0)$. The $x$-intercept is $-8$. The $y$-intercept is the $y$-coordinate of the point where the line crosses the $y$-axis, $(0, -9)$. The $y$-intercept is $-9$.

**d.** Write the equation in standard form.

$4y = 12x - 12$

$-12x = -12x$

$-12x + 4y = -12$

To find the $x$-intercept, substitute 0 for $y$ and solve for $x$.

$-12x + 4y = -12$

$-12x + 4(0) = -12$

$-12x + 0 = -12$

$-12x = -12$

$x = 1$

To find the $y$-intercept, substitute 0 for $x$ and solve for $y$.

$-12x + 4y = -12$

$-12(0) + 4y = -12$

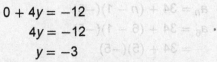
$$0 + 4y = -12$$
$$4y = -12$$
$$y = -3$$

Graph the $x$- and $y$-intercepts, $(1, 0)$ and $(0, -3)$, and draw a line through them.

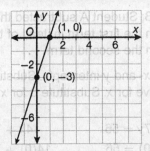

**e.** Substitute 0 for $y$ and solve for $x$.

Substitute 0 for $x$ and solve for $y$.

| | |
|---|---|
| $6x + 12y = 24$ | $6x + 12y = 24$ |
| $6x + 12(0) = 24$ | $6(0) + 12y = 24$ |
| $6x + 0 = 24$ | $0 + 12y = 24$ |
| $6x = 24$ | $12y = 24$ |
| $x = 4$ | $y = 2$ |

The $x$-intercept is 4 and the $y$-intercept is 2. To go 24 miles by one mode, Hirva could run for 4 hours or bike for 2 hours.

## Practice 35

**1.** $\dfrac{-2.25}{x} = \dfrac{9}{6}$

$$9x = -2.25 \cdot 6$$
$$9x = -13.5$$
$$x = -1.5$$

**2.** $\dfrac{y + 2}{y + 7} = \dfrac{11}{31}$

$$11(y + 7) = 31(y + 2)$$
$$11y + 77 = 31y + 62$$
$$11y + 15 = 31y$$
$$15 = 20y$$
$$y = \dfrac{15}{20} \text{ or } \dfrac{3}{4}$$

**3.** $2(f + 3) + 4f = 6 + 6f$

$$2f + 6 + 4f = 6 + 6f$$
$$6 + 6f = 6 + 6f$$
$$6 = 6$$

The equation $6 = 6$ is always true, so it has infinitely many solutions. All real numbers are solutions.

**4.** $3x + 7 - 2x = 4x + 10$

$$x + 7 = 4x + 10$$
$$x = 4x + 3$$
$$-3x = 3$$
$$x = -1$$

**5.** $(m + 6) \div (2 - 5)$

$$(9 + 6) \div (2 - 5)$$
$$(15) \div (-3)$$
$$-5$$

**6.** $-3(x + 12 \cdot 2)$

$$-3(-8 + 12 \cdot 2)$$
$$-3(-8 + 24)$$
$$-3(16)$$
$$-48$$

**7.** $10y^3 + 5y - 4y^3$

$$6y^3 + 5y$$

**8.** $10xy^2 - 5xy^2 + 3y^2x$

$$13xy^2 - 5x^2y$$

**9.** $\sqrt{7}$ is a real number and an irrational number.

**10.**
| | |
|---|---|
| $5x + 10y = -20$ | $5x + 10y = -20$ |
| $5x + 10(0) = -20$ | $5(0) + 10y = -20$ |
| $5x + 0 = -20$ | $0 + 10y = -20$ |
| $5x = -20$ | $10y = -20$ |
| $x = -4$ | $y = -2$ |

The $x$-intercept is $-4$ and the $y$-intercept is $-2$.

**11.** Substitute 0 for $y$ and solve for $x$.

Substitute 0 for $x$ and solve for $y$.

| | |
|---|---|
| $-8x + 20y = 40$ | $-8x + 20y = 40$ |
| $-8x + 20(0) = 40$ | $-8(0) + 20y = 40$ |
| $-8x + 0 = 40$ | $0 + 20y = 40$ |
| $-8x = 40$ | $20y = 40$ |
| $x = -5$ | $y = 2$ |

The $x$-intercept is $-5$ and the $y$-intercept is 2.

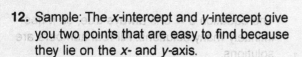

**12.** Sample: The *x*-intercept and *y*-intercept give you two points that are easy to find because they lie on the *x*- and *y*-axis.

**13.** Substitute 0 for *y* and solve for *x*.

$15x + 9y = 45$

$15x + 9(0) = 45$

$15x + 0 = 45$

$15x = 45$

$x = 3$

The answer is **B**.

**14.** Substitute 0 for *y* and solve for *x*.

Substitute 0 for *x* and solve for *y*.

| | |
|---|---|
| $y = 8x$ | $y = 8x$ |
| $0 = 8x$ | $y = 8(0)$ |
| $0 = x$ | $y = 0$ |

The *x*-intercept is 0. The *y*-intercept is 0.

Find two additional points.

| | |
|---|---|
| $y = 8x$ | $y = 8x$ |
| $= 8(1)$ | $= 8(2)$ |
| $= 8$ | $= 16$ |

Graph the points (1, 8) and (2, 16) and draw a line through them.

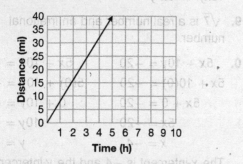

By inspection of the graph, the fish swims 20 miles in 2.5 hours.

**15.** $29 - 34 = -5$

$24 - 29 = -5$

$19 - 24 = -5$

Yes, it is arithmetic. The common difference is −5. The next two terms are

$19 + (-5) = 14$ and $14 + (-5) = 9$.

$a_n = 34 + (n - 1)(-5)$

$a_5 = 34 + (5 - 1)(-5)$

$= 34 + (4)(-5)$

$= 34 + (-20)$

$= 14$

$a_n = 34 + (n - 1)(-5)$

$a_6 = 34 + (6 - 1)(-5)$

$= 34 + (5)(-5)$

$= 34 + (-25)$

$= 9$

**16.** Student B; Student A subtracted the second term from the first term instead of the first term from the second term.

**17.** Find the *x*- and *y*-intercepts. Substitute 0 for *y* and solve for *x*. Substitute 0 for *x* and solve for *y*.

| | |
|---|---|
| $14x + 7y = 56$ | $14x + 7y = 56$ |
| $14x + 7(0) = 56$ | $14(0) + 7y = 56$ |
| $14x + 0 = 56$ | $0 + 7y = 56$ |
| $14x = 56$ | $7y = 56$ |
| $x = 4$ | $y = 8$ |

The *x*-intercept is 4, so the base of the triangle is 4 units. The *y*-intercept is 8, so the height of the triangle is 8 units. Use the formula for the area of a triangle.

$A = \frac{1}{2}bh$

$= \frac{1}{2}(4)(8)$

$= \frac{1}{2}(32)$

$= 16$

The area of the triangle is 16 square units.

**18. a.** $13.5 - 12 = 1.5$

$12 - 10.5 = 1.5$

$10.5 - 9 = 1.5$

$9 - 7.5 = 1.5$

$d = 1.5$

$a_1 = 7.5$

$a_n = a_{n-1} + 1.5$

**b.** $a_8 = 7.5 + (n - 1)1.5$

$a_8 = 7.5 + (8 - 1)1.5$

$a_8 = 7.5 + (7)1.5$

$a_8 = 7.5 + 10.5$

$a_8 = 18$ lb

**Saxon** Algebra 1

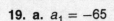 

**19. a.** $a_1 = -65$

**b.** $-72 - (-65) = -7$

$-79 - (-72) = -7$

$-86 - (-79) = -7$

$d = -7$

**c.** $a_n = -65 + (n-1)(-7)$

**20.** The outcome of the first event does not affect the second event. They are independent.

**21.** $a_7 = 25 + (7-1)15$

$= 25 + (6)15$

$= 25 + 90$

$= \$115$

**22.** $P(\text{1st white}) = \dfrac{3}{10}$

$P(\text{2nd white}) = \dfrac{2}{9}$

$P(\text{white and white}) = \dfrac{3}{10} \cdot \dfrac{2}{9} = \dfrac{6}{90} = \dfrac{1}{15}$

**23.** $\dfrac{m^3 n^{-10} p^5}{mn^0 p^{-2}} = m^{3-1} n^{-10-0} p^{5-(-2)}$

$= m^2 n^{-10} p^7$

$= \dfrac{m^2 p^7}{n^{10}}$

The answer is **D**.

**24.** No, the base of 4 was correctly raised to the second power, but the rule for negative exponents was not correctly followed.

The correct solution is $4^{-2} = \dfrac{1}{16}$.

**25.** $\dfrac{\overset{3}{\cancel{45}} \text{ miles}}{1 \text{ hour}} \cdot \dfrac{1 \text{ hour}}{\underset{4}{\cancel{60}} \text{ minutes}}$

$\dfrac{3 \text{ miles}}{4 \text{ minutes}}$

0.75 miles/min

**26.** Sample: Do you prefer SUVs or passenger cars?

**27.** The money earned is dependent and the hours worked is independent.

**28.** $F = \dfrac{9}{5}C + 32$

$F = \dfrac{9}{5}(-12) + 32$

$= -\dfrac{108}{5} + 32$

$= -21.6 + 32$

$= 10.4$

**29.** $f(d) = 1440 - 32d$

**30.** Sample: $f = 8h$; The relation is a function because each $f$ value has exactly one $h$ value.

## LESSON 36

### Warm Up 36

**1.** ratio

**2.** $\dfrac{13}{52} = \dfrac{x}{36}$

$52x = 13 \cdot 36$

$52x = 468$

$x = 9$

**3.** $\dfrac{42}{56} = \dfrac{63}{w}$

$42w = 56 \cdot 63$

$42w = 3528$

$w = 84$

**4.** $15x - 37 = 143$

$15x = 180$

$x = 12$

**5.** $78 + 22y = -230$

$22y = -308$

$y = -14$

### Lesson Practice 36

**a.** Since the triangles are similar,

$m\angle K = m\angle B = 25°$ and

$m\angle M = m\angle C = 20°$.

**b.** $\dfrac{5}{3} = \dfrac{x}{5}$

$3x = 5 \cdot 5$

$3x = 25$

$x = \dfrac{25}{3}$

**c.** $\frac{5}{4} = \frac{x}{21}$

$4x = 5 \cdot 21$

$4x = 105$

$x = 26.25$

The building is 26.25 m tall.

**d.** $\frac{1}{18} = \frac{5}{x}$

$x = 90$

$\frac{1}{18} = \frac{2.5}{x}$

$x = 45$

The table is 90 inches by 45 inches.

**e.** $\frac{1^2}{64^2} = \frac{1}{4096}$

The ratio is 1 sq. in.:4096 sq. in.

**Practice 36**

**1.** $\frac{3}{4} = \frac{x}{100}$

$4x = 3 \cdot 100$

$4x = 300$

$x = 75$

**2.** $\frac{5.5}{x} = \frac{1.375}{11}$

$1.375x = 5.5 \cdot 11$

$1.375x = 60.5$

$x = 44$

**3.** $2^2 + 6(8 - 5) \div 2$

$2^2 + 6(3) \div 2$

$4 + 18 \div 2$

$4 + 9$

$13$

**4.** $\frac{(3 + 2)(4 + 3) + 5^2}{6 - 2^2}$

$\frac{(5)(7) + 5^2}{6 - 2^2}$

$\frac{35 + 25}{6 - 4}$

$\frac{60}{2}$

$30$

**5.** $\frac{14 - 8}{-2^2 + 1}$

$\frac{14 - 8}{-4 + 1}$

$\frac{6}{-3}$

$-2$

**6.** Since both coordinates are positive, the point (3, 5) is in the first quadrant.

**7.** True. Any vertical line intersects the graph of the function in at most one point.

**8.** $\frac{9}{x} = \frac{16}{12}$

$16x = 9 \cdot 12$

$16x = 108$

$x = 6.75$

**9.** The shortest side of one triangle corresponds to the shortest side of the similar triangle.

$\frac{3}{9} = \frac{1}{3}$

The answer is **B**.

**10. a.** See student work.

**b.** $\frac{x}{6} = \frac{5}{2}$

$2x = 30$

$x = 15$

The tree is 15 feet tall.

**11.** $\frac{0.5^2}{10^2} = \frac{0.25}{100}$

The ratio is 0.25 sq. ft:100 sq. ft.

**12.** Substitute 0 for $y$ and solve for $x$.
Substitute 0 for $x$ and solve for $y$.

$2x + 3y = 24 \qquad\qquad 2x + 3y = 24$

$2x + 3(0) = 24 \qquad\quad 2(0) + 3y = 24$

$2x + 0 = 24 \qquad\qquad 0 + 3y = 24$

$2x = 24 \qquad\qquad\quad 3y = 24$

$x = 12 \qquad\qquad\qquad y = 8$

The $x$-intercept is 12 and the $y$-intercept is 8.

**13.** $\frac{20}{8} = \frac{x}{14}$

$8x = 20 \cdot 14$

$8x = 280$

$x = 35$

**14.** Substitute 0 for $y$ and solve for $x$.

$11x - 33y = 99$

$11x - 33(0) = 99$

$11x - 0 = 99$

$11x = 99$

$x = 9$

**15.** Substitute 0 for $x$ and solve for $y$.

$-7x - 8y = 56$

$-7(0) - 8y = 56$

$0 - 8y = 56$

$-8y = 56$

$y = -7$

**16.** Find the $x$- and $y$-intercepts. Substitute 0 for $y$ and solve for $x$. Substitute 0 for $x$ and solve for $y$.

| | |
|---|---|
| $11x - 4y = 22$ | $11x - 4y = 22$ |
| $11x - 4(0) = 22$ | $11(0) - 4y = 22$ |
| $11x = 22$ | $-4y = 22$ |
| $x = 2$ | $y = -5.5$ |

The $x$-intercept is 2, so the base of the triangle is 2 units. The $y$-intercept is –5.5, so the height of the triangle is 5.5 units. Use the formula for the area of a triangle.

$A = \dfrac{1}{2}bh$

$= \dfrac{1}{2}(2)(5.5)$

$= \dfrac{1}{2}(11)$

$= 5.5$

The area of the triangle is 5.5 square units.

**17. a.** $7x = -10y + 280$

$7x + 10y = 280$

**b.** Substitute 0 for $x$ and solve for $y$.

$7x + 10y = 280$

$7(0) + 10y = 280$

$0 + 10y = 280$

$10y = 280$

$y = 28$

Sample: To earn $280 by only washing SUVs, 28 SUVs would have to be washed.

**c.** $7x + 10y = 280$

$7x + 10(0) = 280$

$7x + 0 = 280$

$7x = 280$

$x = 40$

Sample: To earn $280 by washing only cars, 40 cars would have to be washed.

**18.** Find the common difference.

$0.1 - 0.4 = -0.3$

$-0.2 - 0.1 = -0.3$

$-0.5 - (-0.2) = -0.3$

$d = -0.3$

Yes, the sequence is arithmetic. Use the common difference to find the next two terms.

$a_n = 0.4 + (n - 1)(-0.3)$

$a_5 = 0.4 + (5 - 1)(-0.3)$

$= 0.4 + 4(-0.3)$

$= 0.4 - 1.2$

$= -0.8$

$a_n = 0.4 + (n - 1)(-0.3)$

$a_6 = 0.4 + (6 - 1)(-0.3)$

$= 0.4 + 5(-0.3)$

$= 0.4 - 1.5$

$= -1.1$

The next two terms are –0.8 and –1.1.

**19.** Student A; Student B's sequence does not have a common difference so it is not arithmetic.

**20.** There are 4 students left and 2 prizes, 1 of which is a book.

$P(\text{student}) = \dfrac{1}{4}$

$P(\text{book}) = \dfrac{1}{2}$

$P(\text{student and book}) = \dfrac{1}{4} \cdot \dfrac{1}{2} = \dfrac{1}{8}$

**21.** $\dfrac{1}{6} = \dfrac{x}{200}$

$6x = 200$

$x = 33\dfrac{1}{3}$

It weighs about $33\dfrac{1}{3}$ pounds.

**22.** There are 4 A sections and 2 B sections on the spinner. The odds against spinning a B are 4:2 or 2:1.

The answer is **C**.

**23. a.** Steve has $(300 - 10w)$ dollars in the bank. Mario has $(100 + 5w)$ dollars in the bank.

    **b.** Find the sum of the expressions that represents how much they each have in the bank.

$$(300 - 10w) + (100 + 5w)$$
$$400 - 5w$$

    **c.** $400 - 5w$
$$400 - 5 \cdot 6$$
$$400 - 30$$
$$370$$

    After six weeks, they have $370.

**24.** The size of the fire is independent.
The number of firefighters is dependent.

**25.** $3(x + 2) + (x + 2) = 128$
$$3x + 6 + x + 2 = 128$$
$$4x + 8 = 128$$
$$4x = 120$$
$$x = 30$$

**26.** $(250 + 422) \div 42$
$$672 \div 42$$
$$16$$
He will have 16 lessons.

**27.** $\dfrac{4x^2z^0}{2x^3z} = 2x^{2-3}z^{0-1}$
$$= 2x^{-1}z^{-1}$$
$$= \dfrac{2}{xz}$$

**28.** $T_v = T(1 + 0.61r)$
$$285 = 282.5(1 + 0.61r)$$
$$285 = 282.5 + 172.325r$$
$$-282.5 = -282.5$$
$$2.5 = 172.325r$$
$$r = 0.015$$

**29.** Sample: Joe needs to measure out the 5 samples of liquid more precisely than what is shown on the graph. Smaller intervals would better show the differences between the samples.

**30.** $34 - 2(x + 17) = 23x - 15 - 3x$
$$34 - 2x - 34 = 23x - 15 - 3x,$$
    Distributive Property
$$-2x = 20x - 15,$$
    Combine like terms.
$$\underline{-20x} = \underline{-20x},$$
    Subtraction Property of Equality
$$-22x = -15$$
$$-\frac{1}{22} \cdot -22x = -15 \cdot -\frac{1}{22},$$
    Multiplication Property of Equality
$$x = \frac{15}{22},$$
    Multiply.

## LESSON 37

### Warm Up 37

**1.** exponent

**2.** $7^4 = 7 \cdot 7 \cdot 7 \cdot 7 = 2401$

**3.** $(8.34)(-4)(100) = (834)(-4) = -3336$

**4.** $5^{-5} = \dfrac{1}{5^5}$
$$= \dfrac{1}{5 \cdot 5 \cdot 5 \cdot 5 \cdot 5}$$
$$= \dfrac{1}{3125}$$

**5.** $\dfrac{3x^{-3}}{5xy^{-5}} = \dfrac{3x^{-3-1}y^5}{5}$
$$= \dfrac{3x^{-4}y^5}{5}$$
$$= \dfrac{3y^5}{5x^4}$$

### Lesson Practice 37

**a.** Move the decimal 6 places.
$$1,234,000 = 1.234 \times 10^6$$

**Saxon** Algebra 1

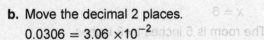
**b.** Move the decimal 2 places.

$0.0306 = 3.06 \times 10^{-2}$

**c.** $(5.82 \times 10^3)(6.13 \times 10^{11})$

$(5.82 \cdot 6.13)(10^3 \cdot 10^{11})$

$35.6766 \times 10^{14}$

$3.56766 \times 10^{15}$

**d.** $\dfrac{7.29 \times 10^{-2}}{8.1 \times 10^{-6}}$

$\dfrac{7.29}{8.1} \times \dfrac{10^{-2}}{10^{-6}}$

$0.9 \times 10^{-2-(-6)}$

$0.9 \times 10^4$

$9.0 \times 10^3$

**e.** $\dfrac{4.56 \times 10^9}{3 \times 10^5}$        $\dfrac{5.2 \times 10^8}{1.3 \times 10^5}$

$\dfrac{4.56}{3} \times \dfrac{10^9}{10^5}$        $\dfrac{5.2}{1.3} \times \dfrac{10^8}{10^5}$

$1.52 \times 10^{9-5}$        $4 \times 10^3$

$1.52 \times 10^4$

Since $1.52 \times 10^4 > 4 \times 10^3$,

$\dfrac{4.56 \times 10^9}{3 \times 10^5} > \dfrac{5.2 \times 10^8}{1.3 \times 10^5}$

**f.** $\dfrac{2.25 \times 10^{11}}{3 \times 10^8}$

$\dfrac{2.25}{3} \times \dfrac{10^{11}}{10^8}$

$0.75 \times 10^{11-8}$

$0.75 \times 10^3$

$7.5 \times 10^2$

**Practice 37**

**1.** $18 \div 3^2 - 5 + 2$

$18 \div 9 - 5 + 2$

$2 - 5 + 2$

$-1$

**2.** $7^2 + 4^2 + 3$

$49 + 16 + 3$

$68$

**3.** $3[-2(8 - 13)]$

$3[-2(-5)]$

$3(10)$

$30$

**4.** $13b^2 + 5b - b^2$

$12b^2 + 5b$

**5.** $-3(8x + 4) + \dfrac{1}{2}(6x - 24)$

$-24x - 12 + 3x - 12$

$-21x - 24$

**6.** Move the decimal 9 places.

$7.4 \times 10^{-9} = 0.0000000074$

**7.** Sample: A number has to be of the form $a \times 10^b$, and $a$ has to be greater than or equal to 1 and less than 10.

**8.** Sample: It quickly shows how large or small a number is without having to count zeros.

**9.** $(3.4 \times 10^{10})(4.8 \times 10^5)$

$(3.4 \cdot 4.8)(10^{10} \cdot 10^5)$

$16.32 \times 10^{15}$

$1.632 \times 10^{16}$

The answer is **B**.

**10.** $4 \times 10^{-5} = 0.00004$

**11.** Write and solve a proportion that relates the corresponding side lengths.

$\dfrac{20}{x} = \dfrac{18}{12}$

$18x = 20 \cdot 12$

$18x = 240$

$x = 13\dfrac{1}{3}$

**12.** $\dfrac{79 + 88 + 94 + x}{4} = 90$

$\dfrac{261 + x}{4} = 90$

$\left(\dfrac{261 + x}{4}\right)4 = 90 \cdot 4$

$261 + x = 360$

$\underline{-261 = -261}$

$x = 99$

**13.** Find the $x$- and $y$-intercepts.

Substitute 0 for $y$ and solve for $x$.

Substitute 0 for $x$ and solve for $y$.

$50x - 100y = 300$   $50x - 100y = 300$
$50x - 100(0) = 300$   $50(0) - 100y = 300$
$50x - 0 = 300$   $0 - 100y = 300$
$50x = 300$   $-100y = 300$
$x = 6$   $y = -3$

Graph (6, 0) and (0, −3) and connect them with a line.

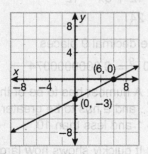

**14. a.** 3 to 6 or 1 to 2

**b.** $P = 4s$
$P = 4 \cdot 3$
$P = 12$
$P = 4 \cdot 6$
$P = 24$

The perimeter of the smaller square is 12 cm. The perimeter of the larger square is 24 cm.

**c.** 12 to 24 or 1 to 2

**d.** $A = s^2$
$A = 3^2$
$A = 9$
$A = 6^2$
$A = 36$

The area of the smaller square is 9 square centimeters. The area of the larger square is 36 square centimeters.

**e.** 9 to 36 or 1 to 4

**15.** Student B; Sample: Corresponding angles of similar triangles are congruent. They are not in proportion.

**16.** $\dfrac{1 \text{ in.}}{2 \text{ ft}} = \dfrac{x \text{ in.}}{10 \text{ ft}}$
$2x = 10$
$x = 5$

$\dfrac{1 \text{ in.}}{2 \text{ ft}} = \dfrac{x \text{ in.}}{12 \text{ ft}}$
$2x = 12$

$x = 6$
The room is 5 inches by 6 inches.

**17.** $\dfrac{\pi(2)^2}{\pi(3)^2}$
$\dfrac{4\pi}{9\pi}$
$\dfrac{4}{9}$

**18.** $2\dfrac{2}{3} - 4 = -\dfrac{4}{3}$
$1\dfrac{1}{3} - 2\dfrac{2}{3} = -\dfrac{4}{3}$ and
$0 - 1\dfrac{1}{3} = -\dfrac{4}{3}$

The sequence is airthmetic with a common difference of $-\dfrac{4}{3}$.

**19.** The outcome of the first event does affect the second event. They are dependent.

**20.** Sample: $\dfrac{21}{x} = \dfrac{3}{13}$

**21.** $a_1$ represents the first term in the sequence. The answer is **B**.

**22.** $10^{-9} = \dfrac{1}{10^9}$
$10^{-7} = \dfrac{1}{10^7}$
$\dfrac{1}{10^9}$ m to $\dfrac{1}{10^7}$ m

**23.**   $\dfrac{13}{14} = \dfrac{x}{10}$
$14x = 13 \cdot 10$
$14x = 130$
$14 \cdot 9 = 126$
$14 \cdot 10 = 140$
The solution is between 9 and 10.

**24.** Sample: The data could be displayed in a circle graph even though the given breeds do not represent the entire data set, which could lead to incorrect conclusions.

**25.** Sample: bar graph; Bar graphs can clearly display information gathered in surveys to compare different categories of data.

     **Saxon** Algebra 1

**26.** $f(w) = 2w + 20$

**27.** $89{,}678 \approx 10^5$

$11{,}004{,}734 \approx 10^7$

$(10^5) \times (10^7) = 10^{12}$

**28.** $7x + 9 = 2(4x + 2)$

| | |
|---|---|
| $7x + 9 = 8x + 4$ | Distributive Property |
| $\underline{-7x} \qquad \underline{-7x}$ | Subtraction Property of Equality |
| $9 = x + 4$ | |
| $\underline{-4} \quad \underline{-4}$ | Subtraction Property of Equality |
| $5 = x$ | |

**29. a.** Look for a relationship between yards and feet in the table.

$-2037 \div -679 = 3$

$-375 \div -125 = 3$

$96 \div 32 = 3$

$237 \div 79 = 3$

The number of yards is 3 times the number of feet.

$f = 3y$

**b.** $f = 3y$

$f = 3 \cdot 27.5$

$f = 82.5$

82.5 ft

**c.** There are 12 inches in 1 foot so there are 36 inches in 1 yard.

$N = 36y$

**30. a.** $P = 2w + 2l$

$38 + x = 2x + 2(3x - 2)$

**b.** $38 + x = 2x + 2(3x - 2)$

$38 + x = 2x + 6x - 4$

$38 + x = 8x - 4$

$42 + x = 8x$

$42 = 7x$

$x = 6$

**c.** $3x - 2$

$3(6) - 2$

$18 - 2$

$16$

16 cm

## LESSON 38

**Warm Up 38**

1. factor

2. $2x(3x - 5) = 6x^2 - 10x$

3. $-3x^2y(4x^2 - 7xy) = -12x^4y + 21x^3y^2$

4. $\dfrac{x^5}{x^{-3}} = x^{5-(-3)} = x^8$

5. $\dfrac{1}{-(-4)^3} = \dfrac{1}{-(-64)} = \dfrac{1}{64}$

**Lesson Practice 38**

**a.** List the factors and then the prime factors.

$100 = 2 \cdot 50$

$\qquad = 2 \cdot 2 \cdot 25$

$\qquad = 2 \cdot 2 \cdot 5 \cdot 5$

**b.** List the factors and then the prime factors.

$51 = 3 \cdot 17$

**c.** $24m^3n^4 + 32mn^5p$

$24m^3n^4 = 2 \cdot 2 \cdot 2 \cdot 3 \cdot m \cdot m \cdot m \cdot n \cdot n$
$\qquad\qquad \cdot n \cdot n$

$32mn^5p = 2 \cdot 2 \cdot 2 \cdot 2 \cdot 2 \cdot m \cdot n \cdot n \cdot n \cdot n$
$\qquad\qquad \cdot n \cdot p$

The GCF is $8mn^4$.

**d.** $5p^2q^5r^2 - 10pq^2r^2$

$5p^2q^5r^2 = 1 \cdot 5 \cdot p \cdot p \cdot q \cdot q \cdot q \cdot q \cdot q \cdot r \cdot r$

$10pq^2r^2 = 2 \cdot 5 \cdot p \cdot q \cdot q \cdot r \cdot r$

The GCF is $5pq^2r^2$.

**e.** Find the GCF. The GCF is $4d^2e^2$.

$8d^2e^3 + 12d^3e^2$

$4d^2e^2(2e + 3d)$

**f.** Find the GCF. The GCF is $6x^3y^2z$.

$12x^4y^2z - 42x^3y^3z^2$

$6x^3y^2z(2x - 7yz)$

**g.** $\dfrac{6x + 18}{6}$

$\dfrac{\cancel{6}(x + 3)}{\cancel{6}}$

$x + 3$

**h.** $\dfrac{18x + 45x^3}{9x}$

$\dfrac{\cancel{9}x(2 + 5x^2)}{\cancel{9}x}$

$2 + 5x^2$

**i.** $h = -16t^2 + 60t + 4$
$h = -4(4t^2 - 15t - 1)$

## Practice 38

**1.** $6 = hj + k$

$6 - k = hj$

$\dfrac{6 - k}{h} = \dfrac{hj}{h}$

$j = \dfrac{6 - k}{h}$

**2.** $\dfrac{a + 3}{b} = c$

$a + 3 = bc$

$a = bc - 3$

**3.** The height of the plant increases over time.

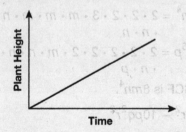

**4.** The slope of the graph will become steeper when the plant begins to grow faster.

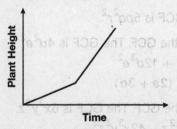

**5.** The slope of the graph will increase slowly, then stay the same, then increase greatly.

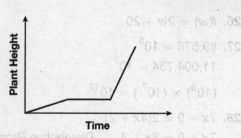

**6.** $\dfrac{144 \text{ lb}}{30 \text{ books}} = 4.8$ lb/book

**7.** $\dfrac{\$43.45}{5.5 \text{ hours}} = \$7.90$/hour

**8.** Move the decimal 6 places.
$2 \times 10^6 = 2,000,000$

**9.** $\dfrac{p}{3} = \dfrac{18}{21}$

$21p = 3 \cdot 18$

$21p = 54$

$p = \dfrac{54}{21} \approx 2.57$

**10.** List the factors and then the prime factors.
$140 = 2 \cdot 70$
$\quad\quad = 2 \cdot 2 \cdot 35$
$\quad\quad = 2 \cdot 2 \cdot 5 \cdot 7$

**11.** $\dfrac{10x + 5}{5}$

$\dfrac{\cancel{5}(2x + 1)}{\cancel{5}}$

$2x + 1$

The answer is **B**.

**12.** $h = 40 - 16t^2$
$h = 8(5 - 2t^2)$

**13.** Sample: They use opposite operations. The Distributive Property uses multiplication to rewrite a product as a polynomial. Factoring divides out the GCF to write a polynomial as a product of its factors.

**14.** Sample: The fraction $\dfrac{6(x - 1)}{6}$ can be reduced because the division of 6 undoes the multiplication of 6 in the numerator. The numerator of the fraction $\dfrac{6x - 1}{6}$ cannot be factored and therefore cannot be reduced because division does not undo subtraction.

**15.** Move the decimal 9 places.
$0.000000002 = 2 \times 10^{-9}$

**Saxon** Algebra 1

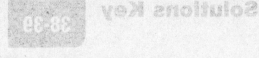
**16.** Move the decimal 9 places.
$0.000000001 = 1 \times 10^{-9}$

**17.** Move the decimal 7 places.
$78,000,000 = 7.8 \times 10^{7}$

**18.** $A = s^2$
$= (6.04 \times 10^{-5})(6.04 \times 10^{-5})$
$= (6.04 \times 6.04)(10^{-5} \times 10^{-5})$
$= 36.4816 \times 10^{-10}$
$= 3.64816 \times 10^{-9}$ square meters

**19.** $\frac{12}{9} = \frac{x}{12}$
$9x = 144$
$x = 16$

**20. a.** Move the decimal 11 places.
100 billion = 100,000,000,000
$= 1.0 \times 10^{11}$

**b.** $\dfrac{3}{1.0 \times 10^{11}}$
$\dfrac{3}{1} \times \dfrac{1}{10^{11}}$
$3 \times 10^{-11}$

**21.** Sample: When $y = 0$, $0 = 12x$, so $0 = x$.
When $x = 0$, $y = 12(0)$, so $y = 0$. The
$x$-intercept and the $y$-intercept are the same
(the origin).

**22.** The odds are 22:18 or 11:9.

**23.** The base of 3 and the exponent of $-2$ were
multiplied. The rule for negative exponents was
not used. The correct solution is $3^{-2} = \frac{1}{9}$.

**24.** Sample: The break in the graph is distorting
the number of books sold.

**25.** Find the common difference.
$2 - \dfrac{5}{4} = \dfrac{8}{4} - \dfrac{5}{4} = \dfrac{3}{4}$
$\dfrac{11}{4} - 2 = \dfrac{11}{4} - \dfrac{8}{4} = \dfrac{3}{4}$
$\dfrac{7}{2} - \dfrac{11}{4} = \dfrac{14}{4} - \dfrac{11}{4} = \dfrac{3}{4}$
$d = \dfrac{3}{4}$

Yes; the sequence is arithmetic. Use the
common difference to find the next two terms.

$a_n = \dfrac{5}{4} + (n - 1)\left(\dfrac{3}{4}\right)$
$a_5 = \dfrac{5}{4} + (5 - 1)\left(\dfrac{3}{4}\right)$
$= \dfrac{5}{4} + 4\left(\dfrac{3}{4}\right)$
$= \dfrac{5}{4} + 3$
$= \dfrac{5}{4} + \dfrac{12}{4}$
$= \dfrac{17}{4}$

$a_n = \dfrac{5}{4} + (n - 1)\left(\dfrac{3}{4}\right)$
$a_6 = \dfrac{5}{4} + (6 - 1)\left(\dfrac{3}{4}\right)$
$= \dfrac{5}{4} + 5\left(\dfrac{3}{4}\right)$
$= \dfrac{5}{4} + \dfrac{15}{4}$
$= \dfrac{20}{4}$
$= 5$

The next two terms are $\frac{17}{4}$ and 5.

**26.** Standard form is $Ax + By = C$.
The only equation in this form
is $9x + 11y = 65$.
The answer is **D**.

**27.** The stems represent tens and the leaves
represent ones.
3|0

**28.** $2v + 20.90 = 2.95v$
$\quad\ \ -2v = -2v$
$20.90 = 2.95v - 2v$
$20.90 = 0.95v$
$v = 22$
The total fees will be the same for 22 visits.

**29.** $p - 5 + 2p = 43$
$3p - 5 = 43$
$+5 = +5$
$3p = 48$
$p = 16$
The starting price was $16.

**30. a.**

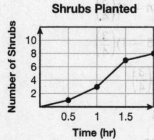

Shrubs Planted

**b.** Yes, the graph is a function because a vertical line will cross it only at one point.

**c.** No, this is not a linear function.

## LESSON 39

**Warm Up 39**

**1.** real

**2.** $-3x^2y(4x^2y^{-1} - xy)$
$-12x^4 + 3x^3y^2$

**3.** $mn(2x - 3my + 5ny)$
$2mnx - 3m^2ny + 5mn^2y$

**4.** $\dfrac{5x - 25x^2}{5x}$

$\dfrac{\cancel{5}x(1 - 5x)}{\cancel{5}x}$

$1 - 5x$

**5.** $3a^2b^3 - 6a^4b + 12ab$
$3ab(ab^2 - 2a^3 + 4)$

**Lesson Practice 39**

**a.** $\dfrac{r^2}{q}\left(\dfrac{r^2}{q^3} + \dfrac{7q^3}{w}\right)$

$\dfrac{r^2 \cdot r^2}{q \cdot q^3} + \dfrac{r^2 \cdot 7q^3}{qw}$

$\dfrac{r^4}{q^4} + \dfrac{7q^3r^2}{qw}$

$\dfrac{r^4}{q^4} + \dfrac{7q^2r^2}{w}, \; q \neq 0, \; w \neq 0$

**b.** $\dfrac{t}{z}\left(\dfrac{uay}{tq} - 2t^3y^2\right)$

$\dfrac{t \cdot uay}{z \cdot tq} - \dfrac{t \cdot 2t^3y^2}{z}$

$\dfrac{uay}{zq} - \dfrac{2t^4y^2}{z}, \; q \neq 0, \; t \neq 0, \; z \neq 0$

**c.** $\dfrac{j^{-2}}{m}\left(\dfrac{j^{-3}}{m^{-2}} + \dfrac{9m^3}{k}\right)$

$\dfrac{j^{-2} \cdot j^{-3}}{m \cdot m^{-2}} + \dfrac{j^{-2} \cdot 9m^3}{mk}$

$\dfrac{j^{-5}}{m^{-1}} + \dfrac{j^{-2} \cdot 9m^2}{k}$

$\dfrac{m}{j^5} + \dfrac{9m^2}{kj^2}, \; j \neq 0, \; k \neq 0, \; m \neq 0$

**d.** $\dfrac{n^{-2}}{z}\left(\dfrac{v^{-2}cb}{nv^{-1}} - 4n^5b^{-3}\right)$

$\dfrac{n^{-2} \cdot v^{-2}cb}{z \cdot nv^{-1}} - \dfrac{n^{-2} \cdot 4n^5b^{-3}}{z}$

$\dfrac{n^{-3} \cdot v^{-1}cb}{z \cdot v^{-1}} - \dfrac{4n^3b^{-3}}{z}$

$\dfrac{cb}{n^3zv} - \dfrac{4n^3}{zb^3}, \; b \neq 0, \; n \neq 0, \; v \neq 0, \; z \neq 0$

**e.** $\dfrac{fs}{d^4}\left(\dfrac{fhs}{d} + 2sk - \dfrac{7}{d^6}\right)$

$\dfrac{fs \cdot fhs}{d^4 \cdot d} + \dfrac{fs \cdot 2sk}{d^4} - \dfrac{fs \cdot 7}{d^4 \cdot d^6}$

$\dfrac{f^2hs^2}{d^5} + \dfrac{2fs^2k}{d^4} - \dfrac{7fs}{d^{10}}, \; d \neq 0$

**f.** $\dfrac{zx}{w^{-2}}\left(\dfrac{zd^{-2}x}{w} + 5tz - \dfrac{2}{w^{-4}}\right)$

$\dfrac{zx \cdot zd^{-2}x}{w^{-2} \cdot w} + \dfrac{zx \cdot 5tz}{w^{-2}} - \dfrac{zx \cdot 2}{w^{-2} \cdot w^{-4}}$

$\dfrac{z^2d^{-2}x^2}{w^{-1}} + \dfrac{5tz^2x}{w^{-2}} - \dfrac{2zx}{w^{-6}}$

$\dfrac{z^2x^2w}{d^2} + 5tz^2xw^2 - 2zxw^6, \; d \neq 0, \; w \neq 0$

**g.** $\dfrac{t^2y}{z}\left(\dfrac{t^{-3}}{y^{-2}} + \dfrac{z^{-4}}{y^5t}\right)$

$\dfrac{t^2y \cdot t^{-3}}{z \cdot y^{-2}} + \dfrac{t^2y \cdot z^{-4}}{z \cdot y^5t}$

$\dfrac{t^{-1}y}{zy^{-2}} + \dfrac{t^2yz^{-4}}{zy^5t}$

**Saxon** Algebra 1

$$\frac{t^{-1}y^3}{z} + ty^{-4}z^{-5}$$

$$\frac{y^3}{tz} + \frac{t}{y^4 z^5}, \; t \neq 0, \; y \neq 0, \; z \neq 0$$

**Practice 39**

1. $4\left(y + \frac{3}{2}\right) = -18$

 $4y + \frac{12}{2} = -18$

 $4y + 6 = -18$

 $4y = -24$

 $y = -6$

 $4\left(-6 + \frac{3}{2}\right) = -18$

 $-24 + 6 = -18$

 $-18 = -18$

2. $x - 4 + 2x = 14$

 $3x - 4 = 14$

 $3x = 18$

 $x = 6$

 $6 - 4 + 2(6) = 14$

 $6 - 4 + 12 = 14$

 $14 = 14$

3. It is false. Sample: $2 \div 3$ is not an integer.

4. Add to get the sum.

 $a + 3$

5. Add.

 $k + 2.5$

6. Subtract.

 $x - 3$

7. Multiply 3 and $y$, then add 2.

 $3y + 2$

8. $\dfrac{d^2}{s^2}\left(\dfrac{d^2}{s} + \dfrac{9s^3}{h}\right)$

 $\dfrac{d^2 \cdot d^2}{s^2 \cdot s} + \dfrac{d^2 \cdot 9s^3}{s^2 h}$

 $\dfrac{d^4}{s^3} + \dfrac{9d^2 s^3}{s^2 h}$

 $\dfrac{d^4}{s^3} + \dfrac{9d^2 s}{h}, \; h \neq 0, \; s \neq 0$

9. Sample: Division by zero is undefined. A number cannot be divided into groups of zero and zero has no reciprocal.

10. $\dfrac{x^{-2}}{n^{-1}}(2x^{-4} + n^{-3})$

 $= \dfrac{2x^{-4} \cdot x^{-2}}{n^{-1}} + \dfrac{x^{-2}n^{-3}}{n^{-1}}$   Distributive Property

 $= \dfrac{2x^{-6}}{n^{-1}} + n^{-2}x^{-2}$   Rules of Exponents

 $= \dfrac{2n}{x^6} + \dfrac{1}{n^2 x^2}$   Rules of Exponents

 $n \neq 0, \; x \neq 0$

11. $\dfrac{g^{-2}s}{b^2}\left(\dfrac{g^{-3}s^{-1}}{b^{-1}} + \dfrac{4}{b^3}\right)$

 $\dfrac{g^{-2}s \cdot g^{-3}s^{-1}}{b^2 \cdot b^{-1}} + \dfrac{g^{-2}s \cdot 4}{b^2 \cdot b^3}$

 $\dfrac{g^{-5}}{b} + \dfrac{4g^{-2}s}{b^5}$

 $\dfrac{1}{bg^5} + \dfrac{4s}{b^5 g^2}$

 The answer is **D**.

12. $\dfrac{w^2 p}{t}\left(\dfrac{4}{w^4} - \dfrac{t^2}{p^5}\right)$

 $\dfrac{w^2 p \cdot 4}{t \cdot w^4} - \dfrac{w^2 p \cdot t^2}{t \cdot p^5}$

 $\dfrac{4w^2 p}{tw^4} - \dfrac{w^2 p t^2}{p^5 t}$

 $\dfrac{4w^{-2}p}{t} - \dfrac{w^2 p^{-4}t}{1}$

 $\dfrac{4p}{tw^2} - \dfrac{w^2 t}{p^4}, \; p \neq 0, \; t \neq 0, \; w \neq 0$

13. List the factors and then the prime factors.

 $918 = 2 \cdot 459$

 $= 2 \cdot 3 \cdot 153$

 $= 2 \cdot 3 \cdot 3 \cdot 51$

 $= 2 \cdot 3 \cdot 3 \cdot 3 \cdot 17$

14. Student B; Sample: The third term of the polynomial is the same as the GCF, and factoring results in a monomial divided by itself, which is 1. Student A represented the third term with 0, not 1.

15. Factor the expression.

$6a^2b + 15ab$

$3ab(2a + 5)$

$3ab$ and $2a + 5$

16. The side lengths of similar figures are in proportion.

The answer is **C**.

17. **a.** $24x^2y^3 + 18xy^2 + 6xy$

$24x^2y^3 = 2 \cdot 2 \cdot 2 \cdot 3 \cdot x \cdot x \cdot y \cdot y \cdot y$

$18xy^2 = 2 \cdot 3 \cdot 3 \cdot x \cdot y \cdot y$

$6xy = 2 \cdot 3 \cdot x \cdot y$

The GCF is $2 \cdot 3 \cdot x \cdot y$

**b.** $24x^2y^3 + 18xy^2 + 6xy$

$6xy(4xy^2 + 3y + 1)$

18. $\dfrac{6(x + 4)}{9 \cdot 15}$

$\dfrac{6(x + 4)}{135}$

$\dfrac{2(x + 4)}{45}$

19. No. Sample: To double the volume of water, you only need to double one of the dimensions.

20. Find the $x$- and $y$-intercepts.

Substitute 0 for $y$ and solve for $x$.

Substitute 0 for $x$ and solve for $y$.

$27x + 9y = 54 \qquad 27(0) + 9y = 54$

$27x + 9(0) = 54 \qquad 0 + 9y = 54$

$27x + 0 = 54 \qquad 9y = 54$

$27x = 54 \qquad y = 6$

$x = 2$

Graph (2, 0) and (0, 6) and connect them with a line.

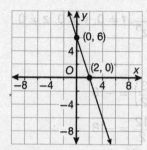

21. $\quad 5x + 8y = 480 \qquad 5(0) + 8y = 480$

$\quad 5x + 8(0) = 480 \qquad 0 + 8y = 480$

$\quad 5x + 0 = 480 \qquad 8y = 480$

$\quad 5x = 480 \qquad y = 60$

$\quad x = 96$

The $x$-intercept is 96 and the $y$-intercept is 60.

22. $\$1500 + 5(\$500)$

$\$1500 + \$2500$

$\$4000$

23. Move the decimal 3 places.

$0.00608 = 6.08 \times 10^{-3}$

24. Student B; Sample: Student A wrote 5 zeros and moved the decimal point 6 places instead of 5.

25. $\dfrac{1}{4\frac{3}{4} - 1} \overset{?}{=} \dfrac{4}{15}$

$4\left(4\frac{3}{4} - 1\right) \overset{?}{=} 15(1)$

$19 - 4 \overset{?}{=} 15$

$15 = 15$

26. $\dfrac{x^2y^{-2}}{z^2}$

$\dfrac{x^2}{y^2z^2}$

$\dfrac{3^2}{4^2(-2)^2}$

$\dfrac{9}{16(4)}$

$\dfrac{9}{64}$

**Saxon** Algebra 1

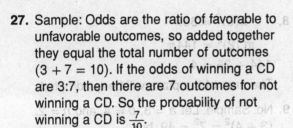
27. Sample: Odds are the ratio of favorable to unfavorable outcomes, so added together they equal the total number of outcomes $(3 + 7 = 10)$. If the odds of winning a CD are 3:7, then there are 7 outcomes for not winning a CD. So the probability of not winning a CD is $\frac{7}{10}$.

28. Sample: The ordered pairs will form a relation but not a function because a given stamp will have more than one possible value.

29. Sample: The vertical axis has a broken scale, making the data appear to increase dramatically. The employer may want the candidate to feel the employer gives large raises.

30. Find the rule. If you subtract 0.5 from each $f(g)$, the resulting $g$ value is 2 times $f(g)$.
$$f(g) = 0.5g + 0.5$$

## LESSON 40

### Warm Up 40

1. exponent

2. $(4x^2y^3)(5x^4y^4)$
$4 \cdot 5 \cdot x^{2+4}y^{3+4}$
$20x^6y^7$

3. $\dfrac{24x^3y^6}{36x^5y^3}$
$\dfrac{2x^{3-5}y^{6-3}}{3}$
$\dfrac{2y^3}{3x^2}$

4. $(-3)^2 - 3^2$
$(-3 \cdot -3) - 3^2$
$9 - 9$
$0$

5. Simplify each expression. Then compare.
$4^2 + \sqrt{36} \qquad -(-3)^2 + \sqrt{25}$
$16 + 6 \qquad\qquad -9 + 5$
$22 \qquad\qquad\quad -4$
Since $22 > -4$, $4^2 + \sqrt{36} > -(-3)^2 + \sqrt{25}$

### Lesson Practice 40

a. $(5^2)^2$
$5^{2\cdot2}$
$5^4$
$625$

b. $(b^4)^7$
$b^{4\cdot7}$
$b^{28}$

c. $(3n^4)^2$
$3^2 \cdot n^{4\cdot2}$
$9n^8$

d. $(9ab^{-2})^2(2a^2b^4)$
$9^2 \cdot a^2 \cdot b^{-2\cdot2} \cdot 2a^2b^4$
$81 \cdot a^2 \cdot b^{-4} \cdot 2a^2b^4$
$162 \cdot a^{2+2} \cdot b^{-4+4}$
$162a^4$

e. $\left(\dfrac{3y^4}{4}\right)^3 = \dfrac{3^3y^{4\cdot3}}{4^3}$
$= \dfrac{27y^{12}}{64}$

f. $\left(\dfrac{-x}{7y^5}\right)^2 = \dfrac{(-1)^2(x)^2}{(7)^2\left(y^5\right)^2}$
$= \dfrac{x^2}{49y^{10}}$

g. $V = s^3$
$= (3x)^3$
$= 3^3 \cdot x^3$
$= 27x^3$

### Practice 40

1. $\dfrac{3}{12} = \dfrac{-24}{m}$
$3m = 12(-24)$
$3m = -288$
$m = -96$

2. $\dfrac{-4}{0.8} = \dfrac{2}{x-1}$
$-4(x-1) = 0.8 \cdot 2$

**Saxon** Algebra 1

$$-4x + 4 = 1.6$$
$$-4x = -2.4$$
$$x = 0.6$$

**3.** $\dfrac{5}{12} = \dfrac{1.25}{k}$

$5k = 12 \cdot 1.25$

$5k = 15$

$k = 3$

**4.** All whole numbers are integers. The statement is true.

**5.** $(4^4)^5$

$4^{4 \cdot 5}$

$4^{20}$

**6.** Simplify each expression.

$(-2x^2y)^2(6y)$

$(-2)^2 \cdot x^{2 \cdot 2} \cdot y^2 \cdot 6y$

$4 \cdot x^4 \cdot y^2 \cdot 6y$

$24x^4y^2$

$-2(x^2y)^2(6y)$

$-2 \cdot x^{2 \cdot 2} \cdot y^2 \cdot 6y$

$-2 \cdot x^4 \cdot y^2 \cdot 6y$

$-12x^4y^2$

$-(2x^2y)^2(6y)$

$-(2^2 \cdot x^{2 \cdot 2} \cdot y^2 \cdot 6y)$

$-(4 \cdot x^4 \cdot y^2 \cdot 6y)$

$-24x^4y^3$

$-(2xy)^3(3)$

$-(2 \cdot x^3 \cdot y^3 \cdot 3)$

$-6x^3y^3$

The answer is **C**.

**7.** $\dfrac{e^3}{r^5}\left(\dfrac{e^2}{4r} + \dfrac{r^9}{k}\right)$

$\dfrac{e^3 \cdot e^2}{r^5 \cdot 4r} + \dfrac{e^3 \cdot r^9}{r^5 \cdot k}$

$\dfrac{e^5}{4r^6} + \dfrac{e^3 r^4}{k},\ k \neq 0,\ r \neq 0$

**8.** $\pi(6)^2 = 36\pi$

$\pi(12)^2 = 144\pi$

$144 \div 36 = 4$

The area of the pizza will be quadrupled.

**9.** No. Sample: Let $a = 3$, $b = 4$, and $n = 2$.

$(3 + 4)^2 = 7^2 = 49$, but

$3^2 + 4^2 = 9 + 16 = 25$.

**10.** Sample: You add exponents when you are multiplying two powers with the same base. You multiply exponents when you are raising a power to a power.

**11.** $\dfrac{wd^{-3}}{c}\left(\dfrac{d}{w^{-4}} + \dfrac{c^{-2}}{wd}\right)$

$\dfrac{wd^{-3} \cdot d}{c \cdot w^{-4}} + \dfrac{wd^{-3} \cdot c^{-2}}{c \cdot wd}$

$\dfrac{wd^{-2}}{cw^{-4}} + \dfrac{wd^{-3}c^{-2}}{cwd}$

$\dfrac{w^5d^{-2}}{c} + \dfrac{d^{-4}c^{-3}}{1}$

$\dfrac{w^5}{d^2c} + \dfrac{1}{d^4c^3},\ c \neq 0,\ d \neq 0,\ w \neq 0$

**12.** $\dfrac{a^2}{d^2}\left(\dfrac{a^{-2}x}{d^{-1}} - \dfrac{2x}{d^{-3}}\right)$

$\dfrac{a^2 \cdot a^{-2}x}{d^2 \cdot d^{-1}} - \dfrac{a^2 \cdot 2x}{d^2 \cdot d^{-3}}$

$\dfrac{x}{d} - 2a^2dx,\ a \neq 0,\ d \neq 0$

**13.** $\dfrac{g^5}{w^{-2}}\left(\dfrac{wx^2}{g^2} + \dfrac{gy^2}{w^2}\right)$

$\dfrac{g^5 \cdot wx^2}{w^{-2} \cdot g^2} + \dfrac{g^5 \cdot gy^2}{w^{-2} \cdot w^2}$

$g^3 w^3x^2 + g^6y^2,\ g \neq 0,\ w \neq 0$

**14. a.** $\dfrac{rt}{w^3}\left(\dfrac{rty}{w} + 2ty - \dfrac{8}{w^2}\right)$

$\dfrac{rt \cdot rty}{w^3 \cdot w} + \dfrac{rt \cdot 2ty}{w^3} - \dfrac{rt \cdot 8}{w^3 \cdot w^2}$

$\dfrac{r^2t^2y}{w^4} + \dfrac{2rt^2y}{w^3} - \dfrac{8rt}{w^5}$

**b.** $w \neq 0$ because it is in the denominator.

**Saxon** Algebra 1

**15.** $4xy^2z^4 = 2 \cdot 2 \cdot x \cdot y \cdot y \cdot z \cdot z \cdot z \cdot z$

$2x^2y^3z^2 = 2 \cdot x \cdot x \cdot y \cdot y \cdot y \cdot z \cdot z$

$6x^3y^4z = 2 \cdot 3 \cdot x \cdot x \cdot x \cdot y \cdot y \cdot y \cdot z$

The GCF is $2xy^2z$.

**16.** Student A; Sample: Student B canceled without first writing the numerator as a product. The factor that is canceled in the denominator must be the same factor that is canceled in the numerator and, therefore, must be a common factor.

**17. a.** $V = lwh$

$2 \cdot 5x(10x + 15)$

**b.** $10x(10x + 15)$

$100x^2 + 150x$

$50x(2x + 3)$

**18.** $0.78 \cdot 250 = n$

$n = 195$

**19.** The domain is the set of possible values for the independent variable. The range is the set of values for the dependent variable.

Domain: $\{2,4,5,9\}$

Range: $\{4,7,9,12\}$

**20. a.**

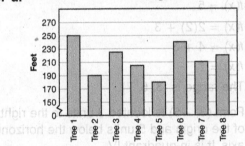

Tree Heights

**b.**

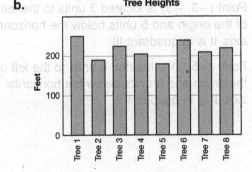

Tree Heights

**c.** Sample: The heights appear to vary greatly in the graph with the broken scale. The heights appear very close to each other in the graph with large increments.

**21.** Sample: $1 \times 10^{-4}$ is a small number, but it is greater than 0, so it is greater than $-10$.

**22.** $\dfrac{1.6 \times 10^7}{6.4 \times 10^2}$

$\dfrac{1.6}{6.4} \times \dfrac{10^7}{10^2}$

$0.25 \times 10^5$

$2.5 \times 10^4$

The answer is **A**.

**23.** Move the decimal 6 places.

$3,480,000 = 3.48 \times 10^6$

**24.** $\dfrac{120}{x} = \dfrac{18}{12}$

$18x = 1440$

$x = 80$

**25.** Find the $x$- and $y$-intercepts. Substitute 0 for $y$ and solve for $x$. Substitute 0 for $x$ and solve for $y$.

$11x - 2y = 110 \qquad 11(0) - 2y = 110$

$11x - 2(0) = 110 \qquad 0 - 2y = 110$

$11x - 0 = 110 \qquad -2y = 110$

$11x = 110 \qquad y = -55$

$x = 10$

Graph $(10, 0)$ and $(0, -55)$ and connect them with a straight line.

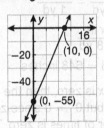

**26.** No, the sequence does not have a common difference.

$2 - 0.2 = 1.8$ but $20 - 2 = 18$.

**27.**

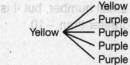

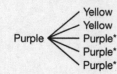

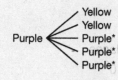

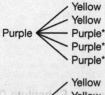

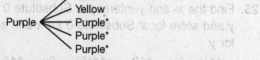

Count the number of ways you can draw a purple sticker and then another purple sticker. There are 12 ways.

**28.** The leaves represent the ones digits.

5

**29.** $\dfrac{12 \text{ in.}}{1 \text{ ft}} \cdot \dfrac{3 \text{ ft}}{1 \text{ yd}} = \dfrac{36 \text{ in.}}{1 \text{ yd}}$

$\dfrac{36 \text{ in.}}{1 \text{ yd}} = \dfrac{x \text{ in.}}{18 \text{ yd}}$

$x = 36 \cdot 18 = 648$ inches

**30.** Sample: If $x$ is zero, then the rule would be $0^{-n} = \dfrac{1}{0^n}$, but $0^n = 0$ since zero multiplied any number of times is zero. This would mean dividing by zero, which is undefined.

## INVESTIGATION 4

**a.** inductive; Sample: It is based on an observed pattern where the friend has an allergic reaction when he eats peanuts.

**b.** deductive; Sample: It is based on the knowledge that a snake bite requires first aid.

**c.** Sample: If it rains today, then the game will be postponed.

**d.** Sample: If $x = 2$, then $x$ is negative.

**e.** Sample: Cats are animals, but not all cats are Siamese.

**f.** Sample: Some female cats are not Siamese.

## LESSON 41

### Warm Up 41

**1.** linear

**2.** The range is the set of values for the dependent variable of a set of ordered pairs. Substitute each value for $x$ to find the range of the function.

$f(x) = 2x + 3$
$f(x) = 2(0) + 3$
$f(x) = 0 + 3$
$f(x) = 3$
$f(x) = 2(1) + 3$
$f(x) = 2 + 3$
$f(x) = 5$
$f(x) = 2(2) + 3$
$f(x) = 4 + 3$
$f(x) = 7$

The range is $\{3, 5, 7\}$.

**3.** Point $(3, -5)$ is located 3 units to the right of the origin and 5 units below the horizontal axis. It is in quadrant IV.

**4.** Point $(-3, -5)$ is located 3 units to the left of the origin and 5 units below the horizontal axis. It is in quadrant III.

**5.** Point $(-5, 3)$ is located 5 units to the left of the origin and 3 units below the horizontal axis. It is in quadrant II.

**Saxon** Algebra 1

## Lesson Practice 41

**a.** Choose two points on the graph and find the ratio of the change in drum kicks to the change in time.

$$\frac{\text{change in drum kicks}}{\text{change in measures}} = \frac{16 - 12}{4 - 3}$$

$$= \frac{4}{1} = 4$$

4 kicks/measure

**b.** $\dfrac{\text{change in feet}}{\text{change in miles}}$

$$= \frac{26{,}400 - 15{,}840}{5 - 3}$$

$$= \frac{10{,}560}{2}$$

$$= 5{,}280$$

5,280 ft/mi

**c.** slope $= \dfrac{\text{rise}}{\text{run}} = \dfrac{6}{2} = 3$

**d.** slope $= \dfrac{\text{rise}}{\text{run}} = \dfrac{-4}{10} = -\dfrac{2}{5}$

**e.** slope $= \dfrac{\text{rise}}{\text{run}} = \dfrac{0}{3} = 0$

**f.** slope $= \dfrac{\text{rise}}{\text{run}} = \dfrac{5}{0}$

The slope is undefined.

**g.** slope $= \dfrac{\text{rise}}{\text{run}} = \dfrac{12 - 8}{4 - 3} = \dfrac{4}{1} = 4$

**h.** The rate of change means that, during each measure, Iliana kicked the drum 4 times.

## Practice 41

**1.** $-2(b + 5) = -6$

$-2b - 10 = -6$

$\underline{+10 = +10}$

$-2b = 4$

$b = -2$

**2.** $4(y + 1) = -8$

$4y + 4 = -8$

$\underline{-4 = -4}$

$4y = -12$

$y = -3$

**3.** $\dfrac{5}{8} = 2m + \dfrac{3}{8}$

$\dfrac{2}{8} = 2m$

$\dfrac{2}{8} \cdot \dfrac{1}{2} = \dfrac{2m}{2}$

$\dfrac{2}{16} = m$

$m = \dfrac{1}{8}$

**4.** slope $= \dfrac{\text{rise}}{\text{run}} = \dfrac{-5}{-4} = 1\dfrac{1}{4}$

**5.** slope $= \dfrac{\text{rise}}{\text{run}} = \dfrac{1}{-3} = -\dfrac{1}{3}$

**6.** slope $= \dfrac{\text{rise}}{\text{run}} = \dfrac{0}{2} = 0$

**7.** slope $= \dfrac{\text{rise}}{\text{run}} = \dfrac{2}{0}$

The slope is undefined.

**8.** Move the decimal 5 places to the left.

$110{,}400 = 1.104 \times 10^5$

**9.** $45a^3b^4c^2 + 30a^2bc^3$

$45a^3b^4c^2 = 15 \cdot 3 \cdot a^2 \cdot a \cdot b \cdot b^3 \cdot c^2$

$30a^2bc^3 = 15 \cdot 2 \cdot a^2 \cdot b \cdot c^2 \cdot c$

The GCF is $15a^2bc^2$.

The answer is **A**.

**10.** No, it is not completely factored. The terms $5x^3$, $6x^2$, and $3x$ all have a common factor of $x$.

$2x(5x^3 + 6x^2 - 3x)$

$2x^2(5x^2 + 6x - 3)$

**11.** $\dfrac{\text{rate of change of balance}}{\text{rate of change of time}} = \dfrac{1400 - 1200}{3 - 0}$

$= \dfrac{200}{3}$

$= 66.67$

$66.67 per year

**12.** Sample: Mindy is descending the mountain.

**13.** $(b^3)^5$

$= b^{3 \cdot 5}$

$= b^{15}$

**14.** Student B; Student A multiplied the coefficient, −2, by the exponent 5. The correct way to simplify is to raise −2 to the fifth power, which is −32.

**15.** $A = s^2$

$A = (4xy)^2$

$\quad = (4)^2 x^2 y^2$

$\quad = 16x^2 y^2$

**16. a.** $(10^2)^3$

$10^{2 \cdot 3}$

$10^6$ cubic centimeters

**b.** $10^6 \times 10^3$

$10^{6+3}$

$10^9$ cubic millimeters

**17.** $V = s^3$

$V = (5ab)^3$

$\quad = (5)^3 a^3 b^3$

$\quad = 125a^3 b^3$ cubic inches

**18.** $\dfrac{fr}{d^3}\left(\dfrac{fsr}{d^2} + 3fs - \dfrac{8}{d}\right)$

$= \dfrac{f^2 sr^2}{d^5} + \dfrac{3f^2 rs}{d^3} - \dfrac{8fr}{d^4}$

**19.** $\dfrac{rt^{-2}}{g^{-3}h}\left(\dfrac{tg^4}{r^3 h^{-2}} - \dfrac{r^3 h}{g^{-2} r^{-2}}\right)$

$= \dfrac{rt^{-1}g^4}{g^{-3}h^{-1}r^3} - \dfrac{r^4 t^{-2}h}{g^{-5}hr^{-2}}$

$= \dfrac{r^{-2}t^{-1}g^7}{h^{-1}} - \dfrac{r^6 t^{-2}}{g^{-5}}$

$= \dfrac{g^7 h}{tr^2} - \dfrac{r^6 g^5}{t^2}$

**20.** There are 12 inches in foot so there are 36 inches in 3 feet.

$\dfrac{1 \text{ in.}}{12 \text{ in.}} = \dfrac{x}{36 \text{ in.}}$

$1 \cdot 36 = 12 \cdot x$

$36 = 12x$

$x = 3$

The height of the chair in the dollhouse is 3 inches.

**21.** The $x$-intercept is the $x$-coordinate of the point where the line crosses the $x$-axis. The point where the line crosses the $x$-axis is (2, 0). The $x$-intercept is 2.

The $y$-intercept is the $y$-coordinate of the point where the line crosses the $y$-axis. The point where the line crosses the $y$-axis is (0, 5). The $y$-intercept is 5.

**22.** $\qquad F = \dfrac{9}{5}C + 32$

$5F = 5\left(\dfrac{9}{5}C + 32\right)$

$5F = 9C + 160$

$5F - 9C = 160$

or

$-9C + 5F = 160$

**23.** Find the common difference.

$19 - 8 = 11$

$d = 11$

$a_n = a_{n-1} + d$

$\quad = a_{n-1} + 11$

$a_1 = 8$

$a_5 = a_1 + (n - 1)11$

$\quad = 8 + 4(11)$

$\quad = 8 + 44$

$\quad = 52$

$a_6 = a_1 + (n - 1)11$

$\quad = 8 + 5(11)$

$\quad = 8 + 55$

$\quad = 63$

The next two terms are 52 and 63.

**24.** Sample: When looking at two events, if they are dependent, the first will affect the probability of the second. If they are independent, the first does not affect the probability of the second.

**25.** $\dfrac{2 \text{ batches}}{\frac{3}{4}\text{cup}} = \dfrac{6 \text{ batches}}{x \text{ cups}}$

$2x = 6 \cdot \dfrac{3}{4}$

$2x = \dfrac{18}{4}$

**Saxon** Algebra 1

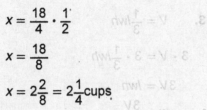
$$x = \frac{18}{4} \cdot \frac{1}{2}$$

$$x = \frac{18}{8}$$

$$x = 2\frac{2}{8} = 2\frac{1}{4}\text{cups}$$

**26.** $y = \$2.50x$

$f(x) = \$2.50x$

**27.** Parabola A is a function. A vertical line cuts the graph in exactly one place. Parabola B is not a function. A vertical line cuts the graph in more than one place.

**28.** $V = \dfrac{d}{t}$

$V = \dfrac{5.8 \text{ m}}{2.5 \text{ s}}$

$V = 2.32 \text{ m/s}$

$E_K = \dfrac{1}{2}(2.5 \text{ kg})(2.32 \text{ m/s})^2$

$E_K = \dfrac{1}{2}(2.5 \text{ kg})(5.3824 \text{ m/s})$

$E_K = 6.728 \text{ kg} \cdot \text{m}^2\text{s}^2$

**29. a.** $d = rt$

$d = 65x$

$65x$

**b.** $d = rt$

$d = 50(x + 1)$

$50(x + 1)$

**c.** $65x = 50(x + 1)$

$65x = 50x + 50$

$15x = 50$

$x = 3\frac{1}{3}$

Car 2 traveled $3\frac{1}{3}$ hours.

**d.** $d = 65x$

$d = 65 \cdot 3\frac{1}{3}$

$d = 216.7$ miles

**30.** $l = 3w - 5$

$w + w + 3w - 5 + 3w - 5 = 14$

$8w - 10 = 14$

$8w = 24$

$w = 3$

$l = 3(3) - 5$

$l = 9 - 5$

$l = 4$

The length of the rectangle is 4 inches.
The width of the rectangle is 3 inches.

## LESSON 42

### Warm Up 42

**1.** proportion

**2.** $3x + 8 = 32$

$3x = 24$

$x = 8$

**3.** $-6y - 7 = 29$

$-6y = 36$

$y = -6$

**4.** $\dfrac{5}{4} = \dfrac{25}{g}$

$5g = 4 \cdot 25$

$5g = 100$

$g = 20$

The team loses 20 games.

**5.** Since the ratio of white marbles to black marbles is 7 to 10, the proportion of white marbles is $\frac{7}{17}$. For every 17 marbles, 7 are white.

$\dfrac{7}{17} = \dfrac{w}{36}$

$17w = 7 \cdot 36$

$17w = 252$

$w = 56$

There are 56 white marbles.

### Lesson Practice 42

**a.** $n = 0.35 \cdot 70$

$n = 24.5$

24.5

**b.** $c = 1.50 \cdot 24$

$c = 36$

36

**c.** $\frac{315}{100} = \frac{x}{21}$

$100x = 315 \cdot 21$

$100x = 6615$

$x = 66.15$

**d.** $\frac{59.5}{17} = \frac{p}{100}$

$17p = 59.5 \cdot 100$

$17p = 5950$

$p = 350$

$350\%$

**e.** $(0.33)(32) = 10.56$ miles per gallon

$32 - 10.56 = 21.44$ miles per gallon

**f.** $\frac{t}{15,432} = \frac{45}{100}$

$100t = 694440$

$t = \$6944.40$

## Practice 42

**1.** $5d - 8 = 3 + 7d$

$5d = 11 + 7d$

$-2d = 11$

$d = \frac{11}{2}$

Check:

$5\left(-\frac{11}{2}\right) - 8 = 3 + 7\left(-\frac{11}{2}\right)$

$-\frac{55}{2} - 8 = 3 - \frac{77}{2}$

$-\frac{55}{2} = 11 - \frac{77}{2}$

$\frac{22}{2} = 11$

$11 = 11$ ✓

**2.** $9 + 2.7t = -4.8t - 6$

$9 + 7.5t = -6$

$7.5t = -15$

$t = -2$

Check:

$9 + 2.7(-2) = -4.8(-2) - 6$

$9 - 5.4 = 9.6 - 6$

$3.6 = 3.6$ ✓

**3.** $V = \frac{1}{3}lwh$

$3 \cdot V = 3 \cdot \frac{1}{3}lwh$

$3V = lwh$

$w = \frac{3V}{lh}$

**4.** $d = rt$

$\frac{d}{r} = \frac{rt}{r}$

$t = \frac{d}{r}$

**5.** $\sqrt{36} = 6$ and $\sqrt{49} = 7$, so $\sqrt{42}$ is between 6 and 7.

**6.** $p = 0.18 \cdot 340$

$p = 61.2$

$61.2$

**7.** $n = 2.7 \cdot 93$

$n = 251.1$

$251.1$

**8.** $(6mn^3)^2$

$6^2m^2n^{3 \cdot 2}$

$36m^2n^6$

**9.** $\frac{54}{100} = \frac{x}{1200}$

$100x = 64800$

$x = 648$

The answer is **C**.

**10.** $n = 2.24 \cdot \$1.36$

$n = \$3.05$

The new price was $3.05 per gallon.

**11.** Sample: Fractions, percentages, and decimals are all used to express a part of a whole.

**12. a.** In a stem-and-leaf plot, the stem represents tens and the leaves represent ones.

**Numbers of Pitches Thrown per Inning**

| Stem | Leaves |
|------|--------|
| 1 | 9, 9 |
| 2 | 0, 1, 2, 3, 5 |
| 3 | 0, 8 |

Key: 1|9 means 19

**Saxon** Algebra 1

**b.** Find the greatest and least number on the stem-and-leaf plot. The greatest number of pitches thrown was 38. The least number of pitches thrown was 19.

**13.** $\$10.50h = \$147$

$h = 14$

She worked 14 hours each week.

**14.** $\dfrac{10^{12}}{10^6}$

$10^{12-6}$

$10^6$

or 1,000,000 times more information.

**15.** It is incorrect. The correct solution for $y$ is

$6x + \dfrac{1}{4}y = 44$

$\dfrac{1}{4}y = 44 - 6x$

$4 \cdot \dfrac{1}{4}y = 4(44 - 6x)$

$y = 176 - 24x$

**16. a.**

| x (Number of Pies) | 2 | 4 | 6 |
|---|---|---|---|
| y (Total Cost) | $5 | $10 | $15 |

**b.**

Any vertical line intersects the graph at only one point, so the graph shows a function.

**c.** Each $y$-value is 2.5 times more than its $x$-value, so $y = 2.50x$.

**d.** Substitute $x = 14$ into the equation in c or look at the graph to see that the price of 14 pies is $35.00.

**17.** Sample: They could draw the graph with a broken axis.

**18. a.** Road 1 is one of three possible roads and Road 4 is one of two possible roads.

$P = \dfrac{1}{3} \cdot \dfrac{1}{2} = \dfrac{1}{6}$

**b.** By taking different roads on the way back, there are fewer possibilities. Road 5 is the only possibility and Road 2 is one of two possible roads.

$P = \dfrac{1}{1} \cdot \dfrac{1}{2} = \dfrac{1}{2}$

**19. a.** $d = 3$

$a_n = a_{n-1} + 3$

**b.** $a_n = a_1 + (n - 1)d$

$a_5 = 52 + (5 - 1)3$

$a_5 = 52 + (4)3$

$a_5 = 52 + 12$

$a_5 = 64$

64 in.

**c.** no; Sample: Humans eventually stop growing.

**20.** The $x$-intercept is the $x$-coordinate of the point where the line crosses the $x$-axis. The point where the line crosses the $x$-axis is $(-8, 0)$. The $x$-intercept is $-8$.

The $y$-intercept is the $y$-coordinate of the point where the line crosses the $y$-axis. The point where the line crosses the $y$-axis is $(0, -7)$. The $y$-intercept is $-7$.

**21.** If two similar figures have a scale factor of $\dfrac{a}{b}$, then the ratio of their volumes is $\dfrac{a^3}{b^3}$.

$\dfrac{a^3}{b^3} = \dfrac{2^3}{1^3} = 8$

**22.** $14p^5qr^2 = 28p^2q^2r^3$

$14p^5qr^2 = 2 \cdot 7 \cdot p \cdot p \cdot p \cdot p \cdot p \cdot q \cdot r \cdot r$

$28p^2q^2r^3 = 2 \cdot 2 \cdot 7 \cdot p \cdot p \cdot q \cdot q \cdot r \cdot r \cdot r$

The GCF is $14p^2qr^2$.

**23.** $\dfrac{r^{-2}}{s^{-3}}\left(\dfrac{rs^{-2}}{sr^{-1}} - \dfrac{s^{-3}r^{-1}}{r^{-3}}\right)$

$= \dfrac{r^{-2+1}s^{-2}}{s^{-3+1}r^{-1}} - \dfrac{r^{-3}s^{-3}}{r^{-3}s^{-3}}$

$$= \frac{r^{-1}s^{-2}}{s^{-2}r^{-1}} - \frac{r^{-3}s^{-3}}{r^{-3}s^{-3}}$$

$$= 1 - 1$$
$$= 0$$

**24.** Move the decimal three places to the right.
$$2 \times 10^{-3}$$

**25.** In a rational expression, the denominator cannot equal zero. So, $s$ cannot equal zero. The answer is **C**.

**26.** $\dfrac{\text{change in miles}}{\text{change in gallons}} = \dfrac{100 - 0}{4 - 0}$

$$= \frac{100}{4}$$

$$= 25 \text{ miles per gallon}$$

**27.** Student A; Sample: Student B raised the base to the second power.

**28.** $\dfrac{\text{change in miles}}{\text{change in inches}} = \dfrac{1 - 0}{4 - 0}$

$$= \frac{1}{4} \text{ mile per inch}$$

**29. a.** $\dfrac{\text{change in cost}}{\text{change in days of rental}} =$

$$\frac{427 - 405}{2 - 1} = \frac{22}{1} = \$22 \text{ per one day}$$

**b.** 3 days · $22 per day = $66
$$\$471 + \$66 = \$537$$

**30.** The rise is the longer base and the run is the shorter base.

$$\text{slope} = \frac{\text{rise}}{\text{run}} = \frac{8}{6} = \frac{4}{3}$$

The rise is the shorter base and the run is the longer base.

$$\text{slope} = \frac{\text{rise}}{\text{run}} = \frac{6}{8} = \frac{3}{4}$$

## LESSON 43

### Warm Up 43

**1.** greatest common factor

**2.** $\dfrac{36}{48} = \dfrac{3}{4}$

**3.** $\dfrac{32x^5}{48x^7}$

$$= \frac{2x^{5-7}}{3}$$

$$= \frac{2x^{-2}}{3}$$

$$= \frac{2}{3x^2}$$

**4.** $\dfrac{7x - 49x^2}{7x}$

$$= \frac{7x(1 - 7x)}{7x}$$

$$= 1 - 7x$$

**5.** $3x^2 + 6x^3$
$$= 3x^2 \cdot 1 + 3x^2 \cdot 2x$$
$$= 3x^2(1 + 2x)$$

### Lesson Practice 43

**a.** $5x = 0$
$$x = 0$$

**b.** $x + 8 = 0$
$$x = -8$$

**c.** $6x - 42 = 0$
$$6x = 42$$
$$x = 7$$

**d.** $\dfrac{7x - 27}{5x}$, $x \neq 0$

**e.** $\dfrac{3x^2 - 3x}{9x^2 + 15x}$

$$\text{GCF} = 3x$$

$$\frac{3x(x - 1)}{3x(3x + 5)} = \frac{x - 1}{3x + 5}$$

$$x \neq 0 \text{ and } x \neq -\frac{5}{3}$$

**f.** $\dfrac{4x + 28}{3x^2 + 21x}$

$$\text{GCF} = 4$$
$$\text{GCF} = 3x$$

$$\frac{4(x + 7)}{3x(x + 7)} = \frac{4}{3x}$$

$$x \neq 0 \text{ and } x \neq -7$$

**Saxon** Algebra 1

**g.** $\dfrac{2\pi rh + 2\pi r^2}{\pi r^2 h}$

$GCF = 2\pi r$

$\dfrac{2\pi r(h + r)}{\pi r^2 h}$

$= \dfrac{2r^{1-2}(h + r)}{h}$

$= \dfrac{2r^{-1}(h + r)}{h}$

$= \dfrac{2(h + r)}{rh}$

$h \neq 0$ and $r \neq 0$

**Practice 43**

**1.** $f(x) = -2x$
$f(x) = -2(-5)$
$f(x) = 10$

**2.** $h(x) = 3x - 1$
$h(x) = 3(7) - 1$
$h(x) = 21 - 1$
$h(x) = 20$

**3.** $a_n = 16 + (n - 1)(-0.5)$
$a_{15} = 16 + (15 - 1)(-0.5)$
$a_{15} = 16 + (14)(-0.5)$
$a_{15} = 16 - 7$
$a_{15} = 9$

**4.** $a_n = -8 + (n - 1)(2)$
$a_{100} = -8 + (100 - 1)(2)$
$a_{100} = -8 + (99)(2)$
$a_{100} = -8 + 198$
$a_{100} = 190$

**5.** $x + 10 = 0$
$x = -10$

**6.** $5 - x = 0$
$x = 5$

**7.** $j = 0.14 \cdot 120$
$j = 16.8$

**8.** $\dfrac{75}{100} = \dfrac{x}{60}$
$100x = 4500$
$x = 45$

**9.** $x + 2x = 2700$
$3x = 2700$
$x = 900$
The students need to raise $900.

**10. a.** $1.8 + 0.05n = 2.55$
**b.** $1.8 + 0.05n = 2.55$
$0.05n = 0.75$
$n = 15$
She has 15 nickels.

**11.** Student B; Sample: Student A confused the dependent and independent variables. If any of the $x$-values were the same, the relation would not be a function.

**12.** Use a vertical line test. If a vertical line passes through more than one point on the graph, the relation is not a function.

**13.** $\dfrac{1 \text{ in.}}{25 \text{ mi.}} = \dfrac{2.5 \text{ in.}}{x \text{ mi.}}$
$x = 2.5 \cdot 25$
$x = 62.5$
The towns are 62.5 miles apart.

**14.** Set each denominator equal to 0 to determine which expression is undefined at $x = -6$.
$12x + 72 = 0$
$12x = -72$
$x = -6$
$2(x + 12) = 0$
$2x + 24 = 0$
$2x = -24$
$x = -12$
$72 - 12x = 0$
$-12x = -72$
$x = 6$
$x = 0$
The answer is **A**.

**15.** $\dfrac{3z^2 + 2.7z}{(z + 0.9)(z - 0.9)}$
$GCF = 3z$
$\dfrac{3z(z + 0.9)}{(z + 0.9)(z - 0.9)}$

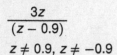 

$$\frac{3z}{(z - 0.9)}$$

$z \neq 0.9,\ z \neq -0.9$

**16.** The reciprocal of $\frac{8x}{2x + 16}$ is $\frac{2x + 16}{8x}$.

Set the denominator equal to 0.

$8x = 0$

$x = 0$

The reciprocal is undefined for $x = 0$.

**17.** The probability of guessing the first of the two numbers correctly on the first try is $\frac{1}{10}$. The probability of guessing the second of the two numbers correctly on the first try is $\frac{1}{9}$ because it is a different number.

$$P = \frac{1}{10} \cdot \frac{1}{9} = \frac{1}{90}$$

**18. a.** $a_n = a_1 + (n - 1)d$

$a_n = 17 + (n - 1)10$

**b.** $a_4 = 17 + (4 - 1)10$

$a_4 = 17 + (3)10$

$a_4 = 17 + 30$

$a_4 = 47$

$a_{11} = 17 + (11 - 1)10$

$a_{11} = 17 + (10)10$

$a_{11} = 17 + 100$

$a_{11} = 117$

**19.** Sample: Multiply both sides by 6. Then add $5x$ to both sides.

$$y = -\frac{5}{6}x - 2$$

$$6 \cdot y = 6\left(-\frac{5}{6}x - 2\right)$$

$6y = -5x - 12$

$+5x = +5x$

$5x + 6y = -12$

**20.** Corresponding sides of similar figures are in proportion. Corresponding angles of similar figures are congruent.

$\overline{MN}$ and $\overline{KL}$; $\overline{MP}$ and $\overline{KJ}$; $\overline{NP}$ and $\overline{LJ}$;

$\angle M$ and $\angle K$; $\angle N$ and $\angle L$; $\angle P$ and $\angle J$

**21.** $(1.6 \times 10^{-5})(2.2 \times 10^{3})$

$(1.6 \cdot 2.2)(10^{-5} \cdot 10^{3})$

$3.52 \times 10^{-2}$

**22. a.** To find the area of a rectangle, multiply length by width.

$8x(6x + 4)$

**b.** $8x(6x + 4)$

$= 8x \cdot 2(3x + 2)$

$= 16x(3x + 2)$

**23.** $(10g^3h^{-4})^2 (3gh^6)^3$

$= 10^3 g^6 h^{-8} \cdot 3^3 g^3 h^{18}$

$= 100g^6 h^{-8} \cdot 27g^3 h^{18}$

$= 2700g^9 h^{10}$

The answer is **A**.

**24.** $(8x^3)(2x)^{-3}$

$= (8x^3)(2^{-3}x^{-3})$

$= \frac{8x^3}{2^3 x^3}$

$= \frac{8x^3}{8x^3} = 1$

They are multiplicative inverses of each other.

**25.** $\frac{k}{g}\left(\frac{rtw}{nk} - 5k^2w^6\right)$

$= \frac{krtw}{gnk} - \frac{5k^3w^6}{g}$

$= \frac{rtw}{gn} - \frac{5k^3w^6}{g}$

**26.** $\frac{r^2}{t}\left(\frac{t}{s} + \frac{s^2}{rt}\right)$

$= \frac{r^2t}{ts} + \frac{r^2s^2}{rt^2}$

$= \frac{r^2}{s} + \frac{rs^2}{t^2}$

**27.** $\frac{\text{change in guests}}{\text{change in tables}} = \frac{60 - 36}{5 - 3}$

$= \frac{24}{2}$

$= 12$ guests/table

**28. a.** Sample: $\frac{x}{100} = \frac{134.4}{42}$

**b.** $\frac{x}{100} = \frac{134.4}{42}$

$42x = 100 \cdot 134.4$

$42x = 13440$

$x = 320$

320%

**Saxon** Algebra 1

**c.** Sample: 320% = 3.2 times a number

42 · 3.2 = 134.4

**29.** $p = 0.10 \cdot 14.5 = 1.45$

$14.5 - 1.45 \approx 13$

The tower leaned about 13 ft past center after the dirt was removed.

**30.** $x = 1.3 \cdot 12$

$x = 15.6$

## LESSON 44

**1.** slope

**2.** (−6, −4)

**3.** (4, −5)

**4.** (5, 3)

**5.** $\dfrac{\text{change in ounces}}{\text{change in servings}} = \dfrac{16 - 8}{4 - 2} = \dfrac{8}{2} = \dfrac{4}{1}$

## Lesson Practice 44

**a.** $m = \dfrac{y_2 - y_1}{x_2 - x_1}$

$= \dfrac{0 - (-4)}{3 - (-3)}$

$= \dfrac{4}{6}$

$= \dfrac{2}{3}$

**b.** $m = \dfrac{y_2 - y_1}{x_2 - x_1}$

$= \dfrac{6 - 8}{5 - (-5)}$

$= \dfrac{-2}{10}$

$= -\dfrac{1}{5}$

**c.** $m = \dfrac{y_2 - y_1}{x_2 - x_1}$

$= \dfrac{12 - 6}{1 - 0}$

$= \dfrac{6}{1}$

$= 6$

**d.** $m = \dfrac{y_2 - y_1}{x_2 - x_1}$

$= \dfrac{-9 - 7}{2 - (-2)}$

$= \dfrac{-16}{4}$

$= -4$

**e.** $m = \dfrac{y_2 - y_1}{x_2 - x_1}$

$= \dfrac{-13 - (-27)}{-2 - (-4)}$

$= \dfrac{14}{2}$

$= 7$

**f.** $m = \dfrac{y_2 - y_1}{x_2 - x_1}$

$= \dfrac{-2 - 5}{4 - (-7)}$

$= \dfrac{-7}{11}$

$= -\dfrac{7}{11}$

**g.** $m = \dfrac{y_2 - y_1}{x_2 - x_1}$

$= \dfrac{4 - (-5)}{5 - (-6)}$

$= \dfrac{9}{11}$

**h.** $m = \dfrac{y_2 - y_1}{x_2 - x_1}$

$= \dfrac{4 - 4}{2 - (-5)}$

$= \dfrac{0}{7}$

$= 0$

**i.** It is a vertical line so its slope is undefined.

**j.** Use the slope formula to find the speed.

$m = \dfrac{y_2 - y_1}{x_2 - x_1}$

$= \dfrac{2640 - 0}{55 - 10}$

$= \dfrac{2640}{45}$

$= 58.7$ ft/s

Saxon Algebra 1

## Practice 44

**1.** Move the decimal 9 places to the left.

$8.2 \times 10^{-9}$

0.0000000082

**2.** Move the decimal 6 places to the right.

$0.23 \times 10^{6}$

230,000

**3.** Move the decimal 5 places to the left.

112,500

$1.125 \times 10^{5}$

**4.** Move the decimal 4 places to the right.

0.00058

$5.8 \times 10^{-4}$

**5.** The domain is the set of possible values for the independent variable of a set of ordered pairs.

domain: {1, 3, 5, 7}

range: {2, 4, 6, 8}

**6.** domain: {3, 4}

range: {4, 5}

**7.** $f(x) = 20x + 180$

**8.** $\dfrac{26}{520} = \dfrac{x}{100}$

$520x = 2600$

$x = 5$

26 is 5% of 520.

**9.** To find 35% more than 90, find 135% of 90.

$p = 1.35 \cdot 90$

$p = 121.5$

**10.** Set the denominator equal to 0.

$16 + 8x = 0$

$8x = -16$

$x = -2$

**11.** $m = \dfrac{y_2 - y_1}{x_2 - x_1}$

$= \dfrac{7 - 1}{5 - (-5)}$

$= \dfrac{6}{10}$

$= \dfrac{3}{5}$

**12.** $m = \dfrac{y_2 - y_1}{x_2 - x_1}$

$= \dfrac{-6 - (-4)}{3 - (-3)}$

$= \dfrac{-2}{6}$

$= -\dfrac{1}{3}$

**13.** $m = \dfrac{y_2 - y_1}{x_2 - x_1}$

$= \dfrac{4 - (-6)}{3 - 3}$

$= \dfrac{10}{0}$

The slope is undefined.

**14.** $\dfrac{\text{change in inches}}{\text{change in months}} = \dfrac{42 - 22}{12 - 2}$

$= \dfrac{20}{10}$

$= \dfrac{2}{1}$

$= 2$ inches per month

**15.** Find the slope.

$m = \dfrac{y_2 - y_1}{x_2 - x_1}$

$= \dfrac{6 - 26}{1 - 3}$

$= \dfrac{-20}{-2}$

$= 10$

Use $m = 10$ in the formula for slope to find the missing $y$-value.

$10 = \dfrac{y_2 - 6}{0 - 1}$

$10 = \dfrac{y_2 - 6}{-1}$

$-1(10) = y_2 - 6$

$-10 = y_2 - 6$

$y_2 = -4$

**16.** $21y = 18(y + 7)$

$21y = 18y + 126$

$3y = 126$

$y = 42$

$21 \cdot 42 = 882$

Each orchard contains 882 trees.

**Saxon** Algebra 1

**17.** $13.80 ÷ 4 = $3.45 per lb

12 · $3.45 + 3 · $3.75

= $41.40 + $11.25

= $52.65

It would cost $52.65.

**18.** 16 + 7(10.5)

= 16 + 73.5

= 89.5

The height of the building is 89.5 feet.

**19. a.** $2y - 500 = -20x$

$2y = 500 - 20x$

$20x + 2y = 500$

**b.** $20x + 2y = 500$

$20(0) + 2y = 500$

$0 + 2y = 500$

$2y = 500$

$y = 250$

Sample: To earn all profits with just pencil sales, 250 boxes of pencils would have to be sold.

**c.** $20x + 2y = 500$

$20x + 2(0) = 500$

$20x + 0 = 500$

$20x = 500$

$x = 25$

Sample: To earn all profits with just T-shirt sales, 25 T-shirts would have to be sold.

**20. a.** Sample: $0.75x = 10.5$

**b.** Sample: To get rid of the decimal, multiply both sides by 100 and then solve, $100 · 0.75x = 10.5 · 100$ or isolate the variable by dividing by 0.75, $0.75x = 10.5$ so $x = 14$ laps.

**21.** $(4.2 \times 10^{12})(3.14 \times 10^{-4})$

$= (4.2 \times 3.14)(10^{12} \times 10^{-4})$

$= 13.188 \times 10^8$

$= 1.3188 \times 10^9$

**22.** $3x^2y^2 + 3xy^3 - 6x^3y^6$

$GCF = 3xy^2$

$3xy^2(x + y - 2x^2y^4)$

**23.** $(-2^3)^3$

$= -2^{3 \cdot 3}$

$= -2^9$

**24. a.** $2^5 \times 2^{10}$

$2^{5+10}$

$2^{15} = 32,768$ ways

**b.** $P = \dfrac{1}{2^5} \times \dfrac{1}{2^{10}}$

$= \dfrac{1}{2^{5+10}}$

$= \dfrac{1}{2^{15}}$

$= \dfrac{1}{32,768}$

**25.** $m = \dfrac{y_2 - y_1}{x_2 - x_1}$

$= \dfrac{2 - 8}{5 - (-5)}$

$= \dfrac{-6}{10}$

$= -\dfrac{3}{5}$

The answer is **B**.

**26.** Sample: The number of ice cream cones sold at a shop from August to November.

**27.** $\dfrac{0.75m}{2.50 + 0.50m}$

$GCF = 0.25$

$\dfrac{0.25(3m)}{0.25(10 + 2m)}$

$\dfrac{3m}{10 + 2m}$

**28.** Student A; Student B did not add the inverse of 3 when solving for the undefined value.

**29. a.** $4(x^2 + 6x)$

$= 4x^2 + 24x$ units

**b.** $\dfrac{x^2}{4x^2 + 24x}$

**c.** $\dfrac{x^2}{4x^2 + 24x}$

$= \dfrac{x \cdot x}{4x(x + 6)}$

$= \dfrac{x}{4(x + 6)}$

**Saxon** Algebra 1

**30.** $\dfrac{2\pi r^2 + 4\pi r}{2\pi r^2}$

$= \dfrac{2\pi r(r + 2)}{2\pi r^2}$

$= \dfrac{\cancel{2\pi r}(r + 2)}{\cancel{2\pi r} \cdot r}$

$= \dfrac{r + 2}{r}$

## LESSON 45

### Warm Up 45

1. algebraic expression

2. $-1 + (-2)^2 - \sqrt{9}$
$= -1 + 4 - 3$
$= 0$

3. $\sqrt{400} + \sqrt{225} - \sqrt{81} - \sqrt{100}$
$= 20 + 15 - 9 - 10$
$= 35 - 19$
$= 16$

4. $\dfrac{x^3 y^2}{xy^4}$
$= x^{3-1} y^{2-4}$
$= x^2 y^{-2}$
$= \dfrac{x^2}{y^2}$

5. $\dfrac{x^3 y^{-3} z}{x^2 y z^5}$
$= x^{3-2} y^{-3-1} z^{1-5}$
$= xy^{-4} z^{-4}$
$= \dfrac{x}{y^4 z^4}$

### Lesson Practice 45

a. $\dfrac{x}{-2} > -9$

b. $0 \le 2n - 8$

c. $\dfrac{1}{2}n + 3 \ne 15$

d. $11n < 121$

e. Sample: The product of 12 and an unknown number is at least $-8$.

f. Sample: The sum of the product of 1.5 and a number and 2.5 is less than 11.5.

g. Sample: 9 is greater than the difference of one-third of a number and 8.

h. Sample: A number divided by 7 is at most 8.

i. $\dfrac{9}{5} C + 32 \ge 140$

### Practice 45

1. 42 ft
$= 42 \, \cancel{ft} \cdot \dfrac{12 \, \cancel{in.}}{1 \, \cancel{ft}} \cdot \dfrac{2.54 \, cm}{1 \, \cancel{in.}}$
$= 1280.16 \, cm$

2. 2 mi
$= 2 \, \cancel{mi} \cdot \dfrac{5280 \, \cancel{ft}}{1 \, \cancel{mi}} \cdot \dfrac{12 \, in.}{1 \, \cancel{ft}}$
$= 126,720 \, in.$

3. $-2(-3 - 3)(-2 - 4) - (-3 - 2) + 3(4 - 2)$
$= -2(-6)(-6) - (-5) + 3(2)$
$= -72 + 5 + 6$
$= -61$

4. $\dfrac{5(-5 + 3) + 7(-5 + 9) + 2}{(4 - 2) + 3 + 5}$
$= \dfrac{5(-2) + 7(4) + 2}{2 + 3 + 5}$
$= \dfrac{-10 + 28 + 2}{2 + 3 + 5}$
$= \dfrac{20}{10}$
$= 2$

5. $6x \le 15$

6. $x > 7$

7. Sample: The product of $-4$ and $b$ is at least 7.

8. Sample: Four less than the quotient of $t$ and 7 is less than 8.

9.

**Saxon** Algebra 1

$$m = \frac{y_2 - y_1}{x_2 - x_1} \qquad m = \frac{y_2 - y_1}{x_2 - x_1}$$

$$= \frac{2 - 3}{3 - 1} \qquad = \frac{-1 - 2}{5 - 3}$$

$$= \frac{-1}{2} \qquad = \frac{-3}{2}$$

$$= -\frac{1}{2} \qquad = -\frac{3}{2}$$

$$m = \frac{y_2 - y_1}{x_2 - x_1} \qquad m = \frac{y_2 - y_1}{x_2 - x_1}$$

$$= \frac{1 - 3}{2 - 1} \qquad = \frac{-1 - 1}{5 - 2}$$

$$= \frac{-2}{1} \qquad = \frac{-2}{3}$$

$$= -2 \qquad = -\frac{2}{3}$$

**10.** $\frac{24}{160} = \frac{x}{100}$

$160x = 24 \cdot 100$

$160x = 2400$

$x = 15$

24 is 15% of 160. The answer is **B**.

**11.** Sample: "4 more" means to add 4. "The quotient of an unknown and 9" can be represented as a fraction with a variable over 9. "No less" can be translated to greater than or equal to. The correct inequality is $\frac{n}{9} + 4 \geq 15$.

**12.** Her third score added to her score after two rounds must be greater than or equal to 83.2. $s + 45.7 \geq 83.2$, where $s$ is the score of the third round.

**13.** "Five less than an unknown is at most seven" translates to $x - 5 \leq 7$. The answer is **C**.

**14.** $m = \frac{y_2 - y_1}{x_2 - x_1}$

$$= \frac{7 - (-6)}{8 - (-5)}$$

$$= \frac{13}{13}$$

$$= 1$$

**15. a.** $\frac{\text{change in stock value}}{\text{change in days}} = \frac{28 - 12}{9 - 0}$

$$= \frac{16}{9}$$

$$= 1.78$$

$1.78 per day

$\frac{\text{change in stock value}}{\text{change in days}} = \frac{24 - 16}{8 - 0}$

$$= \frac{8}{8}$$

$$= 1$$

$1.00 per day

**c.** Sample: Stock A was the better buy. Its graph shows a larger rate of increase in value over the 9 days.

**16.** $\frac{\text{change in parts per million}}{\text{change in years}}$

$$= \frac{320 - 315}{1969 - 1962}$$

$$= \frac{5}{7}$$

$= 0.71$ parts per million per year

**17.** Use two points on the line that forms the hypotenuse.

$$m = \frac{y_2 - y_1}{x_2 - x_1}$$

$$= \frac{9 - 3}{7 - 2}$$

$$= \frac{6}{5}$$

**18.** $5m^2n^4 + 10m^3n$

$GCF = 5m^2n$

$5m^2n(n^3 + 2m)$

**19.** $\frac{x^{-3}}{w^2}\left(\frac{4x^2}{w} - \frac{j^{-3}w}{x}\right)$

$$= \frac{4x^{-3+2}}{w^{2+1}} - \frac{x^{-3}j^{-3}w}{w^2x}$$

$$= \frac{4x^{-1}}{w^3} - \frac{x^{-3}j^{-3}w}{w^2x}$$

$$= \frac{4}{xw^3} - x^{-3-1}j^{-3}w^{1-2}$$

$$= \frac{4}{xw^3} - x^{-4}j^{-3}w^{-1}$$

$$= \frac{4}{xw^3} - \frac{1}{j^3wx^4}$$

**20.** Write the equation in standard form. Then find the intercepts.

$$y = 4x + 12 \qquad\qquad y = 4x + 12$$
$$-4x + y = 12 \qquad\quad -4x + y = 12$$
$$-4x + 0 = 12 \qquad\quad -4(0) + y = 12$$
$$-4x = 12 \qquad\qquad\quad 0 + y = 12$$
$$x = -3 \qquad\qquad\qquad y = 12$$

The intercepts are (–3, 0) and (0, 12).

**21. a.** $\dfrac{1\ in}{16\ mi} = \dfrac{5\ in}{x\ mi}$

$$x = 16 \cdot 5$$
$$x = 80$$

80 miles

**b.** $\dfrac{1\ in}{16\ mi} = \dfrac{17.5\ in}{x\ mi}$

$$x = 16 \cdot 17.5$$
$$x = 280$$

280 miles

**c.** $\dfrac{1\ in}{16\ mi} = \dfrac{20\ in}{x\ mi}$

$$x = 16 \cdot 20$$
$$x = 320$$

320 *miles*

$$80 + 280 = 360$$
$$360 - 320 = 40$$

It is 40 miles shorter.

**d.** No; Sample: The shorter route may have more traffic or a slower speed limit for driving.

**22.** $A = 4\pi r^2$

$$A = 4\pi(1.75 \times 10^3)^2$$
$$A = 4\pi(1.75)^2 \times (10^3)^2$$
$$A = 4\pi\, 3.0625 \times 10^6$$
$$A = 12.25\pi \times 10^6$$
$$A = 1.225\pi \times 10^7$$

**23.** $\dfrac{\text{change in earnings}}{\text{change in hours}}$

$$= \dfrac{27 - 13.50}{4 - 2}$$
$$= \dfrac{13.50}{2}$$
$$= \$6.75/\text{hour}$$

**24.** $V = 803 + (803 \cdot 25\%)$
$$V = 803 + (803 \cdot 0.25)$$
$$V = 803 + 200.75$$
$$V = 1003.75\ in^3$$
See student work.

**25.** $\dfrac{24 + 9x}{x}; x \neq 0$

**26.** Student B; Sample: Student A did not factor the GCF from the numerator correctly.

**27.**

| x | 0 | 1 | –1 | 2 | 4 |
|---|---|---|----|---|---|
| y | 1 | 0.5 | 1.5 | 0 | –1 |

**28. a.** $\dfrac{10^3}{10^{-2}}$

$$= 10^{3-(-2)}$$
$$= 10^5 = 100{,}000 \text{ times longer}$$

**b.** $\dfrac{10^0}{10^{-2}}$

$$= 10^{0-(-2)}$$
$$= 10^2 \text{ times longer}$$
$$= 10^2 \cdot 10^3 = 10^5 = 100{,}000 \text{ times longer}$$

yes

**29.** There are 6 possible first names and 5 possible middle names.

$$P = \dfrac{1}{6} \cdot \dfrac{1}{5} = \dfrac{1}{30};$$

**30.** For 8,000,000, the number of zeros equals the exponent, but that does not hold true for the other examples. The pattern only exists if there is one digit followed by zeros.

# LESSON 46

## Warm Up 46

**1.** perfect square

**2.** yes; $\sqrt{25} = 5$

**3.** No; Sample: There is not a whole number squared that equals 12.

**4.** yes; $\sqrt{49} = 7$

**5.** $5^3 = 5 \cdot 5 \cdot 5 = 125$

**6.** $(-3)^4 = (-3)(-3)(-3)(-3) = 81$

 **Saxon** Algebra 1

## Lesson Practice 46

**a.** $\sqrt{196} = \sqrt{14^2}$
$= \sqrt{14 \cdot 14}$
$= 14$

**b.** $-\sqrt{64} = -\sqrt{8^2}$
$= -\sqrt{8 \cdot 8}$
$= -8$

**c.** $\sqrt{1} = \sqrt{1^2}$
$= \sqrt{1 \cdot 1}$
$= 1$

**d.** $\sqrt{-64}$ has no real solution.

**e.** $\sqrt{\dfrac{81}{144}} = \dfrac{\sqrt{81}}{\sqrt{144}}$
$= \dfrac{\sqrt{9^2}}{\sqrt{12^2}}$
$= \sqrt{\dfrac{9 \cdot 9}{12 \cdot 12}}$
$= \dfrac{9}{12}$
$= \dfrac{3}{4}$

**f.** $\sqrt[3]{1728} = \sqrt[3]{12^3}$
$= \sqrt[3]{12 \cdot 12 \cdot 12}$
$= 12$

**g.** $\sqrt[3]{-343} = \sqrt[3]{(-7)^3}$
$= \sqrt[3]{(-7) \cdot (-7) \cdot (-7)}$
$= -7$

**h.** $\sqrt[4]{160,000} = \sqrt[4]{20^4}$
$= \sqrt[4]{20 \cdot 20 \cdot 20 \cdot 20}$
$= 20$

**i.** $\sqrt[4]{-16}$ has no real solution.

**j.** $(125)^{\frac{1}{3}} = \sqrt[3]{125}$
$= \sqrt[3]{5^3}$
$= 5$

**k.** $(-8)^{\frac{1}{3}} = \sqrt[3]{-8}$
$= \sqrt[3]{(-2)^3}$
$= -2$

**l.** $(81)^{\frac{1}{4}} = \sqrt[4]{81}$
$= \sqrt[4]{3^4}$
$= 3$

**m.** $(-625)^{\frac{1}{4}}$ has no real solution.

**n.** $V = s^3 = 1728$
$s = \sqrt[3]{1728}$
$= \sqrt[3]{12^3}$
$= \sqrt[3]{12 \cdot 12 \cdot 12}$
$= 12$

The side length of the block is 12 feet.

## Practice 46

**1.** $(p - x)(a - px)$
$= [(3 - (-4)][(-3 - 3(-4)]$
$= 7[(3 - (-12)]$
$= 7(9)$
$= 63$

**2.** $-a[-a(x - a)]$
$= -(-2)[-(-2)(3 - (-2)]$
$= 2(2 \cdot 5)$
$= 20$

**3.** $\sqrt{-10,000}$ has no real solution.

**4.** $-\sqrt[4]{10,000} = -\sqrt[4]{10^4}$
$= -\sqrt[4]{10 \cdot 10 \cdot 10 \cdot 10}$
$= -10$

**5.** $xym^2 + 3xy^2m - 4m^2xy + 5mxy^2$
$= m^2xy - 4m^2xy + 3mxy^2 + 5mxy^2$
$= -3m^2xy + 8mxy^2$

**6.** $-\sqrt[3]{-\dfrac{27}{64}} = -\sqrt[3]{-\dfrac{3^3}{4^3}}$
$= -\sqrt[3]{-\dfrac{3 \cdot 3 \cdot 3}{4 \cdot 4 \cdot 4}}$
$= \dfrac{3}{4}$

The answer is **C**.

**7.** $-2 \le x - 7$

**8.** $a \ge 35$

**Saxon** Algebra 1

**9.** $\sqrt[3]{1331} = \sqrt[3]{11^3}$  $\sqrt[3]{1728} = \sqrt[3]{12^3}$
$= \sqrt[3]{11 \cdot 11 \cdot 11}$  $= \sqrt[3]{12 \cdot 12 \cdot 12}$
$= 11$  $= 12$
$\sqrt[3]{1500}$ is between 11 and 12.

**10.** The independent variable is the number of cattle as a multiple of 15. The dependent variable is the number of mineral blocks.

**11.**
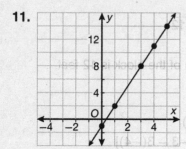

**12.** $\dfrac{5}{7} = \dfrac{h}{49}$
$7h = 5 \cdot 49$
$7h = 245$
$h = 35$

**13. a.** $P(\text{skirt}) = \dfrac{5}{8}$

$P(\text{shirt}) = \dfrac{10}{10}$

$P(\text{vest}) = \dfrac{1}{3}$

$P = \dfrac{5}{8} \cdot \dfrac{10}{10} \cdot \dfrac{1}{3} = \dfrac{50}{240} = \dfrac{5}{24}$

**b.** $P(\text{skirt}) = \dfrac{3}{7}$

$P(\text{shirt}) = \dfrac{9}{9}$

$P(\text{tie}) = \dfrac{2}{3}$

$P = \dfrac{3}{7} \cdot \dfrac{9}{9} \cdot \dfrac{2}{3} = \dfrac{54}{189} = \dfrac{2}{7}$

**14. a.** $10y \geq 180$

**b.** $10y \geq 180$
$y \geq 180 \div 10$
$y \geq 18$

**15.** $\dfrac{gt}{d^2}\left(\dfrac{gth}{d} - 3th + \dfrac{t}{5}\right)$

$= \dfrac{gt \cdot gth}{d^2 \cdot d} - \dfrac{gt \cdot 3th}{d^2} + \dfrac{gt \cdot t}{d^2 \cdot 5}$

$= \dfrac{g^2t^2h}{d^3} - \dfrac{3gt^2h}{d^2} + \dfrac{gt^2}{5d^2}$

**16.** $\left(\dfrac{-8x^4}{3}\right)^2$

$= \dfrac{64x^8}{9}$

**17.** For the circumference to be greater than 5, the diameter $d$ must be greater than the circumference, 5, divided by $\pi$.
$C = \pi d$
$d = \dfrac{C}{\pi}$
$d > \dfrac{5}{\pi}$

**18.** $\dfrac{1 \text{ in.}}{10 \text{ in.}} = \dfrac{9 \text{ in.}}{x \text{ in.}}$
$x = 10 \cdot 9$
$x = 90$ in. or 7.5 ft
$\dfrac{1 \text{ in.}}{10 \text{ in.}} = \dfrac{15 \text{ in.}}{x \text{ in.}}$
$x = 10 \cdot 15$
$x = 150$ in. or 12.5 ft

**19. a.** Move the decimal place 12 places to the right for 4.9 trillion and 8 places to the right for 300 million.
4.9 trillion = 4,900,000,000,000
$= 4.9 \times 10^{12}$
300 million = 300,000,000
$= 3.0 \times 10^8$

**b.** $\dfrac{4.9 \times 10^{12} \text{ dollars}}{3.0 \times 10^8 \text{ people}}$
$\approx \$1.63 \times 10^{12-8}$ per person
$= \$1.63 \times 10^4$ per person

**20.** $27x^2y^3z = 3 \cdot 3 \cdot 3 \cdot x \cdot x \cdot y \cdot y \cdot y \cdot z$ and $12xy^2z = 2 \cdot 2 \cdot 3 \cdot x \cdot y \cdot y \cdot z$, so both terms have $3 \cdot x \cdot y \cdot y \cdot z$ in common and the GCF is $3xy^2z$; $3xy^2z(9xy + 4)$

**21.** $\dfrac{\text{change in water}}{\text{change in time}}$
$= \dfrac{15,072.75 - 15,048.5}{15 - 10}$
$= \dfrac{24.25}{5}$
$= 4.85$ gallons per minute

**Saxon** Algebra 1

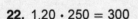
**22.** $1.20 \cdot 250 = 300$

**23.** $x^2$ and $15 - x$ have no common factor, so the rational expression cannot be simplified. The answer is **B**.

**24.** $\dfrac{6 - 6x}{9 - 9x}$

$= \dfrac{6(1 - x)}{9(1 - x)}$

$= \dfrac{6(1 - x)}{9(1 - x)}$

$= \dfrac{6}{9} = \dfrac{2}{3}$

Sample: I factored out a 6 in the numerator and a 9 in the denominator. Then I canceled the $1 - x$ binomial and simplified the remaining fraction.

**25.** $m = \dfrac{y_2 - y_1}{x_2 - x_1}$

$= \dfrac{-5 - (-4)}{8 - 4}$

$= \dfrac{-1}{4} = -\dfrac{1}{4}$

**26.** $m = \dfrac{y_2 - y_1}{x_2 - x_1}$

$= \dfrac{8 - 7}{5 - 1}$

$= \dfrac{1}{4}$

**27.** Student A; Sample: Student B incorrectly translated "at most" as greater than or equal to instead of less than or equal to.

**28.** The perimeter of the flower bed can be 45 feet or less.

$P = w + w + 2w + 2w$

$P = 6w$

$6w \le 45$

**29.** $400 - 255 = 145$

$8r \ge 145$

$r \ge 18.125$

She needs to read about 18 pages each day to complete the assignment on or before time.

**30.**

$V = \pi r^2 h$

$V = \dfrac{128}{9}\pi$

$\pi r^2 h = \dfrac{128}{9}\pi$

$r^2 \cdot 8 = \dfrac{128}{9}$

$9 \cdot r^2 \cdot 8 = 128$

$72r^2 = 128$

$r^2 = \dfrac{128}{72} = \dfrac{16}{9}$

$r = \sqrt{\dfrac{16}{9}}$

$r = \dfrac{4}{3}$

$d = 2r$

$d = 2 \cdot \dfrac{4}{3} = \dfrac{8}{3} = 2\dfrac{2}{3}$ inches

## LESSON 47

**Warm Up 47**

**1.** percent

**2.** $\dfrac{60}{80} = \dfrac{x}{100}$

$80x = 60 \cdot 100$

$80x = 6000$

$x = 75$

60 is 75% of 80.

**3.** $q = 0.20 \cdot 40$

$q = 8$

20% of 40 is 8.

**4.** $\dfrac{7}{x} = \dfrac{5}{100}$

$5x = 7 \cdot 100$

$5x = 700$

$x = 140$

7 is 5% of 140.

**5.** $\dfrac{25}{80} = \dfrac{x}{100}$

$80x = 25 \cdot 100$

$80x = 2500$

$x = 31.25$

25 is 31.25% of 80.

**Saxon** Algebra 1

## Lesson Practice 47

**a.** $630 - 600 = 30$

$\dfrac{30}{600} = 0.05$

The percent of increase is 5%.

**b.** $774 - 1032 = -258$

$\dfrac{-258}{1032} = 0.25$

The percent of decrease is 25%.

**c.** $n = 0.45 \cdot \$44.00 = \$19.80$

The markup is $19.80.

$\$44.00 + \$19.80 = \$63.80$

**d.** $n = 0.22 \cdot \$344,000 = \$75,680$

The discount is $75,680.

$\$344,000 - \$75,680 = \$268,320$

**e.** $125 - 90 = 35$

$\dfrac{35}{90} = 0.388$

The percent of increase is 39%.

**f.** $\$4.95 - \$3.87 = \$1.08$

$\dfrac{\$1.08}{\$4.95} = 0.218$

The percent of decrease is 22%.

## Practice 47

**1.** $-(x - 3) - 2(x - 4) = 7$

$-x + 3 - 2x + 8 = 7$

$-3x + 11 = 7$

$-3x = -4$

$x = \dfrac{-4}{-3} = \dfrac{4}{3}$

**2.** $3p - 4 - 6 = -2(p - 5)$

$3p - 10 = -2p + 10$

$3p = -2p + 20$

$5p = 20$

$p = 4$

**3.** $k + 4 - 5(k + 2) = 3k - 2$

$k + 4 - 5k - 10 = 3k - 2$

$-4k - 6 = 3k - 2$

$-7k - 6 = -2$

$-7k = 4$

$k = -\dfrac{4}{7}$

**4.** $3.6x > 18$

**5.** $a^3 x - |x^3|$

$= (-3)^3(-2) - |(-2)^3|$

$= -27(-2) - |-8|$

$= 54 - 8 = 46$

**6.** $\dfrac{\$67.50}{15} = \$4.50$ per box

**7.** $\sqrt[3]{-512} = \sqrt[3]{(-8)^3}$

$= \sqrt[3]{(-8) \cdot (-8) \cdot (-8)} = -8$

**8.** $\$49 - \$35 = \$14$

$\dfrac{14}{35} = 0.4$

The percent of increase is 40%.

**9.** $88 - 78 = 10$

$\dfrac{10}{78} = 0.128$

The percent of increase is 13%.

The answer is **C**.

**10.** Sample: It is possible to have a percent of increase of more than 100%. This could be when a price more than doubles. However, it is not possible to have a percent decrease more than 100%.

**11.** $30,000 - 12,000 = 18,000$

$\dfrac{18,000}{30,000} = 0.6$

Sample: There is a 60% decrease from one number to the next number.

$4800 - 0.6 (4800) = 1920$

$1920 - 0.6 (1920) = 768$

**12.** $m = \dfrac{y_2 - y_1}{x_2 - x_1}$ $\qquad m = \dfrac{y_2 - y_1}{x_2 - x_1}$

$= \dfrac{10 - 8}{-1 - (-16)}$ $\qquad = \dfrac{6 - (-15)}{18 - (-5)}$

$= \dfrac{2}{15}$ $\qquad = \dfrac{21}{23}$

$m = \dfrac{y_2 - y_1}{x_2 - x_1}$ $\qquad m = \dfrac{y_2 - y_1}{x_2 - x_1}$

**Saxon** Algebra 1

$$= \frac{-1-1}{-1-1} \qquad = \frac{15-(-4)}{-1-(-1)}$$

$$= \frac{-2}{-2} \qquad = \frac{19}{0} \text{ undefined}$$

$$= 1$$

The answer is **D**.

13. Sample: Rise over run refers to a change in the vertical position of a line divided by the corresponding change in the horizontal position.

14.     $0.25 \cdot \$500 = \$125$

    $\$500 - \$125 = \$375$

    $\$375 \cdot 0.25 = \$93.75$

    $\$375 + \$93.75 = \$468.75$

No, it is not correct. The original price is higher. 25% of $500 is $125, but 25% of the discounted price of $375 is only $93.75.

15. Student A; Sample: The expression is equal to the fourth root of 16, which is 2.

16.   $A = \pi r^2$

    $\pi r^2 = 81\pi$

    $r^2 = 81$

    $r = \sqrt{81}$

    $r = \sqrt{9 \cdot 9}$

    $r = 9$

    $C = \pi d$

    $C = \pi(9 + 9)$

    $C = 18\pi$ inches

17. $\sqrt[4]{2 \cdot 4 \cdot 25 \cdot 50}$

  $= \sqrt[4]{10000}$

  $= \sqrt[4]{10 \cdot 10 \cdot 10 \cdot 10}$

  $= 10$

18. $\frac{7}{15} = \frac{x}{45}$      $\frac{8}{15} = \frac{x}{45}$

  $15x = 7 \cdot 45$    $15x = 8 \cdot 45$

  $15x = 315$      $15x = 360$

    $x = 21$        $x = 24$

There were 21 sparrows and 24 doves.

19. $\frac{3n^0}{m^{-2}}$

  $= \frac{3(-8)^0}{(-3)^{-2}}$

$$= \frac{3 \cdot 1}{(-3)^{-2}}$$

$$= 3 \cdot 9$$

$$= 27$$

20. **a.** $a_1 = 9, a_n = a_{n-1} + 13$

  **b.** $a_2 = a_{n-1} + 13$

    $a_2 = 9 + 13$

    $a_2 = 22$

    $a_3 = 22 + 13$

    $a_3 = 35$

    $a_4 = 35 + 13$

    $a_4 = 48$

    9, 22, 35, 48

21. Student B; Sample: Twice a number means 2 times a number. Student A added instead of multiplying.

22. $m = \frac{y_2 - y_1}{x_2 - x_1} \qquad m = \frac{y_2 - y_1}{x_2 - x_1}$

  $= \frac{6 - 0}{0 - (-4)} \qquad = \frac{6 - 0}{0 - 4}$

  $= \frac{6}{4} \qquad\qquad = \frac{6}{-4}$

  $= \frac{3}{2} \qquad\qquad = -\frac{3}{2}$

  $m = \pm\frac{3}{2}$

23. The expression is defined for all values of $x$ because the denominator is never equal to zero.

24. The family wants to put 15% of their monthly income of $3484, or $0.15 \cdot \$3484 = \$522.60$, into retirement savings. They are already putting 6% of their monthly income of $3484, or $0.06 \cdot \$3484 = \$209.04$, into retirement savings. Therefore, they need to put $\$522.60 - \$209.04 = \$313.56$ more into retirement each month.

25. $\frac{\text{change in eggs}}{\text{change in omelets}} = \frac{0 - 16}{4 - 0}$

                    $= \frac{-16}{4}$

                    $= -4$ eggs/omelet

**26.** $(-4ab^2c^2)^3$

$(-4)^3 \cdot a^3 \cdot b^{2\cdot3}c^{2\cdot3}$

$-64a^3b^6c^6$

**27.** Sample: Because if $x = 0$, then $x^2 = 0$, and you cannot have a zero in the denominator.

**28.** Move the decimal 15 places to the left.
0.000000000000002817939

**29. a.** yes; Sample: Using the Distributive Property,
$2(2a + 2ab + 2bc) = 4a + 4b + 4c$, which is the original polynomial.

**b.** no; Sample: The polynomial in parentheses, $2a + 2ab + 2bc$ still has a common factor of 2. The complete factorization would be $4(a + ab + bc)$.

**30.** $854.71 = $220.25 + $318.12 + x + x$

$854.71 = $538.37 + 2x$

$2x = $316.34$

$x = $158.17$

## LESSON 48

### Warm Up 48

**1.** outcome

**2.** Write each fraction as a decimal.

$\frac{4}{9} = 0.44$    $1\frac{2}{3} = 1.67$

$1\frac{4}{5} = 1.8$    $\frac{2}{5} = 0.4$

$\frac{3}{8} = 0.375$

$\frac{3}{8}, \frac{2}{5}, \frac{4}{9}, 1\frac{2}{3}, 1\frac{4}{5}$

**3.** 2.337, 2.5, 2.59, 2.75

**4.** $\frac{6 - 3 + 5}{10 - 2} = \frac{8}{8} = 1$

**5.**  $3x + 7 = 5x + 11$

$-2x + 7 = 11$

$-2x = 4$

$x = -2$

### Lesson Practice 48

**a.** Order the data from least to greatest.
15, 21, 25, 25, 28, 30, 33, 38, 46

mean: $\frac{\text{sum of data}}{9} = \frac{261}{9} = 29$

median: 28

mode: The number 25 occurs more often than any other number.

**b.** Greatest value of trucks: 560

Least value of trucks: 125

Greatest value of convertibles: 810

Least value of convertibles: 600

$560 - 125 = 435$

$810 - 600 = 210$

$435 > 210$

Trucks have the greatest range.

**c.** Write the data from least to greatest.
21, 22, 22, 22, 22, 22, 22, 22, 22, 23,
23, 24, 24, 25, 26, 26, 59, 64
59 and 64 are outliers.

**d.** $\frac{\text{sum of data}}{18} = \frac{415}{18} = 23.1$

$\frac{\text{sum of data}}{20} = \frac{538}{20} = 26.9$

$26.9 - 23.1 = 3.8$

The outliers raise the mean age of the graduating students by 3.8 years.

median: The median without the outliers is 22.

The median with the outliers

is $\frac{22 + 23}{2} = \frac{45}{2} = 22.5$.

$22.5 - 22 = 0.5$

The outliers raise the median by 0.5.

**e.** Write the data in numeric order.

median $= \frac{$2.30 + $2.32}{2} = \frac{$4.62}{2}$

$= $2.31$

The median price was $2.31.

Sample: No, if I lived in 1 of these cities, I would use the mean, which is $2.33, because it might be better to use the higher price when budgeting.

**Saxon** Algebra 1

## Practice 48

**1.** $4ab^2c^4 - 2a^2b^3c^2 + 6a^3b^4c$

$4ab^2c^4 = 2 \cdot 2 \cdot a \cdot b \cdot b \cdot c \cdot c \cdot c \cdot c$

$2a^2b^3c^2 = 2 \cdot a \cdot a \cdot b \cdot b \cdot b \cdot c \cdot c$

$6a^3b^4c = 2 \cdot 3 \cdot a \cdot a \cdot a \cdot b \cdot b \cdot b \cdot b \cdot c$

$GCF = 2 \cdot a \cdot b \cdot b \cdot c$

$GCF = 2ab^2c$

**2.** $5m^2x^2y^5 - 10m^2xy^2 + 15m^2x^2y^4$

$5m^2x^2y^5 = 5 \cdot m^2 \cdot x \cdot x \cdot y^2 \cdot y \cdot y \cdot y$

$10m^2xy^2 = 2 \cdot 5 \cdot m^2 \cdot x \cdot y^2$

$15m^2x^2y^4 = 3 \cdot 5 \cdot m^2 \cdot x \cdot x \cdot y^2 \cdot y \cdot y$

$GCF = 5 \cdot m \cdot m \cdot x \cdot y \cdot y$

$GCF = 5m^2xy^2$

**3.** $4x^2(ax - 2)$

$= 4x^2(ax) - 4x^2(2)$

$= 4ax^3 - 8x^2$

**4.** $\dfrac{6a^{-3}c^{-3}}{a^{-2}cd^0}$

$= \dfrac{6a^{-3-(-2)}c^{-3-1}}{d^0}$

$= \dfrac{6a^{-1}c^{-4}}{1}$

$= \dfrac{6}{ac^4}$

**5.** $P(\text{first green card}) = \dfrac{6}{8} = \dfrac{3}{4}$

$P(\text{second green card}) = \dfrac{5}{7}$

$P = \dfrac{3}{4} \cdot \dfrac{5}{7} = \dfrac{15}{28}$

**6.** mean: $\dfrac{\text{sum of data}}{11} = \dfrac{44}{11} = 4$

median: 1, 2, 2, 3, 4, 4, 5, 5, 6, 6, 6

The median is 4.

mode: The number 6 occurs more often than any other number. The mode is 6.

**7.** Write an equation using the definition of the mean. These six values plus four of the same unknown divided by 10 must equal 19.

$\dfrac{105 + x + x + x + x}{10} = 19$

$\dfrac{105 + 4x}{10} = 19$

$105 + 4x = 190$

$4x = 85$

$x = 21.25$

21.25

**8. a.** $\left(\dfrac{x}{y} - \dfrac{r}{x}\right)^2$

$= \left(\dfrac{x}{y} - \dfrac{r}{x}\right)\left(\dfrac{x}{y} - \dfrac{r}{x}\right)$

**b.** $\dfrac{x}{y}\left(\dfrac{x}{y} - \dfrac{r}{x}\right) - \dfrac{r}{x}\left(\dfrac{x}{y} - \dfrac{r}{x}\right)$

$= \dfrac{x \cdot x}{y \cdot y} - \dfrac{x \cdot r}{x \cdot y} - \dfrac{r \cdot x}{x \cdot y} + \dfrac{r \cdot r}{x \cdot x}$

$= \dfrac{x^2}{y^2} - \dfrac{r}{y} - \dfrac{r}{y} + \dfrac{r^2}{x^2}$

**c.** $\dfrac{x^2}{y^2} - \dfrac{r}{y} - \dfrac{r}{y} + \dfrac{r^2}{x^2}$

$= \dfrac{x^2}{y^2} - \dfrac{2r}{y} + \dfrac{r^2}{x^2}$

**9.** It is true when $n$ is even and false when $n$ is odd. Sample: Multiplying a negative number an even number of times results in a positive number. Multiplying a negative number an odd number of times results in a negative number.

**10. a.** $9 = \dfrac{216}{x + 12}$

$9(x + 12) = 216$

**b.** $9(x + 12) = 216$

$9x + 108 = 216$

$9x = 108$

$x = 12$

**c.** $x + 12 = 12 + 12 = 24$

**11.** mean:

$\dfrac{30 + 90 + 60 + 30 + 90 + 40 + 90 + 50}{8}$

$= \dfrac{480}{8}$

$= 60$

median: 30, 30, 40, 50, 60, 90, 90, 90

$\dfrac{50 + 60}{2} = 55$

The median is 55.

mode: 30, 30, 40, 50, 60, 90, 90, 90

The mode is 90.

The answer is **B**.

**Saxon** Algebra 1

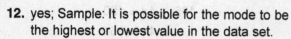

**12.** yes; Sample: It is possible for the mode to be the highest or lowest value in the data set.

**13. a.**
$150 \cdot 0.15 = \$22.50$
$150 + \$22.50 = \$172.50$
$172.50 \cdot 0.08 = \$13.80$
$172.50 - \$13.80 = \$158.70$
$158.70 \cdot 0.25 = \$39.68$
$158.70 + \$39.68 = \$198.38$
$198.38$

**b.** $198.38 - \$150 = \$48.38$

$\dfrac{\$48.38}{\$150} = 0.32$

It increased by 32%.

**14.** $3474 - \$1689 = \$1785$

$\dfrac{\$1785}{\$1689} = 1.06$

There is a percent increase of 106%.

**15.** Sample: The sum of 8 and 7 is 15, which is odd.

**16.** Sample: The mode of the data is 0, but this is not representative of Juan's average score. He may have missed the last three games, so the median or mean would better describe the set.

**17.** Order the data from least to greatest.
2, 2, 2, 2, 2, 2, 2, 3, 3, 3, 3, 4, 4, 4, 4, 4,
5, 5, 5, 5, 5, 5, 5, 5, 5, 6, 7, 7, 8, 12
12; Sample: The outlier represents a goalie who performed very well for the season.

**18. a.**
$10y = 3x + 360$
$-3x + 10y = 360$

**b.**
$-3x + 10y = 360$
$-3(0) + 10y = 360$
$0 + 10y = 360$
$10y = 360$
$y = 36$

Sample: If 0 minutes are used, the bill is $36. In other words, even if the phone has not been used, the person will still be charged $36.

**c.**
$-3x + 10y = 360$
$-3x + 10(0) = 360$
$-3x + 0 = 360$
$-3x = 360$
$x = -120$

Sample: In order to have a 0 bill, $-120$ minutes would have to be used. This is impossible.

**19.** $h = -16t^2 + 12t + 2$
$h = -2(8t^2 - 6t - 1)$

**20.** $\dfrac{93}{100} = \dfrac{x}{24}$
$100x = 93 \cdot 24$
$100x = 2232$
$x = 22.32$

**21.** $\dfrac{xl}{0.5(x^2 + 4x)}$

$= \dfrac{xl}{0.5x(x + 4)}$

$= \dfrac{xl}{0.5x(x + 4)}$

$= \dfrac{l}{0.5(x + 4)} \cdot \dfrac{2}{2}$

$= \dfrac{2l}{x + 4}$

**22.** $m = \dfrac{y_2 - y_1}{x_2 - x_1}$

$= \dfrac{-25 - (-9)}{4 - 2}$

$= \dfrac{-16}{2}$

$= -8$

**23.** $\dfrac{1}{2}x + (-4) < 6$

$\dfrac{1}{2}x - 4 < 6$.

**24.** $45w + \$215 > \$500$
The answer is **A**.

**25.** Since $\sqrt[n]{b} = b^{\frac{1}{n}}$, $\sqrt[8]{m} = m^{\frac{1}{8}}$.

**26.** Since $b^{\frac{1}{n}} = \sqrt[n]{b}$, $-15^{\frac{1}{4}} = -\sqrt[4]{15}$.
The negative sign is not in parentheses with 15, so find the fourth root of 15.
The answer is **B**.

**Saxon** Algebra 1

**27.** $500 - $400 = $100

$\dfrac{$100}{$500} = 0.2$

This is a 20% decrease.

**28.** Student A; Sample: Student B calculated a percent decrease.

**29.** $2 \cdot 0.75 = 1.5$

$2 + 1.5 = 3.5$ in.

A square with sides of 3.5 inches is 75% bigger than the square shown.

**30.** This uses inductive reasoning, because the conclusion is based on an observed pattern.

## LAB 3

### Lab Practice

**a.** Enter the equation into the Y= editor.

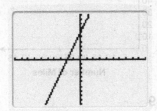

**b.** Place the cursor on the y-intercept of the graph by pressing TRACE. The coordinates are at the bottom of the screen. The y-intercept for $y = 3x + 6$ is (0, 6).

**c.** Press TRACE and use the arrow keys to move the cursor. The coordinates of the cursor are at the bottom of the screen. Sample:
(−0.65, 4.06), (1.29, 9.87), (2.26, 12.77)

**d.** Enter the equation into the Y= editor.

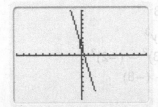

**e.** Place the cursor on the y-intercept of the graph by pressing TRACE. The coordinates are at the bottom of the screen. The y-intercept for $y = -5x + 2$ is (0, 2).

**f.** Press TRACE and use the arrow keys to move the cursor. The coordinates of the cursor are at the bottom of the screen. Sample:
(−1.61, 10.06), (−0.65, 5.23), (0.97, −2.84)

## LESSON 49

### Warm Up 49

**1.** The coordinates of the y-intercept must have an x-coordinate of 0. The answer is **B**.

**2.** $x + 3y - 4 = 0$

$x + 3y = 4$

$3y = -x + 4$

$\dfrac{1}{3} \cdot 3y = \dfrac{1}{3}(-x + 4)$

$y = -\dfrac{1}{3}x + \dfrac{4}{3}$

**3.** $3x - 2y - 7 = 0$

$3x - 2y = 7$

$-2y = -3x + 7$

$-\dfrac{1}{2}(-2y) = -\dfrac{1}{2}(-3x + 7)$

$y = \dfrac{3}{2}x - \dfrac{7}{2}$

**4.** $y = 2x + 10$

$y = 2(4) + 10$

$y = 8 + 10$

$y = 18$

**5.** $y = x^2$

$y = (-9)^2$

$y = 81$

### Lesson Practice 49

**a.** $y = 0.7x - 4.9$

$m = 0.7;\ b = -4.9$

**b.** $-9x + 3y = 12$

$3y = 9x + 12$

$\dfrac{3y}{3} = \dfrac{9x}{3} + \dfrac{12}{3}$

$y = 3x + 4$

$m = 3;\ b = 4$

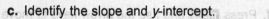

**c.** Identify the slope and $y$-intercept.

$$y = \frac{3}{5}x$$

$$m = \frac{3}{5}, \; b = 0$$

Graph the $y$-intercept on the coordinate plane at point $(0, 0)$. Use the value of the slope to plot another point. Move 3 units up and 5 units to the right from the $y$-intercept.

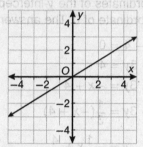

**d.** Write the equation in slope-intercept form.

$$x - 4y - 20 = 0$$

$$-4y = -x + 20$$

$$-\frac{1}{4}(-4y) = -\frac{1}{4}(-x + 20)$$

$$y = \frac{1}{4}x - 5$$

Graph the $y$-intercept on the coordinate plane at point $(0, -5)$. Use the value of the slope to plot another point. Move 1 unit up and 4 units to the right from the $y$-intercept.

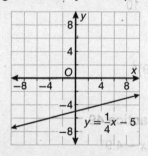

**e.** The $y$-intercept is the $y$-value where the line crosses the $y$-axis.

$y$-intercept: 4

rise $= 1$

run $= 1$

slope $= 1$

$$y = mx + b$$

$$y = x + 4$$

**f.** The $y$-intercept is the $y$-value where the line crosses the $y$-axis.

$y$-intercept: $-2$

rise $= -2$

run $= 6$

slope $= -\frac{1}{3}$

$$y = mx + b$$

$$y = -\frac{1}{3}x - 2$$

**g.** Identify the slope and $y$-intercept. The slope is 0.5 because it is the rate of change. The $y$-intercept is 50 because it is the initial fee.

$$y = 0.5x + 50$$

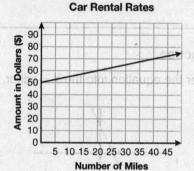

**Car Rental Rates**

Amount in Dollars ($)

Number of Miles

**Practice 49**

**1.** $x^2 y^3(3xy - 5y)$

$= (x^2 y^3 \cdot 3xy) - (x^2 y^3 \cdot 5y)$

$= 3x^3 y^4 - 5x^2 y^4$

**2.** $-2x^3 y^3(4x^2 y - 3xy)$

$= (-2x^3 y^3 \cdot 4x^2 y) - (-2x^3 y^3 \cdot 3xy)$

$= -8x^5 y^4 + 6x^4 y^4$

**3.** $x^2 y^3 z$

$= (3^2)(-2)^3(4)$

$= 9(-8)(4)$

$= -288$

**4.** $-x^2 - y^3$

$= -(-3)^2 - (-2)^3$

$= -9 - (-8)$

$= -1$

**5.** $3x + 2y - 10 = 0$

$3x + 2y = 10$

$3x + 2(0) = 10$

$3x = 10$

$$x = \frac{10}{3}$$

$$\left(\frac{10}{3}, 0\right)$$

**6.** Write the equation in slope-intercept form.

$$2x - 5y - 6 = 0$$
$$2x - 5y = 6$$
$$-5y = -2x + 6$$
$$-\frac{1}{5}(-5y) = -\frac{1}{5}(-2x + 6)$$
$$y = \frac{2}{5}x - \frac{6}{5}$$
$$m = \frac{2}{5}, \quad b = -\frac{6}{5}$$

**7.** The $y$-intercept is $-3$. The slope is $-\frac{1}{3}$.

$$y = -\frac{1}{3}x - 3$$

The answer is **B**.

**8. a.** $90 - 15 = 75$;

$$y = 15x + 75$$

$y$ represents the total cooking time and $x$ represents the number of biscuits.

**b.** 75; no; Sample: You would not cook 0 biscuits for 75 seconds.

**9.** The slope is $\frac{9}{5}$. The $y$-intercept is 32.

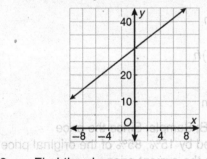

**10. a.** Find the slope.

$$m = \frac{y_2 - y_1}{x_2 - x_1}$$
$$= \frac{1\frac{1}{4} - \frac{3}{4}}{12 - 9}$$
$$= \frac{\frac{1}{2}}{3}$$
$$= \frac{1}{2} \cdot \frac{1}{3}$$
$$= \frac{1}{6}$$

Find the $y$-intercept.

$$y = mx + b$$
$$1\frac{1}{4} = \frac{1}{6}(9) + b$$
$$\frac{5}{4} = \frac{9}{6} + b$$
$$b = \frac{5}{4} - \frac{9}{6}$$
$$b = \frac{30}{24} - \frac{36}{24}$$
$$b = -\frac{6}{24}$$
$$b = -\frac{1}{4}$$

The equation is $y = \frac{1}{6}x - \frac{1}{4}$.

**b.** no; Sample: According to the $x$-intercept, a cat that weighs $1\frac{1}{2}$ lb should get zero cups of food a day.

**11.** mean:

$$\frac{4 + 2 + 0 + 4 + 5 + 4 + 2 + 3}{8}$$
$$= \frac{24}{8}$$
$$= 3$$

median: 0, 2, 2, 3, 4, 4, 4, 5

$$\frac{3 + 4}{2} = \frac{7}{2} = 3.5$$

The median is 3.5.

mode: 0, 2, 2, 3, 4, 4, 4, 5

The number that occurs most often is 4.

The mode is 4.

**12.** Order the data from least to greatest.

median:

35, 42, 42, 45, 45, 50, 55, 55, 58, 61, 63, 68

$$\frac{50 + 55}{2} = \frac{105}{2} = 52.5$$

The median is 52.5. Student B is correct. Sample: Student A did not list the data in numeric order before finding the median.

**Saxon** Algebra 1

**13.** Find the mean, median, and mode.

mean:

$$= \frac{\text{sum of data}}{15}$$

$$= \frac{30}{15}$$

$$= 2$$

median: 0, 0, 1, 1, 1, 1, 1, 2, 2, 2, 2, 3, 3, 4, 7

The median is 2.

mode: 0, 0, 1, 1, 1, 1, 1, 2, 2, 2, 2, 3, 3, 4, 7

The number that occurs most often is 1.

The mode is 1.

no; Sample: The data centers around the values 2 (mean and median) and 1 (mode). It is more likely that the next person surveyed will have 1 or 2 pets.

**14.** $\dfrac{x^2 - 12x}{2x^2 - x}$

$$= \frac{\cancel{x}(x - 12)}{\cancel{x}(2x - 1)}$$

$$= \frac{x - 12}{2x - 1}$$

**15.** $\dfrac{x}{80} = \dfrac{22}{100}$

$100x = 80 \cdot 22$

$100x = 1760$

$x = 17.6$

22% of 80 is 17.6.

**16.** slope $= \dfrac{\text{rise}}{\text{run}} = \dfrac{-6}{1} = -6$

**17.** $\$5 + \$0.15b = \$7 + \$0.05b$

$\$0.15b = \$2 + \$0.05b$

$\$0.10b = \$2$

$b = 20$

The cost of travel is the same for 20 blocks.

**18.** The odds for an event are $m{:}n$, where there are $m$ favorable outcomes and $n$ unfavorable outcomes.

5:10 or 1:2, 10:5 or 2:1

**19.** $a_1 = -3$, $a_n = a_{n-1} + 9$

$a_2 = -3 + 9$

$a_2 = 6$

$a_3 = 6 + 9$

$a_3 = 15$

$a_4 = 15 + 9$

$a_4 = 24$

$-3, 6, 15, 24$

**20. a.** $\angle Q$

**b.** $\angle M = \angle Q$

$\angle M = 110°$

$\angle Q = 110°$

**c.** $\dfrac{6}{4} = \dfrac{3}{2} = 3{:}2$ or $\dfrac{4}{6} = \dfrac{2}{3} = 2{:}3$

**d.** $\dfrac{3}{2} = \dfrac{10}{x}$

$3x = 2 \cdot 10$

$3x = 20$

$x = \dfrac{20}{3}$

**21.** greatest value: 287.1 million

least value: 258.7 million

287.1 million − 258.7 million

$= 28.4$ million

**22.** mean: $\dfrac{7 + 8 + 12 + 6 + 7 + 10 + 6}{7}$

$$= \frac{56}{7}$$

$$= 8$$

$A = \dfrac{1}{2}bh$

$8 = \dfrac{1}{2}(4)h$

$8 = 2h$

$h = 4$ cm

**23.** Student B; Sample: Since the price decreased by 15%, 85% of the original price would be the current price.

**24. a.** $A = s^2$

$2116 = s^2$

$s = \sqrt{2116}$ or 46 inches

**b.** $46 + 3 + 3 = 52$

$A = 52^2$

$A = 2704$ square inches

**c.** $A = 52 \cdot 3 \cdot 2 + 46 \cdot 3 \cdot 2$

$A = 312 + 276$

$A = 588$ square inches

**25.** $\sqrt[4]{256^{\frac{1}{2}}}$

$= \sqrt[4]{16}$

$= \sqrt[4]{2 \cdot 2 \cdot 2 \cdot 2}$

$= 2$

$\sqrt{256^{\frac{1}{4}}}$

$= \sqrt{4}$

$= \sqrt{2 \cdot 2}$

$= 2$

$2 = 2$, so $\sqrt[4]{\sqrt{256}} = \sqrt{\sqrt[4]{256}}$

**26.** $\$23 - \$20 = \$3$

$\frac{3}{20} = 0.15$

15% increase

**27.** $2x + \frac{1}{3} < 1\frac{2}{3}$

**28.** $\dfrac{\text{change in kilometers}}{\text{change in years}} = \dfrac{804 - 826}{1996 - 1980}$

$= \dfrac{-22}{16}$

$= -1.375$ km/yr

**29.** inductive reasoning; The conclusion is based on an observed pattern.

**30. a.** $A = s^2$

$A = (2x)^2$

$= 2^2 x^2$

$= 4x^2$ square inches

**b.** $5(4x^2)$

$= 20x^2$ square inches

## LESSON 50

### Warm Up 50

**1.** inequality

**2.** $137 \geq 2x - 13$

**3.** $8y - 3 = 15$

$8y = 18$

$y = \dfrac{18}{8}$

$y = \dfrac{9}{4}$

**4.** $7 = 5x + 4$

$3 = 5x$

$x = \dfrac{3}{5}$

### Lesson Practice 50

**a.**

| $3x + 4 < 19$ | $x = 0$ |
|---|---|
| $x = -2$ | $3(0) + 4 < 19$ |
| $3(-2) + 4 < 19$ | $0 + 4 < 19$ |
| $-6 + 4 < 19$ | $0 < 19$; true |
| $-2 < 19$; true | |

| $x = 5$ | $x = 11$ |
|---|---|
| $3(5) + 4 < 19$ | $3(11) + 4 < 19$ |
| $15 + 4 < 19$ | $33 + 4 < 19$ |
| $19 < 19$; false | $37 < 19$; false |

−2 and 0 are part of the solution set.

**b.** Represent > with an open circle.

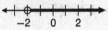

**c.** Represent ≥ with a closed circle.

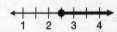

**d.** Represent ≤ with a closed circle.

**e.** Represent < with an open circle.

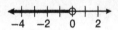

**f.** $m > 0.5$

**g.** $n \geq 12$

**h.** $g < 45$

**i.** $p \leq \dfrac{2}{5}$

**j.** $t \geq 100$

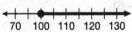

### Practice 50

**1.** $6k^5m^2 - 2k^3m - km$
$= km(6k^4m - 2k^2 - 1)$

**2.** $mx^4y^2 - m^2x^3y^3 + 5m^2x^6y^2$
$= mx^3y^2(x - my + 5mx^3)$

**Saxon** Algebra 1

**3.** $\left(\dfrac{2x}{3y^4}\right)^3$

$= \dfrac{2^3 x^{1 \cdot 3}}{3^3 y^{4 \cdot 3}}$

$= \dfrac{8x^3}{27y^{12}}$

**4.** $(2x^3 y^2)^4$

$= 2^4 x^{3 \cdot 4} y^{2 \cdot 4}$

$= 16x^{12} y^8$

**5.** false; $3 - 5 = -2$, and $-2$ is not a whole number.

**6.** $m = \dfrac{y_2 - y_1}{x_2 - x_1} = \dfrac{6 - (-3)}{6 - (-8)} = \dfrac{9}{14}$

**7.** $5x - 2 = 6y$

$\qquad 5x = 6y + 2$

$5x - 6y = 2$

**8.** Since $\sqrt[n]{b} = b^{\frac{1}{n}}$, $\sqrt[4]{y} = y^{\frac{1}{4}}$.

**9.** $P(P) = \dfrac{1}{7}$

$P(E) = \dfrac{2}{6} = \dfrac{1}{3}$

$P = \dfrac{1}{7} \cdot \dfrac{1}{3} = \dfrac{1}{21}$

**10.** Ten families will be chosen. 4,990 families will not be chosen.

10:4990

1:499

**11.** $a_n = a_1 + (n - 1)d$

$a_n = 32 + (n - 1)(-6)$

$a_5 = 32 + (5 - 1)(-6)$

$a_5 = 32 + 4(-6)$

$a_5 = 32 - 24$

$a_5 = 8$

$a_{12} = 32 + (12 - 1)(-6)$

$a_{12} = 32 + (11)(-6)$

$a_{12} = 32 - 66$

$a_{12} = 32 - 66$

$a_{12} = -34$

**12.** Student A; Sample: Student B solved the equation for $x$ instead of for $y$.

**13.** $\qquad -2y + 3 < 0 \qquad y = 0$

$\qquad\qquad y = -6 \qquad -2(0) + 3 < 0$

$-2(-6) + 3 < 0 \qquad\qquad\qquad 0 + 3 < 0$

$\qquad 12 + 3 < 0 \qquad\qquad\qquad 3 < 0;\text{ false}$

$\qquad\quad 15 < 0;\text{ false}$

$\qquad\quad y = 1 \qquad\qquad\qquad\qquad y = 6$

$-2(1) + 3 < 0 \qquad\qquad -2(6) + 3 < 0$

$\qquad -2 + 3 < 0 \qquad\qquad -12 + 3 < 0$

$\qquad\quad 1 < 0;\text{ false} \qquad\qquad -9 < 0;\text{ true}$

6 is part of the set of solutions for the inequality.

**14.** The circle on 7 is closed so the graph shows $x \le 7$. The answer is **A**.

**15.** Sample: Draw a number line and label several numbers, including 12. Draw a circle at the location of 12 and fill it in. Then shade the section of the number line to the right of the circle.

**16.** $x < 2$, $x > 2$, or the graph of $x \ne 2$ is all values except 2.

**17. a.** Move the decimal 7 places to the left.

$12{,}756{,}000 = 1.2756 \times 10^7$

Move the decimal 8 places to the left.

$695{,}900{,}000 = 6.959 \times 10^8$

**b.** $\dfrac{6.959 \times 10^8}{1.2756 \times 10^7}$

$= \dfrac{6.959}{1.2756} \times \dfrac{10^8}{10^7}$

$5.5 \times 10^1$ or about 55 times

**18.** $E = mc^2$

$E = 2(3 \times 10^8)^2$

$E = 2(3^2 \times 10^{8 \cdot 2})$

$E = 2(9 \times 10^{16})$

$E = 18 \times 10^{16}$

$E = 1.8 \times 10^{17}$ joules

**19. a.** Ivan's rate $= \dfrac{4 - 0}{5 - 0}$

$= \dfrac{4}{5}$

$= 0.8$ pages per minute

**b.** Jed's rate $= \dfrac{4.5 - 0}{5 - 0}$

$= \dfrac{4.5}{5}$

$= 0.9$ pages per minute

**Saxon** Algebra 1

**20.** yes; Sample: Because of the Distributive Property of Multiplication, she can break the problem apart.

**21.** $\dfrac{6x + 30}{36x + 6} = \dfrac{\cancel{6}(x + 5)}{\cancel{6}(6x + 1)} = \dfrac{x + 5}{6x + 1}$

Set the denominator equal to 0.

$6x + 1 = 0$

$6x = -1$

$x = -\dfrac{1}{6}$

$x \neq -\dfrac{1}{6}$

**22.** $5h + 135 \geq 280$, where $h$ is the number of hours

**23.** $49 - 45 = 4$

$\dfrac{4}{45} = 0.08$ or 8%

The answer is **B**.

**24.** $9 - 6 = 3$

$\dfrac{3}{6} = 0.5$ or 50%

$28 - 20 = 8$

$\dfrac{8}{20} = 0.4$ or 40%

Sample: Kwami's collection increased by 3 which is a 50% increase. Lisa's collection increased by 8 which is a 40% increase.

**25.** mean:

$\dfrac{\text{sum of data}}{11}$

$= \dfrac{297}{11}$

$= 27$

median: 15, 15, 18, 20, 21, 25, 26, 27, 28, 32, 70

The median is 25.

mode: 15, 15, 18, 20, 21, 25, 26, 27, 28, 32, 70

The number that appears most often is 15. The mode is 15.

**26.** greatest value: 418

least value: 6

The range is $418 - 6 = 412$.

**27.** Sample: If he creates a table of values using the equation, he can make sure that those ordered pairs are on the line in the original graph.

**28.** $P = 4s$

$y = 4x$

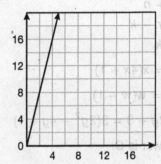

Sample: (0, 0), (1, 4), (2, 8)

**29. a.** $y = 7.5x - 185$

**b.**

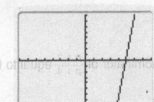

**c.** To make a profit, Jean Claude must sell 25 candles.

**30.** $t \leq 32$

## INVESTIGATION 5

### Investigation Practice

**a.** If it is not cloudy, then it is not raining.

**b.** If it is cloudy, then it is raining.

**c.** If it is not raining, then it is not cloudy.

**d.** true; If the original statement is true, then the contrapositive is true.

**e.** false; If the converse is false, then the inverse is also false.

**f.** contrapositive; The original statement and the contrapositive are true.

**g.** inverse; The original statement is true, but the inverse is false.

**Saxon** Algebra 1

## LESSON 51

### Warm Up 51

1. $\frac{2}{3x}$ is a rational expression because it is an expression with a variable in the denominator.

2. $5n - k + n$
$= 5n + n - k$
$= 6n - k$

3. $4x^2 + x = x(4x + 1)$

4. $w^2 - w = w(w - 1)$

5. $6g^2 - 12g + 3 = 3(2g^2 - 4g + 1)$

The answer is **D**.

### Lesson Practice 51

**a.** Set the denominator of $\frac{9}{4h}$ equal to 0.
$4h = 0$

$h = 0$

**b.** Set the denominator of $\frac{p+2}{p+4}$ equal to 0.
$p + 4 = 0$

$p = -4$

$p \neq -4$

**c.** Set the denominator of $\frac{g-5}{3g-15}$ equal to 0.
$3g - 15 = 0$

$3g = 15$

$g = 5$

$g \neq 5$

**d.** Set the denominator equal to 0.
$2a^2 = 0$

$a^2 = 0$

$a = 0$

$a \neq 0$

0 is the excluded value.
Factor out the GCF and simplify.
$\frac{4a^3}{2a^2}$

$= \frac{2a^2(2a)}{2a^2}$

$= 2a$

**e.** Set the denominator equal to 0.
$d = 0$

$d \neq 0$

0 is the excluded value.
Factor out the GCF and simplify.
$\frac{d + 1}{d}$

The numerator cannot be factored, so the expression cannot be simplified.

**f.** Set the denominator equal to 0.
$5z - 10 = 0$

$5z = 10$

$z = 2$

$z \neq 2$

2 is the excluded value.
Factor and simplify.
$\frac{3z^2 - 6z}{5z - 10}$

$= \frac{3z(z - 2)}{5(z - 2)}$

$= \frac{3z}{5}$

**g.** Set the denominator equal to 0.
$x^2 y^2 = 0$

$x^2 = 0, \; y^2 = 0$

$x = 0, \; y = 0$

$x \neq 0, \; y \neq 0$

Factor and simplify.
$\frac{5xy - 10x}{x^2 y^2}$

$= \frac{5x(y - 2)}{x^2 y^2}$

$= \frac{5(y - 2)}{xy^2}$

**h.** $\frac{4f}{r^2} - \frac{2f}{r^2}$

$= \frac{4f - 2f}{r^2}$

$= \frac{2f}{r^2}$

**i.** $6m^{-2}n^4 + \dfrac{3m^{-2}}{n^{-4}}$

$= \dfrac{6n^4}{m^2} + \dfrac{3n^4}{m^2}$

$= \dfrac{9n^4}{m^2}$

**j.** $P = 2(l + w)$

$P = 2\left(\dfrac{2x + 5}{4y} + \dfrac{6 - x}{4y}\right)$

$= 2\left(\dfrac{x + 11}{4y}\right)$

$= \dfrac{x + 11}{2y}$ in.

**Practice 51**

**1.** $\sqrt[4]{81}$

$= \sqrt[4]{3^4}$

$= \sqrt[4]{3 \cdot 3 \cdot 3 \cdot 3}$

$= 3$

**2.** $\sqrt[3]{-27}$

$= \sqrt[3]{-3^3}$

$= \sqrt[3]{(-3) \cdot (-3) \cdot (-3)}$

$= -3$

**3.** $\sqrt[3]{64}$

$= \sqrt[3]{4^3}$

$= \sqrt[3]{4 \cdot 4 \cdot 4}$

$= 4$

**4.** $\sqrt[3]{-64}$

$= \sqrt[3]{(-4)^3}$

$= \sqrt[3]{(-4) \cdot (-4) \cdot (-4)}$

$= -4$

**5.** $\qquad 7y = \dfrac{3}{8}x - 1$

$8(7y) = 8\left(\dfrac{3}{8}x\right) - 8(1)$

$56y = 3x - 8$

$3x - 56y = 8$

**6.** $\dfrac{12x^2 - 16x}{16xy}$

$= \dfrac{4x(3x - 4)}{4x(4y)}$

$= \dfrac{3x - 4}{4y}$

**7.** $\dfrac{dm^{-2}}{3} + \dfrac{5d}{m^2}$

$= \dfrac{d}{3m^2} + \dfrac{5d}{m^2}$

$= \dfrac{d}{3m^2} + 3\left(\dfrac{5d}{m^2}\right)$

$= \dfrac{d}{3m^2} + \dfrac{15d}{3m^2}$

$= \dfrac{16d}{3m^2}$

**8.** $\dfrac{8h^{-6}}{y^2} + \dfrac{y^{-2}}{h^6}$

$= \dfrac{8}{h^6y^2} + \dfrac{1}{h^6y^2}$

$= \dfrac{9}{h^6y^2}$

**9.** Set the denominator equal to 0.

$2h - 6 = 0$

$2h = 6$

$h = 3$

$h \neq 3$

The excluded value is 3. The answer is **D**.

**10.** $P = 2(l + w)$

$P = 2\left(\dfrac{360 + 360f}{f + 1} + \dfrac{160 + 160f}{f + 1}\right)$

$= 2\left(\dfrac{520 + 520f}{f + 1}\right)$

$= \dfrac{1040 + 1040f}{f + 1}$

$= 1040\left(\dfrac{1 + f}{f + 1}\right)$

$= 1040$ feet

**11.** Set the denominator equal to 0.

$p - 6 = 0$

$p = 6$

$p \neq 6$

Sample: A value of 6 would make the denominator equal to zero, and division by zero is undefined.

**12.** $a_n = a_{n-1} + d$

$a_2 = a_1 + d$

$32 = 21 + d$

$d = 11$

$a_n = a_1 + (n - 1)d$

60 minutes will be the 13th term.

$a_{13} = 21 + (13 - 1)11$

$= 21 + (12)11$

$= 21 + 132$

$= 153$

**13.** In the converse of a conditional statement, the order of the hypothesis and conclusion of the original statement is reversed: "If a number is a natural number, then the number is a whole number." The statement is true because all natural numbers fall into the set of whole numbers.

**14.** Order the data from least to greatest. Then find the difference between the least and greatest values.

56, 57, 58, 59, 62, 62, 64, 66

$66 - 56 = 10$

The range is 10, answer **B**.

**15.** Similar triangles have congruent corresponding angles. Therefore, the corresponding angle in the larger triangle also measures 60°.

**16.** $\dfrac{\text{cost}}{\text{\# of units}} = \dfrac{4.80}{3}$

$= \dfrac{1.60}{1}$

The unit price is $1.60 per pound.

**17. a.** $s = (8 + 150) + 285\% \cdot (8 + 150)$

$= 158 + 285\% \cdot 158$

**b.** $s = 158 + 2.85 \cdot 158$

$= 158 + 450.30$

$= 608.30$

The sale price is $608.30.

**18.** no; Sample: A rational expression is undefined only when the denominator is zero because division by zero is undefined. If the numerator is zero and the denominator is a nonzero number, then the value of the rational expression is zero because zero divided by any nonzero number is zero.

**19.** $m = \dfrac{y_2 - y_1}{x_2 - x_1}$

$m = \dfrac{-3 - 6}{5 - (-2)}$

$m = \dfrac{-9}{7}$

**20.** $\dfrac{\text{amount of increase}}{\text{original amount}} = \%\text{increase}$

The amount of increase is $10,200 − $7000

$= \$3200$

$\dfrac{\$3,200}{\$7,000} \approx 0.457$

The percent of increase is 46%.

**21.** The premise and conclusion use deductive reasoning. The conclusion is based on the definition of a triangle, that the sum of the angles of a triangle is 180°.

**22.** The temperature of the sun's core is greater than 5880 kelvins.

$t > 5880$

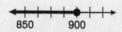

5780    5880

**23.** The sign's area is less than or equal to 900 square feet.

$s \le 900$

850    900

**24. a.** Sample: First I would list the data in numeric order. Then I would count the number of data values (20). Because the number is even, I would find the average of the tenth and eleventh data values to determine the median.

**b.** Order the data from least to greatest.

128, 134, 136, 141, 145, 148, 149, 150, 153, 155, 157, 168, 170, 176, 176, 182, 199, 200, 208, 211

**Saxon** Algebra 1

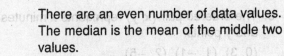
There are an even number of data values. The median is the mean of the middle two values.

$$\frac{155 + 157}{2} = \frac{312}{2} = 156$$

**25.** $5x + 3y = 9$

$$3y = -5x + 9$$

$$y = -\frac{5}{3}x + 3$$

**26.** Write each equation in slope-intercept form.

$4x + 2y + 3 = 0$

$$2y = -4x - 3$$

$$y = -2x - \frac{3}{2}$$

slope of $-2$, $y$-intercept of $-\frac{3}{2}$

$3x + 6y + 6 = 0$

$$6y = -3x - 6$$

$$y = -\frac{1}{2}x - 1$$

slope of $-\frac{1}{2}$, $y$-intercept of $-1$

$5x + 10y + 30 = 0$

$$10y = -5x - 30$$

$$y = -\frac{1}{2}x - 3$$

slope of $-\frac{1}{2}$, $y$-intercept of $-3$

$6x + 2y + 1 = 0$

$$2y = -6x - 1$$

$$y = -3x - \frac{1}{2}$$

slope of $-3$, $y$-intercept of $-\frac{1}{2}$

The answer is **C**.

**27.** Evaluate $x - 1 \geq 4$ for $\{-1, 0, 1, 2\}$.

$-1 - 1 \overset{?}{\geq} 4$  $\quad$ $0 - 1 \overset{?}{\geq} 4$

$-2 \ngeq 4$  $\qquad$ $-1 \ngeq 4$

$1 - 1 \overset{?}{\geq} 4$  $\quad$ $2 - 1 \overset{?}{\geq} 4$

$0 \ngeq 4$  $\qquad$ $1 \ngeq 4$

None of the values are solutions to the inequality.

**28.** Student B; Sample: Student A graphed all numbers less than 0, and "at least 9" means that the number is equal to or greater than 9.

**29. a.** The filled circle indicates "or equal to" so this graph shows a temperature of greater than or equal to $-15°$.

$t \geq -15$

**b.** Sample: The temperature is greater than or equal to negative fifteen.

**30.** The phrase "at least" indicates "greater than or equal to" so an inequality is $l \geq 1\frac{1}{2}$.

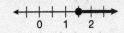

## LESSON 52

### Warm Up 52

**1.** slope

**2.** Substitute 0 for $y$ and solve for $x$.

$3x + y = 6$

$3x + 0 = 6$

$3x = 6$

$x = 2$

**3.** Substitute 0 for $x$ and solve for $y$.

$3x + y = 6$

$3(0) + y = 6$

$0 + y = 6$

$y = 6$

**4.** $\frac{2}{9} = \frac{4}{n}$

$2n = 9 \cdot 4$

$2n = 36$

$n = 18$

**5.** $\frac{5}{x + 10} = \frac{1}{3}$

$5 \cdot 3 = 1(x + 10)$

$15 = x + 10$

$x = 5$

## Lesson Practice 52

**a.** Graph the point (5, 6). From this point, count up two units and to the right one unit. Graph a point there. Sketch the line through the two points (5, 6) and (6, 8).

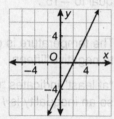

**b.** Graph the point (−1, 1). A line with a slope of zero is a horizontal line. Sketch a horizontal line that passes through the point (−1, 1).

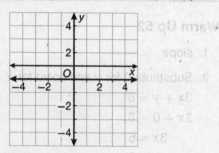

**c.** Write the formula.

$y - y_1 = m(x - x_1)$

Substitute 7 for $x_1$ and 9 for $y_1$.

$y - 9 = 6(x - 7)$

**d.** Write the slope formula.

$$m = \frac{y_2 - y_1}{x_2 - x_1}$$

$$m = \frac{4 - {}^-3}{7 - 2}$$

$$m = \frac{7}{5}$$

Write the point-slope formula.

$y - y_1 = m(x - x_1)$

$y - 4 = \dfrac{7}{5}(x - 7)$

$5y - 20 = 7x - 49$

$5y = 7x - 29$

$y = \dfrac{7}{5}x - \dfrac{29}{5}$

**e.** The ordered pair (x, y) represents x minutes and y points.

(0, 3), (1, −1), (2, −5)

$$m = \frac{y_2 - y_1}{x_2 - x_1}$$

$$m = \frac{-1 - 3}{1 - 0}$$

$$= -\frac{4}{1}$$

$$= -4$$

Write the point-slope formula.

$y - y_1 = m(x - x_1)$

Substitute (0, 3) for $(x_1, y_1)$.

$y - 3 = -4(x - 0)$

$y - 3 = -4x$

$y = -4x + 3$

Substitute 3 for x and solve for y.

$y = -4(3) + 3$

$= -12 + 3$

$= -9$ points

## Practice 52

**1.** $f(x) = 3x - 5$; domain: {0, 1, 2, 3}

$f(x) = 3(0) - 5$

$= 0 - 5$

$= -5$

$f(x) = 3(1) - 5$

$= 3 - 5$

$= -2$

$f(x) = 3(2) - 5$

$= 6 - 5$

$= 1$

$f(x) = 3(3) - 5$

$= 9 - 5$

$= 4$

The range is {−5, −2, 1, 4}.

**2.** $f(x) = \dfrac{1}{2}x + 3$; domain: {−2, 0, 2, 4}

$f(x) = \dfrac{1}{2}(-2) + 3$

$= -1 + 3$

$= 2$

$f(x) = \frac{1}{2}(0) + 3$

$= 0 + 3$

$= 3$

$f(x) = \frac{1}{2}(2) + 3$

$= 1 + 3$

$= 4$

$f(x) = \frac{1}{2}(4) + 3$

$= 2 + 3$

$= 5$

The range is {2, 3, 4, 5}.

**3.** "more than 3 years" is the same as "greater than 3"

$x > 3$

**4.** "the minimum wage" is the same as "greater than or equal to"

$x \geq 5.15$

**5.** $\dfrac{(3 \times 10^{-9})}{(4.8 \times 10^{-1})}$

$= \dfrac{3}{4.8} \times \dfrac{10^{-9}}{10^{-1}}$

$= 0.625 \times 10^{-8}$

$= 6.25 \times 10^{-9}$

**6.** $m = -1(3, 1)$

Graph point(3, 1). From this point, count down 1 unit and to the right 1 unit. Graph a point there. Sketch the line through the two points (3, 1) and (4, 0).

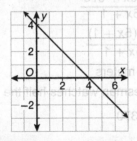

**7.** $\dfrac{\text{map distance}}{\text{actual distance}}$

$\dfrac{1}{20} = \dfrac{4}{x}$

$1x = 20 \cdot 4$

$x = 80$ miles

**8.** $\dfrac{\text{drawing length}}{\text{actual length}}$

$\dfrac{1}{6} = \dfrac{7}{x}$

$1x = 6 \cdot 7$

$x = 42$ inches

**9. a.** $\dfrac{t^3}{y^4}\left(\dfrac{t^2}{y^2} + \dfrac{5y}{m}\right)$

$= \dfrac{t^3}{y^4}\left(\dfrac{t^2}{y^2}\right) + \dfrac{t^3}{y^4}\left(\dfrac{5y}{m}\right)$

$= \dfrac{t^5}{y^6} + \dfrac{5t^3}{my^3}$

**b.** $y^6 = 0 \qquad my^3 = 0$

$\quad y = 0 \qquad\quad m = 0$

$\quad y \neq 0 \qquad\quad m \neq 0$

**10.** $I = prt$

$I = (20{,}000)(6.95\%)(5)$

$= (20{,}000)(0.0695)(5)$

$= \$6950.00$

**11. a.** Set the denominator equal to 0.

$15x^2 - 75x = 0$

$15x(x - 5) = 0$

$15x = 0 \qquad$ or $\qquad x - 5 = 0$

$\quad x = 0 \qquad\qquad\qquad x = 5$

**b.** $x - 5 = 0$

$\quad x = 5$

The numerator is 0 at $x = 5$.

**c.** The expression is undefined when the denominator is equal to zero. It is undefined at $x = 0$ and $x = 5$.

**12.** $y - y_1 = m(x - x_1)$

$y - (-2) = 3(x - (-1))$

$\quad y + 2 = 3(x + 1)$

$\quad y + 2 = 3x + 3$

$\qquad y = 3x + 1$

Substitute 4 for $x$.

$y = 3(4) + 1$

$= 12 + 1$

$= 13$

**Saxon** Algebra 1

**13.** operation: subtraction

inequality: $\leq$

$-4 - x \leq 0$

**14.** $-\sqrt{\dfrac{25}{16}} = -\dfrac{\sqrt{25}}{\sqrt{16}}$

$= -\dfrac{5}{4}$ or $-1\dfrac{1}{4}$

**15.** total profit =

(selling price)(number of bags)−

(total cost + $18 · number of bags)

$2200 = 40x - (1100 + 18x)$

$2200 = 40x - 1100 - 18x$

$2200 = 22x - 1100$

$3300 = 22x$

$x = 150$ bags

**16.** Order the data from least to greatest.

5, 5, 6, 6, 7, 7, 8, 8, 8, 10

mean =

$\dfrac{5 + 5 + 6 + 6 + 7 + 7 + 8 + 8 + 8 + 10}{10}$

$= \dfrac{70}{10}$

$= 7$

median $= \dfrac{7 + 7}{2}$

$= \dfrac{14}{2}$

$= 7$

Since 8 occurs most frequently in this set, 8 is the mode.

**17. a.** Use two points to find the slope.

$m = \dfrac{y_2 - y_1}{x_2 - x_1}$

$m = \dfrac{50 - 30}{4 - 2}$

$= \dfrac{20}{2}$

$= 10$

Write the point-slope formula.

$y - y_1 = m(x - x_1)$

$y - 30 = 10(x - 2)$

$y - 30 = 10x - 20$

$y = 10x + 10$

**b.** Substitute 5 for $x$.

$y = 10(5) + 10$

$= 50 + 10$

$= \$60$

**18. a.** $y = $ total cost

$x = $ pairs of shoes

$m = $ cost per pair of shoes

$b = $ rental fee for two lanes

$y = 2x + 40$

**b.** $y = 2(10) + 40$

$= 20 + 40$

$= \$60$

**19.** circle: closed arrowhead points to the right from $\dfrac{4}{5}$

$y \geq \dfrac{4}{5}$

**20.** Student A; Sample: Student B graphed $b$ as greater than 2.5, but should have graphed 2.5 as greater than $b$. Rewriting the inequality with the variable on the left, such as $b < 2.5$, would have been less confusing.

**21.** Set the denominator equal to 0.

$b^3 = 0$

$b = 0$

$b \neq 0$

**22.** $P = 2(l + w)$

$P = 2\left(\dfrac{525x + 100}{5x + 1} + \dfrac{400x + 85}{5x + 1}\right)$

$= 2\left(\dfrac{925x + 185}{5x + 1}\right)$

$= \dfrac{1850x + 370}{5x + 1}$

$= \dfrac{370(5x + 1)}{5x + 1}$

$= 370$ meters

Each linesman watches half the perimeter.

$= \dfrac{1}{2} \cdot 370$

$= 185$ meters

**23.** If a polygon does not have four sides, then it is not a quadrilateral. The statement is true because, by definition, a quadrilateral is a polygon with four sides.

**Saxon** Algebra 1

**24.** Student B; Sample: Student A forgot to rewrite each term with positive exponents before trying to combine like terms. As a result, the expressions did not appear to be like terms.

**25.** $\dfrac{4x + 8}{x^2 + 2x} = \dfrac{4(x + 2)}{x(x + 2)} = \dfrac{4}{x}$

**26.** $t = 2l + w$

$t = 2\left(\dfrac{6a}{3a - 1}\right) + \dfrac{4}{3a - 1}$

$= \dfrac{12a}{3a - 1} + \dfrac{4}{3a - 1}$

$= \dfrac{12a + 4}{3a - 1}$ meters

**27.** Write two points that represent the relationship between the number of days and the number of tickets sold.

$(1, 4)$ and $(2, 7)$

Find the slope of a line connecting the two points.

$m = \dfrac{y_2 - y_1}{x_2 - x_1}$

$m = \dfrac{7 - 4}{2 - 1}$

$m = \dfrac{3}{1}$

$m = 3$

Write the point-slope formula.

$y - y_1 = m(x - x_1)$

$y - 4 = 3(x - 1)$

$y - 4 = 3x - 3$

$y = 3x + 1$

The answer is **A**.

**28.** $m = \dfrac{y_2 - y_1}{x_2 - x_1}$

$m = \dfrac{2 - 2}{3 - (-1)}$

$= \dfrac{0}{4}$

$= 0$

Sample: It is a horizontal line, which has zero slope.

**29. a.** $y =$ total blanket length

$m =$ rate of Michelle's crocheting

$x =$ days of Michelle's crocheting

$b =$ amount Rachel has crocheted

$y = 8x + 24$

**b.** Enter the equation in the **Y=** editor. Press **Y=**. Then press 8 **X,T,θ,n** **+** 24. Press **ZOOM** and choose **6:ZStandard** to view the graph. Place the cursor on y-intercept by pressing **TRACE**. While the cursor is tracing the y-intercept, press **ENTER**.

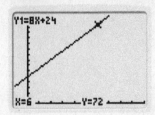

**c.** Substitute 72 for y.

$y = 8x + 24$

$72 = 8x + 24$

$72 - 24 = 8x$

$48 = 8x$

$x = 6$ days

**30. a.** Press **Y=** and enter the equation into the **Y=** editor. Open the Table Setup menu by pressing. **2nd** **WINDOW** TBLSET. TblStart should be 0. Use 1 for Δ Tbl. Press **2nd** **GRAPH** TABLE to view the table of values.

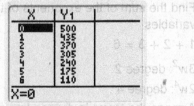

**b.** $d = 500 - 65t$

$d = 500 - (65 \cdot 4)$

$= 500 - 260$

$= 240$ miles

## LESSON 53

### Warm Up 53

1. term

2. $\left(\dfrac{4}{9}\right)^0$

$= \dfrac{4^0}{9^0}$

$= \dfrac{1}{1}$

$= 1$

3. $\left(\dfrac{12}{8}\right)^{-1}$

$= \dfrac{12^{-1}}{8^{-1}}$

$= \dfrac{8}{12}$

$= \dfrac{2}{3}$

4. $25b^3 = 25 \cdot b \cdot b \cdot b$

$50b^2 = 50 \cdot b \cdot b$

$100b = 100 \cdot b$

The GCF is $25b$.

### Lesson Practice 53

a. Find the sum of the exponents of the variables.

$2 + 1 + 6 = 9$

b. Find the sum of the exponents of the variables.

$1 + 1 + 1 = 3$

c. Find the sum of the exponents of the variables.

$1 + 2 + 3 = 6$

d. $3w^2$: degree 2

$2w^4$: degree 4

Arrange the terms in descending order. $-2w^4 + 3w^2$ is in standard form. The leading coefficient is $-2$.

e. Add the exponents of the variables.

$5ab^2$: $1 + 2 = 3$

$3a^2b^2$: $2 + 2 = 4$

$8ab$: $1 + 1 = 2$

$-1$: A constant has a degree of 0.

$3a^2b^2 + 5ab^2 + 8ab - 1$ is in standard form. The leading coefficient is 3.

f. Add the exponents of the variables.

$2ab$: $1 + 1 = 2$

$-7$: A constant has a degree of 0.

$-5a^2b$: $2 + 1 = 3$

$-5a^2b + 2ab - 7$ is in standard form. The leading coefficient is $-5$.

g. Arrange like terms in columns. Then add like terms.

$$\begin{array}{r} 2x^2 + x + 8 \\ +x^2 \qquad + 4 \\ \hline 3x^2 + x + 12 \end{array}$$

The polynomial is in standard form.

h. Arrange like terms in columns. Then add like terms.

$$\begin{array}{r} 3n^2 + 7n - 1 \\ + -2n^2 - n + 1 \\ \hline n^2 + 6n + 0 \\ n^2 + 6n \end{array}$$

The polynomial is in standard form.

i. Find the opposite of the second polynomial.

$(12y^3 + 10) - (18y^3 - 3y^2 + 5)$

$-18y^3 + 3y^2 - 5$

Arrange like terms in columns. Then add like terms.

$$\begin{array}{r} 12y^3 \qquad +10 \\ + -18y^3 + 3y^2 - 5 \\ \hline -6y^3 + 3y^2 + 5 \end{array}$$

The polynomial is in standard form.

j. Find the opposite of the second polynomial.

$(c^2 + 6c - 2) - (c^2 - 2c + 6)$

$-c^2 + 2c - 6$

Arrange like terms in columns. Then add like terms.

$$\begin{array}{r} c^2 + 6c - 2 \\ + -c^2 + 2c - 6 \\ \hline 0c^2 + 8c - 8 \\ 8c - 8 \end{array}$$

The polynomial is in standard form.

Saxon Algebra 1

**k.** Find the opposite of the second polynomial.
$(-16t^2 + 22t + 4) - (-16t^2 + 17t + 6)$
$16t^2 - 17t - 6$

Arrange like terms in columns. Then add like terms.

$$-16t^2 + 22t + 4$$
$$\underline{+16t^2 - 17t - 6}$$
$$5t - 2$$

The polynomial is in standard form.

## Practice 53

**1.** $18 - 12 + 4^2$
$= 18 - 12 + 16$
$= 22$

**2.** $-2[7 + 6(3 - 5)]$
$= -2[7 + 6(-2)]$
$= -2(7 - 12)$
$= -2(-5)$
$= 10$

**3.** $x \leq 8$

circle: filled

arrowhead: points to the left from 8

**4.** circle: open

arrowhead: points to the right of 2.5

$x > 2.5$

**5.** Rewrite the number on the left in scientific notation to compare the two expressions.

$3.04 \times 10^{-3} > 3.04 \times 10^{-4}$

**6.** Factor out the GCF, $9ab^3c$.
$18a^2b^3c - 45ab^6c$
$= 9ab^3c(2a - 5b^3)$

**7.** Factor out the GCF, $-8$.
$h = -16t^2 + 80t + 8$
$h = -8(2t^2 - 10t - 1)$

**8.** $(3a)(6a^2b)^3$
$= (3a)(216a^6b^3)$
$= 648a^7b^3$

**9.** $\dfrac{40 + 6t}{20 + 10t}$
$= \dfrac{2(20 + 3t)}{10(2 + t)}$
$= \dfrac{20 + 3t}{5(2 + t)}$

**10. a.**

Month (2007)

**b.** $m = \dfrac{y_2 - y_1}{x_2 - x_1}$
$m = \dfrac{2.69 - 2.08}{6 - 1}$
$= \dfrac{0.61}{5}$
$= 0.122$

**c.** July is the seventh month, so substitute 7 for $x_1$ and solve for $y_1$.
$y - y_1 = m(x - x_1)$
$y - 2.08 = 0.122(7 - 1)$
$y - 2.08 = 0.122(6)$
$y - 2.08 = 0.732$
$y = 2.812\%$

**11.** Sample: greater than or equal to, at least, no less than

**12.** $-\sqrt{b}$
$= -\left(b^{\frac{1}{2}}\right)$
$= -b^{\frac{1}{2}}$

**13.** $\text{mean} = \dfrac{\text{(Sum of periods)}}{8}$
$= \dfrac{107{,}257}{8}$
$= 13{,}407.125 \text{ days}$
$\text{median} = \dfrac{687 + 4329}{2}$
$= \dfrac{5016}{2}$
$= 2508 \text{ days}$

**Saxon** Algebra 1

**14.** Rewrite $-3 \leq y$ so the variable is on the left.

$y \geq -3$

circle: filled

arrowhead: pointing to the right from $-3$.

The answer is **A**.

**15.** Sample: Locate the number on the number line. If the number is in the region indicated by the shading, then it is part of the solution.

**16.** $48{,}763 - 39{,}400 = 9{,}363$

$\dfrac{9363}{48{,}763} \cdot 100 = 19.2\%$ decrease

**17.** Write the equation in slope-intercept form.

$1.5x + 3y - 6 = 0$

$3y = -1.5x + 6$

$y = \dfrac{1.5x}{3} + \dfrac{6}{3}$

$y = -0.5x + 2$

The slope is $m = -0.5$ and the $y$-intercept is $b = 2$.

**18.** Simplify.

$\dfrac{2k + 6}{k + 2}$

$= \dfrac{2(k + 3)}{k + 2}$

Set the denominator equal to 0.

$k + 2 = 0$

$k = -2$

$k \neq -2$

**19.** $P = 2(l + w)$

$P = 2\left(\dfrac{50x + 150}{3x + 5} + \dfrac{40x}{3x + 5}\right)$

$= 2\left(\dfrac{90x + 150}{3x + 5}\right)$

$= \dfrac{180x + 300}{3x + 5}$

$= \dfrac{(3x + 5)(60)}{3x + 5}$

$= 60$ meters

**20.** Student A; Sample: Student B cancelled parts of a term. Only factors can be cancelled.

**21.**

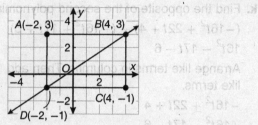

Because a rectangle is a parallelogram with four right angles and equal opposite sides, point $D$ must be at $(-2, -1)$.

Find the slope.

$m = \dfrac{y - y_1}{x_2 - x_1}$

$m = \dfrac{-1 - 3}{-2 - 4}$

$= \dfrac{-4}{-6}$

$= \dfrac{2}{3}$

Write the point-slope formula.

$y - y_1 = m(x - x_1)$

$y - 3 = \dfrac{2}{3}(x - 4)$

$3y - 9 = 2x - 8$

$3y = 2x + 1$

$y = \dfrac{2}{3}x + \dfrac{1}{3}$

**22.** $y =$ unharvested area

$m =$ rate of harvesting

$x =$ days

$b =$ area of field

**a.** $y = -50x + 800$

**b.** $y = -50x + 600$

**c.** $y = -50(10) + 800$

$= -500 + 800$

$= 300$ acres

$y = -50(10) + 600$

$= -500 + 600$

$= 100$ acres

**Saxon** Algebra 1

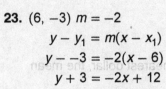
**23.** $(6, -3)$ $m = -2$

$$y - y_1 = m(x - x_1)$$
$$y - -3 = -2(x - 6)$$
$$y + 3 = -2x + 12$$
$$y = -2x + 9$$

**24.** $x^2 + x^{-1}$ is not a polynomial because it has a negative power. The answer is **B**.

**25.**

$$59x^2 - 262x + 3,888$$
$$+ \,-33x^3 + 611x^2 - 1433x + 28,060$$
$$\overline{-33x^3 + 670x^2 - 1695x + 31,948}$$

**26.** $-a^2b^2c^3 + 5x^5$

$2 + 2 + 3 = 7$

The degree is 7.

**27. a.** $m = \dfrac{y_2 - y_1}{x_2 - x_1}$

$$m = \frac{4 - 5}{6 - 4}$$

$$m = -\frac{1}{2}$$

$$y - y_1 = m(x - x_1)$$
$$y - 5 = -\frac{1}{2}(x - 4)$$

**b.** $y - 5 = -\dfrac{1}{2}(x - 4)$

$$y - 5 = -\frac{1}{2}x + 2$$

$$y = -\frac{1}{2}x + 7$$

**c.** Enter the equation in the **Y=** editor. Press the Y= key. Then press $-\frac{1}{2}$ X,T,θ,n + 7. Press ZOOM and choose **6: ZStandard** to view the graph. Place the cursor on the y-intercept by pressing TRACE. While the cursor is tracing the y-intercept, press ENTER.

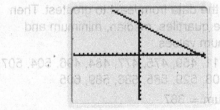

**d.** $4 = -\dfrac{1}{2}x + 7$ 　　$y = -\dfrac{1}{2}(3) + 7$

$$8 = -x + 14 \qquad y = -\frac{3}{2} + 7$$

$$x = 6 \qquad 2y = -3 + 14$$

$$2y = 11$$

$$y = \frac{11}{2}$$

**28.** $y - y_1 = m(x - x_1)$

$$y - 1 = -1(x - 3)$$
$$y - 1 = -(x - 3)$$

**29.** yes; Sample: $x^0 = 1$ and $4 \times 1 = 4$.

**30.** $3x^2 + 7x - 6$

$$+ \qquad \quad + 6$$
$$\overline{3x^2 + 7x + 0}$$
$$3x^2 + 7x$$

## LAB 4

### Practice Lab 4

**a.** 1. Press STAT and choose **1:Edit** to enter data into L1.

2. Clear old data by pressing ▲ key until L1 is selected. Then, press CLEAR and ENTER.

3. Enter data. Press ENTER after keying in each value.

4. Press 2nd Y= (STAT PLOT) and select **1:Plot1…** to open plot setup menu.

5. Press ENTER to turn Plot1 **On**. Then, press ▼ once and ▶ four times. **Xlist** should be L1 and **Freq** should be 1.

6. Press ZOOM and select **9:ZoomStat**.

7. Use TRACE and then, ◀ and ▶ to view statistical data.

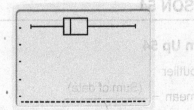

**Saxon** Algebra 1

**b.** 1. Press STAT and choose **1:Edit** to enter data into L1.

2. Clear old data by pressing ▲ key until L1 is selected. Then, press CLEAR and ENTER.

3. Enter data. Press ENTER after keying in each value.

4. Press 2nd Y= (STAT PLOT) and select **1:Plot1...** to open plot setup menu.

5. Press ENTER to turn Plot1 **On**. Then, press ▼ once and ▶ four times. **Xlist** should be L1 and **Freq** should be 1.

6. Press ZOOM and select **9:ZoomStat**.

7. Use TRACE and then, ◀ and ▶ to view statistical data.

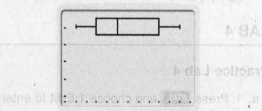

**c.** 59, 60, 61, 61, 62, 63, 64, 66, 67, 68, 69

median = middle of data set

median = 63 inches

**d.** $1^{st}$ quartile = median of lower half of data

59, 60, 61, 61, 62

$1^{st}$ quartile = 61

$3^{rd}$ quartile = median of upper half of data

64, 66, 67, 68, 69

$3^{rd}$ quartile = 67

50% of students fall between 61 and 67 inches

## LESSON 54

### Warm Up 54

1. outlier

2. mean $= \dfrac{(\text{Sum of data})}{7}$

---

$= \dfrac{278.94}{7}$

$= 39.85$

Rounded to the nearest dollar, the mean is $40.00.

**3. a.** Order the data from least to greatest.

128.86, 140.98, 161.05, 167.28, 184.93, 184.93, 185.66, 192.79, 194.77, 195.82

$\text{median} = \dfrac{184.93 + 184.93}{2}$

$= \dfrac{369.86}{2}$

$= 184.93$

**b.** range $= 195.82 - 128.86$

$= 66.96$

**4.** $\dfrac{(8.2 + 3.7 + 9.1 + 3.8)}{4}$

$= \dfrac{24.8}{4}$

$= 6.2$

**5.** $-\dfrac{7}{8} \div \left(-\dfrac{3}{4}\right)$

$= -\dfrac{7}{8} \cdot \left(-\dfrac{4}{3}\right)$

$= \dfrac{7}{6}$

### Lesson Practice 54

**a.** $Q_1 = 30$

$Q_3 = 50$

$IQR = 50 - 30 = 20$

$x < Q_1 - 1.5(IQR)$     $x > Q_3 + 1.5(IQR)$

$x < 30 - 1.5(20)$     $x > 50 + 1.5(20)$

$x < 30 - 30$          $x > 50 + 30$

$x < 0$             $x > 80$

No values are less than 0 or greater than 80, so there are no outliers.

**b.** Order the data from least to greatest. Then find the quartiles, median, minimum and maximum values.

387, 411, 459, 475, 477, 484, 496, 504, 507, 507, 508, 529, 585, 586, 589, 605

minimum = 387

**Saxon** Algebra 1

$Q_1 = \dfrac{475 + 477}{2} = 476$

median $= \dfrac{504 + 507}{2} = 505.5$

$Q_3 = \dfrac{529 + 585}{2} = 557$

maximum = 605

Draw a box-and-whisker plot.

**State Test Scores**

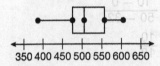

350 400 450 500 550 600 650

Half of the scores are between 476 and 557.

**c.** 1, 18, 19, 19, 21, 22, 23, 27, 28, 34, 37, 43, 44, 89

minimum = 1

$Q_1 = 19$

median $= \dfrac{23 + 27}{2} = 25$

$Q_3 = 37$

maximum = 89

IQR = 37 − 19 = 18

$x < Q_1 - 1.5(\text{IQR})$   $x > Q_3 + 1.5(\text{IQR})$

$x < 19 - 1.5(18)$   $x > 37 + 1.5(18)$

$x < 19 - 27$   $x > 37 + 27$

$x < -8$   $x > 64$

89 is an outlier because it is greater than 64.

Make a box-and-whisker plot. The upper whisker will end at 37, and 89 will be represented by an asterisk.

**Number of Yards Run**

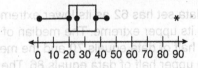

0 10 20 30 40 50 60 70 80 90

**d.** $Q_1 = 0.7$

$Q_3 = 1.75$

IQR = 1.75 − 0.7 = 1.05

$Q_1 - 1.5(\text{IQR}) = 0.7 - 1.5(1.05)$

$= -0.875$

$Q_3 + 1.5(\text{IQR}) = 1.75 + 1.5(1.05)$

$= 3.325$

The outliers are 3.8 and 8.1.

**e. 1.** Press **STAT** and choose **1:Edit** to enter data into L1.

**2.** Clear old data by pressing ⏶ key until L1 is selected. Then, press **CLEAR** and **ENTER**.

**3.** Enter data. Press **ENTER** after keying in each value.

**4.** Press **2nd** **Y=** and select **1:Plot1...** to open plot setup menu.

**5.** Press **ENTER** to turn Plot1 **On**. Then, press ⏷ once and ▶ four times. **Xlist** should be L1 and **Freq** should be **1**.

**6.** Press **ZOOM** and select **9:ZoomStat**.

**7.** Use **TRACE** and then, ◀ and ▶ to view statistical data.

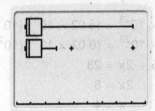

Sample: The plot with the outlier represents the data better. There are no values between 3.8 and 8.1. A whisker makes it look like data are distributed throughout that range. Identifying an outlier shows that most of the data are less than 3.

**Practice 54**

**1.** $\dfrac{1}{2} + \dfrac{3}{8}x - 5 = 10\dfrac{1}{2}$

$\dfrac{1}{2} + \dfrac{3}{8}x = 15\dfrac{1}{2}$

$\dfrac{3}{8}x = 15$

$3x = 120$

$x = 40$

**2.** $0.02x - 4 - 0.01x - 2 = -6.3$

$0.01x - 6 = -6.3$

$0.01x = -0.3$

$x = -30$

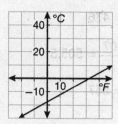

**3.** $x - 5x + 4(x - 2) = 3x - 8$

$x - 5x + 4x - 8 = 3x - 8$

$-8 = 3x - 8$

$0 = 3x$

$x = 0$

**4.** $\dfrac{2x^2 - 10x}{2x}$

$= \dfrac{2x(x - 5)}{2x}$

$= x - 5$

**5.** $\dfrac{b^2}{d^{-3}}\left(\dfrac{db^{-2}}{4} - \dfrac{3f^{-3}d^2}{b^{-2}}\right)$

$= b^2 d^3\left(\dfrac{d}{4b^2} - \dfrac{3b^2 d^2}{f^3}\right)$

$= \dfrac{b^2 d^4}{4b^2} - \dfrac{3b^4 d^5}{f^3}$

$= \dfrac{d^4}{4} - \dfrac{3b^4 d^5}{f^3}$

**6.** $6.02 \times 10^{23} = (6.02 \times 10^{15})(10^{-x})^2$

$6.02 \times 10^{23} = (6.02 \times 10^{15})(10^{2x})$

$15 + 2x = 23$

$2x = 8$

$x = 4$

**7. a.** $-4, 32, 50, 77$

$C = \dfrac{5}{9}(F - 32)$

$C = \dfrac{5}{9}(-4 - 32) = \dfrac{5}{9}(-36) = -20$

$C = \dfrac{5}{9}(32 - 32) = \dfrac{5}{9}(0) = 0$

$C = \dfrac{5}{9}(50 - 32) = \dfrac{5}{9}(18) = 10$

$C = \dfrac{5}{9}(77 - 32) = \dfrac{5}{9}(45) = 25$

| °F | −4 | 32 | 50 | 77 |
|----|-----|----|----|----|
| °C | −20 | 0 | 10 | 25 |

**b.** Graph all the points in the table using °F as the x-axis and °C as the y-axis. Draw a line through the points.

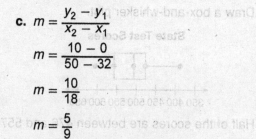

**c.** $m = \dfrac{y_2 - y_1}{x_2 - x_1}$

$m = \dfrac{10 - 0}{50 - 32}$

$m = \dfrac{10}{18}$

$m = \dfrac{5}{9}$

**8.** LE = point at the extreme left = 1

$Q_1$ = point at left end of box = 2

median = point inside the box = 2.5

$Q_3$ = point at right end of box = 3

UE = point at extreme right = 5

IQR = $Q_3 - Q_1$ = 3 − 2 = 1

**9.** LE = point at the extreme left = 12

$Q_1$ = point at left end of box = 18

median = point inside the box = 25

$Q_3$ = point at right end of box = 27

UE = point at extreme right = 30

IQR = $Q_3 - Q_1$ = 27 − 18 = 9

**10.** LE = 62

$Q_1$ = 70

median = 84

$Q_3$ = 86

UE = 95

The data set has 62 as its lower extreme and 95 as its upper extreme. The median of the lower half of data equals 70 and the median of the upper half of data equals 86. The median of the entire set of data equals 84.

Sample: 62, 64, 70, 70, 71, 84, 85, 86, 86, 90, 95

**11.** To determine the mode and mean, you need to see the entire data set. A box-and-whisker plot does not show that. It only shows the range of the data. The answer is **B**.

**Saxon** Algebra 1

**12.** Order the data from least to greatest.

36, 67, 93, 142, 484, 887, 1765, 2791

$$\text{median} = \frac{142 + 484}{2} = 313$$

$$Q_1 = \frac{67 + 93}{2} = 80$$

$$Q_3 = \frac{887 + 1765}{2} = 1326$$

IQR = 1326 − 80 = 1246

$x < Q_1 - 1.5(IQR) \quad x > Q_3 + 1.5(IQR)$

$x < 80 - 1.5(1246) \quad x > 1326 + 1.5(1246)$

$x < -1789 \quad\quad x > 3195$

There are no outliers.

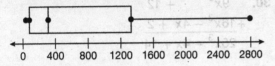

**13.** 2392 − 2175 = 217

$$\frac{217}{2175} = 0.0998$$

It is a 10% increase because the new price is greater than the old price.

**14.** Measure of central tendency can be the mean, median, or mode.

Order the data from least to greatest.

78, 84, 86, 86, 88, 90, 92, 92, 94, 94, 96, 100

$$\text{mean} = \frac{(\text{Sum of data})}{12}$$

$$= \frac{1080}{12}$$

$$= 90\%$$

$$\text{median} = \frac{90 + 92}{2}$$

$$= 91$$

mode = 86, 92, 94

Sample: the mean value of 90; The median value (91) is not a part of the data set and there is more than one mode (86, 92, 94).

**15.** $b = 467$ (number of skateboards in stock)

$m = 115$ (rate of skateboard production)

$x$ = time (in hours)

$y = 115x + 467$

**16.** circle: filled

arrowhead: shaded from −6 to the left

$x \le -6$

**17.** $m = \dfrac{y_2 - y_1}{x_2 - x_1}$

$$m = \frac{16 - 20}{20000 - 10000}$$

$$m = \frac{-4}{-10000}$$

$$m = \left(\frac{1}{2500}\right) \text{ mm/miles}$$

**18. a.** false; Sample: A vehicle can be a standard truck.

**b.** The oval for trucks lies completely within the oval for motor vehicles. The statement is true.

**19.** Sample: The square root of a negative real number is imaginary, whereas the square root of 1 is 1.

**20.** $\dfrac{2g}{2g + 6}$ cannot be simplified to $\dfrac{1}{6}$

because when factoring, the denominator cannot be separated. The GCF of this expression is 2.

$$= \frac{2(g)}{2(g + 3)}$$

$$= \frac{g}{g + 3}$$

**21.** $3rd^{-1} - \dfrac{6}{r^{-1}d}$

$$= \frac{3r}{d} - \frac{6r}{d}$$

$$= \frac{-3r}{d}$$

$$= -3rd^{-1}$$

$$\ne \frac{-3d}{r}$$

The answer is **C**.

**22.** $y = -25x + 500$

$y = -25(9) + 500 = 275$

$y = -25(0) + 500 = 500$

$(9, 275), (0, 500)$

Plot both points and draw a line through them.

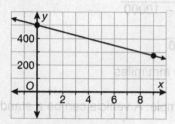

**23.** $m = \dfrac{y_2 - y_1}{x_2 - x_1}$

$m = \dfrac{-4 - 6}{3 - 1}$

$= \dfrac{-10}{2}$

$= -5$

**24.** Sample: a horizontal line passing through $(-1, 1)$

**25.** Find the slope.

$m = \dfrac{y_2 - y_1}{x_2 - x_1}$

$m = \dfrac{9 + 3}{-6 - 14}$

$= \dfrac{12}{-20}$

$= \dfrac{-3}{5}$

Use the point-slope formula to write an equation in slope-intercept form.

$y - y_1 = m(x - x_1)$

$y - 9 = -\dfrac{3}{5}(x + 6)$

$5y - 45 = -3x - 18$

$5y = -3x + 27$

$y = -\dfrac{3}{5}x + \dfrac{27}{5}$

**26.** Student B; Sample: Student A didn't combine like terms.

**27.** $P = s + s + s$

$= (2x + 6) + (3x + 7) + (4x + 3)$

$= 9x + 16$

**28.** $P = 2(l + w)$

$= 2(3x - 16 + 5x + 21)$

$= 2(8x + 5)$

$= 16x + 10$

**29. a.** Because both accounts have the same growth rate $g$, the model for Jane's account will have the same exponents for the corresponding months.

$J = 375g^3 + 410g^2 + 50g + 200$

**b.** $\quad 300g^3 + 400g^2 + 200g + 25$

$\underline{+375g^3 + 410g^2 + 50g + 200}$

$\quad 675g^3 + 810g^2 + 250g + 225$

**30.** $\quad 9x^3 \qquad\quad + 12$

$\quad +16x^3 - 4x + 2$

$\overline{\quad 25x^3 - 4x + 14}$

## LAB 5

### Practice Lab 5

**a. 1.** Enter the equations into the **Y=** editor.

**2.** Graph the equations in a standard viewing window.

**3.** Trace one of the lines by pressing **TRACE**. Use the ▼ and ▲ keys to move to another line. Use the ◀ and ▶ keys to move along the line to the intersection.

**4.** The approximate intersection point (displayed at the bottom of the screen) is $(0.851, 1.298)$.

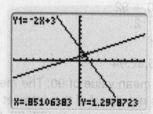

**b. 1.** After completing steps 1–4 above, press **2nd** **TRACE** and select **5:Intersection**. At the prompt "First Curve?," press **ENTER** to select the first line.

**2.** At the prompt "Second Curve?," press **ENTER** to select the second line.

**Saxon** Algebra 1

3. Use the ◀ and ▶ keys to move the cursor near intersection.

4. At the prompt "Guess?," press ENTER.

5. The solution (displayed as a decimal at the bottom of the screen) is (0.8, 1.4).

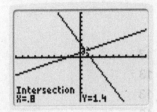

c. 1. Enter the equations into the **Y=** editor.

2. Graph the equations in a standard viewing window.

3. Trace one of the lines by pressing TRACE. Use the ▼ and ▲ keys to move to another line. Use the ◀ and ▶ keys to move along the line to the intersection.

4. The approximate intersection point is displayed at the bottom of the screen.

5. Press 2nd TRACE and select

**5: Intersection**. At the prompt "First Curve?," press ENTER to select the first line.

6. At the prompt "Second Curve?," press ENTER to select the second line.

7. Use the ◀ and ▶ keys to move the cursor near intersection.

8. At the prompt "Guess?," press ENTER.

9. The solution (displayed as a decimal at the bottom of the screen) is (−0.6, 3.2).

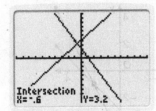

d. 1. Enter the equations into the **Y=** editor.

2. Graph the equations in a standard viewing window.

3. Trace one of the lines by pressing TRACE. Use the ▼ and ▲ keys to move to another line. Use the ◀ and ▶ keys to move along the line to the intersection.

4. The approximate intersection point is displayed at the bottom of the screen.

5. Press 2nd TRACE and select

**5: Intersection**. At the prompt "First Curve?," press ENTER to select the first line.

6. At the prompt "Second Curve?," press ENTER to select the second line.

7. Use the ◀ and ▶ keys to move the cursor near intersection.

8. At the prompt "Guess?," press ENTER.

9. The solution is displayed as a decimal at the bottom of the screen.

10. Press 2nd MODE to return to home screen.

11. Press X,T,θ,n and ENTER, and then press MATH and select **1:>Frac**. Press ENTER.

12. Press ALPHA Y= and ENTER. Then, press MATH and select **1:>Frac**. Press ENTER. The intersection point $\left(-\frac{60}{11}, \frac{335}{11}\right)$.

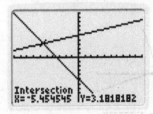

e. 1. Enter the equations into the **Y=** editor.

2. Graph the equations in a standard viewing window.

3. Trace one of the lines by pressing **TRACE**. Use the ⌄ and ⌃ keys to move to another line. Use the ◁ and ▷ keys to move along the line to the intersection.

4. The approximate intersection point is displayed at the bottom of the screen.

5. Press **2nd** **TRACE** and select **5: Intersection**. At the prompt "First Curve?," press **ENTER** to select the first line.

6. At the prompt "Second Curve?," press **ENTER** to select the second line.

7. Use the ◁ and ▷ keys to move the cursor near intersection.

8. At the prompt "Guess?," press **ENTER**.

9. The solution is displayed as a decimal at the bottom of the screen.

10. Press **2nd** **MODE** to return to home screen.

11. Press **X,T,θ,n** and **ENTER**, and then press **MATH** and select **1:▸Frac**. Press **ENTER**.

12. Press **ALPHA** **Y=** and **ENTER**. Then, press **MATH** and select **1:▸Frac**. Press **ENTER**. The intersection point $\left(\frac{4}{9}, \frac{7}{9}\right)$.

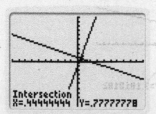

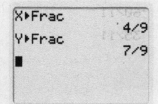

## LESSON 55

**Warm Up 55**

1. solution

2. $18 + 3n$
$= 18 + 3(2)$
$= 18 + 6$
$= 24$

3. $3x + 2y = 13$
$3(3) + 2(2) = 13$
$9 + 4 = 13$
$13 = 13$

Yes, Sample: (3, 2) is a solution to the equation because substituting the values for the variables makes the equation true.

4. $2x + 3y = 6$
$3y = -2x + 6$
$y = -\frac{2}{3}x + 2$

**Lesson Practice 55**

a. $2x + y = 5$    $2x + 2y = 8$
$2(1) + 3 \overset{?}{=} 5$   $2(1) + 2(3) \overset{?}{=} 8$
$2 + 3 \overset{?}{=} 5$    $2 + 6 \overset{?}{=} 8$
$5 = 5$     $8 = 8$

Yes, (1, 3) is a solution to both equations.

b. $2x + y = 5$    $2x + 2y = 8$
$2(3) + 4 \overset{?}{=} 5$   $2(3) + 2(4) \overset{?}{=} 8$
$6 + 4 \overset{?}{=} 5$    $6 + 8 \overset{?}{=} 8$
$10 \neq 5$     $14 \neq 8$

No, (3, 4) is not a solution of either equation.

c. Graph both equations on the same coordinate plane. Find the point of intersection.

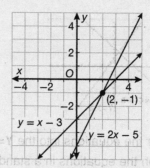

(2, −1) is a solution of the system.

**Saxon** Algebra 1

**d.** Graph both equations on the same coordinate plane. Find the point of intersection.

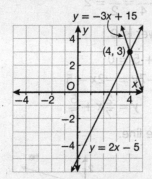

(4, 3) is a solution of the system.

**e.** Write $2x + 3y = 6$ in slope intercept form.

$$2x + 3y = 6$$
$$3y = -2x + 6$$
$$y = -\frac{2}{3}x + 2$$

Graph both equations and then use the intersection command.

The intersection point and the solution of the system is (8.4, −3.6).

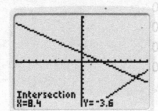

**f.** Jill: $y = 5x + 20$

Jose: $y = 10x + 5$

Graph the equations. Find the intersection of the two lines using a graphing calculator.

intersection point: (3, 35)

After 3 weeks, both Jill and Jose will have $35.

**Practice 55**

**1.** $39.95 + 0.99d = 55.79$
$$0.99d = 15.84$$
$$d = 16$$

**2.** $12.6 = 4p + 1$
$$11.6 = 4p$$
$$p = 2.9$$

**3.** $2(b - 4) = 8b - 11$
$$2b - 8 = 8b - 11$$
$$3 = 6b$$
$$b = \frac{1}{2}$$

**4.** $1.8r + 9 = -5.7r - 6$
$$7.5r = -15$$
$$r = -2$$

**5.** $\dfrac{k^{-4}}{2}$

$$= \frac{1}{2k^4}$$

**6.** $10r^{-3}t^4$

$$= \frac{10t^4}{r^3}$$

**7.** $\dfrac{p^{-9}q^{-4}}{r^2 s^{-3}}$

$$= \frac{s^3}{r^2 p^9 q^4}$$

**8. a.** Sample: Which beverage do you prefer to drink with your lunch?

**b.** Sample: What is your favorite class?

**c.** Sample: When would be the best time for the class to exercise?

**9.** $\dfrac{rs}{z^2}\left(\dfrac{pr^{-5}s^4}{z^{-7}} - 7p^{-2}s^{-1} + \dfrac{5}{z^{-3}}\right)$

$$= \frac{rs}{z^2}\left(\frac{ps^4z^7}{r^5} - \frac{7}{p^2s} + 5z^3\right)$$

$$= \frac{ps^5z^5}{r^4} - \frac{7r}{p^2z^2} + 5rsz$$

**10.** $(2ab^2)^2 (-2b^2)^2$
$$= (4a^2b^4)(4b^4)$$
$$= 16a^2b^8$$

**11.** slope $= \dfrac{\text{change in height}}{\text{change in distance}}$

$$m = \frac{1}{12}$$

**12. a.** $620 =$ total distance

$272.8 =$ distance already hiked

$x =$ percentage already hiked

$620x = 272.8$

**b.** $620x = 272.8$

$$x = \frac{272.8}{620}$$

$$x = 0.44$$

The solution is 44%.

**c.** Sample: Round 272.8 up to 300. Round 620 down to 600. $300 \div 600 = 0.5 = 50\%$. Therefore, 44% is a reasonable answer compared to the estimate of 50%.

**13.** $250 =$ donations Gaby has

$40m =$ donation for each mile $m$

$40m + 250 \geq 500$

**14. a.** The box is half full.

$$\frac{1}{2}V = 5324$$

$$V = 10{,}648 \text{ cubic inches}$$

**b.**     $V = s \cdot s \cdot s$

$$V = s^3$$

$$10{,}648 = s^3$$

$$\sqrt[3]{10{,}648} = s$$

$$s = 22 \text{ inches}$$

**15.**  Vickie    Annie

$\dfrac{48}{60}$     $\dfrac{47}{60}$

0.8       0.78

80%       78%

$80 - 72 = 2$

Vickie's grade was 2% greater than Annie's.

**16.** the mode value of 5; Sample: This represents half of the values that fall below the median (7).

**17. a.** $b = 500$

$m = 20$

$x =$ years

$y = 20x + 500$

**b.** $2005 - 1997 = 8$ years

$$y = 20x + 500$$

$$y = 20(8) + 500$$

$$= 160 + 500$$

$$= 660 \text{ students}$$

**18.** $(4, 0), (6, 4)$

$$m = \frac{4 - 0}{6 - 4} = \frac{4}{2} = 2$$

The answer is **C**.

**19.** $2x - 7y + 5 = 0$

$$-7y = -2x - 5$$

$$y = \frac{2}{7}x + \frac{5}{7}$$

Graph the line.

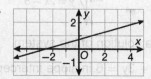

**20.** The phrase "to not score lower" means the same as "greater than or equal to."

$s \geq 13{,}468$

circle: filled

arrowhead: shaded from 13,468 pointing to the right.

**21.** Set the denominator equal to 0.

$$20f^4 = 0$$

$$f^4 = 0$$

$$f = 0$$

$$f \neq 0$$

Simplify.

$$\frac{5f^9}{20f^4}$$

$$= \frac{5f^4(f^5)}{5f^4(4)}$$

$$= \frac{f^5}{4}$$

**22.** Student A; Sample: Student B found the sum of all the exponents of each monomial.

**23.** Evaluate the expression $-16t^2 + 100t$ for each value of $t$.

$t = 3$: $-16(3^2) + 100(3)$
$\qquad -16(9) + 300$
$\qquad -144 + 300$
$\qquad$ 156 feet

$t = 5$: $-16(5^2) + 100(5)$
$\qquad -16(25) + 500$
$\qquad -400 + 500$
$\qquad$ 100 feet

**24.** $\quad 3n^3 + 2n - 7$
$\quad \underline{+\ -n^3 +\ \ n + 2}$
$\qquad 2n^3 + 3n - 5$

**25.** LE = point on the extreme left = 2.32
$Q_1$ = point on left end of box = 2.75
median = point inside the box = 2.89
$Q_3$ = point on right end of box = 2.94
UE = point at the extreme right = 3.02
IQR = $Q_3 - Q_1$ = 2.94 − 2.75 = 0.19

**26.** The interquartile range is the area of the box-and-whisker plot where half of the data falls. So, the probability of a data value falling in the interquartile range is 50%.

**27.** Graph both equations and then use the intersection command.

The intersection point and the solution of the system is (8,0).

Check your answer.

$y = -\dfrac{1}{2}x + 4 \qquad y = \dfrac{1}{4}x - 2$

$0 = -\dfrac{1}{2}(8) + 4 \qquad 0 = \dfrac{1}{4}(8) - 2$

$0 = -4 + 4 \qquad\ \ 0 = 2 - 2$

$0 = 0 \qquad\qquad\ \ 0 = 0$

**28.** Solve each system of equations.

The ordered pair (−4, −2) makes both of the equations true. The answer is **C**.

**29. a.** Talk-A-Lot: $y = 0.25x + 1.25$
Save-N-Talk: $y = 0.50x$

**b.** Graph both equations and then use the intersection command.

The intersection point and the solution of the system is (5, 2.5).

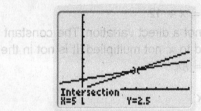

Intersection
X=5        Y=2.5

**c.** Sample: Both phone companies will charge the same amount of $2.50 when 5 minutes are used.

**30. a.** LE = 1
$Q_1 = 3$
median = 5
$Q_3 = 8$
UE = 8
IQR = 8 − 3 = 5

**Fat Grams in Meat**

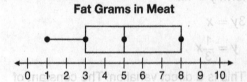

**b.** The upper whisker is missing because the values of the whisker are contained in the upper quartile.

## LESSON 56

### Warm Up 56

**1.** 3

**2.** $3x + 2y = 8$
$\qquad 2y = -3x + 8$
$\qquad\quad y = -\dfrac{3}{2}x + 4$

**3.** $5y = 3x$
$\qquad y = \dfrac{3}{5}x$

**4.** $y = \dfrac{3}{5}(0) = 0$

$y = \dfrac{3}{5}(5) = 3$

$y = \dfrac{3}{5}(10) = 6$

{0, 3, 6}

## Lesson Practice 56

**a.** $y - 12 = x$

$\qquad y = x + 12$

This is not a direct variation. The constant is added to $x$, not multiplied. It is not in the form $y = kx$.

**b.** $\dfrac{y}{-3} = x$

$\qquad y = -3x$

This is a direct variation. The constant of variation is $-3$.

**c.** $2xy = 8$

$\qquad y = \dfrac{8}{2x}$

$\qquad y = \dfrac{4}{x}$

This is not a direct variation. The constant divided by $x$, not multiplied. It is not in the form $y = kx$.

**d.** $3y = x$

$\qquad y = \dfrac{1}{3}x$

This is a direct variation. The constant of variation is $\dfrac{1}{3}$.

**e.** Find the ratio $\dfrac{y}{x}$ for each ordered pair.

$\dfrac{y}{x} = \dfrac{10}{3}$

$\dfrac{y}{x} = \dfrac{40}{12} = \dfrac{10}{3}$

$\dfrac{y}{x} = \dfrac{30}{9} = \dfrac{10}{3}$

The ordered pairs represent a direct variation because the ratio is the same for all pairs.

**f.** Find the ratio $\dfrac{y}{x}$ for each ordered pair.

$\dfrac{y}{x} = \dfrac{4}{10} = \dfrac{2}{5}$

$\dfrac{y}{x} = \dfrac{6}{12} = \dfrac{1}{2}$

$\dfrac{y}{x} = \dfrac{8}{14} = \dfrac{4}{7}$

The ordered pairs do not represent a direct variation because the ratio is not the same for all pairs.

**g.** $\dfrac{y}{x} = \dfrac{72}{9} = 8$

$\qquad y = 8x$

**h.** $\dfrac{y}{x} = \dfrac{18}{6} = 3$

$\qquad y = 3x$

$\qquad y = 3(8)$

$\qquad\ \ = 24$ boys

**i.** $\dfrac{29}{4} = \dfrac{y}{3}$

$\qquad 4y = 87$

$\qquad y = \dfrac{87}{4}$ or $21.75$ cubic centimeters

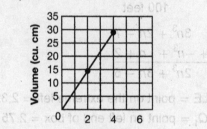

## Practice 56

**1.** $-4\dfrac{3}{4} + 3\dfrac{3}{5}x = 13\dfrac{1}{4}$

$\qquad -\dfrac{19}{4} + \dfrac{18}{5}x = \dfrac{53}{4}$

$\qquad\qquad \dfrac{18}{5}x = \dfrac{72}{4}$

$\qquad\qquad\quad x = \dfrac{72}{4}\left(\dfrac{5}{18}\right)$

$\qquad\qquad\quad x = 5$

**2.** $0.3x - 0.02x + 0.2 = 1.18$

$\qquad\qquad\qquad 0.28x = 0.98$

$\qquad\qquad\qquad\quad\ x = 3.5$

**3.** $7p + 3w = w - 12 - 3p$

$\qquad 10p = -2w - 12$

$\qquad\ \ p = -\dfrac{2}{10}w - \dfrac{12}{10}$

$\qquad\ \ p = -\dfrac{1}{5}w - \dfrac{6}{5}$

**4.** 315

$\quad\ 3 \cdot 105$

$\qquad\ \ 3 \cdot 35$

$\qquad\qquad 5 \cdot 7$

$315 = 3 \cdot 3 \cdot 5 \cdot 7$

**Saxon** Algebra 1

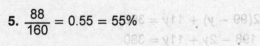
**5.** $\frac{88}{160} = 0.55 = 55\%$

**6.** $1.40(70) = x$

$\quad x = 98$

**7.** "20% of $x$ is 18"

$\quad 0.20x = 18$

$\quad\quad x = 90$

**8.** $\frac{y}{11} = x$

$\quad y = 11x$

This is a direct variation. It is in $y = kx$ form.

**9.** $3y = x$

$\quad y = \frac{1}{3}x$

Yes. It can be written in $y = kx$ form.

**10.** $\left(\frac{10x^3}{y}\right)^2\left(-2x^2y^2\right)^3$

$= \left(100x^6y^{-2}\right)\left(-8x^6y^6\right)$

$= -800x^{12}y^4$

**11.** 63% of $22,000 = x$

$\quad 0.63(22,000) = x$

$\quad\quad x = 13,860$ customers

**12. a.** $A = \pi r^2$

$\quad A = \pi(10x)^2$

$\quad A = \pi100x^2$

**b.** $A = l \cdot w$

$\quad A = (20x)(20x)$

$\quad A = 400x^2$

**c.** $\frac{\pi100x^2}{400x^2}$

$\quad \frac{\pi}{4}$

**13.** Sample: The origin $(0,0)$ will always make the equation $y = kx$ true.

**14.** $3y = -2x$, or $y = -\frac{2}{3}x$, is the only choice that is in $y = kx$ form. The answer is **D**.

**15.** $\frac{3.65}{5.00} = \frac{y}{8.00}$

$\quad 5.00y = 3.65(8.00)$

$\quad 5.00y = 29.20$

$\quad\quad y = 5.84$ euros

**16.** $-4y + x = 2$

$\quad -4y = -x + 2$

$\quad\quad y = \frac{1}{4}x - \frac{1}{2}$

**17.** circle: closed

arrowhead: shaded from 4.6 pointing to the left.

$z \leq 4.6$

**18.** $V = \frac{1}{3}(\text{area of base})(\text{height})$

$\quad V = \frac{1}{3}(l^2)(h)$

$\quad 128 = \frac{1}{3}(l^2)(6)$

$\quad 128 = 2l^2$

$\quad\quad l^2 = 64$

$\quad\quad l = 8$ feet

**19.** Any data set where 9 is the middle value, 9 is the average, and the value 12 appears more than any other value will satisfy the criteria. Sample: 3, 7, 8, 9, 12, 12, 12.

**20.** $P = 2(l + w)$

$\quad P = 2\left(\frac{150x + 200}{2x + 4} + \frac{60x + 220}{2x + 4}\right)$

$\quad = 2\left(\frac{210x + 420}{2x + 4}\right)$

$\quad = \frac{210x + 420}{x + 2}$

$\quad = \frac{210(x + 2)}{x + 2}$

$\quad = 210$ feet

**21.** $y - y_1 = m(x - x_1)$

$\quad y - 8 = \frac{1}{2}(x - 2)$

**22.** Sample: the degree of the highest-degree term in the polynomial

**23.** $a^2b^3 = 2 + 3 = 5$

$\quad a^3b^4 = 3 + 4 = 7$

$\quad 2ab = 1 + 1 = 2$

The degree of the polynomial is 7. The answer is **C**.

**Saxon** Algebra 1

**24.** LE = 66

$Q_1 = \dfrac{70 + 72}{2} = 72.5$

median $= \dfrac{84 + 88}{2} = 86$

$Q_3 = \dfrac{99 + 103}{2} = 101$

UE = 105

IQR = 101 − 72.5 = 28.5

**Average High Temperature in Phoenix, AZ**

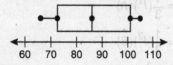

**25.** LE = 201

$Q_1 = 236$

median = 241

$Q_3 = 267$

UE = 360

IQR = 267 − 236 = 31

$Q_1 - 1.5(\text{IQR}) = 236 - 1.5(31) = 189.5$

$Q_3 + 1.5(\text{IQR}) = 267 + 1.5(31) = 313.5$

360 is an outlier.

**Marathon Completion Times (min)**

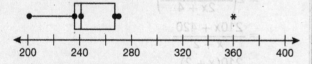

**26.** Student A; Sample: Student B used the median instead of $Q_3$ in the outlier formula.

**27.** $4s = 3(s + 1)$

$4s = 3s + 3$

$s = 3$

**28.** Student A; Sample: The solution of Student B is incorrect because it only satisfied one equation.

**29.** The system is

$81 + x + y = 180$

$2x + 2(5.5y) = 360$

Solve the system.

$81 + x + y = 180$

$x + y = 99$

$x = 99 - y$

$2(99 - y) + 11y = 360$

$198 - 2y + 11y = 360$

$9y = 162$

$y = 18$

$2x + 11(18) = 360$

$2x + 198 = 360$

$2x = 162$

$x = 81$

**30. a.** $t = 5 + m$

$t - 3 = 2m$

$t = 2m + 3$

**b.** $5 + m = 2m + 3$

$2 = m$

$t = 5 + m$

$t = 5 + 2$

$t = 7$

**c.** Sample: If 5 years were taken away from Thomas's age, the result would be 2 years, which is Miguel's age. If 3 years were taken away from Thomas's age, the result would be 4 years, which is equivalent to twice Miguel's age.

## LESSON 57

**Warm Up 57**

**1.** prime

**2.** $18 = 2 \cdot 9$

$18 = 2 \cdot 2 \cdot 3$

**3.** $110 = 2 \cdot 55$

$110 = 2 \cdot 5 \cdot 11$

**4.** $(3x + 27)$

$= 3(x + 9)$

**5.** $(4x^3 + 14x)$

$= 2x(2x^2 + 7)$

**Lesson Practice 57**

**a.** $16 = 2 \cdot 2 \cdot 2 \cdot 2$

$42 = 2 \cdot 3 \cdot 7$

$\text{LCM} = 2 \cdot 2 \cdot 2 \cdot 2 \cdot 3 \cdot 7 = 336$

**Saxon** Algebra 1

**b.** $8 = 2 \cdot 2 \cdot 2$

$12 = 2 \cdot 2 \cdot 3$

$17 = 1 \cdot 17$

$LCM = 2 \cdot 2 \cdot 2 \cdot 3 \cdot 1 \cdot 17 = 408$

**c.** $6c^2d^7 = 2 \cdot 3 \cdot c \cdot c \cdot d \cdot d \cdot d \cdot$
$\quad\quad d \cdot d \cdot d \cdot d$

$15c^5d = 3 \cdot 5 \cdot c \cdot c \cdot c \cdot c \cdot c \cdot d$

$LCM = 2 \cdot 3 \cdot 5 \cdot c \cdot c \cdot c \cdot c \cdot c \cdot$
$\quad\quad d \cdot d \cdot d \cdot d \cdot d \cdot d \cdot d = 30c^5d^7$

**d.** $4k^4p^3n^2 = 2 \cdot 2 \cdot k \cdot k \cdot k \cdot k \cdot p \cdot p \cdot p \cdot n \cdot n$

$5k^2p^3 = 1 \cdot 5 \cdot k \cdot k \cdot p \cdot p \cdot p$

$20n^4k^3 = 2 \cdot 2 \cdot 5 \cdot n \cdot n \cdot n \cdot n \cdot k \cdot k \cdot k$

$LCM = 1 \cdot 2 \cdot 2 \cdot 5 \cdot k \cdot k \cdot k \cdot k \cdot p \cdot p \cdot p \cdot$
$\quad\quad n \cdot n \cdot n \cdot n$

$\quad = 20k^4p^3n^4$

**e.** $(3x + 5) = 1 \cdot (3x + 5)$

$(2x - 7) = 1 \cdot (2x - 7)$

$LCM = 1 \cdot (3x + 5) \cdot (2x - 7)$

$\quad = (3x + 5)(2x - 7)$

**f.** $(15c^2 - 3c) = 1 \cdot 3c \cdot (5c - 1)$

$(35c - 7) = 1 \cdot 7 \cdot (5c - 1)$

$LCM = 1 \cdot 7 \cdot 3c \cdot (5c - 1) = 21c(5c - 1)$

**g.** $(8f^5 - 24f^2) = 8f^2(f^3 - 3)$

$(8f^5 - 24f^2) = 2 \cdot 2 \cdot 2 \cdot f \cdot f \cdot (f^3 - 3)$

$(18f^3 - 54f^4) = 18f^3(1 - 3f)$

$(18f^3 - 54f^4) = 2 \cdot 3 \cdot 3 \cdot f \cdot f \cdot f \cdot (1 - 3f)$

$LCM = 2 \cdot 2 \cdot 2 \cdot 3 \cdot 3 \cdot f \cdot f \cdot f \cdot$
$\quad\quad (f^3 - 3) \cdot (1 - 3f)$

$\quad = 72f^3(f^3 - 3)(1 - 3f)$

**h.** $24 = 2 \cdot 2 \cdot 2 \cdot 3$

$36 = 2 \cdot 2 \cdot 3 \cdot 3$

$60 = 2 \cdot 2 \cdot 3 \cdot 5$

$LCM = 2 \cdot 2 \cdot 2 \cdot 3 \cdot 3 \cdot 5$

$\quad = 360$ backpacks

## Practice 57

**1.** $s + 4t = r$

$\quad s = r - 4t$

**2.** $3m - 7n = p$

$\quad 3m = p + 7n$

$\quad m = \dfrac{p + 7n}{3}$

**3.** $\dfrac{3}{4} = \dfrac{a + 5}{21}$

$\quad 4a + 20 = 63$

$\quad 4a = 43$

$\quad a = 10.75$

**4.** $\dfrac{3}{y - 3} = \dfrac{1}{9}$

$\quad 27 = y - 3$

$\quad y = 30$

**5.** $\dfrac{50 - 20}{50} = x$

$\quad 30 = 50x$

$\quad x = 0.6$

$\quad x = 60\%$

It is a 60% decrease because the new value is less than the original value.

**6.** $\dfrac{96 - 12}{12} = x$

$\quad 84 = 12x$

$\quad x = 7.0$

$\quad x = 700\%$

It is a 700% increase because the new value is greater than the original value.

**7.** The LCM is found by using all the factors of the two numbers the greatest number of times they appear in either number. The GCF is found by determining the greatest single factor that appears in both numbers.

**8.** $24 = 2 \cdot 2 \cdot 2 \cdot 3$

$84 = 2 \cdot 2 \cdot 3 \cdot 7$

$LCM = 2 \cdot 2 \cdot 2 \cdot 3 \cdot 7 = 168$

**9.** $24 = 2 \cdot 2 \cdot 2 \cdot 3$

$84 = 2 \cdot 2 \cdot 3 \cdot 7$

$GCF = 2 \cdot 2 \cdot 3 = 12$

**Saxon** Algebra 1

**10.** Plot the point (6, 5). A horizontal line will go through this point and always have an *x*-value of 6. A vertical line will go through this point and always have a *y*-value of 5.

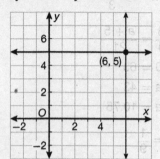

**11. a.** $m = \dfrac{y_2 - y_1}{x_2 - x_1}$

$m = \dfrac{88 - 75}{12 - 6}$

$m = \dfrac{13}{6}$

$m = 2.1\overline{6}°F$ per hour

**b.** $m = \dfrac{y_2 - y_1}{x_2 - x_1}$

$m = \dfrac{82 - 88}{14 - 12}$

$m = \dfrac{-6}{2}$

$m = -3°F$ per hour

**c.** $m = \dfrac{y_2 - y_1}{x_2 - x_1}$

$m = \dfrac{92 - 75}{16 - 6}$

$m = \dfrac{17}{10}$

$m = 1.7°F$ per hour

**12. a.** Draw a number line valued from 26 to 51. Plot each data point above the corresponding number on the line. For values that appear in the data set more than once, place each additional point above the previous.

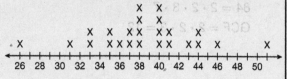

**b.** The shape of the data is a bell curve with a peak at 40.

**c.** Most of the students could hop on one leg for 31 to 46 seconds.

**13.** $\dfrac{900 - 600}{600} = x$

$300 = 600x$

$x = 0.5$

$x = 50\%$

**14.**

$$\begin{array}{r} -9z^3 \qquad\qquad - 3z \\ + \qquad - 8z^2 + 13z \\ \hline -9z^3 - 8z^2 + 10z \end{array}$$

**15. a.** Sample: The domain is made of whole numbers and the range is rational numbers greater than or equal to 5.95.

**b.** $b = 5.95$

$m = 0.04$

$x = $ minutes

$y = 0.04x + 5.95$

**16.** Set the denominator equal to 0.

$7k - 21 = 0$

$7k = 21$

$k = 3$

$k \neq 3$

Simplify.

$\dfrac{k - 3}{7k - 21}$

$= \dfrac{k - 3}{7(k - 3)}$

$= \dfrac{1}{7}, \; k \neq 3$

**17.** circle: filled

arrowhead: shaded from 2 pointing to the right.

$n \geq 2$

**18.** $b = 40$

rate of change = 2

$w = $ weeks

$m = 2w + 40$

Use 60 for *m*.

$60 = 2w + 40$

$20 = 2w$

$w = 10$

Joyce will jog 60 miles in 10 weeks so to jog more than 60 miles, it will take 11 weeks.

**Saxon** Algebra 1

**19.** $Q_1 = \dfrac{127 + 131}{2} = 129$

$Q_3 = \dfrac{162 + 169}{2} = 165.5$

IQR = 165.5 − 129 = 36.5

129 − 1.5(36.5) = 74.25

165.5 + 1.5(36.5) = 220.25

221 is an outlier

**20.** The upper extreme is the point at the extreme right of the box-and-whisker plot. In this plot, it is the same value as $Q_3$(7). The answer is **C**.

**21. a.** Stephen: $y = 2x + 16$

Robert: $y = 3x + 14$

**b.** $2x + 16 = 3x + 14$

$x = 2$ shots

**c.** $y = 2(2) + 16$

$y = 4 + 16$

$y = 20$ points

$y = 3(2) + 14$

$y = 6 + 14$

$y = 20$ points

**22.** Graph both equations and then use the intersection command.

The intersection point and the solution of the system is (0, 4).

**23.** $7 + y = x$

$y = x − 7$

No. This is not a direct variation because the expression is not in $y = kx$ form.

**24.** $\dfrac{63.5}{25} = \dfrac{x}{9}$

$25x = 571.5$

$x = 22.86$ cm

**25.** Student B; Sample: Student A substituted 24 months instead of 24 years.

**26.** $y = $ radius

$x = $ circumference

$y = kx$

$10 = k(20\pi)$

$k = \dfrac{1}{2\pi}$

**29** $= \dfrac{1}{2\pi}(x)$

$x = 58\pi$ feet

**27. a.** $y = $ fluid pressure

$x = $ depth of object

$y = kx$

$124.8 = k(2)$

$k = 62.4$

$y = 62.4x$

**b.** Graph (2, 124.8) and (0, 0) and draw a line through them.

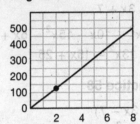

At 9 feet below the surface, there are approximately 560 pounds per square foot.

**c.** Locate 312 lbs on the y-axis and find the approximate depth from the x-axis (5 feet).

**28.** Sample: The LCM is the least common denominator of the fractions.

**29.** $15k^{11} = 3 \cdot 5 \cdot k \cdot k \cdot k \cdot k \cdot k \cdot k \cdot k \cdot k \cdot k \cdot k \cdot k$

$36k^6 = 2 \cdot 2 \cdot 3 \cdot 3 \cdot k \cdot k \cdot k \cdot k \cdot k \cdot k$

LCM $= 2 \cdot 2 \cdot 3 \cdot 3 \cdot 5 \cdot k \cdot k \cdot k \cdot k \cdot k \cdot k \cdot k \cdot k \cdot k \cdot k \cdot k = 180k^{11}$

The answer is **C**.

**30.** $4x^3y^6 = 2 \cdot 2 \cdot x \cdot x \cdot x \cdot y \cdot y \cdot y \cdot y \cdot y \cdot y$

$2xy^2 = 1 \cdot 2 \cdot x \cdot y \cdot y$

$6x^4y = 2 \cdot 3 \cdot x \cdot x \cdot x \cdot x \cdot y$

LCM $= 2 \cdot 2 \cdot 3 \cdot x \cdot x \cdot x \cdot x \cdot y \cdot y \cdot$

$y \cdot y \cdot y \cdot y = 12x^4y^6$

**Saxon** Algebra 1

Solutions Key

# Solutions Key

## LESSON 58

### Warm Up 58

1. trinomial

2. $2xy^2(3x^2y + 5xy - 6x)$
$= 6x^3y^3 + 10x^2y^3 - 12x^2y^2$

3. $-3xy(x^3y^2 - 4xy - 7xy^2)$
$= -3x^4y^3 + 12x^2y^2 + 21x^2y^3$

4. $3x^2 + 2x - 5x + 7$
$= 3x^2 - 3x + 7$

5. $6x^3 + 2x^2 - 10x - 15x^2 - 5x + 25$
$= 6x^3 - 13x^2 - 15x + 25$

### Lesson Practice 58

a. $3x(x^2 + 3x - 7)$
$= 3x^3 + 9x^2 - 21x$

b. $-4x(x^2 + 2x - 3)$
$= -4x^3 - 8x^2 + 12x$

c. $(x + 4)(x + 3)$
$= x(x + 3)$
$= x^2 + 3x$
$= 4(x + 3)$
$= 4x + 12$
$= x^2 + 3x + 4x + 12$
$= x^2 + 7x + 12$

d. $(x - 5)(x - 2)$
$= x(x - 2)$
$= x^2 - 2x$
$= -5(x - 2)$
$= -5x + 10$
$= x^2 - 2x - 5x + 10$
$= x^2 - 7x + 10$

e. $(x + 6)(x + 4)$
$= x^2 + 4x + 6x + 24$
$= x^2 + 10x + 24$

f. $(x - 8)(x - 1)$
$= x^2 - x - 8x + 8$
$= x^2 - 9x + 8$

g. $(2x + 2)(x^2 - 3x - 2)$
$= 2x(x^2 - 3x - 2)$
$= 2x^3 - 6x^2 - 4x$
$= 2(x^2 - 3x - 2)$
$= 2x^2 - 6x - 4$
$= 2x^3 - 6x^2 - 4x + 2x^2 - 6x - 4$
$= 2x^3 - 4x^2 - 10x - 4$

h. $(5x - 2)(x^2 - 3x - 2)$

$$
\begin{array}{r}
x^2 - 3x - 2 \\
5x - 2 \\
\hline
-2x^2 + 6x + 4 \\
+5x^3 - 15x^2 - 10x \\
\hline
5x^3 - 17x^2 - 4x + 4
\end{array}
$$

i. $A = l \cdot w$
$= (x + 6)(x^2 + 4x - 2)$
$x(x^2 + 4x - 2)$
$x^3 + 4x^2 - 2x$
$6(x^2 + 4x - 2)$
$6x^2 + 24x - 12$
$= x^3 + 4x^2 - 2x + 6x^2 + 24x - 12$
$A = x^3 + 10x^2 + 22x - 12$ in.$^2$

## Practice 58

1. $x \le -2$
circle: filled
arrowhead: shaded from $-2$ pointing to the left.

2. $x > 2$
circle: open
arrowhead: shaded from 2 pointing to the right.

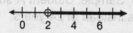

3. $4(2x - 3) = 3 + 8x - 11$
$8x - 12 = 8x - 8$
$0x = 4$
There is no solution for this equation.

4. $-5m + 2 + 8m = 2m + 11$
$3m + 2 = 2m + 11$
$m = 9$

**Saxon** Algebra 1

**5.** $(-2x + 1)(-3x + 2)$
$= 6x^2 - 4x - 3x + 2$
$= 6x^2 - 7x + 2$
The answer is **D**.

**6.** $A = l \cdot w$
$A = (x + 5)(3x^2 + 6x + 4)$
$\quad x(3x^2 + 6x + 4)$
$\quad 3x^3 + 6x^2 + 4x$
$\quad 5(3x^2 + 6x + 4)$
$\quad 15x^2 + 30x + 20$
$A = 3x^3 + 6x^2 + 4x + 15x^2 + 30x + 20$
$A = 3x^3 + 21x^2 + 34x + 20$ in.$^2$

**7.** $(x - 2)(x + 3)$
$= x^2 + 3x - 2x - 6$
$= x^2 + x - 6$

**8.** $(2x - 3)(2x + 3)$
$= 4x^2 + 6x - 6x - 9$
$= 4x^2 - 9$

**9.** No; Sample: He multiplied the exponents instead of adding.

**10.** $5(x^2 + 3x - 7)$
$= 5x^2 + 15x - 35$

**11.** $35 = 5 \cdot 7$
$60 = 2 \cdot 2 \cdot 3 \cdot 5$
$100 = 2 \cdot 2 \cdot 5 \cdot 5$
$LCM = 2 \cdot 2 \cdot 3 \cdot 5 \cdot 5 \cdot 7 = 2100$

**12.** 8 feet = 96 inches
$96 = 2 \cdot 2 \cdot 2 \cdot 2 \cdot 2 \cdot 3$
$16 = 2 \cdot 2 \cdot 2 \cdot 2$
$LCM = 2 \cdot 2 \cdot 2 \cdot 2 \cdot 2 \cdot 3$
$\quad\quad = 96$ inches (8 feet)

**13.** Student B; Sample: Student A only used factors that both expressions had in common–the GCF.

**14.** The angles in a parallelogram add up to 360 degrees, but it is not a rectangle.

**15. a.** $10 = 2 \cdot 5$
$24 = 2 \cdot 2 \cdot 2 \cdot 3$
$15 = 3 \cdot 5$
$LCM = 2 \cdot 2 \cdot 2 \cdot 3 \cdot 5 = 120$
The 120th pair of shoes blinks, glows, and is waterproof, so 119 pairs are made before that happens.

**b.** $2000 \div 120 = 16.6$
16 pairs will blink, glow, and are waterproof.

**16.** Find the ratio $\frac{y}{x}$ for each ordered pair.
$\frac{y}{x} = \frac{6}{9} = \frac{2}{3}$
$\frac{y}{x} = \frac{8}{11}$
$\frac{y}{x} = \frac{19}{22}$
The ordered pairs do not represent a direct variation because the ratio is not the same for all pairs.

**17.** $y$ = seconds
$x$ = kilometers
$y = kx$
$27 = k(9)$
$k = 3$
$51 = 3x$
$x = 17$ kilometers

**18.** Student A; Sample: Student B reversed the original $x$- and $y$-values in the equation.

**19.** LE = point at extreme left = 3
$Q_1$ = point at left end of box = 14
median = point inside of box = 23
$Q_3$ = point at right end of box = 38
UE = point at extreme right = 62
$IQR = 38 - 14 = 24$

**20.** $\frac{81}{108} = x$
$81 = 108x$
$x = 0.75$ or 75%

**21.** $\dfrac{9x - 81}{4x^2 - 36x}$

$= \dfrac{9(x - 9)}{4x(x - 9)}$

$= \dfrac{9}{4x}, x \neq 0$

**22.** $\dfrac{(x - 4)(2x - 3)}{7x - 28}$

$= \dfrac{(x - 4)(2x - 3)}{7(x - 4)}$

$= \dfrac{2x - 3}{7}, x \neq 4, x \neq 9$

**23.** $m^2 = \dfrac{m_0{}^2}{1 - \dfrac{v^2}{c^2}}$

$\dfrac{v^2}{c^2} \neq 1$

The expression is undefined when $\dfrac{v^2}{c^2} = 1$, so $v^2 \neq c^2$ (the velocity cannot equal the speed of light).

**24. a.** "no more than" is the same as "less than or equal to" $5\frac{1}{2} + \frac{1}{2}n \leq 10$

**b.** The sum of $5\frac{1}{2}$ and $\frac{1}{2}n$ is no greater than 10.

**25.** mean $= \dfrac{0.2 + 2.9 + 5.4 + 9.4 + 10.9}{5}$

$= \dfrac{28.8}{5}$

$= 5.76$ inches

mean $= \dfrac{0.2 + 3.6 + 4.3 + 5.5 + 12.6}{5}$

$= \dfrac{26.2}{5}$

$= 5.24$ inches

St. Paul receives less snow.

**26.** $4x - 2y = 10$

$-2y = -4x + 10$

$y = 2x - 5$

$y = 2(0) - 5 = -5$

$y = 2(2) - 5 = 4 - 5 = -1$

$y = 2(3) - 5 = 6 - 5 = 1$

$y = 2(4) - 5 = 8 - 5 = 3$

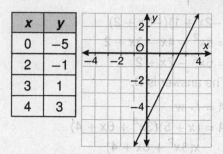

| x | y |
|---|---|
| 0 | −5 |
| 2 | −1 |
| 3 | 1 |
| 4 | 3 |

The pairs of values that satisfy the equation are recorded in the table of values and form coordinates that are points on the line in the graph.

**27.** $\quad 1.521t^2 - 2.304t + 56.659$

$\underline{+ -0.104t^2 + 5.879t + 196.432}$

$\quad 1.417t^2 + 3.575t + 253.091$

**28.** Find the slope.

$m = \dfrac{y_2 - y_1}{x_2 - x_1}$

$m = \dfrac{8 - 9}{16 - 8}$

$m = -\dfrac{1}{8}$

Use the point-slope formula.

$y - y_1 = m(x - x_1)$

$y - 9 = -\dfrac{1}{8}(x - 8)$

$y - 9 = -\dfrac{1}{8}x + 1$

$y = -\dfrac{1}{8}x + 10$

Substitute −8 for x.

$y = -\dfrac{1}{8}(-8) + 10$

$y = 1 + 10$

$y = 11$

**29.** $\dfrac{4m - 8}{2m - 4}$

$= \dfrac{4(m - 2)}{2(m - 2)}$

$= 2, m \neq 2$

**30.** $y$ = number of guests

$m$ = servings per guest

$x$ = number of servings available

$y = mx$

$y = 1(10)$

$y = 10$

10 or fewer guests could come; Sample: A number line shows all the real number solutions for an inequality, and because the number of guests must be a natural number, the graph shows too many possible solutions.

## LESSON 59

### Warm Up 59

**1.** solution

**2.**

| $3x + 2y = 3$ | $x - 3y = -10$ |
|---|---|
| $3(-1) + 2(3) = 3$ | $-1 - 3(3) = -10$ |
| $-3 + 6 = 3$ | $-1 - 9 = -10$ |
| $3 = 3$ | $-10 = -10$ |

Yes, it is a solution to the system.

**3.** $3x + 7 = 5x - 28$

$35 = 2x$

$x = \dfrac{35}{2}$

**4.** $5x + 2 = 3x + 26$

$2x = 24$

$x = 12$

### Lesson Practice 59

**a.** Solve for $x$.

$y = 4x - 3$

$y = 3x - 5$

$4x - 3 = 3x - 5$

$x = -2$

Solve for $y$.

$y = 4(-2) - 3$

$y = -8 - 3$

$y = -11$

**b.** Solve for $y$.

$x = 3y - 11$

$5x + 2y = -4$

$5(3y - 11) + 2y = -4$

$15y - 55 + 2y = -4$

$17y = 51$

$y = 3$

Solve for $x$.

$x = 3(3) - 11$

$x = 9 - 11$

$x = -2$

**c.** Solve for $x$

$4x + 3y = 2$

$2x + y = 6$

$y = -2x + 6$

$4x + 3(-2x + 6) = 2$

$4x - 6x + 18 = 2$

$-2x = -16$

$x = 8$

Solve for $y$.

$y = -2(8) + 6$

$y = -16 + 6$

$y = -10$

**d.** Solve for $y$.

$4x + 3y = 19$

$7x - 6y = -23$

$4x = -3y + 19$

$x = -\dfrac{3}{4}y + \dfrac{19}{4}$

$7\left(-\dfrac{3}{4}y + \dfrac{19}{4}\right) - 6y = -23$

$-\dfrac{21}{4}y + \dfrac{133}{4} - 6y = -23$

$-21y + 133 - 24y = -92$

$-45y = -225$

$y = 5$

Solve for $x$.

$4x + 3(5) = 19$

$4x + 15 = 19$

$4x = 4$

$x = 1$

**e.** Let $x$ = books and $y$ = pencils.

$5x + 10y = 36$

$2x + 40y = 18$

$5x = -10y + 36$

$x = -2y + \dfrac{36}{5}$

183

Solve for $y$.

$$2\left(-2y + \frac{36}{5}\right) + 40y = 18$$

$$-4y + \frac{72}{5} + 40y = 18$$

$$-20y + 72 + 200y = 90$$

$$180y = 18$$

$$y = 0.10$$

Solve for $x$.

$$5x + 10(0.10) = 36$$

$$5x + 1 = 36$$

$$5x = 35$$

$$x = 7$$

Books cost $7 and pencils cost $0.10.

**Practice 59**

**1.** $-[-(-k)] - (-2)(-2 + k) = -k - (4k + 3)$

$$-(k) - (4 - 2k) = -k - 4k - 3$$

$$-k - 4 + 2k = -5k - 3$$

$$k - 4 = -5k - 3$$

$$6k = 1$$

$$k = \frac{1}{6}$$

**2.** $\frac{1}{3} + 5\frac{1}{3}k + 3\frac{2}{9} = 0$

$$5\frac{1}{3}k = -\frac{1}{3} - 3\frac{2}{9}$$

$$\frac{16}{3}k = -\frac{1}{3} - \frac{29}{9}$$

$$48k = -3 - 29$$

$$48k = -32$$

$$k = -\frac{32}{48}$$

$$k = -\frac{2}{3}$$

**3.** $\sqrt{9} + \sqrt{16} - \sqrt{225}$

$3 + 4 - 15$

$7 - 15$

$-8$

**4.** Any fraction that does not simplify into a whole number would meet the criteria. Sample: $\frac{7}{4}$

**5.** $\sqrt{49} = 7$ and 7 is a rational number ($7 = \frac{7}{1}$). The statement is true.

**6.** $y = 3x - 5$

$$y = -2x + 15$$

$$3x - 5 = -2x + 15$$

$$5x = 20$$

$$x = 4$$

$$y = 3(4) - 5$$

$$y = 12 - 5$$

$$y = 7$$

The solution is (4, 7).

**7.** $y = -8x + 21$

$$y = -3x + 6$$

$$-8x + 21 = -3x + 6$$

$$-5x = -15$$

$$x = 3$$

$$y = -8(3) + 21$$

$$y = -24 + 21$$

$$y = -3$$

The solution is (3, −3).

**8.** Sample: The point satisfies every equation in the system.

**9.** $4x + 9y = 75$

$$8x + 6y = 66$$

$$4x = -9y + 75$$

$$x = -\frac{9}{4}y + \frac{75}{4}$$

$$8\left(-\frac{9}{4}y + \frac{75}{4}\right) + 6y = 66$$

$$-18y + 150 + 6y = 66$$

$$-12y = -84$$

$$y = 7$$

$$4x + 9(7) = 75$$

$$4x + 63 = 75$$

$$4x = 12$$

$$x = 3$$

The solution is (3, 7). The answer is **A**.

**10.** $x + y = 64$

$$x - y = 14$$

$$x = -y + 64$$

$$-y + 64 - y = 14$$

$$-2y = -50$$

$$y = 25$$

$$x + 25 = 64$$

$x = 39$

The numbers are 39 and 25.

**11.** Student A; Sample: Student B multiplied the exponents instead of adding them.

**12.** $A = l \cdot w$

$= (4x + 8)(x + 8)$

$= 4x^2 + 32x + 8x + 64$

$= 4x^2 + 40x + 64$ square feet

**13. a.** $A = l \cdot w$

$= (5x + 1)(5x + 1)$

$= 25x^2 + 5x + 5x + 1$

$= 25x^2 + 10x + 1$ square inches

**b.** $V = (5x + 1)(25x^2 + 10x + 1)$

$= 125x^3 + 50x^2 + 5x + 25x^2 + 10x + 1$

$= 125x^3 + 75x^2 + 15x + 1$ inches cubed

**14.** $A = \frac{1}{2}bh$

$= \dfrac{(6x^2 + 8x + 12)(x - 1)}{2}$

$= \dfrac{6x^3 + 8x^2 + 12x - 6x^2 - 8x - 12}{2}$

$= \dfrac{6x^3 + 2x^2 + 4x - 12}{2}$

$= 3x^3 + x^2 + 2x - 6$ square feet

**15.** $4x(x^2 + 2x - 9)$

$= 4x^3 + 8x^2 - 36x$

**16.** $b = -1$

$m = 2$

$y = mx + b$

$y = 2x - 1$

**17.** $4 + 3 = 7$

$1 + 1 = 2$

$2 + 3 = 5$

The degree is 7.

**18.** LE $= 0.380$

$Q_1 = 0.451$

median $= 0.505$

$Q_3 = 0.580$

UE $= 0.604$

IQR $= 0.580 - 0.451 = 0.129$

$0.451 - 1.5(0.129) = 0.258$

$0.580 + 1.5(0.129) = 0.774$

There are no outliers.

**Percentage of Games Won**

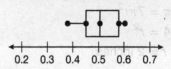

**19.** $y = kx$

$17 = k \cdot 4$

$k = 4.25$

$y = 4.25(18)$

$y = \$76.50$

**20.** The point $(4, -12)$ represents the same direct variation. The answer is **C**.

**21.** $16c^6 = 2 \cdot 2 \cdot 2 \cdot 2 \cdot c \cdot c \cdot c \cdot c \cdot c \cdot c$

$24c^3 = 2 \cdot 2 \cdot 2 \cdot 3 \cdot c \cdot c \cdot c$

LCM $= 2 \cdot 2 \cdot 2 \cdot 2 \cdot 3 \cdot c \cdot c \cdot c \cdot c \cdot c \cdot c$

$= 48c^6$

**22.** $20x^3y = 2 \cdot 2 \cdot 5 \cdot x \cdot x \cdot x \cdot y$

$12xy^3c = 2 \cdot 2 \cdot 3 \cdot x \cdot y \cdot y \cdot y \cdot c$

LCM $= 2 \cdot 2 \cdot 3 \cdot 5 \cdot x \cdot x \cdot x \cdot y \cdot y \cdot y \cdot c$

$= 60x^3y^3c$

**23.** $300d^2 = 2 \cdot 2 \cdot 3 \cdot 5 \cdot 5 \cdot d \cdot d$

$90d^4 = 2 \cdot 3 \cdot 3 \cdot 5 \cdot d \cdot d \cdot d \cdot d$

LCM $= 2 \cdot 2 \cdot 3 \cdot 3 \cdot 5 \cdot 5 \cdot d \cdot d \cdot d \cdot d$

$= 900d^4$

**24.** $\dfrac{3x - 24}{24x + 9}$

$= \dfrac{3(x - 8)}{3(8x + 3)}$

$= \dfrac{x - 8}{8x + 3}$

**25.** $m = \dfrac{y_2 - y_1}{x_2 - x_1}$

$m = \dfrac{-1 - 1}{1 + 1}$

$m = \dfrac{-2}{2}$

$m = -1$

**26.** A bird is an animal that has wings, but it is not an insect.

**27. a.** $V = \pi r^2 h$

$28\pi = \pi r^2 (7)$

$28\pi = 7\pi r^2$

**b.** $28\pi = 7\pi r^2$

$4 = r^2$

$r = 2$ inches

**28.** slope $= \dfrac{\text{gravity on Jupiter}}{\text{gravity on Earth}} = \dfrac{2.34}{1} = 2.34$

$b = 0$

$y = mx + b$

$y = 2.34x$

**29.** If a number is a rational number, then it is an integer; The number 0.5 is a rational number, but it is not an integer.

**30.** Sample: An excluded value is the value of the variable that makes the denominator equal 0. It is excluded because division by 0 is undefined.

## LESSON 60

## Warm Up 60

**1.** The answer is **C**.

**2.** $(2x + 3)(3x - 5)$

$= 6x^2 - 10x + 9x - 15$

$= 6x^2 - x - 15$

**3.** $(3x + 7)(5x + 6)$

$= 15x^2 + 18x + 35x + 42$

$= 15x^2 + 53x + 42$

**4.** $(3x - 2)(3x^2 - x + 7)$

$= 9x^3 - 3x^2 + 21x - 6x^2 + 2x - 14$

$= 9x^3 - 9x^2 + 23x - 14$

## Lesson Practice 60

**a.** $(x + 9)^2$

$= (x)^2 + 2(x)(9) + (9)^2$

$= x^2 + 18x + 81$

**b.** $(3x + 5)^2$

$= (3x)^2 + 2(3x)(5) + (5)^2$

$= 9x^2 + 30x + 25$

**c.** $(x - 1)^2$

$= (x)^2 - 2(x)(1) + (1)^2$

$= x^2 - 2x + 1$

**d.** $(8x - 6)^2$

$= (8x)^2 - 2(8x)(6) + (6)^2$

$= 64x^2 - 96x + 36$

**e.** $(x + 8)(x - 8)$

$= x^2 - 64$

**f.** $(3x + 2)(3x - 2)$

$= 9x^2 - 4$

**g.** $28^2$

$= (30 - 2)^2$

$= (30)^2 - 2(30)(2) + (2)^2$

$= 900 - 120 + 4$

$= 784$

**h.** $58 \cdot 62$

$= (60 - 2)(60 + 2)$

$= (60)^2 - (2)^2$

$= 3600 - 4$

$= 3596$

**i.** $A = (x - 6)(x + 6)$

$A = x^2 - 36$

## Practice 60

**1.** $(3k + 2k^2 - 4) - (k^2 + k - 6)$

$= 3k + 2k^2 - 4 - k^2 - k + 6$

$= k^2 + 2k + 2$

**2.** $(-2m + 1) + (6m^2 - m - 2)$

$= -2m + 1 + 6m^2 - m - 2$

$= 6m^2 - 3m - 1$

**3.** $(x + 4)(x - 5)$

$= x^2 - 5x + 4x - 20$

$= x^2 - x - 20$

**4.** $(x + 2)(6x^2 + 4x + 5)$

$= 6x^3 + 4x^2 + 5x + 12x^2 + 8x + 10$

$= 6x^3 + 16x^2 + 13x + 10$

**5.** $(3t - 1)^2$

$= (3t)^2 - 2(3t)(1) + (1)^2$

$= 9t^2 - 6t + 1$

**Saxon** Algebra 1

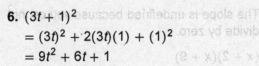
**6.** $(3t + 1)^2$
$= (3t)^2 + 2(3t)(1) + (1)^2$
$= 9t^2 + 6t + 1$

**7.** $(3x + 6)(3x + 6)$
$= (3x + 6)^2$
$= (3x)^2 + 2(3x)(6) + (6)^2$
$= 9x^2 + 36x + 36$ square inches

**8.**
$$y = 2x - 9$$
$$8x - 6y = 34$$
$$8x - 6(2x - 9) = 34$$
$$8x - 12x + 54 = 34$$
$$-4x = -20$$
$$x = 5$$
$$y = 2(5) - 9$$
$$y = 10 - 9$$
$$y = 1$$
The solution is (5, 1).

**9.** $(6x + 7)^2$
$= (6x)^2 + 2(6x)(7) + (7)^2$
$= 36x^2 + 84x + 49$
The answer is **C**.

**10.**
$$y = 2x - 4$$
$$y = x + 5$$
$$x + 5 = 2x - 4$$
$$x = 9$$
$$y = 2(9) - 4$$
$$y = 18 - 4$$
$$y = 14$$
The solutions is (9, 14).

**11.** Sample: You can use the FOIL method to check your work.

**12.** $(9x + 8)(9x + 8) = 81x^2 + 64$
$= (9x + 8)(9x + 8)$
$= 81x^2 + 72x + 72x + 64$
$= 81x^2 + 144x + 64$
The statement is false.

**13.** $P = 2(l + w)$                 $l = 3(9) + 3$
$78 = 2[(3w + 3) + w]$       $l = 27 + 3$
$78 = 6w + 6 + 2w$            $l = 30$ feet
$72 = 8w$
$w = 9$ feet

**14.** Student A; Sample: Student B did not distribute the 6 over the 19.

**15.** Let $x$ = natural light bulb and $y$ = ceiling bulb.
$$5x + 2y = 23$$
$$3x + 4y = 25$$
$$5x = -2y + 23$$
$$x = -\frac{2}{5}y + \frac{23}{5}$$
$$5x = -2(4) + 23$$
$$5x = -8 + 23$$
$$5x = 15$$
$$x = 3$$
$$3\left(-\frac{2}{5}y + \frac{23}{5}\right) + 4y = 25$$
$$-\frac{6}{5}y + \frac{69}{5} + 4y = 25$$
$$-6y + 69 + 20y = 125$$
$$14y = 56$$
$$y = 4$$
Natural light bulbs cost $3 and ceiling bulbs cost $4.

**16.**
$$4g + 7b = 169$$
$$b = 1 + 2g$$
$$4g + 7(1 + 2g) = 169$$
$$4g + 7 + 14g = 169$$
$$18g = 162$$
$$g = 9$$
$$b = 1 + 2(9)$$
$$b = 1 + 18$$
$$b = 19$$
Right now, the girl is 9 years old and the boy is 19 years old. In 10 years, the girl will be 19 years old and the boy will be 29 years old.

**17.** $P = 2(l + w)$
$l = 7w - 4$
$24 = 2(7w - 4 + w)$
$24 = 14w - 8 + 2w$
$32 = 16w$
$w = 2$ cm
$l = 7(2) - 4$
$l = 14 - 4$
$l = 10$ cm

**Saxon** Algebra 1

**18.** LE = 0.84

$$Q_1 = \frac{1.54 + 1.58}{2} = 1.56$$

$$\text{median} = \frac{1.78 + 1.90}{2} = 1.84$$

$$Q_3 = \frac{2.33 + 3.11}{2} = 2.72$$

UE = 6.10

IQR = 2.72 − 1.56 = 1.16

1.56 − 1.5(1.16) = −0.18

2.72 + 1.5(1.16) = 4.46

6.04 and 6.10 are outliers.

**Average Monthly Rainfall in Cloudcroft, NM (in inches)**

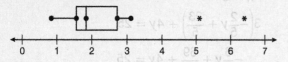

**19.** $6f^4 = 2 \cdot 3 \cdot f \cdot f \cdot f \cdot f$

$4f^2 = 2 \cdot 2 \cdot f \cdot f$

LCM = $2 \cdot 2 \cdot 3 \cdot f \cdot f \cdot f \cdot f = 12f^4$

**20.** $(4x^4 - 14x^3) = 2 \cdot x \cdot x \cdot x \cdot (2x - 7)$

$(6x^2 - 21x) = 3 \cdot x \cdot (2x - 7)$

LCM = $2 \cdot 3 \cdot x \cdot x \cdot x \cdot (2x - 7)$

$= 6x^3(2x - 7)$

The answer is **A**.

**21.** Find the ratio $\frac{y}{x}$ for each ordered pair.

$$\frac{y}{x} = \frac{8}{2} = 4$$

$$\frac{y}{x} = \frac{16}{4} = 4$$

$$\frac{y}{x} = \frac{28}{7} = 4$$

The ordered pairs represent a direct variation because the ratio is the same for all pairs.

**22.** $A = l \cdot w$

$A = (2x + 15)(4x + 25)$

$A = 8x^2 + 50x + 60x + 375$

$A = 8x^2 + 110x + 375$ square feet

**23.** $m = \dfrac{y_2 - y_1}{x_2 - x_1}$

$m = \dfrac{-4 - 5}{-1 + 1}$

$m = \dfrac{-9}{0}$

The slope is undefined because you cannot divide by zero.

**24.** $(x + 2)(x + 9)$

$= x^2 + 9x + 2x + 18$

$= x^2 + 11x + 18$

**25.** Sample: The difference of a number and 2.5 is greater than 4.7.

**26.**     Jose's cards = $t$

Eleanor's cards > $2t$

$$79 > 2t$$

$$2t < 79$$

$$t < 39.5$$

Jose could have 39 cards.

**27. a.** $1^{st}$ week: $x = \dfrac{10}{85} = 0.12 = 12\%$

$2^{nd}$ week: $x = \dfrac{7}{75} = 0.09 = 9\%$

**b.** $x = \dfrac{17}{85} = 0.20 = 20\%$

**28.** Sample: The graph should only include non-negative numbers, because negative speed means moving backward and this cannot happen when driving legally on a road.

**29.** $P = 2(l + w)$

$= 2\left(\dfrac{2a}{3a - 2} + \dfrac{a - 2}{3a - 2}\right)$

$= 2\left(\dfrac{2a + a - 2}{3a - 2}\right)$

$= 2\left(\dfrac{3a - 2}{3a - 2}\right)$

$= 2$ yards

**30.** $y = mx + b$

$y = x - 4$

$m = 1$

$b = -4$

Sample: Using the slope-intercept equation of a line, the slope is the coefficient of $x$ and the $y$-intercept is the number added to or subtracted from $x$.

# INVESTIGATION 6

## Practice Investigation 6

**a.** $f(x) = x$

$f(x) = x + 4$

$f(x) = x + 4$ will have the same slope as $f(x) = x$, but will be shifted up 4 units because of the y-intercept.

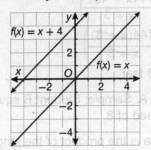

**b.** $f(x) = x$

$f(x) = -x$

$f(x) = -x$ will be a reflection of the original line $f(x) = x$.

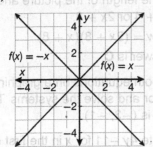

**c.** $f(x) = x$

$f(x) = \frac{1}{2}x$

$f(x) = \frac{1}{2}x$ will have the same y-intercept as $f(x) = x$, but will not be as steep because $\frac{1}{2}$ is less than 1.

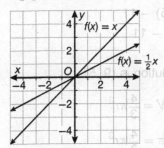

**d.** $f(x) = x$

$f(x) = 4x - 2$

$f(x) = 4x - 2$ will be shifted down 2 units to reflect the y-intercept of –2 and will also be steeper because 4 is greater than 1.

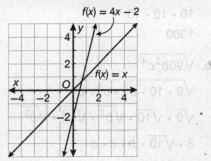

# LESSON 61

## Warm Up 61

1. square root

2. $\sqrt{36} = \sqrt{6^2} = 6$

3. $\sqrt{81} = \sqrt{9^2} = 9$

4. $\sqrt{\frac{1}{4}} = \sqrt{\frac{1^2}{2^2}} = \frac{1}{2}$

5. Since $\sqrt{49} = 7$ and $\sqrt{64} = 8$, $\sqrt{54}$ is between 7 and 8.

## Lesson Practice 61

**a.** $\sqrt{75}$

$\sqrt{25 \cdot 3}$

$\sqrt{25} \cdot \sqrt{3}$

$5\sqrt{3}$

**b.** $\sqrt{63}$

$\sqrt{9 \cdot 7}$

$\sqrt{9} \cdot \sqrt{7}$

$3\sqrt{7}$

**c.** $\sqrt{363}$

$\sqrt{3 \cdot 11 \cdot 11}$

$\sqrt{3} \cdot \sqrt{11} \cdot \sqrt{11}$

$11\sqrt{3}$

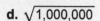

Solutions Key

**d.** $\sqrt{1,000,000}$

$\sqrt{10^6}$

$\sqrt{10^2 \cdot 10^2 \cdot 10^2}$

$\sqrt{10^2} \cdot \sqrt{10^2} \cdot \sqrt{10^2}$

$10 \cdot 10 \cdot 10$

$1000$

**e.** $\sqrt{90b^2c^4}$

$\sqrt{9 \cdot 10 \cdot b^2 \cdot c^2 \cdot c^2}$

$\sqrt{9} \cdot \sqrt{10} \cdot \sqrt{b^2} \cdot \sqrt{c^2} \cdot \sqrt{c^2}$

$3 \cdot \sqrt{10} \cdot b \cdot c \cdot c$

$3bc^2\sqrt{10}$

**f.** $\sqrt{25x^3y^7}$

$\sqrt{25 \cdot x^2 \cdot x \cdot y^2 \cdot y^2 \cdot y^2 \cdot y}$

$\sqrt{25} \cdot \sqrt{x^2} \cdot \sqrt{x} \cdot \sqrt{y^2} \cdot \sqrt{y^2} \cdot \sqrt{y^2} \cdot \sqrt{y}$

$5 \cdot x \cdot \sqrt{x} \cdot y \cdot y \cdot y \cdot \sqrt{y}$

$5xy^3\sqrt{xy}$

**g.** $A = s^2$

$s = \sqrt{A}$

$s = \sqrt{80}$

$s = \sqrt{16 \cdot 5}$

$s = \sqrt{16} \cdot \sqrt{5}$

$s = 4\sqrt{5}$ m

**Practice 61**

**1.** $\sqrt{12}$

$= \sqrt{4 \cdot 3}$

$= 2\sqrt{3}$

**2.** $\sqrt{200}$

$= \sqrt{4 \cdot 25 \cdot 2}$

$= \sqrt{4} \cdot \sqrt{25} \cdot \sqrt{2}$

$= 2 \cdot 5 \cdot \sqrt{2}$

$= 10\sqrt{2}$

**3.** $(-16)^{\frac{1}{4}}$ is not a real number.

**4.** $x^{\frac{1}{3}} = 343^{\frac{1}{3}}$

$= \sqrt[3]{343}$

$= \sqrt[3]{7 \cdot 7 \cdot 7}$

$= \sqrt[3]{7^3}$

$= 7$

**5.** FOIL stands for First, Outer, Inner, Last.

**6.** $P = 2(l + w)$

$P = 2\left(\dfrac{144x}{x + 3} + \dfrac{432}{x + 3}\right)$

$P = 2\left(\dfrac{144x + 432}{x + 3}\right)$

$P = 2\left(\dfrac{144(x + 3)}{x + 3}\right)$

$P = 288$ feet

**7.** Student A; Sample: Student B squared −8 instead of 8.

**8.** The area is the product of the length and the width.

The width of the picture and the mat is $x + 4 + 4$ or $x + 8$.

The length of the picture is twice the width, or $2x$. The length of the picture and the mat is $2x + 4 + 4$ or $2x + 8$.

$A = l \cdot w = (2x + 8)(x + 8)$

The answer is **C**.

**9.** Graph both equations on a graphing calculator and solve the systems. The solution is $(-3, -1)$.

**10.** Substitute $4y - 11$ for $x$ in the first equation.

$2x - 3y = 3$

$2(4y - 11) - 3y = 3$

$8y - 22 - 3y = 3$

$5y = 25$

$y = 5$

Substitute 5 for $y$ in either original equation.

$x = 4(5) - 11$

$x = 20 - 11$

$x = 9$

The solution is $(9, 5)$.

**11.** $V = \dfrac{4}{3}\pi r^3$

$3456\pi = \dfrac{4}{3}\pi r^3$

$10,368\pi = 4\pi r^3$

$2592 = r^3$

$r \approx 13.7$

The diameter is 13.7 · 2 or about 27.5 feet.

**12. a.** Adding the attendance numbers together results in 45,734. Divide by the number of data points to find the mean.

mean

$= \dfrac{45{,}734}{7}$

$= 6482$

**b.** Add the outlier and divide by 8.

mean

$= \dfrac{57{,}368}{8}$

$= 7171$

Sample: The outlier raises the mean attendance value to 7171.

**13.** $(4b - 3)^2$

$(4b)^2 - 2(4b)(3) + 3^2$

$16b^2 - 24b + 9$

**14.** $(-2x + 5)^2$

$(-2x)^2 + 2(-2x)(5) + 5^2$

$4x^2 - 20x + 25$

**15.** Write a system to represent the situation.

$10x + 20y = 1700$

$x + y = 105$

Solve the second equation for $x$.

$x = -y + 105$

Substitute $x = -y + 105$ for $x$ in the first equation and solve for $y$.

$10(-y + 105) + 20y = 1700$

$-10y + 1050 + 20y = 1700$

$10y = 650$

$y = 65$

Substitute 65 for $y$ in either of the original equations.

$x = -65 + 105$

$x = 40$

They wash 40 cars and 65 SUVs.

**16. a.** $m = \dfrac{8 - 3}{2 - 1}$

$m = \dfrac{5}{1}$

$m = 5$

**b.** Graph the two points and draw a smooth line through them.

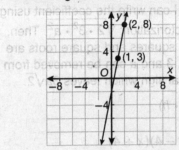

**c.** Use point-slope form, $y - y_1 = m(x - x_1)$.

$y - 3 = 5(x - 1)$ or $y - 8 = 5(x - 2)$

**d.** Use either equation from part c to write an equation in slope-intercept form.

$y - 3 = 5(x - 1)$

$y - 3 = 5x - 5$

$y = 5x - 2$

**e.**  $-3 = 5x - 2$  $\qquad$ $y = 5(-2) - 2$

$\quad -1 = 5x$  $\qquad\qquad$ $y = -10 - 2$

$\quad x = -\dfrac{1}{5}$  $\qquad\qquad$ $y = -12$

**17.** $y = kx$

$y =$ weight on the moon

$x =$ weight on the Earth

$9 = k(60)$

$k = 0.15$

Write and solve an equation of direct variation.

$y = 0.15(25)$

$y = 3.75$ pounds

**18.** Substitute each possible solution into the system to determine which makes both equations true.

**A** $8 - 5(1) = 3$  $\qquad$ $3(1) + 8(8) = 24$

$\quad 8 - 5 = 3$  $\qquad\qquad$ $3 + 64 = 24$

$\quad 3 = 3$  $\qquad\qquad\quad$ $67 \neq 24$

**B** $0 - 5(0) = 3$  $\qquad$ $3(0) + 8(0) = 24$

$\quad 0 \neq 3$  $\qquad\qquad\quad$ $0 \neq 24$

**C** $3 - 5(0) = 3$  $\qquad$ $3(0) + 8(3) = 24$

$\quad 3 = 3$  $\qquad\qquad\quad$ $24 = 24$

**Saxon** Algebra 1

**D** $1.5 - 5(4) = 3$     $3(4) + 8(1.5) = 24$
$1.5 - 20 = 3$          $12 + 12 = 24$
$-18.5 \neq 3$               $24 = 24$
The answer is **C**.

**19.** Sample: I can write the coefficient using prime factorization: $\sqrt{2 \cdot 3^2 \cdot a^2}$. Then, because squares and square roots are inverses, 3 and $a$ can be removed from under the radical sign which leaves $3a\sqrt{2}$.

**20.** $A = \frac{1}{2}(l \cdot h)$

$A = \frac{1}{2}(x - 4)(x + 4)$

$= \frac{1}{2}(x^2 - 16)$

$= \frac{x^2 - 16}{2}$ square inches

**21.**    $4x^2 \qquad\quad - 3$
$+ \; \underline{-x^2 - 5x - 1}$
$\quad\; 3x^2 - 5x - 4$

**22.** $21 = 3 \cdot 7$
$33 = 3 \cdot 11$
$13 = 1 \cdot 13$
$\text{LCM} = 3 \cdot 7 \cdot 11 \cdot 13 = 3003$

**23.** $8 = 2 \cdot 2 \cdot 2$
$32 = 2 \cdot 2 \cdot 2 \cdot 2 \cdot 2$
$12 = 2 \cdot 2 \cdot 3$
$\text{LCM} = 2 \cdot 2 \cdot 2 \cdot 2 \cdot 2 \cdot 3 = 96$

**24. a.** $A = l \cdot w$
$= 3 \cdot 3$
$= 9$

**b.** $A = l \cdot w$
$= x \cdot x$
$= x^2$

**c.** The area is equal to the difference between the area of the large square and the area of the smaller square.
$A = 9 - x^2$

**25.** $A = s^2$
$A = (8x - 16)^2$
$A = 64x^2 - 2(8x)(16) + 256$
$A = 64x^2 - 256x + 256$ square inches

**26. a.** $A = \pi r^2$
$r^2 = \dfrac{A}{\pi}$
$r = \sqrt{\dfrac{A}{\pi}}$

**b.** $r = \sqrt{\dfrac{A}{\pi}}$
$r = \sqrt{\dfrac{20\pi \text{ cm}^2}{\pi}}$
$r = \sqrt{20}$ cm
$r = \sqrt{4 \cdot 5}$ cm
$r = 2\sqrt{5}$ cm

**27.** Sample: The quotient of an unknown and 7 plus 3 is greater than or equal to 5.

**28.** Sample: The product of an unknown and 3 minus 4 is less than $-2$.

**29.** $a = 60$ cm/s$^2$
$r = 15$ cm
$\sqrt{ar} = \sqrt{60 \text{ cm/s}^2 \cdot 15 \text{ cm}}$
$= \sqrt{900}$ cm/s
$= 30$ cm/s

**30.** Order the data from least to greatest.
5, 6, 6.5, 6.5, 7, 7, 7, 7, 7.5, 8, 8.5, 9, 10
minimum $= 5$
$Q_1 = 6.5$
median $= 7$
$Q_3 = 8$
maximum $= 10$
Draw a box-and-whisker plot.

Shoe Sizes
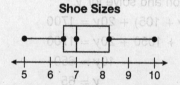

## LAB 6

### Practice Lab 6

**a.** Enter the data into List 1, Press **2nd** **STAT PLOT** **Y=** and select **1:Plot1...** to open the plot setup menu. Press **ENTER** to turn Plot1 **On** and then select the Type at the end of the first row. Create a histogram by pressing **ZOOM** and

**Saxon** Algebra 1

selecting **9:ZoomStat.** Press WINDOW to change the intervals and window settings. To create a histogram with an interval of 5, use Xmin=35, Xmax=75, and Xscl=5.

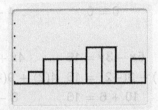

**b.** According to the data, 3 people typed between 55 and 59 words per minute and 3 people typed between 60 and 65 words per minute, so 6 people can type between 55 and 65 words per minute.

**c.** There are 4 musicians between the ages of 10 and 20. The answer is **B**.

**d.** no; Sample: The histogram shows the frequency of ages of musicians, not the number of times musicians in each age group went to rehearsal.

## LESSON 62

### Warm Up 62

**1.** The answer is **A**.

**2.** Order the data from least to greatest.

2, 3, 4, 5, 5, 6, 7, 8

$$\text{mean} = \frac{40}{8} = 5$$

$$\text{median} = \frac{5 + 5}{2} = 5$$

mode = 5
range = 8 − 2 = 6

**3.** Order the data from least to greatest.

12, 13, 14, 15, 16, 20

$$\text{mean} = \frac{90}{6} = 15$$

$$\text{median} = \frac{14 + 15}{2} = 14.5$$

mode = none
range = 20 − 12 = 8

### Lesson Practice 62

**a.** Organize data by each tens value.

40's: 42, 43
50's: 50, 51, 52, 52, 54, 56
60's: 60, 60, 61, 63, 65, 69
70's: 70

Create a stem-and-leaf plot of the data and create a key.

**Low Temperatures (°F)**
**April 2007 for New Orleans, LA**

| Stem | Leaves |
|------|--------|
| 4 | 2, 3 |
| 5 | 0, 1, 2, 2, 4, 6 |
| 6 | 0, 0, 1, 3, 5, 9 |
| 7 | 0 |

Key: 5 | 6 = 56°F

**b.** The data is already organized in four intervals of 10. Create a graph showing the intervals and the number of data points in each interval.

**Low Temperatures in New Orleans**
**First 15 Days of April 2007**

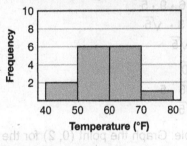

**c.** median = 60
mode = 59, 63, 64, 68
range = 71 − 45 = 26°

**d.** The data value 64 occurs 2 times. There are 15 total values.

$$\frac{2}{15}; 0.1\overline{3}; 13.\overline{3}\%$$

**e.** Enter the data into List 1, Press 2nd Y= STAT PLOT and select **1:Plot1...** to open the plot setup menu. Press ENTER to turn Plot1 **On** and then select the Type at the end of the first row. Create a histogram by pressing ZOOM and selecting **9:ZoomStat.** Press WINDOW to change the intervals and window settings. To create a histogram with an interval of 10, use Xmin=40, Xmax=80, and Xscl=10.

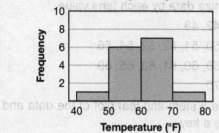

**Low Temperatures in New Orleans First 15 Days of April 2007**

**Practice 62**

1. median $= \dfrac{39 + 41}{2} = 40$ years

2. mode $= 34$ years

3. range $= 64 - 25 = 39$ years

4. relative frequency $= \dfrac{2}{20} = 10\%$

5. $\sqrt{88}$
   $= \sqrt{4 \cdot 22}$
   $= 2\sqrt{22}$

6. $\sqrt{720}$
   $= \sqrt{16 \cdot 9 \cdot 5}$
   $= 4 \cdot 3 \cdot \sqrt{5}$
   $= 12\sqrt{5}$

7. $\sqrt{180}$
   $= \sqrt{36 \cdot 5}$
   $= 6\sqrt{5}$

8. Sample: Graph the point $(0, 2)$ for the $y$-intercept. Then graph the point that is one unit down and 3 units to the right of that, or $(3, 1)$, and draw a line between the two points.

9. Student A; Sample: Student B used the wrong pattern to find the product.

10. Sample: $3x - 2y = 0$
    $3(4) - 2(6) = 0$
    $12 - 12 = 0$
    $0 = 0$

11. Substitute $(2, -2)$ in each system of equations.

    **A** $\quad x + y = 0 \qquad\qquad 2x - 3y = -2$
    $\quad\quad 2 + (-2) = 0 \qquad 2(2) - 3(-2) = -2$
    $\quad\quad\quad\quad 0 = 0 \qquad\qquad\quad 4 + 6 = -2$
    $\quad\quad\quad\quad\quad\quad\quad\quad\quad\quad\quad\quad 10 \neq -2$

    **B** $\quad\quad 5x - 3y = 16 \qquad\qquad 4x + 9y = 10$
    $\quad 5(2) - 3(-2) = 16 \quad 4(2) + 9(-2) = 10$
    $\quad\quad\quad 10 + 6 = 16 \qquad\qquad 8 - 18 = 10$
    $\quad\quad\quad\quad 16 = 16 \qquad\qquad\quad -10 \neq 10$

    **C** $\quad\quad 9x - 2y = 22 \qquad\qquad 3x + 6y = -6$
    $\quad 9(2) - 2(-2) = 22 \quad 3(2) + 6(-6) = -6$
    $\quad\quad\quad 18 + 4 = 22 \qquad\qquad 6 - 12 = -6$
    $\quad\quad\quad\quad 22 = 22 \qquad\qquad\quad\quad -6 = -6$

    **D** $\quad\quad x + 2y = -2 \qquad\qquad 2x + y = -2$
    $\quad 2 + 2(-2) = -2 \quad\quad 2(2) + (-2) = -2$
    $\quad\quad\quad 2 - 4 = -2 \qquad\qquad 4 - 2 = -2$
    $\quad\quad\quad\quad -2 = -2 \qquad\qquad\quad 2 \neq -2$

    The answer is **C**.

12. $-4(x^2 + 4x - 1)$
    $= -4x^2 - 16x + 4$

13. $(b - 8)^2$
    $= b^2 - 2(b)(8) + 8^2$
    $= b^2 - 16b + 64$

14. $\left(x + \dfrac{1}{2}\right)\left(x + \dfrac{1}{4}\right)$
    $= x^2 + \dfrac{1}{4}x + \dfrac{1}{2}x + \dfrac{1}{8}$
    $= x^2 + \dfrac{3}{4}x + \dfrac{1}{8}$

15. $152 - 95 = \$57$ million decrease
    $\dfrac{152}{(152 + 95)} = \dfrac{152}{247} = .615$
    Consumers spend about 62% of the total on mother's day.

16. median diameter $= 19$ inches
    $C = 2\pi r$
    $C = 2 \cdot 3.14 \cdot (19 \div 2)$
    $C = 59.66$ inches

**Saxon** Algebra 1

**17.** Graph the equations,

$y = x + 6$ and $y + 3x = 6$ or $y = -3x + 6$. The solution of the system is the point of intersection.

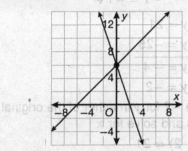

The solution is (0, 6).

Check:

$6 = 0 + 6 \qquad 6 = -3(0) + 6$

$6 = 6 \qquad\quad 6 = 6$

**18.** Sample: the upper and lower quartiles of the data.

**19.** Organize data by each hundreds value.

100's: 106, 108

110's:

120's: 125, 129

130's: 134, 135

140's: 144, 149

150's: 150, 157

Create a stem-and-leaf plot of the data and create a key.

**Money Raised in Homerooms**

| Stem | Leaves |
|------|--------|
| 10 | 6, 8 |
| 11 | |
| 12 | 5, 9 |
| 13 | 4, 5 |
| 14 | 4, 9 |
| 15 | 0, 7 |

Key: 10|5 means $105

**20.** Graph the equation.

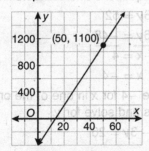

$p = 30n - 400$

$p = 30(50) - 400$

$p = \$1100$

**21.** $\sqrt[4]{x^2} = \sqrt[4]{9^2}$

$\qquad = \sqrt{9}$

$\qquad = 3$

**22.** $\sqrt[3]{x^6} = \sqrt[3]{2^6}$

$\qquad = \sqrt{2^2}$

$\qquad = 4$

**23.** $\quad y = kx$

$-90 = k(10)$

$\quad k = -9$

An equation is $y = -9x$.

**24. a.** $\quad 500 + 1000r + 500r^2$

$\qquad\quad + 600 + 600r$

$\overline{\quad 1100 + 1600r + 500r^2}$

**b.** $1100 + 1600(0.03) + 500(0.03)^2$

$1100 + 48 + 0.45$

$\$1148.45$

**25.** $n = 0.29(68) = \$19.72$ increase

new price $= 68 + 19.72 = \$87.72$

**26.** $100 - 15 = 85\%$

The new price is 85% of the original price.

$98.60 = 0.85n$

$\quad n = \$116$

**27.** $(2r - 2s) = 2 \cdot (r - s)$

$(4r^2 - 4rs) = 2 \cdot 2 \cdot r \cdot (r - s)$

$(8rs - 8s^2) = 2 \cdot 2 \cdot 2 \cdot s \cdot (r - s)$

LCM $= 2 \cdot 2 \cdot 2 \cdot r \cdot s \cdot (r - s)$

$\qquad = 8rs(r - s)$ days

**28.** $\sqrt{2800}$

$\sqrt{100 \cdot 4 \cdot 7}$

$20\sqrt{7} = 2\sqrt{700} = 10\sqrt{28}$

The answer is **D**.

**29.** $A = s^2$

$A = (9x - 20)^2$

$A = 81x^2 - 2(9x)(20) + 400$

$A = 81x^2 - 360x + 400$ square inches

**Saxon** Algebra 1

**30.** $A = 25 \text{ units}^2$

$A = s^2$

$s = \sqrt{A}$

$s = \sqrt{25}$

$s = 5 \text{ units}$

Sample: $(0, 0), (0, 5), (5, 0), (5, 5)$

## LESSON 63

**Warm Up 63**

**1.** linear

**2.** $3(4x - 5)$

$= 3(4x) - 3(5)$

$= 12x - 15$

**3.** $4(7y + 12)$

$= 4(7y) + 4(12)$

$= 28y + 48$

**4.** $ky^2 k^3 k^2 y^5$

$= k \cdot k^3 \cdot k^2 \cdot y^2 \cdot y^5$

$= k^6 y^7$

**5.** $xy - 3xy^2 + 5y^2 x - 4xy$

$= xy - 4xy - 3xy^2 + 5y^2 x$

$= xy - 4xy - 3xy^2 + 5xy^2$

$= (1 - 4)xy + (-3 + 5)xy^2$

$= -3xy + 2xy^2$

**Lesson Practice 63**

**a.** Add the equations to eliminate a variable.

$7x - 4y = -3$

$-3x + 4y = -1$

$\overline{\phantom{-3x} 4x = -4}$

$x = -1$

Substitute $-1$ for $x$ in one of the original equations and solve for $y$.

$7(-1) - 4y = -3$

$-7 - 4y = -3$

$-4y = 4$

$y = -1$

The solution is $(-1, -1)$.

Check:

$7(-1) - 4(-1) = -3$

$-7 + 4 = -3$

$-3 = -3$ ✓

$-3(-1) + 4(-1) = -1$

$3 - 4 = -1$

$-1 = -1$ ✓

**b.** $11x + 6y = 21$

$-11x - 4y = -25$

$\overline{\phantom{-11x} 2y = -4}$

$y = -2$

Substitute $-2$ for $y$ in either of the original equations and solve for $x$.

$11x + 6(-2) = 21$

$11x - 12 = 21$

$11x = 33$

$x = 3$

The solution is $(3, -2)$.

**c.** Write the first equation in standard form. Multiply the second equation by 3. Then add the equations and combine like terms.

$-6x + 15y = 18$

$6x - 2y = 34$

$\overline{\phantom{6x} 13y = 52}$

$y = 4$

Substitute 4 for $y$ in either of the original equations and solve for $x$.

$-2x + 5(4) = 6$

$-2x + 20 = 6$

$-2x = -14$

$x = 7$

The solution is $(7, 4)$.

**d.** Multiply the first equation by 2 and the second equation by $-3$ to get opposite coefficients for the variable $y$.

$2(-8x - 3y) = 2(26)$

$-3(-5x - 2y) = -3(16)$

Add the equations and combine like terms.

$-16x - 6y = 52$

$15x + 6y = -48$

$\overline{\phantom{15x} -x = 4}$

$x = -4$

Substitute $-4$ for $x$ in one of the original equations and solve for $y$.

$-8(-4) - 3y = 26$

$$32 - 3y = 26$$
$$-3y = -6$$
$$y = 2$$

The solution is $(-4, 2)$.

**e.** Let $x =$ the cost of a child ticket
and $y =$ the cost of an adult ticket.
Write and solve a system of linear equations.

$$x + y = 540$$
$$5.50x + 6.00y = 3060$$

Multiply the first equation by $-11$ and
the second equation by 2 to get opposite
coefficients for the variable $x$.

$$-11(x + y) = -11(540)$$
$$2(5.50x + 6.00y) = 2(3060)$$

Add the equations and combine like terms.

$$-11x - 11y = -5940$$
$$\underline{11x + 12y = 6120}$$
$$y = 180 \text{ adult tickets}$$

## Practice 63

**1.** $\sqrt{256}$
$= \sqrt{4 \cdot 64}$
$= 2 \cdot 8$
$= 16$

**2.** $\sqrt{108}$
$= \sqrt{36 \cdot 3}$
$= 6\sqrt{3}$

**3.** $\sqrt{294}$
$= \sqrt{49 \cdot 6}$
$= 7\sqrt{6}$

**4.** $\left(\dfrac{r^{-3}t^{\frac{1}{2}}e}{rg^4t^{\frac{3}{2}}}\right)^2$

$= \left(\dfrac{t^{\frac{1}{2}}e}{r^4g^4t^{\frac{3}{2}}}\right)^2$

$= \dfrac{te^2}{r^8g^8t^3}$

$= \dfrac{e^2}{r^8g^8t^2}$

**5.** $\dfrac{t^3n^{-2}s}{f^7tb^5}\left(\dfrac{t^{-2}}{ns^3} - \dfrac{f^6t^{-1}}{b}\right)$

$= \dfrac{t^2s}{f^7n^2b^5}\left(\dfrac{1}{ns^3t^2} - \dfrac{f^6}{tb}\right)$

$= \dfrac{t^2s}{f^7n^3b^5s^3t^2} - \dfrac{t^2sf^6}{f^7n^2b^6t}$

$= \dfrac{1}{b^5f^7n^3s^2} - \dfrac{st}{b^6fn^2}$

**6.** Order the data from least to greatest.
1450, 1500, 1500, 1630, 1710, 2800
range $= 2800 - 1450 = 1350$

**7.** $\dfrac{5}{12} = 0.41\overline{6}$

$\dfrac{3}{7.2} = 0.41\overline{6}$

$\dfrac{7}{16.8} = 0.41\overline{6}$

Yes, the set of ordered pairs represents a
direct variation.

**8.** $2t^3sv^5 = 2 \cdot t \cdot t \cdot t \cdot s \cdot v \cdot v \cdot v \cdot v \cdot v$
$6v^3t^4 = 2 \cdot 3 \cdot v \cdot v \cdot v \cdot t \cdot t \cdot t \cdot t$
$10v^8s^4 = 2 \cdot 5 \cdot v \cdot v \cdot v \cdot v \cdot v \cdot v \cdot v \cdot v$
$\cdot v \cdot s \cdot s \cdot s \cdot s$
LCM $= 2 \cdot 3 \cdot 5 \cdot s \cdot s \cdot s \cdot s \cdot t \cdot t \cdot t \cdot t$
$\cdot v \cdot v \cdot v \cdot v \cdot v \cdot v \cdot v \cdot v$
$= 30s^4t^4v^8$

**9.** $14dv^3 = 2 \cdot 7 \cdot d \cdot v \cdot v \cdot v$
$7s^2v = 7 \cdot s \cdot s \cdot v$
$28s^7v^5 = 2 \cdot 2 \cdot 7 \cdot s \cdot s \cdot s \cdot s \cdot s \cdot s \cdot s$
$\cdot s \cdot v \cdot v \cdot v \cdot v \cdot v$
LCM $= 2 \cdot 2 \cdot 7 \cdot d \cdot s \cdot s \cdot s \cdot s \cdot s \cdot s \cdot s$
$\cdot s \cdot v \cdot v \cdot v \cdot v \cdot v \cdot v$
$= 28ds^7v^5$

**10.** $(x + 5)(x - 5) = x^2 - 25$
The answer is **A**.

**11.** 4 feet $= 48$ inches
7 feet $= 84$ inches
Write and solve a system of equations.
$16x + 48 = y$
$13x + 84 = y$
Multiply the first equation by $-1$.
$-1(16x + 48) = -1(y)$

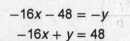 
$-16x - 48 = -y$

$-16x + y = 48$

Add the equations and combine like terms.

$-16x + y = 48$

$\underline{13x - y = -84}$

$-3x = -36$

$x = 12$ years

The two trees will be the same height in 12 years.

**12.** Substitute $-5x + 10$ for $y$ in the second equation.

$6x - 2(-5x + 10) = 12$

$6x + 10x - 20 = 12$

$16x = 32$

$x = 2$

Substitute 2 for $x$ in one of the original equations and solve for $y$.

$y = -5(2) + 10$

$y = -10 + 10$

$y = 0$

The solution is $(2, 0)$.

**13.** Add the equations and combine like terms.

$6x + 4y = 22$

$\underline{-6x + 2y = -16}$

$6y = 6$

$y = 1$

Substitute 1 for $y$ in one of the original equations and solve for $x$.

$6x + 4(1) = 22$

$6x + 4 = 22$

$6x = 18$

$x = 3$

The solution is $(3, 1)$.

**14.** $-x + y = 4$

$2x + y = 1$

$y = x + 4$

$y = -2x + 1$

Graph the equations. The solution is the point of intersection.

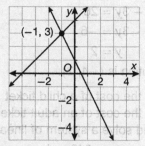

The solution is $(-1, 3)$. Use a graphing calculator to verify the solution.

**15.** $P = 2(l + w)$

$P = 2(2x + 3(x - 2))$

$P = 2(2x + 3x - 6)$

$P = 4x + 6x - 12$

$P = 10x - 12$

**16.** Substitute each possible solution into the system to determine which makes both equations true.

**A** $9\left(-\dfrac{2}{3}\right) - 3(2) = 20 \quad 3\left(-\dfrac{2}{3}\right) + 6(2) = 2$

$\qquad -6 - 6 = 20 \qquad\qquad -2 + 12 = 2$

$\qquad -12 \neq 20 \qquad\qquad\quad 10 \neq 2$

**B** $9(2) - 3\left(\dfrac{2}{3}\right) = 20 \quad 3(2) + 6\left(\dfrac{2}{3}\right) = 2$

$\qquad 18 - 2 = 20 \qquad\qquad 6 + 4 = 2$

$\qquad 16 \neq 20 \qquad\qquad\quad 10 \neq 2$

**C** $9(2) - 3\left(-\dfrac{2}{3}\right) = 20 \quad 3(2) + 6\left(-\dfrac{2}{3}\right) = 2$

$\qquad 18 + 2 = 20 \qquad\qquad 6 - 4 = 2$

$\qquad 20 = 20 \qquad\qquad\quad 2 = 2$

**D** $9(-2) - 3\left(\dfrac{2}{3}\right) = 20 \quad 3(-2) + 6\left(\dfrac{2}{3}\right) = 2$

$\qquad -18 - 2 = 20 \qquad\quad -6 + 4 = 2$

$\qquad -20 \neq 20 \qquad\qquad -2 \neq 2$

The answer is **C**.

**17.** Sample: Substitute the values solved for the variables back into the original equations to ensure that they make both of the original equations true.

**18. a.** Order the data from least to greatest.

2, 4, 4, 4, 4, 5, 5, 5, 6, 6, 6, 6, 6, 6, 6,

7, 7, 7, 7, 8, 8, 8, 8, 8, 8, 8, 8, 8, 9

minimum = 2

$Q_1 = 5$

**Saxon** Algebra 1

median $= \dfrac{6 + 7}{2} = 6.5$

$Q_3 = 8$

maximum $= 9$

Make a box-and-whisker plot.

**Deer Antler Points at 4.5 Years**

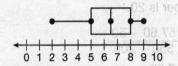

b. no; Sample: There is a wide range on this graph.

19. $A = s^2$

$s = \sqrt{A}$

$s = \sqrt{40,000}$

$s = 200$ m

20. $A = l \cdot w$

$A = (3x + 15)(x + 10)$

$A = 3x^2 + 30x + 15x + 150$

$A = 3x^2 + 45x + 150$ square feet

21. $n = 0.38(1527) = 580.26$ decrease

new price $= 1527 - 580.26 = \$946.74$

22. $n = 0.015(25,720) = 385.80$ increase

new price $= 25,720 + 385.80$

$= \$26,105.80$

23. $n = 2.15(10.25) = 22.04$ increase

new price $= 10.25 + 22.04 = \$32.29$

24. $(a + b)^2 = a^2 + 2ab + b^2$

$(a - b)^2 = a^2 - 2ab + b^2$

25. $A = s^2$

$A = (2x + 6)^2$

$A = 4x^2 + 2(2x)(6) + 36$

$A = 4x^2 + 24x + 36$ square feet

26. $\sqrt{76g^6}$

$\sqrt{4 \cdot 19 \cdot g^2 \cdot g^2 \cdot g^2}$

$2g^3 \sqrt{19}$

The answer is **A**.

27. Student A; Sample: Student B found the stem with the most data points, 17 or 170.

28. Sample: The second equation is the first equation multiplied by $-\frac{3}{2}$, so the equations would be the same line on a graph. There are an infinite number of solutions.

29. The absolute value of that coefficient would be greater than 1.

30. Total number of students is 20, 9 students work 5–10 hours per week $\frac{9}{20} = 0.45 = 45\%$

## LESSON 64

### Warm Up 64

1. inverse operation

2. $y = 7x$

$y = kx$

$k = 7$

3. $-4y = 12x$

$y = -3x$

$k = -3$

4. Sample: $y = 3x$

5. Sample: $y = -0.5x$

### Lesson Practice 64

a. This is not an inverse variation; Sample: The equation solved for $y$ is $y = \frac{x}{4}$. This equation does not match the inverse variation equation $y = \frac{k}{x}$.

b. This is an inverse variation; Sample: The equation solved for $y$ is $y = \frac{3}{x}$. This equation matches the inverse variation equation $y = \frac{k}{x}$.

c. $x_1y_1 = x_2y_2$

$20(3.5) = x_2(10)$

$70 = 10x_2$

$x_2 = 7$

d. $y = \dfrac{k}{x}$

$\dfrac{1}{2} = \dfrac{k}{8}$

$k = 4$

$y = \dfrac{4}{x}$

**Saxon** Algebra 1

To graph, plot several coordinate pairs from the equation and connect the points.

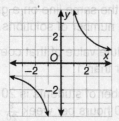

**e.** $x_1y_1 = x_2y_2$

$7(8) = x_2(10)$

$56 = 10x_2$

$x_2 = 5.6$ hours

## Practice 64

**1.** $8mn^4 = 2 \cdot 2 \cdot 2 \cdot m \cdot n \cdot n \cdot n \cdot n$

$12m^5n^2 = 2 \cdot 2 \cdot 3 \cdot m \cdot m \cdot m \cdot m \cdot m \cdot n \cdot n$

$LCM = 2 \cdot 2 \cdot 2 \cdot 3 \cdot m \cdot m \cdot m \cdot m \cdot m \cdot$

$n \cdot n \cdot n \cdot n \cdot$

$= 24m^5n^4$

**2.** List the multiples of $\frac{1}{2}$ and $\frac{1}{4}$.

$\frac{1}{2}: \frac{1}{2}, 1, \frac{3}{2}, 2, \frac{5}{2}...$

$\frac{1}{4}: \frac{1}{4}, \frac{1}{2}, \frac{3}{4}, 1, \frac{5}{4}...$

Their lowest common multiple is one-half. Now, find the LCM of the algebraic part of the expression.

$\frac{1}{2}wx^3 = \frac{1}{2} \cdot w \cdot x \cdot x \cdot x$

$\frac{1}{4}w^2x^6 = \frac{1}{4} \cdot w \cdot w \cdot x \cdot x \cdot x \cdot x \cdot x \cdot x$

$LCM = \frac{1}{2} \cdot w \cdot w \cdot x \cdot x \cdot x \cdot x \cdot x \cdot x$

$= \frac{1}{2}w^2x^6$

**3.** $y = \frac{x}{11}$ ; no

$y \neq \frac{k}{x}$

**4.** $y = \frac{3}{x}$ ; yes

$y = \frac{k}{x}$

**5.** $100(25) = 50(y_2)$

$2500 = 50y_2$

$y_2 = 50$

The value of $y$ would be close to 50.

**6.** Order the data from least to greatest.

1, 8, 8, 9, 9, 10, 10, 10, 11, 20

The minimum number is 1 and the maximum number is 20.

**7.** $m = \dfrac{57.50 - 50}{350 - 200}$

$= \dfrac{7.50}{150}$

$= \$0.05$ charge per minute

$y - 57.50 = 0.05(x - 350)$

$y - 57.50 = 0.05x - 17.50$

$y = 0.05x + 40$

To find the monthly fee, find the value of $y$ when $x = 0$.

$y = 0.05(0) + 40$

$= \$40$

The charge per minute is $0.05.

The monthly fee is $40.

**8.** $(b + 2)^2$

$= b^2 + 2(b)(2) + 2^2$

$= b^2 + 4b + 4$

**9.** $(x - 8)(x + 2)$

$= x^2 + 2x - 8x - 16$

$= x^2 - 6x - 16$

**10. a.** $A = s^2$

$s = \sqrt{A}$

**b.** $s = \sqrt{121}$ cm$^2$

**c.** $s = 11$ cm

**d.** The side length is measured in cm.

**11.** Write and solve a system of equations.

$y = 4x + 5$

$y = 6x + 2$

Subtract the second equation from the first to eliminate a variable.

$\begin{aligned} y &= 4x + 5 \\ y &= 6x + 2 \\ \hline 0 &= -2x + 3 \end{aligned}$

$2x = 3$

$x = 1.5$ hours

**Saxon** Algebra 1

Substitute 1.5 for $x$ in one of the original equations to find $y$, the distance each person will be from the school.

$y = 4(1.5) + 5$

$y = 6 + 5 = 11$ miles

**12.** $12(9) = 4(y_2)$

$\quad 108 = 4y_2$

$\quad y_2 = 27$

The answer is **C.**

**13.** mean $= \dfrac{1537}{8} = 192.125$

mean $= \dfrac{362}{8} = 45.25$

Sample: The mean value for waste generated is 192.125 million tons, and the mean value of materials recovered is 45.25. On average, the United States generates about 150 million tons of waste a year after recycling.

**14.** $P =$ the sum of the three side lengths

$$P = \left(\frac{8}{2a^2 + 3a}\right) + \left(\frac{5a + 1}{2a^2 + 3a}\right)$$

$$+ \left(\frac{3a + 3}{2a^2 + 3a}\right)$$

$$= \frac{8 + 5a + 1 + 3a + 3}{2a^2 + 3a}$$

$$= \frac{8a + 12}{2a^2 + 3a}$$

$$= \frac{4(2a + 3)}{a(2a + 3)} = \frac{4}{a} \text{ centimeters}$$

**15.** median $= \$32,000$

**16.** mode $= \$23,000$

**17.** range $= 68,00 - 21,000 = \$47,000$

**18.** relative frequency $= \frac{2}{23} \approx 0.0869$ about 9%

**19.** Order the data from least to greatest.

103, 112, 116, 118, 120, 130, 140, 145, 155, 157, 170, 175, 180, 190

minimum $= 103$

$Q_1 = 118$

median $= \dfrac{140 + 145}{2} = 142.5$

$Q_3 = 170$

maximum $= 190$

IQR $= 170 - 118 = 52$

$x < 118 - 1.5(52) \qquad x > 170 + 1.5(52)$

$x < 40 \qquad\qquad\quad x > 248$

There are no outliers.

**Weights**

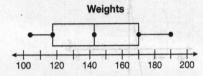

**20.** contrapositive; The original statement and contrapositive are false.

**21.** $\sqrt{24}$

$= \sqrt{4 \cdot 6}$

$= 2\sqrt{6}$

**22.** $\sqrt{75}$

$= \sqrt{5 \cdot 5 \cdot 3}$

$= 5\sqrt{3}$

**23.** Student B; Sample: Student A subtracted to eliminate the variable $x$, but then added the other terms in the equation.

**24.** Write a system of equations.

$x + y = 39$

$2x + \frac{1}{3}y = 33$

Multiply the first equation by $-2$. Add the two equations and combine like terms.

$-2x - 2y = -78$

$2x + \frac{1}{3}y = 33$

$-\frac{5}{3}y = -45$

$5y = 135$

$\quad y = 27$ square units

Substitute 27 for $y$ in one of the original equations and solve for $x$.

$x - 27 = 39$

$\quad x = 12$ square units

The area of Rectangle A is 12 square units. The area of Rectangle B is 27 square units.

**25.** $9x - 1.5y + 12 = 0$

$-1.5y = -9x - 12$

$1.5y = 9x + 12$

$\quad y = 6x + 8$

Graph the equation using the $y$-intercept, 8, and the slope, 6.

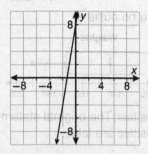

**26.** Add the equations to eliminate a variable.

$$-3x + 2y = -6$$
$$\underline{-5x - 2y = 22}$$
$$-8x = 16$$
$$x = -2$$

Substitute $-2$ for $x$ in one of the original equations and solve for $y$.

$$-3(-2) + 2y = -6$$
$$6 + 2y = -6$$
$$2y = -12$$
$$y = -6$$

The solution is $(-2, -6)$.

**27. a.** Write each equation in terms of $y$.

$$2x - y = 14 \qquad x + 4y = -2$$
$$-y = -2x + 14 \qquad 4y = -x - 2$$
$$y = 2x - 14 \qquad y = -\frac{1}{4}x - \frac{1}{2}$$

Graph the equations using the $y$-intercepts and slopes.

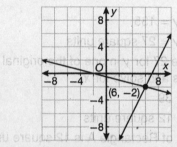

(6, -2)

**b.** Substitute $-\frac{1}{4}x - \frac{1}{2}$

for $y$ in the first equation.

$$2x - \left(-\frac{1}{4}x - \frac{1}{2}\right) = 14$$
$$\frac{9}{4}x = \frac{27}{2}$$

$9x = 54$
$x = 6$

Substitute 6 for $x$ in one of the original equations and solve for $y$.

$$6 + 4y = -2$$
$$4y = -8$$
$$y = -2$$

The solution is $(6, -2)$.

**c.** $2(6) - (-2) = 14 \qquad 6 + 4(-2) = -2$
$12 + 2 = 14 \qquad 6 - 8 = -2$
$14 = 14 \qquad -2 = -2$

**28.** $\qquad V = \dfrac{t}{p}$

$$450 \text{ m}^3 = \frac{t}{95}$$
$$t = 42{,}750$$
$$V = \frac{42{,}750}{475}$$
$$V = 90 \text{ mm}^3$$

**29.** Sample: The number of points varies directly with the number of touchdowns.

**30.** Sample: When $k$ is positive, the graph is in Quadrants I and III; when $k$ is negative, the graph is in Quadrants II and IV.

## LESSON 65

### Warm Up 65

**1.** point-slope

**2.** $2x + y = -5$
$$y = -2x - 5$$

The slope is $m = -2$. The $y$-intercept is $b = -5$.

**3.** $-9x + 3y = 12$
$$3y = 9x + 12$$
$$y = 3x + 4$$

The slope is $m = 3$.
The $y$-intercept is $b = 4$.

**4.** $y - (-5) = \dfrac{2}{3}(x - 0)$

$$y + 5 = \frac{2}{3}x$$

$$y = \frac{2}{3}x - 5$$

**Saxon** Algebra 1

## Lesson Practice 65

**a.** Solve each equation for $y$ to find the slope.

$$y = \frac{2}{3}x + 5\frac{2}{3} \rightarrow m = \frac{2}{3}$$

$$\frac{3}{2}x + y = 1$$

$$y = -\frac{3}{2}x + 1 \rightarrow m = -\frac{3}{2}$$

no; The lines are perpendicular.

**b.** A parallel line has slope $m = \frac{4}{7}$.

$$y - 2 = \frac{4}{7}\left(x - (-3)\right)$$

$$y - 2 = \frac{4}{7}x + \frac{12}{7}$$

$$y = \frac{4}{7}x + 3\frac{5}{7}$$

**c.** $m = \dfrac{-4 - 2}{2 - (-2)}$ $\qquad m = \dfrac{3 - 6}{5 - 3}$

$\quad = -\dfrac{6}{4}$ $\qquad\qquad = -\dfrac{3}{2}$

$\quad = -\dfrac{3}{2}$

no; The lines are parallel.

**d.** A perpendicular line has slope $m = -\dfrac{7}{4}$.

$$y - 3 = -\frac{7}{4}\left(x - (-1)\right)$$

$$y - 3 = -\frac{7}{4}x - \frac{7}{4}$$

$$y = -\frac{7}{4}x + 1\frac{1}{4}$$

**e.** Sample: The slope of $\overline{AB}$ is $-\frac{1}{2}$, the slope of $\overline{BC}$ is 2, and $\left(-\frac{1}{2}\right)(2) = -1$. $\overline{AB} \perp \overline{BC}$. Therefore, $ABC$ is a right triangle.

## Practice 65

**1.** $\sqrt{360}$

$= \sqrt{36 \cdot 10}$

$= 6\sqrt{10}$

**2.** $\sqrt{252}$

$= \sqrt{4 \cdot 9 \cdot 7}$

$= 2 \cdot 3 \cdot \sqrt{7}$

$= 6\sqrt{7}$

**3.** $\sqrt{384}$

$= \sqrt{4 \cdot 4 \cdot 4 \cdot 6}$

$= 2 \cdot 2 \cdot 2 \cdot \sqrt{6}$

$= 8\sqrt{6}$

**4.** $(x^2 + 5)^2$

$= (x^2 + 5)(x^2 + 5)$

$= (x^2)^2 + 5x^2 + 5x^2 + 5^2$

$= x^4 + 10x^2 + 25$

**5.** $(x - 2)(x - 9)$

$= x^2 - 9x - 2x + 18$

$= x^2 - 11x + 18$

**6.** $c \geq -5$

circle: filled

arrowhead: shaded from $-5$ pointing to the right

**7.** Sample: Treat the $(x - 5)$ like a single variable. Then, take each factor the greatest number of times it appears.
LCM $= 2 \cdot 3 \cdot (x - 5)^7 = 6(x - 5)^7$

**8.** The answer is **B**.

**9.** First, organize the data in order from least to greatest. Then, divide the data into groups using seconds to the tenths place as the stem and seconds to the hundredths place as the leaf.

**2007 NCAA Division II**
**Final Results Men's 50M Freestyle**

| Stem | Leaves |
|------|--------|
| 203 | 2, 6, 9 |
| 204 | 3 |
| 206 | 2, 7, 8, 8 |
| 208 | 1 |
| 209 | 7 |
| 210 | 7 |
| 212 | 4, 5 |
| 213 | 1 |
| 214 | 5 |
| 215 | 6 |

Key: 201|7 = 20.17 seconds

**10.** The slope is $m = 4$ and the $y$-intercept is $b = 22$. An equation is $y = 4x + 22$, where $x$ is the number of additional hours. To find the cost of 9 hours of parking, substitute

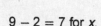

## Solutions Key

$9 - 2 = 7$ for $x$.

$y = 4(7) + 22$

$y = 28 + 22$

$y = \$50$ ·

**11.** Student A; Sample: Student B wrote a direct variation equation.

**12.** Write a system of equations.

$7x + 3y = 108$

$x + y = 20$

Multiply the second equation by $-3$. Add the equations and combine like terms.

$7x + 3y = 108$

$\underline{-3x - 3y = -60}$

$4x = 48$

$x = 12$   7-cm pieces

Solve for $y$.

$12 + y = 20$

$y = 8$   3-cm pieces

$8 \cdot 3 = 24 = 0.24$ m

$0.8$ m $- 0.24$ m $= 0.56$ m left

no; He needs 84 centimeters of wood for the twelve 7-centimeter pieces, and he only has 80 centimeters of wood leftover.

**13.** $2x - y = 3$         $3x + y = 2$

$-y = -2x + 3$     $y = -3x + 2$

$y = 2x - 3$

Graph each equation and determine the point at which the two lines intersect.

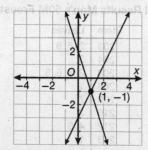

The solution is $(1, -1)$.

**14.** Add the equations to eliminate a variable.

$5x + 7y = 41$

$\underline{-3x - 7y = -47}$

$2x = -6$

$x = -3$

Substitute $-3$ for $x$ in one of the original equations and solve for $y$.

$5(-3) + 7y = 41$

$-15 + 7y = 41$

$7y = 56$

$y = 8$

The solution is $(-3, 8)$.

**15.** Solve the second equation for $y$.

$9x + y = 12$

$y = -9x + 12$

Substitute $-9x + 12$ for $y$ in the first equation and solve for $x$.

$5x - 2(-9x + 12) = 22$

$5x + 18x - 24 = 22$

$23x = 46$

$x = 2$

Substitute 2 for $x$ in one of the original equations and solve for $y$.

$9(2) + y = 12$

$18 + y = 12$

$y = -6$

The solution is $(2, -6)$.

**16.** Write a system of equations.

$y = 3x + 12$

$y = 5x$

Use substitution to solve for $x$.

$5x = 3x + 12$

$2x = 12$

$x = 6$ weeks

**17. a.** Sample: The range of the data is 221.25. To make it easier, I would create 5 intervals that are each 50 points apart.

**b.** 2007 NCAA Division II Championship Women's 3-Meter Diving Results

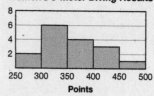

Points

**c.** Sample: A histogram is better. The data is so dispersed across a wide range that a stem-and-leaf plot would not be very useful.

**Saxon** Algebra 1

**18.** The slope is $m = -2$ and the $y$-intercept is $b = 6$. An equation is $y = -2x + 6$.

**19.** $I = prt$

$\quad = (x - 11)(x - 11)(1)$

$\quad = x^2 - 11x - 11x + 121$

$\quad = x^2 - 22x + 121$ dollars

**20.** $A = s^2$

$A = (7x - 24)^2$

$A = (7x)^2 - 2(7x)(24) + 24^2$

$A = 49x^2 - 336x + 576$ square feet

**21.** $WXYZ$ is a parallelogram. The sides $\overline{WX}$ and $\overline{YZ}$ are both vertical, so $\overline{WX} \parallel \overline{YZ}$. The slopes of $\overline{WZ}$ and $\overline{XY}$ are the same, $\frac{3}{5}$, so $\overline{WZ} \parallel \overline{XY}$.

**22.** $5xy = 40$

$\quad xy = 8$

$\quad y = \dfrac{8}{x}$

The equation can be written in the form $y = \frac{k}{x}$. Yes.

**23.** yes; Sample: Choose two points along each line and find the midpoint between the corresponding points on each line. Use this point and the slope of lines $a$ and $b$ to create the line of reflection.

**24.** There are an infinite number of parallel lines for any given slope.

**25.** $6x + 3y = 36$

$\quad\quad 3y = -6x + 36$

$\quad\quad\ y = -2x + 12$

The slope of the parallel line is $-2$.

**26. a.** Graph both points and draw a smooth line through them.

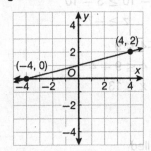

**b.** Find the slope

$m = \dfrac{2 - 0}{4 - (-4)}$

$= \dfrac{2}{8}$

$= \dfrac{1}{4}$

Write an equation.

$\quad y - 0 = \dfrac{1}{4}(x - (-4))$

$\quad\quad\ y = \dfrac{1}{4}x + 1$

**c.** no; Sample: The first line has a slope of $\frac{1}{4}$ and the second line has a slope of $-\frac{1}{4}$. They are not parallel.

**27.** Student B; Sample: Student A tried to add the equations without aligning like terms first.

**28.** Let $x =$ seconds spent racing the initial phase and $y =$ seconds spent racing the second phase. Write a system of equations.

$\quad x + y = 18.1$

$2.7x + 6.6y = 100$

Write the second equation with fractions. Then, multiply the first equation by $-2.7$. Add the equations and combine like terms.

$-2.7x - 2.7y = -48.87$

$\underline{\ 2.7x + 6.6y = 100\ }$

$\quad\quad\ 3.9y = 51.13$

$\quad\quad\quad\ y \approx 13.11$ seconds

Substitute the solution for $y$ into the second equation and solve for $2.7x$.

$2.7x + 6.6y = 100$

$\quad\quad 2.7x \approx 13.5$ meters

It is not necessary to solve for $x$, since the problem asks for distance, not time.

**29.** $x_1y_1 = x_2y_2$

$6(12) = 2(y_2)$

$\quad 72 = 2y_2$

$\quad y_2 = 36$ cm$^2$

**30.** $s = \dfrac{d}{t}$

$t = \dfrac{d}{s}$

$t_1 = \dfrac{8}{16} = 0.5 = 30$ minutes

$t_2 = \dfrac{8}{12} = 0.6 = 40$ minutes

$40 - 30 = 10$ minutes

**Saxon** Algebra 1

## LESSON 66

### Warm Up 66

1. inequality

2. $x + 13 = 21$
$x + 13 - 13 = 21 - 13$
$x = 8$

3. $-26 + x = -9$
$-26 + 26 + x = -9 + 26$
$x = 17$

4. $x < 2$
circle: open
arrowhead: shaded from 2 pointing to the left

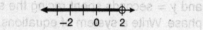
$-2 \quad 0 \quad 2$

5. $x \geq -3$
circle: filled
arrowhead: shaded from $-3$ pointing to the right

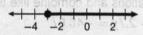
$-4 \quad -2 \quad 0 \quad 2$

### Lesson Practice 66

a. $x - \frac{1}{2} > 3$
$x - \frac{1}{2} + \frac{1}{2} > 3 + \frac{1}{2}$
$x > 3\frac{1}{2}$
circle: open
arrowhead: shaded from $3\frac{1}{2}$ pointing to the right

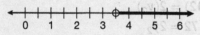
$0 \quad 1 \quad 2 \quad 3 \quad 4 \quad 5 \quad 6$

b. $z - 2 \geq \frac{1}{2}$
$z - 2 + 2 \geq \frac{1}{2} + 2$
$z \geq 2\frac{1}{2}$
circle: open
arrowhead: shaded from $2\frac{1}{2}$ pointing to the right

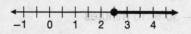
$-1 \quad 0 \quad 1 \quad 2 \quad 3 \quad 4$

c. $y + 1.1 \leq 3.2$
$y + 1.1 - 1.1 \leq 3.2 - 1.1$
$y \leq 2.1$
circle: filled
arrowhead: shaded from 2.1 pointing to the left

$1.5 \quad 1.6 \quad 1.7 \quad 1.8 \quad 1.9 \quad 2.0 \quad 2.1 \quad 2.2 \quad 2.3$

d. $x + 2.5 \geq 4.4$
$x + 2.5 - 2.5 \geq 4.4 - 2.5$
$x \geq 1.9$
She intends to crochet at least 1.9 feet more.

### Practice 66

1. $\dfrac{11p}{6s^4} + \dfrac{p}{6s^4}$
$= \dfrac{12p}{6s^4}$
$= \dfrac{2p}{s^4}$

2. $\dfrac{4x}{5w^4} - \dfrac{5x}{5w^4}$
$= -\dfrac{x}{5w^4}$

3. $\dfrac{7y}{3x^4 + 1} + \dfrac{5y}{3x^4 + 1}$
$= \dfrac{12y}{3x^4 + 1}$

4. $z + 10 \geq 3$
$z + 10 - 10 \geq 3 - 10$
$z \geq -7$

5. $x - 4 \leq 9$
$x - 4 + 4 \leq 9 + 4$
$x \leq 13$

6. $z \leq 1\frac{2}{3}$
circle: filled
arrowhead: shaded from $1\frac{2}{3}$ pointing to the left

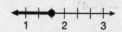
$1 \quad 2 \quad 3$

**Saxon** Algebra 1

**7.** The inequality $x > 5$ does not include 5. The inequality $x \geq 5$ does include 5. When graphing $x > 5$ starts with an open circle and $x \geq 5$ starts with a closed circle.

**8.** $f(x) = x + 3$

**9.** $x < 21.64$

circle: open

arrowhead: shaded from 21.64 down to zero with another open circle at zero

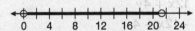

Sample: The graph would only include non negative numbers because there cannot be a negative time.

**10.** $\dfrac{14}{4} = \dfrac{10.5}{x}$

$14x = 42$

$x = 3$ millimeters

**11. a.** $P = M + F$

$M = P - F$

$M = 2387.74t + 155211.46$
$- (1223.58t + 79{,}589.03)$

$M = 1164.16t + 75{,}622.43$

**b.** $M = P - F$

$M = 298{,}475.86 - 153{,}003.83$

$M = 145{,}472.03$

**12.** $3z + 2 \leq z - 4 + 2 + z$

$3z + 2 \leq 2z - 2$

$z \leq -4$

The answer is **A**.

**13.** Sample: $y = 3 - x$ is a line of symmetry for the figure. $y = 3 - x$ has a slope of $-1$ and is perpendicular to $\overline{AB}$ and $\overline{EF}$, which each have a slope of 1.

**14. a.** $12 = 2 \cdot 2 \cdot 3$

$16 = 2 \cdot 2 \cdot 2 \cdot 2$

$28 = 2 \cdot 2 \cdot 7$

$LCM = 2 \cdot 2 \cdot 2 \cdot 2 \cdot 3 \cdot 7$

$= 336$ students

**b.** $1200 \div 336 = 3.57$

3 students

**15.** Solve both equations for $y$.

$x = 10y - 2$        $8 = 2x - 18y$

$y = \dfrac{1}{10}x + \dfrac{1}{5}$        $y = \dfrac{1}{9}x - \dfrac{4}{9}$

Now equate the two equations and solve for $x$.

$\dfrac{1}{10}x + \dfrac{1}{5} = \dfrac{1}{9}x - \dfrac{4}{9}$

$\dfrac{1}{5} + \dfrac{4}{9} = \dfrac{1}{9}x - \dfrac{1}{10}x$

$\dfrac{9}{45} + \dfrac{20}{45} = \dfrac{10}{90}x - \dfrac{9}{90}x$

$\dfrac{29}{45} = \dfrac{1}{90}x$

$x = 58$

Substitute this value of $x$ into either equation to find $y$.

$x = 10y - 2$

$58 = 10y - 2$

$60 = 10y$

$y = 6$

The solution is (58, 6)

**16.** $V = \sqrt{\dfrac{Fr}{m}}$

$V = \sqrt{\dfrac{60(2)}{3}}$

$V = \sqrt{40}$

$V = \sqrt{4 \cdot 10}$

$V = 2\sqrt{10}$ m/s

**17.** Substitute 5 for $y$ in each equation.

**A** $2x + 5y = 16$

$2x + y = -4$

$\underline{\phantom{xx}2x + 5y = 16}$

$-2x - y = 4$

$\phantom{xxxxx}4y = 20$

$\phantom{xxxxxx}y = 5$

The answer is **A**.

**18.** Sample: First I would multiply the first equation by 3, and then I would multiply the second equation by 2. Then I would subtract the second equation from the first, eliminating the variable $x$. After solving for $y$, I would substitute the $y$-value into one of the original equations to solve for $x$.

**19.** *EFHG* is a trapezoid because it has one pair of parallel sides. $\overline{EF} \parallel \overline{GH}$ because they have equal slopes of 0. $\overline{EG}$ and $\overline{FH}$ are not parallel because they have different slopes.

**20.** Student B; Sample: Student A did not write down the product rule correctly.

**21.** $y = kx$
$30 = k(5)$
$k = 6$
$y = 6x$

**22.** $y = \dfrac{k}{x}$
$20 = \dfrac{k}{4}$
$k = 80$
$y = \dfrac{80}{x}$

**23.** $(2x - 3)(2x - 3)$
$= 4x^2 - 6x - 6x + 9$
$= 4x^2 - 12x + 9$

**24.** $(t - 12)(t + 12)$
$= t^2 - 12^2$
$= t^2 - 144$

**25.** $(y^3 - 4)^2$
$= (y^3)^2 - 2(y^3)(4) + 4^2$
$= y^6 - 8y^3 + 16$

**26.** Distributive Property:
$(2y + 4)(3y + 5)$
$= 2y(3y + 5) + 4(3y + 5)$
$= 6y^2 + 10y + 12y + 20$
$= 6y^2 + 22y + 20$
FOIL Method:
$(2y + 4)(3y + 5)$
$= 6y^2 + 10y + 12y + 20$
$= 6y^2 + 22y + 20$

**27.** $y = \dfrac{k}{x}$
$3,571,429 = \dfrac{k}{280}$
$k = 1,000,000,000$
$y = \dfrac{1,000,000,000}{x}$

$y = \dfrac{1,000,000,000}{450}$
$y = 2,222,222$ minutes
$y = 4.2$ years

**28.** $m_{\overline{PQ}} = -2$, $m_{\overline{PR}} = \dfrac{1}{2}$,
and $(-2)(\frac{1}{2}) = -1$; $\overline{PQ} \perp \overline{PR}$.
Therefore, *PQR* is a right triangle.

**29.** $y = \dfrac{x}{3} - 1 \rightarrow m = \dfrac{1}{3}$
$-4 = 12x + 4y$
$4y = -12x + 4$
$y = -3x + 1 \rightarrow m = -3$
false; Sample: The line are perpendicular because their slopes are negative reciprocals: $\frac{1}{3}$, $-3$.

**30.** $x - 5 \geq 25$
$x - 5 + 5 \geq 25 + 5$
$x \geq 30$ miles

## LESSON 67

**Warm Up 67**

1. system

2. The slope is 4 and the *y*-intercept is –7.

3. $6x - 2y = 18$
$-2y = -6x + 18$
$y = 3x - 9$
The slope is 3 and the *y*-intercept is –9.

4. $15x + 3y = 24$
$3y = -15x + 24$
$y = -5x + 8$
$m = -5$
$m_p = -5$

5. $x + 4y = -7$
$4y = -x - 7$
$y = -\dfrac{1}{4}x - \dfrac{7}{4}$
$m = -\dfrac{1}{4}$
$m_\perp = 4$

**Saxon** Algebra 1

## Lesson Practice 67

**a.** $\frac{1}{2}x + \frac{1}{2} = \frac{1}{2}x + 7$

$0x = 6\frac{1}{2}$

no solution

**b.** $x + y = 10$

$-x - y = -10$

There are infinitely many solutions—any ordered pair $(x, y)$ that satisfies the equation $y = -x + 10$.

**c.** $-4y = -4x - 4$

$y = x + 1$

consistent and dependent

**d.** $-2x + y = 3$

$y = 2x + 3$

$y = -x - 2$

$2x + 3 = -x - 2$

$3x = -5$

$x = -1\frac{2}{3}$

$y = -\left(-1\frac{2}{3}\right) - 2$

$y = -\frac{1}{3}$

consistent and independent

**e.** $y = 22x$

$y = 12x + 40$

$22x = 12x + 40$

$10x = 40$

$x = 4$

$y = 22(4)$

$y = \$88$

$y = 12(4) + 40$

$y = \$88$

4 service calls; Both plans cost $88 at 4 service calls.

## Practice 67

**1.** $(2b - 3)^2$

$= (2b)^2 - 2(2b)(3) + 3^2$

$= 4b^2 - 12b + 9$

**2.** $(-b^3 + 5)^2$

$= (-b^3)^2 + 2(-b^3)(5) + 5^2$

$= b^6 - 10b^3 + 25$

**3.** $\sqrt{25x^4}$

$= \sqrt{5 \cdot 5 \cdot x^2 \cdot x^2}$

$= 5x^2$

**4.** $\sqrt{144x^6y}$

$= \sqrt{12 \cdot 12 \cdot x^2 \cdot x^2 \cdot x^2 \cdot y}$

$= 12 \cdot x \cdot x \cdot x \cdot \sqrt{y}$

$= 12x^3\sqrt{y}$

**5.** $\frac{3x}{y^2} + xy^{-2}$

$= \frac{3x}{y^2} + \frac{x}{y^2}$

$= \frac{4x}{y^2}$

**6.** Find the slope.

$m = \frac{21 - 18}{4 - 3}$

$= 3$

Use the slope to write an equation in point-slope form.

$y - 18 = 3(x - 3)$

$y - 18 = 3x - 9$

$y = 3x + 9$

$y = 3(6) + 9$

$y = 27$ pages

**7.** $z - 3 \geq 10$

$z - 3 + 3 \geq 10 + 3$

$z \geq 13$

**8.** $z - 5 < -2$

$z - 5 + 5 < -2 + 5$

$z < 3$

**9.** The modes are 324 cards and 356 cards.

**10.** $44 = 2 \cdot 2 \cdot 11$

$28 = 2 \cdot 2 \cdot 7$

$LCM = 2 \cdot 2 \cdot 7 \cdot 11 = 308$

Saxon Algebra 1

**11. a.** Create a box-and-whisker plot using the data in the table.

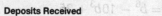

**Deposits Received**

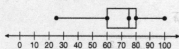

0  10  20  30  40  50  60  70  80  90  100

**b.** LE: 25, Q1: 60, median: 75, Q3: 80, UE: 100

**12.** inverse; The original statement is true, but the inverse is false.

**13.** Student B; Sample: You need to subtract 2 from each side to eliminate 2 from the left side.

**14.** Create a histogram by dividing the data into 5 groups of 4-year blocks.

**Ages of Players on Eastern Conference Team for NBA 2007 All-Star Game**

20  24  28  32  36
Age (years)

**15. a.** $A = l \cdot w$
$A = (2x + 2)(2x + 2)$
$A = 4x^2 + 4x + 4x + 4$
$A = 4x^2 + 8x + 4 \text{ in}^2$

**b.** $V = s \cdot A$
$V = (2x + 2)(4x^2 + 8x + 4)$
$V = 8x^3 + 16x^2 + 8x + 8x^2 + 16x + 8$
$V = 8x^3 + 24x^2 + 24x + 8 \text{ in}^3$

**16.** Sample:
$5(20) - 2(15) = 100 - 30 = 70$ and
$3(20) + 4(15) = 60 + 60 = 120.$

**17.** $y = 1$ and $x = 3$ are both lines of symmetry; $y = 1$ is perpendicular to $\overline{DG}$ and $\overline{EF}$, and $x = 3$ is perpendicular to $\overline{DE}$ and $\overline{GF}$.

**18.**
$y = 0.015x + 32,000$
$y = 0.03x + 26,000$
$0.015x + 32,000 = 0.03x + 26,000$
$6000 = 0.015x$
$x = \$400,000$

**19.** inconsistent

**20.** $y = 3x + 12 \rightarrow m = 3$
$y = 3x - 9 \rightarrow m = 3$
The lines are parallel.

**21.** Add the equations and combine like terms.
$2x - 3y = -17$
$\underline{-2x + 9y = 47}$
$6y = 30$
$y = 5$
Substitute 5 for $y$ in one of the original equations and solve for $x$.
$2x - 3(5) = -17$
$2x - 15 = -17$
$2x = -2$
$x = -1$
The solution is $(-1, 5)$.

**22.** Add the equations and combine like terms.
$y = x - 5$
$y = -2x + 1$
$0 = 3x - 6$
$3x = 6$
$x = 2$
Substitute 2 for $x$ in one of the original equations and solve for $y$.
$y = 2 - 5$
$y = -3$
The solution is $(2, -3)$.

**23.** $7.5 = \dfrac{k}{5}$
$k = 37.5$
The answer is **D**.

**24.** no; Sample: The value of $x$ can never equal 0 because that would mean the product of $x$ and $y$ would equal 0.

**25.** $24 \cdot 3 = 72$ total prizes
$\dfrac{4}{72} = \dfrac{1}{18}$

**26.** $x < 4 + 4$
$x < 8$

**27. a.** $x - 25,000 < 55 + 48 + 72$
**b.** $x < 175 + 25,000$
$x < 25,175$
**c.** $x > 25,000$

**Saxon** Algebra 1

**28.** Student B; Sample: Student A did not classify the graph correctly. Parallel lines have no common solutions.

**29.**
$$y = 65x + 15$$
$$13x - \frac{1}{5}y = -3$$
$$-\frac{1}{5}y = -13x - 3$$
$$y = 65x + 15$$

neither; Sample: These equations form a set of consistent and dependent equations.

**30.** Substitute $8x - 7$ for $y$ and solve for $x$.
$$2(8x - 7) = 4x + 1$$
$$16x - 14 = 4x + 1$$
$$12x = 15$$
$$x = \frac{15}{12} = \frac{5}{4}$$

Substitute $\frac{5}{4}$ for $x$ and solve for $y$.
$$y = 8\left(\frac{5}{4}\right) - 7$$
$$y = 10 - 7$$
$$y = 3$$
The solution is $\left(\frac{5}{4}, 3\right)$.
Check:

$$2y = 4x + 1 \qquad y = 8x - 7$$
$$2(3) = 4\left(\frac{5}{4}\right) + 1 \qquad 3 = 8\left(\frac{5}{4}\right) - 7$$
$$6 = 5 + 1 \qquad 3 = 10 - 7$$
$$6 = 6 \checkmark \qquad 3 = 3 \checkmark$$

## LESSON 68

### Warm Up 68

**1.** independent

**2.** $P(\text{less than } 4) = \frac{3}{6} = \frac{1}{2}$

**3.** $P(\text{multiple of } 3) = \frac{2}{6} = \frac{1}{3}$

**4.** $\frac{2}{3} + \frac{1}{6}$
$$= \frac{2}{3}\left(\frac{2}{2}\right) + \frac{1}{6}$$
$$= \frac{4}{6} + \frac{1}{6}$$
$$= \frac{5}{6}$$

**5.** $\frac{3}{4} - \frac{1}{3}$
$$= \frac{3}{4}\left(\frac{3}{3}\right) - \frac{1}{3}\left(\frac{4}{4}\right)$$
$$= \frac{9}{12} - \frac{4}{12}$$
$$= \frac{5}{12}$$

### Lesson Practice 68

**a.** $P(A) = \frac{1}{36}$

$P(B) = \frac{3}{36}$

$P(A \text{ or } B) = \frac{1}{36} + \frac{3}{36} = \frac{4}{36} = \frac{1}{9}$

**b.** $P(A) = \frac{27}{36}$

$P(B) = \frac{2}{36}$

$P(A \text{ and } B) = \frac{2}{36}$

$P(A) + P(B) - P(A \text{ and } B)$
$$= \frac{27}{36} + \frac{2}{36} - \frac{2}{36}$$
$$= \frac{27}{36}$$
$$= \frac{3}{4}$$

**c.** $12 + 12 + 5 + 3 = 32$ total outcomes

$P(A) = \frac{12}{32}$

$P(B) = \frac{3}{32}$

$P(A \text{ or } B) = \frac{12}{32} + \frac{3}{32} = \frac{15}{32}$

**d.** $P(\text{emp. or} \geq 75)$
$= P(\text{emp.}) + P(\geq 75) - P(\text{emp. and} \geq 75)$

$P(\text{emp. or} \geq 75) = \frac{291}{510} + \frac{29}{510} - \frac{10}{510} = \frac{31}{51}$

$\frac{31}{51} \cdot 200 = \frac{6200}{51} \approx 122$

about 122 people

## Practice 68

**1.** $14x^2y^3z^4$

$2 + 3 + 4 = 9$

**2.** $12q^2r + 4r - 10q^2r^6$

$2 + 6 = 8$

**3.** $5x^4z^3 + 4xz$

$4 + 3 = 7$

**4.** $\sqrt{48}$

$= \sqrt{2 \cdot 2 \cdot 2 \cdot 2 \cdot 3}$

$= 2 \cdot 2 \cdot \sqrt{3}$

$= 4\sqrt{3}$

**5.** $\sqrt{25x^4}$

$= \sqrt{5 \cdot 5 \cdot x^2 \cdot x^2}$

$= 5x^2$

**6.** $y = \dfrac{5}{x}$

$y = \dfrac{k}{x}$

yes

**7.** $y = \dfrac{1}{2}x$

$y \neq \dfrac{k}{x}$

no

**8.** $\quad x + 1 > 1.1$

$x + 1 - 1 > 1.1 - 1$

$x > 0.1$

**9.** $\quad x - 2.3 \leq 7.6$

$x - 2.3 + 2.3 \leq 7.6 + 2.3$

$x \leq 9.9$

**10.** $P(A) = \dfrac{6}{36}$

$P(B) = \dfrac{2}{36}$

---

$P(A \text{ or } B) = \dfrac{6}{36} + \dfrac{2}{36} = \dfrac{8}{36} = \dfrac{2}{9}$

**11.** $\quad P(A) = \dfrac{0}{36}$

$P(B) = \dfrac{0}{36}$

$P(A \text{ or } B) = \dfrac{0}{36} + \dfrac{0}{36} = 0$

**12.** $\quad P(A) = \dfrac{50}{75 + 50 + 75}$

$P(B) = \dfrac{30}{75 + 50 + 75}$

$P(A \text{ or } B) = \dfrac{50}{75 + 50 + 75} + \dfrac{30}{75 + 50 + 75}$

$= \dfrac{80}{75 + 50 + 75}$

$= \dfrac{80}{200} = \dfrac{2}{5}$

**13.** The slope is 0.10 and the $y$-intercept is 50.

$y = 0.10x + 50$

$y = 0.10(100) + 50$

$y = 10 + 50$

$y = \$60$

**14.** Find the slope.

$m = \dfrac{-9 - (-8)}{4 - 0}$

$= -\dfrac{1}{4}$

Use the slope to write and solve an equation in point-slope form.

$B - (-8) = -\dfrac{1}{4}(A - 0)$

$B + 8 = -\dfrac{1}{4}A$

$B = -\dfrac{1}{4}A - 8$

$B = -\dfrac{1}{4}(-4) - 8$

$B = 1 - 8$

$B = -7°F$

**15. a.** Graph the two equations.

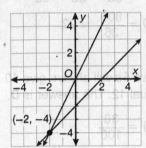

**b.** Substitute $2x$ for $y$ in the first equation and solve for $x$.

$x = 2x + 2$

$x = -2$

Substitute $-2$ for $x$ and solve for $y$.

$2(-2) = y$

$y = -4$

Verify using a graphing calculator.

**16.** $A = l \cdot w$

$A = (2x + 5)(x + 6)$

$A = 2x^2 + 12x + 5x + 30$

$A = 2x^2 + 17x + 30$ square feet

**17.** Write a system of equations.

$6x + 5y = 150$

$2x - 2 = y$

Substitute $2x - 2$ for $y$ in the first equation.

$6x + 5(2x - 2) = 150$

$6x + 10x - 10 = 150$

$16x = 160$

$x = 10$

Substitute 10 for $x$ in one of the original equations and solve for $y$.

$y = 2(10) - 2$

$y = 20 - 2$

$y = 18$

Find the ages.

$10 - 5 = 5$

$18 - 5 = 13$

boy: 5 years old; girl: 13 years old

**18.** false; Sample: $(x + 2)(x + 2) = x^2 + 2^2$

$= x^2 + 4$

Check work by using the FOIL method:

$(x + 2)(x + 2)$

$= x^2 + 2x + 2x + 4$

$= x^2 + 4x + 4 \neq x^2 + 4$

**19.** Write a system of equations.

$30x + 60y = 780$

$x + y = 20 \rightarrow x = -y + 20$

Substitute $-y + 20$ for $x$ in the first equation and solve for $y$.

$30(-y + 20) + 60y = 780$

$-30y + 600 + 60y = 780$

$30y = 180$

$y = 6$ tables

$x = -6 + 20$

$x = 14$ chairs

**20.** Student B; Sample: Student A did not correctly substitute the values of $x$ and $y$ from the known pair.

**21. a.** Plot the coordinate pairs and draw lines through them.

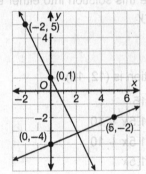

**b.** Find the slope of the first line.

$m = \dfrac{-2 - (-4)}{5 - 0}$

$= \dfrac{2}{5}$

Write an equation for the first line.

$y - (-4) = \dfrac{2}{5}(x - 0)$

$y + 4 = \dfrac{2}{5}x$

$y = \dfrac{2}{5}x - 4$

Find the slope of the second line.

$m = \dfrac{1 - 5}{0 - (-2)}$

$= -2$

Write an equation for the second line.

**Saxon Algebra 1**

$$y - 5 = -2(x - (-2))$$
$$y - 5 = -2x - 4$$
$$y = -2x + 1$$

c. no; Sample: The slopes of Line 1 and Line 2 are not negative reciprocals.

**22.** $x - 2 < 14.99$
$$x - 2 + 2 < 14.99 + 2$$
$$x < 16.99$$

**23.** Student A; Sample: The solution of the equation is $x \leq -3$.

**24.** $y = \frac{3}{4}x + 3$
$$y = x$$
$$0 = -\frac{1}{4}x + 3$$
$$\frac{1}{4}x = 3$$
$$x = 12$$

Substitute this solution into either equation to solve for $y$.

$$y = x$$
$$y = 12$$

The solution is (12, 12).

**25. a.** $y = 15$
$$y = 1.5x + 10$$
$$15 = 1.5x + 10$$
$$5 = 1.5x$$
$$x = 3.\overline{3}$$

3 stations

**b.** consistent and independent

**c.** Systems for equations that are consistent and independent have a common solution. However, because the solution is a decimal, and there can only be a whole number of stations, there is not a point where the plans cost the same amount.

**d.** no; Sample: There is no whole-number solution common to both equations.

**26.** consistent and independent

**27.** $P(A) = \frac{6}{36}$

$$P(B) = \frac{2}{36}$$

$$P(A + B) = \frac{6}{36} + \frac{2}{36} = \frac{8}{36}$$

$$\frac{8}{36} \cdot 100 = \frac{800}{36} \approx 22$$

about 22

**28.** Rolling two 5s will always give 10 and will never equal 12. The answer is **D**.

**29.** $P(A) = \frac{30}{100}$

$$P(B) = \frac{25}{100}$$

$$P(A \text{ or } B) = \frac{30}{100} + \frac{25}{100} = \frac{55}{100} = 55\%$$

**30.** The probability is higher if A and B are mutually exclusive.

## LESSON 69

### Warm Up 69

1. like terms

2. $3s + 4t + 8s - 7t$
$$= 11s - 3t$$

3. $9wv - 4m + 13m - 17wv$
$$= 9m - 8wv$$

4. $\sqrt{72}$
$$= \sqrt{3 \cdot 3 \cdot 2 \cdot 2 \cdot 2}$$
$$= 3 \cdot 2 \cdot \sqrt{2}$$
$$= 6\sqrt{2}$$

5. $\sqrt{50}$
$$= \sqrt{5 \cdot 5 \cdot 2}$$
$$= 5\sqrt{2}$$

### Lesson Practice 69

**a.** $9\sqrt{5} + 8\sqrt{5}$
$$= (9 + 8)\sqrt{5}$$
$$= 17\sqrt{5}$$

**b.** $11\sqrt{ab} - 23\sqrt{ab}$
$$= (11 - 23)\sqrt{ab}$$
$$= -12\sqrt{ab}$$

**c.** $5\sqrt{7} + 3\sqrt{2}$

no simplification is possible since the radicands are not alike.

**Saxon** Algebra 1

**d.** $\dfrac{3\sqrt{2x}}{5} + \dfrac{2\sqrt{2x}}{5} - \dfrac{\sqrt{2x}}{5}$

$\quad = \dfrac{(3 + 2 - 1)\sqrt{2x}}{5}$

$\quad = \dfrac{4\sqrt{2x}}{5}$

**e.** $4\sqrt{3c^2} - 8\sqrt{2c^2}$

$\quad = 4c\sqrt{3} - 8c\sqrt{2}$

**f.** $-11\sqrt{10a} + 3\sqrt{250a} + \sqrt{160a}$

$\quad = -11\sqrt{10a} + 3\sqrt{5 \cdot 5 \cdot 10a} + \sqrt{4 \cdot 4 \cdot 10a}$

$\quad = -11\sqrt{10a} + 15\sqrt{10a} + 4\sqrt{10a}$

$\quad = (-11 + 15 + 4)\sqrt{10a}$

$\quad = 8\sqrt{10a}$

**g.** $P = l + l + l$

$\quad P = \sqrt{12} + \sqrt{48} + 2\sqrt{15}$

$\quad P = \sqrt{2 \cdot 2 \cdot 3} + \sqrt{4 \cdot 4 \cdot 3} + 2\sqrt{15}$

$\quad P = 2\sqrt{3} + 4\sqrt{3} + 2\sqrt{15}$

$\quad P = 6\sqrt{3} + 2\sqrt{15}$ meters

**h.** $P = l + l + w + w$

$\quad P = \sqrt{75a^2} + \sqrt{75a^2} + \sqrt{27a^2} + \sqrt{27a^2}$

$\quad P = 2\sqrt{75a^2} + 2\sqrt{27a^2}$

$\quad P = 2\sqrt{5 \cdot 5 \cdot 3 \cdot a^2} + 2\sqrt{3 \cdot 3 \cdot 3 \cdot a^2}$

$\quad P = 2 \cdot 5 \cdot a \cdot \sqrt{3} + 2 \cdot 3 \cdot a \cdot \sqrt{3}$

$\quad P = 10a\sqrt{3} + 6a\sqrt{3}$

$\quad P = 16a\sqrt{3}$ feet

## PRACTICE 69

**1.** $-6\sqrt{2} + 8\sqrt{2}$

$\quad = 2\sqrt{2}$

**2.** $-4\sqrt{7} - 5\sqrt{7}$

$\quad = -9\sqrt{7}$

**3.** $2\sqrt{3} + 5\sqrt{3}$

$\quad = 7\sqrt{3}$

**4.** The degree is 1.

**5.** The degree is 2.

**6.** $xy + 2 \rightarrow 1 + 1 = 2$

**7.** $\quad P(A) = \dfrac{1}{36}$

$\quad P(B) = \dfrac{1}{36}$

$\quad P(A \text{ or } B) = \dfrac{1}{36} + \dfrac{1}{36} = \dfrac{2}{36} = \dfrac{1}{18}$

**8.** $P(A) = \dfrac{36}{36} = 1$

**9.** $\quad -4.3t^2 + 7.7t + 1.4$

$\quad \underline{\phantom{-}-3t^2 \phantom{+} + 5t \phantom{+} + 6}$

$\quad -7.3t^2 + 12.7t + 7.4$ meters

**10.** Order the data from least to greatest.

$\quad$ 3, 3, 4, 4, 4, 5, 5, 7, 8, 8, 9, 12, 18

$\quad$ min $= 3$

$\quad Q_1 = 4$

$\quad$ median $= 5$

$\quad Q_3 = 8.5$

$\quad$ max $= 18$

$\quad IQR = 8.5 - 4 = 4.5$

$\quad x < 4 - 1.5(4.5)$

$\quad x < 4 - 6.75$

$\quad x < -2.75$

$\quad x > 8.5 + 1.5(4.5)$

$\quad x > 8.5 + 6.75$

$\quad x > 15.25$

$\quad$ 18 is an outlier.

Create a box-and-whisker plot with this data.

**Hours a Candle Burns**

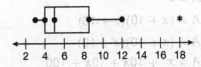

**11. a.** $\quad y = kx$

$\quad 79 = k(5)$

$\quad k = 15.8$

$\quad y = 15.8x$

$\quad$ where $x$ represents inches on a map and $y$ represents miles.

**b.** Plot a point for $y = 15.8x$ when $x = 0$ and (5,79). Draw a line through the points.

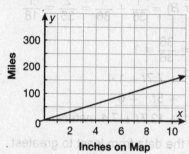

**Inches on Map**

**c.** $y = 15.8x$

$y = 15.8(6.5) = 102.7$

approximately 103 miles

**12.** Write a system of equations.

$$x + y = 35 \rightarrow y = -x + 35$$

$0.10x + 0.25y = 6.80$

Substitute $-x + 35$ for $y$ in the second equation and solve for $x$.

$0.10x + 0.25(-x + 35) = 6.80$

$0.10x - 0.25x + 8.75 = 6.80$

$-0.15x = -1.95$

$x = 13$ bananas

Substitute 13 for $x$ in one of the original equations and solve for $y$.

$y = -13 + 35 = 22$ apples

**13. a.** $A = s^2$

$A = x^2$

**b.** $A = (x + 10)(x + 10)$

**c.** $A = (x + 10)(x + 10)$

$A = x^2 + 10x + 10x + 100$

$A = x^2 + 20x + 100$

**d.** $A = x^2 + 20x + 100 - x^2$

$A = 20x + 100$ square feet

**14.** The square root usually indicates the positive, or principal square root. If a negative number is under the radical sign and is squared, the simplified answer will be the opposite of that value. For example:

$\sqrt{x^2} = -x$

$\sqrt{(-4)^2} = -(-4)$, when $x = -4$

$\sqrt{16} = 4$

$4 = 4$

**15.** Multiply the second equation by $-5$. Add the equations to eliminate a variable. Then, solve for $x$.

$35x - 15y = -15$

$41x = 0$

$x = 0$

Substitute 0 for $x$ in one of the original equations and solve for $y$.

$6(0) + 15y = 15$

$y = 1$

**16.** $y = \dfrac{k}{x}$

$180 = \dfrac{k}{4}$

$k = 720$

$y = \dfrac{720}{12}$

$y = \$60$

**17.** $y = -\dfrac{3}{2}x + 8\dfrac{1}{2} \rightarrow m = -\dfrac{3}{2}$

$y - \dfrac{2}{3}x = 0 \rightarrow y = \dfrac{2}{3}x \rightarrow m = \dfrac{2}{3}$

The lines are perpendicular.

**18.** mean $= \dfrac{85 + 95}{2} = 90$

Because the mean after two tests equals 90, Rachel's third test score must be 90 or greater to maintain a mean of 90.

$x \geq 90$

**19.** $x + 5 > 3$      $x - 6 \leq -8$

$x > -2$         $x \leq -2$

$$-7 \quad -5 \quad -3 \quad -1 \; 0 \; 1$$

Sample: Together they include all real numbers but have no solutions in common.

**20.** $x + 6 \geq 2x - 12$

$x \leq 18$

The answer is **B**.

**21.** $-\dfrac{1}{4}x + y = -2 \rightarrow y = \dfrac{1}{4}x - 2$

$-x + 4y = -8 \rightarrow 4y = x - 8 \rightarrow y = \dfrac{1}{4}x - 2$

**Saxon** Algebra 1

Any ordered pair $(x, y)$ that satisfies the equation $y = \frac{1}{4}x - 2$.

**22.** Student A; Sample: Student B did not interpret the solution correctly.

**23.**
$$y = 75x + 5$$
$$\frac{1}{5}y - 15x = 1$$
$$\frac{1}{5}y = 15x + 1$$
$$y = 75x + 5$$

Sample: The equations are dependent, so the truck is on schedule.

**24.** Student A; Sample: Student B multiplied the individual probabilities instead of adding them.

**25. a.** $36 + 24 + 30 + 28 = 118$ outcomes

$P(\text{pasta}) = \frac{24}{118} = \frac{12}{59}$

**b.** $P(\text{vegetarian}) = \frac{28}{118} = \frac{14}{59}$

**c.** $P(\text{pasta or vegetarian}) = \frac{12}{59} + \frac{14}{59}$

$P(\text{pasta or vegetarian}) = \frac{26}{59}$

**26.**
$$P(\text{black}) = \frac{3}{8}$$
$$P(10) = \frac{4}{8}$$
$$P(\text{black and } 10) = \frac{2}{8}$$
$$\frac{3}{8} + \frac{4}{8} - \frac{2}{8} = \frac{5}{8}$$

**27.** true; Sample: If $n$ is an even number greater than or equal to 2, the radical will be eliminated. If $n$ is an odd number greater than 2, an $x$ will remain under the radical.

**28.** Student B; Sample: The radicals have different radicands and the radicands cannot be further simplified. Therefore, the radicals cannot combine.

**29.** $\sqrt{51} \approx 7$
$\sqrt{63} \approx 8$
$\sqrt{83} \approx 9$
$\sqrt{104} \approx 10$
$7 + 8 + 9 + 10 = 34$
$\sqrt{51} + \sqrt{63} + \sqrt{83} + \sqrt{104} \approx 34$

**30.** $P = 4l$
$P = 4\sqrt{756}$
$P = 4\sqrt{9 \cdot 4 \cdot 21}$
$P = 4 \cdot 3 \cdot 2 \cdot \sqrt{21}$
$P = 24\sqrt{21}$
$P \approx 24 \cdot 4.6$
$P \approx 110$ in.

# LESSON 70

## Warm Up 70

**1.** solution

**2.** $12x = -84$
$x = -7$

**3.** $-7x = -91$
$x = 13$

**4.** $x > -1$
circle: open
arrowhead: shaded from $-1$ pointing to the right

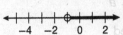

**5.** $x \leq 4$
circle: filled
arrowhead: shaded from 4 pointing to the left

## Lesson Practice 70

**a.** $\frac{1}{3}n < 2$

$(3)\frac{1}{3}n < 2(3)$

$n < 6$
circle: open
arrowhead: shaded from 6 pointing to the left

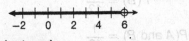

See student work.

**b.** $\frac{-x}{4} < 8$

$-4\left(\frac{-x}{4}\right) < 8(-4)$

$x > -32$

**Saxon** Algebra 1

circle: open

arrowhead: shaded from −32 pointing to the right

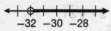
$$-32 \quad -30 \quad -28$$

See student work.

**c.** $6w \le 57$

$$\frac{6w}{6} \le \frac{57}{6}$$

$$w \le 9\frac{1}{2}$$

circle: filled

arrowhead: shaded from $9\frac{1}{2}$ pointing to the left

$$6 \quad 7 \quad 8 \quad 9 \quad 10$$

See student work.

**d.** $\frac{1}{2} \ge -4a$

$$\left(-\frac{1}{4}\right)\frac{1}{2} \ge \left(-\frac{1}{4}\right)(-4a)$$

$$-\frac{1}{8} \le a$$

circle: filled

arrowhead: shaded from $-\frac{1}{8}$ pointing to the right

$$-\frac{1}{8} \quad 0 \quad \frac{1}{8} \quad \frac{2}{8} \quad \frac{3}{8} \quad \frac{4}{8} \quad \frac{5}{8} \quad \frac{6}{8} \quad \frac{7}{8} \quad 1$$

See student work.

**e.** $0.04s \ge 750$

$$\frac{0.04s}{0.04} \ge \frac{750}{0.04}$$

$$s \ge \$18,750$$

**Practice 70**

**1.** $P(A) = \frac{6}{12}$

$P(B) = \frac{2}{12}$

$P(A \text{ and } B) = \frac{1}{12}$

$P(A \text{ or } B) = \frac{6}{12} + \frac{2}{12} - \frac{1}{12} = \frac{7}{12}$

**2.** $P(A) = \frac{6}{12}$

$P(B) = \frac{6}{12}$

$P(A \text{ and } B) = \frac{3}{12}$

$P(A \text{ or } B) = \frac{6}{12} + \frac{6}{12} - \frac{3}{12} = \frac{9}{12} = \frac{3}{4}$

**3.** $P(A) = \frac{1}{2}$

$P(B) = \frac{0}{6}$

$P(A \text{ and } B) = \frac{1}{2} \cdot \frac{0}{6} = 0$

**4.** $y - 2 < \frac{1}{2}$

$$y - 2 + 2 < \frac{1}{2} + 2$$

$$y < 2\frac{1}{2}$$

**5.** $y + \frac{3}{2} < \frac{1}{4}$

$$y + \frac{3}{2} - \frac{3}{2} < \frac{1}{4} - \frac{3}{2}$$

$$y < -1\frac{1}{4}$$

**6.** $18\sqrt{3y} + 8\sqrt{3y}$

$= (18 + 8)\sqrt{3y}$

$= 26\sqrt{3y}$

**7.** $\sqrt{3x} + 2\sqrt{3x}$

$= (1 + 2)\sqrt{3x}$

$= 3\sqrt{3x}$

**8.** $y = \frac{k}{x}$

$4.5 = \frac{k}{18}$

$k = 81$

$y = \frac{81}{x}$

**9.** yes; when dividing by a negative number, the inequality symbol needs to be reversed.

$-2a \ge -5$

$$\frac{-2a}{-2} \ge \frac{-5}{-2}$$

$a \le 2.5$

**Saxon** Algebra 1

**10. a.** Order the data from least to greatest.
22, 42, 43, 44, 49, 51, 55, 56, 60
min = 22
$Q_1 = 42.5$
median = 49
$Q_3 = 55.5$
max = 60
$IQR = 55.5 - 42.5 = 13$
$x < 42.5 - 1.5(13)$
$x < 42.5 - 19.5$
$x < 23$
$x > 55.5 + 1.5(13)$
$x > 55.5 + 19.5$
$x > 75$
22 is an outlier.

**b.**

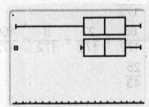

**c.** Sample: about 50 points; Excluding the outlier, both the mean and median of the scores are 50 points.

**11.** Order the data from least to greatest. 1, 5, 6, 11, 29, 29, 30, 33, 36, 38, 40, 42, 44, 61, 63, 82
min = 1
$Q_1 = \dfrac{11 + 29}{2} = 20$
median $= \dfrac{33 + 36}{2} = 34.5$
$Q_3 = \dfrac{42 + 44}{2} = 43$
max = 82
$IQR = 43 - 20 = 23$
$x < 20 - 1.5(23)$
$x < 20 - 34.5$
$x < -14.5$
$x > 43 + 1.5(23)$
$x > 43 + 34.5$
$x > 77.5$
82 is an outlier.

**Ages at a Family Party**

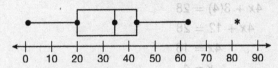

**12.** The solution is $(1, -3)$.

**13. a.** $18 = 2 \cdot 3 \cdot 3$
$15 = 3 \cdot 5$
$30 = 3 \cdot 2 \cdot 5$
$LCM = 2 \cdot 3 \cdot 3 \cdot 5 = 90$

**b.** $15 = 3 \cdot 5$
$30 = 2 \cdot 3 \cdot 5$
$LCM = 2 \cdot 3 \cdot 5 = 30$
2 balls have only two designs.

**14.** $(8x + 18)^2 = (8x)^2 + 2(8x)(18) + 18^2$
$= 64x^2 + 288x + 324$ square feet

**15.** $x + x\sqrt{5}$
$x = \sqrt{5}$
$\sqrt{5} + \sqrt{5}\,(\sqrt{5})$
$\sqrt{5} + 5$

**16. a.** Divide the data into groups by tens. Create a stem-and-leaf plot using the tens place as the stem and the ones place as the leaf.

**Customers Served Per Day**

| Stem | Leaves |
|---|---|
| 8 | 0, 0, 2, 3, 5, 6, 6, 6 |
| 9 | 0, 1, 5 |
| 10 | 1, 5, 9 |
| 11 | 4 |
| 12 | 7, 7, 7 |
| 13 | 5, 6, 7 |
| 14 | 0, 1, 1, 6, 8, 8, 8, 8, 9 |

key: 10|1 means 101

**b.** Sample: The data is not distributed evenly; it is clustered at the upper and lower extremes. This means the diner is usually extremely busy or relatively slow.

**17.** Multiply the second equation by 2 to eliminate a variable. Add the equations and combine like terms.
$-8x - 5y = -52$
$\underline{8x + 6y = 56}$
$y = 4$
Substitute 4 for $y$ in one of the original

**Saxon** Algebra 1

equations and solve for $x$.

$$4x + 3(4) = 28$$
$$4x + 12 = 28$$
$$4x = 16$$
$$x = 4$$

The solution is (4, 4).

**18.** $I = \dfrac{k}{d^2}$

$0.1 = \dfrac{k}{1^2}$

$k = 0.1$

$I = \dfrac{0.1}{d^2}$

$d^2 = \dfrac{0.1}{I}$

$d^2 = \dfrac{0.1}{0.0001}$

$d^2 = 1000$

$d \approx 31.6$

About 32 meters

**19.** $m_{\overleftrightarrow{AB}} = \dfrac{3}{2}$, $m_{\overleftrightarrow{CD}} = \dfrac{3}{2}$, $\overleftrightarrow{AB} \parallel \overleftrightarrow{CD}$.

$m_{\overleftrightarrow{AD}} = -\dfrac{2}{3}$, $m_{\overleftrightarrow{BC}} = -\dfrac{2}{3}$, $\overleftrightarrow{AD} \parallel \overleftrightarrow{BC}$, and

$\overleftrightarrow{AB} \perp \overleftrightarrow{AD} \perp \overleftrightarrow{CD} \perp \overleftrightarrow{BC} \perp \overleftrightarrow{AB}$. Therefore,

$ABCD$ is a rectangle.

**20.** Solve each system to determine which has only one common solution.

**A** $0 = 28x + 6$

$28x = -6$

$x = -\dfrac{6}{28} = -\dfrac{3}{14}$

$y = -7\left(-\dfrac{3}{14}\right) = 1\dfrac{1}{2}$

one solution

**B** $5x - 2y = 0 \rightarrow \dfrac{5}{2}x - y = 0$

$5x - 2y = 0$

same line

**C** $-y = 13x - 6$

$-2y = 26x + 9 \rightarrow -y = 13x + \dfrac{9}{2}$

parallel lines

**D** $x - 7y = 14$

$\dfrac{1}{4}x - \dfrac{7}{4}y = \dfrac{7}{2} \rightarrow x - 7y = 14$

same line

The answer is **A**.

**21.** Sample: The system is consistent and dependent because both equations are the graph of the same line.

**22.** Student B; Sample: Student A treated the events as being mutually exclusive.

**23.** $72 + 65 + 8 + 27 = 172$ outcomes

$P(\text{off}) = \dfrac{65}{172}$

$P(\text{spt}) = \dfrac{27}{172}$

$P(\text{off/def}) = \dfrac{8}{172}$

$P(\text{off or spt}) = \dfrac{65}{172} + \dfrac{27}{172} + \dfrac{8}{172} = \dfrac{100}{172}$

$= \dfrac{25}{43}$

**24.** $P = 4l$

$P = 4\left(2\sqrt{9}\right)$

$P = 8\sqrt{9}$

$P = 8 \cdot 3$

$P = 24$ meters

**25.** The absolute value of that coefficient would be between 0 and 1.

**26.** $P = l + l + w + w$

$P = 6\sqrt{4} + 6\sqrt{4} + 5\sqrt{4} + 5\sqrt{4}$

$P = 22\sqrt{4}$

$P = 22 \cdot 2$

$P = 44$

$44 \cdot 8 = 352$ ft

**27.** $5f > -10$

$\dfrac{5f}{5} > -\dfrac{10}{5}$

$f > -2$

circle: open

arrowhead: shaded from $-2$ pointing to the right

The answer is **A**.

**Saxon** Algebra 1

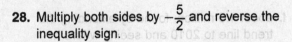
28. Multiply both sides by $-\frac{5}{2}$ and reverse the inequality sign.

29. $4s \le 100$

$$\frac{4s}{4} \le \frac{100}{4}$$

$$s \le 25$$

The solutions are between 0 and 25 and are rational numbers to the hundredths place.

30. $\frac{1}{3}b \le 20$

$(3)\frac{1}{3}b \le 20(3)$

$b \le 60$

She can make at most 60 burgers.

## INVESTIGATION 7

### Investigation Practice

a. $y = kx$

$14 = k(2)$

$k = 7$

$y = 7x$

b. $w = \frac{k}{z}$

$-8 = \frac{k}{3}$

$k = -24$

$w = \frac{-24}{z}$

c. $s = kt$

$9 = k(3)$

$k = 3$

$s = 3t$

$s = 3(5)$

$s = 15$ servings

d. inverse variation because as the pressure goes up, the volume goes down

$P = \frac{k}{v}$

$25 = \frac{k}{2.80}$

$k = 70$

$P = \frac{70}{v}$

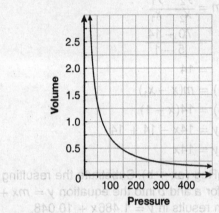

## LESSON 71

### Warm Up 71

1. slope-intercept

2. $-2$

3. $x - 2y = 4$

$x - x - 2y = -x + 4$

$-2y = -x + 4$

$\frac{-2y}{-2} = \frac{-x + 4}{-2}$

$y = \frac{1}{2}x - 2$

4. $\frac{3}{8} = m$ and $-4 = b$.

$y = mx + b$

$y = \frac{3}{8}x - 4$

### Lesson Practice 71

a.
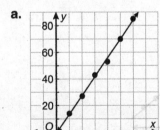

**b.** Sample: $y = 14x$, using data points $(1, 14)$ and $(5, 70)$.

$$m = \frac{y_2 - y_1}{x_2 - x_1}$$

$$= \frac{70 - 14}{5 - 1}$$

$$= 14$$

$$(y - y_1) = m(x - x_1)$$

$$(y - 14) = 14(x - 1)$$

$$y = 14x - 14 + 14$$

$$y = 14x$$

**c.** Use LinReg $(ax + b)$. Substitute the resulting values for $a$ and $b$ into the equation $y = mx + b$, which results in $y = 1.486x + 10.048$.

**d.** There is a negative correlation because the points cluster in a linear pattern and the slope of the trend line is negative.

**e.** There is a positive correlation because as the $x$-values increase, the $y$-values also increase.

**f.** There is a negative correlation because as temperature increases, the need for sweaters decreases.

**g.** There is no correlation because there is no relationship between hair color and height.

**h.** Graph 2 because as time increases, amount of calories burned increases, a positive correlation.

**i.** Graph 1 because as the number of dishes increases the amount of detergent left decreases, a negative correlation.

**j.** Graph 3 because population has no relationship to number of states. There is no correlation.

**k.**

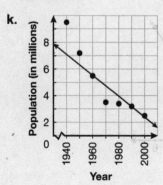

**l.** about 1.5 million, found by extending the trend line to 2010 and seeing where it intersects with the value of $y$ (population).

**m.** Use LinReg $(a + b)$. To the nearest thousandth: $a = -.111$ and $b = 223.782$

$$y = ax + b$$

$$y = -.111x + 223.782$$

The equation for a line of best fit is $y = -.111x + 223.782$.

**n.** $y = -0.111x + 223.782$

$$y = -0.111(2010) + 223.782$$

$$y = -223.11 + 223.782$$

$$y = 0.672$$

The population in 2010 will be about 0.5 million.

## Practice 71

**1.**
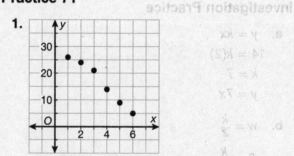

**2.** Substitute 5 for $x$ and 2 for $y$ in each equation.

$$y = 7 - x \qquad y = \frac{1}{5}x + 1$$

$$2 \overset{?}{=} 7 - 5 \qquad 2 \overset{?}{=} \frac{1}{5}(5) + 1$$

$$2 = 2 \checkmark \qquad 2 = 2 \checkmark$$

The ordered pair $(5, 2)$ is a solution.

**3.** Substitute 5 for $x$ and 2 for $y$ in each equation.

$$5y - x = 5 \qquad y = 2x - 8$$

$$5(2) - 5 \overset{?}{=} 5 \qquad 2 \overset{?}{=} 2(5) - 8$$

$$10 - 5 \overset{?}{=} 5 \qquad 2 \overset{?}{=} 10 - 8$$

$$5 = 5 \checkmark \qquad 2 = 2 \checkmark$$

The ordered pair $(5, 2)$ is a solution.

**4.** $31\sqrt{5} - 13\sqrt{5}$

$$= (31 - 13)\sqrt{5}$$

$$= 18\sqrt{5}$$

**5.** $\sqrt{27} - \sqrt{12}$

$= \sqrt{3^2 \cdot 3} - \sqrt{2^2 \cdot 3}$

$= 3\sqrt{3} - 2\sqrt{3}$

$= \sqrt{3}$

**6.** $-y = x + 8$

$y = -x + 1$

Rewrite $-y = x + 8$.

$-1(-y) = (x - 8)-1$

$y = -x + 8$

Use substitution.

$-x + 8 = -x + 1$

$8 = 0x + 1$

There is no solution. The two equations have the same slope, $-x$, and different $y$-intercepts, so the lines are parallel.

**7.** $6y - x = 12$ $\qquad y = \frac{1}{6}x + 2$

$6y = x + 12$

$y = \frac{1}{6}x + 2$

Since the equations are identical, there are infinitely many solutions. Any ordered pair $(x, y)$ that satisfies the equation is a solution.

**8.** $k = xy$

$k = \frac{2}{3}(33)$

$= 22$

$y = \frac{22}{x}$

**9.** $k = xy$

$k = 6(14)$

$= 84$

$y = \frac{84}{x}$

**10.** Student B; Sample: Student A divided the left side by 0.2 instead of −0.2.

**11.** This represents a negative correlation. The answer is **B**.

**12. a.**

**b.** no; Sample: The data appear to show no correlation since data points do not cluster to form a linear pattern.

**13.** Sample: As one set of data values increases, the other set of data values decreases.

**14.** Student A; Sample: The square root of 4 is 2. Student B did not correctly calculate the square root of 4 in the first step of the calculation.

**15.** $\sqrt{27} - \sqrt{3} + \sqrt{12}$

$= \sqrt{3^2 \cdot 3} - \sqrt{3} + \sqrt{2^2 \cdot 3}$

$= 3\sqrt{3} - \sqrt{3} + 2\sqrt{3}$

$= 4\sqrt{3}$

Randy is $4\sqrt{3}$ miles from his starting point.

**16.** **B**, since numbers that comprise a sum of 3 are also factors of 6.

**17.** probability = 1; Sample: A probability of 1 means that the outcome is certain to happen. Since heads and tails are the only outcomes and are mutually exclusive, the coin is certain to land on either heads or tails.

**18.** $x + 15 + 15 + 5 \geq 40$

$x + 35 \geq 40$

$x \geq 5$

Paulo should consume at least 5 more grams of protein.

**19.** Line 1 $\qquad\qquad$ Line 2

$m_1 = \dfrac{y_2 - y_1}{x_2 - x_1} \qquad\qquad m_1 = \dfrac{y_2 - y_1}{x_2 - x_1}$

$= \dfrac{6 - (-6)}{4 - 2} \qquad\qquad = \dfrac{0 - 1}{6 - 0}$

$= \dfrac{12}{2} \qquad\qquad\quad = \dfrac{-1}{6}$

$= 6 \qquad\qquad\qquad = -\dfrac{1}{6}$

Since 6 is the negative reciprocal of $-\frac{1}{6}$, the lines are perpendicular.

**20.**

**21.** No, because the division is by a positive value.

$$11b < 5$$

$$\frac{11b}{11} < \frac{5}{11}$$

$$b < \frac{5}{11}$$

**22.** $3s \le 36$

$$\frac{3s}{3} \le \frac{36}{3}$$

$$s \le 12$$

The side of the banner can be 12 inches or less.

**23. a.** $0.02s \ge 250,000$

   **b.** $0.02s \ge 250,000$

$$\frac{0.02s}{0.02} \ge \frac{250,000}{0.02}$$

$$s \ge 12,500,000$$

To spend $250,000 on marketing, the company must earn at least $12,500,000.

**24.** Sample: If one variable had the same coefficient in each equation, I would eliminate that variable. If one of the coefficients of a variable in one equation is a multiple of a coefficient of the same variable in the other equation, I would multiply to eliminate that variable.

**25.** There is a negative correlation because as the $x$-values in the table increase, the $y$-values decrease.

**26.** no; Sample: A histogram does not show exact values, but rather how the values are distributed within intervals. It would not be possible to determine exact values and find the mode given only a histogram.

**27.** $2\pi\sqrt{\dfrac{l}{g}}$

$$= 2\pi\sqrt{\frac{40\ m}{10\ m/s^2}}$$

$$= 2\pi\sqrt{\frac{4\ m}{1\ m/s^2}}$$

$$= 2\pi\sqrt{4s^2}$$

$$= 2\pi \cdot 2 \cdot s = 4\pi s$$

The period of the pendulum is $4\pi s$.

**28. a.** $y = 921x + 200,770$

$$y = 2419x + 183,106$$

   **b.** Use the intersection feature to find the intersection of the lines of the two equations to determine when the two populations would be equal. The point of intersection shows that the populations would be equal in 2016.

**29.** $y = kx$

$$42 = k \cdot 6$$

$$7 = k$$

$$y = 7x$$

**30. a.** Length times width:

$$(5x + 1)(2x + 2)$$

$$= (5x)(2x) + (5x)(2) + (1)(2x) + (1)(2)$$

$$= 10x^2 + 10x + 2x + 2$$

$$= 10x^2 + 12x + 2 \text{ inches square}$$

   **b.** Height times length times width (from problem a):

$$(6x + 4)(10x^2 + 12x + 2)$$

$$= 6x(10x^2 + 12x + 2) = 60x^3 + 72x^2 + 12x$$

$$= 4(10x^2 + 12x + 2) = 40x^2 + 48x + 8$$

$$= 60x^3 + 72x^2 + 12x + 40x^2 + 48x + 8$$

$$= 60x^3 + 112x^2 + 60x + 8 \text{ inches cubed}$$

The volume of the box is

$$60x^3 + 112x^2 + 60x + 8 \text{ inches cubed}$$

# LESSON 72

## Warm Up 72

**1.** binomial

**2.** $(5x + 3)(2x - 4)$

$$= (5x)(2x) + (5x)(-4) + (3)(2x) + (3)(-4)$$

$$= 10x^2 - 20x + 6x - 12$$

$$= 10x^2 - 14x - 12$$

**3.** $(5x - 6)^2$

$$(a - b)^2 = a^2 - 2ab + b^2$$

$$(5x - 6)^2 = (5x)^2 - 2(5x)(6) + (6)^2$$

$$= 25x^2 - 60x + 36$$

**4.** $(x + 1)(x^2 + 3)$

$$= (x \cdot x^2) + (x \cdot 3) + (1 \cdot x^2) + (1 \cdot 3)$$

**Saxon** Algebra 1

$$= x^3 + 3x + x^2 + 3$$
$$= x^3 + x^2 + 3x + 3$$

**Lesson Practice 72**

a. $x^2 + 3x + 2$

$ax^2 + bx + c$

In this trinomial, $b$ is 3 and $c$ is 2. Because $b$ is positive, $b$ must be the sum of two positive numbers that are factors of $c$.

One pair of positive numbers has a product of 2: (1)(2).

This pair also has a sum of 3.

So, $x^2 + 3x + 2 = (x + 1)(x + 2)$.

b. $x^2 - 10x + 16$

$ax^2 + bx + c$

In this trinomial, $b$ is $-10$ and $c$ is 16. Because $b$ is negative, it must be the sum of two negative numbers that are factors of $c$.

Three pairs of negative numbers have a product of 16.

$$(-1)(-16) \quad (-2)(-8) \quad (-4)(-4)$$

Only one pair has a sum of $-10$:

$(-2)(-8)$.

The constant terms in the binomials are $-2$ and $-8$.

So, $x^2 - 10x + 16 = (x - 2)(x - 8)$.

c. $x^2 + 4x - 12$

$ax^2 + bx + c$

In this trinomial, $b$ is 4 and $c$ is $-12$.

Six pairs of positive and negative numbers have a product of $-12$.

$$(1)(-12) \quad (-1)(12) \quad (2)(-6) \quad (-2)(6)$$
$$(3)(-4) \quad (-3)(4)$$

Only one pair has a sum of 4: $(-2)(6)$.

So, $x^2 + 4x - 12 = (x - 2)(x + 6)$.

d. $x^2 - 5x - 36$

$ax^2 + bx + c$

In this trinomial, $b$ is $-5$ and $c$ is $-36$.

Nine pairs of positive and negative numbers have a product of $-36$.

$$(1)(-36) \quad (-1)(36) \quad (2)(-18) \quad (-2)(18)$$
$$(3)(-12) \quad (-3)(12) \quad (4)(-9) \quad (-4)(9)$$
$$(6)(-6)$$

Only one pair has a sum of $-5$: $(4)(-9)$.

So, $x^2 - 5x - 36 = (x + 4)(x - 9)$.

e. $x^2 + 9xy + 20y^2$

$ax^2 + bx + c$

In this trinomial, $b$ is $9y$ and $c$ is $20y^2$. Because both $b$ and $c$ are positive, $b$ must be the sum of two positive terms that are factors of $c$.

Nine pairs of positive terms have a product of $20y^2$.

$$(1y^2)(20) \quad (1y)(20y) \quad (1)(20y^2)$$
$$(2y^2)(10) \quad (2y)(10y) \quad (2)(10y^2)$$
$$(4y^2)(5) \quad (4y)(5y) \quad (4)(5y^2)$$

Only the pair $4y$ and $5y$ has a sum of $9y$.

So, $x^2 + 9xy + 20y^2 = (x + 4y)(x + 5y)$.

f. $x^2 - xy - 12y^2$

$ax^2 + bx + c$

In this trinomial, $b$ is $-1y$ and $c$ is $-12y^2$. Because both $b$ and $c$ are negative, $b$ must be the sum of negative and positive terms that are factors of $c$.

Eighteen pairs of positive and negative terms have a product of $-12y^2$.

$$(1y^2)(-12) \quad (1y)(-12y) \quad (1)(-12y^2)$$
$$(-1y^2)(12) \quad (-1y)(12y) \quad (-1)(12y^2)$$
$$(2y^2)(-6) \quad (2y)(-6y) \quad (2)(-6y^2)$$
$$(-2y^2)(6) \quad (-2y)(6y) \quad (-2)(6y^2)$$
$$(3y^2)(-4) \quad (3y)(-4y) \quad (3)(-4y^2)$$
$$(-3y^2)(4) \quad (-3y)(4y) \quad (-3)(4y^2)$$

Only the pair $3y$ and $-4y$ has a sum of $-1y$.

So, $x^2 - xy - 12y^2 = (x + 3y)(x - 4y)$.

g. $12x + 20 + x^2$

$ax^2 + bx + c$

Write the trinomial in standard form as $x^2 + 12x + 20$, where $b$ is 12 and $c$ is 20.

Three pairs of positive numbers have a product of 20.

$$(1)(20) \quad (2)(10) \quad (4)(5)$$

Only the pair 2 and 10 has a sum of 12.

So, $x^2 + 12x + 20 = (x + 2)(x + 10)$.

h. $7x + x^2 - 44$

$ax^2 + bx + c$

**Saxon** Algebra 1

Write the trinomial in standard form as $x^2 + 7x - 44$, where $b$ is 7 and $c$ is $-44$.

Six pairs of positive and negative numbers have a product of $-44$.

$(1)(-44)$   $(-1)(44)$   $(2)(-22)$   $(-2)(22)$
$(4)(-11)$   $(-4)(11)$

Only the pair $-4$ and 11 has a sum of 7.
So, $x^2 + 7x - 44 = (x - 4)(x + 11)$.

**i.** Evaluate $x^2 + x - 6$ and its factors for $x = 4$.

$ax^2 + bx + c$

In this trinomial, $b$ is 1 and $c$ is $-6$.

Four pairs of numbers have a product of $-6$.

$(1)(-6)$   $(-1)(6)$   $(2)(-3)$   $(-2)(3)$

Only the pair $-2$ and 3 has a sum of 1.
So, $x^2 + x - 6 = (x - 2)(x + 3)$.

Now evaluate $x^2 + x - 6$ and
$(x - 2)(x + 3)$ for $x = 4$.

| Trinomial | Factors |
|---|---|
| $x^2 + x - 6$ | $(x - 2)(x + 3)$ |
| $= (4)^2 + (1)(4) - 6$ | $= (4 - 2)(4 + 3)$ |
| $= 16 + 4 - 6$ | $= (2)(7)$ |
| $= 14$ | $= 14$ |

The results are the same. The trinomial is equal to the product of its binomial factors.

## Practice 72

**1.** $x + 2 + 3 > 6$

$\quad x + 5 > 6$

$\quad x + 5 - 5 > 6 - 5$

$\quad\quad\quad x > 1$

Check the endpoint.

$x + 2 + 3 > 6$

$\quad 1 + 5 \overset{?}{=} 6$

$\quad\quad 6 = 6$ ✓

Check the direction of the inequality.

Choose a number greater than the value of $x$ for $x$.

$x + 5 > 6$

$2 + 5 \overset{?}{>} 6$

$\quad 7 > 6$ ✓

The solution of $x + 2 + 3 > 6$ is $x > 1$.

**2.** The event has a probability of 1. Since vowels and consonants are the only outcomes and are mutually exclusive, choosing a letter is certain to be either a vowel or a consonant.

**3.** List the possible outcomes for each event.
rolling a sum that is a multiple of 4

$(1, 3), (3, 1), (2, 2), (2, 6), (6, 2), (3, 5),$
$(5, 3), (4, 4), (6, 6)$

rolling a set of doubles

$(1, 1), (2, 2), (3, 3), (4, 4), (5, 5), (6, 6)$

rolling a multiple of 4 and a double

$(2, 2), (4, 4), (6, 6)$

$P(\text{multiple of 4 or double}) = P(\text{multiple of 4})$
$+ P(\text{doubles}) - P(\text{multiple of 4 and double})$

Two cubes: $6 \cdot 6 = 36$ total outcomes.

$= \dfrac{9}{36} + \dfrac{6}{36} - \dfrac{3}{36}$

$= \dfrac{12}{36}$

$= \dfrac{1}{3}$

The probability of rolling a sum that is a multiple of 4 or a set of doubles is $\frac{1}{3}$.

**4.** $x^2 + 11x + 24$

$ax^2 + bx + c$

In this trinomial, $b$ is 11 and $c$ is 24.

Four pairs of positive numbers have a product of 24.

$(1)(24)$   $(2)(12)$   $(3)(8)$   $(4)(6)$

Only the pair 3 and 8 has a sum of 11.
So, $x^2 + 11x + 24 = (x + 3)(x + 8)$.

**5.** $k^2 - 3k - 40$

$ax^2 + bx + c$

In this trinomial, $b$ is $-3$ and $c$ is $-40$.

Eight pairs of positive and negative numbers have a product of $-40$.

$(1)(-40)$   $(-1)(40)$   $(2)(-20)$   $(-2)(20)$
$(4)(-10)$   $(-4)(10)$   $(5)(-8)$   $(-5)(8)$

Only the pair 5 and $-8$ has a sum of $-3$.
So, $k^2 - 3k - 40 = (k + 5)(k - 8)$.

**6.** $m^2 + 9m + 20$

$ax^2 + bx + c$

In this trinomial, $b$ is 9 and $c$ is 20.

**Saxon** Algebra 1

Three pairs of positive numbers have a product of 20.

(1)(20)    (2)(10)    (4)(5)

Only the pair 4 and 5 has a sum of 9.

So, $m^2 + 9m + 20 = (m + 4)(m + 5)$.

**7.** $x^2 + 33 + 14x$

$ax^2 + bx + c$

Write the trinomial in standard form as $x^2 + 14x + 33$, where $b$ is 14 and $c$ is 33.

Two pairs of positive numbers have a product of 33.

(1)(33)    (3)(11)

Only the pair 3 and 11 has a sum of 14.

So, $x^2 + 14x + 33 = (x + 3)(x + 11)$.

**8.** Student A; Sample: Student B incorrectly factored −6 and then subtracted the values rather than adding them to obtain $b$.

**9.** Find the sides of the pan (factors) given the area of the pan (the trinomial).

$x^2 + 15x + 54$

$ax^2 + bx + c$

In this trinomial, $b$ is 15 and $c$ is 54.

Find the pair with a product of 54 and a sum of 15.

(1)(54)    (2)(27)    (3)(18)    (6)(9)

The pair 6 and 9 has a sum of 15. So,

$x^2 + 15x + 54 = (x + 6)(x + 9)$.

Substitute 11 for $x$.

$(11 + 6)(11 + 9) = (17)(20)$

The dimensions of the pan are 17 × 20.

**10.** In $x^2 + bx + 36$, $c$ is 36. There are nine possible number pairs that will result in a product of 36.

(1)(36) (2)(18) (3)(12) (4)(9) (6)(6)

(−1)(−36) (−2)(−18) (−3)(−12)

(−4)(−9) (−6)(−6)

**11.** the term $-1x$

**12.**

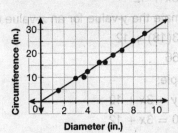

**13.** Student B; Sample: A trend line on a scatter plot does not have to contain any data points. It is used to indicate a trend in the data.

**14. a.**

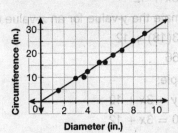

**b.** Use two points on or near the trend line. Find the slope and then the equation for the line. Sample:

Points (3, 9.5) and (8, 25)

$m = \dfrac{y_2 - y_1}{x_2 - x_1}$

$= \dfrac{25 - 9.5}{8 - 3}$

$= \dfrac{15.5}{5}$

$= 3.1$

Slope is 3.1.

$(y - y_1) = m(x - x_1)$

$(y - 9.5) = 3.1(x - 3)$

$y = 3.1x - 9.3 + 9.5$

$y = 3.1x + 0.2$

An equation that models the data is $y = 3.1x + 0.2$.

**c.** Sample: The equation is close to the formula since the slope of the line is approximately $\pi$ and the $y$-intercept is close to zero.

**15. a.** Sample: Use two points on or near the trend line to write an equation for the line.

(2, 18) and (8, 36)

First find the slope.

$m = \dfrac{y_2 - y_1}{x_2 - x_1}$

$= \dfrac{36 - 18}{8 - 2}$

$= \dfrac{18}{6}$

$= 3$

Write the equation for the line.

$(y - y_1) = m(x - x_1)$

**Saxon** Algebra 1

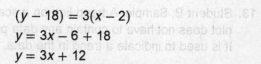

$(y - 18) = 3(x - 2)$
$y = 3x - 6 + 18$
$y = 3x + 12$

Estimate the $y$-value for an $x$-value of 18.

$y = 3(18) + 12$
$y \approx 66$

**b.** Sample:

$y = 3x + 12$
$50 = 3x + 12$
$38 = 3x$
$12.67 = x$
$x \approx 12.67$

The $x$-value for a $y$-value of 50 is about 12.67 or 13.

**16.** yes; Sample: Since the products of two negative numbers is a positive number, the square root of a perfect square can be negative. An example is $-7 \cdot -7 = 49$.

**17.** yes; Sample: The equations for the flight path and runway form a set of consistent and dependent equations. The airplane is on the same path as the runway.

**18.** Since each pair of graphed lines intersect at a single point, each system of paired equations has one solution and is classified as consistent and independent. A consistent system has at least one common solution. An independent system is a consistent system that has exactly one solution.

**19.** parallel. Find the slope of each line.

Line 1: $(-6, 3)$ and $(6, 1)$

$m_1 = \dfrac{y_2 - y_1}{x_2 - x_1}$

$= \dfrac{1 - 3}{6 - (-6)}$

$= \dfrac{-2}{12}$

$= -\dfrac{1}{6}$

Line 2: $(-6, -2)$ and $(6, -4)$

$m_2 = \dfrac{y_2 - y_1}{x_2 - x_1}$

$= \dfrac{-4 - (-2)}{6 - (-6)}$

$= \dfrac{-2}{12}$

$= -\dfrac{1}{6}$

The slopes of the two lines are identical, but the $y$-coordinates are not. Therefore, the lines are parallel, not identical or perpendicular.

**20.** Choose sets of whole numbers whose product is 100. $xy = 100$

| Length | Width | Area |
|--------|-------|------|
| 1 | 100 | 100 |
| 2 | 50 | 100 |
| 4 | 25 | 100 |
| 5 | 20 | 100 |
| 10 | 10 | 100 |
| 20 | 5 | 100 |
| 25 | 4 | 100 |
| 50 | 2 | 100 |
| 100 | 1 | 100 |

**21.** Write and solve a system of linear equations.

$d + q = 124$
$\$0.10d + \$0.25q = \$20.50$

Multiply each equation to get opposite coefficients.

$-10(d + q = 124) \rightarrow$
$-10d - 10q = -1240$
$100(0.10d + 0.25q = 20.50) \rightarrow$
$10d + 25q = 2050$

Add the equations.

$-10d - 10q = -1240$
$\underline{10d + 25q = 2050}$
$15q = 810$
$q = 54$

She has 54 quarters. Since there are four quarters in a dollar, a $10 roll holds 40 quarters. There are $54 - 40$, or 14 quarters left over.

**22.** The binomials are prime. Therefore, the LCM is the product of the binomials $(5x - 9)(3x + 8)$.

**23.** **A.** All the radicals are identical, so simply find the sum of the coefficients.

**24.** To find the median, find the middle value(s). In this plot, the stem represents tens digits and the leaves represent ones digits in the data. The middle number in the leaves is 9. The stems shows 1 opposite 9. So the median is 19. His median time was 19 minutes.

**25.** Write a system of equations.

$a + b = 36$

$a - b = 8$

Rearrange the second equation and use substitution into the first.

$a - b = 8$

$a = b + 8$

$b + 8 + b = 36$

$2b + 8 = 36$

$2b = 28$

$b = 14$

$a + 14 = 36$

$a = 22$

The numbers are 22 and 14. Their product is $22 \cdot 14 = 308$.

**26.** (13, 13)

$y = kx$

$13 = k \cdot 13$

$1 = k$

$y = 1x$

$y = x$

**27.** $\dfrac{3}{105} = \dfrac{5}{m}$

$5 \cdot 105 = 3m$

$525 = 3m$

$175 = m$

An object will travel 175 meters if it travels at 5 m/s for the same amount of time.

**28.** $2 < -4a$

$\dfrac{2}{-4} > \dfrac{-4a}{-4}$

$-\dfrac{1}{2} > a$ or $a < -\dfrac{1}{2}$

**29.** $\dfrac{-1}{3} < \dfrac{-1}{9}p$

$9\left(\dfrac{-1}{3}\right) < 9\left(\dfrac{-1}{9}p\right)$

$-3 < -1p$

$\dfrac{-3}{-1} > \dfrac{-1p}{-1}$

$3 > p$ or $p < 3$

**30.** $0.20x \leq 35{,}000$

$\dfrac{0.20x}{0.20} \leq \dfrac{35{,}000}{0.20}$

$x \leq 175{,}000$

They can buy a house whose sale price is $175,000 or less.

## LESSON 73

### Warm Up 73

**1.** inequality

**2.** $x + 7 < 0$

$\dfrac{-7 \quad -7}{x < -7}$

**3.** $x - 3 \geq -5$

$\dfrac{+3 \quad +3}{x \geq -2}$

**4.** $-x \geq 5$

$(-1)(-1x) \leq 5(-1)$

$x \leq -5$

**5.** $\dfrac{-x}{4} \leq 3$

$(-4)\dfrac{-x}{4} \geq 3(-4)$

$x \geq -12$

### Lesson Practice 73

**a.** $x > 5$ AND $x < 10$ or $5 < x < 10$

**b.** $t \geq 16$ AND $t \leq 20$ or $16 \leq t \leq 20$

**c.** $40 \leq 20 + 0.05x \leq 50$

$20 \leq 0.05x \leq 30$

$400 \leq x \leq 600$

Between 400 and 600 minutes can be used to keep the monthly bill within the desired amounts.

**d.** $x < 1$ OR $x > 6$

**e.** $x \le 0$ OR $x \ge 5$

**f.** $5x > -5$    OR    $6x < -18$

$x < -1$           $x < -3$

The solution is $x < -3$ OR $x > -1$.

**g.** $x \le 1$ OR $x > 2$

**h.** $8 \le x < 12$ or $x \ge 8$ AND $x < 12$

## Practice 73

**1.** $-\frac{1}{2}x + y = 5 \rightarrow y = \frac{1}{2}x + 5$

$x + y = 5 \rightarrow y = -x + 5$

Since they have different slopes, they cannot be inconsistent (parallel). So, use substitution.

$-x + 5 = \frac{1}{2}x + 5$

$-x = \frac{1}{2}x + 0$

$-\frac{3}{2}x = 0$

$x = 0$

$x + y = 5$

$(0) + y = 5$

$y = 5$

The solution is $(0, 5)$. There is exactly one solution, so, the system is consistent and independent.

**2.** $y = 5x - 3$

$2y - 10x = 8 \rightarrow 2y = 10x + 8$

$y = 5x + 4$

Since the equations have the same slope and different y-intercepts, the lines are parallel. The system is inconsistent.

**3.** $x + 2 - 3 \le 6$

$x - 1 \le 6$

**4.** $z + 5 \ge 1.5$

$\underline{-5 \quad -5}$

$z \ge -3.5$

**5.** $-15 \le 2x + 7 \le -9$

$-22 \le 2x \le -16$

$-11 \le x \le -8$

**6.** $x - 3 \ge 4$     OR     $x + 2 < -5$

$x \ge 7$              $x < -7$

The solution is $x < -7$ OR $x \ge 7$.

**7.**

**8.** $x \le 1$ OR $x \ge 6$

**9.** The answer is **A**.

**10.** The compound inequality $x < 0$ OR $x > 120$ describes the decibel levels that human beings cannot hear or that are too painful to hear.

**11.** Sample: Use AND when you are looking for the intersection of two inequalities or where two graphs overlap. Use OR when you are looking for the union of two inequalities or all numbers where two graphs are shaded.

**12.** $x^2 - 12x + 32$

$ax^2 + bx + c$

In this trinomial, $b$ is $-12$ and $c$ is 32.

Three pairs of negative numbers have a product of 32.

$(-1)(-32) \quad (-2)(-16) \quad (-4)(-8)$

Only the pair $-4$ and $-8$ has a sum of $-12$.

So, $x^2 - 12x + 32 = (x - 4)(x - 8)$

**13.** $2x\sqrt[3]{xy}$. Since the radicands are the same, simply add the coefficients.

**14.** $x^2 + 12x + 27$

$ax^2 + bx + c$

In this trinomials, $b$ is 12 and $c$ is 27.

Two pairs of positive numbers have a product of 27. $\quad (1)(27) \quad (3)(9)$

Only the pair 3 and 9 has a sum of 12.

So, $x^2 + 12x + 27 = (x + 3)(x + 9)$

The dimensions of the rectangle are $(x + 3)$ and $(x + 9)$.

**Saxon** Algebra 1

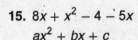

**15.** $8x + x^2 - 4 - 5x$

$ax^2 + bx + c$

Combine like terms and write the trinomial in the standard form as $x^2 + 3x - 4$, where $b$ is 3 and $c$ is $-4$.

Three pairs of positive and negative numbers have a product of $-4$.

$(1)(-4)$ $(-1)(4)$ $(2)(-2)$

Only the pair $-1$ and 4 has a sum of 3.

So, $x^2 + 3x - 4 = (x - 1)(x + 4)$.

**16.** B. $x^2 + 6x + 9$

Two pairs of positive numbers have a product of 9. $(1)(9)$ $(3)(3)$

Only the pair 3 and 3 has a sum of 6.

$x^2 + 6x + 9 = (x + 3)(x + 3)$

**17.** Sample: $y = 0.375x + 5.5$

Use points $(4, 7)$ and $(20, 13)$ to find the slope. Then use the slope to find the equation.

$m = \dfrac{y_2 - y_1}{x_2 - x_1}$

$= \dfrac{13 - 7}{20 - 4}$

$= \dfrac{6}{16}$

$= \dfrac{3}{8}$

$(y - y_1) = m(x - x_1)$

$(y - 7) = \dfrac{3}{8}(x - 4)$

$y - 7 = \dfrac{3}{8}x - \dfrac{3}{2}$

$y = \dfrac{3}{8}x - \dfrac{3}{2} + 7$

$y = \dfrac{3}{8}x + 5\dfrac{1}{2}$ or $0.375 + 5.5$

An equation for the line is $y = 0.375x + 5.5$.

**18.** Student B; Sample: If the data are rearranged so that one set of data values is in ascending order, the corresponding data values in the other set also increase. A scatter plot of the data shows a positive correlation even though the data values are not in increasing order.

**19.**

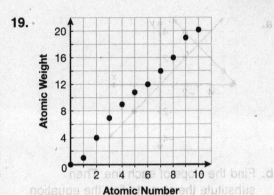

**20.** B. $-\dfrac{n}{12} < 36$

$-12\left(-\dfrac{n}{12}\right) > 36(-12)$

$n > -432$

**21.** Sample: In both cases, divide by $-2$ to solve. For the inequality, the direction of the inequality needs to be switched because you are dividing by a negative number.

**22.** Card 3: $\dfrac{1}{20}$  Card 4: $\dfrac{6}{10} = \dfrac{12}{20}$

$P(A \text{ or } B) = P(A) + P(B)$

$P(3 \text{ or } 4) = P(3) + P(4)$

$= \dfrac{1}{20} + \dfrac{12}{20}$

$= \dfrac{13}{20}$

The probability of getting either Card #3 or Card #4 is $\dfrac{13}{20}$.

**23.** rolling a multiple of 2 outcomes:

2 4 6 8 10 12 14 16 18

rolling a multiple of 3 outcomes:

3 6 9 12 15 18

rolling a multiple of 3 that is also a multiple of 2 outcomes:

6 12 18

$P(A \text{ or } B) = P(A) + P(B) - P(A \text{ and } B)$

$P(2 \text{ or } 3) = P(2) + P(3) - P(2 \text{ and } 3)$

$= \dfrac{10}{20} + \dfrac{6}{20} - \dfrac{3}{20}$

$= \dfrac{13}{20}$

The probability of rolling either a multiple of 2 or a multiple of 3 is $\dfrac{13}{20}$

**Saxon** Algebra 1

**24. a.**

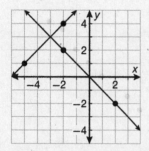

**b.** Find the slope of each line. Then substitute the slope to find the equation.

Line 1: $(-5, 1)$ and $(-2, 4)$

$$m_1 = \frac{y_2 - y_1}{x_2 - x_1}$$

$$= \frac{4 - 1}{-2 - (-5)}$$

$$= \frac{3}{3}$$

$$= 1$$

$$y - y_1 = m(x - x_1)$$

$$y - 1 = 1(x - (-5))$$

$$y - 1 = x + 5$$

$$y = x + 6$$

Line 2: $(-2, 2)$ and $(2, -2)$

$$m_2 = \frac{y_2 - y_1}{x_2 - x_1}$$

$$= \frac{-2 - 2}{2 - (-2)}$$

$$= \frac{-4}{4}$$

$$= -1$$

$$y - y_1 = m(x - x_1)$$

$$y - 2 = -1(x - (-2))$$

$$y - 2 = -1(x + 2)$$

$$y - 2 = -x - 2$$

$$y = -x$$

The equation for line 1 is $y = x + 6$.
The equation for line 2 is $y = -x$.

**c.** yes; Sample: The slopes of line 1 and line 2 are negative reciprocals of each other; they have a product of $-1$.

**25.** Find the value of $k$ in the formula for the first distance.

$$F = \frac{k}{d^2}$$

$$0.512 = \frac{k}{10^2}$$

$$0.512 = \frac{k}{100}$$

$$51.2 = k$$

Substitute for $k$ in the formula to find the second distance.

$$F = \frac{k}{d^2}$$

$$0.0142 = \frac{51.2}{d^2}$$

$$0.0142 \cdot d^2 = 51.2$$

$$d^2 = 3605.63$$

$$d = 60.05$$

The two objects are about 60 centimeters apart when they have an attractive force of 0.0142 newtons.

**26.** To solve: Set up a system of equations.

mass of Gold + mass of Nickel
= 10.3 grams

volume of Gold + volume of Nickel
= 0.7 cm³.

$$G + N = 10.3$$

$$\frac{G}{19} + \frac{N}{9} = 0.7$$

$$171\left(\frac{G}{19} + \frac{N}{9} = 0.7\right) \rightarrow 9G + 19N = 119.7$$

$$-19(G + N = 10.3) \rightarrow -19G - 19N = -195.7$$

$$9G + 19N = 119.7$$

$$\underline{-19G - 19N = -195.7}$$

$$-10G = -76$$

$$G = 7.6$$

Substitute into an original equation.

$$7.6 + N = 10.3$$

$$N = 2.7$$

The solution is $(7.6, 2.7)$.

Find the volume of gold in her ring.

$$\frac{G}{19} = \frac{7.6}{19} = 0.4 \text{ cm}^3$$

Find the volume of nickel in her ring.

$$\frac{N}{9} = \frac{2.7}{9} = 0.3 \text{ cm}^3$$

**Saxon** Algebra 1

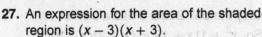

**27.** An expression for the area of the shaded region is $(x - 3)(x + 3)$.

$(a + b)(a - b) = a^2 - b^2$

$(x - 3)(x + 3) = (x)^2 - (3)^2$

$\qquad = x^2 - 9$

The area is $x^2 - 9$ square units.

**28.** $(x + 2)(x^2 + 2x + 2)$

$x(x^2 + 2x + 2) = x^3 + 2x^2 + 2x$

$2(x^2 + 2x + 2) = 2x^2 + 4x + 4$

$\qquad = x^3 + 2x^2 + 2x + 2x^2 + 4x + 4$

$\qquad = x^3 + 4x^2 + 6x + 4$

**29.** Factor each binomial.

The GCF of the terms in $(24r - 6d)$ is 6.

$(24r - 6d) = 2 \cdot 3(4r - d)$

The GCF of the terms in $(20r - 5d)$ is 5.

$(20r - 5d) = 5(4r - d)$

$(4r - d)$ is a common factor.

$\text{LCM} = 2 \cdot 3 \cdot 5(4r - d)$

The LCM is $30(4r - d)$.

**30.** Find the LCM of the two kinds of books. First write each number as a product of prime factors.

$14bn = 2 \cdot 7 \cdot b \cdot n$

$38b^9n = 2 \cdot 19 \cdot b^9 \cdot n$

$\text{LCM} = 2 \cdot 7 \cdot 19 \cdot b^9 \cdot n$

$\text{LCM} = 266b^9n$

$266b^9n$ books have been donated when a new, nonfiction book is donated.

## LESSON 74

### Warm Up 74

**1.** absolute value

**2.** $-5m + 6 = 8$

$\quad \underline{-6 = -6}$

$\quad -5m = 2$

$\quad \dfrac{-5}{-5}m = \dfrac{2}{-5}$

$\quad m = -\dfrac{2}{5}$

**3.** $\dfrac{2}{5}x - \dfrac{3}{10} = \dfrac{1}{2}$

$\quad \dfrac{+\dfrac{3}{10} = +\dfrac{3}{10}}{\dfrac{2}{5}x = \dfrac{8}{10}}$

$\quad \dfrac{5}{2} \cdot \dfrac{2}{5}x = \dfrac{8}{10} \cdot \dfrac{5}{2}$

$\quad x = \dfrac{4}{2}$

$\quad x = 2$

**4.** $\quad 3m - 7m = 8m - 6$

$\quad -4m = 8m - 6$

$\quad \dfrac{-8m = -8m}{-12m = -6}$

$\quad -\dfrac{1}{12} \cdot -12m = -6 \cdot -\dfrac{1}{12}$

$\quad m = \dfrac{1}{2}$

**5.** $-m - 6m + 4 = -2m - 5$

$\quad -7m + 4 = -2m - 5$

$\quad \dfrac{+2m = +2m}{-5m + 4 = -5}$

$\quad \dfrac{-4 = -4}{-5m = -9}$

$\quad -\dfrac{1}{5} \cdot -5m = -9 \cdot -\dfrac{1}{5}$

$\quad m = \dfrac{9}{5}$

### Lesson Practice 74

**a.** $|x| = 11$

$\{11, -11\}$

**b.** $|q + 3| = 6$

$q + 3 = 6 \quad$ or $\quad q + 3 = -6$

$\qquad q = 3 \qquad\qquad q = -9$

$\{3, -9\}$

**c.** $4|y| = 24$

$\dfrac{4|y|}{4} = \dfrac{24}{4}$

$|y| = 6$

$\{6, -6\}$

**d.** $5|z - 3| = 20$

$\dfrac{5|z - 3|}{5} = \dfrac{20}{5}$

$|z - 3| = 4$

**Saxon** Algebra 1

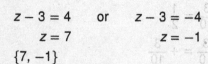
$z - 3 = 4$    or    $z - 3 = -4$

$z = 7$              $z = -1$

$\{7, -1\}$

**e.** $|x - 5| + 3 = 3$

$|x - 5| = 0$

$x - 5 = 0$

$x = 5$

$\{5\}$

**f.** $|x - 5| = -1$

Ø, since an absolute value cannot be equal to a negative number.

**g.** $|x - 30| = 0.4$

$x - 30 = +0.4$    or    $x - 30 = -0.4$

$x = 30.4$             $x = 29.6$

The minimum acceptable weight is 29.6 pounds. The maximum is 30.4 pounds.

## Practice 74

**1.** $x^2 + 12x - 28$

$ax^2 + bx + c$

In this trinomial, $b$ is 12 and $c$ is $-28$.

Six pairs of positive and negative numbers have a product of $-28$.

$(1)(-28)$   $(-1)(28)$   $(2)(-14)$   $(-2)(14)$
$(4)(-7)$   $(-4)(7)$

Only the pair $-2$ and 14 has a sum of 12. So, $x^2 + 12x - 28 = (x - 2)(x + 14)$.

**2.** $15x + 50 + x^2$

$ax^2 + bx + c$

Write the trinomial in the standard form as $x^2 + 15x + 50$, where $b$ is 15 and $c$ is 50.

Three pairs of positive numbers have a product of 50.

$(1)(50)$   $(2)(25)$   $(5)(10)$

Only the pair 5 and 10 has a sum of 15. So, $x^2 + 15x + 50 = (x + 5)(x + 10)$

**3.** $18 + x^2 + 11x$

$ax^2 + bx + c$

Write the trinomial in the standard form as $x^2 + 11x + 18$, where $b$ is 11 and $c$ is 18.

Three pairs of positive numbers have a product of 18.

$(1)(18)$     $(2)(9)$     $(3)(6)$

Only the pair 2 and 9 has a sum of 11. So, $x^2 + 11x + 18 = (x + 2)(x + 9)$.

**4.** $3x - 18 + x^2$

$ax^2 + bx + c$

Write the trinomial in the standard form as $x^2 + 3x - 18$, where $b$ is 3 and $c$ is $-18$.

Six pairs of positive and negative numbers have a product of $-18$.

$(1)(-18)$   $(-1)(18)$   $(2)(-9)$   $(-2)(9)$
$(3)(-6)$   $(-3)(6)$

Only the pair $-3$ and 6 has a sum of 3. So, $x^2 + 3x - 18 = (x - 3)(x + 6)$.

**5.** $|n| = 13$

$\{13, -13\}$

**6.** $|x + 7| = 3$

$x + 7 = +3$    or    $x + 7 = -3$

$x = -4$           $x = -10$

$\{-4, -10\}$

**7.** $-2y + 3x = 4$

$-y + \frac{3}{2}x = 2$

Write each equation in slope-intercept form.

$-2y + 3x = 4 \rightarrow -2y + 3x = 4$

$-2y = -3x + 4$

$y = \frac{3}{2}x - 2$

$-y + \frac{3}{2}x = 2 \rightarrow -y = -\frac{3}{2}x + 2$

$y = \frac{3}{2}x - 2$

The common solution for the system of equations is $y = \frac{3}{2}x - 2$.

**8.** $|h - 12| = 2$

$h - 12 = +2$    or    $h - 12 = -2$

$x = 14$           $h = 10$

The maximum height of a shelf set is 14 inches. The minimum height is 10 inches.

**9.** Sample: When the equation is evaluated at $-3$, the term on the right side of the equation has a value of $-9$. Such a solution would indicate that the absolute value of $|-3 - 6|$ is negative, which is not possible. Calculations:

$|x - 6| = 2x - 3$

$x - 6 = (2x - 3)$ or $x - 6 = -(2x - 3)$

$x - 6 = 2x - 3$     $x - 6 = -2x + 3$

$-6 = x - 3$        $-6 = -3x + 3$

$-3 = x$           $-9 = -3x$

                 $3 = x$

$\{-3, -6\}$

$|-3 - 6| = -9$

**10.** $|x - 3| = 5$

$x - 3 = +5$    or    $x - 3 = -5$

$x = 8$              $x = -2$

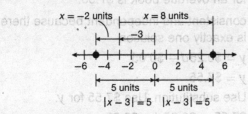

$|x - 3| = 5$    $|x - 3| = 5$

The solution set is $\{-2, 8\}$.

**11. a.** Sample: $|D - 10| = \dfrac{5}{\pi}$ or $\pi|D - 10| = 5$

    **b.** $|D - 10| = \dfrac{5}{\pi}$

       $D - 10 = +\dfrac{5}{\pi}$

          $D = \dfrac{5}{\pi} + 10$

          $D = \dfrac{5}{3.14} + 10$

          $D = 1.59 + 10$

          $D = 11.59$

          or

       $D - 10 = -\dfrac{5}{\pi}$

          $D = -\dfrac{5}{\pi} + 10$

          $D = -\dfrac{5}{3.14} + 10$

          $D = -1.59 + 10$

          $D = 8.41$

The clamp's maximum diameter is 11.6 centimeters. Its minimum diameter is 8.4 centimeters.

**12.**

**13.** $6x < 12$     OR    $3x > 15$

     $x < 2$      OR     $x > 5$

The solution is $x < 2$ OR $x > 5$.

**14.** Student B; Sample: Student A incorrectly isolated the absolute-value term as $z$; the term should be $z + 3$.

**15.** $x > 11 - 6$    AND    $x < 11 + 6$

    $x > 5$       AND      $x < 17$

The possible values for the third side of a triangle is described by $5 < x < 17$.

**16. a.** $3x > 45$     OR     $-2x \geq 24$

       $3x > 45$     OR     $-2x \geq 24$

         $x > 15$     OR      $x \leq -12$

The solution is $x > 15$ OR $x \leq -12$.

    **b.**

**17.** $x^2 - 3x - 40$

$ax^2 + bx + c$

In this trinomial, $b$ is $-3$ and $c$ is $-40$.

Eight pairs of positive and negative numbers have a product of $-40$.

$(1)(-40)$   $(-1)(40)$   $(2)(-20)$   $(-2)(20)$
$(4)(-10)$   $(-4)(10)$   $(5)(-8)$   $(-5)(8)$

Only the pair 5 and $-8$ has a sum of $-3$.

So, $x^2 - 3x - 40 = (x + 5)(x - 8)$.

**18. a.** Use $ax^2 + bx + c$.

Factor the first trinomial.

$x^2 + 9x(\text{ft}) + 20(\text{ft})^2$

In this trinomial, $b$ is 9 and $c$ is 20.

Three pairs of positive numbers have a product of 20.

$(1)(20)$    $(2)(10)$    $(4)(5)$

Only the pair 4 and 5 has a sum of 9.

So, $x^2 + 9x(\text{ft}) + 20(\text{ft})^2$

$= (x + 4 \text{ ft})(x + 5 \text{ ft})$

Factor the second trinomial.

$x^2 + 21x(\text{ft}) + 20(\text{ft})^2$

In this trinomial, $b$ is 21 and $c$ is 20.

Three pairs of positive numbers have a product of 20.

$(1)(20)$    $(2)(10)$    $(4)(5)$

Only the pair 1 and 20 has a sum of 21.

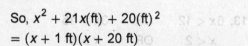
So, $x^2 + 21x(\text{ft}) + 20(\text{ft})^2$

$= (x + 1\text{ ft})(x + 20\text{ ft})$

**b.** the second set; Sample: The dimensions of the rectangles described by this trinomial are much longer than they are wide.

**19.** The answer is **A**.

**20.** Yes, because an inequality is being multiplied by a negative number.

$$-\frac{2}{3}c \le 6$$

$$(-3)(-\frac{2}{3})c \ge 6(-3)$$

$$2c \ge -18$$

$$c \ge -9$$

**21.** $P = 4 \cdot \sqrt{144}$

$P = 4 \cdot \sqrt{12^2}$

$P = 4 \cdot 12$

$P = 48$

The perimeter of the square is 48 inches.

**22.** rolling a sum of 9 outcomes:

(3, 6), (6, 3), (4, 5), (5, 4)

rolling an odd number outcomes:

(1, 1), (1, 2), (1, 3), (1, 4), (1, 5), (1, 6),

(2, 1), (2, 3), (2, 5), (3, 1), (3, 2), (3, 3),

(3, 4), (3, 5), (3, 6), (4, 1), (4, 3), (4, 5),

(5, 1), (5, 2), (5, 3), (5, 4), (5, 5), (5, 6)

(6, 1), (6, 3), (6, 5)

rolling an odd and a sum of 9 outcomes:

(3, 6), (6, 3), (4, 5), (5, 4)

$P(9 \text{ or odd}) = P(9) + P(\text{odd}) - P$

$(9 \text{ and odd})$

$$= \frac{4}{36} + \frac{27}{36} - \frac{4}{36}$$

$$= \frac{27}{36}$$

$$= \frac{3}{4}$$

The probability of rolling either a sum of 9 or an odd number is $\frac{3}{4}$.

**23. a.** $y = \$0.25d + \$0.05$

$= \$0.25(10) + \$0.05$

$= \$2.50 + \$0.05$

$= \$2.55$

The fee for a book that is 10 days overdue is $2.25.

**b.** $y = \$0.25(30) + \$0.05$

$= \$7.50 + \$0.05$

$= \$7.55$

The maximum amount the library charges for an overdue book is $7.55.

**c.** consistent and independent because there is exactly one solution

$y = \$0.25d - \$0.05$

$y = \$7.55$

Use substitution. Use $7.55 for $y$.

$\$7.55 = \$0.25d + \$0.05$

$\$7.50 = \$0.25d$

$\$30 = d$

**24.** $\frac{x}{y}$ will always be greater than $\frac{a}{b}$ because $\frac{x}{y}$ will always have a larger denominator and numerator than $\frac{a}{b}$. Example: $\frac{x}{y} > \frac{a}{b}$

$$\frac{4}{9} > \frac{3}{8}$$

**25.** $\approx 7.9$

**26.** true; Sample: The lines are parallel because they have the same slope of $\frac{1}{4}$ and different $y$-intercepts.

Calculation: Write each equation in $y$-intercept form. Then compare the slopes.

$$y = \frac{x}{4} - 2$$

$$y = \frac{1}{4}x - 2$$

$$4y = x + 8$$

$$y = \frac{x}{4} + 2$$

$$y = \frac{1}{4}x + 2$$

**27.** $x_1 y_1 = x_2 y_2$

$20 \cdot 15 = 5 \cdot y_2$

$300 = 5y_2$

$60 = y_2$

**Saxon** Algebra 1

It would take 60 people to finish the house in 5 days.

28. a. $s = \sqrt{800 \text{ cm}^2}$

$= \sqrt{10^2 \cdot 2 \cdot 2 \cdot 2 \cdot \text{cm}^2}$

$= 10 \cdot 2\sqrt{2} \text{ cm}$

The side length of the container is $20\sqrt{2}$ cm.

b. $20\sqrt{2}$ cm < 30 cm; $20\sqrt{2}$ cm > 25 cm

c. Sample: The book will not fit because one side of the container's dimensions is less than the book's dimensions.

29. $3x + y = 13$

$2x - 4y = 4$

Rearrange the first equation.

$3x + y = 13$

$y = -3x + 13$

Substitute for $y$ in the second equation.

$2x - 4(-3x + 13) = 4$

$2x + 12x - 52 = 4$

$14x - 52 = 4$

$14x = 56$

$x = 4$

Substitute for $x$ in an original equation.

$3(4) + y = 13$

$12 + y = 13$

$y = 1$

The solution to the system is (4, 1).

30. $(x + 8)(6x^2 + 6x + 6)$

$x(6x^2 + 6x + 6) = 6x^3 + 6x^2 + 6x$

$8(6x^2 + 6x + 6) = 48x^2 + 48x + 48$

$= 6x^3 + 6x^2 + 6x + 48x^2 + 48x + 48$

$= 6x^3 + 54x^2 + 54x + 48$

The area of her billboard is $6x^3 + 54x^2 + 54x + 48$.

## LESSON 75

### Warm Up 75

1. trinomial

2. $x^2 + 3 - 10$

$ax^2 + bx + c$

In this trinomial, $b$ is 3 and $c$ is −10.

Four pairs of positive and negative numbers have a product of −10.

$(1)(-10) \quad (-1)(10) \quad (2)(-5) \quad (-2)(5)$

Only the pair −2 and 5 has a sum of 3. So, $x^2 + 3 - 10 = (x - 2)(x + 5)$.

3. $x^2 - x - 42$

$ax^2 + bx + c$

In this trinomial, $b$ is −1 and $c$ is −42.

Six pairs of positive and negative numbers have a product of −42.

$(1)(-42) \quad (-1)(42) \quad (2)(-21) \quad (-2)(21)$

$(6)(-7) \quad (-6)(7)$

Only the pair 6 and −7 has a sum of −1. So, $x^2 - x - 42 = (x + 6)(x - 7)$.

4. $(4x + 5)(3x - 2)$

$(4x)(3x) + (4x)(-2) + (5)(3x) + (5)(-2)$

$12x^2 - 8x + 15x - 10$

$12x^2 + 7x - 10$

5. $(a + b)^2 = a^2 + 2ab + b^2$

$(2x + 5)^2 = (2x)^2 + 2(2x)(5) + (5)^2$

$= 4x^2 + 20x + 25$

### Lesson Practice 75

a. $9x^2 + 38x + 8$

Since $9x^2$ is the product of $(9x)(x)$ and $(3x)(3x)$, write $(9x)(x)$ and $(3x)(3x)$.

List pairs of positive numbers that result in the product of the third term, 8.

$(1)(8) \quad (2)(4)$

Check each pair to see which results in the middle term, $38x$.

| Possibilities | Middle Term |
|---|---|
| $(9x + 1)(x + 8)$ | $72x + x = 73x$ |
| $(9x + 2)(x + 4)$ | $36x + 2x = 38x$ |
| $(x + 1)(9x + 8)$ | $8x + 9x = 17x$ |
| $(x + 2)(9x + 4)$ | $4x + 18x = 22x$ |
| $(3x + 1)(3x + 8)$ | $24x + 3x = 27x$ |
| $(3x + 2)(3x + 4)$ | $12x + 6x = 18x$ |

So, $9x^2 + 38x + 8 = (9x + 2)(x + 4)$.

b. $10x^2 - 23x + 12$

Since $10x^2$ is the product of $(10x)(x)$ and $(2x)(5x)$, write $(10x)(x)$ and $(2x)(5x)$.

List pairs of negative numbers that result in the product of the third term, 12.

$(-1)(-12)$   $(-2)(-6)$   $(-3)(-4)$

Check each pair to see which results in the middle term, $-23x$.

| Possibilities | Middle Term |
|---|---|
| $(10x - 1)(x - 12)$ | $-120x - x = -121x$ |
| $(10x - 2)(x - 6)$ | $-60x - 2x = -62x$ |
| $(10x - 3)(x - 4)$ | $-40x - 3x = -43x$ |
| $(10x - 12)(x - 1)$ | $-10x - 12x = -22x$ |
| $(10x - 6)(x - 2)$ | $-20x - 6x = -26x$ |
| $(10x - 4)(x - 3)$ | $-30x - 4x = -34x$ |
| $(2x - 1)(5x - 12)$ | $-24x - 5x = -29x$ |
| $(2x - 2)(5x - 6)$ | $-12x - 10x = -22x$ |
| $(2x - 3)(5x - 4)$ | $-8x - 15x = -23x$ |
| $(2x - 12)(5x - 1)$ | $-2x - 60x = -62x$ |
| $(2x - 6)(5x - 2)$ | $-4x - 30x = -34x$ |
| $(2x - 4)(5x - 3)$ | $-6x - 20x = -26x$ |

So, $10x^2 - 23x + 12 = (2x - 3)(5x - 4)$.

**c.** $3x^2 + 5x - 2$

Since $3x^2$ is the product of $(3x)(x)$, write $(3x)(x)$.

List pairs of positive and negative numbers that result in the product of the third term, $-2$.

$(1)(-2)$   $(-1)(2)$

Check each pair to see which results in the middle term, $5x$.

| Possibilities | Middle Term |
|---|---|
| $(3x + 1)(x - 2)$ | $-6x + x = -5x$ |
| $(3x - 1)(x + 2)$ | $6x - x = 5x$ |
| $(3x + 2)(x - 1)$ | $-3x + 2x = -x$ |
| $(3x - 2)(x + 1)$ | $3x - 2x = x$ |

So, $3x^2 + 5x - 2 = (3x - 1)(x + 2)$.

**d.** $6x^2 - 5x - 4$

Since $6x^2$ is the product of $(6x)(x)$ and $(2x)(3x)$, write $(6x)(x)$ and $(2x)(3x)$.

List pairs of positive and negative numbers that result in the product of the third term, $-4$.

$(1)(-4)$   $(-1)(4)$   $(2)(-2)$   $(-2)(2)$

$(4)(-1)$   $(-4)(1)$

Check each pair to see which results in the middle term, $-5x$.

| Possibilities | Middle Term |
|---|---|
| $(6x + 1)(x - 4)$ | $-24x + x = -23x$ |
| $(6x - 1)(x + 4)$ | $24x - x = 23x$ |
| $(6x + 2)(x - 2)$ | $-12x + 2x = -10x$ |
| $(6x - 2)(x + 2)$ | $12x - 2x = 14x$ |
| $(6x + 4)(x - 1)$ | $-6x + 4x = -2x$ |
| $(6x - 4)(x + 1)$ | $6x - 4x = 2x$ |
| $(2x + 1)(3x - 4)$ | $-8x + 3x = -5x$ |
| $(2x - 1)(3x + 4)$ | $8x - 3x = 5x$ |
| $(2x + 2)(3x - 2)$ | $-4x + 6x = 2x$ |
| $(2x - 2)(3x + 2)$ | $4x - 6x = -2x$ |
| $(2x + 4)(3x - 1)$ | $-2x + 12x = 10x$ |
| $(2x - 4)(3x + 1)$ | $2x - 12x = -10x$ |

So, $6x^2 - 5x - 4 = (2x + 1)(3x - 4)$.

**e.** $6x^2 + 11xy + 4y^2$

Since $6x^2 = (6x)(x)$ and $(2x)(3x)$, write $(6x)(x)$ and $(2x)(3x)$.

The last term, $4y^2$, is the product of positive factors $(4y)(y)$ and $(2y)(2y)$.

Check each pair to see which results in the middle term, $14xy$.

| Possibilities | Middle Term |
|---|---|
| $(6x + 4y)(x + y)$ | $6xy + 4xy = 10xy$ |
| $(6x + y)(x + 4y)$ | $24xy + xy = 25xy$ |
| $(6x + 2y)(x + 2y)$ | $12xy + 2xy = 14xy$ |
| $(2x + 4y)(3x + y)$ | $2xy + 12xy = 14xy$ |
| $(2x + y)(3x + 4y)$ | $8xy + 3xy = 11xy$ |
| $(2x + 2y)(3x + 2y)$ | $4xy + 6xy = 10xy$ |

So, factors of $6x^2 + 11xy + 4y^2$ are $(3x + 4y)(2x + y)$.

**f.** $-13x + 14x^2 + 3$

Rearrange the terms to $14x^2 - 13x + 3$.

The first term, $14x^2$ can be factored as $(14x)(x)$ and $(7x)(2x)$.

The last term, 3, can be factored as $(-3)(-1)$ and $(-1)(-3)$.

Check each pair to see which results in the middle term, $-13x$.

**Saxon** Algebra 1

| Possibilities | Middle Term |
|---|---|
| $(14x - 3)(x - 1)$ | $-14x - 3x = -17x$ |
| $(14x - 1)(x - 3)$ | $-42x - x = -43x$ |
| $(7x - 3)(2x - 1)$ | $-7x - 6x = -13x$ |
| $(7x - 1)(2x - 3)$ | $-21x - 2x = -23x$ |

So, $14x^2 - 13x + 3 = (7x - 3)(2x - 1)$.

## Practice 75

**1.** $6x^2 + 13x + 6$

The first term, $6x^2$, can be factored as $(6x)(x)$ and $(2x)(3x)$.

The last term, 6, can be factored as $(6)(1)$, and $(2)(3)$.

Check each pair to see which results in the middle term, $13x$.

| Possibilities | Middle Term |
|---|---|
| $(6x + 1)(x + 6)$ | $36x + x = 37x$ |
| $(6x + 6)(x + 1)$ | $6x + 6x = 12x$ |
| $(6x + 2)(x + 3)$ | $18x + 2x = 20x$ |
| $(6x + 3)(x + 2)$ | $12x + 3x = 15x$ |
| $(2x + 1)(3x + 6)$ | $12x + 3x = 15x$ |
| $(2x + 6)(3x + 1)$ | $2x + 18x = 20x$ |
| $(2x + 2)(3x + 3)$ | $6x + 6x = 12x$ |
| $(2x + 3)(3x + 2)$ | $4x + 9x = 13x$ |

So, $6x^2 + 13x + 6 = (2x + 3)(3x + 2)$.

**2.** $3x^2 - 14x - 5$

The first term, $3x^2$, can be factored as $(3x)(x)$.

The last term, $-5$, can be factored as $(1)(-5)$ and $(-1)(5)$.

Check each pair to see which results in the middle term, $-14x$.

| Possibilities | Middle Term |
|---|---|
| $(3x + 1)(x - 5)$ | $-15x + 1 = -14x$ |
| $(3x - 5)(x + 1)$ | $3x - 5x = -2x$ |

So, $3x^2 - 14x - 5 = (3x + 1)(x - 5)$.

**3.** $18 - 15x + 2x^2$

Rearrange the terms to $2x^2 - 15x + 18$.

The first term, $2x^2$ can be factored as $(2x)(x)$.

The last term, 18, can be factored as $(-1)(-18)$, $(-18)(-1)$, $(-2)(-9)$, $(-9)(-2)$, $(-3)(-6)$, and $(-6)(-3)$.

Check each pair to see which results in the middle term, $-15x$.

| Possibilities | Middle Term |
|---|---|
| $(2x - 1)(x - 18)$ | $-36x - x = -37x$ |
| $(2x - 18)(x - 1)$ | $-2x - 18x = -20x$ |
| $(2x - 2)(x - 9)$ | $-18x - 2x = -20x$ |
| $(2x - 9)(x - 2)$ | $-4x - 9x = -13x$ |
| $(2x - 3)(x - 6)$ | $-12x - 3x = -15x$ |
| $(2x - 6)(x - 3)$ | $-6x - 6x = -12x$ |

So, $2x^2 - 15x + 18 = (2x - 3)(x - 6)$.

**4.** $-15 + 7x + 2x^2$

Rearrange the terms to $2x^2 + 7x - 15$.

The first term, $2x^2$ can be factored as $(2x)(x)$.

The last term, $-15$, can be factored as $(1)(-15)$, $(-1)(15)$, $(3)(-5)$, and $(-3)(5)$.

Check each pair to see which results in the middle term, $7x$.

| Possibilities | Middle Term |
|---|---|
| $(2x + 1)(x - 15)$ | $-30x + 1x = -29x$ |
| $(2x - 1)(x + 15)$ | $30x - 1x = 29x$ |
| $(2x + 15)(x - 1)$ | $-2x + 15x = 13x$ |
| $(2x - 15)(x + 1)$ | $2x - 15x = -13x$ |
| $(2x + 3)(x - 5)$ | $-10x + 3x = -7x$ |
| $(2x - 3)(x + 5)$ | $10x - 3x = 7x$ |
| $(2x + 5)(x - 3)$ | $-6x + 5x = -x$ |
| $(2x - 5)(x + 3)$ | $6x - 5x = x$ |

So, $2x^2 + 7x - 15 = (2x - 3)(x + 5)$.

**5.** $22c\sqrt{de} - 9\sqrt{de} = (22c - 9)\sqrt{de}$

**6.** $8\sqrt{7} - 4\sqrt{11} - 3\sqrt{7} + 7\sqrt{11}$
$= (8 - 3)\sqrt{7} + (-4 + 7)\sqrt{11}$
$= 5\sqrt{7} + 3\sqrt{11}$

**7.** Sample: Because the coefficient of the squared term is not 1, $b$ is found by adding the product of factors of $c$ and factors of $a$.

**8.** Sample:
$(7x - 10)(x - 1) = 7x^2 - 17x + 10$
$(7x - 1)(x - 10) = 7x^2 - 71x + 10$

Saxon Algebra 1

$(7x - 5)(x - 2) = 7x^2 - 19x + 10$

$(7x - 2)(x - 5) = 7x^2 - 37x + 10$

These are all the possibilities and none is correct.

**9. C**

$2(-2)^2 - 10(-2) + 14 = 8 + 20 + 14$

$= 42$

**10.** a line

**11.** If $|z| = 5$, then $z = 5$ or $z = -5$. The solution is $\{5, -5\}$.

**12. a.** Sample: $|x - 36| = 4(1.5)$

**b.** $|x - 36| = 4(1.5)$

$x - 36 = +6 \quad$ or $\quad x - 36 = -6$

$x = 42 \qquad\qquad x = 30$

The solution is $\{42 \text{ in.}, 30 \text{ in.}\}$.

The greatest perimeter is 42 inches.

The least perimeter is 30 inches.

**13. a.** $|x + 2| + 6 = 17$

$|x + 2| = 17 - 6$

$|x + 2| = 11$

**b.** $x + 2 = +11 \quad$ or $\quad x + 2 = -11$

**c.** $x + 2 = +11 \quad$ or $\quad x + 2 = -11$

$x = 9 \qquad\qquad x = -13$

The solution is $\{9, -13\}$.

**14.** $400 = 300 + 100$ and

$200 = 300 - 100$

$0.12\% = 0.0012 \quad$ Use $L$ for length.

The absolute-value equation is

$|x - L| = 0.0012L$.

**15.** $\qquad -14 \leq -3x + 10 \leq -5$

$-10 - 14 \leq -3x \leq -5 - 10$

$-24 \leq -3x \leq -15$

$\dfrac{-24}{-3} \geq \dfrac{-3x}{-3} \geq \dfrac{-15}{-3}$

$8 \geq x \geq 5$

or $5 \leq x \leq 8$

**16.** Student A; Sample: If you substitute 0 into the equation, it is a solution. Therefore, the points between the endpoints should be shaded since 0 is a solution.

**17.** $65 \leq x \leq 88 \qquad$ or $\qquad x \geq 65$ AND $x \leq 88$

**18.** The answer is **D**.

Four pairs of numbers have a product of −6.

$(1)(-6) \quad (-1)(6) \quad (2)(-3) \quad (-2)(3)$

Only the pair −1 and 6 has a sum of 5. So,

$x^2 + 5x - 6 = (x - 1)(x + 6)$

**19.** Since $2 < 3$, 2 is a solution of the compound inequality because the inequality uses OR and the solution needs to be true only for one inequality.

**20.** Two points on the trend line are (6, 12) and (16, 3).

Find the slope.

$m = \dfrac{y_2 - y_1}{x_2 - x_1}$

$= \dfrac{3 - 12}{16 - 6}$

$= \dfrac{-9}{10}$ or $-0.9$

Find the equation.

$(y - y_1) = m(x - x_1)$

$(y - 12) = -0.9(x - 6)$

$y = -0.9x + 5.4 + 12$

$y = -0.9x + 17.4$

The equation of the line is $y = -0.9 + 17.4$.

**21.** $\dfrac{1}{4}c \leq 24$

$(4)\dfrac{1}{4}c \leq 24(4)$

$c \leq 96$

He can make 96 or fewer servings.

**22.** 8 minutes = 480 seconds

$x < \dfrac{480}{10}$

$x < 48$

The maximum average time per lap she could swim and still make the team is less than 48 seconds.

**23.** $d = 4t$; direct variation; rate

This is a direct variation because the ratio of the distance and time is always the same. The rate remains constant as the distance and time change.

**24.** choosing an odd number card outcomes:

1 3 5 7 9

**Saxon** Algebra 1

choosing a number 1 outcomes: 1

choosing an odd number and a 1 outcomes: 1

$P(\text{odd or } 1) = P(\text{odd}) + P(1) - P(\text{odd and } 1)$

$$= \frac{5}{9} + \frac{1}{9} - \frac{1}{9}$$

$$= \frac{5}{9}$$

The probability of choosing an odd number or the number 1 is $\frac{5}{9}$.

**25.**  $y = 250 + 50w$

$800 = 250 + 50w$

$550 = 50w$

$11 = w$

The company receives full support for 11 full weeks.

**26.** consistent and independent because the equations have only one solution, (4, 4).

**27. a.** $7a + 5b \le 45$

**b.** $7(4) + 5(4) \overset{?}{\le} 45$

$28 + 20 \not\le 45$

No, she cannot buy 4 DVDs from both bins.

**c.** $7(3) + 5b \le 45$

$21 + 5b \le 45$

$5b \le 24$

$\dfrac{5b}{5} \le \dfrac{24}{5}$

$b \le 4.8$

She can buy 4 DVDs from Bin B.

**28. a.**

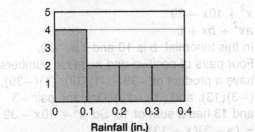

**Measurable Rainfall**

**b.** No; Sample: the histogram only reports the days for which rainfall was measured. The frequency of days without rain would need to be represented as well for the plot to be accurate and fully useful.

**29.**  $(a + b)(a - b) = a^2 - b^2$

$(4y - 4)(4y + 4) = (4y)^2 - (4)^2$

$$= 16y^2 - 16$$

**30.** $5x + 3y = 1$

$8x + 4y = 4$

Rearrange and solve for $y$.

$8x + 4y = 4$

$4y = -8x + 4$

$\dfrac{4y}{4} = \dfrac{-8x}{4} + \dfrac{4}{4}$

$y = -2x + 1$

Substitute for $y$.

$5x + 3(-2x + 1) = 1$

$5x - 6x + 3 = 1$

$-x + 3 = 1$

$-x = -2$

$\dfrac{-1x}{-1} = \dfrac{-2}{-1}$

$x = 2$

Substitute $x = 2$ in an original equation.

$5(2) + 3y = 1$

$10 + 3y = 1$

$3y = -9$

$y = -3$

The solution is (2, −3).

## LESSON 76

### Warm Up 76

**1.** radical expression

**2.** $\sqrt{50{,}000}$

$= \sqrt{10^4 \cdot 5}$

$= \sqrt{10^2 \cdot 10^2 \cdot 5}$

$= \sqrt{10^2} \cdot \sqrt{10^2} \cdot \sqrt{5}$

$= 10 \cdot 10 \cdot \sqrt{5}$

$= 100\sqrt{5}$

**3.** $\sqrt{108}$

$= \sqrt{6^2 \cdot 3}$

$= 6\sqrt{3}$

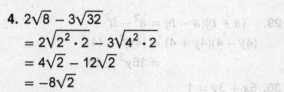
**4.** $2\sqrt{8} - 3\sqrt{32}$
$= 2\sqrt{2^2 \cdot 2} - 3\sqrt{4^2 \cdot 2}$
$= 4\sqrt{2} - 12\sqrt{2}$
$= -8\sqrt{2}$

**5.** $2\sqrt{18} + 4\sqrt{300} - \sqrt{72}$
$= 2\sqrt{3^2 \cdot 2} + 4\sqrt{10^2 \cdot 3} - \sqrt{3^2 \cdot 2^2 \cdot 2}$
$= 6\sqrt{2} + 40\sqrt{3} - 6\sqrt{2}$
$= 40\sqrt{3}$

**Lesson Practice 76**

**a.** $\sqrt{5}\sqrt{3} = \sqrt{15}$

**b.** $3\sqrt{7} \cdot 2\sqrt{3}$
$= 3 \cdot 2\sqrt{7 \cdot 3}$
$= 6\sqrt{21}$

**c.** $(3\sqrt{6})^2$
$= (3)^2(\sqrt{6})^2$
$= 9\sqrt{36}$
$= 54$

**d.** $3\sqrt{3x} \cdot \sqrt{2x}$
$= 3\sqrt{6x^2}$
$= 3x\sqrt{6}$

**e.** $\sqrt{7}(2 + \sqrt{4})$
$= 2\sqrt{7} + \sqrt{28}$
$= 2\sqrt{7} + \sqrt{2^2 \cdot 7}$
$= 2\sqrt{7} + 2\sqrt{7}$
$= 4\sqrt{7}$

**f.** $\sqrt{5}(\sqrt{4} - \sqrt{3})$
$= \sqrt{20} - \sqrt{15}$
$= \sqrt{2^2 \cdot 5} - \sqrt{15}$
$= 2\sqrt{5} - \sqrt{15}$

**g.** $(5 + \sqrt{9})(4 - \sqrt{6})$
$= 20 - 5\sqrt{6} + 4\sqrt{9} - \sqrt{54}$
$= 20 - 5\sqrt{6} + 4\sqrt{3^2} - \sqrt{3^2 \cdot 6}$
$= 20 - 5\sqrt{6} + 12 - 3\sqrt{6}$
$= 32 - 8\sqrt{6}$

**h.** $(4 - \sqrt{7})^2$
$= 16 - 8\sqrt{7} + \sqrt{7^2}$
$= 23 - 8\sqrt{7}$

**i.** $(32 + \sqrt{13})^2$
$= 1024 + 64\sqrt{13} + \sqrt{13^2}$
$= 1037 + 64\sqrt{13}$

**Practice 76**

**1.** $\frac{5}{6} \le -2p$

$(6)\frac{5}{6} \le -2p(6)$

$5 \le -12p$

$-\frac{5}{12} \ge p$

**2.** $|x + 4| = 5$
$x + 4 = +5$    or    $x + 4 = -5$
$x = 1$           $x = -9$
$\{1, -9\}$

**3.** $12x^2 - 25x + 7$
The first term, $12x^2$, can be factored as $(12x)(x)$, $(6x)(2x)$, and $(4x)(3x)$.
The last term, 7, can be factored as $(-7)(-1)$.
Check each pair to see which results in the middle term, $-25x$.

| Possibilities | Middle Term |
| --- | --- |
| $(12x - 7)(x - 1)$ | $-12x - 7x = -19x$ |
| $(12x - 1)(x - 7)$ | $-84x - x = -85x$ |
| $(6x - 7)(2x - 1)$ | $-6x - 14x = -20x$ |
| $(6x - 1)(2x - 7)$ | $-42x - 2x = -44x$ |
| $(4x - 7)(3x - 1)$ | $-4x - 21x = -25x$ |
| $(4x - 1)(3x - 7)$ | $-28x - 3x = -31x$ |

So, $12x^2 - 25x + 7 = (4x - 7)(3x - 1)$.

**4.** $x^2 + 10x - 39$
$ax^2 + bx + c$
In this trinomial, $b$ is 10 and $c$ is $-39$.
Four pairs of positive and negative numbers have a product of $-39$. $(-1)(39)$, $(1)(-39)$, $(-3)(13)$, and $(3)(-13)$. Only the pair $-3$ and 13 has a sum of 10. So, $x^2 + 10x - 39 = (x - 3)(x + 13)$

**5.** $5z^2 + 2z - 7$
The first term, $5z^2$, can be factored as $(5z)(z)$.
The last term, $-7$, can be factored as $(-7)(1)$, and $(7)(-1)$.

Check each pair to see which results in the middle term, 2z.

| Possibilities | Middle Term |
|---|---|
| $(5z - 7)(z + 1)$ | $5z - 7z = -2z$ |
| $(5z + 7)(z - 1)$ | $-5z + 7z = 2z$ |
| $(5z - 1)(z + 7)$ | $35z - z = 34z$ |
| $(5z + 1)(z - 7)$ | $-35z + z = -34z$ |

So, $5z^2 + 2z - 7 = (5z + 7)(z - 1)$.

**6.** $3x^2 + 25x - 18$

The first term, $3x^2$, can be factored as $(3x)(x)$.

The last term, $-18$, can be factored as $(-18)(1)$, $(18)(-1)$, $(-9)(2)$, $(9)(-2)$, $(-6)(3)$, and $(6)(-3)$.

Check each pair to see which results in the middle term, 25x.

| Possibilities | Middle Term |
|---|---|
| $(3x - 18)(x + 1)$ | $3x - 18x = -15x$ |
| $(3x + 18)(x - 1)$ | $-3x + 18x = 15x$ |
| $(3x - 1)(x + 18)$ | $54x - x = 53x$ |
| $(3x + 1)(x - 18)$ | $-54 + x = -53x$ |
| $(3x - 9)(x + 2)$ | $6x - 9x = -3x$ |
| $(3x + 9)(x - 2)$ | $-6x + 9x = 3x$ |
| $(3x - 2)(x + 9)$ | $27x - 2x = 25x$ |
| $(3x + 2)(x - 9)$ | $-27 + 2x = -25x$ |
| $(3x - 6)(x + 3)$ | $9x - 6x = 3x$ |
| $(3x + 6)(x - 3)$ | $-9x + 6x = -3x$ |
| $(3x - 3)(x + 6)$ | $18x - 3x = 15x$ |
| $(3x + 3)(x - 6)$ | $-18x + 3x = -15x$ |

So, $3x^2 + 25x - 18 = (3x - 2)(x + 9)$.

**7.** $4\sqrt{3} \cdot 6\sqrt{6} \cdot 3\sqrt{3} \cdot 2\sqrt{2}$

$= 4 \cdot 6 \cdot 3 \cdot 2\sqrt{3 \cdot 6 \cdot 3 \cdot 2}$

$= 144 \cdot 3 \cdot 2\sqrt{3}$

$= 864\sqrt{3}$

**8.** $-17\sqrt{7s} - 4\sqrt{7s}$

$= -21\sqrt{7s}$

**9.** $(4\sqrt{5})^2$

$= (4)^2(\sqrt{5})^2$

$= 16 \cdot 5$

$= 80$

**10.** $3\sqrt{2} \cdot 4\sqrt{12} - 6\sqrt{54}$

$= 12\sqrt{24} - 6\sqrt{54}$

$= 12\sqrt{4 \cdot 6} - 6\sqrt{9 \cdot 6}$

$= 24\sqrt{6} - 18\sqrt{6}$

$= 6\sqrt{6}$

**11.** $\sqrt{\dfrac{x^2}{60}}$

$= \sqrt{\dfrac{x^2 \cdot x}{2^2 \cdot 15}}$

$= \dfrac{x}{2}\sqrt{\dfrac{x}{15}}$

**12.** $17 \cdot 23$

$= (20 - 3)(20 + 3) = 20^2 - 3^2$

$= 400 - 9$

$= 391$

**13.** An expression for the area is $(8 - \sqrt{4})^2$, since all sides of a square are equal.

$(8 - \sqrt{4})^2$

$= 64 - 16\sqrt{4} + \sqrt{16}$

$= 64 - 32 + 4$

$= 36$

The area of the figure is 36 square feet.

**14.** Sample: Use the Distributive Property to multiply the radicals: $\sqrt{6} \cdot \sqrt{16}$. Then simplify: $\sqrt{6} \cdot 4$.

**15.** Sample: $\sqrt{625} \cdot \sqrt{16} = \sqrt{10,000} = 100$

**16.** The answer is **B**.

**17.** $46x^2 - 9x + 95$

$= 46(3^2) - 9(3) + 95$

$= 414 - 27 + 95$

$= 482$

The cost of a 3-night vacation is $482.

**18.** Student A; Sample: Student B's trinomial would have a middle term of $6x$, not $-6x$.

**19.** $16x^2 - 40x + 25$

The first term, $16x^2$, can be factored as $(16x)(x)$, $(8x)(2x)$, and $(4x)(4x)$.

The last term, 25, can be factored as $(-25)(-1)$, and $(-5)(-5)$.

Check each pair to see which results in the middle term, $-40x$.

243

| Possibilities | Middle Term |
|---|---|
| $(16x - 25)(x - 1)$ | $-16x - 25x = -41x$ |
| $(16x - 1)(x - 25)$ | $-400x - x = -401x$ |
| $(16x - 5)(x - 5)$ | $-80x - 5x = -85x$ |
| $(8x - 25)(2x - 1)$ | $-8x - 50x = -58x$ |
| $(8x - 1)(2x - 25)$ | $-200x - 2x = -202x$ |
| $(8x - 5)(2x - 5)$ | $-40x - 10x = -50x$ |
| $(4x - 25)(4x - 1)$ | $-4x - 100x = -104x$ |
| $(4x - 5)(4x - 5)$ | $-20x - 20x = -40x$ |

So, $16x^2 - 40x + 25 = (4x - 5)(4x - 5)$.

$(4x - 5)^2$

$\sqrt{(4x - 5)^2} = (4x - 5)$

The length of the hypotenuse is $(4x - 5)$.

**20. a.** $2x^2 + 3x - 27$

$2(12^2) + 3(12) - 27$

$= 288 + 36 - 27$

$= 297$

**b.** $2x^2 + 3x - 27$

The first term, $2x^2$, can be factored as $(2x)(x)$.

The last term, $-27$, can be factored as $(-27)(1)$, $(27)(-1)$, $(-9)(3)$, and $(9)(-3)$.

Check each pair to see which results in the middle term, $3x$.

| Possibilities | Middle Term |
|---|---|
| $(2x - 27)(x + 1)$ | $2x - 27x = -25x$ |
| $(2x + 27)(x - 1)$ | $-2x + 27x = 25x$ |
| $(2x - 1)(x + 27)$ | $54x - x = 53x$ |
| $(2x + 1)(x - 27)$ | $-54x + x = -53x$ |
| $(2x - 9)(x + 3)$ | $6x - 9 = -3x$ |
| $(2x + 9)(x - 3)$ | $-6x + 9x = 3x$ |
| $(2x - 3)(x + 9)$ | $18x - 3x = 15x$ |
| $(2x + 3)(x - 9)$ | $-18x + 3x = -15x$ |

So, $2x^2 + 3x - 27 = (2x + 9)(x - 3)$.

**21.** Student B; Sample: Student A incorrectly isolated the absolute-value term by subtracting the coefficient of 3 instead of dividing.

**22.** $|w - 27| = 3$

$w - 27 = +3$ or $w - 27 = -3$

$w = 30$ $w = 24$

The maximum width of window in which a guard will fit is 30 inches. The minimum is 24 inches.

**23.** The answer is **B**.

**24.** all real numbers; Every real number is more than three OR less than five.

**25. a.**

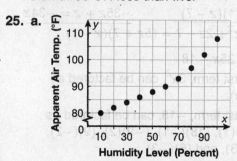

**b.** positive correlation because the points form a linear pattern that rises from left to right.

**26.**

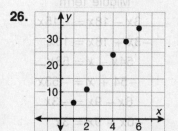

**27.** 12 flying birds + 5 flying insects + 4 land insects + 4 land mammals = 25 chapters.

$\frac{8}{25} = \frac{4}{25} + \frac{4}{25}$ is the only possible combination of chapters. So, the chapters would be about land animals (insects and mammals).

**28. a.** $y = \$20 + \$6x$

$\$32 = \$20 + \$6x$

$12 = 6x$

$2 = x$

New members receive 2 services before paying the same amount as a regular fee.

**b.** An equation describing the regular rate for the facility is $y = \$32 + \$6x$.

**c.** The system of equations is inconsistent because the system has no solution. Graphs of the lines will be parallel since they have the same slope, 6.

**29** $20.5 + x < 235$

$x < 3$

**Saxon** Algebra 1

There could have been less than 3 more inches of snow in 1958.

**30.** $K + D = 30$

$3K - 2D = 5$

$2(K + D = 30) \rightarrow 2K + 2D = 60$

$2K + 2D = 60$

$\dfrac{3K - 2D = 5}{5K = 65}$

$K = 13$

$C = K - 5$

$C = 13 - 5$

$C = 8$

César is 8 years old.

## LESSON 77

### Warm Up 77

**1.** equation

**2.** $x - \dfrac{1}{3} > 2$

$3\left(x - \dfrac{1}{3} > 2\right)$

$3x - 1 > 6$

$3x > 7$

$x > \dfrac{7}{3}$ or $2\dfrac{1}{3}$

**3.** $x + 2.1 < 4.3$

$\dfrac{-2.1 \quad -2.1}{x < 2.2}$

**4.** $\dfrac{1}{2}x \le -3$

$2\left(\dfrac{1}{2}x\right) \le -3(2)$

$x \le -6$

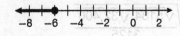

**5.** $-5x \ge 10$

$x \le -2$

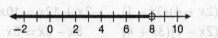

### Lesson Practice 77

**a.** $4x + 29 \le 25$

$4x \le -4$

$x \le -1$

**b.** $-36 - 7k < 6$

$-7k < 42$

$k > -6$

**c.** $-18 + (-3) < -4f + 11$

$-21 < -4f + 11$

$-32 < -4f$

$8 > f$

$f < 8$

**d.** $-5(10 - 5p) > (-10)^2$

$-50 + 25p > 100$

$25p > 150$

$p > 6$

**e.** $\dfrac{1}{12}y + \dfrac{2}{3} \ge \dfrac{5}{6}$

$\dfrac{12(1)}{12}y + \dfrac{2(12)}{3} \ge \dfrac{5(12)}{6}$

$y + 8 \ge 10$

$y \ge 2$

**f.** $180 - 5t \le 150$

$-5t \le -30$

$t \ge 6$

Her time will be at most 150 seconds in 6 weeks.

Saxon Algebra 1

## Practice 77

**1.** 48 lb because it is the middle value.

**2.** 47 lb because it is the most frequent value.

**3.** $6x^2 - 10x - 4$

The first term, $6x^2$, can be factored as $(6x)(x)$ and $(2x)(3x)$.

The last term, $-4$, can be factored as $(-4)(1)$, $(4)(-1)$, and $(-2)(2)$.

Check each pair to see which results in the middle term, $-10x$.

| Possibilities | Middle Term |
|---|---|
| $(6x - 4)(x + 1)$ | $6x - 4x = 2x$ |
| $(6x + 4)(x - 1)$ | $-6x + 4x = -2x$ |
| $(6x - 1)(x + 4)$ | $24x - x = 23x$ |
| $(6x + 1)(x - 4)$ | $-24x + x = -23x$ |
| $(6x - 2)(x + 2)$ | $12x - 2x = 10x$ |
| $(6x + 2)(x - 2)$ | $-12x + 2x = -10x$ |
| $(2x - 4)(3x + 1)$ | $2x - 12x = -10x$ |
| $(2x + 4)(3x - 1)$ | $-2x + 12x = 10x$ |
| $(2x - 1)(3x + 4)$ | $8x - 3x = 5x$ |
| $(2x + 1)(3x - 4)$ | $-8x + 3x = -5x$ |
| $(2x - 2)(x + 2)$ | $4x - 2x = 2x$ |
| $(2x + 2)(x - 2)$ | $-4x + 2x = -2x$ |

So, $6x^2 - 10x - 14 = (6x + 2)(x - 2)$ or $2(3x + 1)$ and $(2x - 4)(3x + 1)$.

**4.**
$$9 > 0.3r$$
$$(10)9 > 0.3r(10)$$
$$90 > 3r$$
$$30 > r$$
$$r < 30$$

**5.** $5 + 4x > 37$
$$4x > 32$$
$$x > 8$$

**6.** $\dfrac{x}{-3} - 2 \le 1$

$$-3\left(\dfrac{x}{-3} - 2\right) \ge (1) - 3$$
$$x + 6 \ge -3$$
$$x \ge -9$$

**7.** $-3x + 2 \le 1$
$$-3x \le -1$$
$$x \ge \dfrac{1}{3}$$

**8.** $\dfrac{x}{5} - 4 > 9$
$$5\left(\dfrac{x}{5} - 4\right) > (9)5$$
$$x - 20 > 45$$
$$x > 65$$

**9.** $-5 < r - 6 < -2$
$$1 < r < 4$$

**10.** $4\sqrt{3x}\,\sqrt{4x}$
$$= 4\sqrt{3x \cdot 4x}$$
$$= 2x \cdot 4\sqrt{3}$$
$$= 8x\sqrt{3}$$

**11.** $\sqrt{400g^6}$
$$= \sqrt{10^2 \cdot 2^2 \cdot g^2 \cdot g^2 \cdot g^2}$$
$$= \sqrt{10^2} \cdot \sqrt{2^2} \cdot \sqrt{g^2} \cdot \sqrt{g^2} \cdot \sqrt{g^2}$$
$$= 10 \cdot 2 \cdot g \cdot g \cdot g$$
$$= 20g^3$$

**12.** Sample: The only difference is having to remember to reverse the inequality sign when you multiply or divide both sides by a negative number.

**13.** The answer is **B**.
$$6 - 7y < 48$$
$$-7y < 42$$
$$y > -6$$

**14.** $2(18) + 2b \le 42$
$$36 + 2b \le 42$$
$$2b \le 6$$
$$b \le 3$$

The bottles can cost at most $3 each.

**15.** $x = \sqrt{\dfrac{HW}{3125}}$

$$x = \sqrt{\dfrac{\sqrt{5184}\,\sqrt{32,400}}{3125}}$$
$$\sqrt{5184} = \sqrt{9^2 \cdot 8^2}$$
$$= 9 \cdot 8$$
$$= 72$$

**Saxon** Algebra 1

$$\sqrt{32,400} = \sqrt{10^2 \cdot 9^2 \cdot 2^2}$$
$$= 10 \cdot 9 \cdot 2$$
$$= 180$$

$$x = \sqrt{\frac{72 \cdot 180}{3125}}$$
$$= \sqrt{4.1472}$$
$$= 2$$

The man's BSA is about 2 square meters.

**16.** $12x^2 - 2x - 4$

The first term, $12x^2$, can be factored as $(12x)(1x)$, $(6x)(2x)$, and $(3x)(4x)$.

The last term, $-4$, can be factored as $(-4)(1)$, $(4)(-1)$, and $(-2)(2)$.

Check each pair to see which results in the middle term, $-2x$.

| Possibilities | Middle Term |
|---|---|
| $(12x - 4)(x + 1)$ | $12x - 4x = 8x$ |
| $(12x + 4)(x - 1)$ | $-12x + 4x = -8x$ |
| $(12x - 1)(x + 4)$ | $48x - x = 47x$ |
| $(12x + 1)(x - 4)$ | $-48x + x = -47x$ |
| $(12x - 2)(x + 2)$ | $24x - 2x = 22x$ |
| $(12x + 2)(x - 2)$ | $-24x + 2x = -22x$ |
| $(6x - 4)(2x + 1)$ | $6x - 8x = -2x$ |
| $(6x + 4)(2x - 1)$ | $-6x + 8x = 2x$ |
| $(6x - 1)(2x + 4)$ | $24x - 2x = 22x$ |
| $(6x + 1)(2x - 4)$ | $-24x + 2x = -22x$ |
| $(6x - 2)(2x + 2)$ | $12x - 4x = 8x$ |
| $(6x + 2)(2x - 2)$ | $-12x + 4x = -8x$ |
| $(3x - 4)(4x + 1)$ | $3x - 16x = -13x$ |
| $(3x + 4)(4x - 1)$ | $-3x + 16x = 13x$ |
| $(3x - 1)(4x + 4)$ | $12x - 4x = 8x$ |
| $(3x + 1)(4x - 4)$ | $-12x + 4x = -8x$ |
| $(3x - 2)(4x + 2)$ | $6x - 8x = -2x$ |
| $(3x + 2)(4x - 2)$ | $-6x + 8x = 2x$ |

So, $12x^2 - 2x - 4 = (6x - 4)(2x + 1)$ and $2(3x - 2)(2x + 1)$.

**17.** Student A; Sample: Student B didn't correctly simplify $\sqrt{150}$.

**18. a.** $S = \sqrt{g \cdot d}$
$$S = \sqrt{9.8 \cdot 1000}$$
$$= \sqrt{9800}$$
$$= \sqrt{7 \cdot 7 \cdot 10 \cdot 10 \cdot 2}$$

$$= 7 \cdot 10\sqrt{2}$$
$$= 70\sqrt{2}$$

The speed of the tsunami is $70\sqrt{2}$ meters per second.

**b.** $S = \sqrt{g \cdot d}$
$$S = \sqrt{9.8 \cdot 2000}$$
$$= \sqrt{19600}$$
$$= \sqrt{7 \cdot 7 \cdot 10 \cdot 10 \cdot 2 \cdot 2}$$
$$= 7 \cdot 10 \cdot 2$$
$$= 140$$

The speed of the tsunami is 140 meters per second.

**19.** $A = \dfrac{bh}{2}$

$$= \frac{(3 + \sqrt{15})(5 - \sqrt{20})}{2}$$
$$= \frac{15 - 3\sqrt{20} + 5\sqrt{15} - \sqrt{300}}{2}$$
$$= \frac{15 - 3\sqrt{2 \cdot 2 \cdot 5} + 5\sqrt{15} - \sqrt{3 \cdot 10 \cdot 10}}{2}$$
$$= \frac{15 - 6\sqrt{5} + 5\sqrt{15} - 10\sqrt{3}}{2}$$

**20.** Student A; Sample: Student B's trinomial would have a middle term of $-16x$, not $16x$.
$$(3x - 5)(5x + 3)$$
$$(3x \cdot 3) - (5 \cdot 5x) = 9x - 25x = -16x$$

**21.** D
$$|x - 3| + 2 = 0$$
$$|x - 3| = -2$$
Because absolute value cannot be equal to a negative number, there is no solution.

**22.** Sample: To solve the equation, the absolute value of $|x + 11|$ would be $-2$. However, an absolute value cannot be less than zero.

**23.** First find the factors of the expression $x^2 + 30x - 400$.
$$ax^2 + bx + c$$

In this trinomial, $b$ is 30 and $c$ is $-400$. Thirteen pairs of positive and negative numbers have a product of $-400$.

| | | |
|---|---|---|
| $(1)(-400)$ | $(-1)(400)$ | $(2)(-200)$ |
| $(-2)(400)$ | $(4)(-100)$ | $(-4)(100)$ |
| $(5)(-80),$ | $(-5)(80)$ | $(8)(-50)$ |

## Solutions Key

77-78

(−50)(8)    (10)(−40)   (−10)(40)
(20)(−20)

Only one pair has a sum of 30 (−10)(40).
So, $x^2 + 30x - 400 = (x - 10)(x + 40)$.
Find the dimensions of the rug if $x$ is 40.
$(x - 10)(x + 40)$
$(40 - 10) = 30$
$(40 + 40) = 80$
The dimensions of the rug are $30 \times 80$.

**24.** positive correlation because the points form a linear pattern that rises from left to right. Both sets of data values are increasing

**25.** $x \geq 4 - 0.03$    AND    $x \leq 4 + 0.03$
$x \geq 3.97$        AND    $x \leq 4.03$
A compound inequality to represent this situation is $3.97 \leq x \leq 4.03$.

**26.** $3gh\sqrt{275g^7h^9}$
$= 3gh\sqrt{275 \cdot g^7 \cdot h^9}$
$= 3gh\sqrt{25 \cdot 11}\sqrt{g^7}\sqrt{h^9}$
$= 3gh \cdot 5\sqrt{11} \cdot g^3\sqrt{g} \cdot h^4\sqrt{h}$
$= 15g^4h^5\sqrt{11gh}$

**27. a.** $57q + 24d + 35n + 60p = 176$
$P(q + d) = P(q) + P(d)$
$= \frac{57}{176} + \frac{24}{176}$
$= \frac{81}{176}$
The probability that the coin is a quarter or dime is $\frac{81}{176}$.

**b.** Since only a quarter or a dime is worth more than 5 cents, the probability is the same as in part a.
$(Pq \text{ or } > 5 \text{ cents}) = (Pq) + P(> 5 \text{ cents})$
$= \frac{57}{176} + \frac{24}{176}$
$= \frac{81}{176}$

**c.** Sample: The answers are the same because the events describe the same set of possible outcomes, but in two different ways.

**28.** Use substitution.
$p = 6x + 24$
$p = 8x + 20$
$6x + 24 = 8x + 20$
$6x = 8x - 4$
$-2x = -4$
$x = 2$
Substitute $x$ in an original equation.
$p = 6(2) + 24$
$p = 36$
The solution is (2, 3). There is exactly one solution, so the system is consistent and independent.

**29.** $l \cdot w = k$
$12 \cdot 3 = 36$
$l = \frac{k}{w}$
Try: $l = \frac{36}{4}$
$= 9$
$4 \cdot 9$ is not a square.
Try $l = \frac{36}{6}$
$= 6$
$6 \cdot 6$ is a square.
The arrangement should be 6 bricks wide and 6 bricks long.

**30.** Student B; Sample: Student A removed the perfect-square factor rather than the square root of that factor.

## LESSON 78

### Warm Up 78

**1.** rational

**2.** true. Make a table of values for $x = -2$.

| x | −2 | −2 | −2 | −2 |
|---|----|----|----|----|
| y | 0 | 1 | 2 | 3 |

The x-values are all the same and the y-values vary. When graphed, a vertical line is formed through −2 on the x-axis and never crosses the y-axis.

© Saxon. All rights reserved.

**Saxon** Algebra 1

**3.** false. Make a table of values for $y = -x$.

| x | 0 | 1 | 2 | 3 |
|---|---|---|---|---|
| y | 0 | −1 | −2 | −3 |

As the $x$-values increase, the $y$-values decrease. When graphed, a line is formed that has a slope of −1.

**4.** Since division by 0 is undefined, start with the denominator.

$$\frac{x+7}{3x}$$

$3x = 0$ when $x = 0$.

The expression is undefined when $x = 0$.

**Lesson Practice 78**

**a.** $y = \dfrac{4}{6m}$

Set the denominator equal to zero and solve.

$6m = 0$

$\dfrac{6m}{6} = \dfrac{0}{6}$

$m = 0$

Excluded value: $m \neq 0$

**b.** $y = \dfrac{6m}{m+2}$

Set the denominator equal to zero and solve.

$m + 2 = 0$

$\dfrac{-2 = -2}{m = -2}$

Excluded value: $m \neq -2$

**c.** $y = \dfrac{m-3}{4m-8}$

Set the denominator equal to zero and solve.

$4m - 8 = 0$

$4(m - 2) = 0$

$\dfrac{4(m-2)}{4} = \dfrac{0}{4}$

$m - 2 = 0$

$m = 2$

Excluded value: $m \neq 2$

**d.** $y = \dfrac{4}{x+1}$

$y = \dfrac{a}{x-b} + c$

$y = \dfrac{4}{x-(-1)} + 0$

Since $b = -1$, the vertical asymptote's equation is $x = -1$.

Since $c = 0$, the horizontal asymptote's equation is $y = 0$.

**e.** $y = \dfrac{2}{x+7} + 6$

$y = \dfrac{a}{x-b} + c$

$y = \dfrac{2}{x-(-7)} + 6$

Since $b = -7$, the vertical asymptote's equation is $x = -7$.

Since $c = 6$, the horizontal asymptote's equation is $y = 6$.

**f.** $y = \dfrac{6}{x+4}$

$y = \dfrac{a}{x-b} + c$

$y = \dfrac{6}{x-(-4)}$

Since $b = -4$, the vertical asymptote's equation is $x = -4$.

Since $c = 0$, the horizontal asymptote's equation is $y = 0$.

Graph the asymptotes.

Make a table of values, plots the points, and connect the points.

| x | 0 | 2 | −3 | −6 | −8 |
|---|---|---|---|---|---|
| y | $1\frac{1}{2}$ | 1 | 6 | −3 | $-1\frac{1}{2}$ |

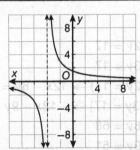

**g.** $y = \dfrac{1}{x-6} - 5$

$y = \dfrac{a}{x-b} + c$

$y = \dfrac{1}{x-(-6)} + (-5)$

Since $b = 6$, the vertical asymptote's equation is $x = 6$.

Since $c = -5$, the horizontal asymptote's equation is $y = -5$.

Graph the asymptotes.

Make a table of values, plots the points, and connect the points.

| $x$ | 0 | 4 | 5 | 7 | 8 |
|---|---|---|---|---|---|
| $y$ | $-5\frac{1}{6}$ | $-5\frac{1}{2}$ | $-6$ | $-4$ | $-4\frac{1}{2}$ |

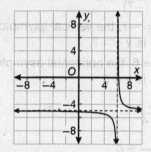

**h.** $y = \dfrac{5500}{x} + 5$

$y = \dfrac{a}{x - b} + c$

Since $b = 0$, the vertical asymptote's equation is $x = 0$.

Since $c = 5$, the horizontal asymptote's equation is $y = 5$.

**i.** $y = \dfrac{5500}{100} + 5$

$y = 55 + 5$
$y = 60$

He will receive 60 clubs.

## Practice 78

**1.**   $3x - 2y = 17$
$-4x - 3y = 17$
$4(3x - 2y = 17) \rightarrow 12x - 8y = 68$
$3(-4x - 3y = 17) \rightarrow -12x - 9y = 51$
$\dfrac{\begin{aligned} 12x - 8y &= 68 \\ -12x - 9y &= 51 \end{aligned}}{\qquad -17y = 119}$
$\qquad\qquad y = -7$

Substitute $-7$ for $y$ in an original equation and solve.

$3x - 2(-7) = 17$
$3x + 14 = 17$
$\qquad 3x = 3$
$\qquad\quad x = 1$

The solution is $(1, -7)$.

**2.** $y = 2x + 4$
$-x - 3y = 9$

Write the first equation in standard form:

$-2x + y = 4$
$-2(-x - 3y = 9) \rightarrow 2x + 6y = -18$
$\quad -2x + y = 4$
$\dfrac{\quad 2x + 6y = -18}{\qquad 7y = -14}$
$\qquad\qquad y = -2$

Substitute $-2$ for $y$ in an original equation and solve.

$-2 = 2x + 4$
$-6 = 2x$
$-3 = x$

The solution is $(-3, -2)$.

**3.** $x^2 + 10xy + 21y^2$
$ax^2 + bx + c$

In this trinomial, $b$ is $10y$ and $c$ is $21y^2$.

Six pairs of positive terms have a product of $21y^2$.

$(1y^2)(21) \quad (1y)(21y) \quad (1)(21y^2)$
$(7y^2)(3) \quad (7y)(3y) \quad (7)(3y^2)$

Only the pair $7y$ and $3y$ has a sum of $10y$.
So, $x^2 + 10xy + 21y^2 = (x + 7y)(x + 3y)$.

**4.** $-30 - 13x + x^2$
$ax^2 + bx + c$

Write the trinomial in standard form as $x^2 - 13x - 30$, where $b$ is $-13$ and $c$ is $-30$.

Eight pairs of positive and negative numbers have a product of $-30$.

$(1)(-30) \quad (-1)(30) \quad (2)(-15) \quad (-2)(15)$
$(3)(-10) \quad (-3)(10) \quad (5)(-6) \quad (-5)(6)$

Only the pair $2$ and $-15$ has a sum of $-13$.
So, $x^2 - 13x - 30 = (x + 2)(x - 15)$.

**5.** $y = \dfrac{4}{7m}$

Set the denominator equal to zero and solve.

$$7m = 0$$
$$\frac{7m}{7} = \frac{0}{7}$$
$$m = 0$$

Excluded value: $m \neq 0$

**6.** $y = \dfrac{m - 2}{3m + 9}$

Set the denominator equal to zero and solve.

$$3m + 9 = 0$$
$$3m = -9$$
$$m = -3$$

Excluded value: $m \neq -3$

**7.** $y = \dfrac{5}{x - 3} + \dfrac{2}{5}$

$$y = \frac{a}{x - b} + c$$

$$y = \frac{5}{x - (3)} + \left(\frac{2}{5}\right)$$

Since $b = 3$, the vertical asymptote's equation is $x = 3$.

**8.** $3 - 9m < 30$
$$-9m < 27$$
$$m > -3$$

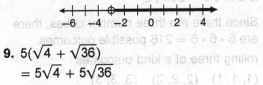

**9.** $5(\sqrt{4} + \sqrt{36})$
$$= 5\sqrt{4} + 5\sqrt{36}$$
$$= 10 + 30$$
$$= 40$$

**10.** $y = \dfrac{20}{x} + 6$

$$y = \frac{a}{x - b} + c$$

Since $b = 0$, the vertical asymptote's equation is $x = 0$.

Since $c = 6$, the horizontal asymptote's equation is $y = 6$.

Graph the asymptotes.

Make a table of values, plots the points, and connect the points.

| x | 2 | 4 | 10 | −10 | −2 |
|---|---|---|----|-----|----|
| y | 16 | 11 | 8 | 4 | −4 |

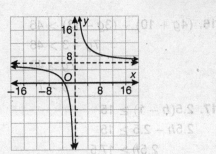

**11.** $y = \dfrac{1}{x} + 5$

$$5 = \frac{1}{x} + 5$$
$$\underline{-5 \qquad -5}$$
$$0 = \frac{1}{x}$$

There is no value $x$ such that $\dfrac{1}{x} = 0$, so, $y$ cannot equal 0.

**12.** $y = \dfrac{2.3}{x + 1.9} + 0.3$

$$y = \frac{a}{x - b} + c$$

$$y = \frac{5}{x - (-1.9)} + (0.3)$$

Since $b = -1.9$, the vertical asymptote's equation is $x = -1.9$.

Since $c = 0.3$, the horizontal asymptote's equation is $y = 0.3$.

**13.** The answer is **C**.

$$y = \frac{6.1}{x + 1.5} + 3.1$$

$$y = \frac{a}{x - b} + c$$

$$y = \frac{6.1}{x - (-1.5)} + 3.1$$

Since $b = -1.5$, the vertical asymptote's equation is $x = -1.5$.

**14.** $30 + 15 \geq 12 + 3c$
$$45 \geq 12 + 3c$$
$$33 \geq 3c$$
$$11 \geq c$$

You can spend at most $11 on each CD.

**15.** Student A; Sample: Student B did not reverse the inequality sign when dividing by −5.

**Saxon** Algebra 1

**16.** $(4g + 10) + (3g - 13) > 46$

$$7g - 3 > 46$$
$$7g > 49$$
$$g > 7$$

**17.** $2.5(h - 1) \geq 15$

$$2.5h - 2.5 \geq 15$$
$$2.5h \geq 17.5$$
$$h \geq 7$$

You will hike at least 7 hours.

**18.** Student B; Sample: Student A multiplied a radical and a whole number.

**19.** $A = lw$

$$\left(7 + \sqrt{32}\right)\left(9 + \sqrt{50}\right)$$
$$= (7 \cdot 9) + 7\sqrt{50} + 9\sqrt{32} + \sqrt{32 \cdot 50}$$
$$= 63 + 7\sqrt{50} + 9\sqrt{32} + \sqrt{1600}$$
$$= 63 + 7\sqrt{5^2 \cdot 2} + 9\sqrt{4^2 \cdot 2} + \sqrt{4^2 \cdot 10^2}$$
$$= 63 + 35\sqrt{2} + 36\sqrt{2} + 40$$
$$= 103 + 71\sqrt{2}$$

The area of his painting is $103 + 71\sqrt{2}$ square inches.

**20.** $10x^2 - 11xy - 6y^2 = (2x - 3y)(5x + 2y)$

Sample: Use FOIL.

$(2x - 3y)(5x + 2y)$
$= (2x \cdot 5x) + (2x \cdot 2y) + (-3y \cdot 5x) +$
$\quad (-3y \cdot 2y)$
$= 10x^2 + 4xy - 15xy - 6y^2$
$= 10x^2 - 11xy - 6y^2$

**21.** The answer is **C**.

$(5x + 1)(4x + 9)$
$= (5x \cdot 4x) + (5x \cdot 9) + (1 \cdot 4x) + (1 \cdot 9)$
$= 20x^2 + 45x + 4x + 9$
$= 20x^2 + 49x + 9$

**22.** $4x^2 - 16x + 16$

$4(-3)^2 - 16(-3) + 16$
$= 36 + 48 + 16$
$= 100$

The area of the tray is 100 square inches.

**23.** $|n| = 12$ means that $n = +12$ or that $n = -12$. So, the solution is $\{12, -12\}$.

**24.** $x \leq 12$ OR $x \geq 65$

**25.** There is no correlation because there is no linear pattern.

**26.** $\dfrac{n}{5} \leq -3$

$(5)\dfrac{n}{5} \leq -3(5)$

$n \leq -15$

Sample verification:

$\dfrac{-20}{5} \overset{?}{\leq} -3$

$-4 \leq -3$

**27.** Since a square has equal length sides, one side will be the square root of the area.

side of large square $= \sqrt{216x^2}$
$$= \sqrt{6 \cdot 6 \cdot 6 \cdot x \cdot x}$$
$$= 6x\sqrt{6}$$
4 sides $= 4(6x\sqrt{6}) = 24x\sqrt{6}$

side of small square $= \sqrt{125x^2}$
$$= \sqrt{5 \cdot 5 \cdot 5 \cdot x \cdot x}$$
$$= 5x\sqrt{5}$$
4 sides $= 4(5x\sqrt{5}) = 20x\sqrt{5}$

The combined perimeter of the two squares is $24x\sqrt{6} + 20x\sqrt{5}$.

**28.** Since there are three number cubes, there are $6 \cdot 6 \cdot 6 = 216$ possible outcomes.

rolling three of a kind outcomes:

(1, 1, 1)  (2, 2, 2)  (3, 3, 3)
(4, 4, 4)  (5, 5, 5)  (6, 6, 6)

rolling a sum that is an odd number outcomes:

(1, 1, 1)  (1, 1, 3)  (1, 1, 5)
(1, 2, 2)  (1, 2, 4)  (1, 2, 6)
(1, 3, 1)  (1, 3, 3)  (1, 3, 5)
(1, 4, 2)  (1, 4, 4)  (1, 4, 6)
(1, 5, 1)  (1, 5, 3)  (1, 5, 5)
(1, 6, 2)  (1, 6, 4)  (1, 6, 6)
(2, 1, 2)  (2, 1, 4)  (2, 1, 6)
(2, 2, 1)  (2, 2, 3)  (2, 2, 5)
(2, 3, 2)  (2, 3, 4)  (2, 3, 6)
(2, 4, 1)  (2, 4, 3)  (2, 4, 5)
(2, 5, 2)  (2, 5, 4)  (2, 5, 6)
(2, 6, 1)  (2, 6, 3)  (2, 6, 5)

Continue this pattern through (6, 6, 5), or compute 6 sets of 18 outcomes = 108 total possible outcomes.

rolling a sum that is an odd number and also three of a kind:

(1, 1, 1)   (3, 3, 3)   (5, 5, 5)

$P$(triples or odd sum)

$= P$(triple) $+ P$(odd) $- P$(triple and odd)

$= \dfrac{108}{216} + \dfrac{6}{216} - \dfrac{3}{216}$

$= \dfrac{111}{216}$

The probability of rolling three of a kind or a sum that is an odd number is $\frac{111}{216}$.

**29.** The answer is **C**.

The slope of this line is 3. Any line that is parallel to it must have the same slope.

**30.** Starting with the 35–39 interval, create more intervals of 5. Count the number of data points that belong in each interval. Create a graph showing the number of data points in each interval.

**Average Milk Production**

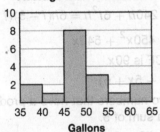

Gallons

## LESSON 79

### Warm Up 79

**1.** polynomial

**2.** $x^2 + 3x - 10$

$ax^2 + bx + c$

In this trinomial, $b$ is 3 and $c$ is $-10$.

Four pairs of positive and negative numbers have a product of $-10$.

(1)(−10)   (−1)(10)   (2)(−5)   (−2)(5)

Only the pair −2 and 5 has a sum of 3.

So, $x^2 + 3x - 10 = (x - 2)(x + 5)$

**3.** $-13p + p^2 + 36$

$ax^2 + bx + c$

Write the trinomial in standard form as $p^2 - 13p + 36$, where $b$ is $-13$ and $c$ is 36.

Five pairs of negative numbers have a product of 36.

(−1)(−36)   (−2)(−18)   (−3)(−12)

(−4)(−9)   (−6)(−6)

Only the pair −4 and −9 has a sum of −13.

So, $p^2 - 13p + 36 = (p - 4)(p - 9)$.

**4.** $-11x - 21 + 2x^2$

Rearrange the terms to $2x^2 - 11x - 21$.

The first term, $2x^2$ can be factored as $(2x)(x)$.

The last term, −21, can be factored as (1)(−21), (−1)(21), (3)(−7), and (−3)(7).

Check each pair to see which results in the middle term, −11x.

| Possibilities | Middle Term |
|---|---|
| $(2x + 1)(x - 21)$ | $-42x + x = -41x$ |
| $(2x - 1)(x + 21)$ | $42x - x = 41x$ |
| $(2x + 21)(x - 1)$ | $-2x + 21x = 19x$ |
| $(2x - 21)(x + 1)$ | $2x - 21x = -19x$ |
| $(2x + 3)(x - 7)$ | $-14x + 3x = -11x$ |
| $(2x - 3)(x + 7)$ | $14x - 3x = 11x$ |
| $(2x + 7)(x - 3)$ | $-6x + 7x = x$ |
| $(2x - 7)(x + 3)$ | $6x - 7x = -x$ |

So, $2x^2 - 11x - 21 = (2x + 3)(x - 7)$.

**5.** $5x^2 - 13x - 6$

The first term, $5x^2$ can be factored as $(5x)(x)$.

The last term, −6, can be factored as (1)(−6), (−1)(6), (2)(−3), and (−2)(3).

Check each pair to see which results in the middle term, −13x.

| Possibilities | Middle Term |
|---|---|
| $(5x + 1)(x - 6)$ | $-30x + x = -29x$ |
| $(5x - 1)(x + 6)$ | $30x - x = 29x$ |
| $(5x + 6)(x - 1)$ | $-5x + 6x = x$ |
| $(5x - 6)(x + 1)$ | $5x - 6x = -x$ |
| $(5x + 2)(x - 3)$ | $-15x + 2x = -13x$ |
| $(5x - 2)(x + 3)$ | $15x - 2x = 13x$ |
| $(5x + 3)(x - 2)$ | $-10x + 3x = -7x$ |
| $(5x - 3)(x + 2)$ | $10x - 3x = 7x$ |

So, $5x^2 - 13x - 6 = (5x + 2)(x - 3)$.

**Saxon** Algebra 1

## Lesson Practice 79

**a.** $p^5 + 13p^4 + 12p^3$

The GCF of the terms is $p^3$.

$p^3(p^2 + 13p + 12)$

Find two numbers that have a product of 12 and a sum of 13.

$12 \cdot 1 = 12$ and $12 + 1 = 13$

$p^3(p^2 + 13p + 12) = p^3(p + 12)(p + 1)$

So,

$p^5 + 13p^4 + 12p^3 = p^3(p + 12)(p + 1)$.

**b.** $6n^4 - 6n^3 - 12n^2$

The GCF of the terms is $6n^2$.

$6n^2(n^2 - n - 2)$

Find two numbers that have a product of $-2$ and a sum of $-1$.

$1(-2) = -2$ and $1 + (-2) = -1$

$6n^2(n^2 - n - 2) = 6n^2(n + 1)(n - 2)$

So,

$6n^4 - 6n^3 - 12n^2 = 6n^2(n + 1)(n - 2)$.

**c.** $-r^2 + r + 30$

Factor out the negative leading coefficient.

$-1(r^2 - r - 30)$

Find two numbers that have a product of $-30$ and a sum of $-1$.

$5(-6)$ and $5 + (-6)$

$-1(r^2 - r - 30) = -1(r + 5)(r - 6)$

So, $-r^2 + r + 30 = -1(r + 5)(r - 6)$.

**d.** $-5d^3 - 25d^2 - 20d$

Factor out the negative leading coefficient.

$-5d(d^2 + 5d + 4)$

Find two numbers that have a product of 4 and a sum of 5.

$4 \cdot 1$ and $4 + 1$

$-5d(d^2 + 5d + 4) = -5d(d + 4)(d + 1)$

So,

$-5d^3 - 25d^2 - 20d = -5d(d + 4)(d + 1)$.

**e.** $y^3x + 3y^2x - 54yx$

The GCF is $yx$, or $xy$.

$xy(y^2 + 3y - 54)$

Find two numbers that have a product of $-54$ and a sum of 3.

$9(-6)$ and $9 + (-6)$

$xy(y^2 + 3y - 54) = xy(y + 9)(y - 6)$

So,

$y^3x + 3y^2x - 54yx = xy(y + 9)(y - 6)$.

**f.** $5bx^3 - 5bx^2 - 60bx$

The GCF is $5bx$.

$5bx(x^2 - x - 12)$

Find two numbers that have a product of $-12$ and a sum of $-1$.

$3(-4)$ and $3 + (-4)$

$5bx(x^2 - x - 12) = 5bx(x + 3)(x - 4)$

So,

$5bx^3 - 5bx^2 - 60bx = 5bx(x + 3)(x - 4)$.

**g.** $18fh - 240h + 6f^2h$

Write in standard form.

$6f^2h + 18fh - 240h$

The GCF is $6h$.

$6h(f^2 + 3f - 40)$

Find two numbers that have a product of $-40$ and a sum of 3.

$-5 \cdot 8$ and $-5 + 8$

$6h(f^2 + 3f - 40) = 6h(f - 5)(f + 8)$

So,

$18fh - 240h + 6f^2h = 6h(f - 5)(f + 8)$.

**h.** $90x^3 + 450x^2 + 540x$

The GCF is $90x$.

$90x(x^2 + 5x + 6)$

Find two numbers that have a product of 6 and a sum of 5.

$3 \cdot 2$ and $3 + 2$

$90x(x^2 + 5x + 6) = 90x(x + 3)(x + 2)$

So,

$90x^3 + 450x^2 + 540x = 90x(x + 3)(x + 2)$.

## Practice 79

**1.** $x_1y_1 = x_2y_2$

$(9)(6) = (12)y_2$

$54 = 12y_2$

$4.5 = y_2$

When $x = 12$, $y = 4.5$.

**2.** $5x = 2y + 10$

$-3y = -2x + 4$

Write each equation in standard form.

$5x - 2y = 10$

$2x - 3y = 4$

$3(5x - 2y = 10) \rightarrow 15x - 6y = 30$

$-2(2x - 3y = 4) \rightarrow -4x + 6y = -8$

$15x - 6y = 30$

$\underline{-4x + 6y = -8}$

$11x = 22$

$x = 2$

Substitute 2 for $x$ in an original equation.

$5(2) - 2y = 10$

$10 - 2y = 10$

$-2y = 0$

$y = 0$

The solution is (2, 0).

**3.** $x - y = 2$

$y + 2x = 1$

Write the second equation in standard form. Then add the equations.

$x - y = 2$

$\underline{2x + y = 1}$

$3x = 3$

$x = 1$

Substitute 1 for $x$ in an original equation.

$2(1) + y = 1$

$y = -1$

The solution is (1, −1).

**4.** $3b - 2 < -8$   OR   $4b + 3 > 11$

$3b < -6$         $4b > 8$

$b < -2$          $b > 2$

The solution is $b < -2$ OR $b > 2$.

**5.** $x^2 - 4x - 45$

$ax^2 + bx + c$

In this trinomial, $b$ is −4 and $c$ is −45.

Six pairs of positive and negative numbers have a product of −45.

$(1)(-45)$   $(-1)(45)$   $(3)(-15)$

$(-3)(15)$   $(5)(-9)$   $(-5)(9)$

Only the pair 5 and −9 has a sum of −4.

So, $x^2 - 4x - 45 = (x + 5)(x - 9)$.

**6.** $k^4 + 6k^3 + 8k^2$

$= k^2(k^2 + 6k + 8)$

Two numbers that have a product of 8 and a sum of 6 are 4 · 2 and 4 + 2.

$k^2(k^2 + 6k + 8) = k^2(k + 4)(k + 2)$

So, $k^4 + 6k^3 + 8k^2 = k^2(k + 4)(k + 2)$.

**7.** $5x^2 + 3x - 2$

The first term, $5x^2$, can be factored as $(5x)(x)$.

The last term, −2, can be factored as $(1)(-2)$ and $(-1)(2)$.

Check each pair to see which results in the middle term, $3x$.

| Possibilities | Middle Term |
|---|---|
| $(5x + 1)(x - 2)$ | $-10x + x = -9x$ |
| $(5x - 1)(x + 2)$ | $10x - x = 9x$ |
| $(5x + 2)(x - 1)$ | $-5x + 2x = -3x$ |
| $(5x - 2)(x + 1)$ | $5x - 2x = 3x$ |

So, $5x^2 + 3x - 2 = (5x - 2)(x + 1)$.

**8.** $2x^3 + 16x^2 + 30x$

$= 2x(x^2 + 8x + 15)$

Two numbers that have a product of 15 and a sum of 8 are 3 · 5 and 3 + 5.

$2x(x^2 + 8x + 15) = 2x(x + 3)(x + 5)$

So, $2x^3 + 16x^2 + 30x = 2x(x + 3)(x + 5)$.

**9.** $abx^2 - 5abx - 24ab$

$= ab(x^2 - 5x - 24)$

Two numbers that have a product of −24 and a sum of −5 are 3(−8) and 3 + (−8).

$ab(x^2 - 5x - 24) = ab(x + 3)(x - 8)$.

So,

$abx^2 - 5abx - 24ab = ab(x + 3)(x - 8)$.

**10.** $15mx^2 + 9mx - 6m$

$= 3m(5x^2 + 3x - 2)$

The first term in the trinomial, $5x^2$, can be factored as $(5x)(x)$.

The last term, −2, can be factored as $(1)(-2)$ and $(-1)(2)$.

Check each pair to see which results in the middle term, $3x$.

| Possibilities | Middle Term |
|---|---|
| $(5x + 1)(x - 2)$ | $-10x + x = -9x$ |
| $(5x - 1)(x + 2)$ | $10x - x = 9x$ |
| $(5x + 2)(x - 1)$ | $-5x + 2x = -3x$ |
| $(5x - 2)(x + 1)$ | $5x - 2x = 3x$ |

So,
$$3m(5x^2 + 3x - 2) = 3m(5x - 2)(x + 1)$$
and
$$15mx^2 + 9mx - 6m = 3m(5x - 2)(x + 1).$$

**11.** $\dfrac{9m}{m + 3}$

$m + 3 = 0$

$\dfrac{-3}{m} = \dfrac{-3}{-3}$

Excluded value: $m \neq -3$

**12.** $16 + (-6) \geq 2(d + 4)$

$\qquad 10 \geq 2d + 8$

$\qquad\quad 2 \geq 2d$

$\qquad\therefore 1 \geq d$

$\qquad\quad d \leq 1$

**13.** yes; Sample: The answer will be the same, but factoring may be more difficult due to larger numbers.

**14.** $3(x + 4)(x + 1) = 3(x^2 + 15x + 44) =$
$3x^2 + 45x + 132$
and
$3(x + 11)(x + 4) = 3(x^2 + 15x + 44) =$
$3x^2 + 45x + 132$

Sample: By the Commutative Property of Multiplication, the order of the factors does not matter.

**15.** The answer is **D**.

**16.** $-16x^2 + 32x - 16$
$= -16(x^2 - 2x + 1)$
Two numbers that have a product of 1 and a sum of $-2$ are $(-1)(-1)$ and $-1 + (-1)$.
$-16(x^2 - 2x + 1) = -16(x - 1)(x - 1)$
$= -16(x - 1)^2$
So, $-16x^2 + 32x - 16 = -16(x - 1)^2$.

**17.** Student A; Sample: Student B wrote the horizontal asymptote.

**18. a.** $y = \dfrac{50,000}{x} + 1$

$\quad y = \dfrac{a}{x - b} + c$

Since $c = 1$, the horizontal asymptote's equation is $y = 1$.

**b.** Since $b = 0$, and the vertical asymptote's equation is $x = 0$.

**c.** $y = \dfrac{50,000}{x} + 1$

$\quad y = \dfrac{50,000}{1000} + 1$

$\quad y = 50 + 1$

$\quad y = 51$

He will receive 51 instruments.

**19. a.** $y = \dfrac{1350}{x} + 15$

$\quad y = \dfrac{a}{x - b} + c$

Since $c = 15$, the horizontal asymptote's equation is $y = 15$.

**b.** Since $b = 0$, and the vertical asymptote's equation is $x = 0$.

**c.** $y = \dfrac{1350}{x} + 15$

$\quad y = \dfrac{1350}{25} + 15$

$\quad y = 54 + 15$

$\quad y = 69$

The planner will receive 69 dinners.

**20.** $\dfrac{5}{x - 8} = \dfrac{y}{1}$

$\quad \dfrac{5}{x - 8} = y$

**21.** $7 + 3g \leq 20$

$\qquad 3g \leq 13$

$\qquad\quad g \leq \dfrac{13}{3}$

$\qquad\quad g \leq 4\dfrac{1}{3}$

He can buy up to $4\dfrac{1}{3}$ gallons.

**22.** Student B; Sample: Student A reversed the inequality sign when dividing by a positive number.

**23.** Sample: Use the FOIL method, simplify radicals, and then combine like terms.

 **Saxon** Algebra 1

**24.** D

$$\sqrt{11 \cdot 11} = \sqrt{121}$$
$$\sqrt{13 \cdot 13} = \sqrt{169}$$
$$\sqrt{121} < \sqrt{124} < \sqrt{169}$$
$$11 < \sqrt{124} < 13$$

**25.** $A = s^2$

$$A = (6\sqrt{36})^2$$
$$= (6)^2(\sqrt{36})^2$$
$$= 36 \cdot 36$$
$$= 1296$$

The area of the sandbox is 1296 square inches.

**26.** $|x - 65| = 8$

$$x - 65 = +8 \quad \text{or} \quad x - 65 = -8$$
$$x = 73 \qquad\qquad x = 57$$

The maximum angle of inclination for the easel is 73°. The minimum angle is 57°.

**27.** Sample: The trend line for a positive correlation rises from left to right. The trend line for a negative correlation falls from left to right. There is no trend line when there is no correlation.

**28. a.** $5100

**b.** $4.80r > 5100$

**c.** $4.80r > 5100$

$$\frac{4.80r}{4.80} > \frac{5100}{4.80}$$
$$r > 1062.5$$

**d.** At least 1063 DVDs per month must be rented in order to make a profit.

**29.** $P = l + l + w + w$

$$P = 2\sqrt{49} + 2\sqrt{49} + \sqrt{81} + \sqrt{81}$$
$$= 2\sqrt{7^2} + 2\sqrt{7^2} + \sqrt{9^2} + \sqrt{9^2}$$
$$= 2(7) + 2(7) + 9 + 9$$
$$= 14 + 14 + 9 + 9$$
$$= 46$$

She will need 46 feet of trimming.

**30. a.** $185 + x \le 750$

$$\frac{-185 \qquad -185}{x \le 565}$$

An inequality representing how much more weight the elevator can carry is $185 + x \le 750$, or $x \le 565$.

**b.** $4(75) + 4(50) + 4(25) + 6(20)$
$$= 300 + 200 + 100 + 120$$
$$= 720$$

No, she will not be able to bring all the weights. Sample: The total weight of the weights is 720 pounds. This would mean that Alicia could weigh no more than 30 pounds, which is not reasonable.

## LESSON 80

**Warm Up 80**

1. measure of central tendency

2. Possible outcomes: 2

   $P(\text{tails}) = \frac{1}{2}$ or 50%

3. Possible outcomes: $3 + 7 = 10$

   $P(\text{yellow}) = \frac{3}{10}$ or 30%.

4. Possible outcomes: 6

   $P(1) = \frac{1}{6}$ or $16\frac{2}{3}$%

5. Possible outcomes: 4

   $P(A) = \frac{1}{4}$ or 25%

**Lesson Practice 80**

**a.**

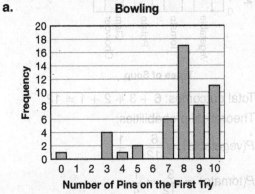

Total outcomes: $1 + 0 + 0 + 4 + 1 + 2 + 0 + 6 + 17 + 8 + 11 = 50$

**Saxon** Algebra 1

Experimental probabilities:

$P(0) = \dfrac{1}{50}$   $P(1) = \dfrac{0}{50} = 0$

$P(2) = \dfrac{0}{50} = 0$   $P(3) = \dfrac{4}{50} = \dfrac{2}{25}$

$P(4) = \dfrac{1}{50}$   $P(5) = \dfrac{2}{50} = \dfrac{1}{25}$

$P(6) = \dfrac{0}{50} = 0$   $P(7) = \dfrac{6}{50} = \dfrac{3}{25}$

$P(8) = \dfrac{17}{50}$   $P(9) = \dfrac{8}{50} = \dfrac{4}{25}$

$P(10) = \dfrac{11}{50}$

**b.**

|        | Tails | Heads |
|--------|-------|-------|
| Tails  | TT    | TH    |
| Heads  | TH    | HH    |

**c.** Total outcomes: 4

Theoretical probabilities:

$P(HH) = \dfrac{1}{4}$   $P(TH) = \dfrac{2}{4} = \dfrac{1}{2}$

$P(TT) = \dfrac{1}{4}$

**d.**

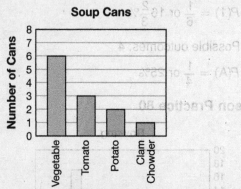

Soup Cans

**e.** Total outcomes: $6 + 3 + 2 + 1 = 12$

Theoretical probabilities:

$P(\text{vegetable}) = \dfrac{6}{12} = \dfrac{1}{2}$

$P(\text{tomato}) = \dfrac{3}{12} = \dfrac{1}{4}$

$P(\text{potato}) = \dfrac{2}{12} = \dfrac{1}{6}$

$P(\text{clam chowder}) = \dfrac{1}{12}$

**Practice 80**

**1.** Sample:

$2y + 10x = -36$

$2y = -10x - 36$

$y = -5x - 18$

Find an equation for a parallel line that passes through $(-1, 4)$.

$y - y_1 = m(x - x_1)$

$y - 4 = -5(x + 1)$

$y - y = -5x - 5$

$y = -5x - 1$

**2.** $y = 108$ and $x = 3$.

Find $x$ when $y = 3$.

$x_1 y_1 = x_2 y_2$

$(3)(108) = x_2(3)$

$324 = 3x_2$

$108 = x_2$

When $y = 3$, $x = 108$.

**3.** $y = 56$ and $x = 7$.

Find $x$ when $y = 4$.

$x_1 y_1 = x_2 y_2$

$(7)(56) = x_2(4)$

$396 = 4x_2$

$98 = x_2$

When $y = 4$, $x = 98$.

**4.** $y = \dfrac{7}{x + 5}$

$y = \dfrac{a}{x - b} + c$

Since there is no $c$, the horizontal asymptote's equation is $y = 0$.

**5.** $y = \dfrac{3}{2x + 3} - 5$

$y = \dfrac{a}{x - b} + c$

Since $c = -5$, the horizontal asymptote's equation is $y = -5$.

**6.** $11|x| = 55$

$\dfrac{11|x|}{11} = \dfrac{55}{11}$

$|x| = 5$

The solution set is $\{5, -5\}$.

**Saxon** Algebra 1

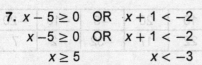

**7.** $x - 5 \geq 0$  OR  $x + 1 < -2$

| $x - 5 \geq 0$ | OR | $x + 1 < -2$ |
|---|---|---|
| $x \geq 5$ | | $x < -3$ |

The solution is $x < -3$ OR $x \geq 5$.

**8.** $c^{12} + 11c^{11} + 24c^{10}$

$c^{10}(c^2 + 11c + 24)$

Two numbers that have a product of 24 and a sum of 11 are $3 \cdot 8$ and $3 + 8$.

$c^{10}(c^2 + 11c + 24) = c^{10}(c + 3)(c + 8)$

So,

$c^{12} + 11c^{11} + 24c^{10} = c^{10}(c + 3)(c + 8)$.

**9.** $42x^4 + 77x^3 - 70x^2$

$7x^2(6x^2 + 11x - 10)$

The first term in the trinomial, $6x^2$, can be factored as $(6x)(x)$ and $(2x)(3x)$.

The last term, $-10$, can be factored as $(1)(-10)$, $(-1)(10)$, $(2)(-5)$, and $(-2)(5)$.

Check each pair to see which results in the middle term, $11x$.

| Possibilities | Middle Term |
|---|---|
| $(6x + 1)(x - 10)$ | $-60x + x = -59x$ |
| $(6x - 1)(x + 10)$ | $60x - x = 59x$ |
| $(6x + 10)(x - 1)$ | $-6x + 10x = 4x$ |
| $(6x - 10)(x + 1)$ | $6x - 10x = -4x$ |
| $(6x + 2)(x - 5)$ | $-30x + 2x = -28x$ |
| $(6x - 2)(x + 5)$ | $30x - 2x = 28x$ |
| $(6x + 5)(x - 2)$ | $-12x + 5x = -7x$ |
| $(6x - 5)(x + 2)$ | $12x - 5x = 7x$ |
| $(2x + 1)(3x - 10)$ | $-20x + 3x = -17x$ |
| $(2x - 1)(3x + 10)$ | $20x - 3x = 17x$ |
| $(2x + 10)(3x - 1)$ | $-2x + 30x = 28x$ |
| $(2x - 10)(3x + 1)$ | $2x - 30x = -28x$ |
| $(2x + 2)(3x - 5)$ | $-10x + 6x = -4x$ |
| $(2x - 2)(3x + 5)$ | $10x - 6x = 4x$ |
| $(2x + 5)(3x - 2)$ | $-4x + 15x = 11x$ |
| $(2x - 5)(3x + 2)$ | $4x - 15x = -11x$ |

So,

$42x^4 + 77x^3 - 70x^2 = 7x^2(2x + 5)(3x - 2)$.

**10.** $-3m^2 - 30m - 48$

$-3(m^2 + 10m + 16)$

Two numbers that have a product of 16 and a sum of 10 are $2 \cdot 8$ and $2 + 8$.

$-3(m^2 + 10m + 16) = -3(m + 2)(m + 8)$

So,

$-3m^2 - 30m - 48 = -3(m + 2)(m + 8)$.

**11.** $(x - 1)x^2 + 7x(x - 1) + 10(x - 1)$

$(x - 1)x^2 + (x - 1)7x + (x - 1)10$

$(x - 1)(x^2 + 7x + 10)$

Two numbers that have a product of 10 and a sum of 7 are $2 \cdot 5$ and $2 + 5$.

$(x - 1)(x^2 + 7x + 10)$
$= (x - 1)(x + 2)(x + 5)$

So,

$(x - 1)x^2 + 7x(x - 1) + 10(x - 1)$
$= (x - 1)(x + 2)(x + 5)$

**12.**

| | Red | Blue | Yellow | Green |
|---|---|---|---|---|
| **1** | R1 | B1 | Y1 | G1 |
| **2** | R2 | B2 | Y2 | G2 |
| **3** | R3 | B3 | Y3 | G3 |
| **4** | R4 | B4 | Y4 | G4 |
| **5** | R5 | B5 | Y5 | G5 |
| **6** | R6 | B6 | Y6 | G6 |

**13.** Sample: Use a table when organizing the data for further calculations. Use a graph to display the data.

**14.** The answer is **D**.

Outcomes for 4 or 5 on one cube: $\frac{2}{6} = \frac{1}{3}$

So, outcomes on three cubes:

$\frac{1}{3} \cdot \frac{1}{3} \cdot \frac{1}{3} = \left(\frac{1}{3}\right)^3$

Outcomes for Heads on one coin: $\frac{1}{2}$

So, outcomes on four coins:

$\frac{1}{2} \cdot \frac{1}{2} \cdot \frac{1}{2} \cdot \frac{1}{2} = \left(\frac{1}{4}\right)^4$

$P = \left(\frac{1}{3}\right)^3 \cdot \left(\frac{1}{2}\right)^4$

**15.**

| | Chemical | Physical |
|---|---|---|
| **Success** | CS | PS |
| **Failure** | CF | PF |

**16.** Total outcomes: $3 + 7 = 10$

$P(\text{red, red, red}) = \left(\frac{3}{10}\right)^3 = \frac{27}{1000}$

Solutions Key

**17.** $-16x^2 + 32x + 48$

$-16(x^2 - 2x - 3)$

Two numbers that have a product of $-3$ and a sum of $-2$ are $-3 \cdot 1$ and $-3 + 1$.

$-16(x^2 - 2x - 3) = -16(x - 3)(x + 1)$

So,

$-16x^2 + 32x + 48 = -16(x - 3)(x + 1)$.

**18.** Student B; Sample: Student A did not factor out the GCF, 2.

**19.** $9m^4 - 54m^3 + 81m^2$

$9m^2(m^2 - 6m + 9)$

Two numbers that have a product of 9 and a sum of $-6$ are $-3(-3)$ and $-3 + (-3)$.

$9m^2(m^2 - 6m + 9) = 9m^2(m - 3)(m - 3)$ or $9m^2(m - 3)^2$

$A = s^2$ One side of the square will be the square root of the area.

$\sqrt{9m^2(m - 3)^2} = 3m(m - 3)$

The side length of the square is $3m(m - 3)$.

**20. a.** $3x^3 + 3x^2 - 18x$

$3x(x^2 + x - 6)$

Two numbers that have a product of $-6$ and a sum of 1 are $-2 \cdot 3$ and $-2 + 3$.

$3x(x^2 + x - 6) = 3x(x - 2)(x + 3)$

So,

$3x^3 + 3x^2 - 18x = 3x(x - 2)(x + 3)$.

**b.** The dimensions of the box are $(3x) \times (x - 2) \times (x + 3)$.

**21.** Student B; Sample: Student A didn't change the sign when subtracting 3 from both sides after setting the denominator equal to 0.

**22.** $y = \dfrac{100}{x} + 12$

$y = \dfrac{a}{x - b} + c$

Since $b = 0$, the vertical asymptote's equation is $x = 0$.

Since $c = 12$, the horizontal asymptote's equation is $y = 12$.

Graph the asymptotes.

Make a table of values, plots the points, and connect the points.

| $x$ | 10 | 20 | $-5$ | $-10$ | $-20$ |
|---|---|---|---|---|---|
| $y$ | 22 | 17 | $-32$ | $-2$ | 7 |

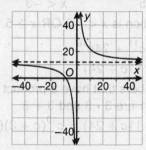

**23.** Sample: In the first inequality, you would solve by dividing both sides by positive 6. In the second, you would solve by dividing both sides by $-6$. It is what you are dividing by, not what is being divided, that determines whether the sign is reversed.

**24.** The answer is **D**.

$5 - 3(2 - m) \geq 29$

$5 - 6 + 3m \geq 29$

$-1 + 3m \geq 29$

$3m \geq 30$

$m \geq 10$

**25.** $\sqrt{4}(3 + \sqrt{6})$

$= 3\sqrt{4} + \sqrt{24}$

$= 3\sqrt{2 \cdot 2} + \sqrt{4 \cdot 6}$

$= 6 + 2\sqrt{6}$

**26.** $9x^2 - 36x - 13$

The first term, $9x^2$, can be factored as $(9x)(x)$ and $(3x)(3x)$.

The last term, $-13$, can be factored as $(1)(-13)$ and $(-1)(13)$.

Check each pair to see which results in the middle term, $-36x$.

| Possibilities | Middle Term |
|---|---|
| $(9x + 1)(x - 13)$ | $-117x + x = -116x$ |
| $(9x - 1)(x + 13)$ | $117x - x = 116x$ |
| $(9x + 13)(x - 1)$ | $-9x + 13x = 4x$ |
| $(9x - 13)(x + 1)$ | $9x - 13x = -4x$ |
| $(3x + 1)(3x - 13)$ | $-39x + 3x = -36x$ |
| $(3x - 1)(3x + 13)$ | $39x - 3x = 36x$ |

So, $9x^2 - 36x - 13 = (3x + 1)(3x - 13)$.

**Saxon** Algebra 1

**27.** Sample: The sum of $5 + 9z^2$ does not contain a factor of $z$, which is necessary for the coefficient $b$, $18z$.

**28. a.** Line of best fit:

$y = ax + b$

$y = 1.556x + 10.6$

**b.** Sample: Look at the value of the slope of the line (the coefficient of the $x$-term). If the slope is positive, then the correlation is positive. If the slope is negative, then the correlation is negative. In this example, there is a positive correlation.

**29.** $0.065x \geq 20,000$

$x \geq 307,692.31$

The house prices that will give the realtor a commission of at least $20,000 are $307,692.31 (or $307,692) or greater.

**30. a.** $d = 40t + 12$

$\frac{1}{4}d = 10t + 3 \rightarrow 4(\frac{1}{4}d = 10t + 3)$

$d = 40t + 12$

The equations are the same. Therefore, the system has infinitely many solutions. The system is consistent and dependent.

**b.** Neither train travels farther; they both travel the same distance because the equations are identical in slope-intercept form.

## INVESTIGATION 8

### Investigation Practice 8

**a.** $s = 4rt$

**b.** $m = \frac{1}{3}n\sqrt{p}$

**c.** $y = \frac{kwx}{z}$

**d.** $36 = \frac{k \cdot 12 \cdot 9}{15}$

$36 = \frac{108k}{15}$

$36 = 7.2k$

$5 = k$

$k = 5$

**e.** $y = \frac{kwx}{z}$

$y = \frac{5 \cdot 16 \cdot 8}{20}$

$y = \frac{640}{20}$

$y = 32$

**f.** $PV = 0.08206nT$

$200 \cdot 30 = 0.08206 \cdot n \cdot 300$

$6000 = 24.618n$

$243.7 = n$

$n = 243.7$

There are 243.7 moles of gas in a 30-liter scuba canister.

**g.** $PV = 0.08206nT$

$\frac{PV}{P} = \frac{0.08206nT}{P}$

$V = \frac{0.08206nT}{P}$

An inverse variation exists between $V$ and $P$. A joint variation exists between $V$ and $n$.

**h.** $V = kr^2h$

**i.** $16.76 = k \cdot 2^2 \cdot 4$

$16.76 = k \cdot 16$

$1.05 = k$

$k = 1.05$

**j.** $V = kr^2h$

$V = 1.05 \cdot 3^2 \cdot 7$

$V = 66.15$

The volume of the cone is 66.15 cubic units.

## LESSON 81

### Warm Up 81

**1.** identity

**2.** $6x \leq 42$

$x \leq 7$

**3.** $-\frac{3k}{4} > \frac{5}{8}$

$(-8) - \frac{3k}{4} < \frac{5}{8}(-8)$

$6k < -5$

$k < -\frac{5}{6}$

261

Saxon Algebra 1

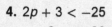 

**4.** $2p + 3 < -25$

$\quad 2p < -28$

$\quad\quad p < -14$

**5.** $5x - 3 - 7x \le -9$

$\quad 5x - 7x \le -6$

$\quad\quad -2x \le -6$

$\quad\quad\quad x \ge 3$

## Lesson Practice 81

**a.** $4x - 8 > -2x + 4$

$\quad 6x - 8 > 4$

$\quad\quad 6x > 12$

$\quad\quad\quad x > 2$

$$\begin{array}{c} \xleftarrow{\quad+\!\!+\!\!+\!\!\oplus\!\!+\!\!+\!\!+\!\!+\quad}\rightarrow \\ 0 \quad 2 \quad 4 \end{array}$$

**b.** $-\dfrac{3a}{5} + \dfrac{7}{10} \ge \dfrac{2a}{5} - \dfrac{9}{10}$

$\quad \dfrac{7}{10} \ge \dfrac{5a}{5} - \dfrac{9}{10}$

$\quad \dfrac{16}{10} \ge \dfrac{5a}{5}$

$\quad \dfrac{16}{10} \ge a$

$\quad a \le 1\dfrac{3}{5}$

$$\begin{array}{c} \xleftarrow{\quad+\!\!+\!\!+\!\!+\!\!+\!\!+\!\!+\!\!+\!\!\bullet\!\!+\!\!+\quad}\rightarrow \\ 0 \quad\quad 1 \quad\quad 2 \end{array}$$

**c.** $4(x - 1) - 2x \le 6 - 5(x + 2)$

$\quad 4x - 4 - 2x \le 6 - 5x - 10$

$\quad\quad 2x - 4 \le -5x - 4$

$\quad\quad 2x \le -5x + 0$

$\quad\quad\quad 7x \le 0$

$\quad\quad\quad\quad x \le 0$

$$\begin{array}{c} \xleftarrow{\quad+\!\!+\!\!+\!\!+\!\!+\!\!+\!\!\bullet\!\!+\!\!+\quad}\rightarrow \\ -4 \;\; -2 \;\;\; 0 \;\;\; 2 \end{array}$$

**d.** $x + 5 + 3x > 4x + 19$

$\quad 4x + 5 > 4x + 19$

$\quad \underline{-4x \quad\quad -4x}$

$\quad\quad\quad 5 > 19$

The inequality is never true.

**e.** $x + 5 > x - 3$

$\quad \underline{-x \quad\; -x}$

$\quad\quad 5 > -3$

The inequality is always true.

**f.** Write an expression for the average number of cell phone minutes for $m$ months after January.

Ara: $4000 + 500m$

Lexi: $12,000 - 500m$

$4000 + 500m \ge 12,000 - 500m$

$4000 + 1000m \ge 12,000$

$\quad\quad 1000m \ge 8000$

$\quad\quad\quad\quad m \ge 8$

Ara's average will be equal to or greater than Lexi's 8 more months after January, which is September.

## Practice 81

**1.** $w^2 - 13w + 36$

$\quad ax^2 + bx + c$

In this trinomial, $b$ is $-13$ and $c$ is 36.

Five pairs of negative numbers have a product of 36.

$(-1)(-36) \quad\quad (-2)(-18) \quad\quad (-3)(-12)$

$(-4)(-9) \quad\quad (-6)(-6)$

Only one pair has a sum of $-13$: $(-4)(-9)$.

So, $w^2 - 13w + 36 = (w - 4)(w - 9)$.

**2.** $-q^2 + q + 42$

Factor out the negative leading coefficient.

$-1(q^2 - q - 42)$

Find two numbers that have a product of $-42$ and a sum of $-1$: $-7 \cdot 6$ and $-7 + 6$.

$-1(q^2 - q - 42) = -1(q - 7)(q + 6)$

So, $-q^2 + q + 42 = -1(q - 7)(q + 6)$.

**3.** $30x^2 - 7xy - 2y^2$

The first term, $30x^2$, can be factored as $(30x)(x)$, $(15x)(2x)$, $(10x)(3x)$, and $(5x)(6x)$

The last term, $-2y^2$, can be factored as $(y)(-2y)$ and $(-y)(2y)$.

Check each pair to see which results in the middle term, $-7xy$.

**Saxon** Algebra 1

Possibilities

$(30x + y)(x - 2y)$
$(30x - y)(x + 2y)$
$(x + y)(30x - 2y)$
$(x - y)(30x + 2y)$

Middle Term

$-60xy + xy = -59xy$
$60xy - xy = 59xy$
$-2xy + 30xy = 28xy$
$2xy - 30xy = -28xy$

Possibilities

$(15x + y)(2x - 2y)$
$(15x - y)(2x + 2y)$
$(2x + y)(15x - 2y)$
$(2x - y)(15x + 2y)$

Middle Term

$-30xy + 2xy = -28xy$
$30xy - 2xy = 28xy$
$-4xy + 15xy = 11xy$
$4xy - 15xy = -11xy$

Possibilities

$(10x + y)(3x - 2y)$
$(10x - y)(3x + 2y)$
$(3x + y)(10x - 2y)$
$(3x - y)(10x + 2y)$

Middle Term

$-20xy + 3xy = -17xy$
$20xy - 3xy = 17xy$
$-6xy + 10xy = 4xy$
$6xy - 10xy = -4xy$

Possibilities

$(5x + y)(6x - 2y)$
$(5x - y)(6x + 2y)$
$(6x + y)(5x - 2y)$
$(6x - y)(5x + 2y)$

Middle Term

$-10xy + 6xy = -4xy$
$10xy - 6xy = 4xy$

---

$-12xy + 5xy = -7xy$ ✓
$12xy - 5xy = 7xy$
So, factors of $30x^2 - 7xy - 2y^2$ are
$(6x + y)(5x - 2y)$.

**4.** $x^2 - 11 + 6x - 44$
$ax^2 + bx + c$
Combine like terms to write the trinomial in standard form as $x^2 + 6x - 55$.
In this trinomial, $b$ is 6 and $c$ is $-55$.
Four pairs of positive and negative numbers have a product of $-55$.
$(1)(-55)$   $(-1)(55)$   $(5)(-11)$   $(-5)(11)$
Only one pair has a sum of 6: $(-5)(11)$.
So, $x^2 + 6x - 55 = (x - 5)(x + 11)$
and $x^2 - 11 + 6x - 44 = (x - 5)(x + 11)$.

**5.** $|x - 3| = 14$
$\quad x - 3 = 14 \quad$ or $\quad x - 3 = -14$
$\qquad x = 17 \qquad\qquad x = -11$
$\{17, -11\}$

**6.** $|x + 4| = 7.5$
$\quad x + 4 = 7.5 \quad$ or $\quad x + 4 = -7.5$
$\qquad x = 3.5 \qquad\qquad x = -11.5$
$\{3.5, -11.5\}$

**7.** $-5 - \dfrac{n}{8} \geq -6$
$\qquad -\dfrac{n}{8} \geq -1$
$\quad (-8) - \dfrac{n}{8} \leq -1(-8)$
$\qquad n \leq 8$

**8.** $12 - 3d \leq -3$
$\qquad -3d \leq -15$
$\qquad d \geq 5$

**9.** $6v + 5 > -2v - 3$
$\quad 8v + 5 > -3$
$\qquad 8v > -8$
$\qquad v > -1$

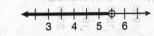

**10.** $y + 4.5 < 10$
$\qquad y < 5.5$

---

**11.** Sample: $y = -\frac{1}{2}x - 1\frac{1}{2}$

Point: $(1, -2)$

The slope of $y = 2x + 6$ is 2. Any line perpendicular to this line has a slope that is the negative reciprocal of 2, which is $-\frac{1}{2}$. Substitute the new slope and the point into the point-slope formula.

$$y - y_1 = m(x - x_1)$$
$$y - (-2) = -\frac{1}{2}(x-1)$$
$$y + 2 = -\frac{1}{2}x + \frac{1}{2}$$
$$y = -\frac{1}{2}x - 1\frac{1}{2}$$

**12.** Sample: $y = -x + 11$

Point: $(6, 5)$

The slope of $y = -x + 4$ is $-1$. Any line parallel to this line has the same slope of $-1$. Substitute the slope and the point into the point-slope formula.

$$y - y_1 = m(x - x_1)$$
$$y - (5) = -1(x - 6)$$
$$y - 5 = -x + 6$$
$$y = -x + 11$$

**13. a.** There are 10 possible outcomes. There are 5 black sections,

so $P(\text{black}) = \frac{5}{10} = \frac{1}{2}$.

**b.** $P(10) = \frac{1}{10}$

**c.** mutually exclusive

**d.** $P(\text{black or } 10) = P(\text{black}) + P(10)$
$$= \frac{5}{10} + \frac{1}{10}$$
$$= \frac{6}{10} = \frac{3}{5}$$

**14.**

**15.** Since $2 < 3$, 2 is a solution of the compound inequality because the inequality uses OR and the solution needs to be true only for one inequality.

**16.** $A = s^2$
$$(8 + \sqrt{8})^2$$
$$= (8 + \sqrt{8})(8 + \sqrt{8})$$
$$= 64 + 8\sqrt{8} + 8\sqrt{8} + \sqrt{8}\sqrt{8}$$
$$= 64 + 16\sqrt{8} + 8$$
$$= 72 + 16\sqrt{2^2 \cdot 2}$$
$$= 72 + 32\sqrt{2}$$

The area of the garden is $72 + 32\sqrt{2}$ square inches.

**17.** $x + (x + 13) + (2x + 12) > 81$
$$x + x + 13 + 2x + 12 > 81$$
$$4x + 25 > 81$$
$$4x > 56$$
$$x > 14$$

**18.** Sample: The vertical asymptote of the graph will be moved horizontally to a value of $b$ on the $x$-axis.

**19.** Total possible outcomes: $6 \cdot 6 = 36$.

$P(2) = \frac{2}{36} = \frac{1}{18}$, $P(3) = \frac{4}{36} = \frac{1}{9}$,

$P(4) = \frac{6}{36} = \frac{1}{6}$, $P(5) = \frac{6}{36} = \frac{1}{6}$,

$P(6) = \frac{6}{36} = \frac{1}{6}$, $P(7) = \frac{6}{36} = \frac{1}{6}$,

$P(8) = \frac{4}{36} = \frac{1}{9}$, $P(9) = \frac{2}{36} = \frac{1}{18}$

**20.** $y = \dfrac{a}{x - b} + c$

$y = \dfrac{7}{x - 2} + 4$

Since $c = 4$, the horizontal asymptote's equation is $y = 4$. The answer is **B**.

**21.** $-5t^2 + 25t - 30$

$-5(t^2 - 5t + 6)$

Two numbers that have a product of 6 and a sum of $-5$ are $-2 \cdot -3$ and $-2 + (-3)$.

$-5(t^2 - 5t + 6) = -5(t - 2)(t - 3)$

So, $-5t^2 + 25t - 30 = -5(t - 2)(t - 3)$.

**Saxon** Algebra 1

**22.** Student A; Sample: Student B did not include the GCF in the final factoring.

**23.** Make a table to show the possible outcomes.

**Cube 1**

| Cube 2 | | 1 | 2 | 3 | 4 | 5 | 6 |
|---|---|---|---|---|---|---|---|
| | 1 | 2 | 3 | 4 | 5 | 6 | 7 |
| | 2 | 3 | 4 | 5 | 6 | 7 | 8 |
| | 3 | 4 | 5 | 6 | 7 | 8 | 9 |
| | 4 | 5 | 6 | 7 | 8 | 9 | 10 |
| | 5 | 6 | 7 | 8 | 9 | 10 | 11 |
| | 6 | 7 | 8 | 9 | 10 | 11 | 12 |

Total possible outcomes: $6 \cdot 6 = 36$
Number of sums of 7 or less: 21

$P(\text{sum} \leq 7) = \dfrac{21}{36} = \dfrac{7}{12}$

**24.** $P(\text{five 3s}) = \left(\dfrac{1}{4}\right)^5 = \dfrac{1}{1024}$

**25.** Student A; Sample: Student B included the sum of 6 but the question asked for less than 6.

**Cube 1**

| Cube 2 | | 1 | 2 | 3 | 4 | 5 | 6 |
|---|---|---|---|---|---|---|---|
| | 1 | 2 | 3 | 4 | 5 | 6 | 7 |
| | 2 | 3 | 4 | 5 | 6 | 7 | 8 |
| | 3 | 4 | 5 | 6 | 7 | 8 | 9 |
| | 4 | 5 | 6 | 7 | 8 | 9 | 10 |
| | 5 | 6 | 7 | 8 | 9 | 10 | 11 |
| | 6 | 7 | 8 | 9 | 10 | 11 | 12 |

Total possible outcomes: $6 \cdot 6 = 36$
Number of sums of less than 6: 10

$P(\text{sum} < 6) = \dfrac{10}{36} = \dfrac{5}{18}$

**26. a.**    **Sum of Two Spins**

| | 1 | 2 | 3 | 4 | 5 | 6 | 7 | 8 |
|---|---|---|---|---|---|---|---|---|
| 1 | 2 | 3 | 4 | 5 | 6 | 7 | 8 | 9 |
| 2 | 3 | 4 | 5 | 6 | 7 | 8 | 9 | 10 |
| 3 | 4 | 5 | 6 | 7 | 8 | 9 | 10 | 11 |
| 4 | 5 | 6 | 7 | 8 | 9 | 10 | 11 | 12 |
| 5 | 6 | 7 | 8 | 9 | 10 | 11 | 12 | 13 |
| 6 | 7 | 8 | 9 | 10 | 11 | 12 | 13 | 14 |

Total possible outcomes: $8 \cdot 6 = 48$

**b.** Number of sums greater than 8: 21

$P(\text{sum} > 8) = \dfrac{21}{48} = \dfrac{7}{16}$

**27.** $2(x + 5) > x + 12$
$2x + 10 > x + 12$
The answer is **C**.

**28.** $40 + 0m < 24 + 0.16m$
$\quad\quad 16 < 0.16m$
$\quad\quad 100 < m$
$\quad\quad\, m > 100$

For the first company to offer a better deal, more than 100 miles per day would have to be driven.

**29.** Sample: Distribute $-3$ through the parentheses on the right side. Then add $3x$ to both sides. Then subtract 5 from both sides. Finally, divide both sides by 5. The solution is $x > 8$.

**30.** Make a table and compute the change between the freshman and sophomore years.

| Player | Freshman (Year 1) | Sophomore (Year 2) | Change (Year 1-2) |
|---|---|---|---|
| Malcolm | 17.3 | 19.1 | 1.8 |
| Frederico | 15.2 | 18.4 | 3.2 |

$15.2 + 3.2y > 17.3 + 1.8y$
$\quad\quad 3.2y > 2.1 + 1.8y$
$\quad\quad 1.4y > 2.1$
$\quad\quad\quad\; y > 1.5$

The variable $y$ represents the number of years after the freshman year (Year 1).

$1 + 1.5 = 2.5$

**Saxon** Algebra 1

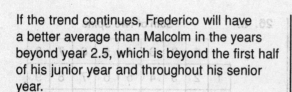 

If the trend continues, Frederico will have a better average than Malcolm in the years beyond year 2.5, which is beyond the first half of his junior year and throughout his senior year.

## LESSON 82

### Warm Up 82

1. compound inequality

2. $8x > 6x - 12$
   $2x > -12$
   $x > -6$

3. $-1 - (-7) \le 3(y - 6)$
   $6 \le 3y - 18$
   $24 \le 3y$
   $8 \le y$
   $y \ge 8$

4. $x - 2 < -7$  OR  $2x \ge 11$
   $x < -5$  OR  $x \ge 5.5$
   The solution is $x < -5$ OR $x \ge 5.5$.

5. The answer is **A**.
   $6 \le -2x < 22$
   $\dfrac{6}{-2} \le \dfrac{-2x}{-2} < \dfrac{22}{-2}$
   $-3 \le x < -11$
   $-11 > x \ge -3$

### Lesson Practice 82

a. $2x + 9 < 8$  OR  $3x + 3 > 12$

   $\dfrac{-9\ \ -9}{\phantom{..}}$  OR  $\dfrac{-3\ -3}{\phantom{..}}$

   $2x < -1$  OR  $3x > 9$

   $\dfrac{2x}{2} < \dfrac{-1}{2}$  OR  $\dfrac{3x}{3} > \dfrac{9}{3}$

   $x < -\dfrac{1}{2}$  OR  $x > 3$

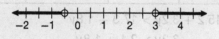

b. $24 \le 2x + 8 < 36$

   $\dfrac{-8\qquad -8\ -8}{\phantom{..}}$

   $16 \le 2x < 28$

   $\dfrac{16}{2} \le \dfrac{2x}{2} < \dfrac{28}{2}$

---

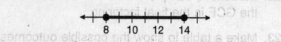 $8 \le x < 14$

8  10  12  14

c. Sample:
   $6 \le 2(x + 12) < 12$
   $6 \le 2x + 24 < 12$   Distributive Prop.
   $\dfrac{-24\quad -24\ -24}{\phantom{..}}$   Subtraction Prop. of Inequality
   $-18 \le 2x < -12$   Simplify.
   $\dfrac{-18}{2} \le \dfrac{2x}{2} < \dfrac{-12}{2}$   Division Prop. of Inequality
   $-9 \le x < -6$   Simplify.

d. Sample:
   $-16 > 2(x - 2)$ OR $27 < 3(x + 2)$
   $-16 > 2x - 4$  OR $27 < 3x + 6$
   Distributive Prop.
   $\dfrac{+4\qquad +4\qquad +(-6)\qquad +(-6)}{\phantom{..}}$
   $-12 > 2x$   OR $21 < 3x$
   Addition Prop. of Inequality
   $\dfrac{12}{2} > \dfrac{2x}{2}$   OR $\dfrac{21}{3} < \dfrac{3x}{3}$
   Division Prop. of Inequality
   $6 > x$   OR $7 < x$   Simplify.

e. Set up a compound inequality.
   $6 \le \dfrac{5.2 + 6.3 + 7.5 + x}{4} \le 8$
   $6 \cdot 4 \le \dfrac{19 + x}{4} \cdot 4 \le 8 \cdot 4$
   $24 \le 19 + x \le 32$
   $5 \le x \le 13$
   The fourth baby's weight could be between 5 and 13 pounds.

### Practice 82

1. $2x^2 + 9xy + 7y^2$
   Since $2x^2 = (2x)(x)$, write $(2x)(x)$.
   The last term, $7y^2$, is the product of positive factors $(7y)(y)$.
   Check the factors to see which order results in the middle term, $9xy$.

Possibilities | Middle Term
$(2x + 7y)(x + y)$ | $2xy + 7xy = 9xy$
$(2x + y)(x + 7y)$ | $14xy + xy = 15xy$

So, $2x^2 + 9xy + 7y^2 = (2x + 7y)(x + y)$.

**2.** $-4m^2 + 8mn + 5n^2$

Since $-4m^2 = (m)(-4m)$, $(-m)(4m)$, and $(2m)(-2m)$, write $(m)(-4m)(-m)(4m)$, and $(2m)(-2m)$.

The last term, $5n^2$, is the product of positive factors $(n)(5n)$.

Check each pair to see which results in the middle term, $8mn$.

Possibilities
$(m + n)(-4m + 5n)$
$(-m + n)(4m + 5n)$
$(m + 5n)(-4m + n)$
$(-m + 5n)(4m + n)$
$(2m + n)(-2m + 5n)$
$(2m + 5n)(-2m + n)$

Middle Term
$5mn - 4mn = mn$
$-5mn + 4mn = -mn$
$mn - 20mn = -19mn$
$-mn + 20mn = 19mn$
$10mn - 2mn = 8mn$
$2mn - 10mn = -8mn$

So, factors of $-4m^2 + 8mn + 5n^2$ are $(2m + n)(-2m + 5n)$.

**3.** $(\sqrt{3} - 12)^2$
$= (-12 + \sqrt{3})^2$
$= 144 - 24\sqrt{3} + \sqrt{9}$
$= 144 - 24\sqrt{3} + 3$
$= 147 - 24\sqrt{3}$

**4.** $(2x + \sqrt{3})(2x - \sqrt{3})$
$= 4x^2 - 2x\sqrt{3} + 2x\sqrt{3} - \sqrt{9}$
$= 4x^2 - \sqrt{9}$
$= 4x^2 - 3$

**5.** $y = \dfrac{m - 6}{2m - 10}$

Simplify the denominator. Then set the denominator equal to zero and solve.

$2(m - 5) = 0$
$\dfrac{2(m - 5)}{2} = \dfrac{0}{2}$
$m - 5 = 0$
$\underline{+5 \quad +5}$
$m = 5$

Excluded value: $m \neq 5$

**6.** $y = \dfrac{y + 4}{-2y - 6}$

Simplify the denominator. Then set the denominator equal to zero and solve.

$-2(y + 3) = 0$
$\dfrac{-2(y + 3)}{-2} = \dfrac{0}{-2}$
$y + 3 = 0$
$\underline{-3 \quad -3}$
$y = -3$

Excluded value: $y \neq -3$

**7.** $2z - 6 \leq z$
$2z \leq z + 6$
$z \leq 6$

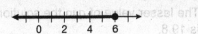

**8.** $2x + 9 > -x + 18$
$2x > -x + 9$
$3x > 9$
$x > 3$

**9.** The two equations have the same slope, 10, and different y-intercepts, $-2$ and 8. Therefore, the lines are parallel and there is no solution. The system is inconsistent.

**10.** $y = 3x$
$2y = 6x \rightarrow y = 3x$
The equations of the lines are identical. Since the graphs would be the same line, there are infinitely many solutions. The system is consistent and dependent.

**11.** $P = 4s$
$48 = 4s$
$12 = s$

The length of each side is 12 feet.

One possible way to express the answer as a radical number is $6\sqrt{4}$.

**12.** $x^2 + 7x + 12$

$ax^2 + bx + c$

In this trinomial, $b$ is 7 and $c$ is 12.

Three pairs of positive numbers have a product of 12.

(1)(12)     (2)(6)     (3)(4)

Only the pair 3 and 4 has a sum of 7.

So, $x^2 + 7x + 12 = (x + 3)(x + 4)$

Longer side: $x + 4 = 20 + 4 = 24$

The longer side is 24 centimeters long.

**13. a.** $x < 12$ OR $x > 15$

**b.**

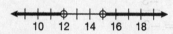

**14.** $|q - 24.9| = 5.1$

$q - 24.9 = 5.1$   or   $q - 24.9 = -5.1$

$q = 30$            $q = 19.8$

$\{19.8, 30\}$

The lesser value of $q$ in the solution set is 19.8.

**15.** $10 + 0.3m \le 20$

$0.3m \le 10$

$m \le 33.33$

$m \le 33\frac{1}{3}$

You can talk for at most 33 minutes.

**16.** Since there are a total of $x$ number of outcomes and only 1 positive outcome, a function to describe the probability is $y = \frac{1}{x}$.

**17.** $-8u^5y + 56u^4y - 80u^3y$

Factor out the GCF.

$-8u^3y(u^2 - 7u + 10)$

Find two numbers that have a product of 10 and a sum of $-7$.

$-5 \cdot -2$ and $-5 + (-2)$.

So, $-8u^3y(u^2 - 7u + 10) =$

$-8u^3y(u - 5)(u - 2)$ and

$-8u^5y + 56u^4y - 80u^3y =$

$-8u^3y(u - 5)(u - 2)$.

**18.** $3x^6 + 6x^5 - 45x^4$

Factor out the GCF.

$3x^4(x^2 + 2x - 15)$

Find two numbers that have a product of $-15$ and a sum of 2.

$-3 \cdot 5$ and $-3 + 5$.

So,

$3x^4(x^2 + 2x - 15) = 3x^4(x - 3)(x + 5)$

and

$3x^6 + 6x^5 - 45x^4 = 3x^4(x - 3)(x + 5)$.

The answer is **A**.

**19.** Total possible outcomes:

$4 + 7 + 9 + 5 + 3 = 28$

$P(A) = \frac{4}{28} = \frac{1}{7}$, $P(B) = \frac{7}{28} = \frac{1}{4}$,

$P(C) = \frac{9}{28}$, $P(D) = \frac{5}{28}$, $P(F) = \frac{3}{28}$

**20.** $P(\text{short pea}) = \frac{0}{4} = 0$; Sample: "tt" does not occur in this chart.

**21.** Student B; Sample: Student A found the probability of rolling a 2 or 3 to be

$\frac{1}{6} \cdot \frac{1}{6} = \frac{1}{36}$ when it is actually $\frac{2}{6} = \frac{1}{3}$.

**22. a.** $75 + 3p < 100 + 2p$

**b.** $75 + 3p < 100 + 2p$

$75 + p < 100$

$p < 25$

**c.** Sample: The solution set is all natural numbers less than 25 since Veejay can only invite whole numbers of people, and at 25, the costs are equal. Therefore, he would have to invite more than 25 people for the bowling alley to cost more than the skating area.

**23.**

| CD | Day 1 | Change |
|-----|-------|--------|
| New | 1 | +2 |
| Old | 7 | −1 |

$1 + 2d > 7 - 1d$

$3d > 6$

$d > 2$

The variable $d$ represents the days after day 1.

day $1 + d = 1 + 2 = 3$ days

If the trend continues, it will take her 3 days to listen to more new CDs than old CDs.

**24.** $4x + 7 > 5x - 2$

$4x + 9 > 5x$

$9 > x$

$x < 9$

The value of $x$ must be less than 9 for the statement that the length is greater than the width to be true.

**25.** Student A; Sample: Student A is correct because $-2 + x > x + 3$ is an inequality that will never be true, while Student B wrote an inequality that is sometimes true.

$-2 + x > x + 3$     $2x + 24 < 3x + 24$

     $x > x + 5$         $24 < x + 24$

     $0 > 5$           $0 < x$

                         $x > 0$

**26.** Sample:

$-17 > -2x - 7$   OR   $27 > 3(x + 6)$

$-17 > -2x - 7$   OR   $27 > 3x + 18$

$\underline{+7 \qquad\qquad +7}$     $\underline{-18 \qquad -18}$

$-10 > -2x$     OR     $9 > 3x$

$\dfrac{-10}{-2} < \dfrac{-2x}{-2}$   OR   $\dfrac{9}{3} > \dfrac{3x}{3}$

$5 < x$      OR      $3 > x$

$x > 5$      OR      $x < 3$

**27.**   $32 < 7x + 11 < 39$

$\underline{-11 \qquad\quad -11 \;\; -11}$

$21 < 7x < 28$

$\dfrac{21}{7} < \dfrac{7x}{7} < \dfrac{28}{7}$

$3 < x < 4$

The answer is **C**.

**28.** $40 \le \dfrac{45 + 52 + 60 + c}{4} \le 60$

$40 \le \dfrac{157 + c}{4} \le 60$

$40 \cdot 4 \le \dfrac{157 + c}{4} \cdot 4 \le 60 \cdot 4$

$160 \le 157 + c \le 240$

$\underline{-157 \;\; -157 \qquad\quad -157}$

$3 \le c \le 83$

The fourth patient's HDL level must be at least 3 and no more than 83.

**29.** $x \ge 90$ OR $x < 70$

**30.**   $90 \le \dfrac{94 + 88 + 91 + x}{4} \le 100$

$90 \le \dfrac{273 + x}{4} \le 100$

$90 \cdot 4 \le \dfrac{273 + x}{4} \cdot 4 \le 100 \cdot 4$

$360 \le 273 + x \le 400$

$\underline{-273 \qquad -273 \qquad\quad -273}$

$87 \le x \le 127$

Since the highest score possible is 100, Felipe must score between 87 and 100 (instead of 127) on his final test.

## LESSON 83

### Warm Up 83

**1.** perfect-square trinomial

**2.** $3x^4 - 12x$

$= 3x \cdot x^3 + 3x \cdot -4$

$= 3x(x^3 - 4)$

**3.** $48y^2 + 16y^3 - 56y^5$

$= 8y^2 \cdot 6 + 8y^2 \cdot 2y + 8y^2 \cdot -7y^3$

$= 8y^2(6 + 2y - 7y^3)$

**4.** $(2b - 3)^2$

$= (2b)^2 - 2(2b)(3) + 3^2$

$= 4b^2 - 12b + 9$

**5.** $(3x + 7)(3x - 7) = (3x)^2 - (7)^2$

$= 9x^2 - 49$

### Lesson Practice 83

**a.** Try to write in perfect-square trinomial form.

$x^2 + 14x + 49$

$= x^2 + 2 \cdot 7x + 7^2$

Yes, this is a perfect-square trinomial.

$= x^2 + 2 \cdot 7x + 7^2$

$= (x + 7)^2$

**b.** Try to write in perfect-square trinomial form.

$6n^4 - 12n^2 + 6$

$= 6(n^4 - 2n^2 + 1)$
$= 6[(n^2)^2 - 2(n)(n) + 1]$
Yes, this is a perfect-square trinomial.
$= 6[(n^2)^2 - 2(n)(n) + 1]$
$= 6(n^2 - 1)^2$

**c.** Try to write in perfect-square trinomial form.
$3g^2 + 9g + 9$
$3[(g)^2 + 3(g) + 3]$
No, because this trinomial cannot be put in the perfect-square trinomial form.

**d.** $\pi r^2 + 12\pi r + 36\pi$
$= \pi(r^2 + 12r + 36)$
$= \pi[r^2 + 2 \cdot (3r)(2) + 6^2]$
$= \pi(r + 6)^2$

The radius of the covered area increased by 6 miles.

**e.** Try to write as a difference of two squares.
$25x^2 - 4$
$= (5 \cdot 5)(x \cdot x) - (2 \cdot 2)$
$= (5x)^2 - 2^2$
Yes, this is a difference of two squares.
$= (5x)^2 - 2^2$
$= (5x + 2)(5x - 2)$

**f.** Try to write as a difference of two squares.
$9b^2 - 100a^2$
$= (3 \cdot 3)(b \cdot b) - (10 \cdot 10)(a \cdot a)$
$= (3b)^2 - (10a)^2$
Yes, this is a difference of two squares.
$= (3b)^2 - (10a)^2$
$= (3b + 10a)(3b - 10a)$

**g.** Try to write as a difference of two squares.
$x^2 - 14$
$= (x \cdot x) - (2 \cdot 7)$
No, this is not a difference of two squares.

**h.** Try to write as a difference of two squares.
$-81 + x^{10}$
$= x^{10} - 81$
$= (x^5)(x^5) - (9 \cdot 9)$
$= (x^5)^2 - 9^2$

Yes this is a difference of two squares.
$= (x^5)^2 - 9^2$
$= (x^5 + 9)(x^5 - 9)$

**i.** $A = lw$
Area of border: $(34)(34)$
Area of pool: $(s)(s)$
$34^2 - s^2 = (34 - s)(34 + s)$
The area of the border is $(34 - s)(34 + s)$ square feet.

**Practice 83**

**1.** $(7 + \sqrt{6})(4 - \sqrt{9})$
$= 28 - 7\sqrt{9} + 4\sqrt{6} - \sqrt{54}$
$= 28 - 7\sqrt{3^2} + 4\sqrt{6} - \sqrt{3^2 \cdot 6}$
$= 28 - 21 + 4\sqrt{6} - 3\sqrt{6}$
$= 7 + \sqrt{6}$

**2.** $(x + \sqrt{12})(x - \sqrt{3})$
$= x^2 - x\sqrt{3} + x\sqrt{12} - \sqrt{36}$
$= x^2 - x\sqrt{3} + x\sqrt{2^2 \cdot 3} - 6$
$= x^2 - x\sqrt{3} + 2x\sqrt{3} - 6$
$= x^2 + x\sqrt{3} - 6$

**3.** $-\dfrac{b}{4} + \dfrac{3}{8} \geq \dfrac{3b}{4} - \dfrac{5}{8}$
$\dfrac{3}{8} \geq \dfrac{4b}{4} - \dfrac{5}{8}$
$\dfrac{8}{8} \geq b$
$b \leq 1$

**4.** $11h + 9 \leq 5h - 21$
$6h + 9 \leq -21$
$6h \leq -30$
$h \leq -5$

**5.** $3x^5 - 3x^4 - 216x^3$
$3x^3(x^2 - x - 72)$
Find two numbers that have a product of $-72$ and a sum of $-1$.
$-9 \cdot 8$ and $-9 + 8$
$3x^3(x^2 - x - 72) = 3x^3(x - 9)(x + 8)$
So,
$3x^5 - 3x^4 - 216x^3 = 3x^3(x - 9)(x + 8)$.

**6.** $-12x^3 - 48x = -12x(x^2 + 4)$

**Saxon** Algebra 1

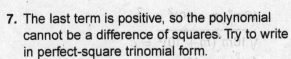

**7.** The last term is positive, so the polynomial cannot be a difference of squares. Try to write in perfect-square trinomial form.

$x^2 + 10x + 25$
$= x^2 + 2 \cdot 5x + 5^2$

This is a perfect-square trinomial.

$= x^2 + 2 \cdot 5x + 5^2$
$= (x + 5)^2$

**8.** The last term is positive, so the polynomial cannot be a difference of squares. Try to write in perfect-square trinomial form.

$x^2 + 12x + 36$
$= x^2 + 2 \cdot 6x + 6^2$

This is a perfect-square trinomial

$= x^2 + 2 \cdot 6x + 6^2$
$= (x + 6)^2$

**9.** *TUV* is a right triangle if $\overline{TU}$ is perpendicular to $\overline{UV}$. Find the coordinates on the endpoints using the graph.

$\overline{TU}$: $(-4, 4)$ and $(1, -1)$

$\overline{UV}$: $(1, -1)$ and $(3, 1)$

Find the slope of each line segment.

slope of $\overline{TU}$

$= \dfrac{y_2 - y_1}{x_2 - x_1} = \dfrac{-1 - 4}{1 - (-4)} = \dfrac{-5}{5} = -1$

slope of $\overline{UV}$

$= \dfrac{y_2 - y_1}{x_2 - x_1} = \dfrac{-1 - 1}{1 - 3} = \dfrac{-2}{-2} = 1$

Since the slopes are negative reciprocals, the two sides are perpendicular and form a right angle at point *U*. Therefore, the triangle is a right triangle because it contains a right angle.

**10.** One factor of a difference of two squares is $-7x + 2y$.

$(-7x + 2y)(-7x - 2y) = 49x^2 - 4y^2$

or

$(2y - 7x)(2y + 7x) = 4y^2 - 49x^2$

**11.** Total hike: 4 miles + off trail for lunch + back to trail and to end

They hiked more than 4 miles, or $x > 4$.

**12.** $y = 2x + 5$

$y - 2x = 1 \rightarrow y = 2x + 1$

Because the two lines have the same slope, $2x$, and different $y$-intercepts, the lines are parallel. Therefore, there is no solution. The system is inconsistent.

**13.** Solve each equation for $y$.

$3y = 2x + 4 \rightarrow$

$y = \dfrac{2}{3}x + \dfrac{4}{3}$

$3x = 4.5y - 6 \rightarrow$

$3x + 6 = 4.5y$

$4.5y = 3x + 6$

$y = \dfrac{3}{4.5}x + \dfrac{6}{4.5}$

$y = \dfrac{2}{3}x + \dfrac{4}{3}$

The two equations are identical. Therefore, they are the same line and have infinitely many solutions. The system is consistent and dependent.

**14.** Total possible outcomes: $6 \cdot 6 = 36$.

rolling a sum of 10 outcomes:

$(4, 6), (6, 4), (5, 5)$

rolling a set of doubles outcomes:

$(1, 1), (2, 2), (3, 3), (4, 4), (5, 5), (6, 6),$

rolling a sum of 10 and a set of doubles outcomes: $(5, 5)$

$P(10 \text{ or double})$
$= P(10) + P(\text{double}) - P(10 \text{ and double})$
$= \dfrac{3}{36} + \dfrac{6}{36} - \dfrac{1}{36}$
$= \dfrac{8}{36}$
$= \dfrac{2}{9}$

The probability of rolling a sum of 10 or a set of doubles is $\frac{2}{9}$.

**15. a.** $0.03d \geq 60$

**b.** $0.03d \geq 60$

$\dfrac{0.03d}{0.03} \geq \dfrac{60}{0.03}$

$d \geq 2000$

**c.** He should deposit at least $2000.

**d.**

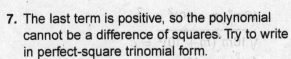

1000  2000  3000

**16.** $8 - 0.2 \leq x \leq 8 + 0.2$
$\qquad 7.8 \leq x \leq 8.2$
$\qquad$ or
$x \geq 8 - 0.2 \;$ AND $\; x \leq 8 + 0.2$
$\qquad x \geq 7.8 \;$ AND $\; x \leq 8.2$

**17. a.** $\dfrac{|x + 3|}{4} = 6$

$\qquad 4 \cdot \dfrac{|x + 3|}{4} = 6 \cdot 4$

$\qquad |x + 3| = 24$

**b.** $|x + 3| = 24$
$\qquad x + 3 = 24 \quad$ or $\quad x + 3 = -24$
$\qquad\qquad x = 21 \qquad\qquad\qquad x = -27$

**c.** $\{21, -27\}$

**18.** Sample: If $c$ is positive, then both are the same sign as $b$: either both positive or both negative. If $c$ is negative, then they have opposite signs.

**19. a.** $y = \dfrac{1000}{x} + 1$ is in the

$\qquad$ form $y = \dfrac{a}{x - b} + c.$

$\qquad$ Since $c = 1$, the horizontal asymptote's equation is $y = 1$.

**b.** Since $b = 0$, the vertical asymptote's equation is $x = 0$.

**c.** $y = \dfrac{1000}{x} + 1$

$\qquad y = \dfrac{1000}{5} + 1$

$\qquad y = 200 + 1$

$\qquad y = 201$

$\qquad$ The preschool will receive 201 toys.

**20.** $(a^2 + b^2) = c^2$
$\qquad (16m^6 + 320m^5 + 1600m^4) = c^2$
$\qquad$ Factor: $16m^6 + 320m^5 + 1600m^4$
$\qquad = 16m^4(m^2 + 20m + 100)$

Two numbers that have a product of 100 and a sum of 20: $10 \cdot 10$ and $10 + 10$.
$16m^4(m^2 + 20m + 100)$
$= 16m^4(m + 10)(m + 10)$
$= 16m^4(m + 10)^2$

Find the length of the hypotenuse.

**21.** $P$(heads, heads) =

$\qquad \left(\dfrac{1}{2}\right) \cdot \left(\dfrac{1}{2}\right) = \left(\dfrac{1}{2}\right)^2 = \dfrac{1}{4}$

$16m^4(m + 10)^2 = c^2$
$\sqrt{16m^4(m + 10)^2} = c$
$4m^2(m + 10) = c$
The length of the hypotenuse is
$4m^2(m + 10)$

**22.** Possible outcomes: $3 \cdot 6 = 18$ even and yellow outcomes: 2Y, 4Y, 6Y even and green outcomes: 2G, 4G, 6G

$P$(even and yellow or green)
$= P$(even, yellow) $+ P$(even, green)
$= \dfrac{3}{18} + \dfrac{3}{18} = \dfrac{6}{18} = \dfrac{1}{3}$

The answer is **A**.

**23.** Sample: The expression is a difference of two squares. Factor as $(45 + 15)(45 - 15)$, which equals $60 \cdot 30 = 1800$.

**24.** No; Sample: The inequality is only true if $x$ is 0 or greater.

**25.** $20h > 10h + \$50$
$\qquad 10h > \$50$
$\qquad\quad h > \$5$

They have to earn more than $5 per hour for Chad to make more money than Juan.

**26.** Student B; Sample: Student A forgot to change the direction of the inequality symbol when using the Multiplication Property of Inequality.

**27. a.** $32 < F \leq 40$

**b.** Set up a compound inequality.

| Minimum Temp. | Mean Temp. | Maximum Temp. |
|---|---|---|

$\qquad 32 < \dfrac{35 + 40 + 20 + 45 + t}{5} \leq 40$

$\qquad 32 < \dfrac{140 + t}{5} \leq 40$

$\qquad 5 \cdot 32 < \dfrac{140 + t}{5} \cdot 5 \leq 40 \cdot 5$

$\qquad 160 < 140 + t \leq 200$
$\qquad \underline{-140 \;\; -140 \qquad\quad -140}$
$\qquad\quad 20 < t \leq 60$

The last temperature should be greater than 20° and no greater than 60°F to be within the proper range.

**28.** $28 < 2(x + 3) < 42$

$28 < 2x + 6 < 42$    Distributive Property of Inequality

$22 < 2x < 36$    Addition Property of Inequality

$11 < x < 18$    Muliplication Property of Inequality

**29.** $49x^2 - 28x + 4$

$= (7x)^2 - 2 \cdot (7x) \cdot 2 + 2^2$

$= (7x - 2)(7x - 2)$

$= (7x - 2)^2$

The answer is **D**.

**30.** Area of deck:

$A = lw$

$= s \cdot s$

Area of shed

$A = lw$

$= 8 \cdot 8$

An expression to find the area to be painted is $s^2 - 8^2$ or $s^2 - 64$.

The factored expression is $(s + 8)(s - 8)$.

## LESSON 84

### Warm Up 84

**1.** function

**2.** $6x^3 = 6(2^3) = 6(8) = 48$

**3.** $x^2 - 4x + 3$

$= (-3^2) - 4(-3) + 3$

$= 9 + 12 + 3$

$= 24$

**4.** $500 - 7x^2$

$= 500 - 7(-10^2)$

$= 500 - 700$

$= -200$

**5.** $7x - y = 2 + 6x$

$7x - y = 6x + 2$

$-y = -x + 2$

$y = x - 2$

The answer is **B**.

### Lesson Practice 84

**a.** $4 - y = x - 2x^2 - 3$

$-y = -2x^2 + x - 7$

$y = 2x^2 - x + 7$

Yes, it is a quadratic function because it can be written in the standard form of a quadratic equation, $f(x) = ax^2 + bx + c$.

**b.** $x = -x^2 + y$

$x^2 + x = y$

$y = x^2 + x$

Yes, it is a quadratic function because it can be written in the standard form of a quadratic equation, $f(x) = ax^2 + bx + c$.

**c.** $4 = y$

$y = 4$

No, this does not represent a quadratic function. It is a linear function.

**d.** $f(x) = 4x^2 - 3$

$y = 4x^2 - 3$

| x | −2 | −1 | 0 | 1 | 2 |
|---|----|----|---|---|---|
| y | 13 | 1 | −3 | 1 | 13 |

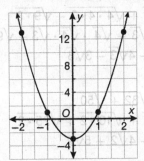

**e.** $f(x) = 2x^2 - 4$

$y = 2x^2 - 4$

$y = ax^2 + bx + c$

In this equation, $a = 2$.

Since $a > 0$, the graph opens upward.

**f.** $f(x) = 2x - 5x^2$

$y = -5x^2 - 2x$

$y = ax^2 + bx + c$

$y = ax^2 + bx + c$

In this equation, $a = -5$.

Since $a < 0$, the graph opens downward.

**Saxon** Algebra 1

**g.** $h = -16t^2 + 16$

$\quad = -16(0.5)^2 + 16$

$\quad = -4 + 16$

$\quad = 12$

The height of the acorn after falling for 0.5 seconds is 12 feet.

## Practice 84

**1.** Try to write in perfect-square trinomial form.

$q^2 + 18q + 81$

$= q^2 + 2 \cdot 9q + 9^2$

This is a perfect-square trinomial.

$= q^2 + 2 \cdot 9q + 9^2$

$= (q + 9)^2$

**2.** Try to write as a difference of two squares.

$36x^2 - 144$

$= (6 \cdot 6)(x \cdot x) - (12 \cdot 12)$

$= (6x)^2 - 12^2$

This is a difference of two squares.

$= (6x)^2 - 12^2$

$= (6x - 12)(6x + 12)$

**3.** $\sqrt{12} + \sqrt{48} - \sqrt{27}$

$= \sqrt{4 \cdot 3} + \sqrt{4 \cdot 4 \cdot 3} - \sqrt{9 \cdot 3}$

$= \sqrt{4} \cdot \sqrt{3} + \sqrt{4} \cdot \sqrt{4} \cdot \sqrt{3} - \sqrt{9} \cdot \sqrt{3}$

$= 2\sqrt{3} + 4\sqrt{3} - 3\sqrt{3}$

$= 3\sqrt{3}$

**4.** $\sqrt{18} + \sqrt{32} + \sqrt{50}$

$= \sqrt{9 \cdot 2} + \sqrt{16 \cdot 2} + \sqrt{25 \cdot 2}$

$= 3\sqrt{2} + 4\sqrt{2} + 5\sqrt{2}$

$= 12\sqrt{2}$

**5.** $2p + 7 > p - 10$

$\quad p + 7 > -10$

$\qquad p > -17$

**6.** $16 < 2x + 8$ OR $15 > 7x + 1$

$\quad \underline{-8} \quad \underline{-8} \qquad \underline{-1} \quad \underline{-1}$

$\quad 8 < 2x \quad$ OR $\quad 14 > 7x$

$\quad \dfrac{8}{2} \quad \dfrac{2x}{2} \qquad \dfrac{14}{7} \quad \dfrac{7x}{7}$

$4 < x$ OR $2 > x$

**7.** $x + 15x^2 - y = 4$

$\quad -y = 4 - x - 15x^2$

$\qquad y = -4 + x + 15x^2$

$\qquad y = 15x^2 + x - 4$

**8.** $P(\text{blue or B})$

$= P(\text{blue}) + P(B) - P(\text{blue and B})$

$= \dfrac{4}{10} + \dfrac{3}{10} - \dfrac{1}{10}$

$= \dfrac{6}{10}$

$= \dfrac{3}{5}$

**9.** $P(\text{gray or D})$

$= P(\text{gray}) + P(D) - P(\text{gray and D})$

$= \dfrac{4}{10} + \dfrac{2}{10} - \dfrac{1}{10} = \dfrac{5}{10} = \dfrac{1}{2}$

**10.** $P(\text{white or C})$

$= P(\text{white}) + P(C) - P(\text{white and C})$

$= \dfrac{2}{10} + \dfrac{2}{10} - \dfrac{0}{10}$

$= \dfrac{4}{10}$

$= \dfrac{2}{5}$

**11.** $P(\text{desktop or notebook})$

$= P(\text{desktop}) + P(\text{notebook})$

$= \dfrac{5}{100} + \dfrac{15}{100}$

$= \dfrac{20}{100}$

$= \dfrac{1}{5}$

The probability that either computer will fail in the first year is $\frac{1}{5}$.

**12. a.** Sample: $y = 40x + 180$, using data points (3, 300) and (8, 500).

$m = \dfrac{y_2 - y_1}{x_2 - x_1}$

$\quad = \dfrac{500 - 300}{8 - 3} = \dfrac{200}{5}$

$m = 40$

**Saxon** Algebra 1

$(y - y_1) = m(x - x_1)$

$(y - 300) = 40(x - 3)$

$y = 40x - 120 + 300$

$y = 40x + 180$

An equation for the trend line is
$y = 40x + 180$.

**b.** The graph shows a correlation because the points cluster to form a line. The correlation is positive because as the x-values increase, the y-values also increase.

**13.** $|w - 162| = 3$

$w - 162 = 3$ or $w - 162 = -3$

$w = 165$ $\qquad$ $w = 159$

{159, 165}

The maximum value of a correct guess is 165. The minimum value is 159 pounds.

**14. a.** $72x^2 - 156x + 72$

$= 72(2)^2 - 156(2) + 72$

$= 288 - 312 + 72$

$= 48$

**b.** $72x^2 - 156x + 72$

$= 12(6x^2 - 13x + 6)$

The first term, $6x^2$, can be factored as $(6x)(x)$ and $(3x)(2x)$.

The last term, 6, can be factored as $(-1)(-6)$ and $(-2)(-3)$.

Check each pair to see which results in the middle term, $-13x$.

| Possibilities | Middle Term |
|---|---|
| $(6x - 1)(x - 6)$ | $-36x - x = -37x$ |
| $(6x - 6)(x - 1)$ | $-6x - 6x = -12x$ |
| $(6x - 2)(x - 3)$ | $-18x - 2x = -20x$ |
| $(6x - 3)(x - 2)$ | $-12x - 3x = -15x$ |
| $(3x - 1)(2x - 6)$ | $-18x - 2x = -20x$ |
| $(3x - 6)(2x - 1)$ | $-3x - 12x = -15x$ |
| $(3x - 2)(2x - 3)$ | $-9x - 4x = -13x$ |
| $(3x - 3)(2x - 2)$ | $-6x - 6x = -12x$ |

So,

$12(6x^2 - 13x + 6) = 12(3x - 2)(2x - 3)$

and $72x^2 - 156x + 72 = 12(3x - 2)(2x - 3)$

**15.** $\sqrt{14} \cdot \sqrt{21}$

$= \sqrt{14 \cdot 21}$

$= \sqrt{2 \cdot 7 \cdot 3 \cdot 7}$

$= 7\sqrt{6}$

**16.** $y = \dfrac{1.6}{x + 2.5 + 7.8}$

Write the equation in the form

$y = \dfrac{a}{x - b} + c$. Then find the vertical asymptote, which occurs at the value of $b$: $x = b$.

$y = \dfrac{1.6}{x + (2.5 + 7.8)}$

$y = \dfrac{1.6}{x + 10.3}$

Since $x = b$, the vertical asymptote's equation is $x = -10.3$.

**17.** $-5t^2 + 40t - 35$

$= -5(t^2 - 8t + 7)$

Find two numbers that have a product of 7 and a sum of $-8$.

$-1 \cdot -7$ and $-1 + (-7)$

$-5(t^2 - 8t + 7) = -5(t - 1)(t - 7)$. So,

$-5t^2 + 40t - 35 = -5(t - 1)(t - 7)$.

**18.**

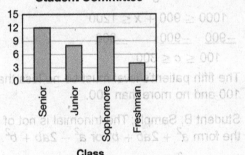

Student Committee

**19.**

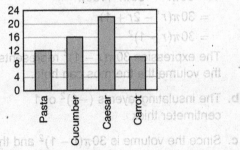

Salad Request

**Saxon** Algebra 1

**20.** Find the constant of variation, $k$, if $a = 18$, $b = 2$, and $c = 3$.

$a = kbc$

$18 = k \cdot 2 \cdot 3$

$18 = 6k$

$3 = k$

$k = 3$

The constant of variation is 3. An equation expressing the relationship is $a = 3bc$.

**21.** $2(x + 9) - 14 > 3x + 7 + 2x$

$2x + 18 - 14 > 5x + 7$

$2x + 4 > 5x + 7$

$-3x > 3$

$x < -1$

**22.** The answer is **B**.

**23.** Set up a compound inequality.

| Minimum Level | Mean Level | Maximum Level |
|---|---|---|

$200 \leq \dfrac{210 + 230 + 225 + 235 + c}{5} \leq 240$

$200 \cdot 5 \leq \dfrac{900 + c}{5} \cdot 5 \leq 240 \cdot 5$

$1000 \leq 900 + x \leq 1200$

$\underline{-900 \quad\quad -900 \quad\quad\quad -900}$

$100 \leq c \leq 300$

The fifth patient's level must be no less than 100 and no more than 300.

**24.** Student B; Sample: The trinomial is not of the form $a^2 + 2ab + b^2$ or $a^2 - 2ab + b^2$.

**25. a.** $V = \pi r^2 h$

$V = 30\pi r^2 - 60\pi r + 30\pi$

$= 30\pi(r^r - 2r + 1)$

$= 30\pi(r - 1)^2$

The expression $30\pi(r - 1)^2$ represents the volume the thermos can hold.

**b.** The insulating layer is $(-1)^2$ or 1 centimeter thick.

**c.** Since the volume is $30\pi(r - 1)^2$ and the inside radius is $r - 1$, the height of the thermos is 30 centimeters.

**26.** A cube has 6 identical faces having identical areas. Surface area of this cube:

$6x^2 + 36x + 54$

$= 6(x^2 + 6x + 9)$

$= 6(x + 3)(x + 3)$

$= 6(x + 3)^2$

Surface area of one face is

$\dfrac{6(x + 3)^2}{6} = (x + 3)^2$.

Therefore, one side of one face is

$\sqrt{(x + 3)^2} = x + 3$ long.

**27.** Sample: Use the data pair $(0, 4)$ from the table. Substitute 0 for $x$ in each equation and solve for $y$.

$y = -x^2 - 3x + 4$

$y = -0^2 - 3(0) + 4$

$y = 4$

$4 = 4$

The answer is **D**.

**28.** Sample function with degree 1 (greatest exponent is 1): $f(x) = -x + 3$

Sample function with degree 2 (greatest exponent is 2): $f(x) = x^2 + x - 3$

**29.** Sample: The shape of the parabolas is the same, but the graph of $y = x^2$ opens upward and the graph of $y = -x^2$ opens downward.

**30.** area of fountain − area of sculpture = area of pool

$A = \pi r^2 - \pi\left(\dfrac{1}{2}r\right)^2$

$= \pi r^2 - \dfrac{1}{4}\pi r^2$

$= \dfrac{3}{4}\pi r^2$

An equation to represent the area of the pool is $A = \dfrac{3}{4}\pi r^2$. This is a quadratic function because it is a polynomial that has a degree of exactly 2 (the term $r^2$).

## LESSON 85

**Warm Up 85**

**1.** perfect square

**2.** $\sqrt{625} = 25$

**Saxon** Algebra 1

**3.** $\sqrt{196} = 14$

**4.** $\sqrt{216} = \sqrt{6 \cdot 6 \cdot 6} = 6\sqrt{6}$

**5.** $\sqrt{389}$ is not a perfect square.

$\sqrt{389}$ is close to the perfect square

$\sqrt{400} = 20$, which is too great a number,
Try $19^2 = 361$. Since 389 is closer to 400
than to 361, try $19.7^2 = 388.09$ and
then $19.8^2 = 392.04$.

To the nearest tenth, $\sqrt{389} = 19.7$.

## Lesson Practice 85

**a.**
$$a^2 + b^2 = c^2$$
$$16^2 + 12^2 = c^2$$
$$256 + 144 = c^2$$
$$400 = c^2$$
$$\sqrt{400} = c$$
$$20 = c$$

The length of side $c$ is 20.

**b.**
$$a^2 + b^2 = c^2$$
$$m^2 + 2^2 = 11^2$$
$$m^2 + 4 = 121$$
$$m^2 = 117$$
$$m = \sqrt{117}$$

$\sqrt{117}$ is between $\sqrt{100} = 10$
and $\sqrt{121} = 11$. Try $10.8^2 = \sqrt{116.64}$.
To the nearest tenth, the length of side
$m$ is 10.8.

**c.**
$$a^2 + b^2 = c^2$$
$$r^2 + 6^2 = \sqrt{85}^2$$
$$r^2 + 36 = 85$$
$$r^2 = 49$$
$$r = \sqrt{49}$$
$$r = 7$$

**d.**
$$a^2 + b^2 = c^2$$
$$3^2 + 9^2 = s^2$$
$$9 + 81 = s^2$$
$$90 = s^2$$
$$\sqrt{90} = s$$
$$\sqrt{9 \cdot 10} = s$$
$$3\sqrt{10} = s$$

**e.** $a^2 + b^2 = c^2$

$$5^2 + 9^2 \overset{?}{=} 11^2$$
$$25 + 81 \overset{?}{=} 121$$
$$106 \neq 121$$

No, the side lengths do not form a
Pythagorean triple.

**f.**
$$a^2 + b^2 = c^2$$
$$8^2 + 15^2 \overset{?}{=} 17^2$$
$$64 + 81 \overset{?}{=} 289$$
$$289 = 289$$

Yes, the side lengths form a Pythagorean
triple.

**g.**
$$a^2 + b^2 = c^2$$
$$4^2 + \sqrt{65}^2 \overset{?}{=} 13^2$$
$$16 + 65 \overset{?}{=} 169$$
$$81 \neq 169$$

No, the side lengths do not form a
Pythagorean triple.

**h.**
$$a^2 + b^2 = c^2$$
$$8^2 + 32^2 = x^2$$
$$64 + 1024 = x^2$$
$$1088 = x^2$$
$$\sqrt{1088} = x$$

$\sqrt{1088}$ is very close to $\sqrt{1089} = 33$.

To the nearest tenth, the length of the ladder
is 33.0 feet.

## Practice 85

**1.** $3\sqrt{45} - \sqrt{5}$
$$= 3\sqrt{9 \cdot 5} - \sqrt{5}$$
$$= 9\sqrt{5} - \sqrt{5}$$
$$= 8\sqrt{5}$$

**2.** $\dfrac{p^{-1}}{w}\left(\dfrac{wx}{cp^{-2}q^{-4}} + 5pq^{-3}\right)$

$$= \dfrac{p^{-1}wx}{wcp^{-2}q^{-4}} + \dfrac{p^{-1} \cdot 5pq^{-3}}{w}$$

$$= \dfrac{p^{-1}x}{cp^{-2}q^{-4}} + \dfrac{5p^0q^{-3}}{w}$$

$$= \dfrac{pq^4x}{c} + \dfrac{5}{q^3w}$$

**3.** $-3t^3 - 27t^2 - 24t$

$-3t(t^2 + 9t + 8)$

Find two numbers that have a product of 8 and a sum of 9.

$8 \cdot 1$ and $8 + 1$

$-3t(t^2 + 9t + 8) = -3t(t + 8)(t + 1)$

So, $-3t^3 - 27t^2 - 24t = -3t(t + 8)(t + 1)$.

**4.** $4x^4 - 16x^2$

$4x^2(x^2 - 4)$

Find two numbers that have a product of $-4$ and a sum of 0.

$-2 \cdot 2$ and $-2 + 2$

$4x^2(x^2 - 4) = 4x^2(x - 2)(x + 2)$

So, $4x^4 - 16x^2 = 4x^2(x - 2)(x + 2)$.

**5.** $2x^2 + 14 - 9x - x^2$

$= x^2 - 9x + 14$

Find two numbers that have a product of 14 and a sum of $-9$.

$-7 \cdot -2$ and $-7 + (-2)$

$x^2 - 9x + 14 = (x - 7)(x - 2)$

So, $2x^2 + 14 - 9x - x^2 = (x - 7)(x - 2)$.

**6.** Try to write as a difference of two squares.

$3g^2 - 12$

$= 3(g^2 - 4)$

This is a difference of two squares.

$= 3(g^2 - 4)$

$= 3(g + 2)(g - 2)$

**7.** Try to write in perfect-square trinomial form.

$9x^2 - 24x + 16$

$= (3x)^2 + 2(3x)(-4) + (-4)^2$

This is a perfect-square trinomial.

$= (3x)^2 + 2(3x)(-4) + (-4)^2$

$= (3x - 4)^2$

**8.** $4 + y = -8 + 16x$

$y = 16x - 12$

This does not represent a quadratic function because it has no term with a degree of exactly 2.

**9.** $y + x^2 = 3x^2 - 10x + 12$

$y = 2x^2 - 10x + 12$

$y = 2x^2 - 10x + 12$ is written in the standard form of a quadratic function.

**10.**

$0.7 + 0.05y = 0.715$

$1000(0.7) + 1000(0.05)y = 1000(0.715)$

$700 + 50y = 715$

$50y = 715 - 700$

$50y = 15$

$y = 0.3$

**11.** $\frac{1}{2} + \frac{3}{4}x = \frac{1}{6}x + 2$

$\frac{6}{12} + \frac{9}{12}x = \frac{2}{12}x + \frac{24}{12}$

$\frac{9}{12}x - \frac{2}{12}x = \frac{24}{12} - \frac{6}{12}$

$\frac{7}{12}x = \frac{18}{12}$

$12\left(\frac{7}{12}\right)x = \left(\frac{18}{12}\right)12$

$7x = 18$

$x = 2\frac{4}{7}$

**12.** $-1.2x \geq -4.8$

$\frac{-1.2x}{-1.2} \leq \frac{-4.8}{-1.2}$

$x \leq 4$

$\begin{array}{c}\xleftarrow{\hspace{1cm}}\bullet\xrightarrow{\hspace{1cm}}\\ \text{-2 \quad 0 \quad 2 \quad 4 \quad 6 \quad 8 \quad 10}\end{array}$

**13.** The slope of the line $y = -3\frac{1}{2}x - 9$ is $-3\frac{1}{2}$. Any line parallel to this line has the same slope . Substitute the slope and the point $(1, 5)$ into the point-slope formula.

$y - y_1 = m(x - x_1)$

$y - 5 = -3\frac{1}{2}(x - 1)$

$y - 5 = -3\frac{1}{2}x + 3\frac{1}{2}$

$y = -3\frac{1}{2}x + 8\frac{1}{2}$

Sample equation of a parallel line:

$y = -3\frac{1}{2}x + 8\frac{1}{2}$.

**14.** $P = l + l + w + w$

$= \sqrt{25} + \sqrt{25} + 2\sqrt{4} + 2\sqrt{4}$

$= 5 + 5 + 4 + 4$

$= 18$

He needs 18 feet of fencing.

**Saxon** Algebra 1

**15.** $\dfrac{x}{-5} + 6 \leq 10$

$\dfrac{x}{-5} \leq 4$

$-5\left(\dfrac{x}{-5}\right) \geq (4)-5$

$x \geq -20$

**16.** $a^2 + b^2 = c^2$

$2^2 + 4^2 = c^2$

$4 + 16 = c^2$

$20 = c^2$

$\sqrt{20} = c$

$\sqrt{2^2 \cdot 5} = c$

$2\sqrt{5} = c$

The missing side length is $2\sqrt{5}$.

**17.** $y = \dfrac{2.4}{x + 4.5} + 6.9$

$y = \dfrac{a}{x - b} + c$

$y = \dfrac{2.4}{x - (-4.5)} + 6.9$

Since $b = -4.5$, the vertical asymptote's equation is $x = -4.5$.

**18.** $xy = k$

$4 \cdot 2 = k$

$k = 8$

**19.**

| State | Population 2005 | Average Change 2000–2005 |
|---|---|---|
| **ND** | 635,000 | $-7000 \div 5 = -1400$ |
| **WY** | 509,000 | $15,000 \div 5 = 3000$ |

$509,000 + 3000y > 635,000 - 1400y$

$3000y > 126,000 - 1400y$

$4400y > 126,000$

$y > 28.6363$

$2005 + 28.6363 = 2033.63$

So, if this trend continues, Wyoming's population will exceed North Dakota's in the last part of the year 2033, or around the year 2034.

**20.** $a^2 + b^2 = c^2$

$10^2 + 27.5^2 = c^2$

$100 + 756.25 = c^2$

$856.25 = c^2$

$\sqrt{856.25} = c$

$30^2 = 900$

$29^2 = 841$

The nearest whole square root of 856.25 is 29. The length of the leach edge is about 29 feet.

**21. a.** An inequality that shows the temperatures that are in the danger zone in degrees Celsius is $5 \leq c \leq 60$.

**b.** $5 \leq c \leq 60$

$5 \leq \dfrac{5}{9}(f - 32) \leq 60$

$9 \cdot 5 \leq 9\left[\dfrac{5}{9}(f - 32)\right] \leq 60 \cdot 9$

$45 \leq 5(f - 32) \leq 540$

$45 \leq 5f - 160 \leq 540$

$\underline{+160 \qquad +160 \qquad +160}$

$205 \leq 5f \leq 700$

$\dfrac{205}{5} \leq \dfrac{5f}{5} \leq \dfrac{700}{5}$

$41 \leq f \leq 140$

An inequality that shows the temperatures that are in the danger zone in degrees Fahrenheit is $41 \leq f \leq 140$.

**c.** An inequality that shows at what temperature food should be kept in degrees Fahrenheit is $f > 41$ OR $f > 140$.

**22.** $24 < 2x + 6 < 36$

$\underline{-6 \qquad -6 \quad -6}$

$18 < 2x < 30$

$\dfrac{18}{2} < \dfrac{2x}{2} < \dfrac{30}{2}$

$9 < x < 15$

Sample: This is an AND inequality since the solution falls within a specific range.

**23.** Student B; Sample: The polynomial is a difference of two squares.

**24.** $A_{\text{(rubber part)}} = A_{\text{(total side)}} - A_{\text{(rim)}}$

$\pi r^2 - 81\pi = \pi r^2 - x$

$-81\pi = -x$

$x = 81\pi$

$A_{(rim)} = 81\pi \doteq 9^2\pi$

Find the diameter of the rim.

$d = 2r$

$\quad = 2 \cdot 9 = 18$ inches

**25.** A cube has 6 square faces, so total surface area of a cube with side edge $x$ is $f(x) = 6x^2$.

Make a table of values, graph the points, and connect the points.

Sample table:

| x | −1 | 0 | 1 | 2 | 3 |
|---|----|----|----|----|----|
| y | 6 | 0 | 6 | 24 | 54 |

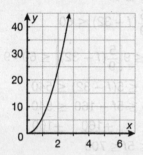

**26.** Sample: The triangle is not a right triangle.

**27.** $a^2 + b^2 = c^2$

$x^2 + (2x)^2 = \sqrt{45}^2$

$x^2 + (2x)^2 = 45$

An equation to find the length of the legs is $x^2 + (2x)^2 = 45$.

$x^2 + 4x^2 = 45$

$\quad\quad 5x^2 = 45$

$\quad\quad\, x^2 = 9$

$\quad\quad\, x = 3$

The shorter leg is 3 centimeters, so the longer leg is $2 \cdot 3$, or 6 centimeters.

**28.** $a^2 + b^2 = c^2$

$x^2 + 5^2 = 13^2$

$x^2 + 25 = 169$

$\quad\quad x^2 = 144$

$\quad\quad\, x = 12$

$P = 12 + 5 + 13 = 30$

The perimeter is 30 inches. The answer is **B**.

**29. a.** $-4x^2 + 48x - 63$

$\quad = (-2x + 3)(2x - 21)$

**b.** $-4x^2 + 48x - 63$

$\quad = -4(4)^2 + 48(4) - 63$

$\quad = -4(16) + 48(4) - 63$

$\quad = -64 + 192 - 63 = 65$

A student earns a grade of 65 when working for 4 hours.

**30.** An expression for the area of the region is $\left(6 + \sqrt{36}\right)^2$.

Find the area.

$\left(6 + \sqrt{36}\right)^2$

$= 36 + 12\sqrt{36} + \sqrt{36 \cdot 36}$

$= 36 + 12 \cdot 6 + 36 = 144$ square meters

## LESSON 86

### Warm Up 86

**1.** $y$-coordinate

**2.** $-3.8 - 5.5 = (-3.8) + (-5.5) = -9.3$

**3.** $(-6 - (-3))^2$

$\quad = (-6 + 3)^2$

$\quad = (-3)^2 = 9$

**4.** $a^2 + b^2 = c^2$

$2^2 + 4^2 = c^2$

$4 + 16 = c^2$

$\quad\, 20 = c^2$

$\sqrt{20} = c$

$\, 4.47 = c$

The length of the ramp is about 4.5 feet.

**5.** The answer is **B**.

### Lesson Practice 86

**a.** Use $A$, $B$, and $C$ as the points of a right triangle. Let $C$ be a right angle.

$(AB)^2 = (BC)^2 + (AC)^2$

$(AB)^2 = (1)^2 + (3)^2$

$\sqrt{(AB)^2} = \sqrt{1^2 + 3^2}$

$\sqrt{(AB)^2} = \sqrt{10}$

$AB \approx 3$

The direct distance from the corner of C St. and 2nd Ave. to the corner of D St. and 5th Ave. is $\sqrt{10}$ or about 3 city blocks.

**b.** Points: $(-3, -2)$ and $(4, 2)$

$d = \sqrt{(x_2 - x_1)^2 + (y_2 - y_1)^2}$

$d = \sqrt{(4 - (-3))^2 + (2 - (-2))^2}$

$= \sqrt{7^2 + 4^2}$

$= \sqrt{49 + 16}$

$= \sqrt{65}$

The distance between the points is $\sqrt{65}$.

**c.** First, determine the coordinates of each point.

$P(-4, 0)$   $Q(1, 3)$   $R(3, -2)$   $S(-1, -5)$

Next, use the distance formula to find the length of each side of PQRS until you find if there are two unequal sides.

$d = \sqrt{(x_2 - x_1)^2 + (y_2 - y_1)^2}$

$PQ = \sqrt{(1 - (-4))^2 + (3 - 0)^2}$

$= \sqrt{5^2 + 3^2}$

$= \sqrt{25 + 9}$

$PQ = \sqrt{34}$

$d = \sqrt{(x_2 - x_1)^2 + (y_2 - y_1)^2}$

$QR = \sqrt{(3 - 1)^2 + (-2 - 3)^2}$

$= \sqrt{2^2 + (-5)^2}$

$= \sqrt{4 + 25}$

$QR = \sqrt{29}$

(You could stop computing the lengths of the remaining sides. Since PQ and QR are not the same lengths, they are not congruent. PQRS is not a rhombus.)

$d = \sqrt{(x_2 - x_1)^2 + (y_2 - y_1)^2}$

$RS = \sqrt{(-1 - 3)^2 + (-5 - (-2))^2}$

$= \sqrt{-4^2 + (-3)^2}$

$= \sqrt{16 + 9}$

$RS = \sqrt{25}$

$d = \sqrt{(x_2 - x_1)^2 + (y_2 - y_1)^2}$

$SP = \sqrt{(-4 - (-1)^2 + (0 - (-5))^2}$

$= \sqrt{-3^2 + 5^2}$

$= \sqrt{9 + 25}$

$SP = \sqrt{34}$

Now, compare the lengths of the four sides of the quadrilateral.

$RS < QR < PQ$ and $SP$

$\sqrt{25} < \sqrt{29} < \sqrt{34}$ and $\sqrt{34}$

So, although two sides are congruent, all four are not congruent. This figure is not a rhombus.

**d.** Endpoints: $(-2, 3)$ and $(4, 7)$

$M = \left(\dfrac{x_1 + x_2}{2}, \dfrac{y_1 + y_2}{2}\right)$

$= \left(\dfrac{-2 + 4}{2}, \dfrac{3 + 7}{2}\right)$

$= \left(\dfrac{2}{2}, \dfrac{10}{2}\right)$

$= (1, 5)$

The midpoint of the line segment is $(1, 5)$.

**e.** The coordinates are $(20, 33)$ and $(58, 15)$. Use the distance formula.

$d = \sqrt{(x_2 - x_1)^2 + (y_2 - y_1)^2}$

$= \sqrt{(58 - 20)^2 + (15 - 33)^2}$

$= \sqrt{38^2 + (-18)^2}$

$= \sqrt{1444 + 324}$

$= \sqrt{1768}$

$= \sqrt{4 \cdot 442}$

$= 2\sqrt{442} \approx 42$

The pass was about 42 yards.

**Practice 86**

**1.** $15y < 60$

$y < 4$

**2.** $16 < 6x + 10$ OR $-16 > 6x - 10$

$\underline{-10 \qquad -10} \qquad \underline{+10 \qquad +10}$

$6 < 6x$ OR $-6 > 6x$

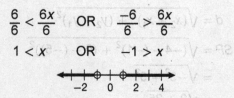
$$\frac{6}{6} < \frac{6x}{6} \quad \text{OR} \quad \frac{-6}{6} > \frac{6x}{6}$$

$$1 < x \quad \text{OR} \quad -1 > x$$

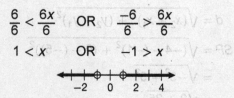

**3.** $-2g^2 - 8g + 90$

$-2(g^2 + 4g - 45)$

Find two numbers that have a product of $-45$ and a sum of 4.

$9 \cdot -5$ and $9 + (-5)$

$-2(g^2 + 4g - 45)$

$= -2(g + 9)(g - 5)$

So, $-2g^2 - 8g + 90 = -2(g + 9)(g - 5)$.

**4.** $20b^2 + 21b - 5$

The first term, $20b^2$, can be factored as $(20b)(b)$, $(10b)(2b)$, and $(5b)(4b)$.

The last term, $-5$, can be factored as $(-5)(1)$, and $(5)(-1)$.

Check each pair to see which results in the middle term, $21b$.

| Possibilities | Middle Term |
|---|---|
| $(20b - 5)(b + 1)$ | $20b - 5b = 15b$ |
| $(20b + 5)(b - 1)$ | $-20b + 5b = -15b$ |
| $(20b - 1)(b + 5)$ | $100b - b = 99b$ |
| $(20b + 1)(b - 5)$ | $-100b + b = -99b$ |
| $(10b - 5)(2b + 1)$ | $10b - 10b = 0$ |
| $(10b + 5)(2b - 1)$ | $-10b + 10b = 0$ |
| $(10b - 1)(2b + 5)$ | $50b - 2b = 48b$ |
| $(10b + 1)(2b - 5)$ | $-50b + 2b = -48b$ |
| $(5b - 5)(4b + 1)$ | $5b - 20b = -15b$ |
| $(5b + 5)(4b - 1)$ | $-5b + 20b = 15b$ |
| $(5b - 1)(4b + 5)$ | $25b - 4b = 21b$ |
| $(5b + 1)(4b - 5)$ | $-25b + 4b = -21b$ |

So, $20b^2 + 21b - 5 = (5b - 1)(4b + 5)$.

**5.** $-13w^2 + 38w - 25$

$= -1(13w^2 - 38w + 25)$

The first term in the trinomial, $13w^2$, can be factored as $(13w)(w)$.

The last term, 25, can be factored as $(-1)(-25)$ and $(-5)(-5)$.

Check each pair to see which results in the middle term, $-38$.

| Possibilities | Middle Term |
|---|---|
| $(13w - 1)(w - 25)$ | $-325w - w = -326w$ |
| $(13w - 25)(w - 1)$ | $-13w - 25w = -38w$ |
| $(13 - 5)(w - 5)$ | $-65w - 5w = -70w$ |

So, $-1(13w^2 - 38w + 25) =$

$-1(13w - 25)(w - 1)$

and

$-13w^2 + 38w - 25 =$

$-1(13w - 25)(w - 1)$.

**6.** $f(x) = ax^2 + bx + c$

$y - 14x = -20x^2$

$\qquad y = -20x^2 + 14x$

This equation can be written in the standard form of a quadratic function.

**7.** $f(x) = ax^2 + bx + c$

$x - 5x = -2x^2 + 7$

$\quad -4x = -2x^2 + 7$

$\quad 0y = -2x^2 + 4x + 7$

This equation cannot be written in the standard form of a quadratic function.

**8.** Points: $(4, -1)$ and $(7, 3)$

$d = \sqrt{(x_2 - x_1)^2 + (y_2 - y_1)^2}$

$d = \sqrt{(7 - 4)^2 + (3 - (-1))^2}$

$\quad = \sqrt{3^2 + 4^2}$

$\quad = \sqrt{9 + 16}$

$\quad = \sqrt{25}$

$\quad = 5$

The distance between the points is 5.

**9.** An inequality is $0.04x \geq 100$.

$0.04x \geq 100$

$\dfrac{0.04x}{0.04} \geq \dfrac{100}{0.04}$

$x \geq 2500$

He will need to make at least $2500 in charges to earn at least $100 cash back.

**10.** There is a positive correlation between the data sets because as the $x$-values increase, the $y$-values also increase.

**Saxon** Algebra 1

**11. a.** $x \le 13$ AND $x \ge 5$

**b.** $x \le 13$ AND $x \ge 5$

$13 \ge x$ AND $x \ge 5$

$5 \le x \le 13$

**c.**

```
←+—+—+●—+—+—+—+—+—●—+—+—→
    4   6   8   10  12  14
```

**12.** $A = lw$

$A = (3 + \sqrt{15})(4 + \sqrt{36})$

$= (3 + \sqrt{15})(4 + 6)$

$= 12 + 18 + 4\sqrt{15} + 6\sqrt{15}$

$= 30 + 10\sqrt{15}$

The area of his new room is $30 + 10\sqrt{15}$ square feet.

**13.** $120 \ge \dfrac{9}{5}C + 32$

$\quad \underline{-32 \quad -32}$

$\quad 88 \ge \dfrac{9}{5}C$

$5 \cdot 88 \ge 5 \cdot \dfrac{9}{5}C$

$440 \ge 9C$

$48\dfrac{8}{9} \ge C$

$C \le 48\dfrac{8}{9}$

The temperature in Texas has never been above $48\dfrac{8}{9}$ degrees Celsius.

**14.** Sample: The value of $c$ determines vertical translation.

**15.**

| | Turkey | Ham | Chicken |
|---|---|---|---|
| **Lettuce** | TL | HL | CL |
| **Tomato** | TT | HT | CT |
| **Cucumber** | TC | HC | CC |
| **Onion** | TO | HO | CO |
| **Peppers** | TP | HP | CP |

**16.** local store: $1.75g + 5$

online store: $2.25g$

$1.75g + 5 \le 2.25g$

$\quad 5 \le 0.5g$

$\quad 10 \le g$

$\quad g \le 10$

Renting from the local store is a better deal when she rents at least $10 + 1$, or 11 or more games from the local store.

**17.** $A = s \cdot s = s^2$

$\sqrt{16} = 4 \quad \sqrt{36} = 6$

The possible lengths of the sides of the third square are $4 < s < 6$ square units.

**18.** $32x^2 - 50y^2$

$= 2(16x^2 - 25y^2)$

$= 2[(4 \cdot 4)(x \cdot x) - (-5 \cdot -5)(y \cdot y)]$

$= 2[(4x)^2 - (-5y)^2]$

$= 2(4x + 5y)(4x - 5y)$

The answer is **C**.

**19.** $y^2 - x^2 - 8x - 41$

$= (y + 5)(y - 5) - (x + 4)^2$

$= (y^2 - 5y + 5y - 25) - (x + 4)(x + 4)$

$= (y^2 - 25) - (x^2 + 4x + 4x + 16)$

$= (y^2 - 25) - (x^2 + 8x + 16)$

**20.** Student A; Sample: Student B did not use the Distributive Property correctly.

$7x^2 + 24 = y - 6x(2 - 3x^2)$

$7x^2 + 24 = y - 12x + 18x^3$

$-18x^3 + 7x^2 + 24 = y - 12x$

$-18x^3 + 7x^2 + 12x + 24 = y$

**21.** Since the coefficient of the quadratic term is negative, the graph opens downward; Sample: If the price of the product is too low, people may buy a lot, but the company will not make much compared to its expenses. If the price of the product is too high, people will not buy it.

**22.** $a^2 + b^2 = c^2$

$n^2 + (\sqrt{84})^2 = 10^2$

$n^2 + 84 = 100$

$n^2 = 16$

$n = \sqrt{16}$

$n = 4$

The missing side length is 4.

**23. a.** $a^2 + b^2 = c^2$

$3^2 + 3^2 = c^2$

$9 + 9 = c^2$

$18 = c^2$

$\sqrt{18} = c$

$3\sqrt{2} = c$

The length of the hypotenuse is $3\sqrt{2}$.

**b.** $a^2 + b^2 = c^2$

$5^2 + 5^2 = c^2$

$25 + 25 = c^2$

$50 = c^2$

$\sqrt{50} = c$

$5\sqrt{2} = c$

The length of the hypotenuse is $5\sqrt{2}$.

**c.** A formula for the hypotenuse of a right isosceles triangle with legs of length $a$ is $c = a\sqrt{2}$.

**24.** Student B; Sample: Student A used $p$ as the hypotenuse; 7 is the length of the hypotenuse.

**25.** Use $A$, $B$, and $C$ as the points of a right triangle. Let $B$ be a right angle.

$(AC)^2 = (AB)^2 + (BC)^2$

$(AC)^2 = (2)^2 + (4)^2$

$\sqrt{(AC)^2} = \sqrt{2^2 + 4^2}$

$\sqrt{(AC)^2} = \sqrt{20}$

$AC = \sqrt{4 \cdot 5}$

$AC = 2\sqrt{5} \approx 4.5$

The direct distance from the corner of A St. and 4th Ave. to the corner of E St. and 2nd Ave. is $2\sqrt{5}$ or about 4.5 city blocks.

**26. a.** $a^2 + b^2 = c^2$

$h^2 + 60^2 = 100^2$

$h^2 + 3600 = 10,000$

$h^2 = 6400$

$h = \sqrt{6400}$

$h = 80$

The length of $h$ is 80 feet.

**b.** $80 + 3 = 83$ The kite is 83 feet off the ground.

**27.** Sample: Dawn's values for $x_2 - x_1$ and $y_2 - y_1$ will be the opposite of Dan's values,

but when the differences are squared, they will be the same positive numbers.

**28.** Sample: Use the distance formula.

between vertices $(-3, 3)$ and $(1, 0)$:

$d = \sqrt{(x_2 - x_1)^2 + (y_2 - y_1)^2}$

$= \sqrt{(1 - (-3))^2 + (0 - 3)^2}$

$= \sqrt{4^2 + (-3)^2}$

$= \sqrt{16 + 9}$

$= \sqrt{25}$

$= 5$

between vertices $(1, 0)$ and $(4, 4)$:

$d = \sqrt{(x_2 - x_1)^2 + (y_2 - y_1)^2}$

$= \sqrt{(4 - 1)^2 + (4 - 0)^2}$

$= \sqrt{3^2 + 4^2}$

$= \sqrt{9 + 16}$

$= \sqrt{25}$

$= 5$

between vertices $(4, 4)$ and $(-3, 3)$

$d = \sqrt{(x_2 - x_1)^2 + (y_2 - y_1)^2}$

$= \sqrt{(-3 - 4)^2 + (3 - 4)^2}$

$= \sqrt{-7^2 + (-1)^2}$

$= \sqrt{49 + 1}$

$= \sqrt{50}$

$= 5\sqrt{2}$

The lengths of the sides of the triangle are 5, 5, and $5\sqrt{2}$.

$a^2 + b^2 = c^2$

$5^2 + 5^2 \stackrel{?}{=} (5\sqrt{2})^2$

$25 + 25 \stackrel{?}{=} (5\sqrt{2})^2$

$50 = 50 \checkmark$

Because the lengths of the sides of the triangle satisfy the equation $a^2 + b^2 = c^2$, the triangle is a right triangle.

**29.** Choice **A**: $(1, 2)$ and $(13, -8)$

$M = \left(\dfrac{1 + 13}{2}, \dfrac{2 - 8}{2}\right)$

$= \left(\dfrac{14}{2}, \dfrac{-6}{2}\right)$

$= (7, -3)$

Choice **B**: $(5, 0)$ and $(9, -5)$

$$M = \left(\frac{5+9}{2}, \frac{0-5}{2}\right)$$

$$= \left(\frac{14}{2}, \frac{-5}{2}\right)$$

$$= \left(7, -2\frac{1}{2}\right)$$

Choice **C**: (2, −9) and (12, 3)

$$M = \left(\frac{2+12}{2}, \frac{-9+3}{2}\right)$$

$$= \left(\frac{14}{2}, \frac{-6}{2}\right)$$

$$= (7, -3)$$

Choice **D**: (4, −2) and (10, −4)

$$M = \left(\frac{4+10}{2}, \frac{-2-4}{2}\right)$$

$$= \left(\frac{14}{2}, \frac{-6}{2}\right)$$

$$= (7, -3)$$

The answer is **B**.

30. coordinates of third base: (0, 90) coordinates of outfielder: (50, 300)

$$d = \sqrt{(x_2 - x_1)^2 + (y_2 - y_1)^2}$$

$$= \sqrt{(50 - 0)^2 + (300 - 90)^2}$$

$$= \sqrt{50^2 + 210^2}$$

$$= \sqrt{2500 + 44{,}100}$$

$$= \sqrt{46{,}600}$$

$$= 215.87 \approx 216$$

The outfielder's throw is 216 feet.

## LESSON 87

### Warm Up 87

1. greatest common factor

2. $90k^4 + 15k^3 = 15k^3(6k + 1)$

3. $x^2 - 8x + 15$

   Find a pair of numbers with a product of 15 and a sum of −8.
   (−3)(−5) and −3 + (−5)
   So, $x^2 - 8x + 15 = (x - 3)(x - 5)$.

4. $4n^2 + 5n - 21$

   The first term, $4n^2$, can be factored as
   (4n)(n) and (2n)(2n).

The last term, −21, can be factored as
(1)(−21), (−1)(21), (3)(−7), and (−3)(7).
Check each pair to see which results in the middle term, 5n.

| Possibilities | Middle Term |
|---|---|
| $(4n + 1)(n - 21)$ | $-84n + n = -83n$ |
| $(4n - 1)(n + 21)$ | $84n - n = 83n$ |
| $(4n + 21)(n - 1)$ | $-4n + 21n = 17n$ |
| $(4n - 21)(n + 1)$ | $4n - 21n = -17n$ |
| $(4n + 3)(n - 7)$ | $-28n + 3n = -25n$ |
| $(4n - 3)(n + 7)$ | $28n - 3n = 25n$ |
| $(4n + 7)(n - 3)$ | $-12n + 7n = -5n$ |
| $(4n - 7)(n + 3)$ | $12n - 7n = 5n$ |
| $(2n + 1)(2n - 21)$ | $-42n + 2n = -40$ |
| $(2n - 1)(2n + 21)$ | $42n - 2n = 40$ |
| $(2n + 3)(2n - 7)$ | $-14n + 6n = -8n$ |
| $(2n - 3)(2n + 7)$ | $14n - 6n = 8n$ |

So, $4n^2 + 5n - 21 = (4n - 7)(n + 3)$.

5. $81x^2 - 64y^2$

$$= (9 \cdot 9)(x \cdot x) - (8 \cdot 8)(y \cdot y)$$

$$= (9x)^2 - (8y)^2$$

$$= (9x + 8y)(9x - 8y)$$

### Lesson Practice 87

a. $3y^2 + 6yz + 4y + 8z$

$$= (3y^2 + 6yz) + (4y + 8z)$$

$$= 3y(y + 2z) + 4(y + 2z)$$

$$= (y + 2z)(3y + 4)$$

Check
$(y + 2z)(3y + 4)$

$$\overset{?}{=} 3y^2 + 4y + 6yz + 8z$$

$$= 3y^2 + 6yz + 4y + 8z \checkmark$$

b. $3y^2 - 4y^3 + 3 - 4y$

$$= 3y^2 + 3 - 4y^3 - 4y$$

$$= 3(y^2 + 1) - 4y(y^2 + 1)$$

$$= (y^2 + 1)(3 - 4y)$$

Check
$(y^2 + 1)(3 - 4y)$

$$= 3y^2 - 4y^3 + 3 - 4y \checkmark$$

c. $99x^3y - 33x^3 + 33x^2y - 11x^2$

$$= 11x^2(9xy - 3x + 3y - 1)$$

$$= 11x^2[(9xy - 3x) + (3y - 1)]$$

$= 11x^2[(3x)(3y - 1) + (3y - 1)]$
$= 11x^2[(3y - 1)(3x + 1)]$
Check
$11x^2[(3y - 1)(3x + 1)]$
$\stackrel{?}{=} 11x^2[(3y + 9xy - 3x - 1)]$
$\stackrel{?}{=} 33x^2y + 99x^3y - 33x^3 - 11x^2$
$= 99x^3y - 33x^3 + 33x^2y - 11x^2$ ✔

**d.** $3a^2b - 4ab + 20 - 15a$
$= (3a^2b - 4ab) + (20 - 15a)$
$= ab(3a - 4) + 5(4 - 3a)$
$= ab(3a - 4) + 5(-1)(3a - 4)$
$= ab(3a - 4) - 5(3a - 4)$
$= (3a - 4)(ab - 5)$
Check
$(3a - 4)(ab - 5)$
$\stackrel{?}{=} -15a + 3a^2b - 4ab + 20$
$= 3a^2b - 4ab + 20 - 15a$ ✔

**e.** $x^2 - 4x - 77$
$ax^2 + bx + c$
$ac = 1 \cdot -77 = -77$
Factors of $-77$ with a sum of $-4$ are 7
and $-11$.
$x^2 - 4x - 77$
$= x^2 + 7x - 11x - 77$
$= x(x + 7) - 11(x + 7)$
$= (x + 7)(x - 11)$

**f.** $6a^2 - 1a - 15$
$ax^2 + bx + c$
$ac = 6 \cdot -15 = -90$
Factors of $-90$ with a sum of $-1$ are 9
and $-10$.
$6a^2 - 1a - 15$
$= 6a^2 + 9a - 10a - 15$
$= 3a(2a + 3) - 5(2a + 3)$
$= (2a + 3)(3a - 5)$

## Practice 87

**1.** $x^2 + 3xy - 54y^2$
$ax^2 + bx + c$
In this trinomial, $b$ is $3y$ and $c$ is $-54y^2$.
The position $b$ must be the sum of two
terms that are factors of $c$.

Twenty-four pairs of terms have a product
of $-54y^2$.

| | | |
|---|---|---|
| $(y^2)(-54)$ | $(y)(-54y)$ | $(y)(-54y^2)$ |
| $(-y^2)(54)$ | $(-y)(54y)$ | $(-y)(54y^2)$ |
| $(2y^2)(-27)$ | $(2y)(-27y)$ | $(2y)(-27y^2)$ |
| $(-2y^2)(27)$ | $(-2y)(27y)$ | $(-2y)(27y^2)$ |
| $(3y^2)(-18)$ | $(3y)(-18y)$ | $(3y)(-18y^2)$ |
| $(-3y^2)(18)$ | $(-3y)(18y)$ | $(-3y)(18y^2)$ |
| $(6y^2)(-9)$ | $(6y)(-9y)$ | $(6y)(-9y^2)$ |
| $(-6y^2)(9)$ | $(-6y)(9y)$ | $(-6y)(9y^2)$ |

Only the pair $-6y$ and $9y$ has a sum of $3y$.
So, $x^2 + 3xy - 54y^2 = (x - 6y)(x + 9y)$.

**2.** $64a^2b - 16a^3 + 18a^2b - 9$
$= (64a^2b - 16a^3) + (18a^2b - 9)$
$= 16a^2(4b - a) + 9(2a^2b - 1)$

**3.** $2g + 9 - 4g < 5 + 6g - 2$
$-2g + 9 < 6g + 3$
$9 < 8g + 3$
$6 < 8g$
$\dfrac{6}{8} < g$
$g > \dfrac{3}{4}$

**4.** $6(k - 5) > 3k - 26$
$6k - 30 > 3k - 26$
$3k - 30 > -26$
$3k > 4$
$k > \dfrac{4}{3}$

**5.** Rolling a 4 on one cube has a probability of
$\frac{1}{6}$, so the probability on two cubes is $\frac{1}{6} \cdot \frac{1}{6}$.
$P(4, 4, \text{heads}) = \left(\dfrac{1}{6}\right)^2 \cdot \dfrac{1}{2}$
$= \dfrac{1}{36} \cdot \dfrac{1}{2}$
$= \dfrac{1}{72}$

**6.** Rolling a number less than 4 on one cube
has a probability of $\frac{3}{6}$ or $\frac{1}{2}$, so the probability
on two cubes is $\left(\frac{1}{2}\right)^2$.
$P(\text{less than 4, less than 4, heads})$
$= \left(\dfrac{1}{2}\right)^2 \cdot \dfrac{1}{2}$

**Saxon** Algebra 1

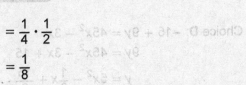

$$= \frac{1}{4} \cdot \frac{1}{2}$$

$$= \frac{1}{8}$$

**7.** Try to write as a difference of two squares.

$100 - c^6$

$= (10 \cdot 10) - (c^3 \cdot c^3)$

$= (10)^2 - (c^3)^2$

This is a difference of two squares.

$= (10)^2 - (c^3)^2$

$= (10 + c^3)(10 - c^3)$

**8.** Try to write in perfect-square trinomial form.

$4x^2 + 20x + 25$

$= (2x)^2 + 2 \cdot 10x + 5^2$

This is a perfect-square trinomial.

$= (2x)^2 + 2 \cdot 10x + 5^2$

$= (2x + 5)^2$

**9.** Points: $(1, 3)$ and $(4, 7)$

$d = \sqrt{(x_2 - x_1)^2 + (y_2 - y_1)^2}$

$d = \sqrt{(4 - 1)^2 + (7 - 3)^2}$

$= \sqrt{3^2 + 4^2}$

$= \sqrt{9 + 16}$

$= \sqrt{25}$

$= 5$

The distance between the points is 5.

**10.** Points: $(2, -1)$ and $(6, 3)$

$d = \sqrt{(x_2 - x_1)^2 + (y_2 - y_1)^2}$

$d = \sqrt{(6 - 2)^2 + (3 - (-1))^2}$

$= \sqrt{4^2 + 4^2}$

$= \sqrt{16 + 16}$

$= \sqrt{32}$

$= \sqrt{16 \cdot 2}$

$= 4\sqrt{2}$

The distance between the points is $4\sqrt{2}$.

**11.** hours of practice and your golf score
The lower the golf score, the better the performance, so as the number of hours of practice increases, the golf score decreases.

**12.**

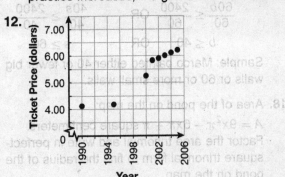

**13. a.** $|x - 50| = 0.5$

**b.** $|x - 50| = 0.5$

$x - 50 = +0.5$  or  $x - 50 = -0.5$

$x = 50.5$  $x = 49.5$

The maximum acceptable weight is 50.5 pounds. The minimum is 49.5 pounds.

**14.** $2m + 5 \leq 9$

$2m \leq 4$

$m \leq 2$

She can hike at most 2 hours before she needs to turn around.

**15. a.** $y = \dfrac{3000}{x} + 100$

$y = \dfrac{a}{x - b} + c$

Since $c = 100$, the horizontal asymptote's equation is $y = 100$.

**b.** Since $b = 0$, the vertical asymptote's equation is $x = 0$.

**c.** $y = \dfrac{3000}{20} + 100$

$= 150 + 100$

$= 250$

The library will receive 250 books.

**16.** Sample: There are no common factors that can be factored out of any grouped terms.

**Saxon** Algebra 1

**17.** $60b + 20 \le 2420$  OR  $40s + 20 \ge 2420$

$\underline{\quad -20 \quad -20}$  $\underline{\quad -20 \quad -20}$

$60b \le 2400$  OR  $40s \ge 2400$

$\dfrac{60b}{60} \le \dfrac{2400}{60}$  OR  $\dfrac{40s}{40} \ge \dfrac{2400}{40}$

$b \le 40$  OR  $s \ge 60$

Sample: Marco painted either 40 or fewer big walls or 60 or more small walls.

**18.** Area of the pond on the map:

$A = 9x^2\pi - 6x\pi + \pi$ square centimeters.
Factor the area trinomial and write in perfect-square trinomial form to find the radius of the pond on the map.

$A = 9x^2\pi - 6x\pi + \pi$

$\quad = \pi(9x^2 - 6x + 1)$

$\quad = \pi[(3x)^2 - 2 \cdot 3x + 1^2]$

$\quad = \pi(3x - 1)^2$

So, if $A = \pi r^2$,

$r^2 = (3x - 1)^2$

$r = \sqrt{(3x - 1)^2} = 3x - 1$ cm.

Find the diameter of the pond on the map:

$d = 2r$

$\quad = 2(3x - 1)$

$\quad = 6x - 2$ cm

Find the diameter of the actual pond using map scale of 1 cm:500 m

$500(6x - 2)$

$= 3000x - 1000$

The actual diameter of the pond is $3000x - 1000$ meters.

**19.** Write each choice in standard quadratic form $y = ax^2 + bx + c$. If $a < 0$, the parabola opens downward.

Choice **A**: $-8y + 3x^2 = 4 + 7x$

$-8y = -3x^2 + 7x + 4$

$y = \dfrac{8}{3}x^2 - \dfrac{7}{8}x - \dfrac{4}{8}$

$\dfrac{8}{3} > 0$

Choice **B**: Since there is no $bx$ term, this is not a quadratic function.

Choice **C**: $-y + 36x = x^2 + 40$

$-y = x^2 - 36x + 40$

$y = -x^2 + 36x - 40$

$-1 < 0$

Choice **D**: $-15 + 9y = 45x^2 - 3x$

$9y = 45x^2 - 3x + 15$

$y = 5x^2 - \dfrac{1}{3}x + \dfrac{15}{9}$

$5 > 0$

The answer is **C**.

**20.** Sample: Rewrite the equation in the standard form of a quadratic function. Use the function to make a table of values. Plot the points from the table in a coordinate plane. Draw a smooth curve through the points.

**21.** $a^2 + b^2 = c^2$

$x^2 + \sqrt{7}^2 = \sqrt{13}^2$

$x^2 + 7 = 13$

$x^2 = 6$

$x = \sqrt{6}$

The missing side length is $\sqrt{6}$.

**22.** lengths: 10, $5\sqrt{5}$, and 15
Use the greatest number for $c$.

$a^2 + b^2 = c^2$

$(10)^2 + (5\sqrt{5})^2 \overset{?}{=} (15)^2$

$100 + 25\sqrt{25} \overset{?}{=} 225$

$100 + (25 \cdot 5) \overset{?}{=} 225$

$225 = 225$

Yes, the lengths form a right triangle

**23.** Check whether the lengths 24, 32, and 42 form a right triangle using the Pythagorean Theorem. Use the greatest number for $c$.

$a^2 + b^2 = c^2$

$(24)^2 + (32)^2 \overset{?}{=} (42)^2$

$576 + 1024 \overset{?}{=} 1764$

$1600 \ne 1764$

No, the lengths do not form a right triangle, so her canvas is not a right triangle.

**24.** Student A; Sample: In calculating $x_2 - x_1$, Student B subtracted 1 instead of $-1$, from 4.

**25. a.** To find the endpoints $M$ and $N$ of the midsegment that joins $\overline{PQ}$ and $\overline{QR}$, find the midpoints of $\overline{PQ}$ and $\overline{QR}$. Endpoints of $\overline{PQ}$ are $P(3, 2)$ and $Q(3, 8)$.

$$M = \left(\frac{x_1 + x_2}{2}, \frac{y_1 + y_2}{2}\right)$$

$$= \left(\frac{3+3}{2}, \frac{2+8}{2}\right)$$

$$= \left(\frac{6}{2}, \frac{10}{2}\right)$$

$$= (3, 5)$$

The midpoint of $\overline{PQ}$ (and endpoint $M$ of $\overline{MN}$) is at $(3, 5)$.

Endpoints of $\overline{QR}$ are $Q(3, 8)$ and $R(7, 6)$.

$$M = \left(\frac{x_1 + x_2}{2}, \frac{y_1 + y_2}{2}\right)$$

$$= \left(\frac{3+7}{2}, \frac{8+6}{2}\right)$$

$$= \left(\frac{10}{2}, \frac{14}{2}\right)$$

$$= (5, 7)$$

The midpoint of $\overline{QR}$ (and endpoint $N$ of $\overline{MN}$) is at $(5, 7)$.

The endpoints $M$ and $N$ of the midsegment that joins sides $\overline{PQ}$ and $\overline{QR}$ are $(3, 5)$ and $(5, 7)$.

**b.** Find the length of $\overline{PR}$. Endpoints of $\overline{PR}$ are $P(3, 2)$ and $R(7, 6)$.

$$d = \sqrt{(x_2 - x_1)^2 + (y_2 - y_1)^2}$$

$$= \sqrt{(7-3)^2 + (6-2)^2}$$

$$= \sqrt{4^2 + 4^2}$$

$$= \sqrt{16 + 16}$$

$$= \sqrt{32}$$

$$= \sqrt{16 \cdot 2}$$

$$= 4\sqrt{2}$$

The length of $\overline{PR}$ is $4\sqrt{2}$.

Find the length of $\overline{MN}$. Endpoints (from part a) of $\overline{MN}$ are $M(3, 5)$ and $N(5, 7)$.

$$d = \sqrt{(5-3)^2 + (7-5)^2}$$

$$= \sqrt{2^2 + 2^2}$$

$$= \sqrt{4 + 4}$$

$$= \sqrt{8}$$

$$= \sqrt{4 \cdot 2}$$

$$= 2\sqrt{2}$$

The length of $\overline{MN}$ is $2\sqrt{2}$, which is half the length of $\overline{PR}$, $4\sqrt{2}$.

**26. a.** $Q(25, 10)$, $R_1(30, 40)$, and $R_2(50, 20)$
Find the distance between $Q$ and the first receiver.

$$d = \sqrt{(x_2 - x_1)^2 + (y_2 - y_1)^2}$$

$$d = \sqrt{(30 - 25)^2 + (40 - 10)^2}$$

$$= \sqrt{5^2 + 30^2}$$

$$= \sqrt{25 + 900}$$

$$= \sqrt{925}$$

Since $30^2 = 900$ and $31^2 = 961$, the quarterback's distance to the receiver at $(30, 40)$ is 30 yards to the nearest yard.

**b.** Find the distance between Q and the second receiver.

$$d = \sqrt{(x_2 - x_1)^2 + (y_2 - y_1)^2}$$

$$d = \sqrt{(50 - 25)^2 + (20 - 10)^2}$$

$$= \sqrt{25^2 + 10^2}$$

$$= \sqrt{625 + 100}$$

$$= \sqrt{725}$$

Since $26^2 = 676$ and $27^2 = 729$, the quarterback's distance to the receiver at $(50, 20)$ is 27 yards to the nearest yard.

**c.** The receiver at $(50, 20)$ is closer to the quarterback.

**27. a.** $A = \frac{1}{2}bh$

**b.**
$$A = \frac{1}{2}bh$$
$$2A = bh$$
$$2(x^2 + 2x) = (x + 2)h$$
$$2x^2 + 4x = (x + 2)h$$

**c.** Factor the area: $2x^2 + 4x = 2x(x + 2)$

**d.** Find the height: $2x(x + 2) = (x + 2)h$
$$\frac{2x(x + 2)}{(x + 2)} = h$$
$$2x = h$$

The length of the height is $2x$.

**28.** yes; Sample: Any number of monomials expressed as a sum or difference is a polynomial.

**29.** $(20 + n) + (20 + n)(n - 5)$

$= (n + 20) + (n + 20)(n - 5)$

$= n + 20 + n^2 + 15n - 100$

$= n^2 + 16n - 80$

Factors of $-80$ with a sum of 16 are $-4$ and 20.

$n^2 + 16n - 80$

$= (n - 4)(n + 20)$

An expression to show the price of 2 discounted books is $(n - 4)(n + 20)$.

**30.** 15 uniforms = first group of 5 plus 2 more groups of 5.

15 uniforms $= (y^2 + 5) + 2(y + 1)$

The uniforms cost $(y^2 + 5) + 2(y + 1)$ dollars.

## LESSON 88

### Warm Up 88

**1.** rational

**2.** $x^6 x^2 = x^8$

**3.** $\dfrac{8b^4}{12b^9}$

$= \dfrac{8}{12b^{9-4}}$

$= \dfrac{2}{3b^5}$

**4.** $\dfrac{12y^4 - 18y^3}{28y^2 - 42y} = \dfrac{6y^3(2y - 3)}{14y(2y - 3)}$

$= \dfrac{6y^3 \cancel{(2y - 3)}^{1}}{14y \cancel{(2y - 3)}} = \dfrac{6y^3}{14y}$

$= \dfrac{\cancel{6}^{3} y^{3-1}}{\cancel{14}y^{7}} = \dfrac{3y^2}{7}$

**5.** $x^2 - 14x + 24$

Four pairs of negative numbers have a product of 24.

$(-1)(-24) \ (-2)(-12) \ (-3)(-8) \ (-4)(-6)$

Only the pair $-2$ and $-12$ has a sum of $-14$.

So, $x^2 - 14x + 24 = (x - 2)(x - 12)$.

### Lesson Practice 88

**a.** $\dfrac{4z^5 q^8}{14qz^7} \cdot \dfrac{14qz^4}{3q^4 z}$

$= \dfrac{56q^9 z^9}{42q^5 z^8}$

$= \dfrac{4q^4 z}{3}$

**b.** $\dfrac{5x^2}{7y^4} \cdot \dfrac{4x^2}{9y^3}$

$= \dfrac{20x^4}{63y^7}$

**c.** $\dfrac{6}{2x - 18} \cdot (x^2 - 6x - 27)$

$= \dfrac{6}{2x - 18} \cdot \dfrac{(x^2 - 6x - 27)}{1}$

$= \dfrac{6}{2(x - 9)} \cdot \dfrac{(x + 3)(x - 9)}{1}$

$= \dfrac{\cancel{6}^{3}}{\cancel{2}_{1} \cancel{(x - 9)}} \cdot \dfrac{(x + 3)\cancel{(x - 9)}}{1}$

$= 3(x + 3)$

**d.** $\dfrac{8m + 6m^2 n}{12} \cdot \dfrac{8m}{24m + 8mn}$

$= \dfrac{\cancel{2}^{1}(4m + 3m^2 n)}{\cancel{12}_{6}} \cdot \dfrac{\cancel{8m}}{\cancel{8m}(3 + n)}$

$= \dfrac{4m + 3m^2 n}{6(3 + n)}$

$= \dfrac{m(4 + 3mn)}{6(3 + n)}$

**e.** $\dfrac{8j^2 k^7}{15k^7 j^4} \div \dfrac{6j^3 k}{5kj^6}$

$= \dfrac{8j^2 k^7}{15k^7 j^4} \cdot \dfrac{5kj^6}{6j^3 k}$

$= \dfrac{8j^2 \cancel{k^7}}{15 \cancel{k^7} j^4} \cdot \dfrac{5 \cancel{k} j^{6^{3}}}{6 j^3 \cancel{k}}$

$= \dfrac{\cancel{8}^{4} j^2}{\cancel{15}_{3} j^4} \cdot \dfrac{\cancel{5} j^{6^{3}}}{\cancel{6}_{3}}$

$= \dfrac{4j}{9}$

**f.** $\dfrac{x^2 + 7x + 12}{x + 5} \div (x + 3)$

$= \dfrac{x^2 + 7x + 12}{x + 5} \div \dfrac{(x + 3)}{1}$

$= \dfrac{x^2 + 7x + 12}{x + 5} \cdot \dfrac{1}{(x + 3)}$

$= \dfrac{(x + 4)(x + 3)}{x + 5} \cdot \dfrac{1}{(x + 3)}$

$= \dfrac{(x + 4)\cancel{(x + 3)}}{x + 5} \cdot \dfrac{1}{\cancel{(x + 3)}}$

$= \dfrac{x + 4}{x + 5}$

**g.** $\dfrac{x^2 + 5x + 6}{x + 2} \div \dfrac{x + 3}{y^2}$

$= \dfrac{x^2 + 5x + 6}{x + 2} \cdot \dfrac{y^2}{x + 3}$

$= \dfrac{(x + 3)(x + 2)}{x + 2} \cdot \dfrac{y^2}{x + 3}$

$= \dfrac{\cancel{(x + 3)}\cancel{(x + 2)}}{\cancel{(x + 2)}} \cdot \dfrac{y^2}{\cancel{(x + 3)}}$

$= y^2$

**h.** $\dfrac{x^2}{20x^2 + 10x} \cdot x^2 + 9x + 20$

$= \dfrac{x^2}{20x^2 + 10x} \cdot \dfrac{x^2 + 9x + 20}{1}$

$= \dfrac{x^2(x^2 + 9x + 20)}{20x^2 + 10x}$

$= \dfrac{x^2(x + 5)(x + 4)}{10x(2x + 1)}$

$= \dfrac{\overset{1}{\cancel{x^2}}(x + 5)(x + 4)}{10\cancel{x}(2x + 1)}$

$= \dfrac{x(x + 5)(x + 4)}{10(2x + 1)}$

**Practice 88**

**1.** $6(x + 2) - 4x > 2 + x + 2$

$6x + 12 - 4x > x + 4$

$2x + 12 > x + 4$

$x > -8$

**2.** $4 \geq 2(x + 3)$ OR $23 < 8x + 7$

$4 \geq 2x + 6$ OR $23 < 8x + 7$

$\underline{-6 \quad -6}$ OR $\underline{-7 \quad -7}$

$-2 \geq 2x$ OR $16 < 8x$

$\dfrac{-2}{2} \geq \dfrac{2x}{x}$ OR $\dfrac{16}{8} < \dfrac{8x}{8}$

$-1 \geq x$ OR $2 < x$

$x \leq -1$ OR $x > 2$

**3.** $f(x) = ax^2 + bx + c$

$x(y - 2x) = 18x^2$

$xy - 2xy = 18x^2$

The equation is not a quadratic equation and cannot be written in the standard form of a quadratic function.

**4.** $f(x) = ax^2 + bx + c$

$2(y - 2x) = 6x^2$

$2y - 4x = 6x^2$

$2y = 6x^2 + 4x$

$y = 3x^2 + 2x$

**5.** Points: $(-4, -5)$ and $(2, -3)$

$d = \sqrt{(x_2 - x_1)^2 + (y_2 - y_1)^2}$

$d = \sqrt{(2 - (-4))^2 + (-3 - (-5))^2}$

$= \sqrt{6^2 + 2^2}$

$= \sqrt{36 + 4}$

$= \sqrt{40}$

$= \sqrt{2^2 \cdot 10}$

$= 2\sqrt{10}$

**6.** Points: $(3, -2)$ and $(1, 0)$

$d = \sqrt{(x_2 - x_1)^2 + (y_2 - y_1)^2}$

$= \sqrt{(1 - 3)^2 + (0 - (-2))^2}$

$= \sqrt{-2^2 + 2^2}$

$= \sqrt{4 + 4}$

$= \sqrt{8}$

$= \sqrt{2^2 \cdot 2}$

$= 2\sqrt{2}$

**7.** Endpoints: $(-4, -5)$ and $(2, -3)$

$$M = \left(\frac{x_1 + x_2}{2}, \frac{y_1 + y_2}{2}\right)$$

$$= \left(\frac{-4 + 2}{2}, \frac{-5 - 3}{2}\right)$$

$$= \left(\frac{-2}{2}, \frac{-8}{2}\right)$$

$$= (-1, -4)$$

The midpoint of the line segment is $(-1, -4)$.

**8.** Endpoints: $(3, -2)$ and $(1, 0)$

$$M = \left(\frac{x_1 + x_2}{2}, \frac{y_1 + y_2}{2}\right)$$

$$= \left(\frac{3 + 1}{2}, \frac{-2 + 0}{2}\right)$$

$$= \left(\frac{4}{2}, \frac{-2}{2}\right)$$

$$= (2, -1)$$

The midpoint of the line segment is $(2, -1)$.

**9.** $\dfrac{2y^2 + 10y}{y + 5} \cdot \dfrac{2x}{2x^3}$

$$= \frac{2y(y + 5)}{y + 5} \cdot \frac{2x}{2x^3}$$

$$= \frac{2y(y + 5)}{y + 5} \cdot \frac{2x}{2x^3{}_2}$$

$$= \frac{2y}{x^2}$$

**10.** $\dfrac{6y}{x} \div \dfrac{x + y}{3y}$

$$= \frac{6y}{x} \cdot \frac{3y}{x + y}$$

$$= \frac{18y^2}{x(x + y)}$$

$$= \frac{18y^2}{x^2 + xy}$$

**11.** $\dfrac{7x}{y} \div \dfrac{4}{y}$

$$= \frac{7x}{y} \cdot \frac{y}{4}$$

$$= \frac{7x}{y} \cdot \frac{y}{4}$$

$$= \frac{7x}{4}$$

**12.** $7x - 60 + x^2$

$$= x^2 + 7x - 60$$

Twelve pairs of positive and negative numbers have a product of $-60$.

$(1)(-60)$  $(-1)(60)$  $(2)(-30)$  $(-2)(30)$
$(3)(-20)$  $(-3)(20)$  $(4)(-15)$  $(-4)(15)$
$(5)(-12)$  $(-5)(12)$  $(6)(-10)$  $(-6)(10)$

Only one pair has a sum of 7: $(-5)(12)$.

So, $x^2 + 7x - 60 = (x - 5)(x + 12)$

and $7x - 60 + x^2 = (x - 5)(x + 12)$.

**13.** $64a^3b - 32a^3 + 16a^2b - 8a^2$

$$= 8a^2(8ab - 4a + 2b - 1)$$

$$= 8a^2(2b - 1)(4a + 1)$$

**14.** $x^2 + 4x - 21$

Four pairs of positive and negative numbers have a product of $-21$.

$(1)(-21)$  $(-1)(21)$  $(3)(-7)$  $(-3)(7)$

Only one pair has a sum of 4: $(-3)(7)$.

So, $x^2 + 4x - 21 = (x - 3)(x + 7)$.

The dimensions of the patterns are
$(x - 3) \times (x + 7)$.

**15.** $-2 < x < 2$

**16. a.** $y = \dfrac{700}{x} + 5$

$$y = \frac{a}{x - b} + c$$

Since $c = 5$, the horizontal asymptote's equation is $y = 5$.

**b.** Since $b = 0$, the vertical asymptote's equation is $x = 0$.

**c.** $y = \dfrac{700}{x} + 5$

$$y = \frac{700}{50} + 5$$

$$y = 14 + 5$$

$$y = 19$$

He will receive 19 uniforms.

**d.** no; Sample: The horizontal asymptote is $y = 5$. The value, 5, for $y$ is undefined. The uniform company would not give away the five free uniforms unless other uniforms were purchased.

**Saxon** Algebra 1

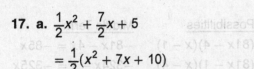

**17. a.** $\frac{1}{2}x^2 + \frac{7}{2}x + 5$

$= \frac{1}{2}(x^2 + 7x + 10)$

Find two numbers that have a product of 10 and a sum of 7.

$2 \cdot 5 = 10$ and $2 + 5 = 7$

$\frac{1}{2}(x^2 + 7x + 10) = \frac{1}{2}(x + 2)(x + 5)$

The area of the triangle is $\frac{1}{2}(x + 2)(x + 5)$.

**b.** $\frac{1}{2}(x + 2)(x + 5)$

$\frac{1}{2}(3 + 2)(3 + 5)$

$= \frac{1}{2}(5)(8)$

$= \frac{1}{2}(40)$

$= 20$

The area of the sail is 20 square feet.

**18.** Sample: They are easier to read than a long list of outcomes.

**19.** $A_{\text{(plot of land)}} = 9s^2 + 54s + 81$

$\qquad = (3s)(3s) + (2)(27s) + (9)(9)$

$\qquad = (3s + 9)(3s + 9)$

The length of a side of the plot of land is $(3s + 9)$ feet. The length of a side of the building is $s$, so the length of a side of the parking lot is $(3s + 9) - 1s = 2s + 9$ greater than the length of the building. Since a side of the parking lot extends outward equally from opposite sides of the building, the distance the parking lot extends from the building is $\frac{2s + 9}{2}$ feet.

**20. a.** $a^2 + b^2 = c^2$

$1^2 + 1^2 = c^2$

$2 = c^2$

$\sqrt{2} = c$

$1^2 + \sqrt{2}^2 = c^2$

$3 = c^2$

$\sqrt{3} = c$

$1^2 + \sqrt{3}^2 = c^2$

$4 = c^2$

$\sqrt{4} = c$

$1^2 + \sqrt{4}^2 = c^2$

$5 = c^2$

$\sqrt{5} = c$

The lengths of hypotenuses of the triangles are $\sqrt{2}, \sqrt{3}, \sqrt{4}, \sqrt{5}$.

**b.** The length of the hypotenuse of the tenth triangle will be $\sqrt{11}$.

**21.** Check whether each set of lengths forms a Pythagorean triple. Use the greatest number as $c$.

Choice A: $3^2 + 4^2 \overset{?}{=} 6^2$

$9 + 16 \overset{?}{=} 36$

$25 \neq 36$

Choice B: $\sqrt{13}^2 + 5^2 \overset{?}{=} 12^2$

$13 + 25 \overset{?}{=} 144$

$38 \neq 144$

Choice C: $\sqrt{15}^2 + 7^2 \overset{?}{=} 8^2$

$15 + 49 \overset{?}{=} 64$

$64 = 64$

Choice D: $6^2 + 8^2 \overset{?}{=} 12^2$

$36 + 64 \overset{?}{=} 144$

$100 \neq 144$

The answer is **C**.

**22.** Student B; Sample: The midpoint formula involves adding the $x$-coordinates of the two points, not subtracting them.

**23.** Find the distance between the points (20, 20) and (114, 70).

$d = \sqrt{(x_2 - x_1)^2 + (y_2 - y_1)^2}$

$= \sqrt{(114 - 20)^2 + (70 - 20)^2}$

$= \sqrt{94^2 + 50^2}$

$= \sqrt{8836 + 2500}$

$= \sqrt{11336}$

$= 106.5$

The length of a diagonal of the court to the nearest tenth is 106.5 units.

**24.** Length of new porch $= x + 5$.

Width of new porch $= x$.

$A_{\text{(new porch)}} = (x + 5)(x)$

$50 = (x + 5)(x)$

$0 = x^2 + 5x - 50$

$0 = (x + 10)(x - 5)$

**Saxon** Algebra 1

The length of the porch is 10 feet and the width is 5 feet.

**25.** $(12x^2 + 3y)(6x^2 + y)$

$= 72x^4 + 12x^2y + 18x^2y + 3y^2$

$= 72x^4 + 30x^2y + 3y^2$

$= 3(24x^4 + 10x^2y + y^2)$

Sample: It is simpler to express the area as the binomials before multiplying $(12x^2 + 3y)(6x^2 + y)$.

**26.** $25x^2 - 81$

$= (5 \cdot 5)(x \cdot x) - (9 \cdot 9)$

$= (5x)^2 - 9^2$

$= (5x + 9)(5x - 9)$

The answer is **D**.

**27.** Sample: Add exponents when multiplying and subtract exponents when dividing.

**28.** $\dfrac{y^2 + 6y + 5}{y^2} \cdot \dfrac{y}{y + 1}$

$= \dfrac{(y + 1)(y + 5)}{y^2} \cdot \dfrac{y}{y + 1}$

$= \dfrac{(\cancel{y+1})(y + 5)}{y^{2\,1}} \cdot \dfrac{\cancel{y}}{\cancel{y+1}}$

$= \dfrac{y + 5}{y}$

The answer is **B**.

**29.** $c^2 + 7c + 10 \cdot \dfrac{1}{c + 5}$

$= \dfrac{c^2 + 7c + 10}{1} \cdot \dfrac{1}{c + 5}$

$= \dfrac{(c + 5)(c + 2)}{1} \cdot \dfrac{1}{c + 5}$

$= \dfrac{(\cancel{c+5})(c + 2)}{\cancel{1}} \cdot \dfrac{\cancel{1}}{\cancel{c+5}}$

$= c + 2$

The mural is $c + 2$ square feet. She will charge $10c + 20$.

**30. a.** $81x^2 - 36x + 4$

The first term, $81x^2$ can be factored as $(81x)(x)$, $(27x)(3x)$, and $(9x)(9x)$.

The last term, 2, can be factored as $(-4)(-1)$ and $(-2)(-2)$.

Check each pair to see which results in the middle term, $-36x$.

| Possibilities | Middle Term |
|---|---|
| $(81x - 4)(x - 1)$ | $-81x - 4x = -85x$ |
| $(81x - 1)(x - 4)$ | $-324x - x = -325x$ |
| $(81x - 2)(x - 2)$ | $-162x - 2x = -164x$ |
| $(27x - 4)(3x - 1)$ | $-27x - 12x = -39x$ |
| $(27x - 1)(3x - 4)$ | $-108x - 3x = -111x$ |
| $(27x - 2)(x - 2)$ | $-54x - 2x = -56x$ |
| $(9x - 4)(9x - 1)$ | $-9x - 36x = -45x$ |
| $(9x - 2)(9x - 2)$ | $-18x - 18x = -36x$ |

So, $81x^2 - 36x + 4 = (9x - 2)(9x - 2)$.

**b.** Sample: It is the product of an expression times itself.

## LAB 8

### Practice Lab 8

**a.**

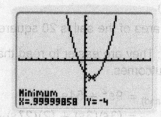

x-intercepts: $(-1, 0)$ and $(3, 0)$

minimum: $(1, -4)$

**b.**

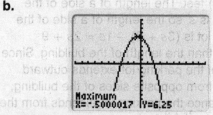

x-intercepts: $(-3, 0)$ and $(2, 0)$

maximum: $(-0.5, 6.25)$

## LESSON 89

### Warm Up 89

1. parabola

2. downward because $a = -3$, so $a < 0$

3. upward because $a = 1$, so $a > 0$

4. $y = x^2 - 4x + 5$

$= (-3)^2 - 4(-3) + 5$

Saxon Algebra 1

$= 9 + 12 + 5$

$= 26$

**5.** Choices **A** and **B** have no quadratic term, so are straight lines.

Choice **D** is a parabola, but has a number for $a$ that is less than 0, so opens downward.

The answer is **C**.

**Lesson Practice 89**

**a.** vertex: $(-1, -4)$; maximum: $-4$; domain: all real numbers; range: all real numbers less than or equal to $-4$

**b.** vertex: $(5, -3)$; minimum: $-3$; domain: all real numbers; range: all real numbers greater than or equal to $-3$

**c.** $y = 0$ when $x = 6$ so, the zero of the function is 6.

**d.** $y = 0$ when $x = -9$ and when $x = -3$, so the zeros of the function are $-9$ and $-3$.

**e.** There are no zeros because the graph does not cross the $x$-axis.

**f.** $\dfrac{2 + 7}{2} = \dfrac{9}{2} = 4.5$

The equation for the axis of symmetry is $x = 4.5$.

**g.** $\dfrac{-8 + 3}{2} = \dfrac{-5}{2} = -2.5$

The equation for the axis of symmetry is $x = -2.5$.

**h.** $y = 3x^2 + 12x + 4$

$x = -\dfrac{b}{2a}$

$= -\dfrac{12}{2(3)}$

$= -\dfrac{12}{6} = -2$

$x = -2$

**i.** $y = -x^2 + 6x + 5$

$x = -\dfrac{b}{2a}$

$= -\dfrac{6}{2(-1)}$

$= -\dfrac{6}{-2} = 3$

$x = 3$

**j.** $y = -16t^2 + 608t + 12{,}447$

Find $t$ at the vertex.

$t = -\dfrac{b}{2a}$

$= -\dfrac{608}{2(-16)}$

$= -\dfrac{608}{-32}$

$t = 19$

Find the $y$-value of the vertex.

$y = -16t^2 + 608t + 12{,}447$

$= -16(19)^2 + 608(19) + 12{,}447$

$= -5776 + 11{,}552 + 12{,}447$

$= 18{,}223$

The highest point the lava reaches is 18,223 feet. It takes 19 seconds to reach the highest point.

**Practice 89**

**1.** $-2|r + 2| = -30$

$\dfrac{-2|r + 2|}{-2} = \dfrac{-30}{-2}$

$|r + 2| = 15$

$r + 2 = 15$ or $r + 2 = -15$

$r = 13$ or $r = -17$

$\{-17, 13\}$

**2.** $3|r + 6| = 15$

$\dfrac{3|r + 6|}{3} = \dfrac{15}{3}$

$|r + 6| = 5$

$r + 6 = 5$ or $r + 6 = -5$

$r = -1$ or $r = -11$

$\{-11, -1\}$

**3.** $35 < 3x + 8$ OR $72 \geq 9(x + 1)$

$35 < 3x + 8$ OR $72 \geq 9x + 9$

$27 < 3x$ OR $63 \geq 9x$

$9 < x$ OR $7 \geq x$

The solution is $x > 9$ OR $x \leq 7$.

**Saxon** Algebra 1

**4.** Try to write in perfect-square trinomial form.

$100y^2 - 80y + 16$

$= 4(25y^2 - 20y + 4)$

$= 4\left[(5y)^2 - 2 \cdot (5y)(2) + 2^2\right]$

Yes, this is a perfect-square trinomial.

$= 4\left[(5y)^2 - 2 \cdot (5y)(2) + 2^2\right]$

$= 4(5y - 2)^2$

**5.** Try to write as a difference of two-squares.

$81x^2 - 1$

$= (9 \cdot 9)(x \cdot x) - (1 \cdot 1)$

$= (9x)^2 - 1^2$

This is a difference of two squares.

$= (9x)^2 - 1^2$

$= (9x + 1)(9x - 1)$

**6.** $9c^2 - 42c + 49$

$ax^2 + bx + c$

$ac = 9 \cdot 49 = 441$

Factors of 441 with a sum of −42 are −21 and −21.

$9c^2 - 42c + 49$

$= 9c^2 - 21c - 21c + 49$

$= (9c^2 - 21c) - (21c + 49)$

$= 3c(3c - 7) - 7(3c - 7)$

$= (3c - 7)(3c - 7)$

$= (3c - 7)^2$

**7.** Points: (2, 2) and (4, 4)

$d = \sqrt{(x_2 - x_1)^2 + (y_2 - y_1)^2}$

$d = \sqrt{(4 - 2)^2 + (4 - 2)^2}$

$= \sqrt{2^2 + 2^2}$

$= \sqrt{4 + 4}$

$= \sqrt{8}$

$= 2\sqrt{2}$

The distance between the points is $2\sqrt{2}$.

**8.** $\dfrac{15a + 5b}{5ab} \div (3a + b)$

$= \dfrac{15a + 5b}{5ab} \cdot \dfrac{1}{3a + b}$

$= \dfrac{5(3a + b)}{5ab} \cdot \dfrac{1}{3a + b}$

$= \dfrac{\cancel{5}(\cancel{3a + b})}{\cancel{5}ab} \cdot \dfrac{1}{\cancel{3a + b}}$

$= \dfrac{1}{ab}$

**9.** $(4x + 2) \div \dfrac{2x + 1}{3y}$

$= \dfrac{4x + 2}{1} \cdot \dfrac{3y}{2x + 1}$

$= \dfrac{2(2x + 1)}{1} \cdot \dfrac{3y}{2x + 1}$

$= \dfrac{2(\cancel{2x + 1})}{1} \cdot \dfrac{3y}{\cancel{2x + 1}}$

$= 6y$

**10.** $y = x^2 + 4x + 6$

$x = -\dfrac{b}{2a}$

$= -\dfrac{4}{2(1)}$

$= -2$

The equation of the axis of symmetry is $x = -2$.

**11.** $y = x^2 - x - 6$

$x = -\dfrac{b}{2a}$

$= -\dfrac{-1}{2(1)}$

$= \dfrac{1}{2}$

The equation of the axis of symmetry is $x = \dfrac{1}{2}$.

**12.** Sample: Use the formula for the axis of symmetry and sketch it on a graph. Substitute the x-value into the equation to find the y-value, and then plot the vertex. Use a table of ordered pairs to find values on the left (or right) side of the vertex, and then use symmetry to find the points that are mirror images of those points.

**13.** $45 \le x \le 65$, or $x \ge 45$ AND $x \le 65$

**14.** $x > 1$ AND $x \le 5$; $1 < x \le 5$

**15.** An expression for the area of the trapezoid is:

$A = \dfrac{1}{2}h(b_1 + b_2)$

$A = \dfrac{1}{2}(2)\left[\left(\sqrt{49} + 4\right) + \left(\sqrt{36} + 8\right)\right].$

**Saxon** Algebra 1

The area of the trapezoid is:

$A = \frac{1}{2}(2)\left[(\sqrt{49} + 4) + (\sqrt{36} + 8)\right]$

$= 1[(7 + 4) + (6 + 8)]$

$= 1[11 + 14]$

$= 25$

The area of the trapezoid is 25 square meters.

**16.** $-16x^2 + 128x - 240$

$= -16(x^2 - 8x + 15)$

Two numbers that have a product of 15 and a sum of $-8$ are $-5$ and $-3$.

$-16(x^2 - 8x + 15) = -16(x - 5)(x - 3)$

So,

$-16x^2 + 128x - 240 = -16(x - 5)(x - 3)$.

**17. a.** $P(\text{brown}) = \frac{50}{100} = \frac{1}{2}$;

$P(\text{red}) = \frac{25}{100} = \frac{1}{4}$;

$P(\text{yellow}) = \frac{25}{100} = \frac{1}{4}$.

**b.** Sample:

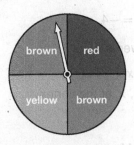

**18.** $35 + 0.09m > 45 + 0.06m$

$0.09m > 10 + 0.06m$

$0.03m > 10$

$m > 333.33$

The first plan is more expensive after 334 minutes.

**19.** $2x + 8 > 2 + 5x + 6$

$2x + 8 > 5x + 8$

$2x > 5x + 0$

$-3x > 0$

$x < 0$

Sample:

$2x + 8 > 2 + 5x + 6$

$2(0) + 8 > 2 + 5(0) + 6$

$8 \not> 8$

$2(-1) + 8 > 2 + 5(-1) + 6$

$-2 + 8 > 2 - 5 + 6$

$6 > 3$

$2(-3) + 8 > 2 + 5(-3) + 6$

$2 > -7$

**20.** Since the x-axis is the ground, the ends of the bridge are along the x-axis at $(x, 0)$ and $(-x, 0)$. Find the two values of $x$.

$y = -\frac{1}{9}x^2 + 1$

$0 = -\frac{1}{9}x^2 + 1$

$-1 = -\frac{1}{9}x^2$

$(-9) - 1 = (-9) - \frac{1}{9}x^2$

$9 = x^2$

$\sqrt{9} = x$

$x = 3$ and $x = -3$

The coordinates of the ends of the bridge are $(-3, 0)$ and $(3, 0)$. Find the distance between the two points. Since the y-coordinates are both 0, only the distance between the x-coordinates needs to be found.

$d = |3 - (-3)|$

$d = 6$

The horizontal distance across the bridge is 6 feet.

**21.** Square prism: $V = lwh$

$= x \cdot x \cdot 10$

$= 10x^2$

Cylinder: $V = \pi r^2 h$

$= 3.14 - x^2 \cdot 10$

$= 31.4x^2$

Make tables of values and use them to plot graphs.

prism: $y = 10x^2$

| x | 0 | 0.2 | 0.3 | 0.4 | 0.5 |
|---|---|-----|-----|-----|-----|
| y | 0 | 0.4 | 0.9 | 1.6 | 2.5 |

cylinder: $y = 31.4x^2$

| $x$ | 0 | 0.2 | 0.3 | 0.4 | 0.5 |
|---|---|---|---|---|---|
| $y$ | 0 | 1.26 | 2.83 | 5.02 | 7.85 |

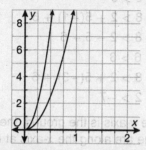

Compare the graphs.

Sample: The volume of the cylinder increases faster than that of the rectangular prism.

**22.**
$$a^2 + b^2 = c^2$$
$$9^2 + 12^2 = p^2$$
$$81 + 144 = p^2$$
$$225 = p^2$$
$$\sqrt{225} = p$$
$$15 = p$$

**23.** Endpoints: (3, 9) and (−1, 2)
$$M = \left(\frac{x_1 + x_2}{2}, \frac{y_1 + y_2}{2}\right)$$
$$= \left(\frac{3-1}{2}, \frac{9+2}{2}\right)$$
$$= \left(\frac{2}{2}, \frac{11}{2}\right)$$
$$= \left(1, \frac{11}{2}\right)$$

The answer is **D**.

**24.** The function is reflected about the x-axis and is vertically stretched by a factor of 4.

**25. a.** $\dfrac{6r^3h^2}{4r^2h} \cdot \dfrac{8rh^2}{3r^2h} \cdot \dfrac{2r^2h}{rh^2}$

$$= \frac{6r^3h^2}{4r^2h} \cdot \frac{8rh^2}{3r^2h} \cdot \frac{2r^2h}{rh^2}$$

$$= \frac{2rh}{2} \cdot \frac{8}{1}$$

$$= 8rh$$

The volume of the box is 8*rh*.

**b.** $\dfrac{4\pi rh}{3} \div 8rh$

$$= \frac{4\pi rh}{3} \cdot \frac{1}{8rh}$$

$$= \frac{4\pi rh}{3} \cdot \frac{1}{8rh}$$

$$= \frac{\pi}{6}$$

The fraction of the box that the globes take up is $\frac{\pi}{6}$.

**26.** $A = \dfrac{3x^2 + x}{y} \cdot (x + 2y)$

$$= \frac{3x^2 + x}{y} \cdot \frac{x + 2y}{1}$$

$$= \frac{(x + 2y)(3x^2 + x)}{y}$$

$$= \frac{3x^3 + x^2 + 6x^2y + 2xy}{y}$$

$$= \frac{3x^3 + 6x^2y + x^2 + 2xy}{y}$$

**27.** Student B; Sample: Student A forgot to put the 1 in the numerator when switching to multiplication.

**28.** $\dfrac{-8 + 0}{2} = -4$

The answer is **A**.

**29.** $y = -5.5x^2 + 44x$

Find time, $x$, at the vertex.

$$x = -\frac{b}{2a}$$

$$= -\frac{44}{2(-5.5)}$$

$$= -\frac{44}{-11}$$

$$x = 4$$

Find the y-value of the vertex.

$$y = -5.5x^2 + 44x$$

$$= -5.5(4)^2 + 44(4)$$

$$= -88 + 176$$

$$= 88$$

It will take the ball 4 seconds to reach the maximum height of 88 meters.

**30.** Sample: If the value of $a$ is positive, the graph opens upward and has a minimum. If the value of $a$ is negative, the graph opens downward and has a maximum.

## LESSON 90

### Warm Up 90

**1.** factor

**2.** $\dfrac{7}{12} + \dfrac{5}{18} = \dfrac{21}{36} + \dfrac{10}{36} = \dfrac{31}{36}$

**3.** $3x^4y + 7y^2 - 4x^4y$
$= 3x^4y - 4x^4y + 7y^2$
$= -x^4y + 7y^2$

**4.** $6r^2(3r - 8) = 18r^3 - 48r^2$

**5.** $(x - 7)(x - 3) = x^2 - 3x - 7x + 21$
$= x^2 - 10x + 21$

### Lesson Practice 90

**a.** $\dfrac{4mn}{24m} + \dfrac{11mn}{24m} = \dfrac{15mn}{24m} = \dfrac{5n}{8}$

**b.** $\dfrac{7y - 2}{y + 6} - \dfrac{y - 38}{y + 6}$

$= \dfrac{7y - 2 - (y - 38)}{y + 6}$

$= \dfrac{7y - 2 - y + 38}{y + 6}$

$= \dfrac{6y + 36}{y + 6}$

$= \dfrac{6(y + 6)}{y + 6}$

$= \dfrac{6\cancel{(y + 6)}}{\cancel{y + 6}}$

$= 6$

**c.** $\dfrac{d^4 + 2d^3}{d^2 - 5d - 36} + \dfrac{2d^3}{d^2 - 5d - 36}$

$= \dfrac{d^4 + 2d^3 + 2d^3}{d^2 - 5d - 36}$

$= \dfrac{d^4 + 4d^3}{d^2 - 5d - 36}$

$= \dfrac{d^3(d + 4)}{(d - 9)(d + 4)}$

$= \dfrac{d^3\cancel{(d + 4)}}{(d - 9)\cancel{(d + 4)}}$

$= \dfrac{d^3}{(d - 9)}$

**d.** $\dfrac{-3p}{6p^2} + \dfrac{2p^3}{p^4}$

$= \dfrac{-3p}{6p^2}\left(\dfrac{p^2}{p^2}\right) + \dfrac{2p^3}{p^4}\left(\dfrac{6}{6}\right)$

$= \dfrac{-3p^3}{6p^4} + \dfrac{12p^3}{6p^4}$

$= \dfrac{9p^3}{6p^4}$

$= \dfrac{3}{2p}$

**e.** $\dfrac{x}{x + 3} - \dfrac{3}{x^2 + 5x + 6}$

$= \dfrac{x}{x + 3} - \dfrac{3}{(x + 3)(x + 2)}$

$= \dfrac{x}{x + 3}\left(\dfrac{x + 2}{x + 2}\right) - \dfrac{3}{(x + 3)(x + 2)}$

$= \dfrac{x^2 + 2x}{(x + 3)(x + 2)} - \dfrac{3}{(x + 3)(x + 2)}$

$= \dfrac{x^2 + 2x - 3}{(x + 3)(x + 2)}$

$= \dfrac{(x + 3)(x - 1)}{(x + 3)(x + 2)}$

$= \dfrac{\cancel{(x + 3)}(x - 1)}{\cancel{(x + 3)}(x + 2)}$

$= \dfrac{x - 1}{x + 2}$

**f.** $\dfrac{-1}{t^4 - 2} + \dfrac{t + 9}{2 - t^4}$

$= \dfrac{-1}{t^4 - 2} + \dfrac{t + 9}{2 - t^4}\left(\dfrac{-1}{-1}\right)$

$= \dfrac{-1}{t^4 - 2} + \dfrac{-t - 9}{t^4 - 2}$

$= \dfrac{-1 - t - 9}{t^4 - 2}$

$= \dfrac{-t - 10}{t^4 - 2}$

**g.** $t = \dfrac{d}{r}$

total time $= \dfrac{5}{1.5 - c} + \dfrac{5}{1.5 + c}$

$= \dfrac{5}{1.5 - c}\left(\dfrac{1.5 + c}{1.5 + c}\right) + \dfrac{5}{1.5 + c}\left(\dfrac{1.5 - c}{1.5 - c}\right)$

$= \dfrac{7.5 + 5c}{(1.5 - c)(1.5 + c)} + \dfrac{7.5 - 5c}{(1.5 - c)(1.5 + c)}$

$= \dfrac{7.5 + 5c + 7.5 - 5c}{(1.5 - c)(1.5 + c)}$

$= \dfrac{15}{(1.5 - c)(1.5 + c)}$

## Practice 90

**1.** Points: $(-3, -1)$ and $(4, 2)$

$d = \sqrt{(x_2 - x_1)^2 + (y_2 - y_1)^2}$

$d = \sqrt{(4 - (-3))^2 + (2 - (-1))^2}$

$= \sqrt{7^2 + 3^2}$

$= \sqrt{49 + 9}$

$= \sqrt{58}$

The distance between the points is $\sqrt{58}$.

**2.** Points: $(1, 1)$ and $(9, 1)$

$d = \sqrt{(x_2 - x_1)^2 + (y_2 - y_1)^2}$

$d = \sqrt{(9 - 1)^2 + (1 - 1)^2}$

$= \sqrt{8^2 + 0^2}$

$= \sqrt{8^2}$

$= 8$

The distance between the points is 8.

**3.** $12 + 17x + 6x^2$

Rearrange the terms to $6x^2 + 17x + 12$.

The first term, $6x^2$, can be factored as $(6x)(x)$ and $(2x)(3x)$.

The last term, 12, can be factored as $(1)(12)$, $(2)(6)$, and $(3)(4)$.

Check each pair to see which results in the middle term, $17x$.

| Possibilities | Middle Term |
|---|---|
| $(6x + 1)(x + 12)$ | $72x + x = 73x$ |
| $(6x + 12)(x + 1)$ | $6x + 12x = 18x$ |
| $(6x + 2)(x + 6)$ | $36x + 2x = 38x$ |
| $(6x + 6)(x + 2)$ | $12x + 6x = 18x$ |
| $(6x + 3)(x + 4)$ | $24x + 3x = 27x$ |
| $(6x + 4)(x + 3)$ | $18x + 4x = 22x$ |
| $(2x + 1)(3x + 12)$ | $24x + 3x = 27x$ |
| $(2x + 12)(3x + 1)$ | $2x + 36x = 38x$ |
| $(2x + 2)(3x + 6)$ | $12x + 6x = 18x$ |
| $(2x + 6)(3x + 2)$ | $4x + 18x = 22x$ |
| $(2x + 3)(3x + 4)$ | $8x + 9x = 17x$ |
| $(2x + 4)(3x + 3)$ | $6x + 12x = 18x$ |

So, $6x^2 + 17x + 12 = (2x + 3)(3x + 4)$
and $12 + 17x + 6x^2 = (2x + 3)(3x + 4)$.

**4.** $21t + 4t^2 - 49$

Rearrange the terms to $4t^2 + 21t - 49$.

The first term, $4t^2$, can be factored as $(t)(4t)$ and $(2t)(2t)$.

The last term, $-49$, can be factored as $(1)(-49)$, $(-1)(49)$, and $(7)(-7)$.

Check each pair to see which results in the middle term, $21t$.

| Possibilities | Middle Term |
|---|---|
| $(t + 1)(4t - 49)$ | $-49t + 4t = -45t$ |
| $(t - 1)(4t + 49)$ | $49t - 4t = 45t$ |
| $(t + 49)(4t - 1)$ | $-t + 196t = 195t$ |
| $(t - 49)(4t + 1)$ | $t - 196t = -195t$ |
| $(t + 7)(4t - 7)$ | $-7t + 28t = 21t$ |
| $(t - 7)(4t + 7)$ | $7t - 28t = -21t$ |
| $(2t + 1)(2t - 49)$ | $-98t + 2t = -96t$ |
| $(2t - 1)(2t + 49)$ | $98t - 2t = 96t$ |
| $(2t + 7)(2t - 7)$ | $-14t + 14t = 0$ |

So, $4t^2 + 21t - 49 = (t + 7)(4t - 7)$
and $21t + 4t^2 - 49 = (t + 7)(4t - 7)$.

**5.** Try to write in perfect-square trinomial form.

$9x^4 + 42x^2y + 49y^2$

$= (3x^2)^2 + 2 \cdot (3x^2)(7y) + (7y)^2$

This is a perfect-square trinomial.

$= (3x^2)^2 + 2 \cdot (3x^2)(7y) + (7y)^2$

$= (3x^2 + 7y)^2$

**6.** Try to write in perfect-square trinomial form.

$x^6 + 16x^3 + 64$

$= (x^3)^2 + 2 \cdot (8x^3) + 8^2$

This is a perfect-square trinomial.

$= (x^3)^2 + 2 \cdot (8x^3) + 8^2$

$= (x^3 + 8)^2$

**Saxon** Algebra 1

**7.** $y = \dfrac{-x^2}{2}$

Make a table of values, graph the points, and connect the points.

Sample table:

| x | 0 | 2 | −2 | 4 | −4 |
|---|---|---|----|---|----|
| y | 0 | −2 | −2 | −8 | −8 |

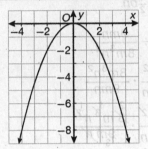

**8.** $\dfrac{2x - 16}{6x^2} - \dfrac{3y^2 + 3x}{3x - 24}$

$= \dfrac{2(x - 8)}{6x^2} \cdot \dfrac{3(y^2 + x)}{3(x - 8)}$

$= \dfrac{\cancel{2}\cancel{(x-8)}}{\cancel{6}x^2} \cdot \dfrac{\cancel{3}(y^2 + x)}{\cancel{3}\cancel{(x-8)}}$

$= \dfrac{y^2 + x}{3x^2}$

**9.** $|n + 3| + 4 = 4$

$|n + 3| = 0$

$n + 3 = 0$

$n = -3$

The solution is {−3}.

**10. a.** $y = -3x^2 + 8x + 1$

$y = ax^2 + bx + c$

$x = -\dfrac{b}{2a}$

$= -\dfrac{8}{2(-3)}$

$= -\dfrac{8}{-6}$

$= 1\tfrac{1}{3}$

The equation of the axis of symmetry is $x = 1\tfrac{1}{3}$.

**11.** $\dfrac{7x}{y} - \dfrac{2}{y}$

$= \dfrac{7x - 2}{y}$

**12.** $\dfrac{4y}{x} - \dfrac{5y}{2x}$

$= \dfrac{4y}{x}\left(\dfrac{2}{2}\right) - \dfrac{5y}{2x}$

$= \dfrac{8y}{2x} - \dfrac{5y}{2x}$

$= \dfrac{8y - 5y}{2x}$

$= \dfrac{3y}{2x}$

**13.** $|x - 210| = 33$

$x - 210 = +33$ or $x - 210 = -33$

$x = 243$ $\qquad\qquad x = 177$

The longest sardine was 243 millimeters. The shortest was 177 millimeters.

**14.** $\dfrac{75 + 90 + x}{3} \geq 80$

$\dfrac{165 + x}{3} \geq 80$

$3 \cdot \dfrac{165 + x}{3} \geq 80 \cdot 3$

$165 + x \geq 240$

$x \geq 75$

Sample: He needs to make at least 75 points on his third test to have an 80 average.

**15.**

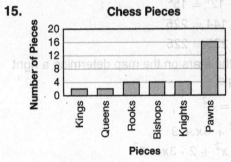

**16. a.** $2f > 20 - 3f$

$5f > 20$

$f > 4$

**b.** Sample: The solution set is all whole numbers greater than 4, so after 4 days there will always be more adult formula than puppy formula.

**Saxon** Algebra 1

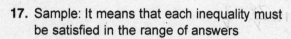

**17.** Sample: It means that each inequality must be satisfied in the range of answers

**18. a.** Sample: The vertical segment joining (2, 2) and (2, −3) is perpendicular to the horizontal segment joining (2, 2) and (5, 2).

**b.** Leg *a:* Find the distance between (2, 2) and (5, 2). Since the *y*-coordinates are the same, only the distance between the *x*-coordinates needs to be found.

$a = |5 − 2|$

$a = 3$

Leg *b:* Find the distance between (2, 2) and (2, −3). Since the *x*-coordinates are the same, only the distance between the *y*-coordinates needs to be found.

$b = |−3 − 2|$

$a = 5$

The lengths of the legs are 3 and 5 units.

**c.** $a^2 + b^2 = c^2$

$3^2 + 5^2 = c^2$

$9 + 25 = c^2$

$34 = c^2$

$\sqrt{34} = c$

The hypotenuse is $\sqrt{34}$ units.

**19.** Use the converse of the Pythagorean Theorem. The sides of the triangle in order of length are 9, 12, 15. Use 15 for *c*.

$9^2 + 12^2 \stackrel{?}{=} 15^2$

$81 + 144 \stackrel{?}{=} 225$

$225 = 225$

Yes, the stars on the map determine a right triangle.

**20. a.** $A = s^2$

**b.** $x^2 + 6x + 9$

$= x^2 + 2 \cdot 3x + 3^2$

$= (x + 3)^2$

**c.** $(x + 3)^2 = s^2$

**d.** $\sqrt{(x + 3)^2} = \sqrt{s^2}$

$(x + 3) = s$

The side length of the square is $x + 3$.

**21.** $k = \dfrac{6}{3 \cdot 4}$

$= \dfrac{6}{12}$

$= \dfrac{1}{2}$

The constant of variation is $\frac{1}{2}$. The area of a triangle is $A = \frac{1}{2} \cdot$ base $\cdot$ height, or $A = \frac{1}{2}bh$.

**22.** $\dfrac{3mn^2}{4m^2n} \div \dfrac{9mn}{8m^3n^2}$

$= \dfrac{3mn^2}{4m^2n} \cdot \dfrac{8m^3n^2}{9mn}$

$= \dfrac{3mn^2}{4m^2 n} \cdot \dfrac{\overset{2}{8} m^{\overset{1}{3}} n^{\overset{1}{2}}}{\underset{3}{9}mn}$

$= \dfrac{2mn^2}{3}$

The answer is **C.**

**23.** $\dfrac{d}{r} = t$

$\dfrac{x^2 − 25}{x + 5}$

$= \dfrac{(x − 5)(x + 5)}{x + 5}$

$= \dfrac{(x − 5)(x + 5)}{x + 5}$

$= x − 5$

It takes $x − 5$ hours to travel the distance.

**24.** Student B; Sample: Student A did not take the opposite of *b*.

**25. a.** Sample: It has a minimum because the value of *a* is positive, which means it opens upward and the vertex is the lowest point.

**b.** Find the axis of symmetry to find the *x*-coordinate of the vertex. Then find the *y*-coordinate by substituting the *x*-coordinate into the function and solving for *y*.

$x = −\dfrac{b}{2a}$

$= −\dfrac{−0.0232}{2(0.000285)}$

**Saxon** Algebra 1

$$= \frac{-0.0232}{0.00057}$$

$x = 40.7 \approx 41$

Sample: The minimum population occurred 41 years after 1900, or during 1941.

$y = 0.000285x^2 - 0.0232x + 3.336$

$= 0.000285(41)^2 - 0.0232(41) + 3.336$

$= 0.000285(1681) - 0.0232(41) + 3.336$

$= 0.479085 - 0.9512 + 3.336$

$= 2.863885$

The population in 1941 was about 2.86 million people.

**c.** Number of years after 1900:

$2020 - 1900 = 120$

$y = 0.000285x^2 - 0.0232x + 3.336$

$= 0.000285(120)^2 - 0.0232(120) + 3.336$

$= 0.000285(14,400) - 0.0232(120) + 3.336$

$= 4.104 - 2.784 + 3.336$

$= 4.656 \approx 4.66$

The population of Ireland in 2020 will be about 4.66 million people.

**26.** Sample: Find the axis of symmetry to find the x-coordinate of the vertex: $x = -\frac{35}{2(-1)} = 17.5$. Substitute 17.5 into the equation for x to find the area, $y$. $y = -x^2 + 35x$

$= -(17.5)^2 + 35(17.5)$

$= 306.25$

**27.** $\dfrac{6}{9q^2} - \dfrac{3q}{9q^2}$

$= \dfrac{6 - 3q}{9q^2}$

$= \dfrac{3(2 - q)}{9q^2}$

$= \dfrac{\cancel{3}(2 - q)}{\underset{3}{\cancel{9}}q^2}$

$= \dfrac{(2 - q)}{3q^2}$

The answer is **C**.

**28.** $\dfrac{(x^2 + 7x + 100) + (17x + 40)}{x^2 + 44x + 420}$

$= \dfrac{x^2 + 24x + 140}{x^2 + 44x + 420}$

$= \dfrac{(x + 10)(x + 14)}{(x + 30)(x + 14)}$

$= \dfrac{(x + 10)\cancel{(x + 14)}}{(x + 30)\cancel{(x + 14)}}$

$= \dfrac{x + 10}{x + 30}$

The fraction of the total profits that come from spring and winter season is $\frac{x + 10}{x + 30}$.

**29.** Sample: Multiplying by these expressions makes each of the denominators equal to the LCD of $n^4 p^5$.

**30.** Sample: Factor the denominator of the first term: $(x + 3)(x + 3)$. Multiply the second expression by $\frac{x + 3}{x + 3}$. The numerator of the second expression becomes $x^2 + 3x$. The sum of the numerators is $x^2 + 3x + 2$, which factors into $(x + 2)(x + 1)$. No common factors cancel, so the answer is $\dfrac{(x + 2)(x + 1)}{(x + 3)(x + 3)} = \dfrac{(x + 2)(x + 1)}{(x + 3)^2}$.

## INVESTIGATION 9

**Practice Investigation 9**

**a.** $x^2 + 2x + 1$

$= (x + 1)(x + 1)$

$= (x + 1)^2$

**b.** $3x^2 + xy - 12x - 4y$

$= x(3x + y) - 4(3x + y)$

$= (3x + y)(x - 4)$

**c.** $9y^4 - 1$

$= (3y^2)(3y^2) - (1)(1)$

$= (3y^2 - 1)(3y^2 + 1)$

**d.** $5x^4 - 5x^2$

First method: GCF

$= 5x^2 (x^2 - 1)$

Second step method: difference of two squares

$= 5x^2 (x + 1)(x - 1)$

**e.** $9x^2 + 30x + 25$

First method: perfect-square trinomial

$= (3x + 5)(3x + 5)$

$= (3x + 5)^2$

**f.** $x^2 - 9$

First method: differences of two squares

$= (x + 3)(x - 3)$

**g.** $3x^2 + 13x + 4$

$= (3x + 1)(x + 4)$

**h.** $x^2 + 9x + 20$

$= (x + 4)(x + 5)$

**i.** $2x^2 + 8x + 6$

$= 2(x + 1)(x + 3)$

## LESSON 91

### Warm Up 91

**1.** absolute-value equation

**2.** $|8 - 15|$

$= |-7|$

$= 7$

**3.** $|-3 + 9|$

$= |6|$

$= 6$

**4.** $|x - 4| = 7$

$x - 4 = -7$    OR    $x - 4 = 7$

$x = -3$           $x = 11$

**5.** $|x + 7| = 2$

$x + 7 = -2$    OR    $x + 7 = 2$

$x = -9$           $x = -5$

### Lesson Practice 91

**a.** $|x| < 12$

$-12 < x < 12$

**b.** $|x| > 19$

$x < -19$ or $x > 19$

**c.** $|x| + 2.8 \le 10.4$

     $\underline{-2.8 \quad -2.8}$

     $|x| \le 7.6$

$-7.6 \le x \le 7.6$

**d.** $\dfrac{|x|}{-5} < -1$

$-5 \cdot \dfrac{|x|}{5} > -5 \cdot (-1)$

$|x| > 5$

$x < -5$ or $x > 5$

**e.** $|x - 10| \le 12$

$x - 10 \ge -12$    AND    $x - 10 \le 12$

$\underline{+10 \quad +10}$          $\underline{+10 \quad +10}$

$x \ge -2$    AND    $x \le 22$

$-2 \le x \le 22$

**f.** $|x + 12| > 18$

$x + 12 < -18$    OR    $x + 12 > 18$

$\underline{-12 \quad -12}$         $\underline{-12 \quad -12}$

$x < -30$    OR    $x > 6$

**g.** $|x| + 21 \le 14$

    $\underline{-21 \quad -21}$

    $|x| \le -7$

$\{ \}$ or $\varnothing$

**h.** $|x| + 33 > 24$

    $\underline{-33 \quad -33}$

    $|x| > -9$ all real numbers

**i.** Let $m$ = the diameter of the machine part.

$|m - 15| \le 0.2$

**j.** $|m - 15| \le 0.2$

$m - 15 \ge -0.2$    AND    $m - 15 \le 0.2$

$\underline{+15 \quad +15}$          $\underline{+15 \quad +15}$

$m \ge 14.8$    AND    $m \le 15.2$

$14.8 \le m \le 15.2$

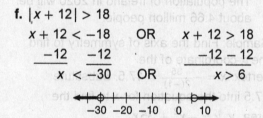

## Practice 91

**1.** $y = -\frac{1}{2}x^2 + x - 3$

$x = -\frac{b}{2a}$

$= -\frac{1}{2\left(-\frac{1}{2}\right)}$

$= 1$

**2.** $\frac{6rs}{r^2s^2} + \frac{18r}{r^2s^2}$

$= \frac{6rs + 18r}{r^2s^2}$

$= \frac{6r(s + 3)}{r^2s^2}$

$= \frac{6(s + 3)}{rs^2}$

**3.** $\frac{b}{2b + 1} - \frac{6}{b - 4}$

$= \frac{b(b - 4)}{(2b + 1)(b - 4)} - \frac{6(2b + 1)}{(b - 4)(2b + 1)}$

$= \frac{b(b - 4) - 6(2b + 1)}{(2b + 1)(b - 4)}$

$= \frac{b^2 - 4b - 12b - 6}{(2b + 1)(b - 4)}$

$= \frac{b^2 - 16b - 6}{(2b + 1)(b - 4)}$

**4.** $-4y^4 + 8y^3 + 5y^2 - 10y$

$= -y(4y^3 - 8y^2 - 5y + 10)$

$= -y[4y^2(y - 2) - 5(y - 2)]$

$= -y(4y^2 - 5)(y - 2)$

**5.** $3a^2 - 27$

$= 3(a^2 - 9)$

$= 3(a^2 - 3^2)$

$= 3(a + 3)(a - 3)$

**6.** $4x^2 + 6x - 4$

$2(2x^2 + 3x - 2)$

$2(2x - 1)(x + 2)$

**7.** $9x^2 - 2x - 32$

$(9x + 16)(x - 2)$

**8.** $|x| < 96$

$-96 < x < 96$

**9.** Sample: $|x| \geq 54$ means that $x$ can be any value that is 54 or more units from 0.

**10.** Sample: No matter what I substitute for $x$, its absolute value is going to be greater than $-5$ because absolute value is always positive.

**11.** The graph shows $x < -9$ or $x > 9$, which can be written as $|x| > 9$. The answer is **B**.

**12.** $|t - 8.54| \leq 0.3$

$t - 8.54 \geq -0.3$   AND   $t - 8.54 \leq 0.3$

$\underline{+8.54 \quad +8.54}$      $\underline{+8.54 \quad +8.54}$

$t \geq 8.24$   AND     $t \leq 8.84$

$8.24 \leq t \leq 8.84$

**13.** Student A; Sample: Student B multiplied the denominator of one of the expressions by $-1$, but forgot to multiply the numerator of that expression by $-1$ also.

**14. a.** $\dfrac{\text{land set aside}}{\text{total land}}$

$= \frac{x^2 + 2x - 8}{x^2 + 22x + 72}$

$= \frac{(x + 4)(x - 2)}{(x + 4)(x + 18)}$

$= \frac{x - 2}{x + 18}$

**b.** Let $x = 30$.

$\frac{30 - 2}{30 + 18}$

$= \frac{28}{48}$

$= 0.58\overline{3}$

about 60%

Saxon Algebra 1

**15.** $\dfrac{\text{area of triangle} + \text{area of small rectangle}}{\text{area of large rectangle}}$

$= \dfrac{\frac{1}{2}(2x)(2x) + 2x(x-2)}{5x(2x + 18)}$

$= \dfrac{2x^2 + 2x^2 - 4x}{5x \cdot 2(x + 9)}$

$= \dfrac{4x^2 - 4x}{10x(x + 9)}$

$= \dfrac{4x(x - 1)}{10x(x + 9)}$

$= \dfrac{2(x - 1)}{5(x + 9)}$

**16.** $(\sqrt{4} - 6)^2$

$= (2 - 6)^2$

$= (-4)^2$

$= 16$

**17.** Sample: Factoring makes it easier to simplify complicated expressions.

**18. a.** (base)(height)

$= (x^2 + y)\left(\dfrac{4x + 2xy}{x^3 + xy}\right)$

$= (x^2 + y)\left[\dfrac{2x(2 + y)}{x(x^2 + y)}\right]$

$= 2(2 + y)$

**b.** $\dfrac{1}{2} \cdot 2(2 + y)$

$= 2 + y$

**19.** Student B; Sample: Student A used the wrong values for $a$ and $b$. The equation in standard form is $y = 2x^2 + 8x$, so $a = 2$ and $b = 8$.

**20.** The time the ball reaches its maximum height is the $x$-coordinate of the maximum.

$x = -\dfrac{b}{2a}$

$= -\dfrac{39}{2(-13)}$

$= \dfrac{3}{2}$

The ball reaches its maximum height in 1.5 seconds. To find the maximum height the ball reaches, find the value of $y$ when $x = 1.5$.

$y = -13x^2 + 39x$

$= -13(1.5)^2 + 39(1.5)$

$= -29.25 + 58.5$

$= 29.25$ feet

**21.** $0.05\sqrt{(7 - 5)^2 + (10 - 3)^2}$

$= 0.05\sqrt{2^2 + 7^2}$

$= 0.05\sqrt{4 + 49}$

$= 0.05\sqrt{53}$

$\approx 0.364$ mile

**22.** $0.25\sqrt{(41 - 5)^2 + (37 - 2)^2}$

$= 0.25\sqrt{36^2 + 35^2}$

$= 0.25\sqrt{1296 + 1225}$

$= 0.25\sqrt{2521}$

$\approx 12.6$ feet

**23.** $t = \sqrt{(\sqrt{3})^2 + 5^2}$

$= \sqrt{3 + 25}$

$= \sqrt{28}$

$\approx 5.3$

**24.** The ladder will touch the house above the windowsill.

$34^2 - 7^2 = 1107$

$33^2 = 1089$

So, $34^2 - 7^2 > 33^2$.

**25.** Plot the points in a coordinate plane and draw a smooth curve through the points.

| $x$ | $-2$ | $-1$ | $0$ | $1$ | $2$ |
|---|---|---|---|---|---|
| $y$ | 16 | 4 | 0 | 4 | 16 |

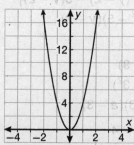

**26.** $a^{2m} + 2a^m b^n + b^{2n}$

$= (a^m)^2 + 2a^m b^n + (b^n)^2$

$= (a^m + b^n)^2$

**Saxon** Algebra 1

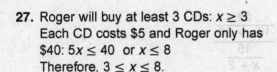

**27.** Roger will buy at least 3 CDs: $x \geq 3$
Each CD costs $5 and Roger only has
$40: $5x \leq 40$ or $x \leq 8$
Therefore, $3 \leq x \leq 8$.

**28. a.** The equation is of the form $y = \dfrac{a}{x-b} + c$.
Since $c = 20$, the horizontal asymptote is
$y = 20$.

**b.** Since $b = 0$, the vertical asymptote is
$x = 0$.

**c.** Find the value of $y$ when $x = 10$.
$$y = \frac{1000}{10} + 20$$
$$= 100 + 20$$
$$= 120 \text{ T-shirts}$$

**29.** Factor the expression.
$4x^2 + 9x + 2 = (4x + 1)(x + 2)$
Therefore, width $= (4x + 1)$ and
height $= (x + 2)$ OR width $= (x + 2)$
and height $= (4x + 1)$.

**30.** $6\sqrt{8} \cdot \sqrt{5}$
$= 6\sqrt{4 \cdot 2} \cdot \sqrt{5}$
$= 6 \cdot 2\sqrt{2} \cdot \sqrt{5}$
$= 12\sqrt{2 \cdot 5}$
$= 12\sqrt{10}$

# LESSON 92

## Warm Up 92

**1.** reciprocal

**2.** $4x - 16 = 4(x - 4)$
LCM $= 4(x - 4)$

**3.** $18x^2 = 2 \cdot 3 \cdot 3 \cdot x \cdot x$
$9x = 3 \cdot 3 \cdot x$
LCM $= 2 \cdot 3 \cdot 3 \cdot x \cdot x = 18x^2$

**4.** $x^2 - 4x - 77$
Find a pair of numbers whose product is
$c = -77$ and sum is $b = -4$.
$(x + 7)(x - 11)$

**5.** $18x^2 + 12x + 2$
$= 2(9x^2 + 6x + 1)$
$= 2\left[(3x)^2 + 2(3x)(1) + (1)^2\right]$
$= 2(3x + 1)(3x + 1)$
$= 2(3x + 1)^2$

## Lesson Practice 92

**a.** $\dfrac{\dfrac{x}{4}}{\dfrac{3(x-3)}{x}}$

$= \dfrac{x}{4} \div \dfrac{3(x-3)}{x}$

$= \dfrac{x}{4} \cdot \dfrac{x}{3(x-3)}$

$= \dfrac{x^2}{12(x-3)}$

**b.** $\dfrac{\dfrac{b}{cd}}{\dfrac{2b}{c}}$

$= \dfrac{\dfrac{b}{cd} \cdot \dfrac{c}{2b}}{\dfrac{2b}{c} \cdot \dfrac{c}{2b}}$

$= \dfrac{\dfrac{bc}{2bcd}}{1}$

$= \dfrac{1}{2d}$

**c.** $\dfrac{\dfrac{4x^2}{x-3}}{\dfrac{x}{3x-9}}$

$= \dfrac{4x^2}{x-3} \div \dfrac{x}{3x-9}$

$= \dfrac{4x^2}{x-3} \cdot \dfrac{3x-9}{x}$

$= \dfrac{4x^2}{x-3} \cdot \dfrac{3(x-3)}{x}$

$= 12x$

**d.** $\dfrac{\dfrac{1}{m} + 5}{\dfrac{2}{m} - \dfrac{x}{m}}$

$= \dfrac{\dfrac{1 + 5m}{m}}{\dfrac{2 - x}{m}}$

$= \dfrac{1 + 5m}{m} \div \dfrac{2 - x}{m}$

$= \dfrac{1 + 5m}{m} \cdot \dfrac{m}{2 - x}$

**Saxon** Algebra 1

$$= \frac{1 + 5m}{2 - x}$$

e. $\dfrac{\dfrac{3x - 27}{x^3}}{\dfrac{5x^2 - 45x}{5x}}$

$$= \frac{3x - 27}{x^3} \div \frac{5x^2 - 45x}{5x}$$

$$= \frac{3x - 27}{x^3} \cdot \frac{5x}{5x^2 - 45x}$$

$$= \frac{3(x - 9)}{x^3} \cdot \frac{5x}{5x(x - 9)}$$

$$= \frac{3}{x^3} \text{ miles per minute}$$

**Practice 92**

1. $\dfrac{15x^4}{x - 4} \cdot \dfrac{x^2 - 10x + 24}{3x^3 + 12x^2}$

$$= \frac{3x^2 \cdot 5x^2}{x - 4} \cdot \frac{(x - 6)(x - 4)}{3x^2(x + 4)}$$

$$= \frac{5x^2(x - 6)}{x + 4}$$

2. $\dfrac{x^2 + 12x + 36}{x^2 - 36} \div \dfrac{1}{x - 6}$

$$= \frac{(x + 6)(x + 6)}{(x + 6)(x - 6)} \cdot \frac{(x - 6)}{1}$$

$$= x + 6$$

3. $-3(r - 2) > -2(-6)$

$$-3r + 6 > 12$$

$$-3r > 6$$

$$\frac{-3r}{-3} < \frac{6}{-3}$$

$$r < -2$$

4. $\dfrac{y}{4} + \dfrac{1}{2} < \dfrac{2}{3}$

$$12\left(\frac{y}{4} + \frac{1}{2}\right) < 12\left(\frac{2}{3}\right)$$

$$12\left(\frac{y}{4}\right) + 12\left(\frac{1}{2}\right) < 12\left(\frac{2}{3}\right)$$

$$3y + 6 < 8$$

$$3y < 2$$

$$y < \frac{2}{3}$$

5. $\dfrac{\dfrac{10x + 20}{15}}{\dfrac{5x}{x + 2}}$

$$= \frac{5x}{10x + 20} \div \frac{15}{x + 2}$$

$$= \frac{5x}{10x + 20} \cdot \frac{x + 2}{15}$$

$$= \frac{5x}{2 \cdot 10(x + 2)} \cdot \frac{x + 2}{15}$$

$$= \frac{x}{30}$$

6. $8\sqrt{9} \cdot 2\sqrt{5}$

$$= 8 \cdot 3 \cdot 2\sqrt{5}$$

$$= 48\sqrt{5}$$

7. Sample: When the denominator equals zero.

8. Sample:

$$\frac{\dfrac{8x^2y}{15a^2b}}{\dfrac{2xy}{5ab^4}}$$

$$= \frac{8x^2y}{15a^2b} \cdot \frac{5ab^4}{2xy}$$

$$= \frac{2 \cdot 4 \cdot 5 \cdot x \cdot x \cdot y \cdot a \cdot b \cdot b^3}{5 \cdot 3 \cdot 2 \cdot x \cdot y \cdot a \cdot a \cdot b}$$

$$= \frac{4xb^3}{3a}$$

and

$$\frac{8x^2y \cdot 5ab^4}{15a^2b \cdot 2xy}$$

$$= \frac{40ab^4x^2y}{30a^2bxy}$$

$$= \frac{4b^3x}{3a}$$

9. $\dfrac{\dfrac{2x}{8x - 8} + \dfrac{x}{4x + 12}}{\dfrac{15}{x^2 + 2x - 3}}$

$$= \frac{\dfrac{x}{4(x - 1)} + \dfrac{x}{4(x + 3)}}{\dfrac{15}{x^2 + 2x - 3}}$$

**Saxon** Algebra 1

$$= \frac{\dfrac{x(x+3)}{4(x-1)(x+3)} + \dfrac{x(x-1)}{4(x+3)(x-1)}}{\dfrac{15}{(x+3)(x-1)}}$$

$$= \frac{x^2 + 3x + x^2 - x}{4(x-1)(x+3)} \div \frac{15}{(x+3)(x-1)}$$

$$= \frac{\overset{1}{2}(x^2 + x)}{\underset{2}{4}(x-1)(x+3)} \cdot \frac{(x+3)(x-1)}{15}$$

$$= \frac{x^2 + x}{30} \text{ miles per minute}$$

**10.** $x^2 + 6x + 9 = (x + 3)^2$

$x^2 - 9 = (x + 3)(x - 3)$

LCD: $(x + 3)^2 (x - 3)$

The answer is **D**.

**11.** $|x| < 65$

$-65 < x < 65$

**12.** Student B; Sample: Student A did not realize that an absolute value can never be less than $-4$ because absolute value is always positive.

**13.** $7 < s < 39$

**14. a.** $|x - 80| \le 15$

**b.** $|x - 80| \le 15$

$x - 80 \ge -15$ AND $x - 80 \le 15$

$\underline{+80 \ +80}$ \qquad $\underline{+80 \ +80}$

$x \ge 65$ AND $x \le 95$

$65 \le x \le 95$

**15.** Student A; Sample: Student B did not fully distribute the negative sign through the numerator of the second expression.

**16.** Find the sum of the time paddled upstream and the time paddled downstream. Use the formula that relates distance, rate, and time: $d = rt$ or $t = \frac{d}{r}$.

$$t = \frac{4}{6-c} + \frac{3}{6+c}$$

$$= \frac{4(6 + c) + 3(6 - c)}{(6 - c)(6 + c)}$$

$$= \frac{24 + 4c + 18 - 3c}{(6 - c)(6 + c)}$$

$$= \frac{c + 42}{(6 - c)(6 + c)}$$

**17.** Since the coefficient $a$ of the $x^2$ term of equations **A**, **B**, and **D** are all positive, the graphs open up and each has a minimum. The graph of **B** has a maximum since $a < 0$. The answer is **B**.

**18.** Sample: One way is to use the zeros of the function. The axis of symmetry goes through the zero when there is 1 zero because the zero is contained in the vertex. It goes through the average of the 2 zeros when there are 2 zeros. The second way is to use the formula $x = -\frac{b}{2a}$. This is the only way to find the axis of symmetry when the function has no zeros.

**19.** Answers will vary. Accept any function that can be written in the standard form of a quadratic function and any function that cannot. Students should explain that they must be able to write the function in standard quadratic form for it to be quadratic.

An example of quadratic function is $y = 3x^2 - 2x + 1$. An example of a function that is not quadratic is $y = \frac{1}{x^2}$.

**20.** Use the Pythagorean theorem.

$a^2 + b^2 = c^2$

$a^2 + 17^2 = 20^2$

$a^2 + 289 = 400$

$a^2 = 111$

$a = \sqrt{111}$

$a \approx 10.5$

**21.** $\dfrac{5f + 6}{f^2 + 7f - 8} - \dfrac{f + 10}{f^2 + 7f - 8}$

$$= \frac{(5f + 6) - (f + 10)}{f^2 + 7f - 8}$$

$$= \frac{5f + 6 - f - 10}{f^2 + 7f - 8}$$

$$= \frac{4f - 4}{f^2 + 7f - 8}$$

$$= \frac{4(f-1)}{(f+8)(f-1)}$$

$$= \frac{4}{f+8}$$

**22.** After plotting the points, it appears that $\overline{AB}$ and $\overline{CD}$ are parallel and that $\overline{AD}$ and $\overline{BC}$ are parallel.

$$AB = \sqrt{[0-(-5)]^2 + (7-3)^2}$$

$$= \sqrt{25 + 16}$$

$$= \sqrt{41}$$

$$CD = \sqrt{(12-7)^2 + (7-3)^2}$$

$$= \sqrt{25 + 16}$$

$$= \sqrt{41}$$

$$AD = \sqrt{(-5-7)^2 + (3-3)^2}$$

$$= \sqrt{144 + 0}$$

$$= 12$$

$$BC = \sqrt{(12-0)^2 + (7-7)^2}$$

$$= \sqrt{144 + 0}$$

$$= 12$$

Since $AB = CD$ and $AD = BC$, $ABCD$ is a parallelogram.

**23.** Athens is at $(10, 10)$. Oneonta is at $(85, 45)$. Use the distance formula to estimate the distance between the two points.

$$\sqrt{(85-10)^2 + (45-10)^2}$$

$$= \sqrt{75^2 + 35^2}$$

$$= \sqrt{6850}$$

about 83 miles

**24.** Student B; Student A did not distribute the negative sign correctly.

**25.** $\dfrac{\text{number of red marbles}}{\text{total number of marbles}}$

$$= \frac{2x + 1}{(2x + 1) + 3x + (x + 2)}$$

$$= \frac{2x + 1}{6x + 3}$$

$$= \frac{\overset{1}{\cancel{2x + 1}}}{3\underset{1}{(\cancel{2x + 1})}}$$

$$= \frac{1}{3}$$

**26. a.** $2x^2 - 8x + 6$

$$= 2(x^2 - 4x + 3)$$

$$= 2(x - 3)(x - 1)$$

**b.** Sample: Since volume = length · width · height, the length is $(x - 1)$ and the width is $(x - 3)$.

**27.** $t$ greater than or equal to $-15°F$ : $t \geq -15$

$t$ less than $-5°F$ : $t < -5$

$$-15 \leq t < -5$$

**28. a.** $2(\text{length}) + 2(\text{width}) = \text{perimeter}$

$$2(2x + 2) + 2(\text{width}) = 8x$$

$$4x + 4 + 2(\text{width}) = 8x$$

$$2(\text{width}) = 4x - 4$$

$$\text{width} = 2x - 2$$

$$\text{length} = 2x + 2$$

**b.** area = length · width

$$= (2x + 2)(2x - 2)$$

$$= 4x^2 - 4$$

**c.** $(x^2)^2 - (4x^2 - 4)$

$$= x^4 - 4x^2 + 4$$

$$= (x^2 - 2)^2$$

**29.** Let $v = 0$ and $s = 14,400$ in the equation.

$$h = -16t^2 + vt + s$$

$$= -16t^2 + 14,400$$

$$= 16(-t^2 + 900)$$

$$= 16(900 - t^2)$$

$$= 16(30 + t)(30 - t)$$

**30.** In the equation, $r$ is jointly proportional to $s$ and $t$, and inversely proportional to $p$.

## LESSON 93

### Warm Up 93

**1.** polynomial

**2.** $\dfrac{72x^2 - 8x}{8x}$

$$= \frac{8x(9x - 1)}{8x}$$

$$= 9x - 1$$

**Saxon** Algebra 1

3. $\dfrac{15x^2 - 3x}{5x - 1}$

$= \dfrac{3x(5x - 1)}{5x - 1}$

$= 3x$

4. $2x^2 + x - 3$
$= (2x + 3)(x - 1)$

5. $25x^2 - 9$
$= (5x)^2 - 3^2$
$= (5x + 3)(5x - 3)$

## Lesson Practice 93

**a.** $(7x^4 + 7x^3 - 84x^2) \div 7x^2$

$= \dfrac{7x^4 + 7x^3 - 84x^2}{7x^2}$

$= \dfrac{7x^4}{7x^2} + \dfrac{7x^3}{7x^2} - \dfrac{84x^2}{7x^2}$

$= x^2 + x - 12$

**b.** $(x^2 - 10x + 25) \div (x - 5)$

$= \dfrac{x^2 - 10x + 25}{x - 5}$

$= \dfrac{(x - 5)(x - 5)}{(x - 5)}$

$= x - 5$

**c.** $(3x^2 - 14x - 5) \div (5 - x)$

$= \dfrac{3x^2 - 14x - 5}{5 - x}$

$= \dfrac{(3x + 1)(x - 5)}{5 - x}$

$= \dfrac{(3x + 1)(x - 5)}{(-1)(x - 5)}$

$= -3x - 1$

**d.** $(8x^2 + x^3 - 20x) \div (x - 2)$

$$
\begin{array}{r}
x^2 + 10x \phantom{xxxxx} \\
x - 2\overline{)x^3 + 8x^2 - 20x} \\
\underline{-(x^3 - 2x^2)} \phantom{xxxx} \\
10x^2 - 20x \\
\underline{-(10x^2 - 20x)} \\
0
\end{array}
$$

The quotient is $x^2 + 10x$.

**e.** $(-3x^2 + 6x^3 + x - 33) \div (-2 + x)$

$$
\begin{array}{r}
6x^2 + 9x + 19 \phantom{xxxx} \\
x - 2\overline{)6x^3 - 3x^2 + x - 33} \\
\underline{-(6x^3 - 12x^2)} \phantom{xxxxxxx} \\
9x^2 + x \phantom{xxxx} \\
\underline{-(9x^2 - 18x)} \phantom{xx} \\
19x - 33 \\
\underline{-(19x - 38)} \\
5
\end{array}
$$

The quotient is $6x^2 + 9x + 19 + \dfrac{5}{x - 2}$.

**f.** $(6x + 5x^3 - 8) \div (x - 4)$

$$
\begin{array}{r}
5x^2 + 20x + 86 \phantom{xxx} \\
x - 4\overline{)5x^3 + 0x^2 + 6x - 8} \\
\underline{-(5x^3 - 20x^2)} \phantom{xxxxxxx} \\
20x^2 + 6x \phantom{xxx} \\
\underline{-(20x^2 - 80x)} \phantom{xx} \\
86x - 8 \\
\underline{-(86x - 344)} \\
336
\end{array}
$$

The quotient is $5x^2 + 20x + 86 + \dfrac{336}{x - 4}$.

**g.** $\dfrac{x^2 - 10x + 24}{x - 4}$

$= \dfrac{(x - 6)(x - 4)}{(x - 4)}$

$= (x - 6)$ feet

## Practice 93

1. $\sqrt{[9 - (-3)]^2 + (-3 - 2)^2}$

$= \sqrt{12^2 + (-5)^2}$

$= \sqrt{169}$

$= 13$

2. $\quad \dfrac{5}{16}y + \dfrac{3}{8} \geq \dfrac{1}{2}$

$16\left(\dfrac{5}{16}y + \dfrac{3}{8}\right) \geq 16\left(\dfrac{1}{2}\right)$

$5y + 6 \geq 8$

$5y \geq 2$

$y \geq \dfrac{2}{5}$

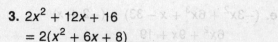

**3.** $2x^2 + 12x + 16$
$= 2(x^2 + 6x + 8)$
Find two factors of $ac = 8$ with a sum of $b = 6$. Replace $6x$ with $4x$ and $2x$.
$2(x^2 + 4x + 2x + 8)$
$= 2[x(x + 4) + 2(x + 4)]$
$= 2(x + 4)(x + 2)$

**4.** $3x^3 - 5x^2 - 9x + 15$
$= x^2(3x - 5) - 3(3x - 5)$
$= (3x - 5)(x^2 - 3)$

**5.** $\dfrac{4x^3 + 42x^2 - 2x}{2x}$
$= \dfrac{4x^3}{2x} + \dfrac{42x^2}{2x} - \dfrac{2x}{2x}$
$= 2x^2 + 21x - 1$

**6.** $y = x^2 - 2x$
$x = -\dfrac{b}{2a}$
$= -\dfrac{-2}{2(1)}$
$= 1$

**7.** $\dfrac{\frac{7x^4}{4x+18}}{\frac{3x^2}{6x+27}}$
$= \dfrac{7x^4}{4x+18} \div \dfrac{3x^2}{6x+27}$
$= \dfrac{7x^4}{4x+18} \cdot \dfrac{6x+27}{3x^2}$
$= \dfrac{7x^{\not4}}{2(2x+9)} \cdot \dfrac{3(2x+9)}{3x^2}$
$= \dfrac{7x^2}{2}$

**8.** $\dfrac{\frac{1}{x^3}}{\frac{1}{x^3}+\frac{1}{x^3}}$
$= \dfrac{\frac{1}{x^3}}{\frac{2}{x^3}}$

$= \dfrac{1}{x^3} \cdot \dfrac{x^3}{2}$
$= \dfrac{1}{2}$

**9.** Sample: Multiply the divisor by the quotient. The product should equal the dividend.

**10. Method 1:**
$\dfrac{x^2-4}{x+2}$
$= \dfrac{(x-2)(x+2)}{(x+2)}$
$= x - 2$

**Method 2:**
$x+2)\overline{x^2+0x-4}$ quotient $x-2$
$\underline{-x^2-2x}$
$-2x-4$
$\underline{+2x+4}$
$0$

**11.** $\dfrac{x^2-16x+63}{x-7}$
$= \dfrac{(x-7)(x-9)}{x-7}$
$= (x-9)$ feet

**12.** $\dfrac{x^3-7x+3x^2-21}{x+3}$
$= \dfrac{x(x^2-7)+3(x^2-7)}{x+3}$
$= \dfrac{(x^2-7)(x+3)}{x+3}$
$= x^2 - 7$
The answer is **A**.

**13.** Student A; Sample: Student B did not write the solution in simplest form.

**14. a.** $\dfrac{7x-42}{4x^2} \div \dfrac{8x^2-48x}{24x^5}$
$= \dfrac{7x-42}{4x^2} \cdot \dfrac{24x^5}{8x^2-48x}$

$$= \frac{7(x-6)}{4x^2} \cdot \frac{x^2 \cdot 8x \cdot 3x^2}{8x(x-6)}$$

$$= \frac{21x^2}{4} \text{ miles per minute}$$

**b.** $\dfrac{21x^2}{4} \div \dfrac{1}{x}$

$$= \frac{21x^2}{4} \cdot \frac{x}{1}$$

$$= \frac{21x^3}{4} \text{ miles per minute}$$

**15.** $\dfrac{m+n}{5} \div \dfrac{m^2+n^2}{15}$

$$= \frac{m+n}{5} \cdot \frac{15}{m^2+n^2}$$

$$= \frac{3(m+n)}{m^2+n^2} \text{ inches}$$

**16.** $|x| > 84$

$x < -84$ or $x > 84$

**17.** $|x - 52{,}041{,}916| \le 104{,}000$

$x - 52{,}041{,}916 \ge -104{,}000$

$$\begin{array}{r} + 52{,}041{,}916 \quad +52{,}041{,}916 \\ \hline x \ge 51{,}937{,}916 \end{array}$$

AND

$x - 52{,}041{,}916 \le \quad 104{,}000$

$$\begin{array}{r} +52{,}041{,}916 \quad +52{,}041{,}916 \\ \hline x \le 52{,}145{,}916 \end{array}$$

$51{,}937{,}916 \le x \le 52{,}145{,}916$

**18.** Student A; Sample: Student B did not realize that all absolute values are greater than $-15$.

**19.** $\dfrac{1}{x^2 - 5x - 50} + \dfrac{1}{2x - 20}$

$$= \frac{1}{(x-10)(x+5)} + \frac{1}{2(x-10)}$$

$$= \frac{2}{2(x-10)(x+5)} + \frac{x+5}{2(x-10)(x+5)}$$

$$= \frac{x+7}{2(x-10)(x+5)}$$

The numerator is $x + 7$. The answer is **D**.

**20.** Sample: Multiply either of the expressions by $\dfrac{-1}{-1}$ because $-1(3 - r) = -3 + r = r - 3$, or $-1(r - 3) = -r + 3 = 3 - r$.

**21.** Three of the five functions have $a > 0$ (a positive $x^2$ term) and therefore have a minimum. The probability is $\frac{3}{5}$.

**22.** Student A; Sample: Student B did not multiply by the reciprocal of the rational expression.

**23.** $6b + b^2 + 3(4b + b^2)$

$$= 6b + b^2 + 12b + 3b^2$$

$$= 4b^2 + 18b$$

$$= 2b(2b + 9) \text{ dollars}$$

**24.** $y = \dfrac{4}{x+2}; \quad y = \dfrac{a}{x-b} + c$

Since $b = -2$, the equation of the vertical asymptote is $x = -2$. Since $c = 0$, the equation of the horizontal asymptote is $y = 0$.

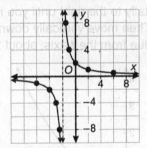

**25.** Area $= 4s^2 + 12s + 9$

$$= (2s)^2 + 2(2s)(3) + 3^2$$

$$= (2s + 3)^2$$

Length of one side of tile $= (2s + 3)$ cm

Difference $= 2s + 3 - s = (s + 3)$ cm

**26. a.**

| $t$ | $h = -16t^2 + 256$ | $(t, h)$ |
|---|---|---|
| 1 | $-16(1)^2 + 256 = 240$ | $(1, 240)$ |
| 2 | $-16(2)^2 + 256 = 192$ | $(2, 192)$ |
| 3 | $-16(3)^2 + 256 = 112$ | $(3, 112)$ |

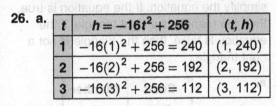

**b.**

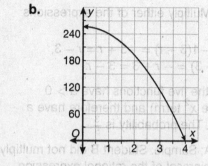

**c.** Let $h = 0$ and solve for $t$.

$$0 = -16t^2 + 256$$
$$16t^2 = 256$$
$$t^2 = 16$$
$$t = 4 \text{ seconds}$$

**27.**

| $t$ | $-10$ | $-5$ | $0$ | $5$ | $10$ |
|---|---|---|---|---|---|
| $l = 2.45 \dfrac{t^2}{\pi^2}$ | 24.8 | 6.2 | 0 | 6.2 | 24.8 |

Find $l = 1$ on the vertical axis and move horizontally to the right until you reach the graph. Then move vertically down and read the $t$-value from the $t$-axis; about 2 seconds.

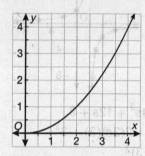

**28.** Sample: Substitute 5 for $a$, 7 for $b$, and 10 for $c$ in the equation $a^2 + b^2 = c^2$ and simplify the equation. If the equation is true, then the triangle is a right triangle. If the equation is false, then the triangle is not a right triangle.

**29. a.**

| Color | Number |
|---|---|
| Red | 3 |
| Blue | 5 |
| Purple | 2 |
| Clear | 4 |

**Marbles**

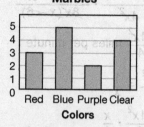

**b.** $\dfrac{\text{number of red or clear marbles}}{\text{total number of marbles}}$

$$= \frac{3 + 4}{3 + 5 + 2 + 4}$$
$$= \frac{7}{14}$$
$$= \frac{1}{2}$$

**30.** $y = \dfrac{kx}{z}$

row 1: $1 = \dfrac{k \cdot 1}{3}$

$k = 3$

row 2: $3 = \dfrac{3 \cdot 2}{z}$

$z = 2$

row 3: $y = \dfrac{3 \cdot 4}{2}$

$y = 6$

row 4: $9 = \dfrac{3 \cdot x}{2}$

$x = 6$

row 5: $2 = \dfrac{3 \cdot x}{12}$

$x = 8$

| $y$ | $x$ | $z$ |
|---|---|---|
| 1 | 1 | 3 |
| 3 | 2 | 2 |
| 6 | 4 | 2 |
| 9 | 6 | 2 |
| 2 | 8 | 12 |

## LESSON 94

### Warm Up 94

**1.** absolute value

**Saxon** Algebra 1

**2.** $|-9| - 5$
$= 9 - 5$
$= 4$

**3.** $|12 - 23|$
$= |-11|$
$= 11$

**4.** $6x - 7 = 11$
$\phantom{6x}+7 \phantom{=} +7$
$\phantom{6x}6x = 18$
$\dfrac{6x}{6} = \dfrac{18}{6}$
$x = 3$

**5.** $11x + 8 = 41$
$\phantom{11x}-8 \phantom{=} -8$
$\phantom{11x}11x = 33$
$\dfrac{11x}{11} = \dfrac{33}{11}$
$x = 3$

## Lesson Practice 94

**a.** $\dfrac{|x|}{7} + 10 = 18$
$\dfrac{|x|}{7} = 8$
$|x| = 56$
$x = 56$ or $x = -56$
$\{-56, 56\}$

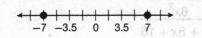

**b.** $3|x| - 11 = 10$
$3|x| = 21$
$|x| = 7$
$x = 7$ or $x = -7$
$\{-7, 7\}$

**c.** $\dfrac{4|x|}{9} + 23 = 11$
$\dfrac{4|x|}{9} = -12$
$4|x| = -108$
$|x| = -27$
Absolute value is never negative; $\varnothing$ or $\{\}$.

**d.** $\dfrac{|x| + 3}{2} - 2 = 1$
$\dfrac{|x| + 3}{2} = 3$
$|x| + 3 = 6$
$|x| = 3$
$x = 3$ or $x = -3$
$\{-3, 3\}$

**e.** $|7x| + 2 = 37$
$|7x| = 35$
$7x = 35$ or $7x = -35$
$x = 5$ $\phantom{or}$ $x = -5$
$\{-5, 5\}$

**f.** $5|x + 1| - 2 = 23$
$5|x + 1| = 25$
$|x + 1| = 5$
$x + 1 = 5$ or $x + 1 = -5$
$x = 4$ $\phantom{or}$ $x = -6$
$\{-6, 4\}$

**g.** $9\left|\dfrac{x}{2} - 1\right| = 45$
$\left|\dfrac{x}{2} - 1\right| = 5$
$\dfrac{x}{2} - 1 = 5$ or $\dfrac{x}{2} - 1 = -5$
$\dfrac{x}{2} = 6$ $\phantom{or}$ $\dfrac{x}{2} = -4$
$x = 12$ $\phantom{or}$ $x = -8$
$\{-8, 12\}$

**h.** $|5x - 100| = 10$
$5x - 100 = 10$ or $5x - 100 = -10$
$5x = 110$ $\phantom{or}$ $5x = 90$
$x = 22$ $\phantom{or}$ $x = 18$
They can produce 18 items or 22 items.

## Practice 94

**1.** $\dfrac{m^2}{m - 4} - \dfrac{16}{m - 4}$
$= \dfrac{m^2 - 16}{m - 4}$
$= \dfrac{(m - 4)(m + 4)}{m - 4}$
$= m + 4$

**2.** $\dfrac{-66}{w^2 - w - 30} + \dfrac{w}{w - 6}$
$= \dfrac{-66}{(w - 6)(w + 5)} + \dfrac{w(w + 5)}{(w - 6)(w + 5)}$
$= \dfrac{-66 + w(w + 5)}{(w - 6)(w + 5)}$
$= \dfrac{w^2 + 5w - 66}{(w - 6)(w + 5)}$

**Saxon** Algebra 1

$$= \frac{(w-6)(w+11)}{(w-6)(w+5)}$$

$$= \frac{w+11}{w+5}$$

**3.** Sample: An absolute value cannot be negative, so any absolute-value equation that sets and absolute value equal to a negative number has no solution.

**4.** Solve each absolute-value equation or substitute $x = -12$ and $x = 60$ in each equation.

$$-5\left|\frac{x}{6} - 4\right| = -30$$

$$\left|\frac{x}{6} - 4\right| = 6$$

$$\frac{x}{6} - 4 = 6 \quad \text{or} \quad \frac{x}{6} - 4 = -6$$

$$\frac{x}{6} = 10 \qquad\qquad \frac{x}{6} = -2$$

$$x = 60 \qquad\qquad x = -12$$

The answer is **D**.

**5.** $0.3(x + y)\left(\dfrac{400 + 100x}{y}\right)$

$$= \frac{0.3(x+y) \cdot 100(4+x)}{y}$$

$$= \frac{0.3(100)(x+y)(4+x)}{y}$$

$$= \frac{30(x^2 + 4x + 4y + xy)}{y} \text{ dollars}$$

**6.** Sample: The droplet is at ground level when $y = 0$. This first occurs at 0 seconds, before the water has shot out from the sprinkler. The maximum value occurs at $x = -\frac{b}{2a} = -\frac{80}{-32} = 2.5$. Because of symmetry, the droplet is at ground level 2.5 seconds before and after its maximum point, so it hits the ground 5 seconds after it shoots up.

**7.** $2a^2 + 8ab + 6a + 24b$

$$= 2(a^2 + 4ab + 3a + 12b)$$

$$= 2[a(a + 4b) + 3(a + 4b)]$$

$$= 2(a + 4b)(a + 3)$$

**8.** $zx^{10} - 4zx^9 - 21zx^8$

$$= zx^8(x^2 - 4x - 21)$$

$$= zx^8(x - 7)(x + 3)$$

**9.** $\dfrac{b-4}{b+9} \cdot (b^2 + 11b + 18)$

$$= \frac{b-4}{b+9} \cdot (b+9)(b+2)$$

$$= (b-4)(b+2)$$

**10.** Student B: Sample: Student A did not put the dividend in descending order or insert a placeholder.

**11.** $\dfrac{\dfrac{-1}{10x - 10}}{\dfrac{x^5}{10x^2 - 10}}$

$$= \frac{-1}{10x - 10} \cdot \frac{10x^2 - 10}{x^5}$$

$$= \frac{-10(x^2 - 1)}{10x^5(x - 1)}$$

$$= \frac{-(x + 1)(x - 1)}{x^5(x - 1)}$$

$$= \frac{-x - 1}{x^5}$$

**12.** $\dfrac{\dfrac{2x}{3x + 12}}{\dfrac{6x^2}{x^2 + 8x + 16}}$

$$= \frac{2x}{3x + 12} \cdot \frac{x^2 + 8x + 16}{6x^2}$$

$$= \frac{2x(x + 4)(x + 4)}{18x^2(x + 4)}$$

$$= \frac{x + 4}{9x}$$

**13.** $|50 - (4x + 10)| = 20$

$$|-4x + 40| = 20$$

$$-4x + 40 = 20$$

$$-4x = -20$$

$$x = 5$$

$$\text{or}$$

$$-4x + 40 = -20$$

$$-4x = -60$$

$$x = 15$$

The minimum is \$5 and the maximum is \$15.

**Saxon** Algebra 1

**14.** $(1 + 4x^4 - 10x^2) \div (x + 2)$

$$
\begin{array}{r}
4x^3 - 8x^2 + 6x - 12 \\
x+2)\overline{4x^4 + 0x^3 - 10x^2 + 0x + 1} \\
\underline{-(4x^4 + 8x^3)} \\
-8x^3 - 10x^2 \\
\underline{-(-8x^3 - 16x^2)} \\
6x^2 + 0x \\
\underline{-(6x^2 + 12x)} \\
-12x + 1 \\
\underline{-(-12x - 24)} \\
25
\end{array}
$$

The quotient is $4x^3 - 8x^2 + 6x - 12 + \frac{25}{x+2}$.

**15.** $\dfrac{25x^3 + 20x^2 - 5x}{5x}$

$= \dfrac{5x(5x^2 + 4x - 1)}{5x}$

$= 5x^2 + 4x - 1$

$= (5x - 1)(x + 1)$

**16.** $\dfrac{|x|}{11} + 9 = 15$

$\dfrac{|x|}{11} = 6$

$|x| = 66$

$x = 66$ or $x = -66$

$\{-6, 6\}$

**17.** Sample: Subtract 1 from both sides to get $\frac{|x|}{-3} = 4$. Then multiply both sides by $-3$ to get $|x| = -12$. Because absolute values cannot be negative, there are no solutions.

**18. a.**
$$
\begin{array}{r}
x^2 - 8x - 1 \\
x+6)\overline{x^3 - 2x^2 - 49x - 98} \\
\underline{-(x^3 + 6x^2)} \\
-8x^2 - 49x \\
\underline{-(-8x^2 - 48x)} \\
-x - 98 \\
\underline{-(-x - 6)} \\
-92
\end{array}
$$

The width is $\left(x^2 - 8x - 1 - \frac{92}{x+6}\right)$ feet.

**b.** $x^2 - 36 = (x + 6)(x - 6)$
The width is $(x - 6)$ feet.

**19.** $10y^2 + 6y$
$= 2y(5y + 3)$
$= \frac{1}{2}(4y)(5y + 3)$

The height is $4y$ centimeters.

**20.** Student B; Sample: Student A did not multiply by the reciprocal.

**21.** $\dfrac{\dfrac{x^2}{6x + 48}}{\dfrac{1}{x^2 + 3x - 40}}$

$= \dfrac{x^2}{6x + 48} \cdot \dfrac{x^2 + 3x - 40}{1}$

$= \dfrac{x^2(x + 8)(x - 5)}{6(x + 8)}$

$= \dfrac{x^2(x - 5)}{6}$ miles per minute

**22.** Sample:
$|0 - 14| = |-14| = 14$ and $14 < 30$.

**23.** The graph represents $-21 \le x \le 21$. The answer is **C**.

**24.** The $y$-values of a horizontal line are the same. Therefore, $(y_2 - y_1)^2 = 0$.

**25. a.** Let $r =$ the hiking rate.

$d = rt$ or $t = \dfrac{d}{r}$

time on easy $+$ time on difficult

$= \dfrac{8}{2.5r} + \dfrac{3}{r}$

$= \dfrac{8 + 3(2.5)}{2.5r}$

$= \dfrac{15.5}{2.5r}$

**b.** Let $r = 2$.

$\dfrac{15.5}{2.5(2)} = 3.1$ hours

**26.** $y = \dfrac{1}{x-2} - 4; \; y = \dfrac{a}{x-b} + c$

Since $b = 2$, the equation of the vertical asymptote is $x = 2$. Since $c = -4$, the equation of the horizontal asymptote is $y = -4$.

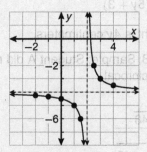

**27. a.** Plan A > Plan B

$12 + 0.06m > 15 + 0.04m$

**b.** $0.06m - 0.04m > 15 - 12$

$0.02m > 3$

$m > 150$

150 minutes

**c.** 
```
←+++++○++++→
  50  100 150 200
```

**28.** $y = 1.9x^2$

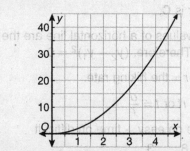

Find 47.5 on the $y$-axis. Move horizontally across the graph. Then move vertically down and read the $x$-value; about 5 feet.

**29. a.** $a^2 + b^2 = c^2$

$a^2 + (25)^2 = (50)^2$

$a^2 + 625 = 2500$

$a^2 = 1875$

$a = \sqrt{1875}$

$a = 25\sqrt{3}$ feet

**b.** $P = 2a + 2b$

$= 2(25\sqrt{3}) + 2(25)$

$= 50\sqrt{3} + 50$

$\approx 136.6$ feet

**30.** The volume of a sphere is directly proportional to the cube of its radius. The constant of variation is equal to $\frac{4}{3}\pi$.

## LESSON 95

### Warm Up 95

**1.** factor

**2.** $8x^4y = 2 \cdot 2 \cdot 2 \cdot x \cdot x \cdot x \cdot x \cdot y$

$12x^3y^2 = 2 \cdot 2 \cdot 3 \cdot x \cdot x \cdot x \cdot y \cdot y$

LCM $= 2 \cdot 2 \cdot 2 \cdot 3 \cdot x \cdot x \cdot x \cdot x \cdot y \cdot y$

$= 24x^4y^2$

**3.** $(9x - 27) = 9(x - 3)$

$(4x - 12) = 4(x - 3)$

LCM $= 9 \cdot 4 \cdot (x - 3) = 36(x - 3)$

**4.** $x^2 + 4x - 21$

$= (x + 7)(x - 3)$

**5.** $10x^2 + 13x - 3$

Find two factors of $ac = 10(-3) = -30$ whose sum is $b = 13$. Replace $13x$ with $15x$ and $-2x$.

$10x^2 + 15x - 2x - 3$

$= 5x(2x + 3) - 1(2x + 3)$

$= (2x + 3)(5x - 1)$

### Lesson Practice 95

**a.** $\dfrac{5x}{5x - 45} - \dfrac{44}{x^2 - 81}$

$= \dfrac{5x}{5(x - 9)} - \dfrac{44}{(x - 9)(x + 9)}$

LCD $= 5(x - 9)(x + 9)$

**b.** $\dfrac{3x}{x + 4} - \dfrac{12}{x^2 + 2x - 8}$

$= \dfrac{3x}{x + 4} - \dfrac{12}{(x + 4)(x - 2)}$

LCD $= (x + 4)(x - 2)$

**Saxon** Algebra 1

**c.** $\dfrac{3x^2}{x^2-25}+\dfrac{x-1}{4x-20}$

$=\dfrac{3x^2}{(x-5)(x+5)}+\dfrac{x-1}{4(x-5)}$

$=\dfrac{3x^2\cdot4}{4(x-5)(x+5)}+\dfrac{(x-1)(x+5)}{4(x-5)(x+5)}$

$=\dfrac{12x^2+x^2+4x-5}{4(x-5)(x+5)}$

$=\dfrac{13x^2+4x-5}{4(x-5)(x+5)}$

**d.** $\dfrac{2x^2}{6x-24}-\dfrac{3x-4}{x^2-16}$

$=\dfrac{2x^2}{6(x-4)}-\dfrac{3x-4}{(x-4)(x+4)}$

$=\dfrac{x^2}{3(x-4)}-\dfrac{3x-4}{(x-4)(x+4)}$

$=\dfrac{x^2(x+4)}{3(x-4)(x+4)}-\dfrac{3(3x-4)}{3(x-4)(x+4)}$

$=\dfrac{x^3+4x^2-9x+12}{3(x-4)(x+4)}$

**e.** $\dfrac{x-1}{x^2-1}+\dfrac{2}{5x+5}$

$=\dfrac{x-1}{(x+1)(x-1)}+\dfrac{2}{5(x+1)}$

$=\dfrac{1}{(x+1)}+\dfrac{2}{5(x+1)}$

$=\dfrac{5}{5(x+1)}+\dfrac{2}{5(x+1)}$

$=\dfrac{5+2}{5(x+1)}$

$=\dfrac{7}{5(x+1)}$

**f.** $\dfrac{2}{x^2-36}-\dfrac{1}{x^2+6x}$

$=\dfrac{2}{(x+6)(x-6)}-\dfrac{1}{x(x+6)}$

$=\dfrac{2x}{x(x+6)(x-6)}-\dfrac{(x-6)}{x(x+6)(x-6)}$

$=\dfrac{2x-(x-6)}{x(x+6)(x-6)}$

$=\dfrac{(x+6)}{x(x+6)(x-6)}$

$=\dfrac{1}{x(x-6)}$

**g.** $\dfrac{4x}{x^2-64}+\dfrac{12}{7x-56}$

$=\dfrac{4x}{(x-8)(x+8)}+\dfrac{12}{7(x-8)}$

$=\dfrac{7\cdot4x}{7(x-8)(x+8)}+\dfrac{12(x+8)}{7(x-8)(x+8)}$

$=\dfrac{28x+12x+96}{7(x-8)(x+8)}$

$=\dfrac{40x+96}{7(x-8)(x+8)}$ miles

**Practice 95**

**1.** $3x^3-9x^2-30x$
$=3x(x^2-3x-10)$
$=3x(x+2)(x-5)$

**2.** $8x^3y^2+4x^2y-12xy^3$
$=4xy(2x^2y+x-3y^2)$

**3.** $32x^3-24x^4+4x^5$
$=4x^5-24x^4+32x^3$
$=4x^3(x^2-6x+8)$
$=4x^3(x-2)(x-4)$

**4.** $mn^3-10mn^2+24mn$
$=mn(n^2-10n+24)$
$=mn(n-6)(n-4)$

**5.** $\dfrac{4m}{17r}\div\dfrac{12m^2}{5r}$
$=\dfrac{4m}{17r}\cdot\dfrac{5r}{12m^2}$
$=\dfrac{4mr\cdot5}{4mr\cdot51m}$
$=\dfrac{5}{51m}$

**6.** $(x^2-16x+64)\div(x-8)$
$=\dfrac{x^2-16x+64}{x-8}$
$=\dfrac{(x-8)(x-8)}{(x-8)}$
$=x-8$

**7.** The graph does not cross the x-axis, so the function has no zeros.

**8.** $\dfrac{4}{x-4} - \dfrac{8}{x^2+6x+8}$

$= \dfrac{4}{x+4} - \dfrac{8}{(x+4)(x+2)}$

LCD $= (x+4)(x+2)$

**9.** $\dfrac{2x}{2x^2-128} + \dfrac{5}{x^2-7x-8}$

$= \dfrac{2x}{2(x^2-64)} + \dfrac{5}{(x-8)(x+1)}$

$= \dfrac{x}{(x-8)(x+8)} + \dfrac{5}{(x-8)(x+1)}$

$= \dfrac{x^2+x+5x+40}{(x-8)(x+8)(x+1)}$

$= \dfrac{x^2+6x+40}{(x-8)(x+8)(x+1)}$

**10.** $9|x| - 22 = 14$

$9|x| = 36$

$|x| = 4$

$x = 4 \text{ or } x = -4$

$\{-4, 4\}$

**11.** Student A; Sample: Student B didn't factor the negative all the way through the second numerator.

**12.** Sample: Factor each denominator. The LCD must contain each factor of each denominator and use each factor the greatest number of times it occurs in either denominator.

**13.** $\dfrac{3x^2}{x^2-100} + \dfrac{x-1}{2x-20}$

$= \dfrac{3x^2}{(x+10)(x-10)} + \dfrac{x-1}{2(x-10)}$

$= \dfrac{2 \cdot 3x^2}{2(x+10)(x-10)} + \dfrac{(x-1)(x+10)}{2(x-10)(x+10)}$

$= \dfrac{6x^2 + x^2 + 9x - 10}{2(x+10)(x-10)}$

$= \dfrac{7x^2 + 9x - 10}{2(x+10)(x-10)}$ miles

**14. a.** $\dfrac{2x}{4x^2-196} + \dfrac{12x}{x^2+x-56}$

$= \dfrac{2x}{4(x-7)(x+7)} + \dfrac{12x}{(x+8)(x-7)}$

$= \dfrac{x(x+8)}{2(x-7)(x+7)(x+8)} +$

$\dfrac{12x \cdot 2 \cdot (x+7)}{(x+8)(x-7)(x+7)}$

$= \dfrac{x^2 + 8x + 24x^2 + 168x}{2(x-7)(x+7)(x+8)}$

$= \dfrac{25x^2 + 176x}{2(x-7)(x+7)(x+8)}$ meters

**b.** $\dfrac{25x^2 + 176x}{2(x-7)(x+7)(x+8)} \div \dfrac{2x}{x+8}$

$= \dfrac{\cancel{x}(25x+176)}{2(x-7)(x+7)\cancel{(x+8)}} \cdot \dfrac{\cancel{x+8}}{2\cancel{x}}$

$= \dfrac{25x + 176}{4(x-7)(x+7)}$ minutes

**15.** Student B; Sample: Student A did not isolate the absolute value and assumed that because the equation was equal to a negative number, the absolute value would be equal to a negative number.

**16.** perimeter $= 4x$

$|34 - 4x| = 2$

$34 - 4x = 2$    or    $34 - 4x = -2$

$-4x = -32$          $-4x = -36$

$x = 8$              $x = 9$

shortest length $= 8$ inches

longest length $= 9$ inches

**17. a.** Let $x =$ the cost of lunch.

$|5 + 5x - 35| = 2$

**b.** $|5x - 30| = 2$

$5x - 30 = 2$    or    $5x - 30 = -2$

$5x = 32$           $5x = 28$

$x = 6.4$          $x = 5.6$

The minimum is $5.60 and the maximum is $6.40.

**18.** Student B; Sample: Student A canceled terms that were not common factors.

**19.** $\dfrac{x^3 - 18x^2 + 81x}{x - 9}$

$= \dfrac{x(x^2 - 18x + 81)}{x - 9}$

$= \dfrac{x\cancel{(x - 9)}(x - 9)}{\cancel{x - 9}}$

$= x(x - 9)$

The width is $(x^2 - 9x)$ feet.

**20.** Sample: $\dfrac{4}{2} \cdot \dfrac{3}{9} = 2 \cdot \dfrac{1}{3} = \dfrac{2}{3}$ and

$\dfrac{4 \cdot 3}{2 \cdot 9} = \dfrac{12}{18} = \dfrac{2}{3}$

**21.** $\dfrac{\dfrac{x^2 - 9}{x^2 - 5x + 6}}{\dfrac{x^2 + 5x + 6}{x^2 - 4}}$

$= \dfrac{x^2 - 9}{x^2 - 5x + 6} \div \dfrac{x^2 + 5x + 6}{x^2 - 4}$

$= \dfrac{x^2 - 9}{x^2 - 5x + 6} \cdot \dfrac{x^2 - 4}{x^2 + 5x + 6}$

$= \dfrac{\cancel{(x + 3)}\cancel{(x - 3)}}{\cancel{(x - 3)}\cancel{(x - 2)}} \cdot \dfrac{\cancel{(x - 2)}\cancel{(x + 2)}}{\cancel{(x + 2)}\cancel{(x + 3)}}$

$= 1$

The answer is **A**.

**22.** $|x| \ge 17$

$x < -17$ or $x > 17$

**23.** $|x - 15.6| \le 0.1$

$x - 15.6 \ge -0.1$ and $x - 15.6 \le 0.1$

$x \ge 15.5 \qquad\qquad x \le 15.7$

$15.5 \le x \le 15.7$

**24. a.** up: $165 - 100 = 65$ degrees

down: $100 - 45 = 55$ degrees

**b.** heat: $t \le 45 + 65$

$t \le 110$ minutes

cool: $t \ge 10 + 2(55)$

$t \ge 120$ minutes

**c.** Since $110 < 120$, to heat up the stew is faster.

**25.** $c^2 = a^2 + b^2$

$c^2 = 25^2 + 50^2$

$c^2 = 3125$

$c \approx 55.9$ meters

**26. a.** $PQ = \sqrt{(124 - 61)^2 + (106 - 43)^2}$

$= \sqrt{63^2 + 63^2}$

$= \sqrt{7938}$

$\approx 89$ pixels

$QR = \sqrt{(155 - 124)^2 + (35 - 106)^2}$

$= \sqrt{31^2 + (-71)^2}$

$= \sqrt{6002}$

$\approx 77$ pixels

$PR = \sqrt{(155 - 61)^2 + (35 - 43)^2}$

$= \sqrt{94^2 + (-8)^2}$

$= \sqrt{8900}$

$\approx 94$ pixels

**b.** $\dfrac{77}{QR} < \dfrac{89}{PQ} < \dfrac{94}{PR}$

**27.** Sample:

$8a^2b + 4a^3 + 12ab + 16ab^2$

$= 4a(2ab + a^2 + 3b + 4b^2)$

**28.** $y = -5x^2 + 10x + 260$

$x = -\dfrac{b}{2a} = -\dfrac{10}{2(-5)} = 1$

1 second

$y = -5(1)^2 + 10(1) + 260 = 265$

265 feet

**29.** Let $x =$ speed to work in miles per hour.

$d = rt$ or $t = \dfrac{d}{r}$

time to work + time from work

$t = \dfrac{15}{x} + \dfrac{15}{x - 5}$

$= \dfrac{15(x - 5)}{x(x - 5)} + \dfrac{15x}{x(x - 5)}$

$= \dfrac{15x - 75 + 15x}{x(x - 5)}$

$= \dfrac{30x - 75}{x(x - 5)} = \dfrac{15(2x - 5)}{x(x - 5)}$ hours

**30.** $\dfrac{\text{number of blue shirts and khaki shirts}}{\text{total number of shirts}}$

$= \dfrac{2}{20}$

$= \dfrac{1}{10}$

## LESSON 96

### Warm Up 96

1. axis of symmetry

2. Evaluate $y = 4x^2 - 6x - 4$ for $x = \frac{1}{2}$.

$y = 4\left(\dfrac{1}{2}\right)^2 - 6\left(\dfrac{1}{2}\right) - 4$

$\quad = 1 - 3 - 4$

$\quad = -6$

3. Evaluate $y = -x^2 + 5x - 6$ for $x = -2$.

$y = -(-2)^2 + 5(-2) - 6$

$\quad = -4 - 10 - 6$

$\quad = -20$

4. $y = -2x^2 + 4x - 5$

$x = -\dfrac{b}{2a}$

$\quad = -\dfrac{4}{2(-2)}$

$\quad = 1$

5. $y = x^2 - 3x - 4$

$x = -\dfrac{b}{2a}$

$\quad = -\dfrac{-3}{2(1)}$

$\quad = \dfrac{3}{2}$

### Lesson Practice 96

**a.** $y = x^2 - 4x + 7$

axis of symmetry: $x = -\dfrac{b}{2a} = -\dfrac{-4}{2(1)} = 2$

vertex: $y = 2^2 - 4(2) + 7 = 3$, or $(2, 3)$
$y$-intercept: $c = 7$, $(0, 7)$
one additional point: Let $x = 1$.
$y = 1^2 - 4(1) + 7 = 4$, or $(1, 4)$

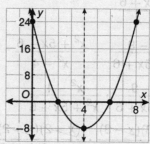

**b.** $y = 2x^2 - 16x + 24$

axis of symmetry: $x = -\dfrac{b}{2a} = -\dfrac{-16}{2(2)} = 4$

vertex: $y = 2(4)^2 - 16(4) + 24 = -8$,
or $(4, -8)$

$y$-intercept: $c = 24$, $(0, 24)$

one additional point: Let $x = 2$.

$y = 2(2)^2 - 16(2) + 24 = 0$, or $(2, 0)$

**c.** $y = 2x^2 - 9$

axis of symmetry: $x = -\dfrac{b}{2a} = -\dfrac{0}{2(2)} = 0$

vertex: $y = 2(0)^2 - 9 = -9$, or $(0, -9)$

$y$-intercept: $c = -9$, $(0, -9)$

one additional point: Let $x = 1$.

$y = 2(1)^2 - 9 = -7$, or $(1, -7)$

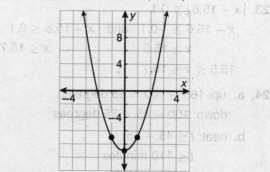

**d.** Use a graphing calculator to graph
$y = x^2 + 10x + 25$. The zero of the
function is $-5$.

322

**Saxon** Algebra 1

e. Use a graphing calculator to graph $y = 3x^2 - 21x + 30$. The zeros of the function are 2 and 5.

f. Use a graphing calculator to graph $y = -\frac{1}{2}x^2 - 1$. There are no zeros for this function.

g. $f(x) = -8x^2 + 24x$
Find the $x$-coordinate of the vertex.

$$x = -\frac{b}{2a} = -\frac{24}{2(-8)} = 1.5$$

1.5 seconds

**Practice 96**

1. The $x$-intercepts appear to be 0 and 4. Check by substituting.

$(0, 0)$            $(4, 0)$

$y = -\frac{1}{2}x^2 + 2x$     $y = -\frac{1}{2}x^2 + 2x$

$0 \stackrel{?}{=} -\frac{1}{2}(0)^2 + 2(0)$    $0 \stackrel{?}{=} -\frac{1}{2}(4)^2 + 2(4)$

$0 = 0$ ✔          $0 = 0$ ✔

The zeros are 0 and 4.

2. $\dfrac{25}{16x^2y} + \dfrac{xy}{32y^5}$

$= \dfrac{25}{16x^2y} \cdot \dfrac{2y^3}{2y^3} + \dfrac{x}{32y^4} \cdot \dfrac{x^2}{x^2}$

$= \dfrac{50y^3}{32x^2y^4} + \dfrac{x^3}{32x^2y^4}$

$= \dfrac{50y^3 + x^3}{32x^2y^4}$

3. $\dfrac{10|x|}{3} + 18 = 4$

$\dfrac{10|x|}{3} = -14$

$10|x| = -42$

$|x| = -4.2$

The absolute value is never negative. The answer is ∅ and there is no graph.

4. $-0.3 + 0.14n = 2.78$

$0.14n = 3.08$

$n = 22$

5. $\dfrac{6}{x-3} = \dfrac{3}{10}$

$6 \cdot 10 = 3(x - 3)$

$60 = 3x - 9$

$69 = 3x$

$23 = x$

6. $\dfrac{6}{x+6} - \dfrac{12}{x^2 + 8x + 12}$

$\dfrac{6}{x+6} - \dfrac{12}{(x+6)(x+2)}$

$LCD = (x + 6)(x + 2)$

7. Since each independent variable, $x$, is paired with exactly one value for the dependent variable, $y$, the relation is a function.

8. $\dfrac{\dfrac{-x^5}{21x + 3}}{\dfrac{5x^9}{28x + 4}}$

$= \dfrac{-x^5}{21x + 3} \div \dfrac{5x^9}{28x + 4}$

$= \dfrac{-x^5}{3(7x + 1)} \cdot \dfrac{4(7x + 1)}{5x^9}$

$= \dfrac{-4}{15x^4}$

9. $y = x^2 - 2x - 8$

axis of symmetry: $x = -\dfrac{b}{2a} = -\dfrac{-2}{2(1)} = 1$

vertex: $y = 1^2 - 2(1) - 8 = -9$, or $(1, -9)$

$y$-intercept: $c = -8$, $(0, -8)$

one additional point: Let $x = 3$.

$y = 3^2 - 2(3) - 8 = -5$, or $(3, -5)$

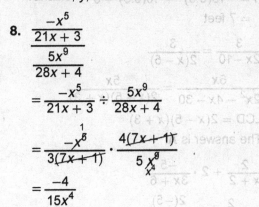

10. Sample: The second point will have the same $y$-value and will be the same horizontal distance from the axis of symmetry, but on the other side.

**Saxon** Algebra 1

**11.** Sample: $x = \frac{-b}{2a} = 3$. Then, substitute 3 into the equation to get

$4(3)^2 - 24(3) + 9 = -27$.

**12.** Find the vertex of each function.

$y = 6x^2 - 72x + 56$

$x = -\frac{b}{2a} = -\frac{-72}{2(6)} = 6$

$y = 6(6)^2 - 72(6) + 56 = -160$

$(6, -160)$

The answer is **A**.

**13.** Evaluate $h = -16t^2 + vt + s$ for $t = 0.5$, $v = 10$, and $s = 6$.

$h = -16(0.5)^2 + 10(0.5) + 6$

$= 7$ feet

**14.** $\dfrac{3}{2x - 10} = \dfrac{3}{2(x - 5)}$

$\dfrac{5x}{2x^2 - 4x - 30} = \dfrac{5x}{2(x - 5)(x + 3)}$

LCD $= 2(x - 5)(x + 3)$

The answer is **A**.

**15.** $\dfrac{2}{x + 2} + 2 \cdot \dfrac{-5}{3x + 6}$

$= \dfrac{2}{x + 2} + \dfrac{2(-5)}{3(x + 2)}$

$= \dfrac{3(2)}{3(x + 2)} + \dfrac{2(-5)}{3(x + 2)}$

$= \dfrac{6 + (-10)}{3(x + 2)}$

$= \dfrac{-4}{3(x + 2)}$ yards

**16.** $\dfrac{3x^2}{9x - 18} - \dfrac{4x - 5}{x^2 - 4}$

$= \dfrac{3x^2}{9(x - 2)} - \dfrac{4x - 5}{(x - 2)(x + 2)}$

$= \dfrac{x^2(x + 2)}{3(x - 2)(x + 2)} - \dfrac{3(4x - 5)}{3(x - 2)(x + 2)}$

$= \dfrac{x^2(x + 2) - 3(4x - 5)}{3(x - 2)(x + 2)}$

$= \dfrac{x^3 + 2x^2 - 12x + 15}{3(x - 2)(x + 2)}$ yards

**17.** $|x - 200| \le 110$

$x - 200 \le 110$ and $x - 200 \ge -110$

$x \le 310$ $\qquad$ $x \ge 90$

$90 \le x \le 310$

**18.** Sample: It helps line up like terms for the dividend and quotient.

**19.** $(-5x + 2x^2 - 3) \div (x - 3)$

$= \dfrac{2x^2 - 5x - 3}{x - 3}$

$= \dfrac{(2x + 1)(x - 3)}{x - 3}$

$= 2x + 1$

The answer is **B**.

**20.** $|2r - 100| = 10$

$2r - 100 = 10$ $\quad$ or $\quad$ $2r - 100 = -10$

$2r = 110$ $\qquad\qquad$ $2r = 90$

$r = 55$ $\qquad\qquad$ $r = 45$

minimum: 45 miles per hour

maximum: 55 miles per hour

**21.** Student A; Sample: Student B graphed all values between $-9$ and $-1$ in addition to the solution set.

**22.** $\dfrac{\text{area of picture} + \text{area of picture}}{\text{area of frame}}$

$\dfrac{\left(\frac{1}{4}x\right)^2 + \left(\frac{1}{2}x\right)^2}{x^2 - 18x + 80}$

$= \dfrac{0.0625x^2 + 0.25x^2}{(x - 8)(x - 10)}$

$= \dfrac{0.3125x^2}{(x - 8)(x - 10)}$

**23.** $\dfrac{3x^2 + 2x}{9y} \div \dfrac{y + 2}{y}$

$= \dfrac{x(3x + 2)}{9y} \cdot \dfrac{y}{y + 2}$

$= \dfrac{x(3x + 2)}{9(y + 2)}$

Sample: Substitute real numbers for the variables $x$ and $y$ before and after dividing.

**Saxon** Algebra 1

**24. a.** $6x^3 + 14x^2 + 4x$

$= 2x(3x^2 + 7x + 2)$

**b.** $2x(3x + 1)(x + 2)$

**25.** Find the distance between $(90, 0)$ and $(150, 80)$.

$$\sqrt{(150 - 90)^2 + (80 - 0)^2}$$

$$= \sqrt{3600 + 6400}$$

$$= \sqrt{10,000}$$

$$= 100 \text{ feet}$$

**26. a.** $a^2 - b^2 = a^2 - 16$

$-b^2 = -16$

$b^2 = 16$

$b = 4 \text{ cm}$

**b.** $36b^2 + 60b + 25$

$= (6b)^2 + 2(6b)(5) + 5^2$

$= (6b + 5)^2$

side length $= 6b + 5$

**c.** $6b + 5$

$6(4) + 5$

$= 29 \text{ cm}$

$(6b + 5)^2$

$(29)^2$

$= 841 \text{ cm}^2$

**27.** $6x > 7x$ is sometimes true; It is true for all negative values of $x$.

**28.** $P(\text{red}) = \frac{6}{24} = \frac{1}{4}$, $P(\text{green}) = \frac{2}{24} = \frac{1}{12}$,

$P(\text{yellow}) = \frac{8}{24} = \frac{1}{3}$, $P(\text{blue}) = \frac{5}{24}$,

$P(\text{orange}) = \frac{2}{24} = \frac{1}{12}$, $P(\text{purple}) = \frac{1}{24}$

**29.** Let $a = 4$, $b = 5$, $c = 2$, and $d = 8$ in.

$$d = \frac{kac}{b}$$

$$8 = \frac{k(4)(2)}{5}$$

$$40 = 8k$$

$$k = 5$$

Let $a = 9$, $b = 15$, and $c = 6$.

$$d = \frac{5(9)(6)}{15}$$

$$= 18$$

**30.** no; If $(x + 10)(x - 2)$ is multiplied, the result is $x^2 + 8x - 20$. Changing the signs to $(x - 10)(x + 2)$ would produce the correct factorization.

# LAB 9

## Practice Lab 9

**a.** Enter $y = 3x + 5$ into the Y = editor. Shade the region below the line. All points in the shaded region are in the solution set of $y < 3x + 5$. Note that the solution set does not include points on the line $y = 3x + 5$. Since the point $(1, 1)$ is in the shaded region, it is a solution of the inequality.

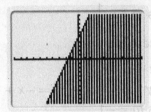

**b.** Enter $y = 2x - 5$ into the Y = editor. Shade the region above the line. All points in the shaded region are in the solution set of $y \geq 2x - 5$. Note that the solution set does include points on the line $y = 2x - 5$. Since the point $(7, 2)$ is not in the shaded region, it is not a solution of the inequality.

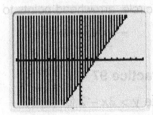

**c.** Enter $y = -2x + 3$ into the Y = editor. Shade the region below the line. All points in the shaded region are in the solution set of $y < -2x + 3$. Note that the solution set does not include points on the line $y = -2x + 3$. Since the point $(0, 0)$ is in the shaded region, it is a solution of the inequality.

**Saxon** Algebra 1

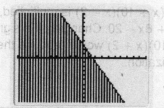

## LESSON 97

**Warm Up 97**

1. slope-intercept form

2. $y = mx + b$

$$y = -\frac{1}{3}x - 5$$

slope is $m = -\frac{1}{3}$

$y$-intercept is $b = -5$

3. $y = mx + b$

$2x + 2y = 6$    or    $y = -x + 3$

slope is $m = -1$

$y$-intercept is $b = 3$

4. $y < 3$

open circle, arrowhead points to the left

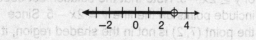

5. $x \geq -2$

closed circle, arrowhead points to the right

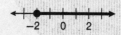

## Lesson Practice 97

**a.** Evaluate $y > 3x - 2$ for $(2, 6)$.

$6 > 3(2) - 2$

$6 > 4$   True

Yes, it is a solution.

**b.** Evaluate $y < -4x + 1$ for $(4, 1)$.

$1 < -4(4) + 1$

$1 < -15$   False

No, it is not a solution.

**c.** Evaluate $y \leq 5$ for $(-6, 2)$.

$2 \leq 5$   True

Yes, it is a solution.

**d.** Graph the boundary line $4x + 5y = -10$ using a solid line because the inequality is $\geq$.

Test: $(0, 0)$.

$4(0) + 5(0) \geq -10$

$0 \geq -10$   True

Shade the half-plane containing $(0, 0)$.

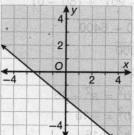

**e.** Graph the boundary line $x = 6$ using a dashed line because the inequality is $<$.

Test: $(0, 0)$.

$0 < 6$   True

Shade the half-plane containing $(0, 0)$.

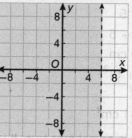

**f.** Solve for $y$.

$4x + 2y \leq 6$

$2y \leq -4x + 6$

$y \leq -2x + 3$

Enter the inequality into the graphing calculator.

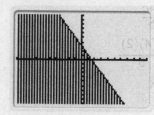

**Saxon** Algebra 1

**g.** Enter $y > 2x + 6$ into the graphing calculator.

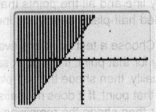

**h.** The boundary line is horizontal with $y$-intercept at 4.

Equation of boundary line: $y = 4$

The inequality symbol is $\leq$ since the graph is shaded below the solid line. $y \leq 4$

**i.** The boundary line has $y$-intercept $-5$ and slope 1.

Equation of boundary line: $y = x - 5$

The inequality symbol is $>$ since the graph is shaded above the dashed line.

$y > x - 5$

**j.** The cost of the series plus the cost of the booth is no more than $25. In other words:

$15x + 5y \leq 25$

Solve for $y$.

$15x + 5y \leq 25$

$5y \leq -15x + 25$

$y \leq -3x + 5$

Since $\leq$ is used, graph the solid boundary line $y = -3x + 5$ and shade below the line.

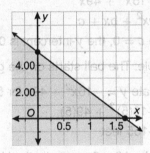

**Practice 97**

1. $\dfrac{30x^{-2}y^{12}}{6y^{-5}}$

$= \dfrac{5y^{12+5}}{x^2}$

$= \dfrac{5y^{17}}{x^2}$

2. $\sqrt{0.09q^2r} + q\sqrt{0.04r}$

$= \sqrt{(0.3q)^2r} + q\sqrt{(0.2)^2r}$

$= 0.3q\sqrt{r} + 0.2q\sqrt{r}$

$= 0.5q\sqrt{r}$

3. $\dfrac{16g^4}{2g+3} - \dfrac{81}{2g+3}$

$= \dfrac{16g^4 - 81}{2g+3}$

$= \dfrac{(4g^2-9)(4g^2+9)}{2g+3}$

$= \dfrac{(2g+3)(2g-3)(4g^2+9)}{2g+3}$

$= (2g-3)(4g^2+9)$

4. order from least to greatest:

7, 18, 23, 27, 31, 35, 39, 44, 66

range $= 66 - 7 = 59$

5. $(4x^2 + 8)(2x - 7)$

$4x^2(2x) + 4x^2(-7) + 8(2x) + 8(-7)$

$8x^3 - 28x^2 + 16x - 56$

6. $\dfrac{9}{9x-36} + \dfrac{-24}{3x^2-48}$

$= \dfrac{9}{9(x-4)} + \dfrac{-24}{3(x-4)(x+4)}$

$= \dfrac{(x+4)}{(x-4)(x+4)} + \dfrac{-8}{(x-4)(x+4)}$

$= \dfrac{x-4}{(x-4)(x+4)}$

$= \dfrac{1}{x+4}$

7. $\dfrac{x}{x^2+2x+1} - \dfrac{x+2}{x+1}$

$= \dfrac{x}{(x+1)(x+1)} - \dfrac{x+2}{x+1}$

$= \dfrac{x}{(x+1)(x+1)} - \dfrac{(x+2)(x+1)}{(x+1)(x+1)}$

$= \dfrac{x - (x^2+3x+2)}{(x+1)(x+1)}$

$= \dfrac{-x^2-2x-2}{(x+1)(x+1)}$ miles

**8.** $(x^2 - 14x + 49) \div (x - 7)$

$= \dfrac{x^2 - 14x + 49}{x - 7}$

$= \dfrac{(x - 7)^2}{x - 7}$

$= x - 7$

**9.** $13 \le 2x + 7 < 15$

$\dfrac{-7}{6} \le \dfrac{-7}{2x} \dfrac{-7}{< 8}$

$\dfrac{6}{2} \le \dfrac{2x}{2} < \dfrac{8}{2}$

$3 \le x < 4$

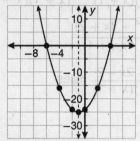

**10.** $\dfrac{|x|}{6} > 8$

$|x| > 48$

$x < -48$ or $x > 48$

**11.** $3x - 4x \ge 6 - x + 8$

$-x \ge 14 - x$

$0 \ge 14$

This is never true.

**12.** Evaluate $y > 3x - 2$ for $(2, 6)$.

$6 > 3(2) - 2$

$6 > 6 - 2$

$6 > 4$

Yes, it satisfies the inequality.

**13.** $y = x^2 + 2x - 24$

axis of symmetry: $x = -\dfrac{b}{2a} = -\dfrac{2}{2(1)} = -1$

vertex: $y = (-1)^2 + 2(-1) - 24 = -25$, or $(-1, -25)$

$y$-intercept: $c = -24$, $(0, -24)$

one additional point: Let $x = 2$.

$y = 2^2 + 2(2) - 24 = -16$, or $(2, -16)$

**14.** Sample: All the points that are on a solid boundary line and all the points that fall in the shaded half-plane satisfy the inequality.

**15.** Sample: Choose a test point and evaluate the inequality for that point. If the point satisfies the inequality, then shade the half-plane that contains that point. If it does not satisfy the inequality, then shade the remaining half-plane.

**16.** The boundary line has $y$-intercept 2 and slope $-\dfrac{2}{3}$.

Equation of boundary line: $y = -\dfrac{2}{3}x + 2$

The inequality symbol is $\le$ since the graph is shaded below the dashed line.

The answer is **B**.

**17.** Let $x =$ the cost of adult tickets and $y =$ the cost of student tickets.

The adult total plus the student total is at least $9000.

$5x + 3y \ge 9000$

**18.** Student B; Sample: Student A did not substitute the $x$-value into the original equation to find the $y$-value.

**19.** $y = 3w^2 - 48$

Graph the function. The zeros of the function are $-4$ and 4 because the graph crosses the $x$-axis at $-4$ and 4.

The width is 4 inches.

**20. a.** $y = -16x^2 + 49x$

$y = ax^2 + bx + c$

Since $c = 0$, the $y$-intercept is 0.

**b.** Sample: The ball starts on the ground.

**c.** Evaluate $y = -16x^2 + 49x$ for 5.

$y = -16(5)^2 + 49(5)$

$= -155$ feet

**d.** Sample: After 5 seconds, the ball has already landed. It cannot have a negative height.

**21.** $\dfrac{1}{x^3 - 2x^2} - \dfrac{1}{2x^2 - 4x}$

$= \dfrac{1}{x^2(x - 2)} - \dfrac{1}{2x(x - 2)}$

$$= \frac{2}{2x^2(x-2)} - \frac{x}{2x^2(x-2)}$$

$$= \frac{2-x}{2x^2(x-2)}$$

$$= \frac{-1(x-2)}{2x^2(x-2)}$$

$$= -\frac{1}{2x^2} \text{ miles}$$

He traveled fewer, not more, miles on Tuesday.

**22.** $\dfrac{3y+2}{y+z} + \dfrac{4}{2y+2z}$

$$= \frac{3y+2}{y+z} + \frac{\overset{2}{\cancel{4}}}{\underset{1}{\cancel{2}}(y+z)}$$

$$= \frac{3y+2}{y+z} + \frac{2}{y+z}$$

$$= \frac{3y+2+2}{y+z}$$

$$= \frac{3y+4}{y+z}$$

The answer is **A**.

**23.** Sample: Evaluate $|3x| - 2 = 31$
for $x = -11$.
$$|3(-11)| - 2 = |-33| - 2 = 33 - 2 = 31$$

**24.** $4|x-8| = 12$
$|x-8| = 3$
$\quad x - 8 = 3 \quad$ or $\quad x - 8 = -3$
$\qquad x = 11 \qquad\qquad\qquad x = 5$
$\{5, 11\}$
The answer is **C**.

**25.** $\left( \dfrac{1}{45x-5} + \dfrac{2x}{25x+5} \right) \div \dfrac{10}{45x^2 + 4x - 1}$

$$\left[ \frac{1}{5(9x-1)} + \frac{2x}{5(5x+1)} \right] \div \frac{10}{(9x-1)(5x+1)}$$

$$\frac{5x+1+2x(9x-1)}{5(9x-1)(5x+1)} \cdot \frac{(9x-1)(5x+1)}{10}$$

$$\frac{5x+1+18x^2-2x}{50}$$

$$\frac{18x^2+3x+1}{50} \text{ miles per minute}$$

**26.** $\left| x - 95\dfrac{5}{8} \right| \le \dfrac{1}{32}$

$x - 95\dfrac{5}{8} \le \dfrac{1}{32}$ and $x - 95\dfrac{5}{8} \ge -\dfrac{1}{32}$

$\qquad x \le 95\dfrac{21}{32} \qquad\qquad x \ge 95\dfrac{19}{32}$

$$95\frac{19}{32} \le x \le 95\frac{21}{32}$$

**27.** Sample: When the vertex is on the $x$-axis, there is 1 zero. When the vertex is not on the $x$-axis, the related function could have either no zeros or 2 zeros. There are no zeros when the vertex is above the $x$-axis and opening upward, or below the $x$-axis and opening downward. There are 2 zeros when the vertex is above the $x$-axis and opening downward or below the $x$-axis and opening upward.

**28.** $\dfrac{2x^4y^2}{15xy^3} \cdot \dfrac{5x^2y}{8x^3y^2}$

$$= \frac{10x^6y^3}{120x^4y^5}$$

$$= \frac{x^2}{12y^2}$$

**29.** $\dfrac{(x^2+30x)\text{oranges}}{1 \text{ hour}} \cdot \dfrac{24 \text{ hours}}{1 \text{ day}}$

$= 24(x^2 + 30x)$ oranges per day

$$\frac{3000}{24(x^2+30x)} = \frac{125}{x(x+30)} \text{ days}$$

**30. a.** $A = \pi r^2$
radius $x$: $A = \pi x^2$
radius $3x$: $A = \pi(3x)^2$ or $A = 9\pi x^2$

**b.**

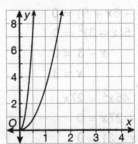

**c.** Sample: The graph of the area of the larger circle is much narrower.

**Saxon** Algebra 1

# LESSON 98

## Warm Up 98

1. zero of a function

2. $x^2 + 3x - 88 = (x + 11)(x - 8)$

3. $6x^2 - 7x - 5 = (3x - 5)(2x + 1)$

4. $4x^2 + 28x + 49$
$= (2x)^2 + 2(2x)(7) + 7^2$
$= (2x + 7)^2$

5. $12x^2 - 27$
$= 3(4x^2 - 9)$
$= 3[(2x)^2 - 3^2]$
$= 3(2x + 3)(2x - 3)$

## Lesson Practice 98

a. $(x - 3)(x + 7) = 0$

$\quad x - 3 = 0 \qquad x + 7 = 0$

$\quad x = 3 \qquad\quad x = -7$

b. $x^2 + 3x - 18 = 0$

$\quad (x - 3)(x + 6) = 0$

$\quad x - 3 = 0 \qquad x + 6 = 0$

$\quad x = 3 \qquad\quad x = -6$

c. $2x^2 + 13x + 15 = 0$

$\quad (2x + 3)(x + 5) = 0$

$\quad 2x + 3 = 0 \qquad x + 5 = 0$

$\quad x = -\dfrac{3}{2} \qquad\quad x = -5$

d. $\quad 5x^2 - 20x = 10x - 45$

$\quad 5x^2 - 30x + 45 = 0$

$\quad 5(x^2 - 6x + 9) = 0$

$\quad 5(x - 3)^2 = 0$

$\quad x - 3 = 0$

$\quad x = 3$

e. $\quad 45x^2 = 27x$

$\quad 45x^2 - 27x = 0$

$\quad 9x(5x - 3) = 0$

$\quad 9x = 0 \qquad 5x - 3 = 0$

$\quad x = 0 \qquad\quad x = \dfrac{3}{5}$

The solution set is $\left\{0, \dfrac{3}{5}\right\}$.

f. $\quad 25x^2 - 16 = 0$

$\quad (5x + 4)(5x - 4) = 0$

$\quad 5x + 4 = 0 \qquad 5x - 4 = 0$

$\quad x = -\dfrac{4}{5} \qquad\quad x = \dfrac{4}{5}$

$\left\{-\dfrac{4}{5}, \dfrac{4}{5}\right\}$

g. Let $w =$ width. Then $3w + 6 =$ length.

$\quad w(3w + 6) = 360$

$\quad 3w^2 + 6w - 360 = 0$

$\quad 3(w^2 + 2w - 120) = 0$

$\quad 3(w - 10)(w + 12) = 0$

$\quad w - 10 = 0 \qquad w + 12 = 0$

$\quad w = 10 \qquad\quad w = -12$

Because the width must be a positive number, the width is 10 feet, and the length is $3(10) + 6 = 36$ feet.

## Practice 98

1. $\quad 11 < 2(x + 5) < 20$

$\quad \dfrac{11}{2} < \dfrac{2(x + 5)}{2} < \dfrac{20}{2}$

$\quad \dfrac{11}{2} < (x + 5) < 10$

$\quad \dfrac{11}{2} - 5 < x + 5 - 5 < 10 - 5$

$\quad \dfrac{1}{2} < \quad x \quad < 5$

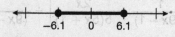

2. $|x| + 1.5 \le 7.6$

$\quad |x| + 1.5 - 1.5 \le 7.6 - 1.5$

$\quad |x| \le 6.1$

$\quad x \le 6.1 \quad$ and $\quad x \ge -6.1$

$\quad -6.1 \le x \le 6.1$

3. $-121 + 9x^2$

$= 9x^2 - 121$

$= (3x)^2 - (11)^2$

Difference of two squares

$(3x + 11)(3x - 11)$

4. $y = 2x^2 + 8x + 6$

axis of symmetry: $x = -\dfrac{b}{2a} = -\dfrac{8}{2(2)} = -2$

**Saxon** Algebra 1

vertex: $y = 2(-2)^2 + 8(-2) + 6 = -2$, or
$(-2, -2)$
$y$-intercept: $c = 6$, $(0, 6)$
one additional point: Let $x = -1$.
$y = 2(-1)^2 + 8(-1) + 6 = 0$, or $(-1, 0)$

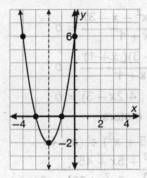

**5.** $S = A + O$
$S = (15x^3 + 17x - 20) + (20x^3 + 11x - 4)$
$= 15x^3 + 20x^3 + 17x + 11x - 20 - 4$
$= 35x^3 + 28x - 24$

**6.** slope of $y = -\dfrac{3}{4}x + 2\dfrac{3}{4}$ is $-\dfrac{3}{4}$.

slope of perpendicular line: $\dfrac{4}{3}$

Substitute $m = \dfrac{4}{3}$ and $(1, 2)$ in
$y - y_1 = m(x - x_1)$
$y - 2 = \dfrac{4}{3}(x - 1)$
$y - 2 = \dfrac{4}{3}x - \dfrac{4}{3}$
$y = \dfrac{4}{3}x + \dfrac{2}{3}$

**7.** $\dfrac{4|x|}{9} + 3 = 11$

$\dfrac{4|x|}{9} = 8$

$4|x| = 72$
$|x| = 18$
$x = 18$  or  $x = -18$
$\{-18, 18\}$

(number line from -18 to 18 marked at -18, -9, 0, 9, 18 with points at -18 and 18)

**8.** $\dfrac{\dfrac{3x + 6}{7x - 7}}{\dfrac{5x + 10}{14x - 14}}$

$= \dfrac{3x + 6}{7x - 7} \div \dfrac{5x + 10}{14x - 14}$

$= \dfrac{3x + 6}{7x - 7} \cdot \dfrac{14x - 14}{5x + 10}$

$= \dfrac{3(x + 2)}{7(x - 1)} \cdot \dfrac{14(x - 1)}{5(x + 2)}$

$= \dfrac{6}{5}$

**9.** $(5xyz)^2(3x^{-1}y)^2$
$= (5^2x^2y^2z^2)(3^2x^{-2}y^2)$
$= 25 \cdot 9x^{2-2}y^{2+2}z^2$
$= 225x^0y^4z^2$
$= 225y^4z^2$

**10.** no; It does not satisfy the inequality.

**11.** Sample: If two numbers multiplied together equal 0, then at least one of the numbers has to be 0.

**12.** Sample: The Zero Product Property

**13.** $0 = (3x - 5)(x + 2)$
$3x - 5 = 0 \qquad\qquad x + 2 = 0$
$x = \dfrac{5}{3} \qquad\qquad x = -2$
$\left\{-2, \dfrac{5}{3}\right\}$ The answer is **A**.

**14.** mother $= m$
girl $= m - 27$
$m(m - 27) = 324$
$m^2 - 27m - 324 = 0$
$(m - 36)(m + 9) = 0$
$m - 36 = 0 \qquad m + 9 = 0$
$m = 36 \qquad m = -9$
The mother is 36 years old and the girl is $36 - 27 = 9$ years old.

**15. a.** Let $x =$ the cost of jeans
and $y =$ the cost of shorts.
The total price of the jeans and the shorts is no more than \$70.
$20x + 10y \le 70$

**b.** Graph the boundary line $20x + 10y = 70$ using a solid line because the inequality is $\leq$.

Test $(0, 0)$.

$$20(0) + 10(0) \leq 70$$
$$0 \leq 70 \qquad \text{True}$$

Shade the half-plane containing $(0, 0)$.

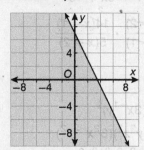

**c.** Find values of $x$ and $y$ that satisfy $20x + 10y = 70$. Sample: 3 pairs of jeans and 1 pair of shorts $(20 \cdot 3 + 10 \cdot 1 = 70)$

**16.** Solve for $y$.

$$4x + 2y > 8$$
$$2y > -4x + 8$$
$$y > -2x + 4$$

Enter the inequality into the graphing calculator.

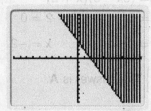

**17.** $(x + 4)(x - 9) = 0$

$$x + 4 = 0 \qquad\qquad x - 9 = 0$$
$$x = -4 \qquad\qquad x = 9$$

**18.** Student A; Sample: Student B wrote an inequality with a solid horizontal line.

**19.** $\dfrac{3x^2 - 15x}{3x} \div \dfrac{2x - 10}{2x^5}$

$$= \dfrac{3x^2 - 15x}{3x} \cdot \dfrac{2x^5}{2x - 10}$$

$$= \dfrac{3x(x - 5)}{3x} \cdot \dfrac{2x^5}{2(x - 5)}$$

$$= x^5 \text{ miles per minute}$$

**20.** $A = \dfrac{1}{2}bh$

$$4x^2 - 2x - 6 = \dfrac{1}{2}b(x + 1)$$

$$\dfrac{2(4x^2 - 2x - 6)}{x + 1} = b$$

$$\dfrac{2 \cdot 2(2x^2 - x - 3)}{x + 1} = b$$

$$\dfrac{4(2x - 3)(x + 1)}{x + 1} = b$$

$$4(2x - 3) = b$$

$$8x - 12 \text{ meters}$$

**21.** $(20x + 5 + x^3) \div (x - 5)$

$$\begin{array}{r} x^2 + 5x + 45 \\ x - 5 \overline{) x^3 + 0x^2 + 20x + 5} \\ \underline{-(x^3 - 5x^2)} \\ 5x^2 + 20x \\ \underline{-(5x^2 - 25x)} \\ 45x + 5 \\ \underline{-(45x - 225)} \\ 230 \end{array}$$

length: $\left( x^2 + 5x + 45 + \dfrac{230}{x - 5} \right)$ inches

**22.** Sample: No, the LCD is found in addition and subtraction problems so that parts of equal size can be added or subtracted.

**23. a.** $\dfrac{4x}{3x + 9} + \dfrac{16}{x^2 + 12x + 27}$

$$= \dfrac{4x}{3(x + 3)} + \dfrac{16}{(x + 9)(x + 3)}$$

$$= \dfrac{4x(x + 9)}{3(x + 3)(x + 9)} + \dfrac{3 \cdot 16}{3(x + 9)(x + 3)}$$

$$= \dfrac{4x(x + 9) + 3 \cdot 16}{3(x + 3)(x + 9)}$$

$$= \dfrac{4x^2 + 36x + 48}{3(x + 3)(x + 9)} \text{ miles}$$

**b.** $\dfrac{4x^2 + 36x + 48}{3(x + 9)(x + 3)} \div \dfrac{4x}{x + 3}$

$$= \dfrac{4(x^2 + 9x + 12)}{3(x + 9)(x + 3)} \cdot \dfrac{(x + 3)}{4x}$$

$$= \dfrac{x^2 + 9x + 12}{3x(x + 9)} \text{ hours}$$

**24.** Evaluate $h = -16t^2 + vt + s$ for $t = 2$, $v = 0$, and $s = 100$.

$h = -16(2)^2 + 0(2) + 100$

$= 36$ feet

**25.** Student B; Sample: Student A found the $y$-intercept.

**26. a.** length $= 26 - 2(1.5) = 23$ cm

width $= 20 - 2(1.5) = 17$ cm

**b.** $c^2 = a^2 + b^2$

$c^2 = 23^2 + 17^2$

$c^2 = 818$

$c \approx 28.6$ cm

**27. a.** $\dfrac{x^{2^x}}{100\,x_1} \cdot (x^2 + 6x + 5)$

$= \dfrac{x(x^2 + 6x + 5)}{100}$

$= \dfrac{x(x + 5)(x + 1)}{100}$ dollars

**b.** $\dfrac{50(50 + 5)(50 + 1)}{100} = \$1402.50$

**28. a.** Let $x =$ length. Then $x - 9 =$ width.

length $\cdot$ width $=$ area $x(x - 9) = 36$

Sample: The formula needs to be set in the form $ax^2 + bx + c = 0$ in order to solve for $x$.

**b.** $x(x - 9) = 36$

$x^2 - 9x - 36 = 0$

$(x - 12)(x + 3) = 0$

$x - 12 = 0 \quad x + 3 = 0$

$x = 12 \qquad x = -3$

The length is 12 feet and the width is $12 - 9 = 3$ feet.

**29.** Sample: Distribute the negative sign so that you are subtracting $x$ and adding 6 to $x^2 - x - 30$. Then combine like terms to get $x^2 - 2x - 24$. Finally, try to factor out $x + 5$ from the numerator. Since you can't, your answer in simplest form is $\dfrac{x^2 - 2x - 24}{x + 5}$

**30.** No. A sign error has occurred. The correct expression would be

$(4x - 6)(8x + 7)$

$= 32x^2 + 28x - 48x - 42$

$= 32x^2 - 20x - 42$.

## LESSON 99

### Warm Up 99

**1.** rational expression

**2.** $7x^2y = 7 \cdot x \cdot x \cdot y$

$3xy^3 = 3 \cdot x \cdot y \cdot y \cdot y$

$\text{LCM} = 7 \cdot 3 \cdot x \cdot x \cdot y \cdot y \cdot y = 21x^2y^3$

**3.** $(3x - 6) = 3 \cdot (x - 2)$

$(9x^2 - 18x) = 3 \cdot 3 \cdot x \cdot (x - 2)$

$\text{LCM} = 9x(x - 2)$

**4.** $\text{LCM} = (x + 3)(2x - 1)$

**5.** $(14x - 7y) = 7 \cdot (2x - y)$

$(10x - 5y) = 5 \cdot (2x - y)$

$\text{LCM} = 7 \cdot 5 \cdot (2x - y) = 35(2x - y)$

### Lesson Practice 99

**a.** $\dfrac{6}{x} = \dfrac{7}{x - 1}$

$6(x - 1) = 7x$

$6x - 6 = 7x$

$-6 = x$

**b.** $\dfrac{2}{x + 4} = \dfrac{x}{6}$

$2(6) = x(x + 4)$

$12 = x^2 + 4x$

$0 = x^2 + 4x - 12$

$0 = (x - 2)(x + 6)$

$x = 2$ or $x = -6$

**c.** $\dfrac{12}{2x} + \dfrac{16}{4x} = 5$

$4x\left(\dfrac{12}{2x}\right) + 4x\left(\dfrac{16}{4x}\right) = 4x(5)$

$24 + 16 = 20x$

$40 = 20x$

$2 = x$

**Saxon** Algebra 1

**d.** $\dfrac{4}{x-2} - \dfrac{2}{x} = \dfrac{1}{3x}$

$\dfrac{4(3x)}{x-2} - \dfrac{2(3x)}{x} = \dfrac{3x}{3x}$

$\dfrac{12x}{x-2} - 6 = 1$

$\dfrac{12x}{x-2} - \dfrac{6(x-2)}{x-2} = 1$

$\dfrac{6x+12}{x-2} = 1$

$6x + 12 = x - 2$

$x = -\dfrac{14}{5}$

**e.** $\dfrac{x+5}{x+4} = \dfrac{x-2}{2x+8}$

$(x+5)(2x+8) = (x+4)(x-2)$

$2x^2 + 18x + 40 = x^2 + 2x - 8$

$x^2 + 16x + 48 = 0$

$(x+12)(x+4) = 0$

$x = -12$ or $x = -4$

$-4$ yields a denominator of 0 in $\dfrac{x+5}{x+4}$,
so $-4$ is extraneous. The solution is $x = -12$.

**f.** (John's r)$h$ + (Sarah's r)$h = 1$

$\dfrac{1}{2}h + \dfrac{1}{3}h = 1$

$6\left(\dfrac{1}{2}h\right) + 6\left(\dfrac{1}{3}h\right) = 6(1)$

$3h + 2h = 6$

$5h = 6$

$h = \dfrac{6}{5}$ or $1\dfrac{1}{5}$

Together, it will take $1\dfrac{1}{5}$ hours.

**Practice 99**

**1.** $\dfrac{4}{x} = \dfrac{8}{x+4}$

$4(x+4) = 8x$

$4x + 16 = 8x$

$16 = 4x$

$4 = x$

**2.** $(x-13)(x+22) = 0$

$x - 13 = 0$ or $x + 22 = 0$

$x = 13 \qquad\qquad x = -22$

$\{-22, 13\}$

**3.** $|10t - 20| = 2$

$10t - 20 = 2$ or $10t - 20 = -2$

$10t = 22 \qquad\qquad 10t = 18$

$t = 2.2 \qquad\qquad\quad t = 1.8$

minimum = 1.8 hours
maximum = 2.2 hours

**4.** Sample: Let $x = 2$ in $y = x^2 + x - 12$.

$y = 2^2 + 2 - 12 = -6$

**5.** $\dfrac{\dfrac{4x}{12x-60} + \dfrac{1}{4x-16}}{\dfrac{-2}{9x-20-x^2}}$

$= \dfrac{\dfrac{4x}{12(x-5)} + \dfrac{1}{4(x-4)}}{\dfrac{2}{x^2-9x+20}}$

$= \dfrac{4x(x-4) + 3(x-5)}{12(x-5)(x-4)} \div \dfrac{2}{(x-5)(x-4)}$

$= \dfrac{4x^2 - 16x + 3x - 15}{12(x-5)(x-4)} \cdot \dfrac{(x-5)(x-4)}{2}$

$= \dfrac{4x^2 - 13x - 15}{24}$

**6.** $x + 4x^2 - 5$

$= 4x^2 + x - 5$

$= (4x + 5)(x - 1)$

**7.** $y = 180 - 2x$ Let $x = 8$.

$y = 180 - 2(8) = 164$ pounds

**8.** Sample: It is an answer that solves
the transformed equation, but not the
original one.

**9.** $\dfrac{2x}{2x^2-72} - \dfrac{12}{x^2+13x+42}$

$\dfrac{2x}{2(x+6)(x-6)} - \dfrac{12}{(x+6)(x+7)}$

LCD $= 2(x-6)(x+6)(x+7)$

**10.** $y = -0.0003x^2 + 0.03x + 1.3$

$x = -\dfrac{b}{2a} = -\dfrac{0.03}{2(-0.0003)} = 50$

$y = -0.0003(50)^2 + 0.03(50) + 1.3 = 2.05$

$(50, 2.05)$; The population reached its
maximum of about 2,050,000 people in 1950.

**11. a.** $P(3, 3)$, $R(11, 3)$

$M\left(\dfrac{3 + 11}{2}, \dfrac{3 + 3}{2}\right)$ or $M(7, 3)$

**b.** $M(7, 3)$, $Q(5, 9)$

$\left(\dfrac{7 + 5}{2}, \dfrac{3 + 9}{2}\right)$ or $(6, 6)$

**12.** $(18x^2 - 120 + 6x^5) \div (x - 2)$

$$
\begin{array}{r}
6x^4 + 12x^3 + 24x^2 + 66x + 132 \\
x - 2 \overline{\smash{)}\,6x^5 + 0x^4 + 0x^3 + 18x^2 + 0x - 120} \\
\underline{-(6x^5 - 12x^4)} \\
12x^4 + 0x^3 \\
\underline{-(12x^4 - 24x^3)} \\
24x^3 + 18x^2 \\
\underline{-(24x^3 - 48x^2)} \\
66x^2 + 0x \\
\underline{-(66x^2 - 132x)} \\
132x - 120 \\
\underline{-(132x - 264)} \\
144
\end{array}
$$

The quotient is

$6x^4 + 12x^3 + 24x^2 + 66x + 132 + \dfrac{144}{x - 2}$

**13.** $\dfrac{\text{volume of a cube with sides of 5 units}}{\text{volume of a cube with sides of 3 units}}$

$= \dfrac{5^3 \text{ cubic units}}{3^3 \text{ cubic units}}$

$= \dfrac{125}{27}$

**14.** Sample: If it would cause one of the denominators to equal 0, the solution is extraneous.

**15.** $x = 5$ and $x = 1$ causes the denominator $(x - 1)(x - 5)$ to equal zero. The answers are **C** and **D**.

**16.** (man's r)$h$ + (friend's r)$h = 1$

$\dfrac{1}{8}h + \dfrac{1}{6}h = 1$

$48\left(\dfrac{1}{8}h\right) + 48\left(\dfrac{1}{6}h\right) = 48(1)$

$6h + 8h = 48$

$14h = 48$

$h = \dfrac{24}{7}$ hours

**17.** Student A; Sample: Sample B has the incorrect signs on both solutions.

**18.** Let $b$ = base. Then $2b + 4$ = height.

$A = \dfrac{1}{2}bh$

$24 = \dfrac{1}{2}b(2b + 4)$

$24 = b^2 + 2b$

$0 = b^2 + 2b - 24$

$0 = (b + 6)(b - 4)$

$b = -6$ or $b = 4$

The base is 4 centimeters and the height is $2(4) + 4 = 12$ centimeters.

**19. a.** length = $2x - 2$

width = $x - 2$

**b.** $(2x - 2)(x - 2) = 144$

$2x^2 - 6x + 4 = 144$

$2x^2 - 6x - 140 = 0$

$2(x - 10)(x - 7) = 0$

$x = 10$ or $x = -7$

The width is 10 feet.

**c.** The length is $2x = 2(10) = 20$ feet.

**20.** Sample: There is no solution when the absolute value is less than 0 because it would be a negative number.

**21.** Area = length · width

$x^2 - 15x + 56 = (x - 7)(x - 8)$

The width is $(x - 8)$ feet.

**22.** $y = 4x^2 + 28x - 72$

$0 = 4(x^2 + 7x - 18)$

$0 = 4(x + 9)(x - 2)$

$x + 9 = 0 \qquad x - 2 = 0$

$x = -9 \qquad x = 2$

The answer is **C**.

**23.** The $y$-intercept is 100 and the slope is $-\dfrac{3}{2}$.

$y = -\dfrac{3}{2}x + 100$

$2y = -3x + 200$

$3x + 2y = 200$

Since the area is shaded above the boundary line, the inequality is $3x + 2y \geq 200$.

**Saxon** Algebra 1

**24.** $(2 + 3x^3 - 8x) \div (x + 4)$

$$x + 4 \overline{)3x^3 + 0x^2 - 8x + 2} \quad \frac{3x^2 - 12x + 40}{}$$

$$\underline{-(3x^3 + 12x^2)}$$
$$-12x^2 - 8x$$
$$\underline{-(-12x^2 - 48x)}$$
$$40x + 2$$
$$\underline{-(40x + 160)}$$
$$-158$$

The length is $\left(3x^2 - 12x + 40 - \frac{158}{x+4}\right)$ inches.

**25.** Student A; Sample: Student B wrote an inequality with a dashed vertical boundary line.

**26.** Graph the boundary line $4x + 5y = -7$ using a solid line because the inequality is $\geq$.

Test: $(0, 0)$.

$4(0) + 5(0) \geq -7$

$0 \geq -7$ True

Shade the half-plane containing $(0, 0)$.

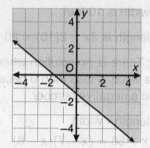

**27. a.** $d = rt$ or $t = \frac{d}{r}$

dirt time + street time

$$t = \frac{6}{0.25x} + \frac{12}{x}$$

$$= \frac{6}{0.25x} + \frac{3}{0.25x}$$

$$= \frac{9}{0.25x}$$

$$= \frac{36}{x}$$

**b.** Sample: the expression for the street time, $\frac{12}{x}$, would be multiplied by $\frac{0.5}{0.5}$ instead of $\frac{0.25}{0.25}$, making the simplified expression $\frac{12}{0.5x} = \frac{24}{x}$.

**28.** $y - 3 = -x^2 + 3$

Write in the form $y = ax^2 + bx + c$.

$y = -x^2 + 6$

Since $a < 0$, the graph opens downward.

Use a table of values to graph the function.

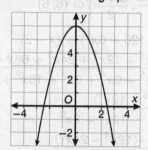

**29.** $A = s^2$

$s^2 + 16x + 64 = (x + 8)^2$

side length $= x + 8$

**30.** $j = \frac{kpq}{mn}$

## LESSON 100

### Warm Up 100

1. parabola

2. Evaluate $3(x - y)^2 - 4y^2$ for $x = -5$ and $y = -2$.

$3[-5 - (-2)]^2 - 4(-2)^2$

$= 3(-5 + 2)^2 - 4(-2)^2$

$= 3(-3)^2 - 4(-2)^2$

$= 3(9) - 4(4)$

$= 27 - 16$

$= 11$

3. Evaluate $-x^2 - 3xy + y$ for $x = 3$ and $y = -1$

$-(3)^2 - 3(3)(-1) + (-1)$.

$= -9 + 9 - 1$

$= -1$

4. $y = ax^2 + bx + c$

$f(x) = 3x^2 + x - 4$

Since $a > 0$, the parabola opens upward.

5. $y = ax^2 + bx + c$

$f(x) = -2x^2 + x + 1$

Since $a < 0$, the parabola opens downward.

## Lesson Practice 100

**a.** $3x^2 - 147 = 0$

Graph the related function $f(x) = 3x^2 - 147$.

axis of symmetry: $x = 0$

vertex: $(0, -147)$

y-intercept: $(0, -147)$

two additional points: $(-4, -99)$, $(3, -120)$

Reflect these two points across the axis of symmetry and connect them with a smooth curve. From the graph, the x-intercepts are $-7$ and $7$. The solutions are $x = -7$ and $x = 7$.

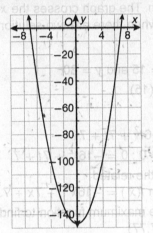

**b.** $5x^2 + 6 = 0$

Graph the related function $f(x) = 5x^2 + 6$.

axis of symmetry: $x = 0$

vertex: $(0, 6)$

y-intercept: $(0, 6)$

two additional points: $(-1, 11)$, $(2, 26)$

Reflect these two points across the axis of symmetry and connect them with a smooth curve. From the graph, there are no x-intercepts. There is no solution.

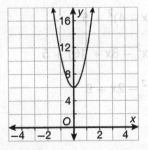

**c.** $x^2 - 10x + 25 = 0$

Graph the related function $f(x) = x^2 - 10x + 25$.

axis of symmetry: $x = 5$

vertex: $(5, 0)$

y-intercept: $(0, 25)$

two additional points: $(2, 9)$, $(6, 1)$

Reflect these two points across the axis of symmetry and connect them with a smooth curve. From the graph, the x-intercept is 5. The solution is $x = 5$.

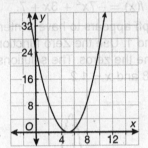

**d.** $x^2 + 64 = 16x$

Write the equation in standard form: $x^2 - 16x + 64 = 0$.

Graph the related function $f(x) = x^2 - 16x + 64$.

The x-intercept appears to be at 8. Use the Table function to determine the zeros. The solutions is 8.

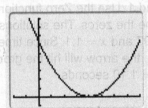

**e.** $x^2 + 4 = 2x$

Write the equation in standard form: $x^2 - 2x + 4 = 0$.

Graph the related function $f(x) = x^2 - 2x + 4$.

The graph opens upward and does not intersect the x-axis. There is no solution.

**Saxon** Algebra 1

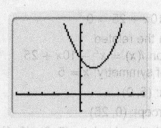

**f.** $-7x^2 + 3x = -7$

Write the equation in standard
form: $-7x^2 + 3x + 7 = 0$.

Graph the related
function $f(x) = -7x^2 + 3x + 7$.

The graph appears to have $x$-intercepts
at $-1$ and $1$. Use the Zero function to
determine the zeros. The solutions are
$x = -0.8$ and $x = 1.2$.

**g.** $h = -16t^2 + 2t + 17$

Let $h = 0 : 0 = -16t^2 + 2t + 17$

Graph the related
function $f(x) = -16x^2 + 2x + 17$.

The graph appears to have $x$-intercepts
at $-1$ and $1$. Use the Zero function to
determine the zeros. The solutions are
$x = -0.97$ and $x = 1.1$. Since time is not
negative, the arrow will hit the ground at
about $t = 1.10$ seconds.

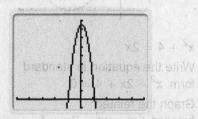

## Practice 100

**1.** $x(2x - 11) = 0$

$x = 0 \qquad 2x - 11 = 0$

$\qquad\qquad 2x = 11$

$\qquad\qquad x = \dfrac{11}{2}$

**2.** $\dfrac{12}{x - 6} = \dfrac{4}{x}$

$12x = 4(x - 6)$

$12x = 4x - 24$

$8x = -24$

$x = -3$

**3.** Sample: The path creates a parabola that
opens downward. The maximum point on the
parabola shows the maximum height. The
positive zero shows the time that the ball hits
the ground (when height is zero).

**4.** Sample: The graph does not cross the $x$-axis
when there is no solution. The graph has
its vertex on the $x$-axis when there is one
solution. The graph crosses the $x$-axis two
times when there are two solutions.

**5.** $y = kx$

Let $x = 15$ and $y = 30$.

$30 = k(15)$

$2 = k$

**6.** $h = -16t^2 + 7t + 7$

Let $h = 0 : 0 = -16t^2 + 7t + 7$

Graph the related
function $f(x) = -16x^2 + 7x + 7$.

Use the maximum function to find the vertex:
$(0.22, 7.77)$

The maximum height is $7.77$ feet.

Use the Zero function to find the zeros.
The solutions are $x = -0.48$ and $x = 0.92$.
Since time is not negative, the basketball hits
the ground at $0.92$ seconds.

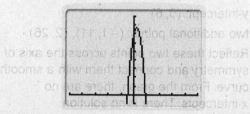

**7.** $y = \dfrac{1}{4}(x - 4)^2 + 5$

$= \dfrac{1}{4}(x^2 - 8x + 16) + 5$

$= \dfrac{1}{4}x^2 - 2x + 9$

**Saxon** Algebra 1

$x = -\dfrac{b}{2a} = \dfrac{-2}{2\left(\frac{1}{4}\right)} = 4$

The answer is **B**.

**8.** $-7x^2 - 10 = 0$

Graph the related
function $f(x) = -7x^2 - 10$.

axis of symmetry: $x = 0$

vertex: $(0, -10)$

$y$-intercept: $(0, -10)$

two additional points: $(-1, -17)$, $(2, -38)$

Reflect these two points across the axis of
symmetry and connect them with a smooth
curve. From the graph, there are no
$x$-intercepts. There is no solution.

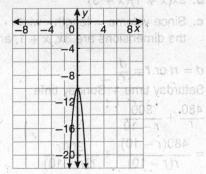

**9.** $\dfrac{6}{x} = \dfrac{8}{x + 7}$

$6(x + 7) = 8x$

$6x + 42 = 8x$

$42 = 2x$

$21 = x$

**10.** $P(\text{black, black, 6}) = \dfrac{1}{2} \cdot \dfrac{1}{2} \cdot \dfrac{1}{6} = \dfrac{1}{24}$

**11.** $\dfrac{x + 5}{6} = \dfrac{6}{x}$

$x(x + 5) = 6 \cdot 6$

$x^2 + 5x = 36$

$x^2 + 5x - 36 = 0$

$(x - 4)(x + 9) = 0$

$x = 4 \quad \text{or} \quad x = -9$

The length is 4 millimeters.

**12. a.** They worked together $t$ hours and Henry
worked for an additional 0.5 hour, so
Henry worked $t + 0.5$ hours.

**b.** $\dfrac{1}{4}(t + 0.5) + \dfrac{1}{3}t = 1$

$12\left[\dfrac{1}{4}(t + 0.5)\right] + 12\left(\dfrac{1}{3}t\right) = 12(1)$

$3(t + 0.5) + 4t = 12$

$3t + 1.5 + 4t = 12$

$7t = 10.5$

$t = 1.5 \text{ hours}$

**c.** $t + 0.5$

$= 1.5 + 0.5$

$= 2 \text{ hours}$

**13.** $\dfrac{a^2 + 10a - 24}{a - 2}$

$= \dfrac{(a + 12)(a - 2)}{a - 2}$

$= a + 12$

**14.** $\sqrt{49y^5}$

$= \sqrt{49y^4 \cdot y}$

$= \sqrt{49y^4} \cdot \sqrt{y}$

$= 7y^2\sqrt{y}$

**15.** $|3x - 270| = 30$

$3x - 270 = 30 \quad \text{or} \quad 3x - 270 = -30$

$3x = 300 \qquad\qquad 3x = 240$

$x = 100 \qquad\qquad\quad x = 80$

minimum = 80 objects

maximum = 100 objects

**16.** $\dfrac{|x - 4 \cdot 85|}{4} = 5$

$|x - 340| = 20$

$x - 340 = 20 \quad \text{or} \quad x - 340 = -20$

$x = 360 \qquad\qquad x = 320$

minimum = 320 objects

maximum = 360 objects

**17.** $|10x| - 3 = 87$

$|10x| = 90$

$10x = 90 \quad \text{or} \quad 10x = -90$

$x = 9 \qquad\qquad x = -9$

$\{-9, 9\}$

**18.** $\dfrac{7x}{x^2 + 3x - 18} - \dfrac{2x + 1}{7x + 42}$

$= \dfrac{7x}{(x - 3)(x + 6)} - \dfrac{2x + 1}{7(x + 6)}$

$= \dfrac{7x \cdot 7}{7(x - 3)(x + 6)} - \dfrac{(2x + 1)(x - 3)}{7(x + 6)(x - 3)}$

$= \dfrac{49x - (2x^2 - 5x - 3)}{7(x - 3)(x + 6)}$

$= \dfrac{-2x^2 + 54x + 3}{7(x - 3)(x + 6)}$ miles

**19.** $y = 5x^2 - 10x + 5$

axis of symmetry: $x = -\dfrac{b}{2a} = -\dfrac{-10}{2(5)} = 1$

vertex: $y = 5(1)^2 - 10(1) + 5 = 0$,
or $(1, 0)$

$y$-intercept: $c = 5$, $(0, 5)$

one additional point: Let $x = 3$.
$y = 5(3)^2 - 10(3) + 5 = 20$, or $(3, 20)$

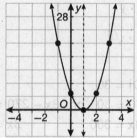

**20.** Sample: Shade the half-plane to the left of the vertical line.

**21.** **A** $(0, 0)$:     $0 + 2(0) < 5$
                $0 < 5$  True

**B** $(2, 1)$:     $2 + 2(1) < 5$
                $4 < 5$  True

**C** $(3, -4)$:   $3 + 2(-4) < 5$
                $-5 < 5$  True

**D** $(-1, 3)$:   $-1 + 2(3) < 5$
                $5 < 5$  False

The answer is **D**.

**22.**         $b(b + 23) = 50$
        $b^2 + 23b - 50 = 0$
        $(b - 2)(b + 25) = 0$
                $b = 2$  or  $b = -25$

The boy is 2 years old and the father is
$2 + 23 = 25$ years old.

**23.** Student B; Sample: Student A did not put the equation in standard form before factoring.

**24.** $y + 2x^2 = 12 + x$
$y = -2x^2 + x + 12$
Since $a = -2$, $a < 0$, the graph opens downward.

**25.**     $a^2 + b^2 = c^2$
      $18^2 + 80^2 = 82^2$
      $324 + 6400 = 6724$
               $6724 = 6724$
Yes.

**26. a.** $3x^3 + 12x^2 + 9x$
        $= 3x(x^2 + 4x + 3)$

**b.** $3x(x + 1)(x + 3)$

**c.** Since volume = length · width · height, the dimensions are $3x$, $x + 1$, and $x + 3$.

**27.** $d = rt$ or $t = \dfrac{d}{r}$

Saturday time + Sunday time

$\dfrac{480}{r} + \dfrac{300}{r - 10}$

$= \dfrac{480(r - 10)}{r(r - 10)} + \dfrac{300r}{r(r - 10)}$

$= \dfrac{480r - 4800 + 300r}{r(r - 10)}$

$= \dfrac{780r - 4800}{r(r - 10)}$

$= \dfrac{60(13r - 80)}{r(r - 10)}$

**28. a.** $|x - 120| \le 5$

**b.**   $x - 120 \le 5$  or  $x - 120 \ge -5$
              $x \le 125$            $x \ge 115$
        $115 \le x \le 125$

**29.** no; Sample: If there are no common factors, then the expression is in the simplest form;

$\dfrac{x^2 - 4}{2x^2 + 12x + 18} = \dfrac{(x - 2)(x + 2)}{2(x + 3)(x + 3)}$

**30.** Let $x$ = the original price.
$x - 0.09x = \$227,500$
$0.91x = \$227,500$
$x = \$250,000$

# INVESTIGATION 10

## Practice Investigation 10

**a.** $f(x) = ax^2 + c$
$f(x) = 2x^2 + 1$

The graph is narrower ($|a| > 1$) and moved 1 unit up ($c = 1$).

**b.** $f(x) = ax^2 + c$
$f(x) = -3x^2 - 2$

The graph is narrower ($|a| > 1$) and opens downward ($a < 0$) and moved 2 units down ($c = -2$).

**c.** $f(x) = ax^2 + c$
$f(x) = \frac{1}{2}x^2 + 2$

The graph is wider ($|a| < 1$) and moved 2 units up ($c = 2$).

**d.** $f(x) = ax^2 + c$
$f(x) = -\frac{1}{2}x^2 - 1$

The graph is wider ($|a| < 1$) and opens downward ($a < 0$) and moved 1 unit down ($c = -1$).

**e.** $f(x) = 2x^2 - 4$
$f(x) = 2x^2 - 4 + 2$
$f(x) = 2x^2 - 2$

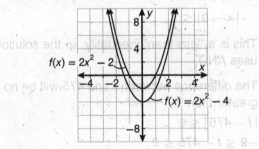

$f(x) = 2x^2 - 2$
$f(x) = 2x^2 - 4$

**f.** $f(x) = 3x^2 + 5$
$f(x) = -3x^2 + 5 - 4$
$f(x) = -3x^2 + 1$

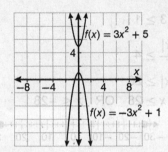

$f(x) = 3x^2 + 5$
$f(x) = -3x^2 + 1$

# LESSON 101

## Warm Up 101

**1.** inequality

**2.** $|-8 + 5| - 7$
$|-3| - 7$
$3 - 7$
$-4$

**3.** $|2 \cdot -6| + 14$
$= |-12| + 14$
$= 12 + 14$
$= 26$

**4.** $3x - 7 > 17$
$3x > 17 + 7$
$3x > 24$
$x > 24 \div 3$
$x > 8$

**5.** $-5x + 12 \geq 37$
$-5x \geq 37 - 12$
$-5x \geq 25$
$x \leq 25 \div -5$
$x \leq -5$

## Lesson Practice 101

**a.** $5|x| + 6 < 31$
$5|x| < 25$
$|x| < 5$
$-5 < x < 5$

**b.** $\dfrac{|x|}{7} - 3 \geq 1$

$\dfrac{|x|}{7} \geq 4$

$|x| \geq 28$

$x \geq 28 \quad \text{OR} \quad x \leq -28$

**c.** $-4|x| + 9 > -1$

$-4|x| > -10$

$|x| < 2.5$

$-2.5 < x < 2.5$

**d.** $|x - 9| + 3 \leq 10$

$|x - 9| \leq 7$

$x - 9 \leq 7 \quad \text{AND} \quad x - 9 \geq -7$

$2 \leq x \leq 16$

**e.** $\left|\dfrac{x}{2} + 5\right| - 9 < -2$

$\left|\dfrac{x}{2} + 5\right| < 7$

$\dfrac{x}{2} + 5 < 7 \quad \text{AND} \quad \dfrac{x}{2} + 5 > -7$

$\dfrac{x}{2} < 2 \quad \text{AND} \quad \dfrac{x}{2} > -12$

$x < 4 \quad \text{AND} \quad x > -24$

$-24 < x < 4$

**f.** $|5x - 5| - 12 > -2$

$|5x - 5| > 10$

$5x - 5 > 10 \quad \text{OR} \quad 5x - 5 < -10$

$5x > 15 \quad \text{OR} \quad 5x < -5$

$x > 3 \quad \text{OR} \quad x < -1$

**g.** The difference between $w$ and 21 ounces must be less than or equal to 1 ounce.

$|w - 21| \leq 1$

$-1 \leq w - 21 \leq 1$

$20 \leq w \leq 22$

The largest acceptable weight is 22 ounces.

**Practice 101**

**1.** $7|x| - 4 \geq 3$

$7|x| \geq 7$

$|x| \geq 1$

$x \geq 1 \quad \text{OR} \quad x \leq -1$

**2.** Student A is correct. Student B did not isolate the absolute-value expression before removing the absolute-value bars.

**3.** Sample: (1) Subtract 11 from each side. (2) Multiply each side by 2. (3) Rewrite as a compound inequality.

**4.** $\dfrac{pt^{-2}}{m^3}\left(\dfrac{p^{-2}wt}{4m^{-1}} + 6t^4 w^{-1} - \dfrac{w}{m^{-3}}\right)$

$= \dfrac{p^{-1}wt^{-1}}{4m^2} + \dfrac{6pt^2 w^{-1}}{m^3} - \dfrac{pt^{-2}w}{1}$

$= \dfrac{w}{4ptm^2} + \dfrac{6pt^2}{wm^3} - \dfrac{pw}{t^2}$

**5.** $-a|x - b| \geq -c$

$|x - b| \leq \dfrac{c}{a}$

This is a "less than" inequality, so the solution uses AND.

**6.** The difference between $t$ and 475 will be no greater than 9.

$|t - 475| \leq 9$

$-9 \leq t - 475 \leq 9$

$466 \leq t \leq 484$

The greatest possible temperature is 484°F.

**7.** Student A is correct. Sample: A parabola can cross the $x$-axis once, twice, or not at all.

**8. a.** Graph the related function $f(t) = -16t^2 + 2t + 9$.

**Saxon** Algebra 1

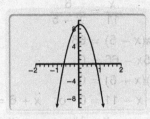

Use the CALC maximum function to find the $y$-coordinate of the vertex. The maximum height of the ball is about 9.1 feet.

b. Use the CALC zero function to find the $x$-intercepts. The ball hits the ground at about 0.82 seconds.

c. Use the CALC maximum to find the $x$-coordinate of the vertex. The time when the ball is at its maximum height is about 0.06 seconds.

9. $(6w^3 - 48w^5)$
$= 6w^3(1 - 8w^2)$
$= 2 \cdot 3 \cdot w \cdot w \cdot w \cdot (1 - 8w^2)$
$(9w - 72w^3)$
$= 9w(1 - 8w^2)$
$= 3 \cdot 3 \cdot w \cdot (1 - 8w^2)$
The LCM is:
$2 \cdot 3 \cdot 3 \cdot w \cdot w \cdot w \cdot (1 - 8w^2)$
$= 18w^3 (1 - 8w^2)$

10. $A = -2t^2 + 5t + 125$
$60 = -2t^2 + 5t + 125$
$0 = -2t^2 + 5t + 65$

Graph the related function on a graphing calculator: $f(t) = -2t^2 + 5t + 65$. Use the CALC zero function to find the $x$-intercepts $t \approx -4.59$ and $t \approx 7.09$.

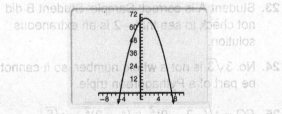

The spill will be 60 square feet at about 7.09 seconds.

11.   $x^2 + 9 = -6x$
$x^2 + 6x + 9 = 0$
axis of symmetry:    $x = -3$
vertex:    $(-3, 0)$
$y$-intercept:    9
additional points:    $(-4, 1), (-5, 4)$

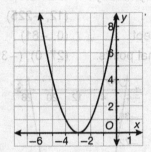

The solution is $x = -3$.

12. $|8x| + 4 = 28$
$|8x| = 24$
$8x = 24$   and   $8x = -24$
$x = 3$   and   $x = -3$
The solution set is $\{-3, 3\}$.

13. $\dfrac{4}{r - 2} + \dfrac{r^2}{2 - r}$

$= \dfrac{4}{r - 2} + \dfrac{r^2}{-(r - 2)}$

$= \dfrac{4}{r - 2}\left(\dfrac{-1}{-1}\right) + \dfrac{r^2}{-(r - 2)}$

$= \dfrac{-4}{-(r - 2)} + \dfrac{r^2}{-(r - 2)}$

$= \dfrac{r^2 - 4}{-(r - 2)}$

$= \dfrac{(r + 2)(r - 2)}{-(r - 2)}$

$= -(r + 2)$

Mia walked $-(r + 2)$ miles.

14. $\dfrac{5}{x - 3} - \dfrac{2}{x - 2}$

$= \dfrac{5}{x - 3}\left(\dfrac{x - 2}{x - 2}\right) - \dfrac{2}{x - 2}\left(\dfrac{x - 3}{x - 3}\right)$

$= \dfrac{5x - 10}{(x - 3)(x - 2)} - \dfrac{2x - 6}{(x - 3)(x - 2)}$

$= \dfrac{3x - 4}{(x - 3)(x - 2)}$

**Saxon** Algebra 1

**15.** $h = -16t^2 + vt + s$

$h = -16(3)^2 + 62(3) + 0$

$h = 42$

The ball is 42 feet above the ground.

**16.** $y = x^2 - 24x - 81$

axis of symmetry: $x = 12$

vertex: $(12, -225)$

$y$-intercept: $(0, -81)$

additional points: $(27, 0), (-3, 0)$

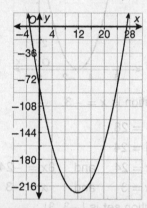

The mother is 27 years old.

**17.** $y \le 3$

$2 \le 3$ is true, so $(-7, 2)$ is a solution of the inequality.

**18.** Sample:

$\left(4 \cdot \dfrac{3}{4} - 3\right)\left(5 \cdot \dfrac{3}{4} + 7\right) = 0$

$(0)\left(5 \cdot \dfrac{3}{4} + 7\right) = 0$

$0 = 0$

**19.** $0 = x^2 - 10x - 39$

$0 = (x - 13)(x + 3)$

$x - 13 = 0$ or $x + 3 = 0$

$x = 13$ $x = -3$

check:

$0 = (13)^2 - 10(13) - 39$

$0 = 169 - 130 - 39$

$0 = 0$ ✓

$0 = (-3)^2 - 10(-3) - 39$

$0 = 9 + 30 - 39$

$0 = 0$ ✓

The roots are $\{13, -3\}$. The answer is **D**.

**20.** $\dfrac{x}{11} = \dfrac{6}{x - 5}$

$x(x - 5) = 66$

$x^2 - 5x - 66 = 0$

$(x - 11)(x + 6) = 0$

$x - 11 = 0$ or $x + 6 = 0$

$x = 11$ $x = -6$

check:

$\dfrac{-6}{11} = \dfrac{6}{-6 - 5}$

$-\dfrac{6}{11} = -\dfrac{6}{11}$ ✓

$\dfrac{11}{11} = \dfrac{6}{11 - 5}$

$1 = 1$ ✓

The solution is $x = -6$ or $x = 11$.

**21.** $-8x^2 - 12 = 3 - y$

$y = 8x^2 + 15$

The coefficient of the quadratic term is positive, so the parabola opens upward.

**22.** Let $h$ be the time for both women to do the copy job together. Maria's rate is 1 copy job per hour. Lachelle's rate is $\frac{1}{2}$ copy job per hour.

(Maria's rate)$h$ + (Lachelle's rate)$h = 1$

$h + \dfrac{1}{2}h = 1$

$2h + 2\left(\dfrac{1}{2}\right)h = 2$

$3h = 2$

$h = \dfrac{2}{3}$

Working together, they can finish the job in $\frac{2}{3}$ of an hour.

**23.** Student A is correct; Sample: Student B did not check to see that $-2$ is an extraneous solution.

**24.** No. $3\sqrt{3}$ is not a whole number, so it cannot be part of a Pythagorean triple.

**25.** $PQ = \sqrt{(-2 - 0)^2 + (1 - 2)^2} = \sqrt{5}$

$QR = \sqrt{(0 - 1)^2 + (2 + 2)^2} = \sqrt{17}$

$RS = \sqrt{(1+1)^2 + (-2+3)^2} = \sqrt{5}$

$PS = \sqrt{(-2+1)^2 + (1+3)^2} = \sqrt{17}$

The length of $PS$ is not equal to the length of $PQ$ and $RS$. $PQRS$ is not a rhombus.

**26. a.** Multiply first:

$$\frac{5x^2y^2}{3x^3y^3} \cdot \frac{9xy^2}{25xy^3}$$

$$= \frac{\overset{3}{45}x^3y^4}{\underset{5}{75}x^4y^6}$$

$$= \frac{3}{5xy^2}$$

**b.** Simplify first:

$$\frac{5x^2y^2}{3x^3y^3} \cdot \frac{9xy^2}{25xy^3}$$

$$= \frac{\cancel{5}x^2y^2}{\cancel{3}x^3y^3} \cdot \frac{\overset{3}{\cancel{9}}xy^2}{\underset{5}{\cancel{25}}xy^3}$$

$$= \frac{3}{5xy^2}$$

**c.** Sample: simplifying before multiplying, because I can cancel out like terms before needing to multiply anything.

**27.** $|x - 974.6| \le 0.1$

$-0.1 \le x - 974.6 \le 0.1$

$974.5 \le x \le 974.7$

974.5 974.6 974.7

**28. a.** $\dfrac{\dfrac{2x^2 - 4x}{7x^3}}{\dfrac{3x - 6}{9x}}$

$$= \frac{2x^2 - 4x}{7x^3} \div \frac{3x - 6}{9x}$$

$$= \frac{2x^2 - 4x}{7x^3} \cdot \frac{9x}{3x - 6}$$

$$= \frac{2x(x-2)}{7x^3} \cdot \frac{3(3x)}{3(x-2)}$$

$$= \frac{6}{7x} \text{ miles per hour}$$

**b.** $\dfrac{\dfrac{6}{7x}}{\dfrac{1}{x^2}}$

$$= \frac{6}{7x} \cdot \frac{x^2}{1}$$

$$= \frac{6x}{7} \text{ miles per hour}$$

**29.** Write the remainder over the divisor.

$$\frac{5}{3x^2 + 7x + 8}$$

**30.** $f(x) = x^2$; Its graph is a parabola opening upward with its vertex at the origin, $(0, 0)$.

## LESSON 102

### Warm Up 102

**1.** square root

**2.** $\sqrt{81} = 9$

**3.** $-\sqrt{25} = -5$

**4.** $\sqrt{24} = \sqrt{4 \cdot 6} = 2\sqrt{6}$

**5.** $\sqrt{\dfrac{9}{49}} = \dfrac{\sqrt{9}}{\sqrt{49}} = \dfrac{3}{7}$

### Lesson Practice 102

**a.** $x^2 = 81$

$\sqrt{x^2} = \pm\sqrt{81}$

$x = \pm 9$

check:

$9^2 = 81 \qquad (-9)^2 = 81$

$81 = 81$ ✓ $\quad 81 = 81$ ✓

**b.** $x^2 = -36$

$\sqrt{x^2} = \pm\sqrt{-36}$

$x \ne \pm\sqrt{-36}$

No real solution exists.

**c.** $x^2 + 5 = 54$

$x^2 = 49$

$\sqrt{x^2} = \pm\sqrt{49}$

$x = \pm 7$

check:

$7^2 + 5 = 54 \qquad (-7)^2 + 5 = 54$

$49 + 5 = 54$      $49 + 5 = 54$

   $54 = 54$ ✓      $54 = 54$ ✓

**d.** $3x^2 - 75 = 0$

     $3x^2 = 75$

      $x^2 = 25$

   $\sqrt{x^2} = \pm\sqrt{25}$

       $x = \pm 5$

check:

$3(5)^2 - 75 = 0$    $3(-5)^2 - 75 = 0$

$3(25) - 75 = 0$    $3(25) - 75 = 0$

     $0 = 0$ ✓        $0 = 0$ ✓

**e.** $\sqrt{x^2} = \pm\sqrt{72}$

  $\sqrt{x^2} = \pm\sqrt{9 \cdot 4 \cdot 2}$

  $\sqrt{x^2} = \pm\sqrt{9} \cdot \sqrt{4} \cdot \sqrt{2}$

     $x = \pm(3)(2)\sqrt{2}$

     $x = \pm 6\sqrt{2}$

     $x \approx \pm 6(1.414213562)$

     $x \approx \pm 8.485$

check:

$(8.485)^2 \approx 72$    $(-8.485)^2 \approx 72$

  $71.99 \approx 72$ ✓     $71.99 \approx 72$ ✓

**f.** $5x^2 - 60 = 0$

     $5x^2 = 60$

      $x^2 = 12$

   $\sqrt{x^2} = \pm\sqrt{12}$

      $x \approx \pm 3.464$

check:

$5(3.464)^2 - 60 \approx 0$

$5(11.999296) - 60 \approx 0$

$59.99648 - 60 \approx 0$

        $-0.003 \approx 0$ ✓

$5(-3.464)^2 - 60 \approx 0$

$5(11.999296) - 60 \approx 0$

$59.99648 - 60 \approx 0$

        $-0.003 \approx 0$ ✓

**g.** $16t^2 - 1600 = 0$

    $16t^2 = 1600$

      $t^2 = 100$

   $\sqrt{t^2} = \pm\sqrt{100}$

      $t = \pm 10$

The ball takes 10 seconds to hit the ground.

check:

$16(10)^2 - 1600 = 0$

$16(100) - 1600 = 0$

         $0 = 0$ ✓

## Practice 102

**1.** $4(2p^{-2}q)^2(3p^3q)^2$

$= 4\left(2^2(p^{-2})^2q^2\right)\left(3^2(p^3)^2q^2\right)$

$= 4(4p^{-4}q^2)(9p^6q^2)$

$= 144p^2q^4$

**2.** $(7\sqrt{8})^2$

$= 7^2(\sqrt{8})^2$

$= 49 \cdot 8$

$= 392$

**3.** Student B is correct. Sample: Both have worked the problem correctly, but Student A did not realize that a negative measurement is impossible in this situation.

**4. a.** $x^2 = 12600 + 1800$

  **b.**   $x^2 = 14400$

    $\sqrt{x^2} = \pm\sqrt{14400}$

       $x = \pm 120$

  The property is 120 feet on each side.

  **c.** $P = 4s$

    $P = 4(120)$

    $P = 480$

  Dominic will need 480 feet of fencing.

**5.** $1000(1 + r)^2 = 1123.6$

     $(1 + r)^2 = 1.1236$

  $\sqrt{(1 + r)^2} = \pm\sqrt{1.1236}$

      $1 + r = \pm 1.06$

         $r = 0.06$   or   $r = -2.06$

The interest rate is 6%.

check:

$1000(1 + 0.06)^2 = 1123.6$

   $1000(1.1236) = 1123.6$

        $1123.6 = 1123.6$ ✓

**6.** $8x^2 - 72 = 0$

    $8x^2 = 72$

     $x^2 = 9$

**Saxon** Algebra 1

$$\sqrt{x^2} = \pm\sqrt{9}$$
$$x = \pm 3$$

The statement is true.

check:

| $8(3)^2 - 72 = 0$ | $8(-3)^2 - 72 = 0$ |
|---|---|
| $72 - 72 = 0$ | $72 - 72 = 0$ |
| $0 = 0$ ✓ | $0 = 0$ ✓ |

**7.**
$$A = s^2$$
$$680 = s^2$$
$$\pm\sqrt{680} = \sqrt{s^2}$$
$$\pm 26.077 \approx s$$

The length of a side is about 26.077 km.

**8.** $\dfrac{|x|}{3} + 6 < 13$

$$\dfrac{|x|}{3} < 7$$
$$|x| < 21$$
$$-21 < x < 21$$

```
      ◁──┼─○─┼────┼────┼────┼─○─┼──▷
        -20  -10   0    10   20
```

**9. a.** $|x + 1| - 8 \leq -4$
$$|x + 1| \leq 4$$
$$-4 \leq x + 1 \leq 4$$
$$-5 \leq x \leq 3$$

**b.** $|y - 4| + 6 \leq 9$
$$|y - 4| \leq 3$$
$$-3 \leq y - 4 \leq 3$$
$$1 \leq y \leq 7$$

**c.** The coordinates of the vertices are $(-5, 7)$, $(3, 7)$, $(3, 1)$, and $(-5, 1)$.

**10.**
$$
\begin{array}{r}
-7x^2 - x + 7 \\
\underline{x - 7} \\
49x^2 + 7x - 49 \\
\underline{-7x^3 - x^2 + 7x} \\
-7x^3 + 48x^2 + 14x - 49
\end{array}
$$

**11.** $x = -\dfrac{0}{2(4)} = 0$

The axis of symmetry is $x = 0$.

$$y = 4x^2 + 6$$
$$= 4(0)^2 + 6 = 6$$

The vertex is $(0, 6)$.

The $y$-intercept, $c$, is 6.

$$y = 4x^2 + 6$$
$$= 4(1)^2 + 6 = 10$$

A point on the parabola is $(1, 10)$.

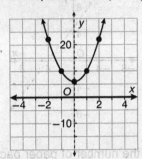

**12.** $h = -16t^2 + 30$
$$= -16(1)^2 + 30$$
$$= 14$$

After 1 second, the balloon is 14 feet above the ground.

**13. a.** $|t - (-187.65)| < 1.65$
$$-1.65 < t + 187.65 < 1.65$$
$$-189.3 < t < -186$$

```
    ◁─┼┼┼┼┼○┼┼┼┼┼┼┼┼┼┼┼┼○┼┼┼┼┼▷
     -190      -188      -186
```

**b.** $-186°C$; $-189.3°C$

**14. a.** For a perfect square trinomial, $a^2 + 2ab + b^2$, the factors are $(a + b)^2$. Where $a = x$ and $b = 5$:
$$x^2 + 10x + 25$$
$$= (x + 5)^2$$

**b.** For the difference of two squares, $a^2 - b^2$, the factors are $(a + b)(a - b)$. Where $a = x$ and $b = 5$:
$$x^2 - 25$$
$$= (x + 5)(x - 5)$$

**15.** The boundary line is:
$$5x + 4y = 20$$
$$4y = -5x + 20$$
$$y = -\dfrac{5}{4}x + 5$$

Test $(0, 0)$:
$$y > -\dfrac{5}{4}x + 5$$
$$0 > -\dfrac{5}{4}(0) + 5$$
$$0 \not> 5$$

Shade the side of the boundary line that does NOT contain (0, 0).

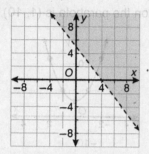

16. Let $x$ be the number of paper packs Tim buys at \$2 each and let $y$ be the number of paint packs he buys at \$10 each. The total cost must be less than or equal to \$40.

$$2x + 10y \leq 40$$
$$10y \leq -2x + 40$$
$$y \leq -\frac{1}{5}x + 4$$

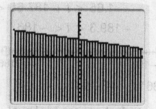

17. By the Zero Product Property,

$$x(x + 12) = 0$$
$$x = 0$$

or $x + 12 = 0$

$$x = -12$$

The solution set is {0, −12}.

18. Sample: $\dfrac{1}{1-1} = \dfrac{3}{2(1)-2}$

$$\frac{1}{0} = \frac{3}{0}$$

which is undefined. This shows that 1 is an extraneous solution.

19. $\dfrac{2}{x-3} = \dfrac{x}{9}$

$$2(9) = x(x - 3)$$
$$18 = x^2 - 3x$$
$$0 = x^2 - 3x - 18$$
$$0 = (x + 3)(x - 6)$$

$x + 3 = 0$  or  $x - 6 = 0$

$x = -3$  $x = 6$

Check:

$$\frac{2}{-3-3} = -\frac{3}{9} \quad \text{or} \quad \frac{2}{6-3} = \frac{6}{9}$$
$$-\frac{2}{6} = -\frac{3}{9} \qquad \frac{2}{3} = \frac{2}{3} \checkmark$$
$$-\frac{1}{3} = -\frac{1}{3} \checkmark$$

The answer is **B**.

20. $\dfrac{m}{m^2 - 4} + \dfrac{2}{3m + 6}$

$$= \frac{m}{(m+2)(m-2)} + \frac{2}{3(m+2)}$$
$$= \frac{m}{(m+2)(m-2)}\left(\frac{3}{3}\right) + \frac{2}{3(m+2)}\left(\frac{m-2}{m-2}\right)$$
$$= \frac{3m}{3(m+2)(m-2)} + \frac{2m-4}{3(m+2)(m-2)}$$
$$= \frac{5m - 4}{3(m+2)(m-2)}$$

21. Graph $f(x) = x^2 - 3x + 12$.

axis of symmetry  $x = \dfrac{3}{2}$

vertex  $\left(\dfrac{3}{2}, \dfrac{37}{4}\right)$

$y$-intercept  12

additional points  (1, 10) and (2, 10)

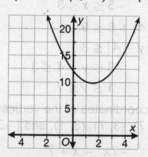

Graph $f(x) = x^2 + 11x + 11$.

axis of symmetry: $x = -\dfrac{11}{2}$

vertex: $\left(-\dfrac{11}{2}, -\dfrac{77}{4}\right)$

$y$-intercept: 11

additional points: (−6, −19) and (−5, −19)

**Saxon** Algebra 1

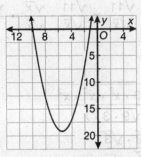

Student A is correct. Sample: Student B wrote an equation that forms a parabola that crosses the x-axis twice, so it has two solutions.

**22.** Graph the related function on a graphing calculator, $f(t) = -16t^2 + 4t + 10$.

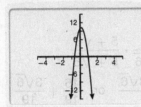

Use the CALC maximum function to find the vertex. Use the CALC zero function to find the x-intercepts.

Maximum height is 10.25 feet. The rocket hits the ground at about 0.93 seconds.

**23.** Graph $x^2 + 12x + 40 = 0$.

axis of symmetry:  $x = -6$
vertex:  $(-6, 4)$
y-intercept:  40
additional points:  $(-5, 5), (-7, 5)$

The graph does not cross the x-axis. The equation has no solution.

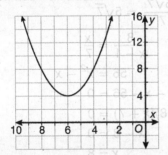

**24.** $M = \left(\dfrac{x_1 + x_2}{2}, \dfrac{y_1 + y_2}{2}\right)$

$= \left(\dfrac{13 + (-7)}{2}, \dfrac{-3 + (-3)}{2}\right)$

$= (3, -3)$

**25.** $-3y^3 - 9yz + 5y^2 + 15z$
$= (-3y^3 - 9yz) + (5y^2 + 15z)$
$= -3y(y^2 + 3z) + 5(y^2 + 3z)$
$= (-3y + 5)(y^2 + 3z)$
Check:
$(-3y + 5)(y^2 + 3z)$
$= -3y^3 + 5y^2 - 9yz + 15z$
$= -3y^3 - 9yz + 5y^2 + 15z$ ✓

**26. a.** Let $x$ be the width of the yard. Let $x + 7$ by the length.
Area = width · length
$144 = x(x + 7)$
Sample: the formula needs to be set in the form $ax^2 + bx + c = 0$ in order to solve for $x$.

**b.**  $144 = x^2 + 7x$
$x^2 + 7x - 144 = 0$
$(x + 16)(x - 9) = 0$
$x + 16 = 0$
$x = -16$
or
$x - 9 = 0$
$x = 9$
The yard is 9 feet wide and 16 feet long.

**27.** $3^2 + 7^2 = 8^2$
$9 + 49 = 64$
$58 \neq 64$
3, 7, and 8 are not a Pythagorean triple.

**28.** $r = \dfrac{d}{t}$

$= \dfrac{\dfrac{9x}{4x - 10} + \dfrac{5x^2}{3x + 9}}{\dfrac{x}{2x^2 + x - 15}}$

$= \left(\dfrac{9x}{4x - 10} + \dfrac{5x^2}{3x + 9}\right)\left(\dfrac{2x^2 + x - 15}{x}\right)$

$= \left(\dfrac{9x}{2(2x - 5)} + \dfrac{5x^2}{3(x + 3)}\right)\left(\dfrac{(2x - 5)(x + 3)}{x}\right)$

$= \left(\dfrac{27x(x + 3) + 10x^2(2x - 5)}{6(2x - 5)(x + 3)}\right)\left(\dfrac{(2x - 5)(x + 3)}{x}\right)$

$$= \frac{20x^2 + 23x + 81}{6}$$

**29. a.** $\dfrac{x^2 - 64}{x + 8}$

$$= \frac{(x + 8)(x - 8)}{(x + 8)}$$

The width is $x - 8$ feet.

**b.**

$$\begin{array}{r} x^2 + 6x - 16 \\ x - 8 \overline{\smash{\big)}\ x^3 - 2x^2 - 64x + 128} \\ \underline{x^3 - 8x^2} \\ 6x^2 - 64x \\ \underline{6x^2 - 48x} \\ -16x + 128 \\ \underline{-16x + 128} \end{array}$$

The length is $x^2 + 6x - 16$ feet.

**30.** Sample: When the operations are on the inside, write two equations to represent the absolute-value equation and solve them. When the operations are on the outside, isolate the absolute value first, then write two equations to represent the absolute-value equation and solve them.

## LESSON 103

### Warm Up 103

**1.** radicand

**2.** $\sqrt{150}$

$$= \sqrt{2 \cdot 3 \cdot 5 \cdot 5} = 5\sqrt{6}$$

**3.** $3\sqrt{72}$

$$= 3\sqrt{2 \cdot 2 \cdot 2 \cdot 3 \cdot 3} = 18\sqrt{2}$$

**4.** $\sqrt{48x^3}$

$$= \sqrt{2 \cdot 2 \cdot 2 \cdot 2 \cdot 3} \cdot \sqrt{x^3}$$

$$= 4\sqrt{3} \cdot x\sqrt{x} = 4x\sqrt{3x}$$

**5.** $\sqrt{12} \cdot \sqrt{15}$

$$= \sqrt{2 \cdot 2 \cdot 3} \cdot \sqrt{3 \cdot 5}$$

$$= \sqrt{2 \cdot 2 \cdot 3 \cdot 3 \cdot 5} = 6\sqrt{5}$$

### Lesson Practice 103

**a.** $\sqrt{\dfrac{5}{3}} = \dfrac{\sqrt{5}}{\sqrt{3}} = \dfrac{\sqrt{5}}{\sqrt{3}} \cdot \dfrac{\sqrt{3}}{\sqrt{3}} = \dfrac{\sqrt{15}}{3}$

**b.** $\sqrt{\dfrac{11}{x}} = \dfrac{\sqrt{11}}{\sqrt{x}} = \dfrac{\sqrt{11}}{\sqrt{x}} \cdot \dfrac{\sqrt{x}}{\sqrt{x}} = \dfrac{\sqrt{11x}}{x}$

**c.** $\dfrac{\sqrt{6x^6}}{\sqrt{27x}}$

$$= \frac{\sqrt{2 \cdot 3 \cdot x^2 \cdot x^2 \cdot x^2}}{\sqrt{9 \cdot 3 \cdot x}}$$

$$= \frac{x^3\sqrt{2} \cdot \sqrt{3}}{3\sqrt{3} \cdot \sqrt{x}}$$

$$= \frac{x^3\sqrt{2}}{3\sqrt{x}} \cdot \frac{\sqrt{x}}{\sqrt{x}}$$

$$= \frac{x^3\sqrt{2x}}{3x} = \frac{x^2\sqrt{2x}}{3}$$

**d.** $\dfrac{3}{5 - \sqrt{6}}$

$$= \frac{3}{5 - \sqrt{6}} \cdot \frac{5 + \sqrt{6}}{5 + \sqrt{6}}$$

$$= \frac{15 + 3\sqrt{6}}{19} \quad \text{or} \quad \frac{15}{19} + \frac{3\sqrt{6}}{19}$$

**e.** $\dfrac{3}{\sqrt{7} - 1}$

$$= \frac{3}{\sqrt{7} - 1} \cdot \frac{\sqrt{7} + 1}{\sqrt{7} + 1}$$

$$= \frac{3\sqrt{7} + 3}{6}$$

$$= \frac{\sqrt{7} + 1}{2} \quad \text{or} \quad \frac{\sqrt{7}}{2} + \frac{1}{2}$$

### Practice 103

**1.** $\dfrac{35}{\sqrt{7}} = \dfrac{35}{\sqrt{7}} \cdot \dfrac{\sqrt{7}}{\sqrt{7}}$

$$= \frac{35\sqrt{7}}{7} = 5\sqrt{7}$$

**2.**

$$\frac{8}{x - 1} = \frac{x}{7}$$

$$56 = x^2 - x$$

$$x^2 - x - 56 = 0$$

$$(x - 8)(x + 7) = 0$$

$$x - 8 = 0$$

$$x = 8$$

$x = 8$

or

$x + 7 = 0$

$x = -7$

check:

$\frac{8}{8 - 1} = \frac{8}{7}$ or $\frac{8}{-7 - 1} = \frac{-7}{7}$

$\frac{8}{7} = \frac{8}{7}$ ✓ $-1 = -1$ ✓

The solutions are is $x = -7$ and $x = 8$.

**3.** Student A is correct. Sample: Student B did not use a conjugate to rationalize the denominator.

**4.** $V = \sqrt{\dfrac{2(150)}{0.0063}}$

$= \sqrt{\dfrac{\frac{300}{63}}{10,000}}$

$= \sqrt{300 \cdot \dfrac{10,000}{63}}$

$= \sqrt{\dfrac{3 \cdot 10^6}{3 \cdot 3 \cdot 7}}$

$= 1000\left(\dfrac{\sqrt{1}}{\sqrt{21}}\right)$

$= 1000\left(\dfrac{\sqrt{1}}{\sqrt{21}} \cdot \dfrac{\sqrt{21}}{\sqrt{21}}\right)$

$= \dfrac{1000\sqrt{21}}{21}$ ft/s

**5.** $\dfrac{c}{40} = \dfrac{400}{100}$

$100c = 16000$

$c = 160$

400% of 40 is 160.

**6.** No; Sample: The radical in the denominator needs to be rationalized.

**7.** $\sqrt{239}$

Check:

$\dfrac{239}{\sqrt{239}} = \sqrt{239}$

$239 = \sqrt{239} \cdot \sqrt{239}$

$239 = 239$

**8. a.** $s + 32 = 47$

$s = 15$

One side is 15 units long.

**b.** $A = s^2$

$A = 15^2 = 225$

The square is 225 square units in area.

**c.** $9x^2 = 225$

$x^2 = 25$

$x = 5$

**9.** $25t^2 - 450 = 0$

$25t^2 = 450$

$t^2 = 18$

$t = \sqrt{18}$

$t \cong 4.243$

The stone will hit the ground in about 4.243 seconds.

**10.** $4x + 2y = 22$

$6x - 5y = 9$

Solve the first equation for $y$.

$2y = 22 - 4x$

$y = 11 - 2x$

Substitute $11 - 2x$ for $y$ in the second equation.

$6x - 5(11 - 2x) = 9$

$6x - 55 + 10x = 9$

$16x = 64$

$x = 4$

Substitute 4 for $x$ in the first equation and solve for $y$.

$4(4) + 2y = 22$

$16 + 2y = 22$

$2y = 6$

$y = 3$

Check:

$4(4) + 2(3) = 22 \qquad 6(4) - 5(3) = 9$

$16 + 6 = 22 \qquad\qquad 24 - 15 = 9$

$22 = 22$ ✓ $\qquad\qquad 9 = 9$ ✓

The solution is (4, 3).

**11.** $5x^2 + 125 = 0$

$5x^2 = -125$

$x^2 = -25$

$$\sqrt{x^2} = \sqrt{-25}$$
$$x = \pm 5\sqrt{-1}$$
False; The solution is $\pm 5\sqrt{-1}$.

**12.** $-6|x| + 20 \geq 2$
$$-6|x| \geq -18$$
$$|x| \leq 3$$
$$-3 \leq x \leq 3$$

**13.** $14x + 2y > 6$
$$2y > -14x + 6$$
$$y > -7x + 3$$

Graph the boundary line with dotted line
$y = -7x + 3$.
Test (0, 0).
$$0 > -7(0) + 3$$
$$0 \not> 3$$
Shade the half-plane that does NOT include
(0, 0).

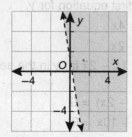

**14.** Student B is correct; Sample: Student A
did not reverse the inequality symbol when
dividing each side by $-12$.

**15.** $\left| \dfrac{x}{7} + 6 \right| - 5 \leq 4$
$$\left| \dfrac{x}{7} + 6 \right| \leq 9$$
$$-9 \leq \dfrac{x}{7} + 6 \leq 9$$
$$-15 \leq \dfrac{x}{7} \leq 3$$
$$-105 \leq x \leq 21$$
The length is the absolute value of the
difference between the endpoints of the
graph.
$|-105 - 21| = 126$
The distance is 126 units.

**16.** The difference between the diameter of a
given tennis ball and $2\frac{5}{16}$ inches must be less
than or equal to $\frac{1}{16}$ of an inch.
$$\left| d - 2\frac{5}{16} \right| \leq \frac{1}{16}$$
$$-\frac{1}{16} \leq d - 2\frac{5}{16} \leq \frac{1}{16}$$
$$2\frac{1}{4} \leq d \leq 2\frac{3}{8}$$
The largest acceptable diameter is $2\frac{3}{8}$ inches.

**17.** $f(x) = 10x^2 - 20$
axis of symmetry: $x = 0$
vertex: $(0, -20)$
$y$-intercept: $(0, -20)$
additional points: $(-1, -10)$, $(1, -10)$,
$\qquad\qquad\qquad\quad (-2, 20)$, $(2, 20)$

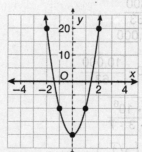

**18.** The ball is on the ground when $h = 0$.
$$0 = -5t^2 + 20t$$
$$0 = -5t(t - 4)$$
$$-5t = 0$$
$$t = 0$$
or
$$t - 4 = 0$$
$$t = 4$$
Check:
$$0 = -5(0)^2 + 20(0) \qquad 0 = -5(4)^2 + 20(4)$$
$$0 = 0 \checkmark \qquad\qquad\quad 0 = -80 + 80$$
$$\qquad\qquad\qquad\qquad\qquad 0 = 0 \checkmark$$
The ball is on the ground at 0 seconds and at
4 seconds.

**19.** $\qquad 0 = x^2 - 170x + 7000$
$$0 = (x - 70)(x - 100)$$
$$x - 70 = 0$$
$$x = 70$$

**Saxon** Algebra 1

or

$x - 100 = 0$

$x = 100$

Check:

$0 = (70)^2 - 170(70) + 7000$

$0 = 4900 - 11900 + 7000$

$0 = 0$ ✔

$0 = (100)^2 - 170(100) + 7000$

$0 = 10,000 - 17,000 + 7000$

$0 = 0$ ✔

**20.** Sample: zeroes or roots

**21.** Rule out choice **A** because $(-2, 6)$ does not satisfy equation **A**.

Rule out choice **B** because $(-2, 6)$ does not satisfy equation **B**.

Rule out choice **C** because the $y$-intercept of equation **C** is $-2$.

Check choice **D**:

$2 = \frac{1}{2}(0)^2 - 0 + 2$

$2 = 2$

$6 = \frac{1}{2}(-2)^2 - (-2) + 2$

$6 = 6$

$14 = \frac{1}{2}(6)^2 - 6 + 2$

$14 = 14$

The answer is **D**.

**22.** $2x^2y + 4xy - 7xyz - 14yz$

$= 2xy(x + 2) - 7yz(x + 2)$

$= (2xy - 7yz)(x + 2)$

**23.** $\frac{90}{24a} \cdot \frac{6a^2b^2}{25b}$

$= \frac{2 \cdot 3 \cdot 3 \cdot 5}{2 \cdot 3 \cdot 4_2 \cdot a} \cdot \frac{2 \cdot 3 \cdot a^2 \cdot b^2}{5 \cdot 5 \cdot b}$

$= \frac{9ab}{10}$

**24.** $15^2 + 36^2 = 39^2$

$225 + 1296 = 1521$

$1521 = 1521$

The side lengths 15, 36, and 39 form a Pythagorean triple.

**25. a.** west: $\frac{300}{230 + w}$; east: $\frac{220}{230 - w}$;

Sample; The numerators represent distance and the denominators represent rate. Add the wind speed to the rate when the plane is going with the wind and subtract it from the rate when the plane is going against the wind.

**b.** $\frac{300}{230 + w} + \frac{220}{230 - w}$

$= \frac{300(230 - w) + 220(230 + w)}{(230 + w)(230 - w)}$

$= \frac{69,000 - 300w + 50,600 + 220w}{(230 + w)(230 - w)}$

$= \frac{119600 - 80w}{(230 + w)(230 - w)}$

**c.** Sample: the total time the plane flew in both directions

**26.** $w = \frac{A}{l}$

$= \frac{x^2 - 14x + 45}{x - 5}$

$= \frac{(x - 5)(x - 9)}{(x - 5)}$

$= x - 9$

The garden is $x - 9$ feet wide.

**27. a.** $|2(8 + 10x) - 66| = 10$

**b.** $|2(8 + 10x) - 66| = 10$

$|16 + 20x - 66| = 10$

$|20x - 50| = 10$

$20x - 50 = 10$

$20x = 60$

$x = 3$

or

$20x - 50 = -10$

$20x = 40$

$x = 2$

The couple can ride for a minimum of 2 hours and a maximum of 3 hours.

**28.** Write each term of the numerator separately over the common denominator, then simplify as needed.

$\frac{4y - 5}{6}$

**Saxon** Algebra 1

$$= \frac{4y}{6} - \frac{5}{6}$$

$$= \frac{2y}{3} - \frac{5}{6}$$

29. The expression cannot be factored. It cannot be written in the form $x^2 + (a + b)x + ab$, because the only possible values of $a$ and $b$ are $a = b = 1$ and $a = b = -1$.

30. $f(x) = ax^2$, where $a > 1$ stretches the parent function vertically and narrows it.

## LESSON 104

### Warm Up 104

1. perfect-square trinomial

2. $\left(\frac{8}{3}\right)^2 = \frac{8}{3} \cdot \frac{8}{3} = \frac{64}{9}$

3. $\left(\frac{12}{3}\right)^2 - 5$

$$= 4^2 - 5$$
$$= 16 - 5$$
$$= 11$$

4. $x^2 + 6x + 9 = 0$

$$(x + 3)(x + 3) = 0$$
$$x + 3 = 0$$
$$x = -3$$

Check:
$$(-3)^2 + 6(-3) + 9 = 0$$
$$9 - 18 + 9 = 0$$
$$0 = 0 \checkmark$$

5. $x^2 - 18x + 81 = 0$

$$(x - 9)(x - 9) = 0$$
$$x - 9 = 0$$
$$x = 9$$

Check:
$$9^2 - 18(9) + 81 = 0$$
$$81 - 162 + 81 = 0$$
$$0 = 0 \checkmark$$

### Lesson Practice 104

a. $\left(\frac{24}{2}\right)^2 = 12^2 = 144$, so the completed square is $x^2 + 24x + 144$

b. $x^2 + 2x = 8$

$$x^2 + 2x + \left(\frac{2}{2}\right)^2 = 8 + \left(\frac{2}{2}\right)^2$$
$$x^2 + 2x + 1 = 9$$
$$(x + 1)^2 = 9$$
$$\sqrt{(x + 1)^2} = \sqrt{9}$$
$$x + 1 = \pm 3$$
$$x + 1 = 3 \quad \text{or} \quad x + 1 = -3$$
$$x = 2 \quad \text{or} \quad x = -4$$

Check:
$$2^2 + 2(2) = 8 \qquad (-4)^2 + 2(-4) = 8$$
$$4 + 4 = 8 \qquad \qquad 16 - 8 = 8$$
$$8 = 8 \checkmark \qquad \qquad 8 = 8 \checkmark$$

c. $x^2 - 14x = 15$

$$x^2 - 14x + \left(\frac{14}{2}\right)^2 = 15 + \left(\frac{14}{2}\right)^2$$
$$x^2 - 14x + 49 = 64$$
$$(x - 7)^2 = 64$$
$$\sqrt{(x - 7)^2} = \sqrt{64}$$
$$x - 7 = \pm 8$$
$$x - 7 = 8 \quad \text{or} \quad x - 7 = -8$$
$$x = 15 \quad \text{or} \quad x = -1$$

Check:
$$(15)^2 - 14(15) = 15$$
$$225 - 210 = 15$$
$$15 = 15 \checkmark$$
$$(-1)^2 - 14(-1) = 15$$
$$1 + 14 = 15$$
$$15 = 15 \checkmark$$

d. $3x^2 + 24x = -27$

$$x^2 + 8x = -9$$
$$x^2 + 8x + \left(\frac{8}{2}\right)^2 = -9 + \left(\frac{8}{2}\right)^2$$
$$x^2 + 8x + 16 = 7$$
$$(x + 4)^2 = 7$$
$$\sqrt{(x + 4)^2} = \sqrt{7}$$
$$x + 4 = \pm\sqrt{7}$$
$$x + 4 = \sqrt{7} \quad \text{or} \quad x + 4 = -\sqrt{7}$$
$$x = -4 + \sqrt{7} \quad \text{or} \quad x = -4 - \sqrt{7}$$
$$x \approx -1.354 \quad \text{or} \quad x \approx -6.646$$

354

Check:

$3(-1.354)^2 + 24(-1.354) \approx -27$

$5.450 - 32.496 \approx -27$

$-27.046 \approx -27$ ✔

$3(-6.646)^2 + 24(-6.646) \approx -27$

$132.508 - 159.504 \approx -27$

$-26.996 \approx -27$ ✔

e. 
$$2x^2 + 6x = -6$$
$$x^2 + 3x = -3$$
$$x^2 + 3x + \left(\frac{3}{2}\right)^2 = -3 + \left(\frac{3}{2}\right)^2$$
$$x^2 + 3x + \frac{9}{4} = -\frac{3}{4}$$
$$\left(x + \frac{3}{2}\right)^2 = -\frac{3}{4}$$
$$\sqrt{\left(x + \frac{3}{2}\right)^2} = \sqrt{-\frac{3}{4}}$$
$$x + \frac{3}{2} = \pm\sqrt{-\frac{3}{4}}$$
$$x = -\frac{3}{2} \pm \frac{\sqrt{-3}}{2}$$

No solution.

f. Let $h$ be the height and $8 + h$ be the length of the base.

$$b \cdot h = A$$
$$(8 + h)h = 20$$
$$h^2 + 8h = 20$$
$$h^2 + 8h + \left(\frac{8}{2}\right)^2 = 20 + \left(\frac{8}{2}\right)^2$$
$$h^2 + 8h + 16 = 36$$
$$(h + 4)^2 = 36$$
$$\sqrt{(h + 4)^2} = \sqrt{36}$$
$$h + 4 = \pm 6$$
$$h + 4 = 6 \quad \text{or} \quad h + 4 = -6$$
$$h = 2 \quad \text{or} \quad h = -10$$

Height must be positive, so the height of the parallelogram is 2 centimeters. The length of the base is $8 + 2$, or 10 centimeters.

**Practice 104**

1. $\left(\frac{100}{2}\right)^2 = 50^2 = 2500$

2. $\left(\frac{-26}{2}\right)^2 = (-13)^2 = 169$

3. $\left(\frac{-30}{2}\right)^2 = (-15)^2 = 225$

The answer is **D**.

4. 
$$6x^2 - 12x - 18 = 0$$
$$x^2 - 2x - 3 = 0$$
$$x^2 - 2x = 3$$
$$x^2 - 2x + \left(\frac{-2}{2}\right)^2 = 3 + \left(\frac{-2}{2}\right)^2$$
$$x^2 - 2x + 1 = 4$$
$$(x - 1)^2 = 4$$
$$\sqrt{(x - 1)^2} = \sqrt{4}$$
$$x - 1 = \pm 2$$
$$x - 1 = 2 \quad \text{or} \quad x - 1 = -2$$
$$x = 3 \quad \text{or} \quad x = -1$$

Check:

$6(3)^2 - 12(3) - 18 = 0$

$54 - 36 - 18 = 0$

$0 = 0$ ✔

$6(-1)^2 - 12(-1) - 18 = 0$

$6 + 12 - 18 = 0$

$0 = 0$ ✔

5. 
$$w \cdot l = A$$
$$x(x + 5) = 24$$
$$x^2 + 5x = 24$$
$$x^2 + 5x + \left(\frac{5}{2}\right)^2 = 24 + \left(\frac{5}{2}\right)^2$$
$$x^2 + 5x + 6.25 = 30.25$$
$$(x + 2.5)^2 = 30.25$$
$$\sqrt{(x + 2.5)^2} = \sqrt{30.25}$$
$$x + 2.5 = \pm 5.5$$
$$x + 2.5 = 5.5 \quad \text{or} \quad x + 2.5 = -5.5$$
$$x = 3 \quad \text{or} \quad x = -8$$

Width must be positive, so the width of the box is 3 inches, and the length is $3 + 5$, or 8 inches. The height is 3 inches.

6. $\frac{\sqrt{3}}{\sqrt{11}} \cdot \frac{\sqrt{11}}{\sqrt{11}} = \frac{\sqrt{33}}{11}$

7. 
$$P(\text{green}) = \frac{6}{8}$$
$$P(\text{yellow}) = \frac{2}{7}$$

**Saxon** Algebra 1

$P(\text{green, then yellow}) = \dfrac{6}{8} \cdot \dfrac{2}{7}$

$= \dfrac{12}{56} = \dfrac{3}{14}$

**8. a.** $A = \pi r^2$

$r^2 = \dfrac{A}{\pi}$

$r = \sqrt{\dfrac{A}{\pi}}$

**b.** $r = \sqrt{\dfrac{A}{\pi}}$

$\approx \sqrt{\dfrac{A}{\frac{22}{7}}}$

$\approx \sqrt{\dfrac{7A}{22}}$

**c.** $r \approx \sqrt{\dfrac{7(6)}{22}} \approx \sqrt{\dfrac{42}{22}} \approx \dfrac{\sqrt{21}}{\sqrt{11}} \cdot \dfrac{\sqrt{11}}{\sqrt{11}} \approx \dfrac{\sqrt{231}}{11}$

**9.** $D = \sqrt{(x_2 - x_1)^2 + (y_2 - y_1)^2}$

$= \sqrt{\left(\dfrac{2\sqrt{5}}{3} - \dfrac{\sqrt{5}}{3}\right)^2 + \left(\dfrac{\sqrt{3}}{4} - \dfrac{3\sqrt{3}}{4}\right)^2}$

$= \sqrt{\left(\dfrac{\sqrt{5}}{3}\right)^2 + \left(\dfrac{-\sqrt{3}}{2}\right)^2}$

$= \sqrt{\dfrac{5}{9} + \dfrac{3}{4}} = \sqrt{\dfrac{47}{36}} = \dfrac{\sqrt{47}}{6}$

**10.** $l = 10 - 2\left(\dfrac{1}{2}\right) = 9$

$w = 8 - 2(1) = 6$

$A = w \cdot l = 6 \cdot 9 = 54$

Let $s$ be the measure of a side of an image. The area of an image is $s^2$, and the area of six images is $6s^2$.

$6s^2 = 54$

$s^2 = 9$

$s = \pm 3$

Each image is 3 inches by 3 inches.

**11.** $18\pi r^2 - 339.12 = 0$

$18(3.14)r^2 \approx 339.12$

$r^2 \approx 6$

$r \approx \pm 2.449$

The interior radius is about 2.449 meters.

**12.** Student A; Sample: Student B didn't correctly factor the GCF of −3 in the second denominator.

**13.** The expression is undefined when the denominator has a value of 0. Division by 0 is undefined, so the expression is undefined when $x = 0$.

**14.** $\qquad 32x - 3x = 24 - 4x^2$

$4x^2 + 29x - 24 = 0$

$(4x - 3)(x + 8) = 0$

$4x - 3 = 0 \quad$ or $\quad x + 8 = 0$

$4x = 3 \quad$ or $\qquad x = -8$

$x = \dfrac{3}{4}$

Check:

$32\left(\dfrac{3}{4}\right) - 3\left(\dfrac{3}{4}\right) = 24 - 4\left(\dfrac{3}{4}\right)^2$

$24 - \dfrac{9}{4} = 24 - \dfrac{9}{4}$

$21\dfrac{3}{4} = 21\dfrac{3}{4} \; \checkmark$

$32(-8) - 3(-8) = 24 - 4(-8)^2$

$-256 + 24 = 24 - 256$

$24 = 24 \; \checkmark$

**15.** $x^2 = 100$

$\sqrt{x^2} = \sqrt{100}$

$x = \pm 10$

**16.** The ball lands on the ground when $h = 0$.

$-32t^2 + 12t + 2 = 0$

$-2(16t^2 - 6t - 1) = 0$

$-2(8t + 1)(2t - 1) = 0$

$8t + 1 = 0 \quad$ or $\quad 2t - 1 = 0$

$8t = -1 \quad$ or $\qquad 2t = 1$

$t = -\dfrac{1}{8} \quad$ or $\qquad t = \dfrac{1}{2}$

The ball lands at $\dfrac{1}{2}$ second.

**17.** Pedro's building rate is $\dfrac{1}{10}$ fence per hour and his partner's is $\dfrac{1}{12}$ fence per hour. Let $h$ be the number of hours it takes for them to build 1 fence together.

**Saxon** Algebra 1

$\frac{1}{10}h + \frac{1}{12}h = 1$

$(60)\frac{1}{10}h + (60)\frac{1}{12}h = 60$

$6h + 5h = 60$

$11h = 60$

$h = \frac{60}{11}$

Together, they can build the fence in $\frac{60}{11}$ or $5\frac{5}{11}$ hours.

18. Write in standard form.

$x^2 + 81 = 18x$

$x^2 - 18x + 81 = 0$

axis of symmetry: $x = 9$

vertex: $(9, 0)$

$y$-intercept: $81$

additional points: $(7, 4)$, $(11, 4)$, $(18, 81)$

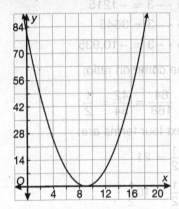

19. $\frac{x}{10} = \frac{x - 20}{2}$

$2x = 10x - 200$

$200 = 8x$

$25 = x$

The flagpole is 25 feet tall.

20. **a.** $-8|x + 7| \geq -24$

$|x + 7| \leq 3$

$-3 \leq x + 7 \leq 3$

$-10 \leq x \leq -4$

**b.** Let $x = -5$        Let $x = -7$

$-8|-5 + 7| \geq -24$    $-8|-7 + 7| \geq -24$

$-8|2| \geq -24$      $-8|0| \geq -24$

$-16 \geq -24$       $0 \geq -24$

21. $|5x - 2| < 9$

$-9 < 5x - 2 < 9$

Since $n$ is a solution of the inequality, the quantity $5x - 2$ is less than 9 when $x = n$.

The answer is **B**.

22. The $x$-intercepts appear to be $-6$ and $2$.

Check:

$0 = \frac{1}{2}(-6)^2 + 2(-6) - 6$

$0 = 18 - 12 - 6$

$0 = 0$ ✔

$0 = \frac{1}{2}(2)^2 + 2(2) - 6$

$0 = 2 + 4 - 6$

$0 = 0$ ✔

The zeroes of the function are $-6$ and $2$.

23. $\dfrac{49x^2 + 21xy}{5x^2} \div \dfrac{14x}{25xy^2}$

$= \dfrac{49x^2 + 21xy}{5x^2} \cdot \dfrac{25xy^2}{14x}$

$= \dfrac{7x(7x + 3y)}{5x^2} \cdot \dfrac{25^5xy^2}{^2 14x}$

$= \dfrac{7x + 3y}{x} \cdot \dfrac{5y^2}{2}$

$= \dfrac{35xy^2 + 15y^3}{2x}$

24. $(6y - 3)(6y + 3)$

$= 36y^2 + 18y - 18y - 9$

$= 36y^2 - 9$

25. $4x^4 - 64$

$= 4(x^4 - 16)$

$= 4(x^2 + 4)(x^2 - 4)$

$= 4(x^2 + 4)(x + 2)(x - 2)$

26. **a.** Let $x$ be the amount the student spends. The difference between $x$ and \$3000 must be less than or equal to \$200.

$|x - 3000| \leq 200$

**b.** $|x - 3000| \leq 200$

$-200 \leq x - 3000 \leq 200$

$2800 \leq x \leq 3200$

The student might pay \$2800–\$3200.

**Saxon** Algebra 1

**27.** $M = \left(\dfrac{x_1 + x_2}{2}, \dfrac{y_1 + y_2}{2}\right)$

$= \left(\dfrac{-4 + 2}{2}, \dfrac{3 + 4}{2}\right)$

$= \left(-1, \dfrac{7}{2}\right)$

**28.** Let $m$ be the number of minutes the student talks. The bill will be $10 + 0.05m$. The difference between the bill and \$25 must be less than or equal to \$5.

$|(10 + 0.05m) - 25| \le 5$

$|-15 + 0.05m| \le 5$

$-5 \le -15 + 0.05m \le 5$

$10 \le 0.05m \le 20$

$200 \le m \le 400$

The minimum is 200 minutes and the maximum is 400 minutes.

**29.** $\dfrac{a}{x} + \dfrac{a}{b}$

$= \dfrac{ab}{bx} + \dfrac{ax}{bx}$

$= \dfrac{ab + ax}{bx}$

Sample: The common denominator should be $bx$. Also, you have to have like denominators to be able to add numerators without writing equivalent fractions.

**30.** Sample: It only has one zero when its vertex is on the $x$-axis.

## LESSON 105

### Warm Up 105

**1.** sequence

**2.** $-2^5$

$= -2 \cdot -2 \cdot -2 \cdot -2 \cdot -2$

$= -32$

**3.** $(-3)^4$

$= (-3) \cdot (-3) \cdot (-3) \cdot (-3)$

$= 81$

**4.** $15(-0.4)^2$

$= 15(0.16)$

$= 2.4$

**5.** $3^{-3}$

$= \dfrac{1}{3^3}$

$= \dfrac{1}{27}$

### Lesson Practice 105

**a.** $\dfrac{16}{2} = \dfrac{128}{16} = \dfrac{1024}{128} = 8$

**b.** $\dfrac{54}{-162} = \dfrac{-18}{54} = \dfrac{6}{-18} = -\dfrac{1}{3}$

**c.** $\dfrac{4.9}{0.7} = \dfrac{34.3}{4.9} = \dfrac{240.1}{34.3} = 7$

**d.** Find the common ratio:

$\dfrac{-15}{5} = \dfrac{45}{-5} = \dfrac{-135}{45} = -3$

The next four terms are:

$-135 \cdot -3 = 405$

$405 \cdot -3 = -1215$

$-1215 \cdot -3 = 3645$

$3645 \cdot -3 = -10{,}935$

**e.** Find the common ratio:

$\dfrac{168}{336} = \dfrac{84}{168} = \dfrac{42}{84} = \dfrac{1}{2}$

The next four terms are:

$42 \cdot \dfrac{1}{2} = 21$

$21 \cdot \dfrac{1}{2} = 10\dfrac{1}{2}$

$10\dfrac{1}{2} \cdot \dfrac{1}{2} = 5\dfrac{1}{4}$

$5\dfrac{1}{4} \cdot \dfrac{1}{2} = 2\dfrac{5}{8}$

**f.** $A(6) = -3(4)^{6-1}$

$= -3(4)^5$

$= -3072$

**g.** Find the common ratio:

$\dfrac{\frac{1}{8}}{-\frac{1}{2}} = \dfrac{-\frac{1}{32}}{\frac{1}{8}} = \dfrac{\frac{1}{512}}{-\frac{1}{32}} = -\dfrac{1}{4}$

Find the 7th term:

$A(7) = \left(-\dfrac{1}{2}\right)\left(-\dfrac{1}{4}\right)^{7-1}$

**Saxon** Algebra 1

$$= \left(-\frac{1}{2}\right)\left(-\frac{1}{4}\right)^6$$

$$= \left(-\frac{1}{2}\right)\left(\frac{1}{4096}\right)$$

$$= -\frac{1}{8192}$$

**h.** Find the common ratio:

$$\frac{-8\frac{1}{2}}{4\frac{1}{4}} = \frac{17}{-8\frac{1}{2}} = \frac{-34}{17} = -2$$

Find the 8th term:

$$A(8) = \left(4\frac{1}{4}\right)(-2)^{8-1}$$

$$= \left(4\frac{1}{4}\right)(-128)$$

$$= -544$$

**i.** Find the common ratio:

$$\frac{32}{40} = \frac{25.6}{32} = 0.8$$

Find the 6th term:

$$A(6) = 40(0.8)^{6-1}$$

$$= 40(0.32768)$$

$$= 13.1072$$

**j.** Each minute, the tank loses $\frac{1}{3}$ of its water. So, the water left in the tank at the end of each minute is $\frac{2}{3}$ of the previous amount. The common ratio is $\frac{2}{3}$. The first term is $\frac{9}{10} \cdot \frac{2}{3} = \frac{3}{5}$.

Fifth term:

$$A(5) = \frac{3}{5}\left(\frac{2}{3}\right)^{5-1}$$

$$= \frac{16}{135}$$

After 5 minutes, the tank holds $\frac{16}{135}$ of a gallon of water.

**Practice 105**

**1.** $\frac{20}{-80} = \frac{-5}{20} = \frac{1\frac{1}{4}}{-5} = -\frac{1}{4}$

**2.** Common ratio:

$$\frac{6}{4} = \frac{9}{6} = \frac{13.5}{9} = 1.5$$

$n$th term:

$$A(n) = 4(1.5)^{n-1}$$

The correct answer is choice **B**.

**3.** Each year, the car loses 18% of its value. So, the value of the car each year is 82% of the previous year's value. The common ratio is 0.82. The first term of the sequence is $20,000 \cdot 0.82 = 16,400$. The 5th term is:

$$A(5) = 16,400(0.82)^{5-1}$$

$$\approx 7414.80$$

In 2012, the car will be worth about \$7414.80.

**4.** Sample: The formula to find the third term of a geometric sequence is $A(3) = a(r)^2$. If the third term is 0 and the first term is not 0, the ratio must be 0. But the first and second terms are not 0, so their ratio cannot be zero. Therefore, the sequence cannot be geometric.

**5.** The recursive formula for an arithmetic sequence with a common difference of $\frac{1}{2}$ is $a_n = a_{n-1} + \frac{1}{2}$. If the first term is $\frac{1}{2}$:

$$a_1 = \frac{1}{2}$$

$$a_2 = \frac{1}{2} + \frac{1}{2} = 1$$

$$a_3 = 1 + \frac{1}{2} = 1\frac{1}{2}$$

$$a_4 = 1\frac{1}{2} + \frac{1}{2} = 2$$

The first four terms of the sequence are $\frac{1}{2}, 1, 1\frac{1}{2}, 2, \ldots$

**6.** $A(n) = a_1 r^{n-1}$

$$605 = 5r^{3-1}$$

$$121 = r^2$$

$$\pm 11 = r$$

The rules are $5(11)^{n-1}$ or $5(-11)^{n-1}$.

**7.** $\left(\frac{b}{2}\right)^2 = \left(\frac{18}{2}\right)^2 = 9^2 = 81$

**8.** $\left(\frac{b}{2}\right)^2 = \left(\frac{28}{2}\right)^2 = 14^2 = 196$

Dominic is incorrect. He did not square the quantity $\frac{b}{2}$.

**9. a.** $l \cdot w = A$

$$(2x + 4)(x + 4) = 880$$

**b.** $2x^2 + 12x + 16 = 880$

$x^2 + 6x + 8 = 440$

$x^2 + 6x = 432$

**c.** $x^2 + 6x + \left(\dfrac{6}{2}\right)^2 = 432 + 9$

$x^2 + 6x + 9 = 441$

$(x + 3)^2 = 441$

$x + 3 = \pm21$

$x = 18 \quad \text{or} \quad x = -24$

The interior of the flower bed is 18 feet wide.

**d.** The area of the border is the total area minus the interior area.

$A = 880 - 18(2 \cdot 18)$

$= 232$

The area of the border is 232 square feet.

**10.** $\dfrac{11x + 22}{22x^2 + 44x}$

$= \dfrac{\cancel{11}(x + 2)}{2\;\cancel{22}x(x + 2)}$

$= \dfrac{1}{2x}, \; x \neq 0, -2$

**11.** $\dfrac{\sqrt{63}}{\sqrt{18}} = \dfrac{\cancel{3}\sqrt{7}}{\cancel{3}\sqrt{2}} = \dfrac{\sqrt{7} \cdot \sqrt{2}}{\sqrt{2} \cdot \sqrt{2}} = \dfrac{\sqrt{14}}{2}$

**12.** By the Pythagorean Theorem:

$h^2 + (h + 14)^2 = 26^2$

$h^2 + h^2 + 28h + 196 = 676$

$2h^2 + 28h = 480$

$h^2 + 14h = 240$

$h^2 + 14h + \left(\dfrac{14}{2}\right)^2 = 240 + \left(\dfrac{14}{2}\right)^2$

$h^2 + 14h + 49 = 289$

$(h + 7)^2 = 289$

$h + 7 = \pm17$

$h = 10 \quad \text{or} \quad h = -24$

The triangle's height is 10 units and the base is 10 + 14, or 24 units.

**13.** Student B; Student A did not multiply by an expression equivalent to 1 to rationalize the denominator.

**14.** $\sqrt{\dfrac{337\frac{1}{2}}{6}} = \sqrt{\dfrac{\overset{225}{\cancel{675}}}{2} \cdot \dfrac{1}{\cancel{6}_2}} = \dfrac{15}{2}$

The edge length is $\dfrac{15}{2}$ meters.

**15.** $14x^2 - 2x = 3 - 21x$

$14x^2 + 19x - 3 = 0$

$(7x - 1)(2x + 3) = 0$

$7x - 1 = 0 \quad \text{or} \quad 2x + 3 = 0$

$7x = 1 \quad \text{or} \quad 2x = -3$

$x = \dfrac{1}{7} \quad \text{or} \quad x = -\dfrac{3}{2}$

Check:

$14\left(\dfrac{1}{7}\right)^2 - 2\left(\dfrac{1}{7}\right) = 3 - 21\left(\dfrac{1}{7}\right)$

$\dfrac{2}{7} - \dfrac{2}{7} = 3 - 3$

$0 = 0 \checkmark$

$14\left(-\dfrac{3}{2}\right)^2 - 2\left(-\dfrac{3}{2}\right) = 3 - 21\left(-\dfrac{3}{2}\right)$

$\dfrac{63}{2} + 3 = 3 + \dfrac{63}{2}$

$\dfrac{69}{2} = \dfrac{69}{2} \checkmark$

**16.** The woman's building rate is $\frac{1}{3}$ doghouse per hour and her husband's is $\frac{1}{4}$ doghouse per hour. Let $h$ be the number of hours it takes for them to build 1 doghouse together.

$\dfrac{1}{3}h + \dfrac{1}{4}h = 1$

$12\left(\dfrac{1}{3}h + \dfrac{1}{4}h\right) = 1(12)$

$4h + 3h = 12$

$7h = 12$

$h = \dfrac{12}{7}$

They can build the doghouse in $\frac{12}{7}$ hours.

**17.** $29^2$

$= (30 - 1)^2$

$= 30^2 - 2(30)(1) + 1^2$

$= 900 - 60 + 1$

$= 841$

**18.** Graph the related function $f(t) = -16t^2 + 6t + 6$:

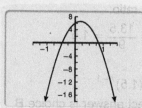

**Saxon** Algebra 1

Use the CALC zero function to find the
*x*-intercepts. Use the CALC maximum
function to find the vertex. The maximum
height is about 6.56 feet and the time when
the horseshoe hits the ground is about
0.83 seconds.

**19.** $55 = 3t^2 + 8t - 70$

$0 = 3t^2 + 8t - 125$

Graph the related function

$f(t) = 3t^2 + 8t - 125$

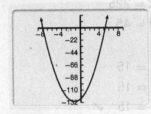

Use the CALC zero function to find the
*x*-intercepts. The puddle reaches 55 square
feet at about 5.26 seconds.

**20.** $2|x| - 12 > -5$

$2|x| > 7$

$|x| > 3.5$

$x < -3.5 \quad \text{or} \quad x > 3.5$

**21.** False. The correct answer is:

$4x^2 - 64 = 0$

$4(x^2 - 16) = 0$

$4(x + 4)(x - 4) = 0$

$x + 4 = 0 \quad \text{or} \quad x - 4 = 0$

$x = \pm 4$

**22.** Student A; Student B should have subtracted
460 from each side of the equation to isolate
the variable.

**23.** The vertex appears to be (0, 0); The
maximum value appears to be 0.

**24.** $\dfrac{d}{d - 10} + \dfrac{10}{10 - d}$

$= \dfrac{d}{d - 10} + \dfrac{10}{-1(-10 + d)}$

$= \dfrac{d}{d - 10} - \dfrac{10}{d - 10}$

$= \dfrac{d - 10}{d - 10}$

$= 1$

**25.** $\dfrac{18}{2x} - 4 = \dfrac{15}{3x}$

$6x\left(\dfrac{18}{2x} - 4\right) = 6x\left(\dfrac{15}{3x}\right)$

$\dfrac{\overset{3}{6}x(18)}{2x} - 24x = \dfrac{\overset{2}{6}x(15)}{3x}$

$54 - 24x = 30$

$-24x = -24$

$x = 1$

Check:

$\dfrac{18}{2(1)} - 4 = \dfrac{15}{3(1)}$

$9 - 4 = 5$

$5 = 5 ✓$

**26. a.** $\dfrac{\dfrac{4x - 16}{x^3}}{\dfrac{6x^2 - 24x}{6x}}$

$= \dfrac{4x - 16}{x^3} \cdot \dfrac{6x}{6x^2 - 24x}$

$= \dfrac{4(x - 4)}{x^3} \cdot \dfrac{6x}{6x(x - 4)}$

$= \dfrac{4}{x^3}$

Louis' rate is $\dfrac{4}{x^3}$ miles per minute.

**b.** $\dfrac{\dfrac{4}{x^3}}{\dfrac{1}{x}}$

$= \dfrac{4}{x^3} \cdot \dfrac{x}{1}$

$= \dfrac{4x}{x^{3\,2}}$

$= \dfrac{4}{x^2}$

Louis' new rate is $\dfrac{4}{x^2}$ miles per minute.

**27.** $\dfrac{8x^2}{x^2 - 11x + 18} - \dfrac{2}{8x - 72}$

$= \dfrac{8x^2}{(x - 2)(x - 9)} - \dfrac{\overset{}{2}}{\underset{4}{8}(x - 9)}$

$$= \frac{8x^2}{(x-2)(x-9)} \cdot \frac{8}{8} - \frac{1}{(x-9)} \cdot \frac{x-2}{x-2}$$

$$= \frac{32x^2 - x + 2}{4(x-2)(x-9)}$$

team has $\frac{32x^2 - x + 2}{4(x-2)(x-9)}$ miles left to travel.

**28.** $M = \left( \frac{x_1 + x_2}{2}, \frac{y_1 + y_2}{2} \right)$

$\quad = \left( \frac{-5+1}{2}, \frac{0+14}{2} \right)$

$\quad = (-2, 7)$

**29. a.** $f(t) = -16t^2 + 32t + 0$

$\quad f(2) = -16(2)^2 + 32(2)$

$\quad\quad = -64 + 64$

$\quad\quad = 0$

After 2 seconds the ball is at 0 feet.

**b.** Sample: This is the height of the ball relative to the top of the cliff.

**c.** Sample: 48 feet below the top of the cliff.

**30.** Sample: Inequalities with $<$ and $>$ are graphed with dashed boundary lines. Inequalities with $\leq$ and $\geq$ are graphed with solid boundary lines.

## LESSON 106

### Warm Up 106

**1.** The expression $\sqrt{x+1} + 2$ contains a radical. The answer is **B**.

**2.** $\left(\sqrt{5}\right)^2 = \sqrt{5} \cdot \sqrt{5} = 5$

**3.** $\left(\sqrt{x+2}\right)^2 = \sqrt{x+2} \cdot \sqrt{x+2} = x+2$

**4.** $\quad x^2 + 5x + 6 = 0$

$\quad (x+2)(x+3) = 0$

$\quad\quad x + 2 = 0 \quad$ or $\quad x + 3 = 0$

$\quad\quad\quad x = -2 \quad$ or $\quad\quad x = -3$

**5.** $\quad\quad x^2 - 5x = 14$

$\quad x^2 - 5x - 14 = 0$

$\quad (x-7)(x+2) = 0$

$\quad\quad x - 7 = 0 \quad$ or $\quad x + 2 = 0$

$\quad\quad\quad x = 7 \quad$ or $\quad\quad x = -2$

### Lesson Practice 106

**a.** $\quad \sqrt{x} = 6$

$\quad \left(\sqrt{x}\right)^2 = (6)^2$

$\quad\quad x = 36$

Check:

$\sqrt{36} = 6$

$\quad 6 = 6$ ✓

**b.** $\quad \sqrt{5x} = 15$

$\quad \left(\sqrt{5x}\right)^2 = (15)^2$

$\quad\quad 5x = 225$

$\quad\quad x = 45$

Check:

$\sqrt{5 \cdot 45} = 15$

$\sqrt{225} = 15$

$\quad 15 = 15$ ✓

**c.** $\quad \sqrt{x+3} = 12$

$\quad \left(\sqrt{x+3}\right)^2 = (12)^2$

$\quad\quad x + 3 = 144$

$\quad\quad x = 141$

Check:

$\sqrt{141 + 3} = 12$

$\sqrt{144} = 12$

$\quad 12 = 12$ ✓

**d.** $\quad \sqrt{4x - 15} = 7$

$\quad \left(\sqrt{4x - 15}\right)^2 = (7)^2$

$\quad\quad 4x - 15 = 49$

$\quad\quad 4x = 64$

$\quad\quad x = 16$

Check:

$\sqrt{4(16) - 15} = 7$

$\sqrt{49} = 7$

$\quad 7 = 7$ ✓

**e.** $\quad \sqrt{x} - 8 = 5$

$\quad\quad \sqrt{x} = 13$

$\quad \left(\sqrt{x}\right)^2 = (13)^2$

$\quad\quad x = 169$

Check:

$\sqrt{169} - 8 = 5$

$\quad 13 - 8 = 5$

$\quad\quad 5 = 5$ ✓

**f.** $\sqrt{x} + 8 = 15$
$\sqrt{x} = 7$
$(\sqrt{x})^2 = (7)^2$
$x = 49$

Check:
$\sqrt{49} + 8 = 15$
$7 + 8 = 15$
$15 = 15$ ✓

**g.** $6\sqrt{x} = 24$
$\sqrt{x} = 4$
$(\sqrt{x})^2 = (4)^2$
$x = 16$

Check:
$6\sqrt{16} = 24$
$6 \cdot 4 = 24$
$24 = 24$ ✓

**h.** $\dfrac{\sqrt{x}}{3} = 15$
$\sqrt{x} = 45$
$(\sqrt{x})^2 = (45)^2$
$x = 2025$

Check:
$\dfrac{\sqrt{2025}}{3} = 15$
$\dfrac{45}{3} = 15$
$15 = 15$ ✓

**i.** $\sqrt{x+4} = \sqrt{2x-1}$
$(\sqrt{x+4})^2 = (\sqrt{2x-1})^2$
$x + 4 = 2x - 1$
$x = 5$

Check:
$\sqrt{5+4} = \sqrt{2(5)-1}$
$\sqrt{9} = \sqrt{9}$
$3 = 3$ ✓

**j.** $\sqrt{x+5} - \sqrt{6x} = 0$
$\sqrt{x+5} = \sqrt{6x}$
$(\sqrt{x+5})^2 = (\sqrt{6x})^2$
$x + 5 = 6x$
$5x = 5$
$x = 1$

Check:
$\sqrt{1+5} - \sqrt{6(1)} = 0$
$\sqrt{6} - \sqrt{6} = 0$
$0 = 0$ ✓

**k.** $\sqrt{x-2} = x - 4$
$(\sqrt{x-2})^2 = (x-4)^2$
$x - 2 = x^2 - 8x + 16$
$x^2 - 9x + 18 = 0$
$(x - 6)(x - 3) = 0$
$x - 6 = 0$ or $x - 3 = 0$
$x = 6$ or $x = 3$

Check:
$\sqrt{6-2} = 6 - 4$ $\qquad$ $\sqrt{3-2} = 3 - 4$
$\sqrt{4} = 2$ $\qquad\qquad$ $\sqrt{1} = -1$
$2 = 2$ ✓ $\qquad\qquad$ $1 \neq -1$

**l.** $\sqrt{x} + 8 = -3$
$\sqrt{x} = -11$

The square root cannot be negative. The equation has no real solution.

**m.** Area = width · length
$42 = \sqrt{x} \cdot (\sqrt{x} + (7 - \sqrt{x}))$
$42 = (\sqrt{x})(\sqrt{x}) + (\sqrt{x})(7 - \sqrt{x})$
$42 = x + 7\sqrt{x} - x$
$42 = 7\sqrt{x}$
$6 = \sqrt{x}$
$(6)^2 = (\sqrt{x})^2$
$36 = x$

Area = width · length
$= (\sqrt{x})(7 - \sqrt{x})$
$= (\sqrt{36})(7 - \sqrt{36})$
$= 6(7 - 6)$
$= 6$

The area of the planter is 6 square yards.

**Practice 106**

**1.** $x^2 = 64$
$\sqrt{(x^2)} = \sqrt{64}$
$x = \pm 8$

Check:
$8^2 = 64$ $\qquad$ $(-8)^2 = 64$
$64 = 64$ ✓ $\qquad$ $64 = 64$ ✓

**2.** The product of −4 and −5 is 20, and the sum of −4 and −5 is −9.

$x^2 - 9x + 20$

$= (x - 5)(x - 4)$

**3.** Sample: The sum of three times a number and 4 is less than 10.

**4.** The answer is **D**. To isolate the radical, divide both sides of the equation by 14.

**5.** $\sqrt{x - 1} = \sqrt{3x + 2}$

$(\sqrt{x - 1})^2 = (\sqrt{3x + 2})^2$

$x - 1 = 3x + 2$

$2x = -3$

$x = -\dfrac{3}{2}$

Check:

$\sqrt{-\dfrac{3}{2} - 1} = \sqrt{3\left(-\dfrac{3}{2}\right) + 2}$

$\sqrt{-\dfrac{5}{2}} = \sqrt{-\dfrac{5}{2}}$

The radicand cannot be negative. The equation has no real solution.

**6.** $\dfrac{\sqrt{x}}{4} = 32$

$\sqrt{x} = 128$

$(\sqrt{x})^2 = (128)^2$

$x = 16{,}384$

Check:

$\dfrac{\sqrt{16{,}384}}{4} = 32$

$\dfrac{128}{4} = 32$

$32 = 32$ ✓

**7.** $\dfrac{-9}{18} = \dfrac{4\frac{1}{2}}{-9} = \dfrac{-2\frac{1}{4}}{4\frac{1}{2}} = -\dfrac{1}{2}$

**8.** $A(n) = a_1 r^{n-1}$

$A(6) = 5(2)^{6-1}$

$= 5(2)^5$

$= 160$

**9. a.** $A(1) = 1 \cdot 0.75 = 0.75$

**b.** $A(n) = 0.75(0.75)^{n-1}$

$= (0.75)^n$

**c.** $A(6) = (0.75)^6$

$\approx 0.18$

The height of the sixth bounce is about 0.18 meters.

**10.** The number of squares per figure forms a geometric sequence: 1, 4, 16, …. The first term is 1. The common ratio is:

$\dfrac{4}{1} = \dfrac{16}{4} = 4$

The ninth term is:

$A(n) = a_1 r^{n-1}$

$A(9) = 1(4)^{9-1}$

$= 4^8$

$= 65{,}536$

The area of each figure is 5 times the number of squares. The area of the ninth figure is $5 \cdot 65{,}536$ or 327,680 square feet.

**11.** $2\sqrt{x - 4} = 20$

$\sqrt{x - 4} = 10$

$(\sqrt{x - 4})^2 = (10)^2$

$x - 4 = 100$

$x = 104$

The ivy will take 104 days to reach 20 feet.

**12.** $3(-5x + 4y = -37)$

$5(3x - 6y = 33)$

$-15x + 12y = -111$

$\underline{15x - 30y = 165}$

$-18y = 54$

$y = -3$

$-5x + 4(-3) = -37$

$-5x - 12 = -37$

$-5x = -25$

$x = 5$

Check:

$-5(5) + 4(-3) = -37$

$-25 - 12 = -37$ ✓

$-37 = -37$ ✓

$3(5) - 6(-3) = 33$

$15 + 18 = 33$

$33 = 33$ ✓

**Saxon** Algebra 1

**13.** The number of unshaded triangles per figure forms a geometric sequence: 1, 3, 9, .... The first term is 1. The common ratio is:

$$\frac{3}{1} = \frac{9}{3} = 3$$

The sixth term is:

$$A(6) = a_1 r^{n-1}$$
$$= 1(3)^{6-1}$$
$$= 3^5$$
$$= 243$$

The sixth figure will have 243 unshaded triangles.

**14.**
$$x^2 + 9x = 4.75$$
$$x^2 + 9x + \left(\frac{9}{2}\right)^2 = 4.75 + \left(\frac{9}{2}\right)^2$$
$$x^2 + 9x + 20.25 = 25$$
$$(x + 4.5)^2 = 25$$
$$\sqrt{(x + 4.5)^2} = \sqrt{25}$$
$$x + 4.5 = \pm 5$$
$$x + 4.5 = 5 \quad \text{or} \quad x + 4.5 = -5$$
$$x = 0.5 \quad \text{or} \quad x = -9.5$$

Check:
$$(0.5)^2 + 9(0.5) = 4.75$$
$$0.25 + 4.5 = 4.75$$
$$4.75 = 4.75 \; \checkmark$$
$$(-9.5)^2 + 9(-9.5) = 4.75$$
$$90.25 - 85.5 = 4.75$$
$$4.75 = 4.75 \; \checkmark$$

**15.** Student A; Student B did not divide all terms by 2 in the initial step.

**16.**
$$u^2 - 0.8u = 0.33$$
$$u^2 - 0.8u + \left(\frac{0.8}{2}\right)^2 = 0.33 + \left(\frac{0.8}{2}\right)^2$$
$$u^2 - 0.8u + 0.16 = 0.49$$
$$(u - 0.4)^2 = 0.49$$
$$\sqrt{(u - 0.4)^2} = \sqrt{0.49}$$
$$u - 0.4 = \pm 0.7$$
$$u - 0.4 = 0.7 \quad \text{or} \quad u - 0.4 = -0.7$$
$$u = 1.1 \quad \text{or} \quad u = -0.3$$

The number of units to be sold is $1000 \cdot 1.1$, or 1100 units.

**17.**
$$\frac{\overset{15}{60}}{\underset{4}{4}x} + \frac{\overset{9}{45}}{\underset{5}{5}x} = 3$$
$$\frac{15}{x} + \frac{9}{x} = 3$$
$$\frac{24}{x} = 3$$
$$24 = 3x$$
$$8 = x$$

Check:
$$\frac{\overset{15}{60}}{\underset{4}{4}(8)} + \frac{\overset{9}{45}}{\underset{5}{5}(8)} = 3$$
$$\frac{15}{8} + \frac{9}{8} = 3$$
$$\frac{24}{8} = 3$$
$$3 = 3 \; \checkmark$$

**18.**
$$\sqrt{x} = 9$$
$$(\sqrt{x})^2 = (9)^2$$
$$x = 81$$

Check:
$$\sqrt{81} = 9$$
$$9 = 9 \; \checkmark$$

**19.** Graph the related function on a graphing calculator $f(t) = -16t^2 + 9t + 4$

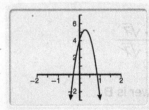

Use the CALC maximum and CALC zero functions to find the vertex and the $x$-intercepts.

Maximum height of the path is about 5.27 feet and the egg hits the ground at about 0.85 seconds.

**20.** Graph the related function $f(x) = x^2 - 16$.

axis of symmetry: $x = 0$

vertex: $(0, -16)$

$y$-intercept: $-16$

additional points: $(4, 0), (-4, 0)$

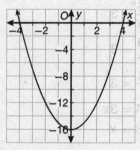

The x-intercepts appear to be 4 and −4.

Check:

$(4)^2 − 16 = 0$      $(−4)^2 − 16 = 0$

$16 − 16 = 0$      $16 − 16 = 0$

$0 = 0$ ✓       $0 = 0$ ✓

The solution is $x = ±4$.

**21.** Let $w$ be the weight of an actual tennis ball. The difference between $w$ and $2\frac{1}{12}$ must be less than or equal to $\frac{1}{12}$.

$$\left| w − 2\frac{1}{12} \right| \le \frac{1}{12}$$

$$-\frac{1}{12} \le w − 2\frac{1}{12} \le \frac{1}{12}$$

$$2 \le w \le 2\frac{1}{6}$$

The smallest acceptable weight is 2 ounces.

**22.** $\dfrac{18\sqrt{7}}{3\sqrt{28}}$

$= \dfrac{\cancel{3} \cdot \overset{3}{\cancel{6}} \cdot \sqrt{7}}{\cancel{3} \cdot \cancel{2} \cdot \sqrt{7}}$

$= 3$

The answer is **B**.

**23.** Sample: Since 145 is close to 144, Anton should find the square root of 144 for the numerator (12) and multiply the square root of 9 (3) by 2 for the denominator (6). The estimated quotient would be 2.

**24.** $\dfrac{2r}{r − 4} − \dfrac{6}{12 − 3r}$

$= \dfrac{2r}{r − 4} − \dfrac{6}{3(4 − r)}$

$= \dfrac{2r}{r − 4} + \dfrac{2}{(r − 4)}$

$= \dfrac{2r + 2}{r − 4}$

$= \dfrac{2(r + 1)}{r − 4}$

**25.** $|x − 16| \le 12$

$-12 \le x − 16 \le 12$

$4 \le x \le 28$

**26.** $l = \dfrac{A}{w}$

$= \dfrac{9x^2 + 44x − 5}{x + 5}$

$= \dfrac{(x + 5)(9x − 1)}{x + 5}$

$= 9x − 1$

The length is $(9x − 1)$ feet.

**27.** $h = −16(1)^2 + 23(1) + 3$

$= −16 + 23 + 3$

$= 10$

After 1 second, the ball's height is 10 feet.

**28. a.** Let $x$ be the number of adult tickets sold and $y$ be the number of student tickets sold.

$5x + 4y \ge 2500$

**b.**

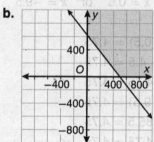

**c.** Yes. The point (200, 400) is in the shaded area.

**29.** Use the Zero Product Property. Set each factor equal to zero and solve for $x$.

$x − 5 = 0$  or  $x + 8 = 0$

$x = 5$  or  $x = −8$

**30.** The axis of symmetry is:

$x = −\dfrac{b}{2a}$

$4 = −\dfrac{b}{2(1)}$

$−8 = b$

**107**

## LESSON 107

### Warm Up 107

1. parent function

2. $3 \cdot 2 + 2|-5|$
   $= 3 \cdot 2 + 2(5)$
   $= 6 + 10$
   $= 16$

3. $5 \cdot 8 - 4|-6|$
   $= 5 \cdot 8 - 4(6)$
   $= 40 - 24$
   $= 16$

4. $4|x - 2| = 60$
   $|x - 2| = 15$
   $x - 2 = 15$    OR    $x - 2 = -15$
       $x = 17$               $x = -13$

5. $-3|x + 4| = 36$
   $|x + 4| = -12$
   The absolute value of a number cannot be negative. There is no solution.

### Lesson Practice 107

a.

| x | −8 | −4 | 0 | 4 | 8 |
|---|----|----|---|---|---|
| y | 10 | 6 | 2 | 6 | 10 |

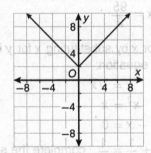

The graph of the parent function is translated up 2 units. The vertex is (0, 2).

b.

| x | −8 | −4 | −2 | 4 | 8 |
|---|----|----|----|---|---|
| y | 6 | 2 | 0 | 6 | 10 |

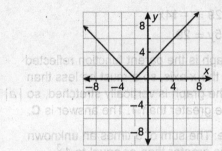

The graph of the parent function is translated 2 units to the left.

c.

| x | −2 | 0 | 1 | 2 | 4 |
|---|----|---|---|---|---|
| y | 5 | 3 | 2 | 3 | 5 |

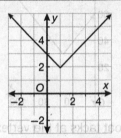

The graph of the parent function is translated 1 unit to the right and 2 units up.

d. Since $|4| > 1$, the graph is stretched vertically.

e. Since $-2 < 0$, the graph is reflected across the x-axis. Since $|-2| > 1$, the graph is stretched vertically.

f. Since $-0.5 < 0$, the graph is reflected across the x-axis. Since $|-0.5| < 1$, the graph is compressed vertically.

g. $f(t) = 2|t| + 25$

### Practice 107

1. $k < 0$, so the graph of the parent function shifts 6 units down.

2. $\sqrt{2x} = 14$
   $(\sqrt{2x})^2 = (14)^2$
   $2x = 196$
   $x = 98$
   Check:
   $\sqrt{2(98)} = 14$
   $\sqrt{196} = 14$
   $14 = 14$

**Saxon** Algebra 1

**3.** $5y - 29 = -14x$

$14x + 5y = 29$

**4.** The graph is the parent function reflected across the x-axis, so a must be less than zero. The graph is vertically stretched, so $|a|$ must be greater than 1. The answer is **C**.

**5.** Sample: The sum of 3 times an unknown and $\frac{2}{5}$ is greater than or equal to $1\frac{3}{5}$.

**6.**

| x | 0 | 25 | 50 | 75 | 100 |
|---|---|----|----|----|-----|
| y | 60 | 45 | 30 | 45 | 60 |

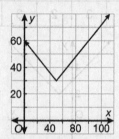

The sailboat tacks at the vertex of the graph, (50, 30).

**7.** Sample: The absolute-value function has a minimum value and that is the y-value at the vertex.

**8.** Solve for y.

$4y = -3x - 4$

$4x + 6 = -5y$

$4(3x + 4y = -4)$

$-3(4x + 5y = -6)$

$2x + 16y = -16$

$-12x - 15y = 18$
_____

$y = 2$

Solve for x.

$4(2) = -3x - 4$

$12 = -3x$

$x = -4$

Check:

$4(2) = -3(-4) - 4$

$8 = 12 - 4$

$8 = 8$ ✓

$4(-4) + 6 = -5(2)$

$-16 + 6 = -10$

$-10 = -10$ ✓

**9.** $P = 4s$

$20 = 4\sqrt{x}$

$5 = \sqrt{x}$

$(5)^2 = (\sqrt{x})^2$

$25 = x$

The length of a side is 25 centimeters.

**10.** Student A; Student B squared incorrectly and should have subtracted seven from both sides first.

**11.** $l = \frac{A}{w}$

$= \frac{-20x + 100 + x^2}{x - 10}$

$= \frac{x^2 - 20x + 100}{x - 10}$

$= \frac{(x - 10)^2}{x - 10}$

$= x - 10$

The length of the deck is $(x - 10)$ feet.

**12. a.** By the Pythagorean Theorem:

$l^2 = (\sqrt{x})^2 + (\sqrt{x + 5})^2$

**b.** $l^2 = x + (x + 5)$

$l^2 = 2x + 5$

**c.** $(10)^2 = 2x + 5$

$100 = 2x + 5$

$95 = 2x$

$x = \frac{95}{2}$

**13.** Solve for x by substituting x for y in the second equation:

$x = \sqrt{x}$

$x^2 = x$

$x^2 - x = 0$

$x^2 - x + \frac{1}{4} = \frac{1}{4}$   complete the square

$\left(x - \frac{1}{2}\right)^2 = \frac{1}{4}$

$\sqrt{\left(x - \frac{1}{2}\right)^2} = \sqrt{\frac{1}{4}}$

$x - \frac{1}{2} = \pm\frac{1}{2}$

$x = 1$ or $x = 0$

Solve for y by substituting each value of x in the first equation:

**Saxon** Algebra 1

$y = 1$ or $y = 0$

The graphs intersect at (1, 1) and (0, 0).

**14.** The terms form a geometric sequence with common ratio:

$$\frac{25}{125} = \frac{5}{25} = \frac{1}{5} = 0.2$$

The next three terms are:

$A(5) = 125(0.2)^4 = 0.2$

$A(6) = 125(0.2)^5 = 0.04$

$A(7) = 125(0.2)^6 = 0.008$

**15.** The percent of carbon-14 remaining after each half-life forms a geometric sequence with the common ratio 0.5. After the first half-life, 50% of the original amount of carbon-14 remains, so the first term of the sequence is 0.5.

$A(9) = 0.5(0.5)^8$

$\approx 0.002$

After nine half-lives, about 0.2% of the original amount of carbon-14 remains.

**16.** Student A; Student B incorrectly multiplied by 4 rather than using 4 as an exponent.

**17.** Graph the related function on a graphing calculator $f(x) = -11x^2 + x + 4$.

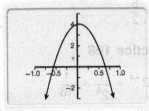

Use the [CALC] zero function to find the x-intercepts.

The solutions are $x \approx -0.6$ and $x \approx 0.7$.

**18.** $|x - 4| + 15 \geq 21$

$|x - 4| \geq 6$

$x - 4 \leq -6$ OR $x - 4 \geq 6$

$x \leq -2$ OR $x \geq 10$

**19.** $|x| + 45 \leq 34$

$|x| \leq -11$

The absolute value cannot be a negative number. The equation has no solution.

**20.** $|c - 21| \leq 0.25$

$-0.25 \leq c - 21 \leq 0.25$

$20.75 \leq c \leq 21.25$

The smallest acceptable circumference is 20.75 inches.

**21. a.** $A = \pi r^2$

$200.96 = \pi(r + 3)^2$

**b.** $\dfrac{200.96}{3.14} = (r + 3)^2$

$\sqrt{64} = \sqrt{(r + 3)^2}$

$8 = r + 3$

$r = 5$

**c.** $d = 2r$

$= 2(5 + 3)$

$= 16$

The new diameter is 16 meters.

**22.**

| $x$ | $-4$ | $-2$ | 0 | 4 | 2 |
|---|---|---|---|---|---|
| $y$ | 7 | 5 | 3 | 5 | 7 |

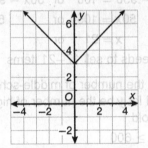

**23.** $-3x^2 + 24x = 36$

$x^2 - 8x = -12$

$x^2 - 8x + \left(\dfrac{-8}{2}\right)^2 = -12 + \left(\dfrac{8}{2}\right)^2$

$(x - 4)^2 = 4$

$\sqrt{(x - 4)^2} = \sqrt{4}$

$x - 4 = \pm 2$

$x = 6$ or $x = 2$

The answer is **C**.

**24.** $x^2 - 50x = c$

$x^2 - 50x + \left(\dfrac{50}{2}\right)^2 = c + \left(\dfrac{50}{2}\right)^2$

$x^2 - 50x + 625 = c + 625$

$(x - 25)^2 = c + 625$

$\sqrt{(x - 25)^2} = \sqrt{c + 625}$

The quantity $c + 625$ cannot be less than zero. The equation has no real solution for values of $c$ less than $-625$.

**25.** $\dfrac{\dfrac{\overset{2}{\cancel{4}x}}{\cancel{2x + 12}^{6}} + \dfrac{x}{3x + 18}}{\dfrac{8x^2}{x^2 + 8x + 12}}$

$= \dfrac{\left(\dfrac{2x}{x + 6}\right)\left(\dfrac{3}{3}\right) + \dfrac{x}{3(x + 6)}}{\dfrac{8x^2}{(x + 2)(x + 6)}}$

$= \dfrac{7\cancel{x}}{3\cancel{(x + 6)}} \cdot \dfrac{(x + 2)\cancel{(x + 6)}}{8x^{\cancel{2}}}$

$= \dfrac{7(x + 2)}{24x}$

**26.** $\sqrt{\dfrac{20}{3}} = \dfrac{2\sqrt{5}}{\sqrt{3}} \cdot \dfrac{\sqrt{3}}{\sqrt{3}} = \dfrac{2\sqrt{15}}{3}$

**27. a.** Let $x$ be the number of items sold.

$|50x - 950| = 100$

**b.** $50x - 950 = 100$ or $50x - 950 = -100$

$50x = 1050$ or $\quad 50x = 850$

$x = 21 \quad$ or $\quad\quad x = 17$

He needs to sell 17–21 items.

**28.** Let $x$ be the number of middle-school tickets sold and let $y$ be the number of high-school tickets sold.

$4x + 6y \geq 600$

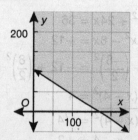

**29. a.** The length is $5 + 2x$, and the width is $4 + 2x$.

**b.** $w = \dfrac{A}{l}$

$4 + 2x = \dfrac{42}{5 + 2x}$

$(4 + 2x)(5 + 2x) = 42$

$20 + 18x + 4x^2 = 42$

$4x^2 + 18x - 22 = 0$

$2(2x^2 + 9x - 11) = 0$

$2(2x + 11)(x - 1) = 0$

$2x + 11 = 0 \quad$ or $\quad x - 1 = 0$

$2x = -11$ or $\quad\quad x = 1$

$x = -\dfrac{11}{2}$

The frame is 1 inch wide.

**30.** Transform the equation by cross-multiplying.

$\dfrac{x}{x - 3} = \dfrac{4}{x}$

$(x)(x) = 4(x - 3)$

$x^2 = 4x - 12$

## LESSON 108

### Warm Up 108

**1.** exponent

**2.** $4^2 = 4 \cdot 4 = 16$

**3.** $6^{-3} = \dfrac{1}{6^3} = \dfrac{1}{216}$

**4.** $2 \cdot 5^{-2} = \dfrac{2}{5^2} = \dfrac{2}{25}$

**5.** $5 \cdot 2^{-1} = \dfrac{5}{2}$

### Lesson Practice 108

**a.** $f(-4) = 2^{-4} = \dfrac{1}{2^4} = \dfrac{1}{16}$

$f(0) = 2^0 = 1$

$f(5) = 2^5 = 32$

**b.** $f(-3) = -3(3)^{-3} = \dfrac{-3}{3^3} = -\dfrac{1}{9}$

$f(1) = -3(3)^1 = -9$

$f(3) = -3(3)^3 = -81$

**c.** $\{(3, -12), (6, -24), (9, -36), (12, -48)\}$

$\dfrac{-24}{-12} \neq \dfrac{-36}{-24}$

The $x$-values increase by a constant amount $(+3)$, but the $y$-values do not have a common ratio. The set does not satisfy a geometric function.

**Saxon** Algebra 1

**d.** {(1, 12), (2, 36), (3, 108), (4, 324)}

$$\frac{36}{12} = \frac{108}{36} = \frac{324}{108} = 3$$

The *x*-values increase by a constant amount (+1), and the *y*-values have a common ratio (3). The set satisfies a geometric function.

**e.**

| x | y |
|---|---|
| −2 | $\frac{2}{9}$ |
| −1 | $\frac{2}{3}$ |
| 0 | 2 |
| 1 | 6 |
| 2 | 18 |

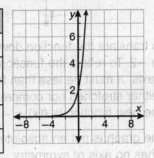

**f.**

| x | y |
|---|---|
| −2 | −1 |
| −1 | −2 |
| 0 | −4 |
| 1 | −8 |
| 2 | −16 |

**g.**

| x | y |
|---|---|
| −2 | 32 |
| −1 | 8 |
| 0 | 2 |
| 1 | $\frac{1}{2}$ |
| 2 | $\frac{1}{8}$ |

**h.**

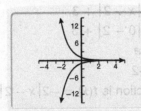

Alike: Both graphs are symmetric about the *x*-axis, and for a given *x*-value, the absolute values of the *y*-values are the same.

Different: When *a* is positive, all the range values are positive. When *a* is negative, all the range values are negative.

**i.**

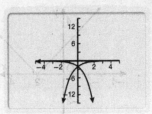

Alike: Both graphs are below the *x*-axis and symmetric about the *y*-axis.

Different: When *b* is 3, the *y*-values decrease as the *x*-values increase. When *b* is $\frac{1}{3}$, the *y*-values increase as the *x*-values increase.

**j.** Enter 8.05(1.01683)$^x$ in the Y = editor. Use the CALC function to find the *y*-value that corresponds to *x* = 6.

| X | Y₁ |
|---|---|
| 0 | 8.05 |
| 1 | 8.1855 |
| 2 | 8.3232 |
| 3 | 8.4633 |
| 4 | 8.6058 |
| 5 | 8.7506 |
| 6 | 8.8979 |

X=6

In 2006, the population will be about 8,897,900.

| X | Y₁ |
|---|---|
| 7 | 9.0476 |
| 8 | 9.1999 |
| 9 | 9.3547 |
| 10 | 9.5122 |
| 11 | 9.6723 |
| 12 | 9.835 |
| 13 | 10.001 |

X=13

The population should reach 10 million in about 2013.

**Practice 108**

**1.** $f(-2) = 2(5)^{-2} = \frac{2}{25}$

$f(0) = 2(5)^0 = 2$

$f(2) = 2(5)^2 = 50$

**2.**

| x | −2 | 0 | 2 | 3 | 4 |
|---|---|---|---|---|---|
| y | 4 | 2 | 0 | 1 | 2 |

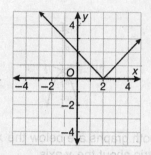

**3.** The value 1 raised to any power equals 1, so the equation really is $f(x) = 4$, a linear equation.

**4.** The graph is above the $x$-axis, so $a$ must be positive. The $y$-values decrease as the $x$-values increase, so $b$ must be less than 1. The answer is **B**.

**5.**

X=9

31.7191968338

−25.7166337996
─────────────
6.0025630342

The difference between the Texas population in 2010 and 2020 should be about 6,002,600.

**6.** $\{(2, -1), (3, -4), (4, -16), (5, -64)\}$

$$\frac{-4}{-1} = \frac{-16}{-4} = \frac{-64}{-16} = 4$$

The $x$-values increase by a constant amount ($+1$), and the $y$-values have a common ratio, $b = 4$. The set satisfies a geometric function.

**7.** The corresponding sides are $\overline{RS}$ and $\overline{NV}$, $\overline{ST}$ and $\overline{VQ}$, and $\overline{RT}$ and $\overline{NQ}$. The corresponding angles are $\angle R$ and $\angle N$, $\angle S$ and $\angle V$, and $\angle T$ and $\angle Q$.

**8.**

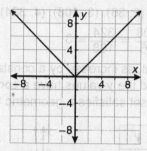

To translate the function down 2 units, $k$ must be $-2$. To reflect the function across the $x$-axis, $a$ must be less than 0. The function is neither stretched nor compressed, so $|a| = 1$. The new function is $f(x) = -|x| - 2$.

**9.** The graph is not an absolute-value function. It has no axis of symmetry.

**10.** $\sqrt[3]{(-4)^3} = \sqrt[3]{(-4) \cdot (-4) \cdot (-4)} = -4$

**11.** Each value of $x$ produces the same $y$-value as $-x$ produces.

**12.** Student B is correct. Student A squared the number 3, instead of the expression $\sqrt{x+3}$.

**13.** $\sqrt{x} - 2 = 8$

$\sqrt{x} = 10$

$(\sqrt{x})^2 = (10)^2$

$x = 100$

Check:

$\sqrt{100} - 2 = 8$

$10 - 2 = 8$

$8 = 8$ ✔

**14.** The function is translated 3 units up and 2 units to the right, so $h$ is 3 and $k$ is 2. The graph passes through $(0, -1)$. Solve for $a$.

$f(x) = a|x - 2| + 3$

$-1 = a|0 - 2| + 3$

$-4 = 2a$

$a = -2$

The function is $f(x) = -2|x - 2| + 3$.

**15.** Solve for $k$.

$xy = k$

$55(11.6) = 638$

Solve for $y$.

$y = \dfrac{k}{x}$

**Saxon** Algebra 1

$= \dfrac{638}{8}$

$= 79.75$

**16.** $a = 12\sqrt{x}$

$108 = 12\sqrt{x}$

$9 = \sqrt{x}$

$81 = x$

When the accumulation is equal to 108 inches, $x = 81$.

**17.** $\dfrac{|x|}{8} - 10 < -9$

$\dfrac{|x|}{8} < 1$

$|x| < 8$

$-8 < x < 8$

**18.** $x^2 = -9$

No real number can be squared to produce a negative number. The equation has no solution.

**19.** $12|x + 9| - 11 = 1$

$12|x + 9| = 12$

$|x + 9| = 1$

$x + 9 = 1$ or $x + 9 = -1$

$x = -8$ or $x = -10$

**20.** $A = l \cdot w$

$338 = 2x \cdot x$

$169 = x^2$

$\pm 13 = x$

The original rooms were 13 feet by 13 feet.

**21.** $\dfrac{\frac{24a^2 b}{7c^2}}{\frac{8ab^2}{49c^2}}$

$= \dfrac{\overset{3}{\cancel{24}} a^2 \cancel{b}}{\cancel{7} \cancel{c^2}} \cdot \dfrac{\overset{7}{\cancel{49}} \cancel{c^2}}{\cancel{8} a \cancel{b^2}}$

$= \dfrac{21a}{b}$

**22.** $x^2 + 7x + \left(\dfrac{7}{2}\right)^2$

$= x^2 + 7x + 12.25$

The missing term is 12.25.

**23.** $\dfrac{-\frac{5}{16}}{-\frac{5}{8}} = \dfrac{-\frac{5}{32}}{-\frac{5}{16}} = \dfrac{-\frac{5}{64}}{-\frac{5}{32}} = \dfrac{1}{2}$

The answer is **C**.

**24.** By the Pythagorean Theorem:

$\left(\dfrac{23}{12}\right)^2 + \left(\dfrac{29}{12}\right)^2 = c^2$

$\dfrac{1370}{144} = c^2$

$\sqrt{\dfrac{1370}{144}} = \sqrt{c^2}$

$\dfrac{\sqrt{1370}}{12} = c$

Li should buy $\dfrac{\sqrt{1370}}{12}$ meters of edging.

**25.** Find the ratio of consecutive pairs of terms.

$\dfrac{|-57.6|}{|-72|} = \dfrac{4}{5}$

$\dfrac{|46.08|}{|-57.6|} = \dfrac{4}{5}$

$\dfrac{|36.864|}{|46.08|} = \dfrac{4}{5}$

The sequence is not geometric.

Sample: The absolute values of the terms have a common ratio of $\dfrac{4}{5}$, but the signs of the terms do not follow a geometric pattern.

**26.** $\dfrac{12x^2 + 36x + 15}{2x + 1}$

$= \dfrac{3(4x^2 + 12x + 5)}{2x + 1}$

$= \dfrac{3(2x + 1)(2x + 5)}{2x + 1}$

$= 3(2x + 5)$

**27. a.** $\dfrac{7x^2}{x^2 - 49} + \dfrac{x - 1}{4x + 28}$

$= \dfrac{7x^2}{(x + 7)(x - 7)} + \dfrac{x - 1}{4(x + 7)}$

$= \dfrac{4(7x^2) + (x - 1)(x - 7)}{4(x + 7)(x - 7)}$

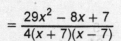
$$= \frac{29x^2 - 8x + 7}{4(x + 7)(x - 7)}$$

Amber drove $\frac{29x^2 - 8x + 7}{4(x + 7)(x - 7)}$ miles.

**b.** $t = \frac{d}{r}$

$$= \frac{\dfrac{29x^2 - 8x + 7}{4(x + 7)(x - 7)}}{\dfrac{7}{7x + 49}}$$

$$= \frac{29x^2 - 8x + 7}{4(x + 7)(x - 7)} \cdot \frac{7(x + 7)}{7}$$

$$= \frac{29x^2 - 8x + 7}{4(x - 7)}$$

Amber spent $\frac{29x^2 - 8x + 7}{4(x - 7)}$ hours delivering pizzas.

**28.**
$$w \cdot l = A$$
$$w(w + 3) = 88$$
$$w^2 + 3w = 88$$
$$w^2 + 3w + \left(\frac{3}{2}\right)^2 = 88 + \left(\frac{3}{2}\right)^2$$
$$\left(w + \frac{3}{2}\right)^2 = \frac{361}{4}$$
$$w + \frac{3}{2} = \frac{19}{2}$$
$$w = 8$$

The width is 8 inches and the length is 8 + 3, or 11 inches.

**29. a.** $9\frac{36}{60} = 9.6$

**b.** $9.6\left(\frac{1}{16}\right) + 9.6\left(\frac{1}{K}\right) = 1$

**c.** Solve for $K$.

$$9.6K + 9.6(16) = 16K$$
$$6.4K = 153.6$$
$$K = 24$$

Kim would need 24 hours to enter the data by herself.

**30.** The $x$-coordinate represents the time it takes the ball to reach its maximum height.

## LESSON 109

### Warm Up 109

1. inequality

2. Graph the dashed boundary line $y = 2x + 3$. Point (0, 0) satisfies the inequality, so shade the side of the boundary that contains (0, 0).

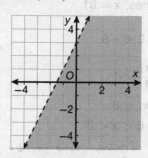

3. The boundary is solid because the inequality includes "or equal to."

4. Graph the solid boundary line $y \geq 2x - 6$. The point (0, 0) satisfies the inequality, so shade the side of the boundary that contains (0, 0).

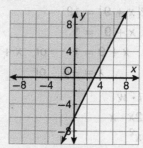

### Lesson Practice 109

**a.** Graph each inequality.

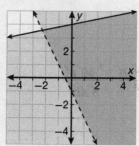

Use (0, 0) to check.

$$0 > -2(0) - 1 \qquad 0 \le \frac{1}{5}(0) + 4$$

$$0 > -1 \qquad\qquad 0 \le 4$$

**b.** Write the first inequality in slope-intercept form:

$$6y + 6 > -2x$$

$$6y > -2x - 6$$

$$y > -\frac{1}{3}x - 1$$

Graph the inequalities.

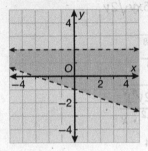

Use (0, 0) to check.

$$6(0) + 6 > -2(0) \qquad y < 2$$

$$6 > 0 \qquad\qquad 0 < 2$$

**c.** Enter the inequalities in the Y= editor. Check (0, 0) in each inequality to choose which half-plane to shade.

$$0 \ge 0 - 6 \qquad 0 \le -(0) + 3$$

$$0 \ge -6 \qquad\quad 0 \le 3$$

Shade above $y \ge x - 6$ and below $y \le -x + 3$.

**d.** Graph each inequality.

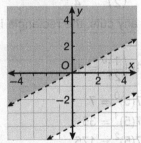

The solution of $y > \frac{1}{2}x$ is a subset of the

solution of $y > \frac{1}{2}x - 4$. The solution of the system is $y > \frac{1}{2}x$.

**e.** Graph each inequality.

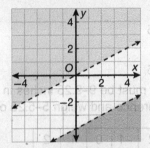

The solution sets do not intersect. The system has no solution.

**f.** Graph the inequalities.

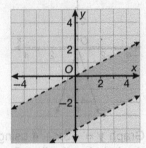

The solution set is the region between the parallel lines.

**g.** Let $x$ be the number of pounds of strawberries and $y$ be the number of pounds of pineapple.

$x \ge 2$       Brett needs at least 2 lbs of strawberries.

$y \ge 3.5$      Brett needs at least 3.5 lbs of pineapple.

$3x + 2y \le 30$   Brett has a total of $30 to spend on dried fruit.

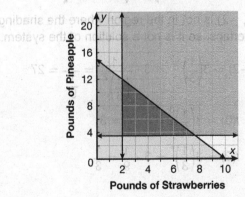

**Saxon** Algebra 1

## Practice 109

**1.** (0, 0) satisfies both the inequalities in choice **A**. The answer is **A**.

**2.** $x \geq 9$
$x \leq 9.25$
$y \geq 5$
$y \leq 5.25$
The ball must be 9–9.25 inches in circumference and weigh 5–5.25 ounces.

**3.**

| x | −2 | −1 | 0 | 1 | 2 |
|---|----|----|----|----|----|
| y | −6 | −3 | 0 | −3 | −6 |

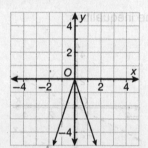

**4.** Sample: Graph $y = -3x + 4$ using a solid line and shade below the line. On the same plane, graph $y < 2x - 1$ using a dashed line and shade below the line. The solution set is the region where the shadings overlap.

**5.**

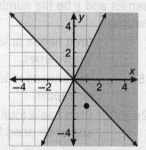

(1, −2) is not in the region where the shading overlaps, so it is not a solution of the system.

**6.** $f(-2) = 3\left(\frac{1}{3}\right)^{-2} = 3 \cdot \dfrac{1}{\left(\frac{1}{3}\right)^2} = \dfrac{3}{\frac{1}{9}} = 27$

$f(0) = 3\left(\frac{1}{3}\right)^0 = 3 \cdot 1 = 3$

$f(2) = 3\left(\frac{1}{3}\right)^2 = 3 \cdot \dfrac{1}{9} = \dfrac{1}{3}$

**7.** Let $p$ be the original price. The original price plus the markup equals the new price.
$p + 0.44p = 900$
$1.44p = 900$
$p = \dfrac{900}{1.44}$
$p = 625$
The original price was $625.

**8.** $10\sqrt{8x^2y^3} - 5y\sqrt{98x^2y}$
$= 20xy\sqrt{2y} - 35xy\sqrt{2y}$
$= -15xy\sqrt{2y}$

**9.** $\sqrt{\dfrac{24y^8}{6x^3}}$

$= \sqrt{\dfrac{(2y^4)^2}{x^2 \cdot x}}$

$= \dfrac{2y^4}{x\sqrt{x}}$

$= \dfrac{2y^4\sqrt{x}}{x^2}$

**10.** Student B; Sample: The $x$-values do not increase by a constant amount.

**11.** $4.8(1.25)^{10} - 4.8(1.25)^5$
$\approx 44.7034 - 14.648$
$\approx 30.06$
The difference is about $30.06.

**12.** After being cut in half 4 times, the rectangle is 1 inch long.
$f(4) = 16\left(\frac{1}{2}\right)^4 = 1$

After being cut in half 6 times, the rectangle is $\frac{1}{4}$ inch long.
$f(6) = 16\left(\frac{1}{2}\right)^6 = \dfrac{1}{4}$

Before any cuts, the rectangle is 16 inches long.
$f(0) = 16\left(\frac{1}{2}\right)^0 = 16$

**13.** $f(0) = 7(5)^0 = 7$
$f(1) = 7(5)^1 = 35$
$f(2) = 7(5)^2 = 175$

**Saxon** Algebra 1

$f(3) = 7(5)^3 = 875$

$f(4) = 7(5)^4 = 4375$

$f(5) = 7(5)^5 = 21,875$

Two of these six possible $x$-values produce $f(x)$ between 100 and 1000.

$\frac{2}{6} = \frac{1}{3}$

The probability is $\frac{1}{3}$.

**14.** No; Sample: An absolute value function is in the shape of a V.

**15.** Graph each inequality.

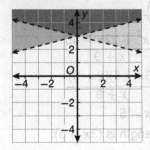

Use (0, 4) to check:

$4 > \frac{1}{4}(0) + 3 \qquad 4 > -\frac{1}{4}(0) + 3$

$4 > 3 \qquad\qquad 4 > 3$

**16.** Find the vertex of each graph.

$0 = |90t - 120|$

$0 = 90t - 120 \quad \text{or} \quad 0 = 120 - 90t$

$t = \frac{4}{3}$

$0 = |90t - 100|$

$0 = 90t - 100 \quad \text{or} \quad 0 = 100 - 90t$

$t = \frac{10}{9}$

$(\frac{10}{9}, 0)$ is to the left of $(\frac{4}{3}, 0)$. The graph shifts to the left.

**17.** Assuming the tiles measure 6 inches by 6 inches, 12 inches by 12 inches, or 13 inches by 13 inches:

$48x^2 = 6912$

$x^2 = 144$

$x = 12$

The tiles measuring 12 inches by 12 inches will work best.

**18.**

$0 = -4.9t^2 - 53.9t + 127.4$

$0 = -4.9(t^2 + 11t - 26)$

$0 = -4.9(t + 13)(t - 2)$

$t + 13 = 0 \quad \text{or} \quad t - 2 = 0$

$t = -13 \quad \text{or} \qquad t = 2$

The object will strike the ground at 2 seconds.

**19.** The terms form a geometric sequence with a common ratio of 0.9.

$\frac{4.5}{5} = \frac{4.05}{4.5} = \frac{3.645}{4.05} = 0.9$

The next three terms are:

$A(5) = 5(0.9)^4 = 3.2805$

$A(6) = 5(0.9)^5 = 2.95245$

$A(7) = 5(0.9)^6 = 2.657205$

**20.** $\sqrt{x} + 7 = -2$

$\sqrt{x} = -9$

The value of a square root cannot be negative. The answer is **C**.

**21.** Sample: The equation is easier to solve if the radical is by itself, because squaring the equation then eliminates the radical.

**22.** $w = \frac{A}{l}$

$= \frac{x^2 - 144}{x - 12}$

$= \frac{(x + 12)(x - 12)}{x - 12}$

$= x + 12$

The gym's width is $(x + 12)$ feet.

**23.** $4|x + 2| - 9 = 19$

$4|x + 2| = 28$

$|x + 2| = 7$

$x + 2 = 7 \quad \text{or} \quad -x - 2 = 7$

$x = 5 \quad \text{or} \qquad x = -9$

The solution is $\{-9, 5\}$.

**24.** $x^2 = -49$

$\sqrt{x^2} = \sqrt{-49}$

The radicand cannot be a negative number. The equation has no real solution.

**25.** $2\left|\frac{x}{4} - 6\right| = 8$

$\left|\frac{x}{4} - 6\right| = 4$

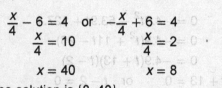

$\frac{x}{4} - 6 = 4$ or $-\frac{x}{4} + 6 = 4$

$\frac{x}{4} = 10$ $\frac{x}{4} = 2$

$x = 40$ $x = 8$

The solution is {8, 40}.

**26. a.** $h = -16(1)^2 + 47(1) + 5$

$= -16 + 47 + 5$

$= 36$

The ball is 36 feet high after 1 second.

**b.** $h = -16(0)^2 + 47(0) + 5$

$= 5$

The ball is released at 5 feet high.

**c.** $v = 47$

The initial velocity is 47 feet per second.

**27.** The boy's work rate is $\frac{1}{2}$ garden per hour, and his sister's rate is $\frac{1}{4}$ garden per hour. Let $h$ be the number of hours they need to work the garden together:

$\frac{1}{2}h + \frac{1}{4}h = 1$

$\frac{3}{4}h = 1$

$h = \frac{4}{3}$

Working together, the boy and his sister will need $\frac{4}{3}$ hours to weed the garden.

**28. a.** Graph the related function

$f(t) = -16t^2 + 31t + 7.$

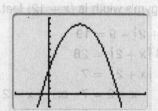

Use the CALC maximum function to find the $x$-value at the graph's vertex. The ball reaches its maximum height at about 0.97 seconds.

**b.** Use the CALC zero function to find the $x$-intercepts. The ball hits the ground at about 2.14 seconds.

**c.** Use the CALC maximum function to find the $y$-value at the graph's vertex. The maximum height of the arc of the ball is about 22.02 feet.

**29.** Sample: Similarities—Solve each inequality by subtracting 1 and dividing by 2 on both sides. Differences—For the first inequality, subtract and divide before removing the absolute-value bars. For the second inequality, write it as a compound inequality first, then subtract and divide.

**30.** $l = \frac{A}{W}$

$= \frac{3x^2 + 22x - 45}{x + 9}$

$= \frac{(3x - 5)(x + 9)}{x + 9}$

$= 3x - 5$

The length is $(3x - 5)$.

## LESSON 110

### Warm Up 110

**1.** quadratic

**2.** $c = \left(\frac{8}{2}\right)^2 = 16$

**3.** $c = \left(\frac{9}{2}\right)^2 = \frac{81}{4}$

**4.** $x^2 + 10x = 24$

$x^2 + 10x + \left(\frac{10}{2}\right)^2 = 24 + \left(\frac{10}{2}\right)^2$

$x^2 + 10x + 25 = 49$

$(x + 5)^2 = 49$

$x + 5 = \pm 7$

$x + 5 = 7$ or $x + 5 = -7$

$x = 2$ or $x = -12$

Check:

$(2)^2 + 10(2) = 24$

$4 + 20 = 24$

$24 = 24$ ✓

$(-12)^2 + 10(-12) = 24$

$144 - 120 = 24$

$24 = 24$ ✓

Saxon Algebra 1

## Lesson Practice 110

**a.** $x = \dfrac{-3 \pm \sqrt{3^2 - 4(1)(-18)}}{2(1)}$

$\quad = \dfrac{-3 \pm \sqrt{81}}{2}$

$\quad = \dfrac{-3 \pm 9}{2}$

$x = -6$ or $x = 3$

Check:

$(-6)^2 + 3(-6) - 18 = 0$

$\qquad 36 - 18 - 18 = 0$

$\qquad\qquad\qquad 0 = 0$ ✓

$(3)^2 + 3(3) - 18 = 0$

$\qquad 9 + 9 - 18 = 0$

$\qquad\qquad 0 = 0$ ✓

**b.** $0 = x^2 - 14x - 72$

$x = \dfrac{14 \pm \sqrt{(-14)^2 - 4(1)(-72)}}{2(1)}$

$\quad = \dfrac{14 \pm \sqrt{484}}{2}$

$\quad = \dfrac{14 \pm 22}{2}$

$x = 18$ or $x = -4$

Check:

$-72 - 14(18) + (18)^2 = 0$

$-72 - 252 + 324 = 0$

$\qquad\qquad\quad 0 = 0$ ✓

$-72 - 14(-4) + (-4)^2 = 0$

$-72 + 56 + 16 = 0$

$\qquad\qquad 0 = 0$ ✓

**c.** $0 = x^2 - 21x + 80$

$x = \dfrac{21 \pm \sqrt{(-21)^2 - 4(1)(80)}}{2(1)}$

$\quad = \dfrac{21 \pm \sqrt{121}}{2}$

$\quad = \dfrac{21 \pm 11}{2}$

$x = 5$ or $x = 16$

Check:

$(5)^2 + 80 = 21(5)$

$\quad 25 + 80 = 105$

$\qquad 105 = 105$ ✓

$(16)^2 + 80 = 21(16)$

$\quad 256 + 80 = 336$

$\qquad\quad 336 = 336$ ✓

**d.** $x = \dfrac{-6 \pm \sqrt{(6)^2 - 4(9)(-1)}}{2(9)}$

$\quad = \dfrac{-6 \pm \sqrt{72}}{18}$

$\quad = \dfrac{-6 \pm 6\sqrt{2}}{18}$

$\quad = \dfrac{-1 \pm \sqrt{2}}{3}$

$x \approx 0.1381$ or $x \approx -0.8047$

Check by graphing the related function
$f(x) = 9x^2 + 6x - 1$.

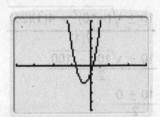

Use the CALC zero function to check the
$x$-intercepts.

**e.** $x = \dfrac{-5 \pm \sqrt{(5)^2 - 4(4)(3)}}{2(4)}$

$\quad = \dfrac{-5 \pm \sqrt{-23}}{8}$

The radicand cannot be negative. The
equation has no real solution.

**f.** $0 = -4.9x^2 + 6x + 50$

$x = \dfrac{-6 \pm \sqrt{(6)^2 - 4(-4.9)(50)}}{2(-4.9)}$

$\quad = \dfrac{-6 \pm \sqrt{1016}}{-9.8}$

$x \approx -2.6403$ or $x \approx 3.8648$

Check:

$-4.9(3.8648)^2 + 6(3.8648) + 50$

$\approx -73.1897 + 23.1888 + 50$

$\approx 0$

The ball hits the ground at about
3.8648 seconds.

379

## Practice 110

**1.** $x = \dfrac{2 \pm \sqrt{(2)^2 - 4(1)(-35)}}{2(1)}$

$= \dfrac{2 \pm \sqrt{144}}{2}$

$= \dfrac{2 \pm 12}{2}$

$x = -5$ or $x = 7$

Check:

$(-5)^2 - 2(-5) - 35 = 0$

$25 + 10 - 35 = 0$

$0 = 0$ ✓

$(7)^2 - 2(7) - 35 = 0$

$49 - 14 - 35 = 0$

$0 = 0$ ✓

**2.** $x = \dfrac{10 \pm \sqrt{(-10)^2 - 4(1)(25)}}{2(1)}$

$= \dfrac{10 \pm \sqrt{100 - 100}}{2}$

$= \dfrac{10 \pm 0}{2}$

$x = 5$

Check:

$(5)^2 - 10(5) + 25 = 0$

$25 - 50 + 25 = 0$

$0 = 0$ ✓

**3. a.** $16h^2 - 40h + 25 = 0$

**b.** $b^2 - 4ac$

$= (40)^2 - 4(16)(25)$

$= 0$

The quantity equals zero.

**c.** $b^2 - 4ac = 0$

$b^2 = 4ac$

The equation will have only one solution when $b^2 = 4ac$.

**4.** Rewrite the right-hand side without scientific notation.

$1.2 \times 10^3 = 1200$

Since $12{,}000 > 1200$, $12{,}000 > 1.2 \times 10^3$.

**5.** Graph the related function $f(x) = x^2 + 12x + 36$.

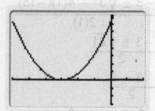

Check the $x$-intercept.

$0 = (-6)^2 + 12(-6) + 36$

$0 = 36 - 72 + 36$

$0 = 0$

The zero of the function is $-6$.

**6.** When $xy = k$ and $k$ is positive, $x$ and $y$ must both be positive or both be negative. The graph will be a hyperbola in Quadrants I and III.

**7.** The one household with 6 cars has many more cars than the other fifteen households. The data value 6 is an outlier.

**8.** The equation cannot be factored. Completing the square would mean having to work with a fractional constant. The quadratic formula is necessary.

$x = \dfrac{-15 \pm \sqrt{(15)^2 - 4(3)(-20)}}{2(3)}$

$= \dfrac{-15 \pm \sqrt{465}}{6}$

**9.** $0 = -4.9t^2 + 7t + 1.5$

$t = \dfrac{-7 \pm \sqrt{(7)^2 - 4(-4.9)(1.5)}}{2(-4.9)}$

$= \dfrac{-7 \pm \sqrt{78.4}}{-9.8}$

$\approx \dfrac{-7 \pm 8.9}{-9.8}$

$t \approx 1.6$ or $t \approx -0.2$

The ball will hit the ground in about 1.6 seconds.

**10.** Student A; Sample: $(1, -4)$ is in the region where the solution sets intersect. Student B chose a point, $(4, 2)$, that is only in one solution set.

**Saxon** Algebra 1

**11.** Graph each inequality.

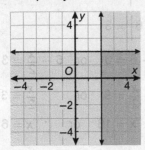

Check (3, 0):

$y \le 2$ $\qquad$ $x \ge 2$

$0 \le 2$ $\qquad$ $3 \ge 2$

**12.** Let $x$ be the number of $5, 10-minute washes. Let $y$ be the number of $15, 30-minute washes. Eight hours is equivalent to 480 minutes.

$5x + 15y \ge 300$

$10x + 30y \le 480$

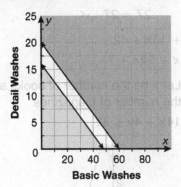

The solution sets do not intersect, so the system has no solution. The students will not be able to raise at least $300 in 8 hours.

**13.** $2l + 2w < 50$

$\qquad w > 5$

Graph the inequalities.

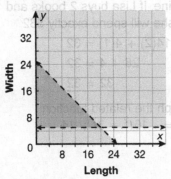

Sample: The point (14, 9) is in the solution set. The rectangle could be 14 units long and 9 units wide.

Check:

$$2l + 2w < 50 \qquad\qquad w > 5$$
$$2(14) + 2(9) < 50 \qquad\quad 9 < 5$$
$$28 + 18 < 50$$
$$46 < 50$$

**14.** $f(-2) = -3(6)^{-2} = -\dfrac{3}{(6)^2} = -\dfrac{3}{36} = -\dfrac{1}{12}$

$f(0) = -3(6)^0 = -3(1) = -3$

$f(2) = -3(6)^2 = -3(36) = -108$

**15.** Student B; Student A should not multiply 2 and 3 because 3 is the base of an exponent.

**16.** Make a table of values.

| $x$ | −1 | 0 | 1 | 2 | 3 |
|-----|-----|-----|-----|-----|-----|
| $y$ | 20 | 10 | 5 | 2.5 | 1.25 |

Graph **A** contains the points (−1, 20), (0, 10), (1, 5), (2, 2.5), and (3, 1.25). The answer is **A**.

**17.** $\dfrac{\sqrt{15xy}}{3\sqrt{10xy^3}} \cdot \dfrac{\sqrt{10xy^3}}{\sqrt{10xy^3}}$

$= \dfrac{\sqrt{150x^2y^4}}{3(10xy^3)}$

$= \dfrac{5xy^2\sqrt{6}}{30xy^3}$

$= \dfrac{\sqrt{6}}{6y}$

**18.** $\dfrac{5x^2}{10x - 30} - \dfrac{2x - 5}{x^2 - 9}$

$= \dfrac{5x^2}{10(x - 3)} - \dfrac{2x - 5}{(x + 3)(x - 3)}$

$= \dfrac{x^2(x + 3) - 2(2x - 5)}{2(x + 3)(x - 3)}$

$= \dfrac{x^3 + 3x^2 - 4x + 10}{2(x + 3)(x - 3)}$

**19.** $T = \sqrt{d^3}$

$= \sqrt{\left(\dfrac{3}{2}\right)^3}$

**Saxon** Algebra 1

$= \dfrac{\sqrt{3^3}}{\sqrt{2^3}}$

$= \dfrac{3\sqrt{3}}{2\sqrt{2}}$

$= \dfrac{3\sqrt{3}}{2\sqrt{2}} \cdot \dfrac{\sqrt{2}}{\sqrt{2}}$

$= \dfrac{3\sqrt{6}}{4}$

Mars takes about $\dfrac{3\sqrt{6}}{4}$ earth years to orbit the Sun.

**20.** The graph shows the parent function $f(x) = |x|$ translated 2 units to the right, or $f(x) = |x - 2|$. The answer is **B**.

**21.**
$p^2 + 13p = -50$

$p^2 + 13p + \left(\dfrac{13}{2}\right)^2 = -50 + \left(\dfrac{13}{2}\right)^2$

$p^2 + 13p + 42.25 = -7.75$

$(p + 6.5)^2 = -7.75$

$\sqrt{(p + 6.5)^2} = \sqrt{-7.75}$

The radicand cannot be negative. The equation has no real solutions.

**22.** $A_n = P\left(1 + \dfrac{r}{n}\right)^{nt}$

$A_1 = 1500\left(1 + \dfrac{0.045}{1}\right)^{1(1)} = 1567.50$

$A_2 = 1500\left(1 + \dfrac{0.045}{1}\right)^{1(2)} = 1638.0375$

$A_3 = 1500\left(1 + \dfrac{0.045}{1}\right)^{1(3)} = 1711.749188$

$A_4 = 1500\left(1 + \dfrac{0.045}{1}\right)^{1(4)} = 1788.777901$

Gretchen's balances at the end of each year for the first four years are $1567.50, $1638.04, $1711.75, and $1788.78.

**23.**
$\sqrt{x + 11} = 16$

$\left(\sqrt{x + 11}\right)^2 = (16)^2$

$x + 11 = 256$

$x = 245$

Check:

$\sqrt{245} + 11 = 16$

$\sqrt{256} = 16$

$16 = 16 \ \checkmark$

**24.** yes; Sample: Because multiplication does not change the absolute value like addition and subtraction do.

**25.** $9\left|\dfrac{x}{2} - 6\right| = 27$

$\left|\dfrac{x}{2} - 6\right| = 3$

$\dfrac{x}{2} - 6 = 3 \quad$ or $\quad 6 - \dfrac{x}{2} = 3$

$\dfrac{x}{2} = 9 \quad$ or $\quad \dfrac{x}{2} = 3$

$x = 18 \quad$ or $\quad x = 6$

Check:

$9\left|\dfrac{18}{2} - 6\right| = 27$

$9|3| = 27$

$9 \cdot 3 = 27$

$27 = 27 \ \checkmark$

$9\left|\dfrac{6}{2} - 6\right| = 27$

$9|-3| = 27$

$9 \cdot 3 = 27$

$27 = 27 \ \checkmark$

**26.** $x^2 + 13x + 42$

$= (x + 6)(x + 7)$

**27. a.** Let $x$ be the number of books and let $y$ be the number of magazines.

$14x + 4y \le 32$

**b.**

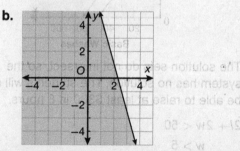

**c.** Sample: The pair (2, 1) is on the boundary line. If Lisa buys 2 books and 1 magazine, she will spend exactly $32.

$14(2) + 4(1) = 32$

$28 + 4 = 32$

$32 = 32$

**28.** Graph the related function $f(t) = -16t^2 + 3t + 14$.

**Saxon** Algebra 1

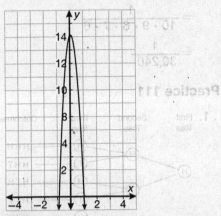

Use the [CALC] maximum function to find the y-value of the vertex. The maximum height of the path is about 14.14 feet.

Use the [CALC] zero function to find the x-intercepts. The ball hits the ground at 1.03 seconds.

**29. a.** $|t - (-247.35)| < 1.25$

$$-1.25 < t + 247.35 < 1.25$$

$$-248.6 < t < -246.1$$

‹++++++++++++++++●++++++●++++++++›
  −250      −248      −246

**b.** The boiling point of neon is −246.1°C. The melting point of neon is −248.6°C.

**30.** $\pi r^2 - 165.05 = 0$

$$\pi r^2 = 165.05$$

$$r^2 = \frac{165.05}{\pi}$$

$$r \approx \sqrt{\frac{165.05}{3.14}}$$

$$r \approx 7.249$$

The radius is about 7.249 meters.

## INVESTIGATION 11

### Investigation Practice 11

**a.** $\frac{32}{8} = 4$

The amount in the account will double 4 times.

$$y = 500(2)^x$$

$$= 500(2)^4$$

$$= 8000$$

In 32 years, the balance will be $8000.

**b.** $\frac{1440}{100} = 14.4$

The glucose has 14.4 half-lives in 24 hours.

$$y = 100\left(\frac{1}{2}\right)^x$$

$$= 100\left(\frac{1}{2}\right)^{14.4}$$

$$\approx 0.0046$$

After 24 hours, about 0.0046 milligrams of the sample will remain.

**c.** The equation models exponential decay. The value of $b$ is $\frac{1}{2}$, which is greater than zero and less than one.

**d.** Both graphs have y-intercept (0, 1) and neither crosses the x-axis. Both graphs show exponential decay. The graph of $y = \left(\frac{1}{3}\right)^x$ curves downward more sharply than the graph of $y = \left(\frac{1}{2}\right)^x$.

**e.** Both graphs have y-intercept (0, 1) and neither crosses the x-axis. The graph of $f(x) = \left(\frac{1}{2}\right)^x$ represents exponential decay. The graph of $h(x) = 2^x$ represents exponential growth. The graphs are mirror images of each other reflected over the y-axis.

**f.** Graph C; The y-intercept is 3 because $k = 3$. The value of $b$ is 0.5, which is greater than zero and less than one, so the equation is exponential decay—as x increases, y decreases.

**g.** Graph A; The y-intercept is 3 because $k = 3$. The value of $b$ is 2, which is greater than one, so the equation is exponential growth—as x increases, y increases.

**h.** Graph B; The y-intercept is 1 because $k = 1$. The value of $b$ is 4, which is greater than one, so the equation is exponential growth—as x increases, y increases.

**i.** Graph D; The y-intercept is 2 because $k = 2$. The value of $b$ is 0.25, which is greater than zero and less than one, so the equation is exponential decay—as x increases, y decreases.

**Solutions Key**

111

## LESSON 111

### Warm Up 111

1. theoretical

2. $P(\text{greater than } 3) = \dfrac{3}{6} = \dfrac{1}{2}$

3. $P(\text{greater than } 7) = \dfrac{0}{6} = 0$

4. independent; Rolling one number cube does not affect the outcome of rolling another number cube.

5. dependent; By not replacing the first marble, the outcome of the second draw is affected. There are fewer marbles to choose from.

### Lesson Practice 111

a. 2 departures · 4 turns = 8 ways

b. 6 hair · 6 faces · 6 attitudes
   · 6 oufits · 2 gender
   = 2592 characters

c. $5! = 5 \cdot 4 \cdot 3 \cdot 2 \cdot 1 = 120$

d. $\dfrac{6!}{3!} = \dfrac{6 \cdot 5 \cdot 4 \cdot 3 \cdot 2 \cdot 1}{3 \cdot 2 \cdot 1} = 6 \cdot 5 \cdot 4 = 120$

e. $_7P_7 = \dfrac{7!}{(7-7)!}$

   $= \dfrac{7!}{0!}$

   $= \dfrac{7 \cdot 6 \cdot 5 \cdot 4 \cdot 3 \cdot 2 \cdot 1}{1}$

   $= 5040$

f. $_{10}P_3 = \dfrac{10!}{(10-3)!}$

   $= \dfrac{10!}{7!}$

   $= 10 \cdot 9 \cdot 8$

   $= 720$

g. $\dfrac{\text{number of ways to choose 1, 2, 3, 4, 5}}{\text{number of ways to choose 5 seasons}}$

   $= \dfrac{1}{_{10}P_5}$

---

$= \dfrac{1}{10 \cdot 9 \cdot 8 \cdot 7 \cdot 6}$

$= \dfrac{1}{30,240}$

### Practice 111

1.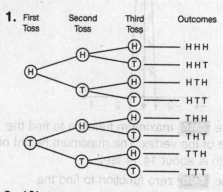

First Toss   Second Toss   Third Toss   Outcomes

HHH
HHT
HTH
HTT
THH
THT
TTH
TTT

2. 10!
   $= 10 \cdot 9 \cdot 8 \cdot 7 \cdot 6 \cdot 5 \cdot 4 \cdot 3 \cdot 2 \cdot 1$
   $= 3,628,800$
   The answer is **A**.

3. 5 drama · 6 comedy · 3 science
   = 90 combinations

4. $\dfrac{3d}{2x^3} - \dfrac{5d}{2x^3}$

   $= \dfrac{3d - 5d}{2x^3}$

   $= \dfrac{-2d}{2x^3}$

   $= -\dfrac{d}{x^3}$

5. Graph $y = x^2 - 8x + 16$.
   The x-intercept is (4, 0).
   Therefore, the zero is 4.

6. Graph $y = 3x^2 + 36x - 39$.
   The x-intercepts are (−13, 0) and (1, 0).
   Therefore, the zeros are −13 and 1.

---

**Saxon** Algebra 1

**7.** History English Math Outcomes

```
              A ── A-A-A
        A ──── B ── A-A-B
              C ── A-A-C
              A ── A-B-A
  A ──── B ── B ── A-B-B
              C ── A-B-C
              A ── A-C-A
        C ──── B ── A-C-B
              C ── A-C-C
              A ── B-A-A
        A ──── B ── B-A-B
              C ── B-A-C
              A ── B-B-A
  B ──── B ──── B ── B-B-B
              C ── B-B-C
              A ── B-C-A
        C ──── B ── B-C-B
              C ── B-C-C
              A ── C-A-A
        A ──── B ── C-A-B
              C ── C-A-C
              A ── C-B-A
  C ──── B ──── B ── C-B-B
              C ── C-B-C
              A ── C-C-A
        C ──── B ── C-C-B
              C ── C-C-C
```

**8.** Sample: Multiply 5 times 4 to get 20 possible outfits.

**9.** $c^2 + 16c - 36 = 0$

$c = \dfrac{-b \pm \sqrt{b^2 - 4ac}}{2a}$

$= \dfrac{-16 \pm \sqrt{16^2 - 4(1)(-36)}}{2(1)}$

$= \dfrac{-16 \pm \sqrt{256 + 144}}{2}$

$= \dfrac{-16 \pm \sqrt{400}}{2}$

$= \dfrac{-16 \pm 20}{2}$

$= 2$ and $-18$

**10.** $70 - 52x = -x^2$

$x^2 - 52x + 70 = 0$

$x = \dfrac{-b \pm \sqrt{b^2 - 4(1)(70)}}{2(1)}$

$x = \dfrac{-(-52) \pm \sqrt{(-52)^2 - 4(1)(70)}}{2(1)}$

$x = \dfrac{52 \pm \sqrt{2424}}{2}$

$x \approx 1$ and $x \approx 51$

**11.** Sample: The student should have made both lines dashed because the points on the boundary lines are not solutions.

**12.** $4x - 2y < 6$ $\qquad$ $y + 1 \geq 2x$

$y > 2x - 3$ $\qquad$ $y \geq 2x - 1$

Graph each inequality on the same plane. The solutions of the system are the same as the solutions of $y \geq 2x - 1$.

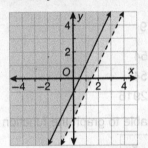

**13.** $\qquad r^2 - 24r = -144$

$r^2 - 24r + \left(\dfrac{24}{2}\right)^2 = -144 + \left(\dfrac{24}{2}\right)^2$

$r^2 - 24r + 144 = -144 + 144$

$(r - 12)^2 = 0$

$r - 12 = 0$

$r = 12$

**14.** Student B; Sample: Student A did not substitute the correct values for $a$, $b$, and $c$ and did not rearrange the equation correctly.

**15.** no, Sample: The formula involves the initial velocity and height.

**16.** $\dfrac{15}{2.54} \leq l \leq \dfrac{17}{2.54}$ $\qquad$ or $\qquad$ $5.91 \leq l \leq 6.69$

$\dfrac{9}{2.54} \leq w \leq \dfrac{11}{2.54}$ $\qquad$ $3.54 \leq w \leq 4.33$

**17.** $\qquad p^2 - 7p = 23,750$

$p^2 - 7p + \left(\dfrac{7}{2}\right)^2 = 23,750 + \left(\dfrac{7}{2}\right)^2$

$(p - 3.5)^2 = 23,762.25$

$p - 3.5 = \pm\sqrt{23,762.25}$

**Saxon** Algebra 1

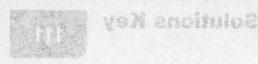
$p = 3.5 \pm 154.2$

$p \approx -150.7$ or $p \approx 157.5$

Since the number of units cannot be negative, 157,700 units need to be sold.

**18.** $\dfrac{1}{2187}, \dfrac{1}{729}, \dfrac{1}{243}, \dfrac{1}{81}, K$

The common ratio is 3.

The next three terms are:

$\dfrac{1}{81} \cdot 3 = \dfrac{1}{27}$

$\dfrac{1}{27} \cdot 3 = \dfrac{1}{9}$

$\dfrac{1}{9} \cdot 3 = \dfrac{1}{3}$

**19.** $\dfrac{\sqrt{x}}{6} = 9$

$\sqrt{x} = 54$

$x = 54^2$

$x = 2916$

**20.** Use a table to graph the function $f(x) = 3|x|$.

| x | y |
|----|---|
| -2 | 6 |
| -1 | 3 |
| 0 | 0 |
| 1 | 3 |
| 2 | 6 |

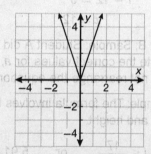

**21.** $y = 4^3 x$ is not an exponential function because it is not of the form $y = ab^x$.

The answer is **C**.

**22.** Sample: To show that the exponent of $x$ only applies to the value of 3, and not to the product of 5 and 3.

**23.** $\sqrt{2}$ is in the irrational set of numbers.

**24.** trinomial

$x^2 - 8x + 15$

$= (-2)^2 - 8(-2) + 15$

$= 4 + 16 + 15$

$= 35$

Factors

$x^2 - 8x + 15$

$= (x - 3)(x - 5)$

$= (-2 - 3)(-2 - 5)$

$= (-5)(-7)$

$= 35$

**25.** $|t - 350| \le 9$

$t - 350 \le 9$ and $-9 t - 350 \ge -9$

$t \le 359$ $t \ge 341$

The solution is $341 \le t \le 359$.

The lowest possible temperature is $341°$ F.

**26. a.** width $= x + 3$

length $= x + 2$

**b.** $(x + 3)(x + 2) = 110$

$x^2 + 5x + 6 = 110$

$x^2 + 5x - 104 = 0$

$(x + 13)(x - 8) = 0$

$x = -13$ or $x = 8$

Since length cannot be negative, $x = 8$.

length $= x + 2 = 8 + 2 = 10$

The original photo is 8 inches by 10 inches.

**27. a.** $x^2 = 21,000 + 1500$

**b.** $x^2 = 22,500$

$x = \pm\sqrt{22,500}$

$x = -150$ or $x = 150$

Since length cannot be negative, $x = 150$ ft.

**c.** $150 \text{ ft} \cdot \dfrac{2 \text{ bulbs}}{1 \text{ ft}} + 1$ bulb on last corner

301 bulbs

**28.** Sample: First, multiply by a factor of 1 using the conjugate of $\sqrt{5} - 7$, which is $\sqrt{5} + 7$. Then use the Distributive Property to multiply across the numerators, and the FOIL method to multiply across the denominators. Finally, combine like terms and simplify.

**29.** $\dfrac{2x^2}{x^2 - 49} - \dfrac{x - 7}{x^2 - 6x - 7}$

$= \dfrac{2x^2}{(x - 7)(x + 7)} - \dfrac{x - 7}{(x - 7)(x + 1)}$

$= \dfrac{2x^2(x + 1) - (x - 7)(x + 7)}{(x - 7)(x + 7)(x + 1)}$

$= \dfrac{2x^3 + 2x^2 - (x^2 - 49)}{(x - 7)(x + 7)(x + 1)}$

$= \dfrac{2x^3 + x^2 + 49}{(x - 7)(x + 7)(x + 1)}$

**30.** $g(x)$ represents exponential growth and $f(x)$ represents exponential decay.

## LESSON 112

### Warm Up 112

**1.** system

**2.** $\quad 2x^2 = -x + 8$

$\quad 2x^2 + x - 8 = 0$

**3.** $5x - y = 4 + 9x$

$\quad -y = 4 + 4x$

$\quad y = -4x - 4$

**4.** Evaluate $50 - 2x^2$ for $x = -5$.

$= 50 - 2(-5)^2$

$= 50 - 2(25)$

$= 50 - 50$

$= 0$

**5.** Substitute each ordered pair in each equation of the system.

$x - y = 7 \qquad\qquad 2x + y = -1$

$2 - (-5) \overset{?}{=} 7 \qquad 2(2) + (-5) \overset{?}{=} -1$

$7 = 7 \qquad\qquad 4 + (-5) \overset{?}{=} -1$

$\qquad\qquad\qquad -1 = -1$

The answer is **A**.

### Lesson Practice 112

**a.** The graphs of $y = x^2$ and $y = 16$ show two points of intersection. The solutions are $(-4, 16)$ and $(4, 16)$.

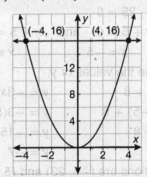

**b.** The graphs of $y = x^2$ and $y = 6x - 9$ intersect at only one point. The solution is $(3, 9)$.

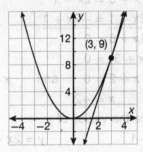

**c.** The graphs of $y = x^2$ and $y = -2x + 3$ show two points of intersection. The solutions are $(-3, 9)$ and $(1, 1)$.

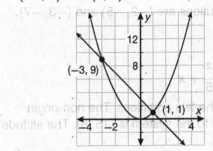

**d.** Enter $Y_1 = \dfrac{x^2}{2} + 1$ and $Y_2 = -\dfrac{3x}{2}$. Use TRACE and the intersect option. The points of intersection and therefore the solutions are $(-1, 1.5)$ and $(-2, 3)$.

**e.** Enter $Y_1 = -2x^2 - 1$ and $Y_2 = -x - 2$. Use TRACE and the intersect option. The points of intersection (and the solutions) are $(1, -3)$ and $(-0.5, -1.5)$.

**Saxon** Algebra 1

**f.**
$$y = x^2 - 3x - 17$$
$$y = -3x + 8$$
$$x^2 - 3x - 17 = -3x + 8$$
$$\underline{+3x - 8 = +3x - 8}$$
$$x^2 - 25 = 0$$
$$x + 5 = 0 \quad \text{and} \quad x - 5 = 0$$
$$x = -5 \qquad\qquad x = 5$$

Determine the values of $y$.

$$y = -3x + 8 \qquad\qquad y = -3x + 8$$
$$y = -3(-5) + 8 \qquad y = -3(5) + 8$$
$$y = 15 + 8 \qquad\qquad y = -15 + 8$$
$$y = 23 \qquad\qquad\quad y = -7$$

The solutions are $(-5, 23)$ and $(5, -7)$.

**g.**
$$y = x^2 + 7x + 5$$
$$y = 2x - 1$$
$$x^2 + 7x + 5 = 2x - 1$$
$$\underline{-2x + 1 = -2x + 1}$$
$$x^2 + 5x + 6 = 0$$
$$(x + 2)(x + 3) = 0$$
$$x + 2 = 0 \quad \text{and} \quad x + 3 = 0$$
$$x = -2 \qquad\qquad x = -3$$

Determine the values of $y$.

$$y = 2x - 1 \qquad\qquad y = 2x - 1$$
$$y = 2(-2) - 1 \qquad y = 2(-3) - 1$$
$$y = -4 - 1 \qquad\qquad y = -6 - 1$$
$$y = -5 \qquad\qquad\quad y = -7$$

The solutions are $(-2, -5)$ and $(-3, -7)$.

**h.** $y = \dfrac{2x}{5}$

$$y = -\dfrac{x^2}{25} + x$$

Graph the two equations. The non-origin solution to the system is $(15, 6)$. The altitude is 6 feet.

## Practice 112

**1.** The graphs of $y = -x^2 + 12$ and $y = -x + 6$ show two points of intersection. The solutions are $(-2, 8)$ and $(3, 3)$.

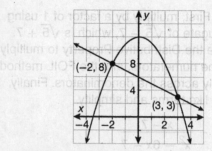

**2.** Graph each system.
$$y = -x^2 + 2$$
$$y = 3$$
The system has no solution because the graphs do not intersect. The answer is **C**.

**3.** $c^{-2}f^{-5} + \dfrac{6}{c^2 f^5}$

$$= \dfrac{1}{c^2 f^5} + \dfrac{6}{c^2 f^5}$$

$$= \dfrac{1 + 6}{c^2 f^5}$$

$$= \dfrac{7}{c^2 f^5}$$

**4.** $x > -4$ and $x < 8$ or $-4 < x < 8$

**5.** $y = -x^2 + 4$
$$y = -2x + 5$$
$$-x^2 + 4 = -2x + 5$$
$$\underline{+x^2 - 4 = +x^2 - 4}$$
$$0 = x^2 - 2x + 1$$
$$0 = (x - 1)^2$$
$$0 = x - 1$$
$$x = 1$$

Find the value of $y$.
$$y = -2x + 5$$
$$y = -2(1) + 5$$
$$y = 3$$

The point of intersection is $(1, 3)$.

**6.** one; Sample: Because the two linear equations can only intersect at one point, that point must also be the point where they both intersect the parabola. So, the maximum number of points of intersection for all three equations is one.

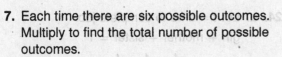
**7.** Each time there are six possible outcomes. Multiply to find the total number of possible outcomes.

$6 \cdot 6 \cdot 6$

216

**8.** Student B; Sample: $0! = 1$, not 0.

**9. a.** angle possibilities $\cdot$ side possibilities

$3 \cdot 3$

9

**b.** 2; equilateral obtuse triangle and equilateral right triangle

**10. a.** $_7P_4$

$= \dfrac{7!}{(7-4)!}$

$= \dfrac{7 \cdot 6 \cdot 5 \cdot 4 \cdot 3 \cdot 2 \cdot 1}{3 \cdot 2 \cdot 1}$

$= 840$ relay teams

**b.** $\dfrac{\text{number on team}}{\text{total runners}} = \dfrac{4}{7}$

**11.** $x^2 - 60 + 17x = 0$

$x^2 + 17x - 60 = 0$

$x = \dfrac{-b \pm \sqrt{b^2 - 4ac}}{2a}$

$x = \dfrac{-17 \pm \sqrt{529}}{2}$

$x = \dfrac{-17 \pm 23}{2}$

$x = 3$ or $x = -20$

Check:

$x^2 - 60 + 17x = 0$

$3^2 - 60 + 17(3) \overset{?}{=} 0$

$9 - 60 + 51 \overset{?}{=} 0$

$0 = 0$ ✔

$x^2 - 60 + 17x = 0$

$(-20)^2 - 60 + 17(-20) \overset{?}{=} 0$

$400 - 60 - 340 \overset{?}{=} 0$

$0 = 0$ ✔

**12.** $2a^2 + 20a - 30 = 0$

$a = \dfrac{-b \pm \sqrt{b^2 - 4ac}}{2a}$

$a = \dfrac{-20 \pm \sqrt{(20)^2 - 4(2)(-30)}}{2(2)}$

$a = \dfrac{-20 \pm \sqrt{640}}{4}$

$a = \dfrac{-20 \pm 8\sqrt{10}}{4}$

$a = -5 \pm 2\sqrt{10}$

The answer is **C**.

**13.** Sample: She is using measurements, therefore, negative values of $x$ are irrelevant.

**14.** Let $x =$ width and $y =$ length.

Perimeter: $2x + 2y = 200$

Cost: $5x + 3x + 3y + 3y = 720$

or

$x + y = 100$

$4x + 3y = 360$

Substitute $x = 100 - y$ for $x$ in the second equation.

$4(100 - y) + 3y = 360$

$400 - 4y + 3y = 360$

$-y = -40$

$y = 40$

$x = 100 - y$

$x = 100 - 40$

$x = 60$

The dimensions are 40 feet by 60 feet.

**15.** The common ratio is $-5$.

The next three terms are:

$4 \cdot (-5) = -20$

$-20 \cdot (-5) = 100$

$100 \cdot (-5) = -500$

**16.** 2, 4, 8, …

$A(n) = ar^{n-1}$

$A(12) = 2(2)^{12-1}$

$= 2 \cdot 2^{11}$

$= 2^{12}$

$= 4096$ rectangles

**17.** $\dfrac{\sqrt{x}}{6} = 12$

$\sqrt{x} = 72$

$x = 5184$

Check: $\dfrac{\sqrt{5184}}{6} \overset{?}{=} 12$

**Saxon** Algebra 1

$\frac{72}{6} \stackrel{?}{=} 12$

$12 = 12$ ✓

**18.** $y = 11.35(1.00183)^x$

Let $x = 2003 - 2000 = 3$.

$y = 11.35(1.00183)^3 \approx 11.412$

11,412,000 people

**19.** $f(x) = -2(4)^x$

$x = -2$: $f(-2) = -2(4)^{-2} = \frac{-2}{16} = -\frac{1}{8}$

$x = 0$: $f(0) = -2(4)^0 = -2 \cdot 1 = -2$

$x = 2$: $f(2) = -2(4)^2 = -2(16) = -32$

The two towns are 62.5 miles apart.

**20.** The system

$y > 2$

$y < 1$

has no solution because the two solution sets do not intersect.

The answer is **D**.

**21.** The first inequality should have $<$ and the second inequality should have $>$.

**22.** $y = x^2 - 6x - 72$

Graph the function. The $x$-intercepts are $(12, 0)$ and $(-6, 0)$. Therefore, the zeros of the function are 12 and $-6$.

**23.** Graph the boundary line $4x - y = -5$ or $y = 4x + 5$ using a solid line because the inequality is $\leq$.

Test: $(0, 0)$

$4(0) - 0 \leq -5$

$0 \leq -5$   False

Shade the half-plane that does not contain $(0, 0)$.

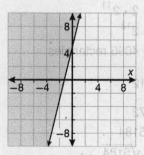

**24. a.** Let $t =$ time to complete job.

girl + mother + sister = 1

$\frac{t}{4} + \frac{t}{3} + \frac{t}{6} = 1$

**b.** $12\left(\frac{t}{4} + \frac{t}{3} + \frac{t}{6}\right) = 12(1)$

$3t + 4t + 2t = 12$

$9t = 12$

$t = \frac{4}{3}$ hours

**c.** $\frac{4}{3}$ hours $\cdot \frac{60 \text{ minutes}}{1 \text{ hour}} = 80$ minutes

**25.** $(49)^2 + (81)^2 = x^2$

$2401 + 6561 = x^2$

$8962 = x^2$

$94.567 \approx x$

**26.** $y = x^2 - 3$

$y = a$

The graph of $y = x^2 - 3$ has vertex $(0, -3)$ and opens up. Any line $y = a$, where $a > -3$, will intersect the parabola in two places, and therefore the system will have two solutions.

**27. a.** $d = r \cdot t$ or $t = \frac{d}{r}$

$t = \frac{85}{\sqrt{10,800}}$

**b.** $t = \frac{85}{\sqrt{10,800}}$

$= \frac{85}{60\sqrt{3}}$

$= \frac{17}{12\sqrt{3}} \cdot \frac{\sqrt{3}}{\sqrt{3}}$

$= \frac{17\sqrt{3}}{12 \cdot 3}$

$= \frac{17\sqrt{3}}{36}$

**28.** Sample: Divide each term of the quadratic equation by the coefficient of the quadratic term. The coefficient of the quadratic term must be 1 in order to complete the square.

**29.** The graph of the function is reflected about the $x$-axis (opens downward) and is shifted up two units.

**Saxon** Algebra 1

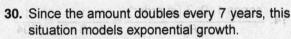
**30.** Since the amount doubles every 7 years, this situation models exponential growth.

$f(x) = 1000 \cdot 2^x$

After 42 years, the balance will have doubled $\frac{42}{7} = 6$ times.

$f(6) = 1000 \cdot 2^6$

$= 1000 \cdot 64$

$= \$64,000$

## LESSON 113

### Warm Up 113

**1.** radicand

**2.** Evaluate $-x^2 - xy - y$ for $x = -5$ and $y = -1$.

$= -(-5)^2 - (-5)(-1) - (-1)$

$= -25 - 5 + 1$

$= -29$

**3.** Evaluate $b^2 + 3ab - a$ for $a = -7$ and $b = -2$.

$= (-2)^2 + 3(-7)(-2) - (-7)$

$= 4 + 42 + 7$

$= 53$

**4.** Evaluate $ab - 5b^2$ for $a = 3$ and $b = 4$.

$= 3(4) - 5(4)^2$

$= 3(4) - 5(16)$

$= 12 - 80$

$= -68$

**5.** Evaluate $7y^2z + 9$ for $y = -3$ and $z = -1$.

$= 7(-3)^2(-1) + 9$

$= 7(9)(-1) + 9$

$= -63 + 9$

$= -54$

### Lesson Practice 113

**a.** $x^2 - 2x - 35 = 0$

$b^2 - 4ac = (-2)^2 - 4(1)(-35)$

$= 4 + 140$

$= 144$

There are two real solutions, so the graph has two x-intercepts.

**b.** $4x^2 + 20x + 25 = 0$

$b^2 - 4ac = (20)^2 - 4(4)(25)$

$= 400 - 400$

$= 0$

There is one real solution, so the graph has one x-intercept.

**c.** $2x^2 - 3x + 7 = 0$

$b^2 - 4ac = (-3)^2 - 4(2)(7)$

$= 9 - 56$

$= -47$

There are no real solutions, so the graph has no x-intercepts.

**d.**

$y = -16t^2 + 60t + 2$

$45 = -16t^2 + 60t + 2$

$0 = -16t^2 + 60t - 43$

$b^2 - 4ac = (60)^2 - 4(-16)(-43)$

$= 3600 - 2752$

$= 848$

Since the discriminant is positive, there are two real solutions. The ball will reach a height of 45 feet.

Alternate solution: Find the vertex.

$x = -\frac{b}{2a} = \frac{60}{2(-16)} = \frac{15}{8} = 1.875$

$y = -16\left(\frac{15}{8}\right)^2 + 60\left(\frac{15}{8}\right) + 2 = 58.25$

(1.875, 58.25)

The ball will reach a height of 45 feet because its maximum height is 58.25 feet.

### Practice 113

**1.** $3x^2 - x + 2 = 0$

$b^2 - 4ac = (-1)^2 - 4(3)(2)$

$= 1 - 24$

$= -23$

**2.** $2w + 2l$

$= 2(9x^2 + x + 36) + 2(4x^2 + 2x + 2)$

$= 18x^2 + 2x + 72 + 8x^2 + 4x + 4$

$= (18x^2 + 8x^2) + (2x + 4x) + (72 + 4)$

$= 26x^2 + 6x + 76$

**3.** $6|z - 3| = 18$

$|z - 3| = 3$

$z - 3 = -3$ or $z - 3 = 3$

**Saxon** Algebra 1

$z = 0$     $z = 6$

{0, 6}

**4.** $8! = 8 \cdot 7 \cdot 6 \cdot 5 \cdot 4 \cdot 3 \cdot 2 \cdot 1 = 40{,}320$

**5.** The graph does not have any x-intercepts, so there are no real real solutions, and the discriminant is negative. The answer is **A**.

**6.** The graph should be a parabola that has two x-intercepts.

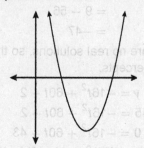

**7.** Sample: all positive values of $b^2 - 4ac$

**8.**

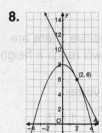

**9.** Student A; Sample: Student B added the linear equation to the quadratic equation rather than substituting it for y.

**10.** $y = -\dfrac{x^2}{25} + 2x$

$y = -x + 14$

Graph the two equations. The solution to the system is (5, 9). The altitude should be 9 feet.

**11.** Enter $Y_1 = \dfrac{x^2}{2}$ and $Y_2 = \dfrac{x}{6} + 6$.

The points of intersection to the nearest whole numbers are (−3, 5) and (4, 7).

**12.** Student A; Sample: Student B did not use the correct formula for permutations.

**13.** sandwich choices · chip choices · drink choices

$3 \cdot 3 \cdot 5$

45

**14.** $\dfrac{\text{songs 1, 2, 3 (in order)}}{{}_9P_3} = \dfrac{1}{9 \cdot 8 \cdot 7} = \dfrac{1}{504}$

**15.** $\sqrt{x} + 2 = 8$

$\dfrac{-2 = -2}{\sqrt{x} = 6}$

$x = 36$

Check:

$\sqrt{36} + 2 \overset{?}{=} 8$

$6 + 2 \overset{?}{=} 8$

$8 = 8$ ✓

**16.** $\sqrt{x + 2} = \sqrt{2x - 4}$

$(\sqrt{x + 2})^2 = (\sqrt{2x - 4})^2$

$x + 2 = 2x - 4$

$x = 6$

**17.** Use a table to graph the function $f(x) = |x + 4|$.

| x | y |
|----|---|
| −6 | 2 |
| −4 | 0 |
| −2 | 2 |
| 0 | 4 |
| 2 | 6 |

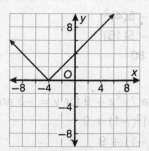

**18. a.** $x(x + 2) = 143$

$x^2 + 2x = 143$

$x^2 + 2x - 143 = 0$

$x = \dfrac{-b \pm \sqrt{b^2 - 4ac}}{2a}$

$x = \dfrac{-2 \pm \sqrt{2^2 - 4(1)(-143)}}{2(1)}$

$x = \dfrac{-2 \pm \sqrt{576}}{2(1)}$

**Saxon** Algebra 1

$$x = \frac{-2 \pm 24}{2}$$

$x = -13$ or $x = 11$

Since length is not negative, the dimensions are 11 feet by $x + 2 = 13$ feet.

**b.** $2l + 2w$

$2(13) + 2(11)$

$26 + 22$

48 feet

**19. a.** Graph $h = -16t^2 + 14t + 50$ on the graphing calculator by entering $Y_1 = -16t^2 + 14t + 50$. Use the maximum function to find the vertex $(0.44, 53.06)$. The maximum height is reached at 0.44 seconds.

**b.** Use the Zero function to determine the zeros. Since time cannot be negative, the ball hits the ground at $t = 2.26$ seconds.

**c.** From the vertex in part a, the maximum height is $h = 53.1$ feet.

**20.** Evaluate $= \sqrt{\dfrac{3h}{2}}$ for $h = 5176$.

$$d = \sqrt{\frac{3 \cdot 5176}{2}}$$

$$= \sqrt{\frac{15{,}528}{2}}$$

$$= \sqrt{7764}$$

$$= 2\sqrt{1941} \text{ feet}$$

**21.** $y \geq -\dfrac{3}{5}x + 3$

$y \geq \dfrac{3}{4}x + 3$

Graph each inequality on the same plane. The solutions of this system is the overlapping shaded region.

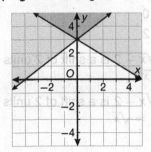

**22.** Sample: The first equation has a variable for the initial height while the second equation assumes that the initial height is 0.

**23.** The boundary line has a $y$-intercept of $-6$ and slope of 1. Therefore, the equation of the boundary line is $y = x - 6$. The inequality symbol is $>$ since the graph is shaded above the dashed line.

$y > x - 6$

**24.** $y = -16t^2 + 84t$

Use the equation $200 = -16t^2 + 84t$.

$0 = -16t^2 + 84t - 200$

$b^2 - 4ac = (84)^2 - 4(-16)(-200) = -5744$

Since the discriminant is negative, the projectile will not reach 200 feet.

**25.** $36x = 9x^2 + 36$

$0 = 9x^2 - 36x + 36$

$0 = 9(x^2 - 4x + 4)$

$0 = 9(x - 2)^2$

$x - 2 = 0$

$x = 2$

**26.** Since the exponential function $f(x) = 100(1.065)^x$ is of the form $y = ab^x$ where $b > 1$, the answer is **B**.

**27. a.** $-4.9t^2 - 29.4t + 34.3 = 0$

$-4.9t^2 - 29.4t = -34.3$

$\dfrac{-4.9t^2 - 29.4t}{-4.9} = \dfrac{-34.3}{-4.9}$

$t^2 + 6t = 7$

**b.** $t^2 + 6t + \left(\dfrac{6}{2}\right)^2 = 7 + \left(\dfrac{6}{2}\right)^2$

$t^2 + 6t + 9 = 7 + 9$

$(t + 3)^2 = 16$

$t + 3 = \pm\sqrt{16}$

$t = -3 \pm 4$

$t = -7$ or $t = 1$

**c.** 1 minute; Time cannot be negative.

**28.** yes; Sample: If the common ratio is $\dfrac{1}{3}$, the fifth term is $-81\left(\dfrac{1}{3}\right)^4 = -1$. If the common ratio is $-\dfrac{1}{3}$, the fifth term is $-81\left(-\dfrac{1}{3}\right)^4 = -1$.

**Saxon** Algebra 1

**29.** If a quadratic function has been vertically compressed, it means the parabola is wider than the parent quadratic function $f(x) = x^2$.

**30.** They are mirror images of each other reflected about the $y$-axis.

## LAB 10

### Practice Lab 10

**a.** Enter $Y = 3\sqrt{x + 2}$ in the graphing calculator. Graph the function by pressing ZOOM and choosing 6:Standard.

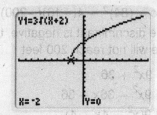

Press TRACE and . Investigate the actual points on the graph using the Table feature.

The graph starts at $(-2, 0)$.

**b.** Enter $Y = 2\sqrt{x + 2}$ in the graphing calculator. Graph the function by pressing ZOOM and choosing 6:Standard.

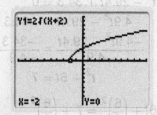

Press TRACE and the . Investigate the actual points on the graph using the Table feature. The graph starts at $(-2, 0)$.

## LESSON 114

### Warm Up 114

**1.** like radicals, unlike radicals

**2.** $-6\sqrt{2} + 8\sqrt{2}$
$= \sqrt{2}(-6 + 8)$
$= 2\sqrt{2}$

**3.** $31\sqrt{5} - 13\sqrt{5}$
$= \sqrt{5}(31 - 13)$
$= 18\sqrt{5}$

**4.** $(7 + \sqrt{6})(4 - \sqrt{9})$
$= (7 + \sqrt{6})(4 - 3)$
$= (7 + \sqrt{6})(1)$
$= 7 + \sqrt{6}$

**5.** $(\sqrt{3} - 12)^2$
$= (\sqrt{3})^2 - 2\sqrt{3}(12) + 12^2$
$= 3 - 24\sqrt{3} + 144$
$= 147 - 24\sqrt{3}$

### Lesson Practice 114

**a.**

| $x$ | $y = 3\sqrt{x + 1}$ | $y$ |
|---|---|---|
| $-1$ | $3\sqrt{-1 + 1} = 3(0)$ | 0 |
| 0 | $3\sqrt{0 + 1} = 3(1)$ | 3 |
| 3 | $3\sqrt{3 + 1} = 3(2)$ | 6 |
| 8 | $3\sqrt{8 + 1} = 3(3)$ | 9 |
| 15 | $3\sqrt{15 + 1} = 3(4)$ | 12 |

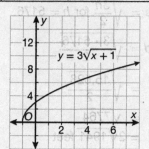

**b.** $f(x) = \sqrt{\dfrac{x}{3}}$

$\dfrac{x}{3} \geq 0$

$x \geq 0$

**c.** $f(x) = \sqrt{x - 2}$

$x - 2 \geq 0$

$x \geq 2$

**d.** $f(x) = \sqrt{x} - 2$ is a shift of 2 units down from $f(x) = \sqrt{x}$.

**e.** $f(x) = \sqrt{x - 2}$ is a shift of 2 units to the right from $f(x) = \sqrt{x}$.

**Saxon** Algebra 1

**f.** $f(x) = -\sqrt{x + 3}$ is a reflection over the
*x*-axis, then a shift of 3 units to the left
from $f(x) = \sqrt{x}$.

**g.** $f(x) = \sqrt{-x} - 4$ is a reflection over the
*y*-axis, then a shift of 4 units down from
$f(x) = \sqrt{x}$.

**h.** Evaluate $t = 0.45\sqrt{x}$ for $x = 8$.
$$t = 0.45\sqrt{8}$$
Sample: about 1.27 seconds

## Practice 114

**1.** $|z + 5| + 11 = 10$
$$|z + 5| = -1$$
Since the absolute value is never negative,
the solution set is { } or $\emptyset$.

**2.** $\qquad 10x^2 = 70x$
$$10x^2 - 70x = 0$$
$$10x(x - 7) = 0$$
$$10x = 0 \quad \text{or} \quad x - 7 = 0$$
$$x = 0 \qquad\qquad x = 7$$

**3.** $\qquad 24x = 32x^2$
$$-32x^2 + 24x = 0$$
$$-8x(4x - 3) = 0$$
$$-8x = 0 \quad \text{or} \quad 4x - 3 = 0$$
$$x = 0 \qquad\qquad x = \frac{3}{4}$$

**4.**
$$\frac{5}{x + 1} - \frac{2}{x} = \frac{5}{10x}$$
$$10x\left(\frac{5}{x + 1}\right) - 10x\left(\frac{2}{x}\right) = 10x\left(\frac{5}{10x}\right)$$
$$(x + 1)\left(\frac{50x}{x + 1}\right) - (x + 1)(20) = 5(x + 1)$$
$$50x - 20x - 20 = 5x + 5$$
$$30x - 20 = 5x + 5$$
$$25x = 25$$
$$x = 1$$

**5.** Evaluate $y = \sqrt{x + 6} - 1$ for $x = 2$.
$$y = \sqrt{2 + 6} - 1$$
$$= \sqrt{8} - 1$$
$$= 2\sqrt{2} - 1$$
The answer is **C**.

**6.** Evaluate $y = \sqrt{10d}$ for $d = 400$.
$$y = \sqrt{10 \cdot 400}$$
$$y = \sqrt{4000}$$
$$y \approx 63 \text{ meters per second}$$

**7.** $x > 19.5$; Sample:
$$(f(x))^2 < \left(\sqrt{\frac{4x}{3} - 1}\right)^2$$
$$5^2 < \frac{4x}{3} - 1$$
$$25 < \frac{4x}{3} - 1$$
$$26 < \frac{4x}{3}$$
$$78 < 4x$$
$$19.5 < x$$

**8.** Sample: Translate the parent function, $f(x) = \sqrt{x}$, 2 units to the right and then translate
the resulting graph 3 units up.

**9.** $2x^2 - 5x - 4 = 0$
$$b^2 - 4ac = (-5)^2 - 4(2)(-4)$$
$$= 25 + 32$$
$$= 57$$

**10.** Student B; Sample: The values of *a*, *b*, and *c*
are found when the equation is set equal to 0.

**11.** yes; Sample: The equation $50 = (x + 12)$
$(x + 8)$ represents the area of the rectangle.
Then $50 = x^2 + 20x + 96$ and $0 = x^2 + 20x + 46$. The discriminant of this equation is
216. Since the discriminant is positive,
there is a value for *x* that makes the
equation true.

**12. a.** $288 = (3 + x)(6 - x)$
$$288 = 18 - 3x + 6x - x^2$$
$$0 = -270 + 3x - x^2$$
or $0 = -x^2 + 3x - 270$

**b.** $a = -1$, $b = 3$, $c = -270$

**c.** $b^2 - 4ac = 3^2 - 4(-1)(-270)$
$$= 9 - 1080$$
$$= -1071$$

**d.** no; There is no base possible because
the discriminant of the equation is
negative.

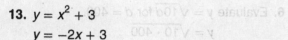
**13.** $y = x^2 + 3$

$y = -2x + 3$

The graphs show two points of intersection. The solutions are $(-2, 7)$ and $(0, 3)$.

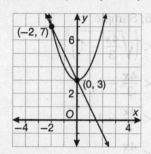

**14.** Student B; Sample: Student A did not add 4 to both sides when setting the equation equal to zero.

**15.** $y = -x^2 + 7x$

$y = x$

Graph the two equations. The non-origin solution to the system is $(6, 6)$ The altitude is 6 feet.

**16.** $y = \dfrac{x^2}{2}$

$y = 4x - 6$

Graph the two equations. The two points of intersections and therefore the solutions are $(6, 18)$ and $(2, 2)$

$6 - 2 = 4$; $8$ cm $= 2(4$ cm$)$, so 1 unit = 2 cm.

**17.** Use a table to graph the function $f(x) = |x| - 2$.

| x | y |
|----|----|
| -4 | 2 |
| -2 | 0 |
| 0 | -2 |
| 2 | 0 |
| 4 | 2 |

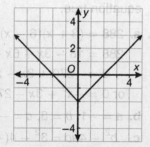

**18.** $x - 65 = |5|$

$x - 65 = 5$ or $x - 65 = -5$

$x = 65 + 5$ or $x = 65 - 5$

$x = 70°$ $x = 60°$

**19.** Arrange the ordered pairs so that the $x$-values are increasing.

$\{(2, 1),(4, 2),(6, 3),(8, 4)\}$

The $x$-values increase by 2.

$2 \div 1 = 2$

$3 \div 2 = 1\dfrac{1}{2}$

$4 \div 3 = 1\dfrac{1}{3}$

Because the ratios are not the same, the ordered pairs do not satisfy an exponential function.

**20.** Let $x$ = number of cars and $y$ = number of motorcycles.

$1800x + 600y \le 8000$

$x + y \ge 5$

$x \ge 1$

$y \ge 4$

Graph the inequalities. The region where all four solution sets intersect shows the possible combinations. Sample: 2 cars and 6 motorcycles or 3 cars and 4 motorcycles

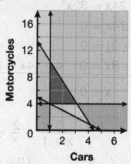

**21.** $x^2 = 19x - 60$

$x^2 - 19x + 60 = 0$

$x = \dfrac{-b \pm \sqrt{b^2 - 4ac}}{2a}$

$x = \dfrac{-(-19) \pm \sqrt{(-19)^2 - 4(1)(60)}}{2(1)}$

$x = \dfrac{19 \pm \sqrt{121}}{2} = \dfrac{19 \pm 11}{2}$

$x = 4$ or $x = 15$

**22.** $_3P_3 = \dfrac{3!}{(3 - 3)!} = \dfrac{3!}{0!} = \dfrac{3 \cdot 2 \cdot 1}{1} = 6$

The answer is **B**.

**Saxon** Algebra 1

**23.** Sample: When you are trying to find the number of ways to pick items and the order of the items matters.

**24. a.** $60 \text{ feet} \cdot \dfrac{12 \text{ inches}}{1 \text{ foot}} = 720 \text{ inches}$

    **b.** $|d - 720| \le \dfrac{1}{2}$

$$d - 720 \ge -\dfrac{1}{2} \text{ and } d - 720 \le \dfrac{1}{2}$$

$$d \ge 719\dfrac{1}{2} \qquad d \le 720\dfrac{1}{2}$$

$$719\dfrac{1}{2} \le d \le 720\dfrac{1}{2}$$

    **c.** $719\dfrac{1}{2} - \left(4\dfrac{1}{8} \div 2\right)$

$$719\dfrac{1}{2} - 2\dfrac{1}{16}$$

$$717\dfrac{7}{16} \text{ inches}$$

**25.** Evaluate $y = \sqrt{2x} + 3$ for $x = 8$.

$$y = \sqrt{2 \cdot 8} + 3$$
$$y = \sqrt{16} + 3$$
$$y = 4 + 3$$
$$y = 7$$

**26.** Let $h$ = height. Then $h + 30$ = base.

$$A = \dfrac{1}{2}bh$$

$$900 = \dfrac{1}{2}(h + 30)(h)$$

$$1800 = h^2 + 30h$$

$$0 = h^2 + 30h - 1800$$

$$0 = (h - 30)(h + 60)$$

$$h = 30 \text{ or } h = -60$$

Since length cannot be negative, height = 30 yards and base = 60 yards.

**27. a.** $A_{(n)} = ab^n$

      $A_{(n)} = 32{,}000(1.04)^n$

    **b.** $40{,}000 = 32{,}000(1.04)^n$

      $1.25 = 1.04^n$

      $6 \approx n$

    **c.** Let $n = 12$.

      $32{,}00(1.04)^{12} \approx \$51{,}233.03$

**28.**
$$\sqrt{x + 3} = 2x$$
$$(\sqrt{x + 3})^2 = (2x)^2$$
$$x + 3 = 4x^2$$
$$0 = 4x^2 - x - 3$$
or $4x^2 - x - 3 = 0$

**29.** Because the coefficient of $x^2$ (i.e., 4) is greater than 1, the graph has been vertically stretched (which means the graph is narrower than the parent quadratic function).

**30.** Both are exponential functions with the same shape, but $g(x)$ has been vertically stretched by a factor of four.

## LESSON 115

### Warm Up 115

**1.** standard

**2.** degree: 2 (degree of the greatest-degree term)

$$8 + x^2 + 2x = x^2 + 2x + 8$$

**3.** degree: 4 (degree of the greatest-degree term)

$$2x^3 - 6x + x^4 = x^4 + 2x^3 - 6x$$

**4.** $(125)^{\frac{1}{3}}$

$$= \sqrt[3]{125}$$
$$= \sqrt[3]{5^3}$$
$$= 5$$

**5.** $\sqrt[3]{-343}$

$$= \sqrt[3]{(-7)^3}$$
$$= -7$$

The answer is **B**.

### Lesson Practice 115

**a.** Use a table to graph the function $y = x^3 + 1$.

| $x$ | $-3$ | $-2$ | $-1$ | 0 | 1 | 2 | 3 |
|-----|------|------|------|---|---|---|----|
| $y$ | $-26$ | $-7$ | 0 | 1 | 2 | 9 | 28 |

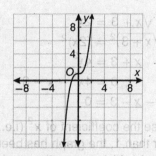

**b.** Graph $y = -4x^3$.
Find the $x$-intercept.
The solution is $x = 0$.

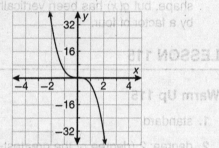

**c.**
$$3 = -x^3 + 8$$
$$0 = -x^3 + 5$$
Graph $y = -x^3 + 5$.
Find the $x$-intercept.
The solution is $x \approx 1.70998$.

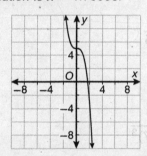

**d.** $x^2 - \frac{1}{4} = \frac{1}{4}x^3$

Enter $Y = \frac{1}{4}x^3 - x^2 + \frac{1}{4}$

The graph shows there are three $x$-intercepts.
Use CALC and the zero command to find the solutions:

$x \approx -0.47$, $x \approx 0.54$, $x \approx 3.94$

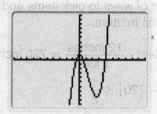

**e.** $V = x^3 + 4$

Enter $Y = x^3 + 4$

in a graphing calculator. Use TRACE
function to find $y$-value when $x \approx 25.5$.
$V \approx 16{,}648$ cubic units

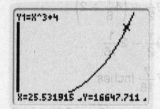

### Practice 115

**1.**
$$\frac{x-2}{x+7} = \frac{x-6}{3x+21}$$
$$(x-2)(3x+21) = (x+7)(x-6)$$
$$3x^2 + 15x - 42 = x^2 + 1x - 42$$
$$2x^2 + 14x = 0$$
$$2x(x+7) = 0$$

$2x = 0$    or    $x + 7 = 0$
$x = 0$            $x = -7$

Check:
$$x = 0$$
$$\frac{0-2}{0+7} \overset{?}{=} \frac{0-6}{3(0)+21}$$
$$-\frac{2}{7} \overset{?}{=} -\frac{6}{21}$$
$$-\frac{2}{7} = -\frac{2}{7} \checkmark$$
$$x = -7$$
$$\frac{-7-2}{-7+7} \overset{?}{=} \frac{-7-6}{3(-7)+21}$$
$$-\frac{9}{0} \overset{?}{=} -\frac{13}{0}$$

undefined
The solution is $x = 0$.

**Saxon** Algebra 1

**2.**
$$\frac{x-4}{x+1} = \frac{x+5}{2x+2}$$
$$(x-4)(2x+2) = (x+1)(x+5)$$
$$2x^2 - 6x - 8 = x^2 + 6x + 5$$
$$x^2 - 12x - 13 = 0$$
$$(x-13)(x+1) = 0$$

$$x - 13 = 0 \quad \text{or} \quad x + 1 = 0$$
$$x = 13 \qquad\qquad x = -1$$

Check:

$$x = 13$$

$$\frac{13-4}{13+1} \stackrel{?}{=} \frac{13+5}{2(13)+2}$$

$$\frac{9}{14} \stackrel{?}{=} \frac{18}{28}$$

$$\frac{9}{14} = \frac{9}{14} \checkmark$$

$$x = -1$$

$$\frac{-1-4}{-1+1} \stackrel{?}{=} \frac{-1+5}{2(-1)+2}$$

$$\frac{-5}{0} \stackrel{?}{=} \frac{4}{0}$$

undefined
The solution is $x = 13$.

**3.** Graph $y = \frac{1}{3}x^3$.

To find the x-intercept to solve $0 = \frac{1}{3}x^3$.
The solution is $x = 0$.

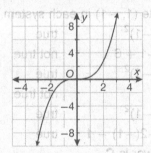

**4.** A cubic function is a polynomial function of degree 3. $y = x^3 - 4x + 1$ is a cubic function. The answer is **C**.

**5.** $V = x^3 - 4$

| x | 1 | 2 | 3 |
|---|---|---|---|
| V | -3 | 4 | 23 |

$x = 3$ when $V = 23$ cubic units.

**6.** $V = \frac{4}{3}\pi r^3$

Enter $Y = \frac{4}{3}\pi r^3$ in a graphing calculator.
Use the [TRACE] function to find y-value when $x = 2$.
$V \approx 33.51$ cubic inches

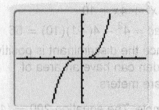

**7.** Sample: The ends of the graph go in opposite directions, it is a smooth curve, and the graph crosses the x-axis at least once and at most 3 times.

**8.** Sample: $y = 10x^3$

**9.** Evaluate $y = \sqrt{4x} - 5$ for $x = 3$.
$$y = \sqrt{4 \cdot 3} - 5$$
$$y = \sqrt{12} - 5$$
$$y = 2\sqrt{3} - 5$$
$$y \approx -1.5$$

**10.** Student B; Sample: Student A incorrectly subtracted the 5 from 6.

**11. a.** $t = 0.45\sqrt{x}$

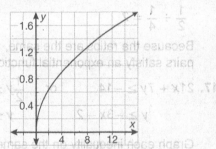

**b.** Find $x = 12$ on the x-axis. Move vertically up to graph, then horizontally left to y-axis. Sample: $\approx 1.6$ seconds

**12.** $6x^2 + 2x - 1 = 0$
$$b^2 - 4ac = (2)^2 - 4(6)(-1)$$
$$= 4 + 24$$
$$= 28$$

Since the discriminant is positive, there are two real solutions.

**Saxon** Algebra 1

**13.** Student B; Sample: The value of $c$ is $-4$, not 4.

**14.** $A = lw$

$A = (6 + x)(10 - x)$

$A = 60 + 4x - x^2$

$50 = 60 + 4x - x^2$

$0 = -x^2 + 4x + 10$

$b^2 - 4ac = 4^2 - 4(-1)(10) = 56$

Yes, since the discriminant is positive, the garden can have an area of 50 square meters.

**15.** no; Sample: The equation $200 = (15 - x)(12 + x)$ represents the area of the rectangle; $200 = 180 + 3x - x^2$ and $0 = -x^2 + 3x - 20$. The discriminant of this equation is $3^2 - 4(-1)(-20) = 9 - 80 = -71$. Since the discriminant is negatve, there is no value for $x$ that makes the equation true.

**16.** Arrange the ordered pairs so that the $x$-values are increasing.

$$\left\{\left(-4, \frac{1}{16}\right), \left(-3, \frac{1}{8}\right), \left(-2, \frac{1}{4}\right), \left(-1, \frac{1}{2}\right)\right\}$$

The $x$-values increase by 1.

$\dfrac{1}{8} \div \dfrac{1}{16} = 2$

$\dfrac{1}{4} \div \dfrac{1}{8} = 2$

$\dfrac{1}{2} \div \dfrac{1}{4} = 2$

Because the ratios are the same, the ordered pairs satisfy an exponential function.

**17.** $21x + 7y \geq -14$    or    $\dfrac{1}{2}y \leq -x + 2$

$\qquad\qquad y \geq -3x - 2 \qquad\qquad y \leq -2x + 4$

Graph each inequality on the same plane. The solutions of the system is the overlapping shaded region.

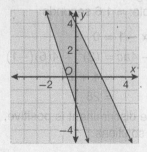

**18.** $A = \dfrac{1}{2}bh$

$48 = \dfrac{1}{2}(x + 4)(x)$

$96 = x^2 + 4x$

$0 = x^2 + 4x - 96$

$0 = (x + 12)(x - 8)$

$x + 12 = 0$    or    $x - 8 = 0$

$x = -12$    or    $x = 8$

Since length cannot be negative, $h = 8$ units and $b = 12$ units.

**19.** Graph $y = 3x^3$. Find the $x$-intercept to solve $0 = 3x^3$. The solution is $x = 0$.

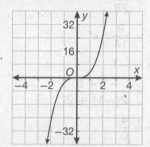

**20.** There are 4 possibilities for the first digit, 2 possibilities for the second digit, and 9 possibilities for the third digit. Multiply to find the total number of possibilities.

$4 \cdot 2 \cdot 9$

72 area codes

**21.** Substitute $(1, -1)$ in each system.

**A.** $1 = (-1)^2$        true

$\quad 1 = -1 + 6$       not true

**B.** $1 = (-1)^2$        true

$\quad 1 = 6$               not true

**C.** $1 = (-1)^2$        true

$\quad 1 = -2(-1) - 1$    true

The answer is **C**.

**22.** none; Sample: The second parallel line could intersect the parabola, at least once. However, since it never intersects the other linear equation, there can be no solution to the system.

**Saxon** Algebra 1

**23.** Let $x$ = the number of big bows and $y$ = the number of small bows.

$5x + 2y \le 20$

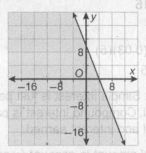

**24.** $-x^2 + 2 = -7x$

Enter $Y = x^2 - 7x - 2$ in a graphing calculator. Find the $x$-intercepts. The solutions are $x = -0.3$ and $x = 7.3$.

**25.** $x^2 + 7 = -42$

$x^2 = -49$

$x = \pm\sqrt{-49}$

There are no real-number solutions.
The answer is **C**.

**26.** The sequence is 1, 3, 6, 12, ...

Extend the sequence by doubling the previous term.

1, 3, 6, 12, 24, 48, 96, ...

After 6 sets of calls, 96 people are notified.

**27. a.** $P = 4s = 4\sqrt{x+1}$ units

**b.** $8 = 4\sqrt{x+1}$

$2 = \sqrt{x+1}$

$2^2 = \sqrt{x+1}^2$

$4 = x + 1$

$3 = x$

**28.** $f(x) = -0.5\,|x|$

Sample: The negative sign indicates that the "V" will open downward.

**29.** $d = |60t - 90|$

If the ball were kicked at 80 feet per second, the graph would be compressed.

**30.** linear, quadratic, exponential

## LESSON 116

### Warm Up 116

**1.** proportion

**2.** $24\% = \dfrac{24}{100} = \dfrac{6}{25}$

$24\% = 0.24$

**3.** $\dfrac{1}{40} = 0.025 = 2.5\%$

**4.** 25% of 250

$0.25 \cdot 250$

$62.5$

**5.** $36 = p \cdot 1125$

$\dfrac{36}{1125} = \dfrac{1125p}{1125}$

$p = 0.032$

$3.2\%$

### Lesson Practice 116

**a.** $I = Prt$

$= 5600(0.04)(10)$

$= \$2240$

**b.** $I = Prt$

$= 25{,}000(0.06)(12)$

$= \$18{,}000$

Total $= 25{,}000 + 18{,}000$

$= \$43{,}000$

**c.** $I = Prt$

$562.5 = 4500(0.025)t$

$562.5 = 112.5t$

$5 = t$

5 years

**d.** $I = Prt$

$130 = 2600(r)\left(\dfrac{15}{12}\right)$

$130 = 3250r$

$0.04 = r$

$4\%$

**e.** $A = P\left(1 + \dfrac{r}{n}\right)^{nt}$

$= 12{,}000\left(1 + \dfrac{0.04}{1}\right)^{1 \cdot 30}$

$= 12,000(1.04)^{30}$

$= \$38,920.77$

f. $A = P\left(1 + \dfrac{r}{n}\right)^{nt}$

$= 12,000\left(1 + \dfrac{0.04}{4}\right)^{4 \cdot 30}$

$= 12,000(1.01)^{120}$

$= \$39,604.64$

g. Applying the formula $I = Prt$, the interest each year is $300.

| Years | $Prt = I$ | Total Amount in Account |
|-------|-----------|-------------------------|
| 1 | $300 | $2800 |
| 2 | $600 | $3100 |
| 5 | $1500 | $4000 |
| 10 | $3000 | $5500 |

h. Use the formula $A = P(1 + r)^t$ to complete the table.

| Principal | Rate | Years | $A = P(1 + r)^t$ |
|-----------|------|-------|------------------|
| $2500 | 12% | 1 | $2800 |
| $2500 | 12% | 2 | $3136 |
| $2500 | 12% | 3 | $4405.85 |
| $2500 | 12% | 4 | $7764.62 |

The account earning compound interest increases more rapidly.

i.

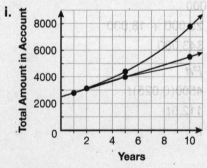

j. $A = P(1 + r)^t$

30-year-old:

$A = 4000(1 + 0.05)^{30}$

$= 17,287.77$

40-year-old:

$A = 6000(1 + 0.05)^{20}$

$= 15,919.79$

$17,287.77 - 15,919.79 = 1367.98$

The 30-year-old man's investment will be worth more by $1367.98.

**Practice 116**

1. $I = Prt$

$= 900(0.03)(5)$

$= \$135$

2. Sample: Simple interest is just paid on the principal. Compound interest is paid on the principal and interest earned.

3. The total amount in account ($y$-axis) at 0 years ($x$-axis) is $200.

4. Enter $Y = 3.45(1.00617)^x$ in a graphing calculator. Access the TABLE function. To find when the population will reach 4 million, scroll down until $y = 4$. It occurs during the 25th year, or in 2025.

5. $I = Prt$

$= 600(0.11)(14)$

$= 924$

Total $= 600 + 924 = \$1524$

The answer is **B**.

6. $A = P(1 + r)^t$

$= 3000(1 + 0.10)^{20}$

$= \$20,182.50$

7. Graph $y = -3x^3$.

Find the $x$-intercept.

The solution is $x = 0$.

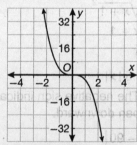

8. Student A; Sample: The word "cubed" means to the third power, not to the second power.

9. $V = s^3$

Graph $y = x^3$ and find the value for $y$ when $x = 2$.

8 cubic units

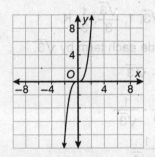

**10. a.**

| $x$ | $y = x^3 + 5$ | $y$ |
|---|---|---|
| $-2$ | $(-2)^3 + 5 = -8 + 5$ | $-3$ |
| $-1$ | $(-1)^3 + 5 = -1 + 5$ | $4$ |
| $0$ | $(0)^3 + 5 = 0 + 5$ | $5$ |
| $1$ | $(1)^3 + 5 = 1 + 5$ | $6$ |
| $2$ | $(2)^3 + 5 = 8 + 5$ | $13$ |

**b.**

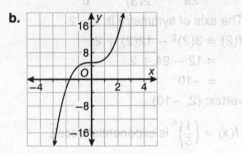

**c.** Find $y$ when $x = 3$.

$y = 3^3 + 5 = 27 + 5 = 32$

The volume is 32 cubic feet.

**11.** Evaluate $y = 3\sqrt{7x + 2} - 7$ for $x = 2$.

$$y = 3\sqrt{7 \cdot 2 + 2} - 7$$
$$= 3\sqrt{14 + 2} - 7$$
$$= 3\sqrt{16} - 7$$
$$= 3(4) - 7$$
$$= 12 - 7$$
$$= 5$$

**12.** Evaluate $y = 8\sqrt{x}$ for $x = 8$.

$y = 8\sqrt{8}$

$y \approx 22.6$ feet per second

**13.** Student B; Sample: Student A just removed the radical sign and then set the entire right side greater than or equal to zero.

**14.** Evaluate $s = \sqrt{A}$ for $A = 625$.

$s = \sqrt{625}$

$s = 25$ feet

**15.** $y \geq \dfrac{2}{5}x - 4$

$y \leq 0$

Graph each inequality on the same plane. The solution of the system is the overlapping shaded region.

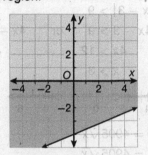

**16.** $46 + 16x = -x^2$

$x^2 + 16x + 46 = 0$

$$x = \frac{-b \pm \sqrt{b^2 - 4ac}}{2a}$$

$$x = \frac{-16 \pm \sqrt{16^2 - 4(1)(46)}}{2(1)}$$

$$x = \frac{-16 \pm \sqrt{72}}{2}$$

$x = -3.7574$ or $x = -12.2426$

**17.** $5! = 5 \cdot 4 \cdot 3 \cdot 2 \cdot 1 = 120$

**18.** $y = 2x^2 - 6x + 1$

$y = -x - 4$

The graphs show no points of intersection. There is no solution.

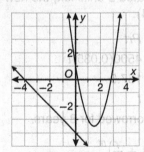

**19.** Graph the function $y = 4x^2 + 8x - 2$. It crosses the $x$-axis at two points. The answer is **C**.

**20.** Sample: The discriminant tells how many times the graph of a quadratic equation crosses or touches the $x$-axis.

**Saxon** Algebra 1

**21.** $4x^2 + 8 = -6x$

Enter $y = 4x^2 + 6x + 8$ in a graphing calculator. The graph does not cross the $x$-axis.

**22.** $|4x - 3| + 1 > 10$

$$|4x - 3| > 9$$

| $4x - 3 > 9$ | or | $4x - 3 < -9$ |
|---|---|---|
| $4x > 12$ | | $4x < -6$ |
| $x > 3$ | | $x < -1.5$ |

**23.**
$$p = 4905\sqrt{x}$$
$$44,145 = 4905\sqrt{x}$$
$$9 = \sqrt{x}$$
$$(9)^2 = (\sqrt{x})^2$$
$$81 = x$$

**24.** Graph $f(x) = |x| - 4$.

| $x$ | $y$ |
|---|---|
| $-3$ | $-1$ |
| $-2$ | $-2$ |
| $-1$ | $-3$ |
| $0$ | $-4$ |
| $1$ | $-3$ |
| $2$ | $-2$ |
| $3$ | $-1$ |

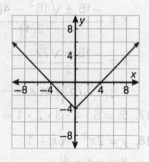

The vertex is $(0, -4)$. When the function is translated 2 units left, the new vertex is $(-2, -4)$.

**25.**
$$I = Prt$$
$$1260 = 4500(0.035)t$$
$$1260 = 157.5$$
$$8 = t$$

It was borrowed for 8 years.

**26.** $A = P\left(1 + \dfrac{r}{n}\right)^{nt}$

$$A = 1200\left(1 + \dfrac{0.22}{12}\right)^{12 \cdot 1}$$

$$= \$1492.32$$

**27.** Because $b$ is negative; Sample: The range values are not all positive or all negative. For example, $f(2) = 16$ and $f(3) = -32$.

**28. a.** $3, \sqrt{3}, 1, \dfrac{\sqrt{3}}{3}, \dfrac{1}{3}, K$

Divide each term by $\sqrt{3}$.

**b.** $\dfrac{1}{3} \div \sqrt{3}$

$$= \dfrac{1}{3} \cdot \dfrac{1}{\sqrt{3}}$$

$$= \dfrac{1}{3\sqrt{3}}$$

$$= \dfrac{1 \cdot \sqrt{3}}{3\sqrt{3} \cdot \sqrt{3}}$$

$$= \dfrac{\sqrt{3}}{9}$$

**29.** $f(x) = 3x^2 - 12x + 2$

$$x = \dfrac{-b}{2a} = \dfrac{-(-12)}{2(3)} = \dfrac{12}{6} = 2$$

The axis of symmetry is $x = 2$.

$$f(2) = 3(2)^2 - 12(2) + 2$$
$$= 12 - 24 + 2$$
$$= -10$$

vertex: $(2, -10)$

**30.** $f(x) = \left(\dfrac{1}{5}\right)^x$ is exponential decay,

$h(x) = 5^x$

is exponential growth, and $j(x) = 5x$ is linear. None of these are quadratics.

## LESSON 117

**Warm Up 117**

**1.** division

**2.** $c^2 = a^2 + b^2$
$$c^2 = 9^2 + 12^2$$
$$c^2 = 81 + 144$$
$$c^2 = 225$$
$$c = 15 \text{ inches}$$

**3.** $c^2 = a^2 + b^2$
$$17^2 = 10^2 + b^2$$
$$289 = 100 + b^2$$
$$189 = b^2$$
$$\sqrt{189} = b$$
$$3\sqrt{21} = b$$
$3\sqrt{21}$ inches or $\approx 13.75$ inches

**Saxon** Algebra 1

**4.** $c^2 = a^2 + b^2$
$10^2 \overset{?}{=} 6^2 + 8^2$
$100 \overset{?}{=} 36 + 64$
$100 = 100$

**5.** $c^2 = a^2 + b^2$
$20^2 \overset{?}{=} 8^2 + 12^2$
$400 \overset{?}{=} 64 + 144$
$400 \neq 208$
No

## Lesson Practice 117

**a.** $\sin A = \dfrac{\text{opposite leg}}{\text{hypotenuse}} = \dfrac{24}{26} = \dfrac{12}{13}$

$\cos A = \dfrac{\text{adjacent leg}}{\text{hypotenuse}} = \dfrac{10}{26} = \dfrac{5}{13}$

$\tan A = \dfrac{\text{opposite leg}}{\text{hypotenuse}} = \dfrac{24}{10} = \dfrac{12}{5}$

**b.** $c^2 = a^2 + b^2$
$5^2 = 3^2 + b^2$
$25 = 9 + b^2$
$16 = b^2$
$4 = b$

$\sin B = \dfrac{b}{c} = \dfrac{4}{5}$

$\cos B = \dfrac{a}{c} = \dfrac{3}{5}$

$\tan B = \dfrac{b}{a} = \dfrac{4}{3}$

$\csc B = \dfrac{c}{b} = \dfrac{5}{4}$

$\sec B = \dfrac{c}{a} = \dfrac{5}{3}$

$\cot B = \dfrac{a}{b} = \dfrac{3}{4}$

**c.** $\angle A = 49°$
Use a calculator.
$\sin A = \sin 49° \approx 0.7547$
$\cos A = \cos 49° \approx 0.6561$
$\tan A = \tan 49° \approx 1.1504$

**d.** $\angle A = 67°$
Use a calculator.
$\csc A = \csc 67° \approx 1.0864$

$\sec A = \sec 67° \approx 2.5593$
$\cot A = \cot 67° \approx 0.4245$

**e.** $\tan 36° = \dfrac{x}{40}$
$40 \tan 36° = x$
$29.06 \approx x$

**f.** $\sin 48° = \dfrac{x}{17}$
$17 \sin 48° = x$
$12.63 \approx x$
$\cos 48° = \dfrac{y}{17}$
$17 \cos 48° = y$
$11.38 \approx y$

**g.** $\tan A = \dfrac{12}{19}$
$\tan^{-1}(\tan A) = \tan^{-1}\left(\dfrac{12}{19}\right)$
$A = 32.28°$
$\tan B = \dfrac{19}{12}$
$\tan^{-1}(\tan B) = \tan^{-1}\left(\dfrac{19}{12}\right)$
$B \approx 57.72°$

**h.** $\cos A = \dfrac{4}{10}$
$\cos^{-1}(\cos A) = \cos^{-1}\left(\dfrac{4}{10}\right)$
$A \approx 66.42°$

## Practice 117

**1.** $\sin A = \dfrac{\text{opposite leg}}{\text{hypotenuse}} = \dfrac{20}{29}$

$\cos A = \dfrac{\text{adjacent leg}}{\text{hypotenuse}} = \dfrac{21}{29}$

$\tan A = \dfrac{\text{opposite leg}}{\text{hypotenuse}} = \dfrac{20}{21}$

**2.** $\sin A = \dfrac{\text{opposite leg}}{\text{hypotenuse}} = \dfrac{15}{17}$

$\cos A = \dfrac{\text{adjacent leg}}{\text{hypotenuse}} = \dfrac{8}{17}$

$\tan A = \dfrac{\text{opposite leg}}{\text{hypotenuse}} = \dfrac{15}{8}$

**3.** $y = kx$

Substitute (24, 3) in the equation.

$3 = k \cdot 24$

$\dfrac{3}{24} = k$

$\dfrac{1}{8} = k$

$y = \dfrac{1}{8}x$

**4.** $\sin A = \sin 77° \approx 0.9744$

$\cos A = \cos 77° \approx 0.2250$

$\tan A = \tan 77° \approx 4.3315$

**5.** Student A; Sample: The tangent ratio is the opposite leg over the adjacent leg and Student B used adjacent over opposite.

**6.** acute angles each measure: $\dfrac{90}{2} = 45°$

$\sin 45° = \dfrac{\text{leg length}}{5}$

$5 \sin 45° = \text{leg length}$

leg length $= 3.54$ cm

**7. a.** $c^2 = a^2 + b^2$

$c^2 = 70^2 + 240^2$

$c^2 = 4900 + 57{,}600$

$c^2 = 62{,}500$

$c = 250$ feet

**b.** $\sin A = \dfrac{70}{250}$

$\sin^{-1}(\sin A) = \sin^{-1}\left(\dfrac{70}{250}\right)$

$A = 16.26°$

**8.** $\tan 45° = \dfrac{\text{tree height}}{25}$

$25 \tan 45° = \text{tree height}$

$25$ feet $= \text{tree height}$

**9.** $I = Prt$

$= 1100(0.09)(2)$

$= \$198$

**10.** $\sin 7° = \dfrac{x}{3.4}$

$3.4 \sin 7° = x$

$0.41 = x$

about 0.41 miles below the water's surface

**11.** Sample: The opposite leg is the leg of a right triangle that is opposite the acute angle and the adjacent leg is the leg that is next to the acute angle, but not the hypotenuse.

**12.** Student B; Sample: Student A found the interest earned, not the account's value.

**13.** $A = P(1 + r)^t$

10% account:

$A = 100(1 + 0.10)^{10}$

$= 100(1.1)^{10}$

$= \$259.37$

20% account:

$A = 100(1 + 0.20)^5$

$= 100(1.2)^5$

$= \$248.83$

$\$259.37 - \$248.83 = \$10.54$

The 10% account for 10 years earns $10.54 more.

**14.** Graph $y = x^3 + 3$.

At $x = 0$, $y = 3$.

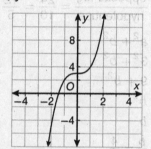

**15.** Student B; Sample: Student A graphed the parent function.

**16.**

| $x$ | 1 | 2 | 3 | 4 |
|---|---|---|---|---|
| $V = x^3 + 3$ | 4 | 11 | 30 | 67 |

$x = 3$ corresponds to a volume of 30 cubic units.

**17.** $2x^2 + 9 = 9x$

$2x^2 - 9x + 9 = 0$

$x = \dfrac{-b \pm \sqrt{b^2 - 4ac}}{2a}$

$= \dfrac{-(-9) \pm \sqrt{(9)^2 - 4(2)(9)}}{2(2)}$

$= \dfrac{9 \pm \sqrt{9}}{4}$

$= \dfrac{9 \pm 3}{4}$

$x = 3$ or $x = 1.5$

**Saxon** Algebra 1

Check:

$x = 3$

$2(3)^2 + 9 \stackrel{?}{=} 9(3)$

$18 + 9 \stackrel{?}{=} 27$

$27 = 27$ ✓

$x = 1.5$

$2(1.5)^2 + 9 \stackrel{?}{=} 9(1.5)$

$4.5 + 9 \stackrel{?}{=} 13.5$

$13.5 = 13.5$ ✓

**18.** $_{12}P_3 = \dfrac{12!}{(12-3)!}$

$= \dfrac{12!}{9!}$

$= 12 \cdot 11 \cdot 10$

$= 1320$

**19.** $x^2 + 5 = 9$

$x^2 = 4$

$\sqrt{x^2} = \pm\sqrt{4}$

$x = \pm 2$

**20.** Graph $y = \dfrac{x^2}{8} + \dfrac{7}{4}$ and $y = -\dfrac{9x}{8}$.

Find the coordinates of the intersections.

$\left(-2, \dfrac{9}{4}\right)$ and $\left(-7, \dfrac{63}{8}\right)$

**21.** $x^2 + 2x - 2 = 0$

$b^2 - 4ac = 2^2 - 4(1)(-2)$

$= 4 + 8$

$= 12$

Since the discriminant is positive, there are two real solutions.

**22.** $f(x) = 2\sqrt{x+6} - 1$

$x + 6 \geq 0$

$x \geq -6$

The answer is **B**.

**23.** Sample: The graph of $f(x) = \sqrt{x+4}$ can be rewritten in the form $f(x) = \sqrt{x-c}$ by changing $+4$ to $-(-4)$. The function is now $y = \sqrt{x-(-4)}$, which is a translation 4 units left of the parent function.

**24.** $3|8x+2| < 12$

$|8x+2| < 4$

$8x + 2 < 4$ and $8x + 2 > -4$

$8x < 2$ $\qquad\qquad 8x > -6$

$x < \dfrac{1}{4}$ $\qquad\qquad x > -\dfrac{3}{4}$

$-0.75 < x < 0.25$

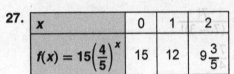

**25. a.** Let $x =$ the first odd number. Then $x + 2 =$ the next consecutive odd number.

**b.** The sum of the squares is 74.

$x^2 + (x+2)^2 = 74$

**c.** $x^2 + x^2 + 4x + 4 = 74$

$2x^2 + 4x - 70 = 0$

$2(x^2 + 2x - 35) = 0$

$2(x+7)(x-5) = 0$

$x = -7$ or $x = 5$

$x + 2 = -5$ $\quad x + 2 = 7$

The solutions are 5 and 7 or −5 and −7.

**26.** $\csc A = \csc 81° \approx 1.0125$

$\sec A = \sec 81° \approx 6.3925$

$\cot A = \cot 81° \approx 0.1584$

**27.**

| $x$ | 0 | 1 | 2 |
|---|---|---|---|
| $f(x) = 15\left(\dfrac{4}{5}\right)^x$ | 15 | 12 | $9\dfrac{3}{5}$ |

$f(0) = 15$, $f(1) = 12$, $f(2) = 9\dfrac{3}{5}$

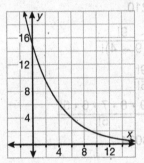

**28.** Sample: In the second system, the points on the boundary line are solutions to the system, and the boundary lines, which intersect, are solid. In the first system, the boundary line is dashed because the points on that line are not solutions. They do not intersect.

**29.** A half-life is the amount of time it takes for half of a substance to remain.

$\dfrac{150}{25} = 6$ half-lives

**Saxon** Algebra 1

**30. a.** $y = \dfrac{a}{x - b} + c$

$y = \dfrac{2000}{x} + 2$

$a = 2000$, $b = 0$, $c = 2$

horizontal asymptote: $y = 2$

**b.** vertical asymptote: $x = 0$

**c.** Evaluate $y = \dfrac{2000}{x} + 2$ for $x = 200$.

$y = \dfrac{2000}{200} + 2 = 12$ rackets

## LESSON 118

### Warm Up 118

**1.** permutation

**2.** $7! = 7 \cdot 6 \cdot 5 \cdot 4 \cdot 3 \cdot 2 \cdot 1 = 5040$

**3.** $\dfrac{6!}{4!} = \dfrac{6 \cdot 5 \cdot 4 \cdot 3 \cdot 2 \cdot 1}{4 \cdot 3 \cdot 2 \cdot 1}$

$= 6 \cdot 5 = 30$

**4.** $_7P_3 = \dfrac{7!}{(7 - 3)!}$

$= \dfrac{7!}{4!}$

$= \dfrac{7 \cdot 6 \cdot 5 \cdot 4 \cdot 3 \cdot 2 \cdot 1}{4 \cdot 3 \cdot 2 \cdot 1}$

$= 210$

**5.** $_9P_4 = \dfrac{9!}{(9 - 4)!}$

$= \dfrac{9!}{5!}$

$= \dfrac{9 \cdot 8 \cdot 7 \cdot 6 \cdot 5!}{5!}$

$= 3024$

### Lesson Practice 118

**a.** $_5P_2 = \dfrac{5!}{(5 - 2)!}$

$= \dfrac{5!}{3!}$

$= \dfrac{5 \cdot 4 \cdot 3!}{3!}$

$= 20$ permutations

**b.** $_5C_2 = \dfrac{5!}{2!(5 - 2)!}$

$= \dfrac{5!}{2!3!}$

$= \dfrac{5 \cdot 4 \cdot 3!}{2 \cdot 1 \cdot 3!}$

$= 10$ combinations

**c.** $_8C_4 = \dfrac{8!}{4!(8 - 4)!}$

$= \dfrac{8!}{4!4!}$

$= \dfrac{8 \cdot 7 \cdot 6 \cdot 5 \cdot 4!}{4 \cdot 3 \cdot 2 \cdot 1 \cdot 4!}$

$= 70$

**d.** $_{22}C_9 = \dfrac{22!}{9!(22 - 9)!}$

$= \dfrac{22!}{9!13!}$

$= \dfrac{1.124 \times 10^{21}}{362{,}880 \times 6{,}227{,}020{,}800}$

$= 497{,}420$

**e.** probability $= \dfrac{1}{_{18}C_4} = \dfrac{1}{\dfrac{18!}{4!(18 - 4)!}} = \dfrac{1}{3060}$

### Practice 118

**1.** $_{15}C_4 = \dfrac{15!}{4!(15 - 4)!}$

$= \dfrac{15!}{4!11!}$

$= \dfrac{15 \cdot 14 \cdot 13 \cdot 12 \cdot 11!}{4 \cdot 3 \cdot 2 \cdot 1 \cdot 11!}$

$= 1365$

**2.** $_{11}C_4 = \dfrac{11!}{4!(11 - 4)!}$

$= \dfrac{11!}{4!7!}$

$= \dfrac{11 \cdot 10 \cdot 9 \cdot 8 \cdot 7!}{4 \cdot 3 \cdot 2 \cdot 1 \cdot 7!}$

$= 330$

**3.** $_9C_7 = \dfrac{9!}{7!(9 - 7)!}$

$= \dfrac{9!}{7!2!}$

$= \dfrac{9 \cdot 8 \cdot 7!}{7!2 \cdot 1}$

$= 36$

**Saxon** Algebra 1

**4.** $_{12}C_5 = \dfrac{12!}{5!(12-5)!}$

$= \dfrac{12!}{5!7!}$

$= \dfrac{12 \cdot 11 \cdot 10 \cdot 9 \cdot 8 \cdot 7!}{5 \cdot 4 \cdot 3 \cdot 2 \cdot 1 \cdot 7!}$

$= 792$

**5.** Sample: With permutations order matters, and with combinations, order does not matter.

**6.** Sample:

$_8C_3 = \dfrac{8!}{3!(8-3)!}$

$= \dfrac{8!}{(8-3)!} \cdot \dfrac{1}{3!}$

$= \dfrac{\dfrac{8!}{(8-3)!}}{3!}$

$= \dfrac{_8P_3}{\text{number of ways to order 3 items}}$

**7.** $_5C_3 = \dfrac{5!}{3!(5-3)!} = \dfrac{5!}{3!2!} = \dfrac{5 \cdot 4 \cdot 3!}{3!2 \cdot 1} = 10$

The answer is **A**.

**8.** $_{10}C_3 = \dfrac{10!}{3!(10-3)!}$

$= \dfrac{10!}{3!7!}$

$= \dfrac{10 \cdot 9 \cdot 8 \cdot 7!}{3 \cdot 2 \cdot 1 \cdot 7!}$

$= 120$

**9.** $15x - 10 = 5(3x - 2)$

$3x - 2 = 3x - 2$

$LCM = 5(3x - 2)$

**10.** $_8C_2 = \dfrac{8!}{2!(8-2)!}$

$= \dfrac{8!}{2!6!}$

$= \dfrac{8 \cdot 7 \cdot 6!}{2 \cdot 1 \cdot 6!}$

$= 28$

**11. a.** $_{25}C_9 = \dfrac{25!}{9!(25-9)!} = \dfrac{25!}{9!16!} = 2{,}042{,}975$

**b.** Probability

$= \dfrac{\text{number of ways to choose 8 favorite}}{\text{total number of ways to choose any 8}}$

$= \dfrac{1}{_{24}C_8}$

$= \dfrac{1}{\dfrac{24!}{8!(24-8)!}}$

$= \dfrac{1}{735{,}471}$

**12.** $\sin A = \dfrac{\text{opposite leg}}{\text{hypotenuse}} = \dfrac{24}{25}; \csc A = \dfrac{25}{24}$

$\cos A = \dfrac{\text{adjacent leg}}{\text{hypotenuse}} = \dfrac{7}{25}; \sec A = \dfrac{25}{7}$

$\tan A = \dfrac{\text{opposite leg}}{\text{hypotenuse}} = \dfrac{24}{7}; \cot A = \dfrac{7}{24}$

**13. a.** $c^2 = a^2 + b^2$

$20^2 = 12^2 + b^2$

$400 = 144 + b^2$

$256 = b^2$

$16 \text{ feet} = b$

**b.** $\sin A = \dfrac{\text{opposite leg}}{\text{hypotenuse}}$

$\sin A = \dfrac{12}{20}$

$\sin^{-1}(\sin A) = \sin^{-1}\left(\dfrac{12}{20}\right)$

$A \approx 36.87°$

**14.** $AC = 6, BC = 8$

$\tan A = \dfrac{BC}{AC}$

$\tan A = \dfrac{8}{6}$

$\tan^{-1}(\tan A) = \tan^{-1}\left(\dfrac{8}{6}\right)$

$A = 53.13°$

**Saxon** Algebra 1

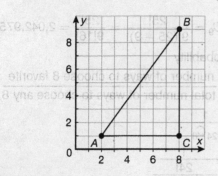

**15.** $I = Prt$

$= 9200(0.05)(3)$

$= 1380$

Money paid $= \$9200 + \$1380$

$= \$10,580$

**16.** $A = P(1 + r)^t$

$= 20,000(1 + 0.06)^5$

$\doteq 26,764.51$

Interest $= \$26,764.51 - \$20,000$

$= \$6764.51$

**17.** Student A; Sample: Student B used interest compounded annually, not quarterly.

**18.** $\dfrac{10!}{5!} = \dfrac{10 \cdot 9 \cdot 8 \cdot 7 \cdot 6 \cdot 5!}{5!} = 30,240$

**19.** $\dfrac{4}{\sqrt{3} - 2} = \dfrac{4}{\sqrt{3} - 2} \cdot \dfrac{\sqrt{3} + 2}{\sqrt{3} + 2}$

$= \dfrac{4(\sqrt{3} + 2)}{3 - 4}$

$= \dfrac{4(\sqrt{3} + 2)}{-1}$

$= -4\sqrt{3} - 8$

**20.**

$y = x^2 - 5$

$y = 4x$

$x^2 - 5 = 4x$

$x^2 - 4x - 5 = 0$

$(x + 1)(x - 5) = 0$

$x + 1 = 0$    or    $x - 5 = 0$

$x = -1$ or    $x = 5$

Determine the values of $y$.

$y = 4(-1)$    $y = 4(5)$

$y = -4$      $y = 20$

The solutions are $(-1, -4)$ and $(5, 20)$.

**21.** Use the equation $45 = -16t^2 + 75t + 2$. Then $0 = -16t^2 + 75t - 43$ and the discriminant is 2873, so the ball will reach a height of 45 feet.

**22.** $y = \sqrt{\dfrac{3}{6} + 2}$

$y = \sqrt{\dfrac{1}{2} + \dfrac{4}{2}}$

$y = \sqrt{\dfrac{5}{2}}$

$y \approx 1.6$

**23.** $x^3 - 27 = 0$

$x^3 = 27$

$\sqrt[3]{x^3} = \sqrt[3]{27}$

$x = 3$

The answer is **A**.

**24.** The parent function of a cubic equation is $y = x^3$.

**25.** $x^2 = 45$

$\sqrt{x^2} = \pm\sqrt{45}$

$x \approx \pm 6.708$

**26. a.** The first term is $a = 500$; the common ratio is $r = 5$.

Find the $n = 5th$ term (Friday).

$A(n) = ar^{n-1}$

$A(5) = 500(5)^4 = 312,500$

**b.**    $r = 5 \cdot \dfrac{3}{4} = 3\dfrac{3}{4}$

$A(n) = ar^{n-1}$

$A(n) = 500\left(3\dfrac{3}{4}\right)^{n-1}$

**c.** $A(5) = 500\left(3\dfrac{3}{4}\right)^{5-1} \approx 98,877$

**27. a.** Let $x =$ the number of teacher tickets and $y =$ the number of student tickets.

$\begin{cases} 3x + \dfrac{1}{2}y \geq 200 \\ x + y \leq 250 \end{cases}$

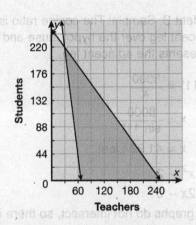

**b.** No; Sample: There is no ordered pair with 15 teachers that is in the solution set.

**28.** $2v^2 + 20v = 21$

$2v^2 + 20v - 21 = 0$

$v = \dfrac{-b \pm \sqrt{b^2 - 4ac}}{2a}$

$v = \dfrac{-20 \pm \sqrt{(20)^2 - 4(2)(-21)}}{2(2)}$

$v = \dfrac{-20 \pm \sqrt{568}}{4}$

$v \approx 1$ and $v \approx -11$

**29.** $-88z^3 - 2r^2z^3 - 30rz^3$

$= -2z^3(44 + r^2 + 15r)$

$= -2z^3(r^2 + 15r + 44)$

$= -2z^3(r + 11)(r + 4)$

**30.** half-lives in 10 hours

$= \dfrac{10 \text{ hr}}{1} \cdot \dfrac{60 \text{ min}}{1 \text{ hr}} \cdot \dfrac{1 \text{ half-life}}{100 \text{ min}}$

$= 6$ half-lives

$320\left(\dfrac{1}{2}\right)^6 = 5 \text{ mg}$

## LESSON 119

### Warm Up 119

**1.** vertex

**2.** $y = 2x^2 + 8x + 2$

$x = -\dfrac{b}{2a} = -\dfrac{8}{2(2)} = -2$

axis of symmetry: $x = -2$

**3.** $y = 0.5x - 3.5$

$y = mx + b$

$m = 0.5, \ b = -3.5$

**4.** $-8x + 2y = 10$

$y = 4x + 5$

$y = mx + b$

$m = 4, \ b = 5$

**5.** $y = x^2 + x - 2$

$0 = x^2 + x - 2$

$0 = (x + 2)(x - 1)$

$x + 2 = 0 \quad$ or $\quad x - 1 = 0$

$x = -2 \quad$ or $\quad x = 1$

The answer is **B**.

### Lesson Practice 119

**a.** The graph has the shape of a linear function.

**b.** The graph has the shape of a quadratic function.

**c.** The graph has the shape of an exponential function.

**d.** Plot the points and connect with a smooth curve. From the graph you can tell that the function belongs to the linear function family.

**e.** Plot the points and connect with a smooth curve. From the graph you can tell that the function belongs to the quadratic function family

**f.** The function family is linear.

**g.** The function family is quadratic.

**h.** The function family is exponential.

**i.** The appropriate model is quadratic.

**j.** The appropriate model is exponential.

**k.** The appropriate model is linear.

### Practice 119

**1.** Student A; Sample: Student B wrote an equation that does not have an $x^2$-term in it.

**2.** The graph has the shape of an exponential function.

**3.** The graph has the shape of a quadratic function.

**Saxon** Algebra 1

**4.** Sample: Graph the parent function and then graph a series of transformations of it.

**5.** If $x$ = the length in feet, then $x^2$ = the number of square feet.

Cost: $f(x) = 12x^2 + 500$

The function family is quadratic and the parent function is $f(x) = x^2$.

**6.** Student A; Sample: Student A used the formula for permutations.

**7. a.** The rate of change is always the same. The function is linear.

**b.** Let $x$ = the number of toppings.
$f(x) = 1.5x + 16$

**8.** The rate of change is always the same. The function family is linear.

**9.** The graph of $y = 5^x$ is exponential. The answer is **C**.

**10.** $A = \frac{1}{2}bh$

$A = \frac{1}{2}b(b - 4)$

$A = \frac{1}{2}b^2 - 2b$

The function family is quadratic.

**11.** The function family to which $y = 2 - 1100x$ belongs is linear.

**12.** $P(\text{all heads}) = \frac{1}{2}^x$ belongs to the exponential function family.

**13. a.** $_{22}C_4 = \frac{22!}{4!(22 - 4)!}$

$= \frac{22!}{4!18!}$

$= 7315$

**b.** probability

$= \frac{\text{number of ways to choose these 4}}{\text{total number of ways to choose}}$

$= \frac{1}{7315}$

**14.** $\sin A = \sin 14° \approx 0.2419$

$\cos A = \cos 14° \approx 0.9703$

$\tan A = \tan 14° \approx 0.2493$

**15.** Student B; Sample: The cosine ratio is the adjacent leg over the hypotenuse and $x$ represents the adjacent leg.

**16.** $\sin 11° = \frac{8000}{x}$

$x = \frac{8000}{\sin 11°}$

$x \approx 41{,}927$ feet

**17.** $y = x^2 - 2$
$y = 2x - 5$

The graphs do not intersect, so there is no solution to the system.

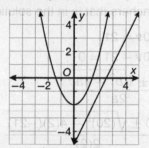

**18.** $9x^2 - 24x + 16 = 0$
$b^2 - 4ac = (-24)^2 - 4(9)(16)$
$= 576 - 576$
$= 0$

Since the discriminant is 0, there is one real solution.

**19.** $n \geq 0$; Sample: The domain is $n \geq -30$, but in the context of the problem the number of cards cannot be negative.

**20.**

| $x$ | −2 | −1 | 0 | 1 | 2 |
|---|---|---|---|---|---|
| $y = x^3 - 2$ | −10 | −3 | −2 | −1 | 6 |

For $x = 0$, $y = -2$.

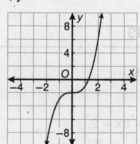

**Saxon** Algebra 1

**21.** Sample: The amount for simple interest results in $I = 500(0.06)(3) = 90$ for an account balance of $590, but compound interest is $A = 500(1.06)^3 = 595.51$ for an account balance of $595.51.

**22.** $A = P\left(1 + \dfrac{r}{n}\right)^{nt}$

$= 1000\left(1 + \dfrac{0.05}{4}\right)^{4 \cdot 20}$

$= 1000(2.70148)$

$= \$2701.48$

The answer is **D**.

**23.** $_8C_3 = \dfrac{8!}{3!(8-3)!}$

$= \dfrac{8!}{3!5!}$

$= \dfrac{8 \cdot 7 \cdot 6 \cdot 5!}{3 \cdot 2 \cdot 1 \cdot 5!}$

$= 56$

**24.** $\dfrac{6}{\sqrt{7} - 3\sqrt{5}} = \dfrac{6}{\sqrt{7} - 3\sqrt{5}} \cdot \dfrac{\sqrt{7} + 3\sqrt{5}}{\sqrt{7} + 3\sqrt{5}}$

$= \dfrac{6(\sqrt{7} + 3\sqrt{5})}{(\sqrt{7})^2 - (3\sqrt{5})^2}$

$= \dfrac{6(\sqrt{7} + 3\sqrt{5})}{7 - 9 \cdot 5}$

$= \dfrac{6(\sqrt{7} + 3\sqrt{5})}{-38}$

$= -\dfrac{3\sqrt{7}}{19} - \dfrac{9\sqrt{5}}{19}$

**25.** $-2m^2 - 12m = 10$

$m^2 + 6m = -5$

$m^2 + 6m + \left(\dfrac{6}{2}\right)^2 = -5 + \left(\dfrac{6}{2}\right)^2$

$m^2 + 6m + 9 = -5 + 9$

$(m + 3)^2 = 4$

$m + 3 = \pm\sqrt{4}$

$m + 3 = \pm 2$

$m = -3 \pm 2$

$m = -1 \quad \text{or} \quad m = -5$

**26. a.** $-4 = -\sqrt{x - 4}$

$4 = \sqrt{x - 4}$

$16 = x - 4$

$20 = x$

**b.** Sample: To isolate the radical, both sides of any equation must be multiplied by $-1$.

**c.**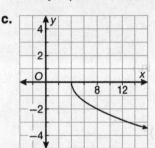

**27.** $y = 100^{(-3x)}$ belongs to the exponential function family.

**28.** Sample: It can easily be factored so the quadratic formula would be unnecessary work.

**29.** $_6P_2 = \dfrac{6!}{(6-2)!}$

$= \dfrac{6!}{4!}$

$= \dfrac{6 \cdot 5 \cdot 4 \cdot 3 \cdot 2 \cdot 1}{4 \cdot 3 \cdot 2 \cdot 1}$

$= 6 \cdot 5$

$= 30$

**30.** $f(x) = ax^2 + bx + c$

**a.** $a \neq 0$ and $b \neq 0$;
$f(x) = ax^2 + bx + c$; parabola

**b.** $a = 0$ and $b \neq 0$;
$f(x) = bx + c$; line

**c.** $a \neq 0$ and $b = 0$;
$f(x) = ax^2 + c$; parabola

**d.** $a = 0$ and $b = 0$;
$f(x) = c$; horizontal line

## LESSON 120

### Warm Up 120

**1.** complement

**2.** complement $= 1 - \dfrac{3}{4} = \dfrac{1}{4}$

**3.** probability

$= \dfrac{\text{number of ways to get a number} > 4}{\text{total number of outcomes}}$

**Saxon** Algebra 1

b. **Sample:** To isolate the radical, both sides of any equation must be multiplied by −1.

$$= \frac{2}{6}$$

$$= \frac{1}{3}$$

4. $A = lw$

$$= (25 \text{ in.})(5 \text{ in.})$$

$$= 125 \text{ in.}^2$$

5. $A = \pi r^2$

$$= 3.14(2 \text{ in.})^2$$

$$= 12.56 \text{ in.}^2$$

### Lesson Practice 120

a. $\dfrac{\text{favorable outcomes}}{\text{total outcomes}} = \dfrac{\text{area of raft}}{\text{area of pool}}$

$$= \frac{2 \cdot 3}{30 \cdot 15}$$

$$= \frac{6}{450}$$

$$= \frac{1}{75}$$

b. $\dfrac{\text{favorable outcomes}}{\text{total outcomes}}$

$$= \frac{\text{area of 6-in. circle}}{\text{area of 10-in. circle}}$$

$$= \frac{\pi \cdot 6^2}{\pi \cdot 10^2}$$

$$= \frac{36}{100}$$

$$= \frac{9}{25}$$

c. $1 - \dfrac{\text{area of square}}{\text{area of circle}} = 1 - \dfrac{2^2}{\pi \cdot 4^2}$

$$= 1 - \frac{4}{16\pi}$$

$$\approx 0.92$$

d. $1 - \dfrac{\text{area of garden}}{\text{area of yard}} = 1 - \dfrac{\frac{1}{2}(5)(6)}{(15)(10)}$

$$= 1 - \frac{15}{150}$$

$$= 0.9$$

e. $\dfrac{\text{favorable outcomes}}{\text{total outcomes}}$

$$= \frac{\text{area not including square}}{\text{area of rug}}$$

---

$$= \frac{8 \cdot 6 - 2 \cdot 2}{8 \cdot 6}$$

$$= \frac{48 - 4}{48}$$

$$= \frac{44}{48}$$

$$= \frac{11}{12}$$

### Practice 120

1. $\dfrac{\text{favorable outcomes}}{\text{total outcomes}} = \dfrac{\text{area of triangle}}{\text{area of square}}$

$$= \frac{\frac{1}{2}(5)(6)}{(8)^2}$$

$$= \frac{15}{64}$$

2. **Sample:** Using geometric formulas to calculate the favorable and total outcomes.

3. Since there are no intersection points, the system has no solution.

4. **Sample:**

$$1 - \frac{\text{area of triangle}}{\text{area of square}} = 1 - \frac{\frac{1}{2} \cdot 8 \cdot 8}{8 \cdot 8}$$

$$= 1 - \frac{32}{64}$$

$$= \frac{32}{64}$$

$$= \frac{1}{2}$$

5. $_7C_2 = \dfrac{7!}{2!(7-2)!}$

$$= \frac{7!}{2!5!}$$

$$= \frac{7 \cdot 6 \cdot 5!}{2 \cdot 1 \cdot 5!}$$

$$= 21$$

6. $V = s^3$

$$= (5 \text{ cm})^3$$

$$= 125 \text{ cm}^3$$

7. $\dfrac{\text{area of circle}}{\text{area of rectangle}} = \dfrac{\pi(15)^2}{45 \cdot 56} \approx 0.28$

The answer is **B**.

**8.** $_{20}C_8 = \dfrac{20!}{8!(20-8)!}$

$\quad = \dfrac{20!}{8!12!}$

$\quad = 125{,}970$

**9.** $\dfrac{\text{shaded area}}{\text{circle area}} = \dfrac{6^2 - \frac{1}{2} \cdot 4 \cdot 5}{\pi \cdot 8^2}$

$\quad\quad\quad\quad = \dfrac{36 - 10}{64\pi}$

$\quad\quad\quad\quad \approx 0.13$

**10.** Any right triangle with sides that are similar to a 3-4-5 right triangle is valid where the shorter leg is opposite angle $A$.

**11.** $f(x) = 3\sqrt{x} - 5$

domain: $\sqrt{x} \geq 0$ or $x \geq 0$

**12.** $A(n) = ar^{n-1}$

$A(4) = 7(-1.1)^{4-1} = -9.317$

**13.** $\dfrac{\text{favorable outcomes}}{\text{total outcomes}}$

$= 1 - \dfrac{\text{area of biscuits}}{\text{area of pan}}$

$= 1 - \dfrac{12(\pi \cdot 1.5^2)}{12 \cdot 9}$

$\approx 1 - 0.785$

$\approx 0.21$

**14.** Student B; Sample: Student A found the probability of landing on the triangle.

**15.** Sample: Using $A = s^2$, the area of the square is 49 square centimeters. The radius of the circle is half the diameter or 3 centimeters. Using $A = \pi r^2$, the area of the circle is $9\pi$. Find the probability of not landing in the circle by finding the complement of the probability of landing in the circle. The formula is $1 - \frac{9\pi}{49}$ which is approximately 0.42.

**16.** $1 - \dfrac{\text{area of red sector}}{\text{total area}} = 1 - \dfrac{1}{3} = \dfrac{2}{3}$

**17.** $\dfrac{\text{favorable outcomes}}{\text{total outcomes}} = \dfrac{\text{area of square}}{\text{area of triangle}}$

$\quad\quad\quad\quad\quad\quad = \dfrac{4^2}{\frac{1}{2}(15)(8)}$

$\quad\quad\quad\quad\quad\quad = \dfrac{16}{60}$

$\quad\quad\quad\quad\quad\quad = \dfrac{4}{15}$

**18. a.** 1 – probability of landing on a square

$= 1 - \dfrac{1}{4}$

$= \dfrac{3}{4}$

**b.** 4(area of small square)

$= 4(49)$

$= 196 \text{ mm}^2$

**19.** Student B; Sample: A linear function must have a constant rate of change. Student A's graph does not have a constant rate of change; it gets steeper as $x$ increases.

**20. a.** quadratic; Sample: The graph is a parabola.

**b.** The vertex appears to be (1, 14). Therefore, the maximum height is 14 feet.

**21.** $y = 4x^2 + 2$ belongs to the quadratic function family.

**22.** Student A; Sample: Student B made order count.

**23.** $-x^2 + 2x + 1 = 0$

$b^2 - 4ac = 2^2 - 4(-1)(1)$

$\quad\quad\quad\quad = 4 + 4$

$\quad\quad\quad\quad = 8$

Since the discriminant is positive, there are two real solutions.

**24.** $\dfrac{\text{favorable outcomes}}{\text{total outcomes}} = \dfrac{\text{area of circle}}{\text{area of square}}$

$\quad\quad\quad\quad\quad\quad = \dfrac{\pi(4)^2}{11^2}$

$\quad\quad\quad\quad\quad\quad \approx 0.42$

**25.** $I = Prt$

$I = 2600(0.08)(7)$

$I = 1456$

Total = \$2600 + \$1456 = \$4056

**26.** $f(x) = |x + 2|$
translated up by 3
is $f(x) = |x + 2| + 3$.

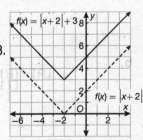

**Saxon** Algebra 1

**27.** $\cos A = \dfrac{5}{7}$

$\cos^{-1}(\cos A) = \cos^{-1}\left(\dfrac{5}{7}\right)$

$A \approx 44.4°$

The answer is **A**.

**28.** $3x^2 + 9x = 5.25$

$\dfrac{3x^2 + 9x}{3} = \dfrac{5.25}{3}$

$x^2 + 3x = 1.75$

$x^2 + 3x + \left(\dfrac{3}{2}\right)^2 = 1.75 + \left(\dfrac{3}{2}\right)^2$

$\left(x + \dfrac{3}{2}\right)^2 = 4$

$x + \dfrac{3}{2} = \pm\sqrt{4}$

$x = -1.5 \pm 2$

$x = 0.5 \text{ or } x = -3.5$

**29.** $1 - \dfrac{\text{area of square}}{\text{area of circle}} = 1 - \dfrac{2^2}{\pi(10)^2}$

$\approx 1 - 0.01$

$= 0.99$

**30. a.** $6! = 720$

**b.** $\dfrac{\text{favorable outcomes}}{\text{total outcomes}} = \dfrac{1}{720}$

## LAB 11

### Practice Lab 11

Use a graphing calculator. Enter each element of matrix A as [A]. Enter each element of matrix B as [B]. Then perform the indicated matrix operation.

**a.**

```
[A]+[B]
     [[5 10 1]
      [4 -5 2]]
```

**b.**

```
[A]-[B]
     [[1  -6 7 ]
      [-6 13 -2]]
```

**c.**

```
3[B]
   [[6  24  -9]
    [15 -27 6 ]]
```

**d.**

```
[B]-[A]
    [[-1 6   -7]
     [6  -13 2 ]]
```

**e.**

```
-2[A]
    [[-6 -4 -8]
     [2  -8 0 ]]
```

## INVESTIGATION 12

### Practice Investigation 12

**a.** Put the data in each table above into a matrix. Label the first table matrix A and the second matrix B. Subtract the data in matrix A from matrix B.

**b.** $\begin{bmatrix} 25 & 60 & 10 \\ 85 & 20 & 35 \\ 30 & 60 & 40 \end{bmatrix} - \begin{bmatrix} 15 & 55 & 0 \\ 75 & 10 & 30 \\ 20 & 40 & 35 \end{bmatrix} = \begin{bmatrix} 10 & 5 & 10 \\ 10 & 10 & 5 \\ 10 & 20 & 5 \end{bmatrix}$

Paul's earnings are represented in the second row. $10 + 10 + 5 = \$25$

**c.** $A(-2, 3)$, $B(-4, -1)$, $C(4, -2)$, $D(3, 3)$

$A = \begin{bmatrix} -2 & -4 & 4 & 3 \\ 3 & -1 & -2 & 3 \end{bmatrix}$

$\dfrac{1}{2}A = \begin{bmatrix} \frac{1}{2}(-2) & \frac{1}{2}(-4) & \frac{1}{2}(4) & \frac{1}{2}(3) \\ \frac{1}{2}(3) & \frac{1}{2}(-1) & \frac{1}{2}(-2) & \frac{1}{2}(3) \end{bmatrix}$

$= \begin{bmatrix} -1 & -2 & 2 & 1.5 \\ 1.5 & -0.5 & -1 & 1.5 \end{bmatrix}$

## APPENDIX

### Appendix Lesson Practice 1

**a.** Graph $y = x^2 - 6x + 8$ as a boundary line. Use a dashed curve because the inequality symbol is $>$.

Shade inside the parabola since the solution consists of y-values greater than the y-values on the parabola for the corresponding x-values.

Test a point in the solution region. Substitute $(3, 0)$ into the inequality.

$y > x^2 - 6x + 8$

$0 \overset{?}{>} (3)^2 - 6(3) + 8$

$0 \overset{?}{>} 9 - 6(3) + 8$

$0 \overset{?}{>} 9 - 18 + 8$

$0 \overset{?}{>} 9 - 18 + 8$

$0 > -1$ ✓

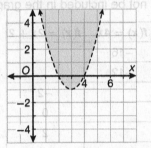

**b.** Graph $y = x^2 - 4x - 5$ as a boundary line. Use a solid curve because the inequality symbol is $\leq$.

Shade below the parabola since the solution consists of y-values less than the y-values on the parabola for the corresponding x-values.

To verify the solution region test a point. Substitute $(-4, 0)$ into the inequality.

$y \leq x^2 - 4x - 5$

$0 \overset{?}{\leq} (-4)^2 - 4(-4) - 5$

$0 \overset{?}{\leq} 16 - 4(-4) - 5$

$0 \overset{?}{\leq} 16 - (-16) - 5$

$0 \overset{?}{\leq} 27$ ✓

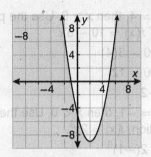

**c.** Write the inequality as $x^2 - 3x - 4 \leq 0$.

Make a table of values.

| $x$ | $-5$ | $-4$ | $-3$ | $-2$ | $-1$ | 0 | 1 | 2 | 3 | 4 | 5 |
|---|---|---|---|---|---|---|---|---|---|---|---|
| $x^2 - 3x - 4$ | 36 | 24 | 14 | 6 | 0 | $-4$ | $-6$ | $-6$ | $-4$ | 0 | 6 |

The inequality $x^2 - 3x - 4 \leq 0$ is true for values of x between $-1$ and 4 inclusively. The solution of the inequality is $-1 \leq x \leq 4$.

**d.** Use a graphing calculator to graph each side of the inequality. Set Y1 equal to $x^2 - 5x + 10$ and set Y2 equal to 4.

View the table comparing the two equations.

Identify the values of x where Y1 = $x^2 - 5x + 10$ are less than or equal to the values of Y2 = 4.

The solution set is $2 \leq x \leq 3$.

**e.** Use a graphing calculator to graph each side of the inequality. Set Y1 equal to $x^2 - 6x - 5$ and set Y2 equal to 2.

Calculate the points of intersection.

Identify the values of x where Y1 < Y2.

The solution set is $-1 < x < 7$.

### Appendix Lesson Practice 2

**a.** When $x = -3$, then $f(-3) = -2$ because $-3 \leq 1$.

When $x = 10$, then $f(10) = 4$ because $10 > 1$.

**b.** When $x = 8$, then $f(8) = 6$ because $8 < 9$.

When $x = 9$, then $f(9) = -11$ because $9 \geq 9$.

**Saxon** Algebra 1

**c.** When $x = 4$, then $x \geq 0$. Use the piece of the function, $f(x) = 10 - 3x$.

$f(4) = 10 - 3(4)$

$\quad = 10 - 12$

$\quad = -2$

When $x = -1$, then $x < 0$. Use the piece of the function, $f(x) = 2x^3$.

$f(-1) = 2(-1)^3$

$\quad = 2(-1)$

$\quad = -2$

**d.** When $x = -5$, then $x \leq -1$. Use the piece of the function, $f(x) = 3x$.

$f(-5) = 3(-5)$

$\quad = -15$

When $x = 1$, then $x > -1$. Use the piece of the function, $f(x) = x - 5$.

$f(1) = 1 - 5$

$\quad = -4$

**e.** Consider the function at $x = 5$. Because $f(5) = 2$, graph the point $(5, 2)$ with a closed circle. $f(x) = 2$ for $x \geq 5$. Draw a ray from the point extending to the right, along the line $y = 2$.

Consider $f(x) = 7$ for $x < 5$. At $(5, 7)$, draw an open circle because $f(5) \neq 7$. Draw a ray going to the left.

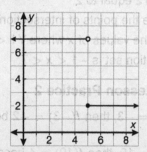

**f.** Consider the function at $x = -3$. Because $f(-3) = 0$, graph the point $(-3, 0)$ with a closed circle. $f(x) = 0$ for $-3 \leq x < 3$. Draw a ray from the point $(-3, 0)$ extending to the right, along the line $y = 0$, to the point $(3, 0)$. Because $f(3) \neq 0$, graph the point $(3, 0)$ with an open circle.

Consider $f(x) = -3$ for $x \geq 3$. At $(3, -3)$, draw a closed circle because $f(3) = -3$. Draw a ray from the point $(3, -3)$ extending to the right, along the line $y = -3$.

Consider $f(x) = 3$ for $x < -3$. At $(-3, 3)$, draw an open circle because $f(-3) \neq 3$. Draw a ray from the point $(-3, 3)$ extending to the left, along the line $y = 3$.

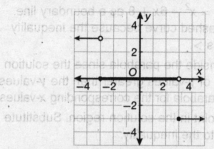

**g.** The function is made of two linear pieces with a domain divided at $x = -2$. Find the value of the two surrounding functions for this value to see if the graph is continuous.

Use a table to find points and graph each piece. The shaded regions are coordinates that will not be included in the graph of $f(x)$.

| $x$ | $f(x) = 4x$ | $f(x) = 2x + 2$ |
|-----|-------------|-----------------|
| $-4$ | $-16$ | |
| $-3$ | $-12$ | |
| $-2$ | | $-2$ |
| $-1$ | | $0$ |
| $0$ | | $2$ |
| $1$ | | $4$ |

Graph each value. There will be an open circle at $(-2, -8)$ and a closed circle at $(-2, -2)$ to clearly show the value of the function at $x = -2$.

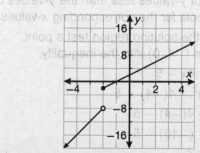

**h.** The function is made of two linear pieces and a quadratic piece with a domain divided at $x = 1$ and $x = 2$. Find the value of the two surrounding functions for these values to see if the graph is continuous.

**Saxon** Algebra 1

Use a table to find points and graph each piece. The shaded regions are coordinates that will not be included in the graph of $f(x)$.

| $x$ | $f(x) = 3x$ | $f(x) = 6x - 3$ | $f(x) = -x^2$ |
|-----|------|------|------|
| −1 | −3 | | |
| 0 | 0 | | |
| 1 | 3 | | |
| 1.5 | | 6 | |
| 2 | | | −4 |
| 3 | | | −9 |
| 4 | | | −16 |

Graph each value. There will be an open circle at $(2, 9)$ and a closed circle at $(2, -4)$ to clearly show the value of the function at $x = 2$. No open circle is needed at $x = 1$ because the function is continuous at that point.

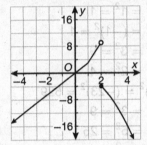

**i.** First, identify the intervals for the independent variables. Let $x$ represent age in years.

under five                          $x < 5$

ages 5 to less than 10        $5 \leq x < 10$

age 10 and older                $x \geq 10$

Then, write the function rule. $f(x)$ is the amount of allowance.

$$f(x) = \begin{cases} 0 \text{ if } x < 5 \\ 3x \text{ if } 5 \leq x < 10 \\ 4x \text{ if } x \geq 10 \end{cases}$$

Graph the function.

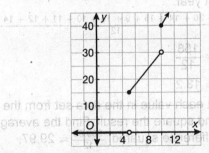

**j.** First, identify the intervals for the independent variables. Let $x$ represent height in feet.

under 4 feet                          $x < 4$

at least 4 feet but shorter than 4.5 feet

$4 \leq x < 4.5$

over 4.5 feet                          $x \geq 4.5$

Then, write the function rule. $f(x)$ is the number of rides in the park.

$$f(x) = \begin{cases} 15 \text{ if } x < 4 \\ 20 \text{ if } 4 \leq x < 4.5 \\ 24 \text{ if } x \geq 4.5 \end{cases}$$

Graph the function.

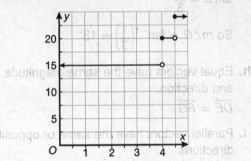

## Appendix Lesson Practice 3

**a.** The horizontal change from $A$ to $B$ is 4.

The vertical change from $A$ to $B$ is 8.

The component form of $\vec{AB}$ is $\langle 4, 8 \rangle$.

**b.** The horizontal change from $C$ to $D$ is −4.

The vertical change from $C$ to $D$ is −5.

The component form of $\vec{CD}$ is $\langle -4, -5 \rangle$.

**c.** $\vec{PQ} = \langle x_2 - x_1, y_2 - y_1 \rangle$

$= \langle 1 - 2, -1 - (-6) \rangle$

$= \langle -1, 5 \rangle$

**d.** $\vec{JK} = \langle x_2 - x_1, y_2 - y_1 \rangle$

$= \langle 8 - 3, -2 - 7 \rangle$

$= \langle 5, -9 \rangle$

**e.** $|\langle a, b \rangle| = \sqrt{a^2 + b^2}$

$|\langle 2, -9 \rangle| = \sqrt{2^2 + (-9)^2}$

$= \sqrt{4 + 81}$

$= \sqrt{85}$

$\approx 9.2$

**f.** $|\langle a, b \rangle| = \sqrt{a^2 + b^2}$

$|\langle 6, 12 \rangle| = \sqrt{6^2 + 12^2}$

$= \sqrt{36 + 144}$

$= \sqrt{180}$

$\approx 13.4$

**g.** First, draw the vector on a coordinate plane. Use the origin as the initial point. The horizontal change and the vertical change make a right triangle, with $\angle G$ formed by the vector and the x-axis.

$\tan G = \dfrac{1}{3}$

So $m\angle G = \tan^{-1}\left(\dfrac{1}{3}\right) \approx 18°$

**h.** Equal vectors have the same magnitude and direction.

$\overrightarrow{DE} = \overrightarrow{FG}$

**i.** Parallel vectors have the same or opposite directions.

$\overrightarrow{DE} \parallel \overrightarrow{FG}$ and $\overrightarrow{NM} \parallel \overrightarrow{LK}$

## Appendix Lesson Practice 4

**a.** First, find the mean of the data by adding the data and dividing by 10.

$\dfrac{900}{15} = 60$

Next, subtract each value in the data set from the mean and square the result.

$(60 - 20)^2 = 40^2 = 1600$

$(60 - 100)^2 = (-40)^2 = 1600$

$(60 - 20)^2 = 40^2 = 1600$

$(60 - 200)^2 = (-140)^2 = 19,600$

$(60 - 20)^2 = 40^2 = 1600$

$(60 - 20)^2 = 40^2 = 1600$

$(60 - 100)^2 = (-40)^2 = 1600$

$(60 - 20)^2 = 40^2 = 1600$

$(60 - 80)^2 = (-20)^2 = 400$

$(60 - 20)^2 = 40^2 = 1600$

$(60 - 20)^2 = 40^2 = 1600$

$(60 - 40)^2 = 20^2 = 400$

$(60 - 100)^2 = (-40)^2 = 1600$

$(60 - 40)^2 = 20^2 = 400$

$(60 - 100)^2 = (-40)^2 = 1600$

Now, find the average of the difference squared.

$\dfrac{1600 + \dots + 1600}{15} = \dfrac{38,400}{15} = 2560$

Finally, take the square root to get the standard deviation.

$\sqrt{2560} \approx 50.6$

**b.** First, find the mean of the data by adding the data and dividing by 10.

$$\dfrac{4 + 10 + 6 + 8 + 4 + 5 + 30 + 4 + 2 + 3 + 1}{11}$$

$= \dfrac{77}{11} = 7$

Next, subtract each value in the data set from the mean and square the result.

$(7 - 4)^2 = 3^2 = 9$

$(7 - 10)^2 = (-3)^2 = 9$

$(7 - 6)^2 = 1^2 = 1$

$(7 - 8)^2 = (-1)^2 = 1$

$(7 - 4)^2 = 3^2 = 9$

$(7 - 5)^2 = 2^2 = 4$

$(7 - 30)^2 = (-23)^2 = 529$

$(7 - 4)^2 = 3^2 = 9$

$(7 - 2)^2 = 5^2 = 25$

$(7 - 3)^2 = 4^2 = 16$

$(7 - 1)^2 = 6^2 = 36$

Now, find the average of the difference squared.

$\dfrac{9 + 9 + 1 + 1 + 9 + 4 + 529 + 9 + 25 + 16 + 36}{11} = \dfrac{648}{11}$

$= 58.9$

Finally, take the square root to get the standard deviation.

$\sqrt{58.9} \approx 7.68$

**c.** First, find the mean of the number of books read last year.

$$\dfrac{12 + 15 + 30 + 14 + 13 + 9 + 10 + 10 + 11 + 12 + 14 + 8}{12}$$

$= \dfrac{158}{12}$

$\approx 13.2$

Subtract each value in the data set from the mean and square the result. Find the average of the difference squared, $\dfrac{359.68}{12} \approx 29.97$,

**Saxon** Algebra 1

and take the square root to get the standard deviation.

$\sqrt{29.97} \approx 5.47$

An outlier is any number more than 3 standard deviations from the mean, $13.2 \pm 3(5.47)$

Negative numbers of books would not make sense, so check to see if any student read more than $13.2 + 3(5.47) = 29.61$ books.

30 is an outlier and it makes the mean larger.

d. First, find the mean of the test scores.

$mean = \dfrac{90 + \ldots + 100}{15}$

$= \dfrac{1285}{15}$

$\approx 85.7$

Subtract each value in the data set from the mean and square the result.
Find the average of the difference squared, $\dfrac{2743.3}{15} \approx 182.9$, and take the square root to get the standard deviation.

$\sqrt{182.9} \approx 13.5$

40 is an outlier and it makes the mean smaller.

e. Because it is a normal distribution, 68% of the data fall within 1 standard deviation of the mean.

$85 \pm 1(5) = 85 \pm 5$

68% of the results fall between 80 and 90.

f. Because it is a normal distribution, 99.7% of the data fall within 3 standard deviations of the mean.

$\$35,000 \pm 3(\$10,000)$

$\$35,000 \pm \$30,000$

99.7% of the salaries fall between $5,000 and $65,000.

## Appendix Lesson Practice 5

**a.** Press **Y=**. Enter $-x^2 - 7x + 9$ for $Y_1$.
Press **2nd** **WINDOW** **TBLSET** to set the table values.

Enter the value of $x$, 22, for **TblStart**. Press **TABLE**
**2nd** **GRAPH** The value of the expression is −629.

**b.** Press **Y=**. Enter $-x^2 - 7x + 9$ for $Y_1$.
Press **2nd** **WINDOW** **TBLSET** to set the table values.
Enter the value of $x$, 42, for **TblStart**. Press **TABLE**
**2nd** **GRAPH** The value of the expression is −2049.

**c.** Press **Y=**. Enter $-x^2 - 7x + 9$ for $Y_1$.
Press **2nd** **WINDOW** **TBLSET** to set the table values.
Enter the value of $x$, 62, for **TblStart**. Press **TABLE**
**2nd** **GRAPH** The value of the expression is −4269.

**d.** Press **Y=**. Enter $6x^2 + x - 13$ for $Y_1$.
Press **2nd** **WINDOW** **TBLSET** to set the table values.
Enter the value of $x$, 48, for **TblStart**. Press **TABLE**
**2nd** **GRAPH** The value of the expression is 13,859.

**e.** Press **Y=**. Enter $6x^2 + x - 13$ for $Y_1$.
Press **2nd** **WINDOW** **TBLSET** to set the table values.
Enter the value of $x$, 78, for **TblStart**. Press **TABLE**
**2nd** **GRAPH** The value of the expression is 36,569.

**f.** Press **Y=**. Enter $6x^2 + x - 13$ for $Y_1$.
Press **2nd** **WINDOW** **TBLSET** to set the table values.
Enter the value of $x$, 108, for **TblStart**. Press **TABLE**
**2nd** **GRAPH** The value of the expression is 70,079.

**g.** Enter 6 in the first column, A1. Enter the expression in cell B1, using A1 instead of a variable. The expression should be typed as $= -2 \times A1^2 + 8 \times A1 - 4$ After pressing **enter**, the value of the expression, −28, appears in the cell.

**h.** Enter 12 in the first column, A1. Enter the expression in cell B1, using A1 instead of a variable. The expression should be typed as $= -2 \times A1^2 + 8 \times A1 - 4$ After pressing **enter**, the value of the expression, −196, appears in the cell.

**i.** Enter 18 in the first column, A1. Enter the expression in cell B1, using A1 instead of a variable. The expression should be typed as

**Saxon** Algebra 1

$= -2 \times A1^2 + 8 \times A1 - 4$ After pressing **enter**, the value of the expression, −508, appears in the cell.

**j.** Enter 4 in the first column, A1. Enter the expression in cell B1, using A1 instead of a variable. The expression should be typed as $= A1^2 + 14 \times A1 - 21$ After pressing **enter**, the value of the expression, 51, appears in the cell.

**k.** Enter 9 in the first column, A1. Enter the expression in cell B1, using A1 instead of a variable. The expression should be typed as $= A1^2 + 14 \times A1 - 21$ After pressing **enter**, the value of the expression, 186, appears in the cell.

**l.** Enter 14 in the first column, A1. Enter the expression in cell B1, using A1 instead of a variable. The expression should be typed as $= A1^2 + 14 \times A1 - 21$ After pressing **enter**, the value of the expression, 371, appears in the cell.

## SKILLS BANK

### Skills Bank Practice 1

**a.** Multiply the denominators to find a common denominator.

$8 \times 12 = 96$

Write the fractions with a common denominator.

$\frac{5}{8} \times \frac{12}{12} \bigcirc \frac{7}{12} \times \frac{8}{8}$

$\frac{60}{96} > \frac{56}{96}$, so $\frac{5}{8} > \frac{7}{12}$.

**b.** Multiply the denominators to find a common denominator.

$11 \times 10 = 110$

Write the fractions with a common denominator.

$\frac{3}{11} \times \frac{10}{10} \bigcirc \frac{3}{10} \times \frac{11}{11}$

$\frac{30}{110} < \frac{33}{110}$, so $\frac{3}{11} < \frac{3}{10}$.

**c.** Multiply the denominators to find a common denominator.

$7 \times 5 = 35$

Write the fractions with a common denominator.

$-\frac{3}{7} \times \frac{5}{5} \bigcirc -\frac{4}{5} \times \frac{7}{7}$

$-\frac{15}{35} > -\frac{28}{35}$, so $-\frac{3}{7} > -\frac{4}{5}$.

**d.** Write each fraction as a decimal.

$\frac{7}{8} = 0.875$

$1\frac{1}{3} = 1.33\overline{3}$

The numbers in order from least to greatest are −2, 0.8, $\frac{7}{8}$, $1\frac{1}{3}$, 2.1.

**e.** Write each fraction as a decimal.

$-\frac{5}{4} = -1.25$

$\frac{4}{3} = 1.33\overline{3}$

$-\frac{9}{2} = -4.5$

The numbers in order from least to greatest are $-\frac{9}{2}$, −2.3, $-\frac{5}{4}$, −1, 0.7, $\frac{4}{3}$.

### Skills Bank Practice 2

**a.** 19.30   Write the problem vertically.
+ 24.54   Align the decimal points.
43.84

**b.** 55.755   Write the problem vertically.
− 30.930   Align the decimal points.
24.825

**c.** 0.216   Write the problem vertically.
× 4.28
0.92448   Since the factors have a total of 5 decimal places, there should be 5 decimal places in the product.

**d.** 6)75.6   Multiply the divisor and dividend by 100 so the divisor is a natural number.

12.6

**e.** 176.40   Write the problem vertically.
− 23.72   Align the decimal points.
152.68

**f.** 24.60   Write the problem vertically.
+ 18.76   Align the decimal points.
43.36

**Saxon** Algebra 1

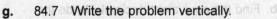

**g.**   84.7   Write the problem vertically.
   × 6.2
   525.14   Since the factors have a total of
              2 decimal places, there should be
              2 decimal places in the product.

       5.3
**h.** 15)79.5   Multiply the divisor and dividend
                 by 10 so the divisor is a natural
                 number.

## Skills Bank Practice 3

**a.** Multiply to find a common denominator.

$12 \times 8 = 96$

$\frac{7}{12}\left(\frac{8}{8}\right) + \frac{3}{8}\left(\frac{12}{12}\right)$   Multiply by fractions
                                          equal to 1.

$= \frac{56}{96} + \frac{36}{96}$   Add.

$= \frac{92}{96}$ or $\frac{23}{24}$

**b.** The LCD of the fractions is 10.

$\frac{9}{10} - \frac{4}{5}\left(\frac{2}{2}\right)$   Multiply by fractions
                                          equal to 1.

$= \frac{9}{10} - \frac{8}{10}$   Add.

$= \frac{1}{10}$

**c.** Multiply the numerators and denominators.
Then simplify.

$\frac{5}{9} \times \frac{3}{4} = \frac{15}{36}$

$= \frac{5}{12}$

**d.** Write the reciprocal of $\frac{9}{8}$ and then multiply.

$\frac{2}{16} \times \frac{8}{9} = \frac{16}{144}$   Multiply by $\frac{8}{9}$.

$= \frac{1}{9}$

**e.** The LCD of the fractions is 16.

$\frac{5}{8}\left(\frac{2}{2}\right) - \frac{5}{16}$   Multiply by fractions equal to 1.

$= \frac{10}{16} - \frac{5}{16}$   Add.

$= \frac{5}{16}$

**f.** The LCD of the fractions is 30.

$\frac{7}{10}\left(\frac{3}{3}\right) + \frac{8}{15}\left(\frac{2}{2}\right)$   Multiply by fractions equal
                                          to 1.

$= \frac{21}{30} + \frac{16}{30}$   Add.

$= \frac{37}{30}$ or $1\frac{7}{30}$

## Skills Bank Practice 4

**a.** Use the Divisibility Rules to determine if 90 is
divisible by each number.

| 2 | The last digit is even. | 90 | divisible |
|---|---|---|---|
| 3 | The sum of the digits is divisible by 3. | 9 + 0 = 9 | divisible |
| 4 | The last two digits are not divisible by 4. | 90 | not divisible |
| 5 | The last digit is 0. | 90 | divisible |
| 6 | It is divisible by both 2 and 3. | | divisible |
| 9 | The sum of the digits is divisible by 9. | 9 + 0 = 9 | divisible |
| 10 | The last digit is 0. | 90 | divisible |

**b.** Use the Divisibility Rules to determine if
830 is divisible by each number.

| 2 | The last digit is even. | 830 | divisible |
|---|---|---|---|
| 3 | The sum of the digits is not divisible by 3. | 8 + 3 + 0 = 11 | not divisible |
| 4 | The last two digits are not divisible by 4. | 30 | not divisible |
| 5 | The last digit is 0. | 830 | divisible |
| 6 | It is not divisible by 3. | | not divisible |
| 9 | The sum of the digits is not divisible by 9. | 8 + 3 + 0 = 11 | not divisible |
| 10 | The last digit is 0. | 830 | divisible |

**Saxon** Algebra 1

**c.** Use the Divisibility Rules to determine if 1024 is divisible by each number.

| 2 | The last digit is even. | 1024 | divisible |
|---|---|---|---|
| 3 | The sum of the digits is not divisible by 3. | $1 + 0 + 2 + 4 = 7$ | not divisible |
| 4 | The last two digits are divisible by 4. | 24 | divisible |
| 5 | The last digit is not 0 or 5. | 1024 | not divisible |
| 6 | It is not divisible by 3. | | not divisible |
| 9 | The sum of the digits is not divisible by 9. | $1 + 0 + 2 + 4 = 7$ | not divisible |
| 10 | The last digit is not 0. | 1024 | not divisible |

**d.** Use the Divisibility Rules to determine if 12 and 54 are both divisible or not both divisible by each number.

| 2 | The last digit is even. | 12 | 54 | both divisible |
|---|---|---|---|---|
| 3 | The sum of the digits is divisible by 3. | $1 + 2 = 3$ | $5 + 4 = 9$ | both divisible |
| 4 | The last two digits in 54 are not divisible by 4. | | | not divisible |
| 5 | The last digit in 12 and the last digit in 54 are not 0. | 12 | 54 | not divisible |
| 6 | It is divisible by both 2 and 3. | 12 | 54 | divisible |

## Skills Bank Practice 5

**a.** Find the equivalent decimal. Divide the numerator by the denominator.

$$5\overline{)3.0}$$ gives $0.6$

Find the equivalent percent. Move the decimal two places to the right.

$0.6 = 60\%$

$\frac{3}{5}$ is equivalent to 0.6 and 60%.

**b.** Find the equivalent decimal. Divide the numerator by the denominator.

$$10\overline{)4.0}$$ gives $0.4$

Find the equivalent percent. Move the decimal two places to the right.

$0.4 = 40\%$

$\frac{4}{10}$ is equivalent to 0.4 and 40%.

**c.** Find the equivalent decimal. Divide the numerator by the denominator.

$$8\overline{)3.000}$$ gives $0.375$

Find the equivalent percent. Move the decimal two places to the right.

$0.375 = 37.5\%$

$\frac{3}{8}$ is equivalent to 0.375 and 37.5%.

**d.** Find the equivalent decimal. Divide the numerator by the denominator.

$5 \div 11 = 0.45\overline{45}$

Find the equivalent percent. Move the decimal two places to the right.

$0.45\overline{45} = 45.\overline{45}\%$

$\frac{5}{11}$ is equivalent to 0.$\overline{45}$ and 45.$\overline{45}$%.

**e.** Find the equivalent decimal. Divide the numerator by the denominator.

$7 \div 9 = 0.77\overline{7}$

Find the equivalent percent. Move the decimal two places to the right.

$0.77\overline{7} = 77.\overline{7}\%$

$\frac{7}{9}$ is equivalent to 0.$\overline{7}$ and 77.$\overline{7}$%.

**f.** Find the equivalent decimal. Divide the numerator by the denominator.

$$4\overline{)3.00}$$ gives $0.75$

Find the equivalent percent. Move the decimal two places to the right.

$= \%$

$\frac{3}{4}$ is equivalent to 0.75 and 75%.

## Skills Bank Practice 6

**a.** The decimal is in the hundredths place, so use 100 as the denominator. Then simplify.

$0.85 = \frac{85}{100} = \frac{17}{20}$

**Saxon** Algebra 1

**b.** The decimal is in the hundredths place, so use 100 as the denominator. Then simplify.

$$1.75 = 1\frac{75}{100} = 1\frac{3}{4}$$

**c.** To eliminate the repeating decimal, subtract the same repeating decimal.

| | |
|---|---|
| $n = 0.\overline{57}$ | Let $n$ represent the fraction equivalent to $0.5757...$ |
| $100n = 57.\overline{57}$ | Since 2 digits repeat, multiply both sides of the equation by $10^2$ or 100. |

$$\begin{array}{r} 100n = 57.\overline{57} \\ - \quad n = 0.\overline{57} \\ \hline 99n = 57 \end{array}$$ Subtract the original equation.

$n = \dfrac{57}{99}$ or $\dfrac{19}{33}$    Divide both sides by 99 and simplify.

$0.575757$ is equivalent to $\frac{19}{33}$.

**d.** To eliminate the repeating decimal, subtract the same repeating decimal.

| | |
|---|---|
| $n = 0.\overline{81}$ | Let $n$ represent the fraction equivalent to $0.\overline{81}$ |
| $100n = 81.\overline{81}$ | Since 2 digits repeat, multiply both sides of the equation by $10^2$ or 100. |

$$\begin{array}{r} 100n = 81.\overline{81} \\ - \quad n = 0.\overline{81} \\ \hline 99n = 81 \end{array}$$ Subtract the original equation.

$n = \dfrac{81}{99}$ or $\dfrac{9}{11}$    Divide both sides by 99 and simplify.

$0.\overline{81}$ is equivalent to $\frac{9}{11}$.

**e.** The decimal is in the hundredths place, so use 100 as the denominator. Then simplify.

$$0.48 = \frac{48}{100} = \frac{12}{25}$$

**f.** The decimal is in the hundredths place, so use 100 as the denominator. Then simplify.

$$1.25 = 1\frac{25}{100} = 1\frac{1}{4}$$

**g.** To eliminate the repeating decimal, subtract the same repeating decimal.

| | |
|---|---|
| $n = 0.\overline{36}$ | Let $n$ represent the fraction equivalent to $0.\overline{36}$ |
| $100n = 36.\overline{36}$ | Since 2 digits repeat, multiply both sides of the equation by $10^2$ or 100. |

$$\begin{array}{r} 100n = 36.\overline{36} \\ - \quad n = 0.\overline{36} \\ \hline 99n = 36 \end{array}$$ Subtract the original equation. Combine like terms.

$n = \dfrac{36}{99}$ or $\dfrac{4}{11}$    Divide both sides by 99 and simplify.

$0.\overline{36}$ is equivalent to $\frac{4}{11}$.

**h.** To eliminate the repeating decimal, subtract the same repeating decimal.

| | |
|---|---|
| $n = 0.44\overline{4}$ | Let $n$ represent the fraction equivalent to $0.\overline{4}$ |
| $10n = 4.44\overline{4}$ | Since 1 digit repeats, multiply both sides of the equation by $10^1$ or 10. |

$$\begin{array}{r} 10n = 4.44\overline{4} \\ - \quad n = 0.44\overline{4} \\ \hline 9n = 4 \end{array}$$ Subtract the original equation. Combine like terms.

$n = \dfrac{4}{9}$    Divide both sides by 9 and simplify.

$0.44\overline{4}$ is equivalent to $\frac{4}{9}$.

**Skills Bank Practice 7**

**a.** Choose any whole number. Multiply the numerator and the denominator by that number.

$$\frac{3}{7} = \frac{3 \times 2}{7 \times 2} = \frac{6}{14}$$

$$\frac{3}{7} = \frac{3 \times 5}{7 \times 5} = \frac{15}{35}$$

**b.** Choose any whole number. Multiply the numerator and the denominator by that number.

$$\frac{1}{5} = \frac{1 \times 5}{5 \times 5} = \frac{5}{25}$$

$$\frac{1}{5} = \frac{1 \times 7}{5 \times 7} = \frac{7}{35}$$

**c.** Find a number that is a factor of the numerator and the denominator. Divide both by that number.

**Saxon** Algebra 1

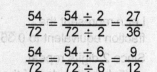

$$\frac{54}{72} = \frac{54 \div 2}{72 \div 2} = \frac{27}{36}$$

$$\frac{54}{72} = \frac{54 \div 6}{72 \div 6} = \frac{9}{12}$$

**d.** Find a number that is a factor of the numerator and the denominator. Divide both by that number.

$$\frac{120}{360} = \frac{120 \div 10}{360 \div 10} = \frac{12}{36}$$

$$\frac{120}{360} = \frac{120 \div 120}{360 \div 120} = \frac{1}{3}$$

**e.** Find the GCF of 14 and 24. The GCF is 2.

$$\frac{14}{24} = \frac{14 \div 2}{24 \div 2} = \frac{7}{12}$$

**f.** Find the GCF of 30 and 36. The GCF is 6.

$$\frac{30}{36} = \frac{30 \div 6}{36 \div 6} = \frac{5}{6}$$

**g.** Find the GCF of 75 and 100. The GCF is 25.

$$\frac{75}{100} = \frac{75 \div 25}{100 \div 25} = \frac{3}{4}$$

**h.** Find the GCF of 48 and 60. The GCF is 12.

$$\frac{48}{60} = \frac{48 \div 12}{60 \div 12} = \frac{4}{5}$$

**i.** Find the GCF of 90 and 360. The GCF is 90.

$$\frac{90}{360} = \frac{90 \div 90}{360 \div 90} = \frac{1}{4}$$

## Skills Bank Practice 8

**a.** Rico should overestimate. If his estimate is more than the actual cost, then he has enough money to buy the supplies.

To overestimate, round each number up.

$2 \times \$2.75 + \$12.50 + 4 \times \$1.99$

$2 \times \$3 + \$13 + 4 \times \$2$

$\$6 + \$13 + \$8$

$\$27$

The actual cost will be less than $27. So Rico has enough money.

**b.** Jordan should underestimate the amount of gas his car will use. Round 32 miles per gallon of gas down to 30.

$120 \div 30 = 4$

Jordan will use about 4 gallons of gas.

## Skills Bank Practice 9

**a.** List the factors of each number.

72: 1, 2, 3, 4, 6, 8, 9, 12, 18, 24, 36, 72

60: 1, 2, 3, 4, 5, 6, 10, 12, 15, 20, 30, 60

The common factors are 2, 3, 4, 6, and 12.

The GCF is 12.

**b.** List the factors of each number.

54: 1, 2, 3, 6, 9, 18, 27, 54

89: 1, 89

The GCF is 1.

**c.** List the factors of each number.

21: 1, 3, 7, 21

56: 1, 2, 4, 7, 8, 14, 28, 56

The GCF is 7.

**d.** List the factors of each number.

120: 1, 2, 3, 4, 5, 6, 8, 10, 12, 15, 20, 24, 30, 40, 60, 120

960: 1, 2, 3, 4, 5, 6, 8, 10, 12, 15, 16, 20, 24, 30, 32, 40, 48, 60, 64, 80, 96, 120, 160, 192, 240, 320, 480, 960

The common factors are 2, 3, 4, 5, 6, 8, 10, 12, 15, 20, 24, 30, 40, 60, and 120

The GCF is 120.

**e.** List the factors of each number.

3: 1, 3

6: 1, 2, 3, 6

12: 1, 2, 3, 4, 6, 12

The GCF is 3.

**f.** List the factors of each number.

7: 1, 7

21: 1, 3, 7, 21

49: 1, 7, 49

The GCF is 7.

**g.** List the factors of each number.

4: 1, 2, 4

22: 1, 2, 11, 22

40: 1, 2, 4, 5, 8, 10, 20, 40

The GCF is 2.

**h.** List the factors of each number.

20: 1, 2, 4, 5, 10, 20

45: 1, 3, 5, 9, 15, 45

80: 1, 2, 4, 5, 8, 10, 16, 20, 40, 80
The GCF is 5.

**i.** Divide 8 and 12 by the GCF, 4.

$$\frac{8}{12} = \frac{8 \div 4}{12 \div 4} = \frac{2}{3}$$

**j.** Divide 15 and 25 by the GCF, 5.

$$\frac{15}{25} = \frac{15 \div 5}{25 \div 5} = \frac{3}{5}$$

**k.** Divide 16 and 64 by the GCF, 16.

$$\frac{16}{64} = \frac{16 \div 16}{64 \div 16} = \frac{1}{4}$$

**l.** Divide 110 and 150 by the GCF, 10.

$$\frac{110}{150} = \frac{110 \div 10}{150 \div 10} = \frac{11}{15}$$

**m.** Divide 52 and 65 by the GCF, 13.

$$\frac{52}{65} = \frac{52 \div 13}{65 \div 13} = \frac{4}{5}$$

### Skills Bank Practice 10

**a.** List the multiples of each number.
Multiples of 9: 9, 18, 27, 36, 45, 54, ...
Multiples of 15: 15, 30, 45, 60, ...
The LCM is 45.

**b.** List the multiples of each number.
Multiples of 20: 20, 40, 60, 80, 100, 120, 140, 160, ...
Multiples of 25: 25, 50, 75, 100, 125, 150, 175, 200, ...
The LCM is 100.

**c.** List the multiples of each number.
Multiples of 24: 24, 48, 72, 96, ...
Multiples of 48: 48, 96, 144, 192, ...
The LCM is 48.

**d.** List the multiples of each number.
Multiples of 14: 14, 28, 42, 56, 70, ...
Multiples of 21: 21, 42, 63, 84, 105, ...
The LCM is 42.

**e.** List the multiples of each number
Multiples of 25: 25, 50, 75, 100, 125, 150, 175, 200, ...
Multiples of 50: 50, 100, 150, 200, 250, 300, 350, 400, ...

Multiples of 100: 100, 200, 300, 400, 500, 600, 700, 800, ...
The LCM is 100.

**f.** List the multiples of each number.
Multiples of 8: 8, 16, 24, 32, 40, 48, ...
Multiples of 16: 16, 32, 48, 64, 80, 96, ...
Multiples of 48: 48, 96, 144, 192, 240, 268, ...
The LCM is 48.

**g.** List the multiples of each number.
Multiples of 2: 2, 4, 6, 8, 10, 12, 14, 16, 18, 20, 22, 24, 26, 28, 30, 32, 34, 36, 38, 40, 42, 44, 46, 48, 50, 52, 54, 56, 58, 60, 62, 64, 66, 68, 70, ...
Multiples of 3: 3, 6, 9, 12, 15, 18, 21, 24, 27, 30, 33, 36, 39, 42, 45, 48, 51, 54, 57, 60, 63, 66, 69, 72, ...
Multiples of 20: 20, 40, 60, 80, 100, ...
The LCM is 60.

**h.** The LCM of 2 and 15 is 30, so 30 is the LCD. Write equivalent fractions using a denominator of 30.

$$\frac{1}{2} = \frac{1 \times 15}{2 \times 15} = \frac{15}{30}$$

$$\frac{7}{15} = \frac{7 \times 2}{15 \times 2} = \frac{14}{30}$$

$\frac{1}{2}$ and $\frac{7}{15}$ are equivalent to $\frac{15}{30}$ and $\frac{14}{30}$, respectively.

### Skills Bank Practice 11

**a.** $24 + 15 + 16 + 15$
$= 24 + 16 + 15 + 15$
$= (24 + 16) + (15 + 15)$
$= 40 + 30 = 70$

**b.** $6 \times 12 \times 5$
$= 6 \times 5 \times 12$
$= (6 \times 5) \times 12$
$= 30 \times 12$
$= 360$

**c.** $58 \times 4$
$= (50 + 8) \times 4$
$= (50 \times 4) + (8 \times 4)$
$= 200 + 32$
$= 232$

**Saxon** Algebra 1

**d.** $6 + 31 + 34 + 9$
$= 6 + 34 + 31 + 9$
$= (6 + 34) + (31 + 9)$
$= 40 + 40$
$= 80$

**e.** $34 \times 7$
$= (30 + 4) \times 7$
$= (30 \times 7) + (4 \times 7)$
$= 210 + 28$
$= 238$

**f.** $4 \times 62 \times 25$
$= 4 \times 25 \times 62$
$= (4 \times 25) \times 62$
$= 100 \times 62$
$= 6200$

**g.** $8 + 67 + 12 + 3$
$= 8 + 12 + 67 + 3$
$= (8 + 12) + (67 + 3)$
$= 20 + 70 = 90$

**h.** $33 \times 9$
$= (30 + 3) \times 9$
$= (30 \times 9) + (3 \times 9)$
$= 270 + 27$
$= 297$

## Skills Bank Practice 12

**a.** List the factors of 17.
1, 17
17 is a prime number.

**b.** List the factors of 15.
1, 3, 5, 15
15 is a composite number.

**c.** List the factors of 32.
1, 2, 4, 8, 16, 32
32 is a composite number.

**d.** List the factors of 29.
1, 29
29 is a prime number.

**e.** Choose any two factors of 72. Continue to factor until each branch ends in a prime number.

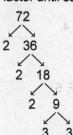

The prime factorization of 72 is
$2 \times 2 \times 2 \times 3 \times 3$ or $2^3 \times 3^2$.

**f.** Choose any two factors of 28. Continue to factor until each branch ends in a prime number.

The prime factorization of 28 is
$2 \times 2 \times 7$ or $2^2 \times 7$.

**g.** Choose any two factors of 34. Continue to factor until each branch ends in a prime number.

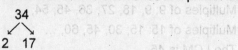

The prime factorization of 34 is $2 \times 17$.

**h.** Choose any two factors of 24. Continue to factor until each branch ends in a prime number.

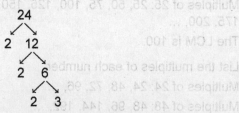

The prime factorization of 24 is
$2 \times 2 \times 2 \times 3$ or $2^3 \times 3$.

**i.** Choose any two factors of 76. Continue to factor until each branch ends in a prime number.

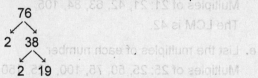

The prime factorization of 76 is
$2 \times 2 \times 19$ or $2^2 \times 19$.

**Saxon** Algebra 1

**j.** Choose any two factors of 32. Continue to factor until each branch ends in a prime number.

The prime factorization of 32 is $2 \times 2 \times 2 \times 2 \times 2$ or $2^5$.

**k.** Choose any two factors of 45. Continue to factor until each branch ends in a prime number.

```
    45
   /  \
  3   15
      /  \
     3    5
```

The prime factorization of 45 is $3 \times 3 \times 5$ or $3^2 \times 5$.

**l.** Choose any two factors of 52. Continue to factor until each branch ends in a prime number.

```
    52
   /  \
  2   26
      /  \
     2   13
```

The prime factorization of 52 is $2 \times 2 \times 13$ or $2^2 \times 13$.

## Skills Bank Practice 13

**a.** This is a right angle because the angle measure is equal to 90°.

**b.** This is an obtuse angle because the angle measure is greater than 90° but less than 180°.

**c.** This is an acute angle because the angle measure is less than 90°.

**d.** The figure has three acute angles and no congruent sides. So, this is an acute scalene triangle.

**e.** The figure has one right angle and at least 2 congruent sides. So, this is a right isosceles triangle.

**f.** The right has one obtuse angle and no congruent sides. So, this is an obtuse scalene triangle.

## Skills Bank Practice 14

**a.** A square has opposite sides that are parallel and congruent. Its opposite angles are congruent. Also, a square has four congruent sides. Therefore, a square is also a rectangle or rhombus.

**b.** A square is a parallelogram that has four congruent sides and four right angles. Therefore, a rhombus is sometimes a square.

**c.** All trapezoids are two-dimensional figures with four sides and four angles. Therefore, all trapezoids are also quadrilaterals.

**d.** By definition, a quadrilateral is any two-dimensional figure with four straight sides and four angles.

## Skills Bank Practice 15

**a.** $66° + m\angle x = 90°$

$$\underline{-66° = -66°}$$

$$m\angle x = 24°$$

66° and $\angle x$ are complementary.

**b.** $28° + m\angle x = 180°$

$$\underline{-28° = -28°}$$

$$m\angle x = 152°$$

28° and $\angle x$ are supplementary.

**c.** $134° + m\angle x = 180°$

$$\underline{-134° = -134°}$$

$$m\angle x = 46°$$

134° and $\angle x$ are supplementary.

**d.** $m\angle D + m\angle E = 90°$

$$50° + m\angle E = 90°$$

$$\underline{-50° = -50°}$$

$$m\angle E = 40°$$

**e.** $m\angle W + m\angle T = 180°$

$$50° + m\angle T = 180°$$

$$\underline{-50° = -50°}$$

$$m\angle T = 130°$$

## Skills Bank Practice 16

**a.** Find the congruent angles and sides.

$\angle L \cong \angle P$     $\overline{LK} \cong \overline{PQ}$

$\angle K \cong \angle Q$     $\overline{KJ} \cong \overline{QT}$

$\angle J \cong \angle T$     $\overline{JL} \cong \overline{TP}$

Write a congruence statement.

$\triangle LKJ \cong \triangle PQT$

**b.** Find the congruent sides and angles.

$\angle J \cong \angle L \cong \angle D \cong \angle Y$

$\angle T \cong \angle B \cong \angle P \cong \angle K$

$\overline{JL} \cong \overline{DY} \cong \overline{YD}$

$\overline{LT} \cong \overline{YP} \cong \overline{DK}$

$\overline{TB} \cong \overline{PK} \cong \overline{KP}$

$\overline{JB} \cong \overline{DK} \cong \overline{YP}$

Write a congruence statement.

Quadrilateral $JLTB \cong$ Quadrilateral $DYPK$

or

Quadrilateral $JLTB \cong$ Quadrilateral $YDKP$

### Skills Bank Practice 17

**a.** Estimate the length of the top, sides, and bottom of the figure.

left: $\approx 6$ feet

right: $\approx 3$ feet

bottom: $\approx 4$ feet

top: 9 feet

$P \approx 6 + 3 + 4 + 9 = 22$

The perimeter is about 22 feet.

**b.** Estimate the area by counting the squares.

18 full squares

2 almost full squares

6 half full squares: $\approx 3$

2 corners: $\approx 0$

The area of the figure is about 23 units$^2$

### Skills Bank Practice 18

**a.**

**b.**

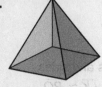

### Skills Bank Practice 19

**a.** center $Z$, radii $\overline{ZY}$, $\overline{ZT}$, $\overline{ZU}$, $\overline{ZV}$, $\overline{ZW}$, $\overline{ZX}$, diameters $\overline{TW}$, $\overline{YV}$, $\overline{XU}$, chords $\overline{TW}$, $\overline{YV}$, $\overline{XU}$, $\overline{YT}$, $\overline{WV}$

**b.** center $T$, radii $\overline{WT}$, $\overline{XT}$, $\overline{YT}$, $\overline{ZT}$, diameters $\overline{WY}$, $\overline{XZ}$, chords $\overline{WX}$, $\overline{WY}$, $\overline{WZ}$, $\overline{XY}$, $\overline{XZ}$, $\overline{YZ}$

### Skills Bank Practice 20

**a.** From the front and all side views, there appears to be three rows of cubes, with 5 cubes on the bottom row, 3 cubes in the middle row, and 1 cube on top. The top view shows an array of 5 cubes by 5 cubes.

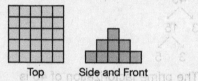

Top        Side and Front

### Skills Bank Practice 21

**a.** $S = 2B + Ph$

$= 2(12.4 \times 15.3) + [2(12.4 + 15.3)](18.0)$

$= 2(189.72) + (55.4)(18.0)$

$= 379.44 + 997.2$

$= 1379.64 \text{ ft}^2$

**b.** $S = B + \frac{1}{2}Pl$

$= (9.6 \times 8.4) + \frac{1}{2}[2(9.6 + 8.4)](9)$

$= 80.64 + \frac{1}{2}[2(18)](9)$

$= 80.64 + \frac{1}{2}[36](9)$

$= 80.64 + (18)(9)$

$= 80.64 + 162$

$= 242.64 \text{ m}^2$

### Skills Bank Practice 22

**a.** No, an oval cannot create a tessellation because there will be gaps.

**Saxon** Algebra 1

**b.** Yes, a regular hexagon can create a tessellation. There are no gaps or overlays.

**c.** No, a regular octagon cannot create a tessellation because there will be overlays.

## Skills Bank Practice 23

**a.** Yes, this shape is a polyhedron. There are 6 faces, 12 edges, and 8 vertices.

**b.** No, this shape is not a polyhedron.

## Skills Bank Practice 24

**a.** The *y*-axis is a line of symmetry.

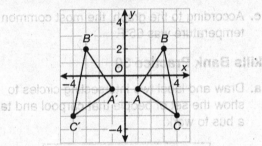

**b.** The coordinates of *ABCD* are *A*(3, 1), *B*(2, −3), *C*(4, −4), and *D*(4, −1). Subtract 5 from each *x*-value to find the coordinates for the points that describe the translation 5 units left. *A'*(−2, 1), *B'*(−3, −3), *C'*(−1, −4), *D'*(−1, −1)

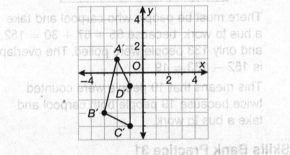

## Skills Bank Practice 25

**a.** ∠*AEB* and ∠*CED*; ∠*BEC* and ∠*DEA*

**b.** ∠*ABQ* and ∠*QBR* are supplementary.
$m\angle ABQ + m\angle QBR = 180°$
$m\angle ABQ + 100° = 180°$

$m\angle ABQ = 80°$
Vertical angles have the same measure.
$m\angle ABC = m\angle QBR$
$m\angle ABC = 100°$
Vertical angles have the same measure.
$m\angle CBR = m\angle ABQ$
$m\angle CBR = 80°$

**c.** ∠*EFG* and ∠*EFI* are supplementary.
$m\angle EFG + m\angle EFI = 180°$
$m\angle EFG + 20° = 180°$
$m\angle EFG = 160°$
Vertical angles have the same measure.
$m\angle GFH = m\angle EFI$
$m\angle GFH = 20°$
Vertical angles have the same measure.
$m\angle HFI = m\angle EFG$
$m\angle HFI = 160°$

**d.** ∠*BAC* and ∠*CAD* are supplementary.
$m\angle BAC + m\angle CAD = 180°$
$m\angle BAC + 140° = 180°$
$m\angle BAC = 40°$
Vertical angles have the same measure.
$m\angle DAE = m\angle BAC$
$m\angle DAE = 40°$
Vertical angles have the same measure.
$m\angle EAB = m\angle CAD$
$m\angle EAB = 140°$

## Skills Bank Practice 26

**a.** $V = Bh$
$= (11 \times 4) \times 2$
$= 44 \times 2$
$= 88$ m³

**b.** $V = \pi r^2 h$
$\approx 3.14 \times (7)^2 \times 8$
$\approx 3.14 \times (49) \times 8$
$\approx 1230.88$ m³

## Skills Bank Practice 27

**a.** Find the appropriate scale. Use the data to determine the length of the bars. Title the graph and label the axes.

**Saxon** Algebra 1

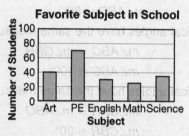

**Favorite Subject in School**

**b.** Find the appropriate scale. Make a point for each data value. Connect the points with line segments. Title the graph and label the axes.

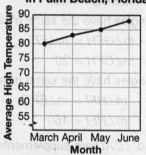

**Average High Temperature in Palm Beach, Florida**

## Skills Bank Practice 28

**a.** Find the angle measures by multiplying each percent by 360°

Dog: 36% × 360° = 0.36 × 360° = 129.60°

Cat: 25% × 360° = 0.25 × 360° = 90°

Fish: 15% × 360° = 0.15 × 360° = 54°

No pets: 24% × 360° = 0.24 × 360° = 86.4°

Use a compass to draw a circle.

Draw a circle and radius with a compass and straightedge. Then use a protractor to draw the first angle, 129.60°. Then draw the second, third, and fourth angles: 90°, 54°, and 86.4°.

Label the graph and give it a title.

**Pet Owners**

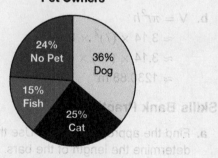

## Skills Bank Practice 29

**a.** Draw a number line that includes the minimum and maximum temperature. Use an *x* to represent each temperature reading. Title the graph and the axis.

**Lowest Temperature Each Day For Two Weeks**

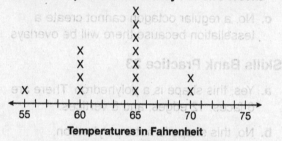

**b.** The minimum temperature recorded was 55°F. The maximum temperature recorded was 70°F.

**c.** According to the graph, the most common temperature was 65°F.

## Skills Bank Practice 30

**a.** Draw and label two intersecting circles to show the set of people that carpool and take a bus to work.

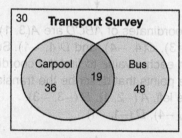

**Transport Survey**

There must be people who carpool and take a bus to work, because 55 + 67 + 30 = 152, and only 133 people were polled. The overlap is 152 − 133 = 19.

This means that 19 people were counted twice because 19 people both carpool and take a bus to work.

## Skills Bank Practice 31

Example 1

**a.** You need to find the area of the deck surrounding the pool. The deck and the pool are both rectangles.

Pool: 40 ft × 30 ft

Deck: 6 ft wide

Draw and label a diagram of the pool with the surrounding deck. Subtract the area of the pool from the area of the entire plot.

Find the length and width of the entire plot.

length: 6 ft + 40 ft + 6 ft = 52 ft

width: 6 ft + 30 ft + 6 ft = 42 ft

Find the area of the entire plot.

$A = lw$

$= 52 \times 42$

$= 2184 \text{ ft}^2$

Find the area of the pool.

$A = lw$

$= 40 \times 30$

$= 1200 \text{ ft}^2$

Find the area of the deck. Subtract the area of the pool from the area of the plot.

$A = 2184 \text{ ft}^2 - 1200 \text{ ft}^2 = 984 \text{ ft}^2$

The area of the deck is 984 ft$^2$.

**Example 2**

**a.** Use the information in the table to determine a pattern. Subtract the time of the first shuttle stop from the time of the second shuttle stop. A possible pattern is to add 25 minutes to the time of each shuttle stop.

Shuttle stop 2:

5:45 a.m. + 25 min = 6:10 a.m.

Shuttle stop 3:

6:10 a.m. + 25 min = 6:35 a.m.

Shuttle stop 4:

6:35 a.m. + 25 min = 7:00 a.m.

Shuttle stop 5:

7:00 a.m. + 25 min = 7:25 a.m.

Shuttle stop 6:

7:25 a.m. + 25 min = 7:50 a.m.

The shuttle should make its 6th stop at 7:50 a.m.

**b.** Shuttle stop 7:

7:50 a.m. + 25 min = 8:15 a.m.

Shuttle stop 8:

8:15 a.m. + 25 min = 8:40 a.m.

Shuttle stop 9:

8:40 a.m. + 25 min = 9:05 a.m.

Shuttle stop 9:

9:05 a.m. + 25 min = 9:30 a.m.

The shuttle should make its 10th stop at 9:30 a.m.

**Example 3**

**a.** Find the number of each type of ticket sold.

Number of tickets sold: 65

Cost of senior citizen ticket: $10

Cost of regular ticket: $15

Total sales: $855

Make a first guess for each type of ticket. The sum of tickets must be 65 and the total cost must be $855. Multiply each guess by the cost of each ticket. Compare the total to $855. Adjust your guess until you find the solution.

| | Senior Citizen Ticket | Regular Ticket | Total Tickets | Total Cost |
|---|---|---|---|---|
| 1st guess | 32 | 33 | 65 | 32($10) + 33($15) = $815 |
| 2nd guess | 45 | 20 | 65 | 45($10) + 20($15) = $750 |
| 3rd guess | 24 | 41 | 65 | 24($10) + 41($15) = $855 |

24 senior citizen tickets and 41 regular-priced tickets were sold.

**Example 4**

**a.** Find the total amount of gas in each tank when the tanks hold equal amounts of gas.

The starting amounts are 8550 ft$^3$ and 7200 ft$^3$.

Subtract 475 ft$^3$ and 250 ft$^3$, respectively.

Make a table with the starting amounts and the total amount subtracted at the end of each day. Continue building the table until the amounts are equal.

**Saxon** Algebra 1

| End of Day | Gas Amount in First Tank (in ft³) | Gas Amount in Second Tank (in ft³) |
|---|---|---|
| 0 | 8550 | 7200 |
| 1 | 8075 | 6950 |
| 2 | 7600 | 6700 |
| 3 | 7125 | 6450 |
| 4 | 6650 | 6200 |
| 5 | 6175 | 5950 |
| 6 | 5700 | 5700 |

There will be 5700 ft³ of gas in each tank when the two tanks hold equal amounts of gas.

**Example 5**

**a.** Find Frank's time.

Distance: 9 laps each 1312 feet long

Rate: 4 mi/hr

Find Frank's time by using simpler numbers to compute.

| $(9)(1312)$ | Find the total distance walked. |
|---|---|
| $= (10 - 1)(1312)$ | Write 9 as $10 - 1$. |
| $= 10(1312) - 1(1312)$ | Use the Distributive Property. |
| $= 13{,}120 - 1312$ | |
| $= 11{,}808$ ft | |

Convert the distance to miles.

$$\frac{11{,}808 \cancel{ft}}{1} \times \frac{1 \text{ mi}}{5280 \cancel{ft}} \approx 2.2 \text{ mi}$$

Use the distance formula to find Frank's time.

$d = rt$

$2.2 = 4 \times t$

$t = \dfrac{2.2}{4} \approx 0.55$

It took Frank 0.55 minutes, or about 33 minutes, to walk 9 laps.

**Example 6**

**a.** Find the color of each person's eyes. There are 4 people and 4 eye colors. Some information on who has what color eyes is given.

Organize the information in a table. Start with the fact that Terry has green eyes and Marc does not have hazel eyes.

Terry has green eyes, so no other person has green eyes.

The person who has blue eyes is Bill's brother and Marc's uncle, so neither Bill nor Marc has blue eyes.

Enter a Y for *yes* or N for *no* in the table. Once you enter a Y in a cell, enter an N in the remaining cells for that row or that column.

| | Green | Brown | Blue | Hazel |
|---|---|---|---|---|
| **Bill** | N | N | N | Y |
| **John** | N | N | Y | N |
| **Marc** | N | Y | N | N |
| **Terry** | Y | N | N | N |

Bill has hazel eyes. John has blue eyes. Marc has brown eyes. Terry has green eyes.

**Example 7**

**a.** Find the time the bus left San Francisco. You know when the bus arrived in Dallas, Texas, the length of the stops that were made, and the time difference between California and Oklahoma and Texas.

Work backward from the time the bus arrived in Dallas.

Then apply the time difference between the cities.

Subtract the length of time it took to drive from Tulsa to Dallas.

11:00 − 6 hours = 5 a.m.   Saturday

Subtract the length of time it took to drive from San Francisco to Tulsa.

5:00 − 16 hours = 1 p.m.   Friday

Since San Francisco is 2 hours ahead of Tulsa time, subtract the difference.

1:00 − 2 hours = 11 a.m.   Friday

The bus left San Francisco at 11:00 a.m. on Friday.